# Advancing Corporate Governance Research

## ADVANCING BUSINESS AND MANAGEMENT

The Advancing Business and Management series aims to provide a forum for advancing theory and practice in business and management. Its books will build on existing theory to move an aspect of business research forward towards relevance in the contemporary world. The series aims to test and advance theory in a contemporary context, whether that be digital disruption, populism, covid 19, climate change or the changing geo-political landscape.

Advancing Business and Management showcases groundbreaking authors that build on previous research to advance their topic. This might be through the integration of perspectives from other fields or even other disciplines or through the application of theory to a new context. While each book takes its own approach, all the titles in the series will aim to advance the subject and bridge the gap between theory and practice.

For a full list of Edward Elgar published titles, including the titles in this series, visit our website at www.e-elgar.com.

# Advancing Corporate Governance Research

## Emerging New Structures and Directions

*Edited by*

Brian Bolton

*Professor of Finance and the Endowed Chair in Finance, University of Louisiana at Lafayette, USA*

Jung Park

*Associate Professor of Entrepreneurship and Innovation, ISG Business School, France and Adjunct Researcher, HES-SO/ HEG-Geneve, Switzerland*

ADVANCING BUSINESS AND MANAGEMENT

Edward Elgar PUBLISHING

Cheltenham, UK • Northampton, MA, USA

Published with the support of the Swiss National Science Foundation



Published by

Edward Elgar Publishing Limited
The Lypiatts
15 Lansdown Road
Cheltenham
Glos GL50 2JA
UK

Edward Elgar Publishing, Inc.
William Pratt House
9 Dewey Court
Northampton
Massachusetts 01060
USA

Authorised representative in the EU for GPSR queries only: Easy Access System Europe – Mustamäe tee 50, 10621 Tallinn, Estonia, gpsr.requests@easproject.com

A catalogue record for this book is available from the British Library

Library of Congress Control Number: 2025950613

This book is available electronically in the Elgaronline
Business subject collection
https://doi.org/10.4337/9781035324965

MIX
Paper | Supporting responsible forestry
FSC® C013604

ISBN 978 1 0353 2495 8 (hardback)
ISBN 978 1 0353 2496 5 (eBook)
ISBN 978 1 0353 8503 4 (ePub)

Printed and bound by CPI Group (UK) Ltd, Croydon, CR0 4YY

# Contents

# List of contributors

**Taib Berrada El Azizi** is a certified public accountant and holds a PhD in finance from Montesquieu-Bordeaux IV University. He has 20 years of experience in teaching finance and auditing, as well as in research, particularly in the fields of family business management, organizational governance, and finance. He also has confirmed expertise in consulting, auditing, and accounting. He is currently a professor at ESCA Ecole de Management and an associate researcher in the Chair of Family Businesses, Casablanca, Morocco.

**Brian Bolton** is Professor of Finance and the Endowed Chair in Finance at the University of Louisiana at Lafayette. He has spent the past 20 years studying different aspects of corporate governance, including board structures, executive compensation and ownership dynamics, focusing on how environmental, social, and governance issues create long-term economic value. His work has been published in the *Journal of Quantitative and Financial Analysis*, *Journal of Corporate Finance*, *Columbia Law Review* and other leading journals.

**Christos Cabolis** is Chief Economist and Head of Operations at the IMD World Competitiveness Center and Adjunct Professor of Economics and Competitiveness at IMD. Formerly at Yale and ALBA Graduate Business School, his research has been published in top journals such as *The Review of Financial Studies* and *Journal of Law and Economics*, among others. He holds a PhD in economics from the University of California Santa Barbara.

**Jinsuk Choi** is the Head of Sustainable Investment at Korea Investment Corporation (KIC), where he leads Environmental, Social, and Governance (ESG) integration, corporate governance analysis, and sustainable fund management. He also serves on various government committees, including the Presidential Commission on Carbon Neutrality. A frequent speaker at global events hosted by organizations such as the World Bank, he holds a PhD in international management from Yonsei University, specializing in sustainability and finance. He co-authored Era of ESG Investing and has received official commendations from the President of the Bank of Korea and the Deputy Prime Minister & Minister of Economy and Finance.

**Demetris Christopoulos** completed his PhD studies in 2017 at the National and Kapodistrian University of Athens. He has worked as a maths tutor, market researcher, multimedia producer, and his research field is noisy numerical analysis. His work at ResearchGate sets him at the upper 4% of all members.

**Agnes Dyvik Clark** is currently a Doctoral Research Fellow at the University of Oslo, Department of Informatics, with a background from Copenhagen Business School and the Norwegian University of Science and Technology. This background of both business and engineering led to her starting her own tech venture after graduation, later joining other startups and scaleups as a business development consultant, before returning to academia for a PhD in Digitalization and Entrepreneurship with a special focus on entrepreneurs as managers and different governance structures in early technology startups.

**Cinzia Dessì** is an Associate Professor of Management in the Department of Economics and Business at the University of Cagliari, Italy. She holds a PhD in Management and a master's degree in economics from the same institution. Last year she spent a period of visiting at the Hanyang University in Seoul, South Korea. She has extensive experience teaching Project Management and Entrepreneurship and Business Creation. Her research has been published in esteemed journals such as *Family Business Review*, *Journal of Small Business and Enterprise Development*, *Journal of Family Business Strategy*, *Journal of Family Business Management*, and *The TQM Journal*. She has received notable grants and awards, including the Academy of Management Best Paper (2009, 2015), Carolyn Dexter Award (2015), IFERA and STEP Best Paper on Conference Theme (2019), De Visscher and Co. Scholarship for the FFI Family Firm Institute Boston (2017), and the FFI Best Unpublished Paper Award (San Diego, 2013). Her primary research interests are in entrepreneurship, SMEs and family firms, and sustainability.

**Truls Erikson** is a Professor of Entrepreneurship at the Department of Informatics at the University of Oslo, in Norway. Beyond being a close to practice entrepreneurship centre director for more than 10 years, he has spent the past 30 years studying different topics related to innovation and entrepreneurship, including venture capital, informal venture capital, and NVT dynamics. His work has been published widely in research journals, such as the *Journal of Business Venturing*, *Journal of Business Venturing Design*, *Journal of Business Venturing Insights*, *Venture Capital*, *Long Range Planning*, *Technological Forecasting* and *Social Change*, *Technovation*, and other national and international leading research outlets.

**Dennis Gan** is a scholar and engaging educator with over five years of experience in research management across corporate and academic domains. He has a PhD in Innovation and Entrepreneurship from University of Oslo and has experience working in global technology firms and start-ups before returning to academia. His hands-on experience in the corporate world and start-ups provides him with interesting insights in his research. His work is interdisciplinary, and he draws on insights from sociology and organizational theory to address novel questions in entrepreneurship, innovation, and strategy research. Currently, he focuses on the use of artificial intelligence in research at the Social Science Faculty, University of Oslo.

**Badr Habba** graduated from the Institut de Gestion des Entreprises in Bordeaux and holds a PhD in Management Sciences from Montesquieu-Bordeaux IV University, France. He is a professor at ESCA Ecole de Management and Director of the Chair of Family Businesses in Morocco. His research focuses primarily on the evaluation of banking institutions as well as the financial policies of family businesses.

**Zhaozhao He** is the Dwayne Wrightsman Associate Professor of Finance at the University of New Hampshire's Paul College of Business and Economics. Dr He's research interests lie in empirical corporate finance, with a focus on firm financial policy, innovation, labor mobility, and corporate governance. Her work has been published in prestigious journals such as the *Journal of Financial and Quantitative Analysis*, *Journal of Corporate Finance*, *Journal of Empirical Finance*, and *Financial Review*, among others. Dr He's research has received numerous awards in the profession, such as the McGraw-Hill/Irwin Distinguished Paper Award at the Southwestern Finance Association, Best Paper Award in Empirical Finance at the Southern Finance Association, Best Doctoral Student Paper Awards at Southwestern Finance Association and Southern Finance Association, and best paper by a young scholar in the annual issues of *Review of Industrial Organization*.

**Flora Huang** is Professor of Law and Business at the University of Derby in the UK, and Central Asian Legal Research Fellow at the Tashkent State University of Law in Uzbekistan. Her extensive academic and professional background has given her a profound understanding of economic systems, sustainability, business law, and trade and investment policies. Her most recent monograph is *Chinese and Global Financial Integration through Stock Connect* (Hart, 2023), which explores a novel market trading mechanism, giving mutual market access to Chinese and international investors.

**Ji-Hee Kim** is a Distinguished Visiting Professor at Hanyang University in Korea and an Associate Professor of Entrepreneurship at Canisius University in the USA. She holds a PhD in Entrepreneurship and Family Business. She has research and teaching experience in the USA, Germany, and Korea. She serves as a Vice President at the Academy of Entrepreneurship and Korean Family Business Association. She has received the best teaching awards and the best faculty advisor awards at her university several times in entrepreneurship. Her primary research interests are in entrepreneurship, family business, and small business management.

**Maude Lavanchy** is a Project Manager in corporate strategy at Transports publics de la région lausannoise SA. She was previously a Research Fellow at IMD Business School in Lausanne, Switzerland, and a semi-professional volleyball player. Passionate about sports, economics, and new technologies, her research is part of the field of economics and organizational behavior.

**Arjya B. Majumdar** is a Professor at OP Jindal Global University, India where he has taught courses on company law, corporate governance, mergers and acquisitions, and securities regulation for over 10 years. He spent the initial part of his career as a corporate lawyer, advising large corporations and the Government of India on matters relating to mergers and acquisitions, capital markets, foreign investments into India, joint ventures and private equity. His present research involves corporate governance and environmental, social, and governance standards.

**Rod B. McNaughton** is a Professor of Entrepreneurship and Academic Director of the Centre for Innovation and Entrepreneurship at the University of Auckland School of Business, New Zealand. His research interests include international new ventures, developing university entrepreneurship ecosystems, and venture financing.

**Nava Michael-Tsabari**, PhD, is the founder and director of the Raya Strauss Center for Family Firm Research at the Coller School of Management, Tel Aviv University. Her dissertation from the Technion is the first one on family firms in Israel. Nava's research examines emotions, organizational culture and employment in family firms, looking at family and non-family members. Her research has been awarded the 2012 Family Firm Institute Best Unpublished Paper, 2014 Family Business Review Best Article, and 2020 IFERA Best Paper with Contribution to Practice. For the last 15 years Nava has taught executive courses for family firm owners. In her work she combines academic rigor with real life experiences coming from a family business. She is herself a third generation member of the Strauss family firm, a multinational, multi-business food and beverage company, active in 20 countries, with 17,500 employees and 2022 revenues of US$2.6 billion, headquartered in Israel.

**David Midgley** joined INSEAD in 1999 as Professor of Marketing and is now Emeritus. Previously he was Foundation Chair at the Australian Graduate School of Management and he has also held visiting positions at the University of California, the University of Pennsylvania and Stanford University. Professor Midgley is a graduate in science, management and marketing from the Universities of Salford and Bradford. He has over 120 publications, including papers in leading journals such as the *Journal of Consumer Research*, *Journal of Information Technology*, *Journal of International Business*, *Journal of Marketing Research*, *Journal of Marketing*, *Marketing Science*, *Management Science*, *Organization Science* and *Research Policy*. He has also written several books, including *The Innovation Manual*, *Strategic Marketing for the C-Suite*, and most recently *A New Theory of Cultural Archetypes*. His principal areas of research are innovation, strategy and international business.

**Mihail K. Miletkov** is an Associate Professor of Finance and Co-Director of the Peter T. Paul Financial Policy Center at the University of New Hampshire. Dr Miletkov's research interests are in empirical corporate finance with a focus on international finance and corporate governance. His research has been published in leading academic journals including *Management Science*, *Journal of International Business Studies*, *Financial Review*, *Journal of Corporate Finance*, and *Journal of Empirical Finance*, among others. His research has also been featured in several media outlets and has been recognized with Best Paper Awards at national and international finance conferences.

**Séverine Mulliez** has successfully evolved in two complementary professional fields: operational and non-operational. In her operational responsibilities as controller, manager, and then executive, she has held key positions in companies of all sizes, from 200 to over 10,000 employees. This experience has given her a solid understanding of the inner workings of organizations and the day-to-day challenges they face. At the same time, she has also taken on board responsibilities, mainly on an international scale, in various business sectors such as retail, personal services, and commercial real estate. This dual role has enabled her to acquire a holistic perspective on companies, understanding both concrete operational challenges and long-term strategic considerations. Séverine sees her career path as an opportunity for continuous learning. Today, with her strong entrepreneurial culture, she devotes her time to her role as supervisor on the Supervisory Board of the Mulliez Family Association, as well as to supporting entrepreneurial families in France and abroad in matters of governance, succession, and onboarding NextGen.

**Nguyen Thi Kim Oanh** is a lecturer in Accounting and Management at International School, Vietnam National University Hanoi. She obtained her PhD from Newcastle University Business School in the United Kingdom. Her research interest is in performance management systems and firm performance towards sustainability. She has over 15 years of consulting experience for MSMEs operating in various sectors. In 2022, she was the project manager for "Building Credibility Index and Training on Writing a Business Plan for Entrepreneurs and SMEs in Vietnam, Laos, and Cambodia" (215,525.18 USD), funded by the Japan-ASEAN Integration Fund via the ASEAN Secretariat (2020–2022). In 2021, she managed the project "Introduction to Codes of Conduct in Business and Internal Control at International School, Vietnam National University Hanoi" (17,488 USD), under the implementation of "the Business-Government Integrity Initiative" – a component of the UN Development Programme's FairBiz project for "Promoting a Fair Business Environment in ASEAN," funded by the UK government via the Office for Business Sustainable Development, Vietnam Chamber of Commerce and Industry. She is also a member of the Consulting Committee on IFRS Translation under the Ministry of Finance of Vietnam.

**Jung Park** is Associate Professor of Entrepreneurship and Innovation at ISG Paris and an adjunct researcher at HES-SO/HEG-Geneve. Holding a PhD in Engineering, he led technological advancements in global high-tech companies before returning to academia. Throughout his career, Jung has been dedicated to interdisciplinary research, evidenced by his scholarly publications, practitioner articles, and patents in various fields. Currently, he focuses on exploring the transformation of venture governance amid data-driven changes, particularly in the context of technology startups.

**Huong-Trang Pham** is a lecturer at the Business School, RMIT University Vietnam. She holds a doctoral degree in Tourism from Vietnam National University Hanoi, a Diploma in Tourism Management from Austria, and two MBA degrees from the University of Applied Sciences Bremen, Germany, with distinction. She obtained Austrian and German scholarships for her studies. With over 15 years of experience, she has a strong network with tourism administration boards at the national level as well as international organizations like PATA, ASEAN, and Swiss-funded sustainable tourism projects. She has offered training programs for diverse stakeholders in Vietnam, including companies or government staff, which positions her to provide practical strategies for enhancing digitalization, managerial knowledge, and sustainable practices, which is also her field of research. Her primary areas of teaching and research encompass international strategic management, sustainability, sustainable tourism, destination marketing, and tourism management.

**Oumaima Quiddi** is a professor of finance at ESCA Ecole de Management in Casablanca, Morocco. She holds a PhD in management sciences from Cadi Ayyad University in Marrakech. Her teaching areas include corporate finance, accounting, management control, and research methodology. She is also an associate researcher at the Chair of Family Businesses in Morocco. Her scientific research focuses on the financial behavior of family businesses in the Arab world and the MENA region, with a particular emphasis on their investment, financing, and dividend payout policies.

**Philip T. Roundy** is the Mary Harris Distinguished Professor of Entrepreneurship at the University of Tennessee at Chattanooga (UTC). Prior to UTC, he was a Postdoctoral Scholar in the McCombs School of Business at the University of Texas at Austin. He received his PhD in Corporate Strategy from UT: Austin. His research focuses on understanding how entrepreneurship can be a tool for economic and community revitalization. He is particularly interested in how entrepreneurs assist in the renewal of struggling regions, "dying" industries, and displaced technologies. He has published over 70 articles and book chapters, is the associate editor of *Journal of Business Venturing Insights*, and serves on several editorial boards, including *Strategic Entrepreneurship Journal*, *Small Business Economics*, *Strategic Organization*, and *Entrepreneurship Research Journal*.

**Karl Schmedders** is Professor of Finance at IMD. He has published numerous research articles in international academic journals such as *Econometrica*, the *Review of Economic Studies*, the *Journal of Financial Economics*, the *Journal of Finance*, the *Review of Financial Studies*, *Management Science*, and *Operations Research*. He received a PhD in Operations Research from Stanford University. He is a fellow of the Game Theory Society and an SAET Economic Theory Fellow.

**Pramodita Sharma** is the University of Vermont's Distinguished Professor and Schlesinger-Grossman Chair of Family Business at the Grossman School of Business. She received her PhD from the University of Calgary in Canada and has received honorary doctorates from the Jönköping University in Sweden, and the University of Witten/Herdecke in Germany. Among the highest cited scholars in family business studies, her research on succession, governance, innovation, next generation commitment, entrepreneurial leadership and sustainability in/by family enterprises has appeared in journals like the *Academy of Management Learning and Education*, *Entrepreneurship Theory and Practice*, *Family Business Review*, *Journal of Business Ethics*, and *Journal of Business Venturing*, among others. She has co-authored eleven books, including the *SAGE Handbook of Family Business*, *Entrepreneurs in Every Generation*, *Patient Capital: The Role of Family Firms in Sustainable Business*, and *Pioneering Business Families of Sustainable Development*. Dita served as the editor of *Family Business Review* from 2008 to 2017 and co-founded the Family Enterprise Research Conference (FERC), and the Schlesinger Global Family Enterprise Case Competition (SG-FECC). A recipient of the prestigious Barbara Hollander award of the Family Firm Institute, she is a frequent speaker at gatherings of family business leaders around the world.

**Małgorzata Smulowitz** is a Researcher and Senior Advisor in family philanthropy, affiliated with the Debiopharm Chair for Family Philanthropy at IMD and Selenza Generations LLC. She has published articles in peer-reviewed academic journals such as *Human Relations* and *Research Policy*, as well as practitioner-oriented work on numerous topics, including cohesive giving, the use of blockchain in philanthropy, and impact. She co-authored the award-winning book *Family Philanthropy Navigator*. She holds a PhD in economics, management, and organization from Universitat Autònoma de Barcelona in Spain.

**Viktoriya Staneva** is an Associate Professor of Finance at the University of New Hampshire. Her research interests lie in the empirical corporate finance field with a focus on capital structure, corporate governance, environmental, social, and governance, and diversity and inclusion. She has authored articles in leading academic journals including the Journal of Banking and Finance, Journal of Empirical Finance, and Journal of Business Ethics, among others. Her research has also been featured in several media outlets and at numerous national and international conferences.

**Sunil Venaik** is Associate Professor at University of Queensland Business School, where his research focuses on international business for small and large firms. He is one of the leading business researchers worldwide, based on his extensive research publications and silver medal from the *Journal of International Business Studies*.

**Léa Zhe Wang** is the Director of the Research Program at Transmission Lab and Professor of Organizational Psychology at the International School of

Cologne, Germany. A specialist in the psychological dynamics of family businesses during succession, her research spans over 3,000 family enterprises, and has been recognized in international journals and French media. She has co-authored multiple publications and is actively involved in large-scale training sessions and seminars, providing leaders with valuable tools to prepare for succession. By promoting open communication and encouraging early anticipation of business successions, Dr Wang helps leaders untangle psychological barriers that often hinder smooth transitions. Her expertise extends to training the next generation of family leaders and fostering entrepreneurial skills. Her research highlights the importance of solid governance and open communication practices, which are essential for ensuring long-term development and success in family-run organisations.

**Richard S. Warr** is a Professor of Finance and the Associate Dean for Faculty and Research in the Poole College of Management at NC State University. He received his PhD in Finance from the University of Florida in 1998. His research focuses on information transmission in markets, equity valuation, endogeneity of corporate events such as option listings, short selling, capital structure and market microstructure. He has published papers in several top finance and accounting journals including the *Journal of Accounting and Economics*, the *Journal of Financial and Quantitative Analysis*, *Financial Management* and the *Journal of Corporate Finance*. He served as the co-editor of the *Financial Review* from 2015 to 2021. His teaching is in the area of investments, portfolio management, and security analysis.

**Marta Widz** is a Professor of Practice at SDA Bocconi School of Management, Milan, Italy. She is also the founder and CEO of the Family Silver Institute – a boutique advisory for family businesses and family offices. She serves as Affiliated Faculty at the Family Business Institute at the Grossman Business School of the University of Vermont, USA; Director in Residence at the INSEAD's Wendel International Centre for Family Enterprise; Affiliated Faculty at the Stewardship Asia Center in Singapore, and is Regional Governance Partner at the International Board Foundation and is a member of Female Board Pool. Family Capital has recognized Marta as Top 100 Family Influencers and as Top 20 Family Business Advisors and "those nominating Widz say she has made a significant impact in family enterprise across Europe, America and Asia." She has also been included in the Family Business Hall of Fame by the Family Business United. Marta obtained her PhD at the Centre for Family Business at the University of St. Gallen, Switzerland, was the Research Fellow at IMD Business School, Switzerland, and the leading contributor to the research and the Global-Asia Family Office Circle at the Wealth Management Institute, Singapore.

**Horace Yeung** is Associate Professor in Commercial Law at the University of Leicester in the UK, and Central Asian Legal Research Fellow at the Tashkent State University of Law in Uzbekistan. His research interests lie closely with the teaching he is doing surrounding commercial law (very broadly defined). His research has a distinctive global comparative and interdisciplinary approach especially underlining the role of law in economic development. He was a recipient of the Confucius Institute Highly Commended Prize for his research in Chinese law.

**Jing Zhao** is an Associate Professor and Cameron Professor of Finance in The School of Business at Portland State University. She received her PhD in Finance from Smeal College of Business at Penn State in 2007. Her research focuses on empirical corporate finance, particularly executive compensation and contracts, corporate governance, innovation, institutional ownership, the board of directors, and corporate social responsibility. She is also interested in real estate and urban economics research with a focus on how school choice programs impact real estate development and the environment. She has published articles in top finance and real estate journals including the *Review of Financial Studies*, *Journal of Corporate Finance*, *Financial Management*, and *Real Estate Economics*. Her research has won several best paper awards and national grants, as well as being featured in leading news media. She teaches in the areas of investments, applied econometrics and financial analytics.

# Acknowledgement

The editors are grateful for the support provided by the Dwight W. Andrus, Jr. / BORSF Endowed Chair in Finance at the Moody College of Business, University of Louisiana at Lafayette, and the Swiss National Science Foundation through research funding under grant CRSK-1_220996, both of which contributed to the advancement of this book project and facilitated open access publication.

## DISCLAIMER ON THE USE OF GENERATIVE AI

The authors declare that they either did not use a generative AI tool or used it responsibly. While such a tool may have been employed to refine thoughts or phrases, the authors have carefully reviewed the resulting text and take full responsibility for its content. They have ensured the removal of any irrelevant or non-value-adding phrases for brevity, as well as any fake or unverified information.

# INTRODUCTION

# 1. Introduction to new directions and new perspectives on corporate governance research

**Brian Bolton and Jung Park**

This book is about the future of corporate governance research.

But, in order to imagine what that future might be, we need to begin with understanding the past. In one way or another, business scholars have been studying corporate governance as long as we have been doing research – even if we didn't know that we were studying corporate governance.[1] The modern era of corporate governance research probably began in 1976 when Jensen and Meckling formally introduced scholars to their agency theory. This seminal work, for our purposes, was about incentive alignment; when principals and agents (or owners and managers) do not have the same incentives, agency costs arise and can be very costly. Thus, corporations should structure incentives – in both financial and non-financial terms – such that principals and agents work towards the same goals.

For most of the next 25 years, corporate governance scholars addressed this issue: studying how principals and agents work – either in alignment or in conflict – to advance the state of the firm. In 1997, finance professors Andrei Shleifer and Robert Vishny summarized this work with what, we believe, is a nice, all-encompassing definition of the field:

> Corporate governance deals with the ways in which suppliers of finance to corporations assure themselves of getting a return on their investment. (Shleifer and Vishny, 1997)

Well, this definition is mostly all-encompassing: if we change the word "finance" to "capital," this definition can work for scholars in all business fields – strategy, economics, entrepreneurship, law, accounting, and, of course, finance. Capital can be money, but capital can also be human capital, intellectual capital, or legal capital.

Agency theory may be the most common foundation of corporate governance research, but it is not the only one scholars have used. Stakeholder theory is based on the premise that the corporation exists to serve many diverse stakeholder groups, and long-term success comes from prioritizing and balancing the preferences of all stakeholders (Freeman, 1984). A similar perspective is provided by stewardship, which argues that business leaders are motivated by serving the needs and preferences of other stakeholders and will intrinsically align their own interests with the needs of the overall organization; they are motivated by being stewards of others rather than being motivated by their own self-interest (see, for example, Davis, Schoorman, and Donaldson, 1997). And resource dependency theory posits that each firm is part of an integrated value chain of many firms; because each firm depends on interaction with other firms and is dependent on resources it does not completely control, it succeeds optimally by making decisions that maximize the long-term benefit of the entire system through investment and collaboration (see, for example, Pfeiffer and Salancik, 1978). And there are also other theories scholars have studied. The purpose of the research is not necessarily to determine which theory is "best" – as making such a claim about human behavior and motivation is likely impossible; the purpose is to provide the foundation for asking questions and seeking explanations for how leaders in organizations behave and what motivates them.

This modern era research was dominated by two characteristics: it focused on US-based stories, and it focused on publicly listed corporations. The US had the most publicly available data with which to study corporate stories; in a field that is principally empirical analysis of human behavior, the most informative stories relied on this data and these large samples to obtain power and significance. Thus, our understanding of modern corporate governance was based largely on what we learned about US listed firms. That's neither right nor wrong, neither good nor bad. But that practice leaves out a plethora of stories, perspectives, and knowledge from many other regions and many other types of firms (Figure 1.1).

In 2001, the study of corporate governance changed from a niche field for law, strategy, finance, and other business scholars to a major legal, societal, and scholarly pursuit following one event: the collapse of Enron Corporation in the US. At the end of 2000, Enron was the seventh largest corporation in the United States; by the end of 2001, due to financial statement manipulation, some lax auditing, a few greedy executives, and a correcting stock market, Enron was bankrupt. Scholars, executives, and policymakers around the world took note: how could this happen? Who was in charge of the company? Why did the auditors allow this? Where were the politicians and policymakers? What was the board of directors' role? Who was looking out for employees

*Notes:* A timeline of major theoretical and regulatory developments in the field. This timeline is not exhaustive but is limited to those discussed in this chapter.

*Figure 1.1 Key milestones in corporate governance research*

(current and former), suppliers, communities, and other stakeholders? Enron became the poster child of failed corporate governance.

Enron certainly was not alone. Over the following years, other high-profile firms around the world became examples of failed corporate governance when they experienced their own challenges with ensuring suppliers of capital received a return on their investment – including Parmalat in Italy, Tyco and HealthSouth in the United States, British Petroleum, Satyam in India, and Volkswagen in Germany.

Regulators have responded to these failures with, predictably, regulation: notably the Sarbanes–Oxley (2002) and Dodd–Frank (2010) Acts in the United States. Investors respond by selling their stock; employees respond by quitting their jobs (and sharing their stories online); and the offending corporations apologize for their failures and vow they will never happen again. While most individual companies have avoided becoming repeat offenders, corporate governance researchers have enjoyed a robust supply of failures to study, analyze, and learn from. Natural experiments are our currency, and corporate governance failures have been very good for the research industry.

As we have moved into the 2010s and 2020s, the number of high-profile natural experiments has diminished – good for society, less good for corporate governance researchers. During this period, there have been two primary approaches to advancing corporate governance research. First, the field has moved from crisis management or crisis analysis in corporate governance towards corporate governance as a mechanism for marginal improvements in how firms behave, perform, and manage themselves. For example, in 2008, Norway became the first large country to mandate gender quotas for corporate boards, requiring every board to be comprised of at least 40% women and 40% men. Other countries have followed Norway's lead. And, predictably, corporate governance researchers retreated to their laboratories to see if such quotas are good or bad for the businesses. This is just one example; overall, scholars became much more creative in thinking about corporate governance issues and in how they studied them. Second, while the number of natural experiments we have to study may be few, the data and technologies we can use to study corporate governance have exploded. Much of the earlier research has been exclusively about the United States – not (just) because it's the largest economy in the world, but because the data we need to study corporate governance has been most readily available for US firms.[2] Eventually, many other nations began making their corporate reports easier to access. And, just as the availability of data was increasing worldwide, the technology available to use and to create new data was proliferating as well. Textual analysis and machine learning introduced a whole new world of corporate governance research, as we could now parse out a CEO's tone and sentiment during a conference call in addition to just identifying an earnings beat or miss.

Data limitations were no longer an excuse for not pushing the research further; we have the data to address just about any corporate governance question we can imagine.[3] To us, access to data and the advent of modern corporate governance institutions around the world allow us to fill the gaps in knowledge that were frequently overlooked by much of the prior research.

As we fast forward to 2025, the state of corporate governance research is at another inflection point; crises have become rare, and while technology available to us continues to grow, we generally have plenty of data. The primary limitation for advancing our work is our imagination. We have to think about corporate governance in new ways. We have to think more broadly about which suppliers or capital can be affected by corporate structures and how. We have to recognize that not all companies are the same – whether due to national institutional context, the stage and maturity of the firm, the structure of the firm, the mission of the firm, and everything else. We have to think about new corporate governance structures and new directions for corporate governance research.

And that's what this book is about: new structures and directions for corporate governance research. This book is about the future of corporate governance research. Of course, the future of corporate governance research might be nearly infinite; we had to set some boundaries and focus on a few priority areas. We chose to focus on the following four areas:

Part I: Cultural Dynamics of Corporate Governance.

Part II: Start-up & Venture Governance.

Part III: Corporate Governance of Family Firms.

Part IV: Governance of Social Purpose, Mission & Impact.

Each part contains 4–5 chapters, authored by a diverse group of scholars, including early-career academics, seasoned faculty, and practitioners. The contributors offer global perspectives, with representation from Asia, Africa, Europe, America, and Oceania. We are especially proud of this diversity – in topics, in regions, and in contributors. Corporate governance research is no longer just about studying the largest firms in the largest economies. Each corporation is unique, with unique incentives and constraints; understanding how diverse corporate governance systems operate in a wide variety of environments is essential to advancing the world of corporate governance research. Each chapter has been peer-reviewed by multiple referees who are experts in the topic area and who understand the purpose of this book. These four parts and priority areas are both independent and related; the individual chapters can stand on their own, as can the thematic parts, and the four parts are also related to one another in meaningful and interesting ways. Different international and cultural contexts may lead to different family governance structures and different firm purposes. Family firms that are start-ups might need different governance than mature family firms. Start-up firms may have evolving missions as the company grows (and potentially as it transitions from family ownership to broad ownership). And start-up firms will be heavily influenced by their cultural contexts and national institutions. We are confident that this approach to telling the story of these new structures and dimensions in corporate governance research helps to tell a more integrated and holistic story … while also highlighting narrow areas of interest that scholars can pursue in more depth (Figure 1.2).

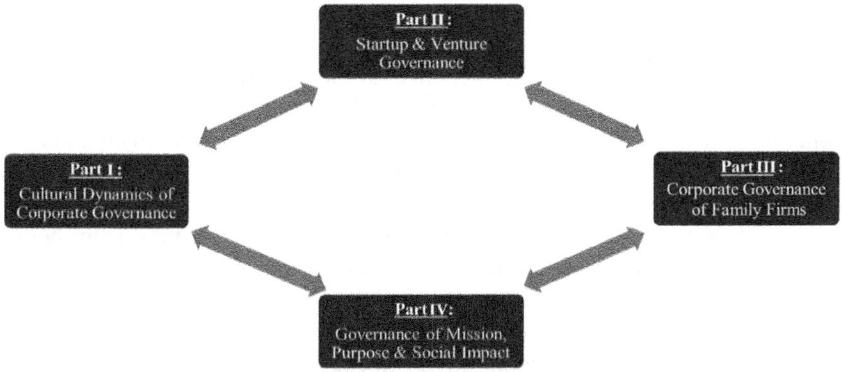


*Figure 1.2* *A diagram highlighting central themes in corporate governance, covering topics explored in the book and shaping future research directions*

Part I on "Cultural dynamics of corporate governance" begins with an overview of how cultural dimensions impact the behaviors of individual agents and the priorities of governance structures. Chapter 1 studies how cultural differences both between countries and within countries influence how firms' corporate governance structures are designed. This is followed by deep dives into new agents and novel structures. These chapters are not intended to address all new agents and structures that will impact governance in the future, but rather are intended to highlight a few of the most impactful dynamics that we expect to shape corporate leadership in the near future. Chapter 3 explores the role of board members from Generation X, the generation that is likely to be the foundation of governance over the next 10–20 years, and Chapter 4 introduces the unique role of dual private and state-government ownership of firms in China. Part I concludes with a study of the governance of Indian unicorns, a fascinating type of firm in a unique context that can help us all think about corporate governance in new ways.

This chapter also provides the perfect segue into Part II on "Start-up and venture governance." These may be firms that have succeeded because they refuse to follow the status quo; their leaders and directors may be even younger than Generation X, and the structure and mission of the firm might be changing dramatically every few months. Systems and structures that help suppliers of capital earn a return on their investments in these firms are essential – but potentially elusive and seemingly impossible to design.

We start Part II with a study of entrepreneurial ecosystems. Many successful start-ups succeed because they have identified market failures but need the support and guidance of other firms that are similarly trying to disrupt the status quo; understanding incentive alignment within these entrepreneurial ecosystems is critical. Chapter 7 explores the idea of ecosystems and collaboration from a novel perspective: "suprateams," or how firms balance both internal and external leadership attitudes within firms in a constantly evolving environment. Chapter 8 studies this evolution within a firm, looking at how advisory boards can assist firms in making the transition from being pure start-ups that succeed because they fight the status quo to becoming more established, mature, and formal structures (that is, to becoming the new status quo). Chapter 9 concludes the section with another, different take on corporate governance in a transitional environment – acquisition – as ownership changes, incentives change, and people change. Again, these perspectives are not intended to be exhaustive; small firm and venture governance is probably more diverse than any other area of corporate governance, as each firm, founder, and mission is unique. These four chapters are included to introduce some of the key venture governance issues we see shaping small firm systems in the near future – and to encourage scholars to open their minds to how these issues might affect all firms.

Part III is about corporate governance in family firms. Just as venture governance provides unique perspectives because every start-up is unique, so does the study of family firms – because every family is unique. By just about any definition,[4] most firms begin as family firms – small start-ups founded by a small group of innovators and disruptors. Sometimes the ownership structure changes as the firm grows, as the government becomes more or less involved, and as it is acquired. But many family firms stay family firms for the long term. Many firms that were initially 100% owned by the founding entrepreneurs remain owned by the founding family through any transitions and challenges. These firms, both when they're new and when they're mature, experience their own unique corporate governance challenges. Thinking of a firm providing a return on investment to suppliers of capital takes on entirely new perspectives when those suppliers of capital are family members.

Chapter 10 introduces a typology of family firms, characterizing firms across different structures and life cycles. Chapter 11 explores how families manage a key event in the life of every family firm: transition planning. The key to any transition is brave communication, allowing for vulnerability, psychological safety, and family harmony. Chapter 12 connects our discussion of family firms with our Part I foundation on cultural dynamics in corporate governance, focusing on family firm priorities with unique cultural dimensions in Morocco. Chapter 13 extends our portfolio of international perspectives on culture and looks at corporate governance in one of the most unique types of family firms in the world: the Korean chaebol. This chapter gives us another glimpse into our Part IV study of mission, purpose, and impact as it considers how governance within Korean chaebols addresses the challenges associated with advancing corporate social responsibility. And Chapter 14 further extends this connection between family firms and purpose and impact with a deep dive into the corporate governance dimensions of family foundations with modern philanthropy as their mission.

The five chapters in Part III could just as easily fit into any of the other themes in this book, which highlights the interconnectedness of these themes. Do family firms have unique cultural governance dynamics? Or do they have unique venture issues? Or are they driven by their own mission or purpose? Of course, they do. Corporate governance research is no longer myopic or linear; we are able to tell more intricate stories and dissect more complex relationships. These five different perspectives on family firm governance help us do that – and they help us understand how culture, venture, and family firm dynamics can both enhance and complicate corporate governance systems.

After these Part III perspectives on the governance of family firm mission, purpose and impact, Part IV begins with two chapters that take a higher-level view of the connection between corporate governance and mission, purpose and impact. Chapter 15 takes a contrarian view of the strategy (fad?) towards prioritizing environmental, social and governance (ESG) issues in both investing strategies and corporate governance structures. Chapter 16 continues the theme of exercising caution and professional skepticism, studying how boards of directors can amplify or moderate greenwashing, or ESG as a marketing scheme rather than an approach to creating value. Chapter 17 further explores ESG strategies, taking the unique perspective of institutional investors in Asia, highlighting the benefits and opportunities associated with incorporating ESG priorities, in contrast to the prior two chapters. Chapters 18 and 19 continue this theme, but primarily focus on the social dynamics by looking at the role gender plays in governance mechanisms. Chapter 18 connects back to our Part II venture governance work and studies female founders, considering both formal and informal governance mechanisms. Finally, Chapter 19 extends this gender dynamic and looks at corporate innovation, showing how pro-social policies can also be economically value-creating policies.

And this introduction of innovation as a goal segues perfectly into our final chapter, in which we conclude the book by focusing exclusively on the future of corporate governance research. In Chapter 20, we consider the role that artificial intelligence is likely to play in corporate governance in the future. For this discussion, we – the editors – surveyed all contributors to the previous 18 chapters and asked them to share their thoughts on how they see AI affecting corporate governance issues with respect to their content chapters. As you might imagine, these perspectives are enormously diverse, ranging from "currently, AI is not at all considered in the family business governance" to "we should also consider the corporate governance of AI as it becomes implemented more and more into corporate structure, operations, and management" and many fascinating perspectives in between. Appropriately, just as the previous 19 chapters highlighted the diverse and interconnected influence of culture, form, owners, and mission on corporate governance research, AI's influence is likely to vary widely based on all of these factors, too. We initially connect these AI issues to each of the four sections related to culture, start-ups, family firms, and mission; AI will have different roles in each context, so we thought it was important to connect this revolutionary technology to these different governance perspectives. Chapter 20 introduces best practices for governance leaders, both from a macro perspective and at the micro level. We then discuss the ethics of AI in governance; as governance mechanisms manage the tensions between managers and owners – principally through a board of directors – understanding the ethical responsibilities and priorities of different parties that may implement AI is critical. Finally, as this book is about advancing corporate governance research, we explore the future avenues for scholarly research related to AI's role and usage in corporate governance.

While no single message can summarize all of the perspectives, opportunities, and challenges for corporate governance with respect to AI, one of our contributors provides simple advice that may need to be the foundation for how companies use AI: "the organization should build a culture of trust so all stakeholders understand the benefits that AI brings the firms." Trust is a common theme throughout this book, being a critical aspect of corporate governance policy for all firms. How firms establish this culture of trust, and how scholars define, measure, and analyze any firm's culture of trust, is left, as we say, as an opportunity for future research.

This is a book about corporate governance research, designed to highlight current and future issues in research. But, as we said at the beginning of this chapter, corporate governance is an applied practice – it is about what happens in real companies with real stakeholders and real economic effects. We care about the research because it impacts what real corporate leaders do. As such, we will conclude this chapter – and we will conclude the introduction to the four following sections – with a short list of implications for the practice of corporate governance. As the first one suggests, none of these lists can capture all issues for all companies and all situations, but we hope that they will serve as guidance or ideas that readers – both scholars and practitioners – can use to better understand and implement the practice of corporate governance.

1. There is no such thing as "one-size-fits-all." Corporate governance is unique for each company, with unique stakeholders and unique regulations. Adapt your governance to what is best for you and for your business.
2. Culture matters – both external regional culture and internal corporate culture. External culture will determine laws and compliance issues; internal culture will determine values, preferences and relationships. Understand how culture makes your company unique.
3. Corporate governance is a dynamic process; it is not a destination and it cannot be static. The governance your business needs in the start-up and growth stages will be very different from the governance your business needs and the expansion and maturity stages. Adapt your governance structures and systems for what your business needs today and in the future.
4. Corporate governance needs to be about people and for people. You need to understand who your stakeholders are, what their incentives and preferences are and the relationships between different stakeholders. The corporate governance systems and strategies you implement must be designed to maximize the economic value of the business across all of your stakeholders.
5. Corporate governance in the future will look very different from how it looks today and has looked in the past. That's okay. Adjust your standards and practices to what your business needs for the future. We will return to this issue when we discuss artificial intelligence in Chapter 20.

If nothing else, we hope that something in the book triggers your imagination and curiosity and ignites some of your own future research. Corporate governance research advances from the work that we do – and by us continuing to ask important questions and trying to find answers to those questions. For us, the beauty of corporate governance is that it will always – probably – be a function of human behavior, priorities, and preferences. It is dynamic; as such, as scholars, we will always have work to do. And, for us, that work begins with Part I and our exploration of the impact of cultural dynamics in corporate governance structures and in corporate governance research.

Thank you for reading, and we hope that you enjoy this compilation of amazing and important corporate governance research.

## NOTES

1. The study of the tension between corporate ownership and corporate control probably gained its foothold with Berle and Means in 1932 (Berle and Means, 1932, *The Modern Corporation and Private Property*. New York: Macmillan).
2. The US Securities and Exchange Commission has provided online access to every publicly traded company's financial statements since the mid-1990s. Moreover, because it's the US, this gave rise to numerous private firms that took to aggregating and selling the data provided by these reports.
3. Of course, more data doesn't automatically lead to advancing the research; data can indeed be a four-letter word if used irresponsibly or inappropriately.
4. In most corporate governance literature, a family firm is defined as one in which the founder or a descendant of the founder currently holds a 5% equity stake in the firm. Shleifer and Vishny (1986), Anderson, Duru, and Reeb (2009) and Anderson, Reeb, and Zhao (2012) and others have used this definition. The 5% threshold generally applies to cash flow rights, not voting rights.

## REFERENCES

Anderson, R., Duru, A., & Reeb, D. (2009). Founders, heirs, and corporate opacity in the United States. *Journal of Financial Economics* 92(2), 205–222.

Anderson, R., Reeb, D., & Zhao, W. (2012). Family-controlled firms and informed trading: Evidence from short sales. *The Journal of Finance* 67(1), 351–385.

Berle, A., & Means, G. (1932). *The modern corporation and private property.* Macmillan.

Davis, J., Schoorman, F., & Donaldson, L. (1997). Toward a stewardship theory of management. *Academy of Management Review* 22(1), 20–47.

Dodd–Frank Wall Street Reform and Consumer Protection Act (2010). Public Law 111-203, 124 Stat. 1376. U.S. Government Publishing Office.

Freeman, R. (1984). *Strategic management: A stakeholder approach.* Cambridge University Press.

Jensen, M., & Meckling, W. (1976). Theory of the firm: Managerial behavior, agency costs, and ownership structure. *Journal of Financial Economics* 3, 305–360.

Pfeffer, J., & Salancik, G. R. (1978). *The external control of organizations: A resource dependence perspective.* Harper & Row.

Sarbanes–Oxley Act of 2002 (2002). Public Law 107-204, 116 Stat. 745. U.S. Government Publishing Office.

Shleifer, A., & Vishny, R. (1986). Large shareholders and corporate control. *Journal of Political Economy* 94(3), 461–488.

Shleifer, A., & Vishny, R. (1997). A survey of corporate governance. *Journal of Finance* 52(2), 737–783.

# PART I

# Cultural Dynamics of Corporate Governance

# Introduction to Part I

For decades, scholars have been reporting that "one size does NOT fit all" with respect to corporate governance structures and mechanisms. All firms are different because they are composed of different people and because they are operating in different contexts. The term "culture" means many things to many people, but to us, it refers to these different people and these different contexts. Culture represents the external factors, institutions, and behaviors that shape how firms are structured and how they pursue their goals. Cultural dynamics can be as institutional as political and legal systems, or cultural dynamics can be the nuanced differences in preferences between individuals. Of course, no single corporate governance structure will be best for all firms, and that's because each firm has unique cultural influences influencing how it provides a return on investment to suppliers of human, natural, and financial capital.

We begin our exploration of new structures and directions in corporate governance research with a macro-level study of how regional or national cultural dynamics determine how firms are structured and governed. In Chapter 2, David Midgley, Sunil Venaik, Demetris Christopoulos, and Jung Park explain how cultural values impact corporate governance strategies across 75 different countries (appropriately, these four authors come from four very different countries) – and within 75 different countries, as intra-culture variations can be just as significant as between-culture variations are. We see this explicitly in Chapter 3: Zhaozhao He, Mihail Miletkov, and Viktoriya Staneva explore the unique perspectives that Generation X directors bring to corporate governance. Gen Xers have historically been characterized as slackers, cynical, and apathetic.[1] Yet, they also came of age during a period of immense technological advancement, social transition, and economic turbulence; as a result, these now 40- and 50-something corporate leaders are characterized as tough, independent, flexible, and practical. This chapter delves into why this matters, both in the boardroom and C-suite.

From these foundational and personal perspectives on culture, we move to considering cultural dynamics in the two most populous nations in the world: China and India. These countries have unique political institutions and cultural histories; exploring how these unique dynamics influence corporate governance structures nicely illuminates why it is so important to conduct our research within the broader social and cultural contexts.

In Chapter 4, Flora Huang and Horace Yeung provide an intricate study of corporate governance for dual public and private companies in China. Corporate ownership in China may seem different from corporate ownership in any other culture, but that doesn't mean the implications of this work are isolated to Chinese companies. Quite the contrary, we can all learn about our own corporate governance contexts and research by better understanding this unique dynamic; after all, many economies have multiple class shares, government ownership of private firms, and global, institutional investors (who want to know that their investments are protected). Finally, in Chapter 5, Arjya Majumdar explores the corporate governance of Indian unicorns – or start-ups that have quickly attained extreme market valuations. In this work, we see that cultural foundations, government policy, and ownership structure are all critical dynamics for corporate governance. We trust that this novel type of firm in a unique context can help us all advance our corporate governance research in new and meaningful ways.

As we have been saying since the start of this book, corporate governance is an applied practice. So, as we transition from this introduction to the Part I content, we want to introduce a few ideas for the practical implementation of corporate governance. We hope these ideas will help you think about how to better implement governance at different firms – and we hope these ideas will introduce novel research paths to truly explore the future of corporate governance.

1. Your firm's corporate governance must be adapted to the national and regional cultures in which you operate. This relates to laws and compliance, but also to habits and behavior. You cannot change this culture, but you can adapt to it and embrace it.
2. Your firm's internal corporate culture is a choice – and it is created by your governance, your ownership, and your leadership. Be intentional with the corporate culture that you create.
3. Know who your stakeholders are and create the governance system that serves them best. Around the world, the average director's age is over 60 years, and approximately 20% of directors are women. Just because those are the averages, it does not mean it's what's best for you. Establish the leadership team and the board of directors that best serve your business.
4. Different companies will grow at different rates and in different ways. Be sure to manage your corporate governance systems to meet what your business will need in the future – not to what made sense in the past. Change is inevitable; embrace it and adapt to it.

You will be able to connect these practical implications to each of the four chapters in this first part – and we hope that they will help scholars generate new avenues and perspectives for research. With that introduction, we now begin advancing corporate governance research by digging deeper into culture and why it is so critical for corporate governance.

## NOTE

1. For full disclosure, both of the editors who wrote this characterization belong to Generation X.

# 2. The impact of within-country heterogeneity in cultural values on global corporate governance

**David Midgley, Sunil Venaik, Demetris Christopoulos and Jung Park**

## 1. INTRODUCTION

There is a well-known association between national culture, particularly cultural values, and corporate governance. Firms operate within the cultural, economic, legal, and political environments of countries in which they are based, and hence their systems of corporate governance are both influenced by these environments and in turn may also influence them, especially through the actions of large firms. This association has been extensively studied: Clarke (2007) explores the global corporate governance crisis, comparing systems across Anglo-Saxon, European, and Asian cultures. The work highlights how cultural diversity impacts corporate structures, using Enron and WorldCom as case studies. Roe and Vatiero (2018) emphasize the pivotal role of politics in corporate governance. Their research examines the historical context of ownership fragmentation in the US, the impact of postwar labor movements in Europe, and the ongoing influence of American executives and boards on governance structures. Together, these studies underscore the dynamic interplay between cultural values, political landscapes, and corporate governance systems worldwide.

However, past research has primarily utilized the standard perspective on national culture established in the 1970s by Hofstede (1984; 2001), that is, a nation can be represented by its averages on some set of values. In this standard perspective, what then becomes interesting for researchers to study is the differences between nations on these averages, and there are many such studies, including those focusing on the association with corporate governance (Hofstede, Hofstede, & Minkov, 2010).

In contrast, the purpose of this chapter is to ask whether this "national average" view is adequate, since other studies have shown considerable heterogeneity of cultural values exists within as well as between countries (Dheer, Lenartowicz, & Peterson, 2015; Steel & Taras, 2010; McSweeney, 2002). We believe it is important to recognize this within-country heterogeneity, since the differences in values among the citizens of a country can potentially impact the environment in which firms operate, as well as their ability to implement corporate governance practices through their employees.

To do so, we utilize the archetypal analysis approach to modeling heterogeneity introduced to the international business literature by Venaik and Midgley (2015) and recently employed by Midgley, Venaik, and Christopoulos (MVC, 2023) to study the evolution of within- and between-country heterogeneity in cultural values for 117 countries over four decades from 1981 to 2021.[1]

MVC's study used Welzel's (2013) secular and emancipative meta-values, drawn from the World Values Survey, rather than the more widely cited Hofstede (1984; 2001) values of power distance, individualism, masculinity, uncertainty avoidance, long-term orientation, and indulgence. Their rationale is that: (i) Welzel's values are available for more countries and years than the Hofstede values, and (ii) unlike Hofstede, they are available at the individual level, which is necessary for archetypal analysis. We will later argue that Welzel's values are also more appropriate for governance research since they directly address the issue of whether individuals will accept or question authority.

In the alternative "archetypal" perspective, a small number of archetypes (specific configurations of cultural values) are calculated using the totality of the data, thus providing a common frame of reference with which to measure the heterogeneity of countries. This common frame of reference is then used to represent individual respondents and countries as weighted compositions of the archetypes. Such compositions can then be analyzed by other statistical techniques such as regression to test the associations between them and outcomes like governance.

The first critical distinction between this alternative perspective and the standard view is that because the compositions are built on a common frame of reference, the alternative perspective reveals not just the differences between countries but also the similarities between them. The second critical distinction is that the archetypes themselves are found at the edges of the data, not the center as with the standard perspective. This makes them much sharper and more distinct than averages, and as a consequence, greatly facilitates interpretation of the resulting compositions. Here, we analyze the associations between the MVC country compositions and an index of corporate governance practices built from items in surveys conducted for the Global Competitiveness Report (Schwab, 2018) between 2007 and 2017. We were able to match 80 countries and 111 observations between the two studies, providing the initial dataset for addressing our research question, but subsequent analysis identified six observations as outliers, so our key results are based on 75 countries and 105 observations. Looked at in terms of cultural research, this is a typical sample size; from the perspective of the governance literature, it may appear small.[2] However, it should be noted that these observations are derived from surveys of large numbers of respondents. The MVC country cultural averages and compositions are based on the analysis of over half a million respondents from the World Values Survey (Inglehart et al., 2020), and the index of governance is derived from the annual global executive surveys conducted for the Global Competitiveness Report, each of which typically has over 10,000 respondents. Hence, we believe the sample of 75 countries and 105 observations is adequate for our purposes here.

To control for the institutional environment of the countries, which might have a more direct influence on corporate governance than culture per se, we built a measure of this environment from three of the World Bank's Worldwide Governance Indicators (Kaufmann, Kraay, & Mastruzzi, 2011), namely *control of corruption*, *regulatory quality*, and *rule of law*. Finally, we added *gross domestic product per capita* (at purchasing power parity), also sourced from the World Bank, as a control for any other unobserved factors in our analyses.

And we used a combination of necessary condition analysis (Dul, 2016) and generalized linear models as the main statistical techniques with which to test the associations between all our constructs and corporate governance, including a comparison of the performance of both the standard and alternative perspectives. These two statistical techniques complement each other since they test different aspects of these associations, and we follow the template provided by Richter et al. (2020) to form overall conclusions on the strength and nature of these associations, as seen through the two techniques, conclusions that allow us to establish the necessary and sufficient conditions for good corporate governance to emerge.

To foreshadow our results, we show that the alternative perspective is clearly superior to the standard perspective in explanatory power and insight. Specifically, it indicates that country cultural compositions are necessary and sufficient conditions for governance, after controlling for the strength of the country's institutions and level of gross domestic product. We further show that two components of our compositions will, on average, increase perceptions of governance, while one will, on average, decrease this. Follow-on analyses also suggest equifinality; that is different configurations for these compositions can result in the same level of governance. Finally, these conclusions are robust to different definitions of governance, whether narrowly focused on value maximization for the firm or more broadly to include elements of social responsibility.

## 2. CONSTRUCTS, DATA, AND MEASUREMENT

In this section, we describe the constructs, analytical approach, and data sources utilized in our study. We adopt Welzel's two meta-values – secular and emancipative – as our primary framework for understanding cultural values. Next, we explain the application of archetypal analysis to assess cultural diversity within and among countries. Subsequently, we elaborate on the two data sources central to our analysis: the World Economic Forum's Global Competitiveness Report and the World Bank's Worldwide Governance Indicators.

### Cultural Values: The Welzel Meta-values

The MVC study is based on Christian Welzel's two meta-values for culture, namely secular and emancipative values (Welzel, 2013), which have been measured by the World Values Survey (Inglehart et al., 2020) since 1981. Hence, it is important to justify why these values are relevant to corporate governance and not the better-known Hofstede values. From a theoretical perspective, Welzel's meta-values "go to the heart of the relationships between individuals, and between individuals and the traditions and institutions of their society" (MVC, 2023, p. 8). "Secular" encompasses sets of values relating to defiance, disbelief, relativism, and skepticism. "Emancipative" encompasses sets of values relating to autonomy, equality, choice, and voice. For interpretive purposes, the two meta-values are generally characterized as representing *sacred to secular*, and *obedient to emancipated* dimensions. Two dimensions that are prima facie related to corporate governance since they potentially impact both the role of firms in their society and the relationships between firms and their employees. For one example, individuals who are high on secular values are inherently skeptical of authority, and if they are also high on emancipative values, they expect to have their opinions heard by decision-makers. In contrast, individuals who are low on both values are more trusting and reluctant to question decisions made by those in authority.

The Welzel values are measured by 24 items in the World Values Survey and combined into the two formative indices, whose construct validity Welzel establishes through extensive testing (Inglehart & Welzel, 2005; 2010). From an empirical perspective, Welzel demonstrates that these two meta-values have power in predicting important societal level outcomes, notably the association between emancipative values and democratization, but also others. Finally, from a practical perspective, Welzel's meta-values have been measured for a larger number of countries, more frequently, and over a longer period of time than other value models such as Hofstede, and this enables us to maximize the amount of data for the current analysis.

## Archetypes and Country Compositions

MVC uses geometry to argue that, given data with two orthogonal dimensions, four archetypes are adequate as a frame of reference with which to represent the heterogeneity present in this data. They also demonstrate empirically that a three-archetype solution is inferior and that a five-archetype solution clearly shows diminishing returns. The four archetypes, which are logically the four combinations of low and high on the two Welzel meta-traits, are shown in Table 2.1, along with their short form labels (e.g., *SacObe* for sacred and obedient). These are based on an archetypal analysis (Cutler & Breiman, 1994) of 587,079 respondents to the World Values Survey between 1981 and 2021. Note, however, that in order to give each country observation an equal weight in the calculation of the four archetypes, MVC used subsampling techniques (Politis, Romano, & Wolf, 1999), full details of which are provided in their book.

Given these four archetypes, every individual in the data can then be described as a four-component composition, where each component is the relative weight of one of the archetypes in their values. The mean of these individual values for a country then provides a composition at the country level of analysis.

We illustrate the contrasting ideas of country cultural averages and country cultural compositions in Figure 2.1, using data for the two largest global

*Table 2.1* *Four archetypes for two Welzel meta-values*

| Archetype* | Secular values** | Emancipative values*** |
|---|---|---|
| 1. Sacred and obedient (*SacObe*) | 0.00 | 0.01 |
| 2. Sacred and emancipative (*SacEma*) | 0.09 | 0.90 |
| 3. Secular and obedient (*SecObe*) | 0.89 | 0.16 |
| 4. Secular and emancipated (*SecEma*) | 0.89 | 0.97 |
| Average individual | 0.38 | 0.44 |

*Note:* * The Welzel meta-values were reproduced from MVC (2023) with permission. ** Continuous scale from 0 = sacred values to 1 = secular values. *** Continuous scale from 0 = obedient values to 1 = emancipated values.

economies, China and the USA. The figure shows both their mean secular and emancipative values (the standard view) and their mean compositions (the alternative perspective). The standard perspective demonstrates that the values of the two countries are different as we would expect, with China being higher on secular values than the USA and lower on emancipative values. In the alternative perspective, the largest components of the two compositions are consistent with this pattern, with China being those holding secular and obedient values (*SecObe* at 0.36) and the USA being those holding sacred and emancipated values (*SacEma* at 0.34). However, note the differences in the other components, which provide a deeper insight not only into the differences between the two countries but also their similarities. For example, in both countries, we can find people holding each of the four sets of combined values.

Note also that the two perspectives are strictly mathematically related. If we multiply the archetype values in Table 2.1 by the compositional weights for each country in Figure 2.1 and then sum these across their four components, we will recover the averages of the standard view. Hence, the first difference between the two perspectives is one of mindset. The standard view regards countries as homogeneous and focuses on differences; the alternative perspective regards countries as heterogeneous and focuses on both differences and similarities.

MVC studies such inter-country differences and similarities in more detail. Here we examine whether the compositional perspective can also provide a *different explanation* for the association between national cultural values and corporate governance than that provided by the standard perspective. That is:

1. In general, does the alternative perspective predict country levels of corporate governance better than the standard view, and
2. In particular, how do the various components of the country compositions relate to the country levels of governance?

Note though that compositions, since they are relative and constrained to sum to a constant (here 1), cannot be directly used in statistical analyses such as

| | Alternative perspective | | | | Standard view | |
|---|---|---|---|---|---|---|
| **Country** | **SacObe** | **SacEma** | **SecObe** | **SecEma** | **Secular** | **Emancipative** |
| China | 0.29 | 0.15 | 0.36 | 0.20 | 0.51 | 0.39 |
| USA | 0.25 | 0.34 | 0.16 | 0.25 | 0.39 | 0.58 |

*Figure 2.1 Country compositions for China, 2013, and USA, 2017*

regression; instead, they need to be transformed (Aitchison, 1982). Here we use the simplest such transformation, the additive log ratio, where three of the component weights for each country observation are divided by the fourth and then natural log transformed, resulting in three log ratios for each country. Mathematically, the choice of the divisor does not matter, but here we choose the *SacObe* component as this is both logical (being the low-low combination) and has the greatest mean weight across our 111 country observations (0.34). More critically, the choice of *SacObe* makes theoretical sense because people with this combination of values are least likely to exert pressure for improved corporate governance. Thus, the three log ratios potentially describe the pressure for improved governance that may come from people with other combinations of values.

In our results, the three additive log ratios describing the composition are labeled as *SacEma/SacObe*, *SecObe/SacObe*, and *SecEma/SacObe*, to make it clear they should be interpreted as ratios. They also need to be seen as a related group of variables and not as three independent variables, since by definition they are connected through the sum constraint (that is, as one increases, others must decrease). Here we use them to test whether county compositions are a necessary and sufficient determinant of corporate governance, and having found they are, we then interpret the meaning of this result through other analyses.

## Corporate Governance: Global Competitiveness Report

We define corporate governance as the system of rules, practices, and processes by which a company is directed and controlled. Basically, it involves balancing the interests of a company's many stakeholders, such as shareholders, management, customers, suppliers, financiers, government, and the community in a way that promotes accountability, transparency, and fairness. The key components of an effective system of corporate governance typically include:

1. *Board of Directors*: is responsible for setting the company's strategic objectives, ensuring that the necessary resources are in place to achieve these objectives, and monitoring management's performance.
2. *Shareholders*: corporate governance seeks to protect their interests by ensuring transparency, accountability, and fair treatment of all shareholders.
3. *Management*: corporate governance establishes a framework for the responsibilities and accountabilities of the company's executives. It includes mechanisms to ensure that management acts in the best interests of the shareholders and the company.

4. *Ethical Behavior and Corporate Social Responsibility*: corporate governance involves promoting ethical behavior and responsible decision-making. This includes considerations for social impacts, not just financial performance.
5. *Transparency and Disclosure*: companies are expected to provide accurate and timely information about their financial situation, performance, ownership, and governance processes. This transparency helps stakeholders make informed decisions.
6. *Risk Management*: an effective corporate governance system includes processes for identifying, managing, and mitigating risks that the company may face.
7. *Legal and Regulatory Compliance*: corporate governance helps ensure that companies adhere to legal and regulatory requirements.
8. *Stakeholder Relations*: corporate governance recognizes the interests of various stakeholders and aims to manage relationships with them in a way that is fair and beneficial to all parties.
9. *Internal Controls and Auditing*: establishing internal controls and conducting regular audits are essential components of corporate governance to ensure the accuracy of financial reporting and the integrity of internal processes.

With this definition in mind, we searched for data that was publicly available at a country level and over multiple time periods. The best match we found was with some of the survey questions in the annual executive survey, which forms one input to the Global Competitiveness Report. We chose 2007 as the starting year since that was the year in which the survey methodology changed, namely by calculating smoothed values over two years, thus ensuring a larger sample base and more robust estimation of country values. While we could not match all items in the definition above, we found seven items that did have a good fit, and these are detailed in Table 2.2. Note that while there have been other items in this survey that might fit the definition, the seven items in Table 2.2 have been written in the same way from 2007 to our cut-off date of 2017, providing consistent measurement over time. Also note the Global Competitiveness Reports have publication dates spanning two years (e.g., 2007–2008), but the executive survey is conducted during the first of these two years, so we use that as the year of the reported values for the seven items.

The executive survey reports *perceptions* of standards and practices in the country, so we conceptualize corporate governance as a reflective construct and simply sum the scores for the seven items for each country and year, all of which are measured on a 7-point scale (and we then divide the sum by seven for easier interpretation). This choice of a reflective construct is supported by

*Table 2.2 Survey items used to construct the index of corporate governance*

| Variable name | Measures | Survey question |
|---|---|---|
| Audit | Strength of auditing and accounting standards | In your country, how strong are financial and auditing standards? [1 = extremely weak; 7 = extremely strong] |
| Board | Efficacy of corporate boards | How would you characterize corporate governance by investors and boards of directors in your country? [1 = management has little accountability to investors and boards; 7 = investors and boards exert strong supervision of management decisions] |
| Delegate | Willingness to delegate | In your country, how do you assess the willingness to delegate authority to subordinates? [1 = low – top management controls all important decisions; 7 = high – authority is mostly delegated to business unit heads and other lower-level managers] |
| Ethical | Ethical behavior of firms | How would you compare the corporate ethics (ethical behavior in interactions with public officials, politicians, and other enterprises) of firms in your country with those of other countries in the world? [1 = among the worst in the world; 7 = among the best in the world] |
| Management | Reliance on professional management | In your country, who holds senior management positions? [1 = usually relatives or friends without regard to merit; 7 = mostly professional managers chosen for merit and qualifications] |
| Shareholder | Protection of minority shareholders' interests | In your country, to what extent are the interests of minority shareholders protected by the legal system? [1 = not protected at all; 7 = fully protected] |
| Training | Extent of staff training | To what extent do companies in your country invest in training and employee development? [1 = hardly at all; 7 = to a great extent] |

the high correlations both within the seven items (ranging from 0.69 to 0.94) and with the sum itself (ranging from 0.88 to 0.94). When analyzed by principal component analysis, the first component explains 83% of the variance in the seven items, demonstrating that the index is essentially unidimensional as desired here, and the Cronbach alpha is 0.96, indicating high internal consistency for the construct. For brevity, in our results we label this construct *governance.*

*Governance* scores range from a low of 3.26 (Bosnia and Herzegovina, 2008) to a high of 6.14 (Sweden, 2011). The median score is 4.31 (India, 2012 and Spain, 2017). Most of the 80 countries have a single year of data, but 27 have either two or three years of data, representing at most 2.7% of the available data, suggesting no country dominance. Nonetheless, we checked the range of scores and the shape of the distribution of the index for countries with single years against that of those with multiple years. Both were highly similar, so in the following analyses, we use the total data set to maximize statistical power.

For this data, the distribution of governance scores is noticeably right-skewed, which has implications for the appropriate choice of regression method, as will be discussed subsequently.

As a final point here, we note that these seven items provide a broad definition of corporate governance, covering ethical behavior, board effectiveness, shareholder protection, auditing standards, management practices, and human capital development. As such, it is more aligned with stakeholder theory than the alternative value maximization theory. Stakeholder theory argues that managers should take into account multiple stakeholders in their decisions, including customers, employees, and society at large (Donaldson & Preston, 1995). In contrast, value maximization argues that the sole focus of managerial decisions should be on profitability and shareholder value (Friedman, 1970; Jensen, 2001). The debate between these two views has been present in the literature for several decades and essentially contrasts organizational efficiency with organizational legitimacy (Filatotchev & Nakajima, 2014).

To test the two views, we also defined a narrower construct, *value maximization*, from the four items relating to board effectiveness, accounting and auditing standards, professional management, and protection of minority shareholders.[3] We included the last of these on the rationale that protecting minority shareholders can boost the long-term financial stability and profitability of the firm. The four-item construct is also unidimensional and has a Cronbach alpha of 0.94.

## Institutional Environment: World Bank Governance Indicators

We selected three of these well-known indicators to represent the institutional environment in which the firms of a country operate, namely *control of corruption*, *regulatory quality*, and *rule of law*. The World Bank's definition of these items is shown in Table 2.3, and they are based on data from over 30 sources (see Kaufmann et al., 2011 for the methodology used to construct these indicators). One of these sources is the Executive Survey of the Global Competitiveness Report, but there is no overlap between the survey items used by the World Bank and those we use for our Governance index, since the World Bank selects items that focus on governance by the government and other institutions of the country, while we select items that focus on the governance of private sector firms. And while there might be a common method bias, the executive survey is only one of several surveys that go into building each of these institutional indicators, suggesting this is unlikely.

The three indicators are highly correlated ($\geq$ 0.90), based on perceptions from surveys and defined by the World Bank as reflective; hence, we formed a single reflective construct from them. This construct is unidimensional (the first principal component explains 96% of the variance among the three items) and has a Cronbach alpha of 0.97, indicating high internal consistency. In our results, we label this construct *institutions*.

### Gross Domestic Product Per Capita

We obtained values for Gross Domestic Product Per Capita from the World Bank for each country and year, using the 2017 international dollar, and purchasing power parity values.[4] Purchasing power parity values are then used as a general control in our regression models, representing many other unobserved factors and, for brevity, labeled *GDP* in our results.

*Table 2.3 Definitions of the World Bank governance indicators*

| Indicator | Definition |
|---|---|
| Control of corruption | Reflects perceptions of the extent to which public power is exercised for private gain, including both petty and grand forms of corruption, as well as "capture" of the state by elites and private interests. |
| Regulatory quality | Reflects perceptions of the ability of the government to formulate and implement sound policies and regulations that permit and promote private sector development. |
| Rule of law | Reflects perceptions of the extent to which agents have confidence in and abide by the rules of society, and in particular the quality of contract enforcement, property rights, the police, and the courts, as well as the likelihood of crime and violence. |

# 3. ANALYSIS METHODS

Our objective here is to analyze the relationship between cultural averages, cultural compositions, and controls as exogenous factors and corporate governance as the dependent outcome. The typical way to do so is through a linear regression, an approach that has an *additive logic*. That is, each factor is assumed to independently contribute to the governance outcome, and since the absence of one factor can be compensated by another, they can be thought of as sufficient but not necessary conditions for the outcome. However, the additive logic is not the only analytical approach possible. Richter and Hauff (2022) discuss two other causal logics: *configurational* and *necessity*. In the configurational logic, it is assumed that the outcome is produced by certain combinations or configurations of the factors, configurations that are identified through methods such as qualitative comparative analysis (Ragin, 1987). In contrast, the necessity logic does not attempt to explain how changes in a factor change the outcome; rather, it seeks to identify the conditions in which an outcome can occur, through a method called necessary condition analysis (Dul, 2016). Here we employ the additive and necessity logics since they complement each other by establishing both the *necessary and sufficient conditions for good governance*. The configurational approach we leave for future research.

Necessary condition analysis can be thought of as (1) identifying "must have" factors, that is factors which must be present for the outcome (governance) to manifest, and (2) the level of governance at which this connection emerges. It does so by examining the behavior of governance against each exogenous factor (cultural values, controls) separately and through an analysis of the bivariate scatter plot. In contrast, regression can be thought of as identifying "should have" factors, focusing on average effects, and in the multivariate case looking at the additive effects of all the exogenous factors on governance. We next discuss necessary condition analysis before discussing generalized linear models, which is the regression method we adopted here because of the skewed distribution of the governance scores.

## Necessary Condition Analysis

We first examined the associations between governance and the other constructs through the lens of necessary condition analysis (NCA). For two variables, X and Y, this technique seeks to determine which level of X must be present for a certain level of Y to be achieved. It does so from the scatter plot of the two variables, as shown in Figure 2.2, for the association of the additive log-ratio transformed high-sacred, high emancipative component of the cultural composition (*SacEma/SacObe*) and the corporate governance index (governance). A ceiling line is drawn on the data in one of two possible ways, called, respectively, the ceiling regression – free disposal hull (CR-FDH) and the ceiling envelopment – free disposal hull (CE-FDH). Here we use the latter as there is no theoretical reason to expect a linear ceiling with our data. The area of the empty space above and to the left of this line is calculated, and the ratio of this area to that of the entire space then provides an estimate of the effect size. For the example in Figure 2.2, this is 0.25, which is a medium-sized effect for NCA (Dul, 2016, p. 30) and potentially allows us to conclude that the *SacEma/SacObe* component of the country's cultural composition is necessary for corporate governance. (Note here that to draw more substantive conclusions on the compositional approach requires us to assess whether all three components are necessary.) NCA also provides a permutation test to

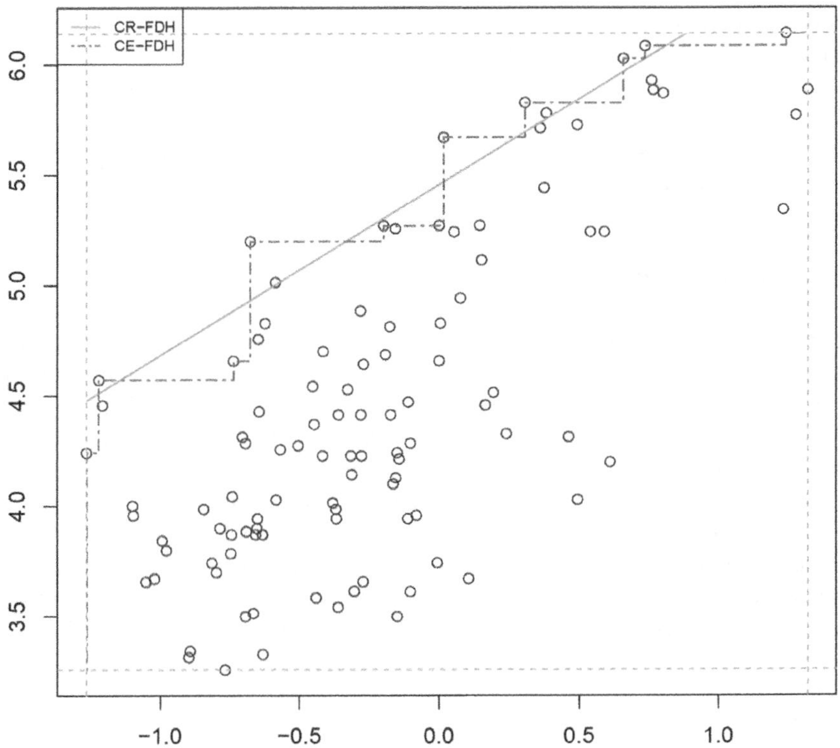


*Figure 2.2* *Scatter plot and ceiling lines for the component SacEma/SacObe (X) and governance (Y)*

assess the statistical significance of the effect size; for this example, the effect is significant at the $p = 0.00$ level (based on 10,000 permutations).

An additional visualization provided by NCA is the bottleneck table, which is a tabular representation of the ceiling. This is useful because it shows whether the condition is necessary for any given level of the dependent variable. For the example, across the bottom 40% of the range of the governance construct, *SacEma/SacObe* is not necessary; for the top 60% of the range, it is necessary.

## Generalized Linear Models

Governance has only positive values, and the right tail of its distribution is noticeably much longer than the left (i.e., a right-skewed distribution). Hence, a generalized linear model, using the Gamma error distribution and an inverse linking function ($Y \sim 1/X$), is more appropriate than an ordinary least squares model ($Y \sim X$). For completeness, we ran both, and they are generally consistent in terms of the sign and approximate magnitude of the coefficients. However, diagnostic tests on the ordinary least squares models reveal the expected problems with the skewed dependent variable, whereas diagnostic tests on the generalized linear model are satisfactory, so we report the latter here.

## Combining the Two Techniques

Richter et al. (2020) discuss the complementary nature of NCA and partial least squares structural equation modeling (PLS-SEM) and provide a template for drawing conclusions from possible result scenarios. We employ that template here since PLS-SEM is built on linear modeling techniques, and their advice is also consistent with a more general discussion on NCA and regression by Dul (2021). The three possible scenarios they discuss focus on scenarios where one or other or both analyses yield positive results. Each scenario leads to a different conclusion on the nature of the relationship between the exogenous and endogenous constructs. It is obvious there is a fourth scenario where both analyses yield negative results, which would lead to the conclusion that there is no association between the constructs under consideration.

## Outliers

Preliminary analyses using both NCA and linear models identified six potentially influential outliers. For NCA, Qatar is an outlier because its extreme value for the base *SacObe* component in the additive log ratio (0.66) distorts the relationship of the other three components with governance. South Africa is an outlier because its high level of governance (86th percentile) is not consistent with a much lower value for institutions (44th percentile). Luxembourg has a GDP value that is highly inflated due to flows of capital from global firms. For generalized linear models, Singapore, Zimbabwe, and the USA (for one of the two observations of this country in our data) appear as outliers on various diagnostic plots.

We ran our analyses both with and without these outliers, and the results are broadly similar, particularly the signs of coefficients. However, we report the results without outliers, as these have better fits with the data and more satisfactory diagnostic tests. Hence, our final results are based on 75 countries and 105 observations.

## 4. RESULTS

Figure 2.3 summarizes the results of the NCA tests and leads to the simple conclusion that cultural values are a necessary condition for governance, as are the two control constructs, institutions and GDP. This conclusion holds for both the standard perspective of secular and emancipative meta-values and for the alternative perspective of three compositional components. It is true that the effect for one of these components, *SecObe/SacObe*, is not significant at the 0.05 level with an estimated probability of 0.09; however, these three components have to be considered as a group, and the other two components are highly significant. Overall, these results indicate a medium to large effect size for the alternative perspective, which is marginally greater than the effects shown for the standard view. The bottlenecks shown in Table 2.4 indicate that these effects mainly manifest themselves at 40% of the range of governance; below this they are not necessary.

The regression results are shown in Figure 2.4. This figure shows the results for four generalized linear models, since we ran models for the standard perspective (country average values) and the alternative perspective (country

| X | Y | Effect size | p-level | Necessary? ($p < 0.05$) | Effect Magnitude |
|---|---|---|---|---|---|
| **Standard Perspective (Country Value Averages)** | | | | | |
| *Secular Values* | *Governance* | 0.27 | 0.02 | Yes | Medium |
| *Emancipative Values* | | 0.27 | 0.00 | Yes | Medium |
| **Alternative Perspective (Country Value Compositions)** | | | | | |
| *SacEma/SacObe* | | 0.25 | 0.00 | Yes | Medium |
| *SecObe/SacObe* | *Governance* | 0.32 | 0.09 | No | Large |
| *SecEma/SacObe* | | 0.33 | 0.00 | Yes | Large |
| **Controls** | | | | | |
| *Institutions* | | 0.42 | 0.00 | Yes | Large |
| *GDP* | *Governance* | 0.28 | 0.00 | Yes | Medium |

*Figure 2.3* *Necessary condition analysis results*

*Table 2.4* *Bottleneck table*

| Governance Index | SacEma/ SacObe* | SecObe/ SacObe | SecEma/ SacObe | Institutions | Secular Values | Emancipative values | GDP per capita (PPP) |
|---|---|---|---|---|---|---|---|
| 0 | NN | NN | NN | NN | NN | NN | NN |
| 10 | NN | NN | NN | NN | NN | NN | NN |
| 20 | NN | NN | NN | NN | NN | NN | 0.8 |
| 30 | NN | NN | NN | 7.3 | NN | NN | 2.5 |
| 40 | 1.7 | NN | NN | 21.4 | NN | 0.0 | 7.9 |
| 50 | 22.7 | 39.5 | 38.2 | 44.5 | 31.0 | 25.3 | 30.8 |
| 60 | 22.7 | 51.4 | 42.7 | 44.5 | 41.8 | 25.3 | 30.8 |
| 70 | 49.5 | 61.6 | 70.3 | 84.7 | 55.8 | 57.2 | 55.2 |
| 80 | 49.5 | 64.2 | 72.0 | 89.4 | 56.9 | 57.2 | 55.2 |
| 90 | 74.4 | 64.2 | 75.8 | 89.4 | 56.9 | 78.5 | 69.3 |
| 100 | 96.9 | 90.5 | 100.0 | 97.6 | 82.0 | 97.7 | 71.4 |

*Note:* * Values are the percentage ranges of the variables; NN = not necessary; PPP = purchasing power parity.

value compositions) on two different data sets: first, on the complete data (N=105), and second on data where the levels of governance exceeded 40% of its range, as indicated by the bottleneck table. This second set of models provides a robustness check on conclusions drawn across the two methods, NCA and regression (Richter et al., 2020).

For the models run on complete data, the fit of the alternative perspective is notably better than that of the model for the standard perspective. The Akaike Information Criterion for the alternative model is 74.15 versus 81.00 for the standard model, where lower values of this criterion are preferred, and the difference between the two criterion values implies the standard model is 0.03 times as probable to minimize information loss as the alternative model, that is, highly unlikely. However, even more striking is that the only significant coefficient for the standard model is that for the institutional control; the coefficients for secular and emancipative values are not significant. In contrast, while the institutional control remains significant in the alternative perspective, so do the coefficients for the compositional components. In the presence of controls, the standard model of culture does not add to the explanation of governance, whereas the alternative model does.

With one exception, these conclusions also hold for the results of the robustness check shown in the right-hand columns of Figure 2.4. The coefficients for secular and emancipative values in the standard model remain insignificant,

| | Generalized Linear Model* | | | | | | | |
|---|---|---|---|---|---|---|---|---|
| | Complete data, N = 105** | | | | *Governance* > Bottleneck Level of 40%, N = 47 | | | |
| **Construct** | **Coefficient** | **t value** | **Pr(>\|t\|)** | **@ 0.05** | **Coefficient** | **t value** | **Pr(>\|t\|)** | **@ 0.05** |
| **Standard Perspective (Country Value Averages)** | | | | | | | | |
| Intercept | 0.25 | 23.48 | 0.00 | yes | 0.24 | 25.82 | 0.00 | yes |
| *Secular Values* | -0.01 | -0.46 | 0.65 | no | -0.03 | -1.16 | 0.25 | no |
| *Emancipative Values* | 0.00 | 0.06 | 0.95 | no | 0.04 | 1.77 | 0.08 | no |
| *Institutions* | 0.03 | 8.08 | 0.00 | yes | 0.02 | 3.52 | 0.00 | yes |
| *GDP* | 1.88E-7 | 0.91 | 0.37 | no | 3.28E-7 | 1.74 | 0.09 | no |
| | AIC*** = 81.00<br>Null deviance 2.77 on 104 degrees of freedom<br>Residual deviance 0.61 on 100 degrees of freedom | | | | AIC = 15.65<br>Null deviance 0.53 on 46 degrees of freedom<br>Residual deviance 0.12 on 42 degrees of freedom | | | |
| **Alternative Perspective (Country Value Compositions)** | | | | | | | | |
| Intercept | 0.25 | 43.09 | 0.00 | yes | 0.23 | 39.74 | 0.00 | yes |
| *SacEma/SacObe* | 0.08 | 2.98 | 0.00 | yes | 0.07 | 2.68 | 0.01 | yes |
| *SecObe/SacObe* | 0.09 | 2.88 | 0.01 | yes | 0.07 | 2.28 | 0.03 | yes |
| *SecEma/SacObe* | -0.09 | -2.98 | 0.00 | yes | -0.08 | 2.41 | 0.02 | yes |
| *Institutions* | 0.03 | 7.89 | 0.00 | yes | 0.02 | 3.74 | 0.00 | yes |
| *GDP* | 3.68E-7 | 1.77 | 0.08 | no | 4.50E-7 | 2.43 | 0.02 | yes |
| | AIC = 74.15<br>Null deviance 2.77 on 104 degrees of freedom<br>Residual deviance 0.56 on 99 degrees of freedom | | | | AIC = 11.11<br>Null deviance 0.53 on 46 degrees of freedom<br>Residual deviance 0.10 on 41 degrees of freedom | | | |

*Note:* * Estimated with the Gamma error family and an inverse link function for a positive and skewed dependent variable (i.e., Y ~ 1/X). Signs for coefficients and t-values are reversed here for interpretability (i.e., Y ~ X). ** With six outliers excluded. *** Akaike's information criterion (AIC). These can only be compared when based on the same data, that is, between the two perspectives, and not between the complete data and the data above the bottleneck level.

*Figure 2.4* *Regression results*

and hence, as before institutions is the sole significant predictor of governance in this model. For the alternative model, the coefficients for the three compositional components and institutions remain significant and have the same signs as for the complete data. The one exception is that the coefficient for the *GDP* control becomes significant at these higher levels of governance.

Figure 2.5 contrasts the complete data results from Figure 2.4 with those derived from a generalized linear model using the same data but with the dependent outcome based on the narrower value maximization definition of governance. Essentially, the results for value maximization are identical to those for governance in terms of the conclusions that would be drawn from the coefficients and the comparison of the standard and alternative perspectives on culture. As before, the coefficients for secular and emancipative value averages are not significant in the standard perspective, whereas they are for the value compositions in the alternative perspective, albeit with probabilities < 0.05 as opposed to < 0.01 for the broader definition. Since the dependent variables of the two models are defined differently, we cannot use the AIC to compare their relative fit, so we use the log likelihood instead, with the least negative likelihood preferred. These show that the value compositions, while statistically significant, provide a weaker explanation of value maximization than they do

| | *Governance** | | | *Value Maximization*** | | |
|---|---|---|---|---|---|---|
| **Construct** | **Coefficient** | **t value** | **Pr (>\|t\|)** | **Coefficient** | **t value** | **Pr (>\|t\|)** |
| **Standard Perspective (Country Value Averages)** | | | | | | |
| *Intercept* | 0.25 | 23.48 | 0.00 | 0.23 | 22.33 | 0.00 |
| *Secular Values* | -0.01 | -0.46 | 0.65 | -0.00 | -0.02 | 0.98 |
| *Emancipative Values* | 0.00 | 0.06 | 0.95 | -0.01 | -0.29 | 0.78 |
| *Institutions* | 0.03 | 8.08 | 0.00 | 0.03 | 8.22 | 0.00 |
| *GDP* | 1.88E-7 | 0.91 | 0.37 | -6.76E-8 | -0.33 | 0.74 |
| | | | | | | |
| Log Likelihood | -34.50 | | | -41.20 | | |
| **Alternative Perspective (Country Value Compositions)** | | | | | | |
| *Intercept* | 0.25 | 43.09 | 0.00 | 0.23 | 39.77 | 0.00 |
| *SacEma/SacObe* | 0.08 | 2.98 | 0.00 | 0.06 | 2.13 | 0.04 |
| *SecObe/SacObe* | 0.09 | 2.88 | 0.01 | 0.07 | 2.14 | 0.04 |
| *SecEma/SacObe* | -0.09 | -2.98 | 0.00 | -0.07 | -2.17 | 0.03 |
| *Institutions* | 0.03 | 7.89 | 0.00 | 0.03 | 7.97 | 0.00 |
| *GDP* | 3.68E-7 | 1.77 | 0.08 | 6.23E-8 | 0.30 | 0.77 |
| | | | | | | |
| Log Likelihood | -30.08 | | | -38.82 | | |

*Note:* * Defined on the full set of seven items shown in Table 2.2. 2** Defined on a narrower set of four items, namely auditing and accounting standards, efficacy of corporate boards, reliance on professional boards, and protection of minority shareholders.

*Figure 2.5 Comparison between the two alternative definitions of the dependent variable*

for governance (log likelihood of –38.82 for the narrower definition versus –30.08 for the broader).

One possible reason for this weaker explanation is that the bottleneck table for value maximization (not shown) identifies a threshold of 60% for the country value compositions compared with 40% for governance as discussed above. Hence the connection between the compositions and governance manifests itself over a smaller range for value maximization than for governance. Notwithstanding this, the two definitions produce essentially identical results, suggesting the identified effects are robust.

## 5. DISCUSSION

In Figure 2.6 we summarize the results for NCA and the generalized linear model on the template we adapted from Richter et al. (2020). We also follow their advice on drawing overall conclusions from the various result scenarios we have here. Overall, these indicate that secular and emancipative values are a necessary condition for governance above 40% of its range. However, there is no impact of these cultural values in the regressions, suggesting that the standard perspective simply provides a threshold at which national averages on these values matter.

In contrast, with the alternative compositional perspective, the three components have an average and additive regression effect throughout the range of

| **Construct** | **Regression Results** | **NCA Results** | **Conclusion** |
|---|---|---|---|
| **Standard Perspective (Country Value Averages)** | | | |
| *Secular Values* are a | nonsignificant determinant* | but a necessary condition** | a level above 40% is necessary for *Governance* to manifest.*** |
| *Emancipative Values* are a | nonsignificant determinant | but a necessary condition | a level above 40% is necessary for *Governance* to manifest. |
| **Alternative Perspective (Country Value Compositions)** | | | |
| *SacEma/SacObe* | significant determinant | and a necessary condition | On average, an increase in *SacEma/SacObe* or *SecObe/SacObe* will increase *Governance*. Whereas an increase in *SecEma/SacObe* will decrease *Governance*.**** For *SacEma/SacObe* and *SecEma/SacObe* levels of above 40% are necessary for *Governance* to manifest. For *SecObe/SacObe* no minimum level is needed. |
| *SecObe/SacObe* | significant determinant | but not a necessary condition | |
| *SecEma/SacObe* | significant determinant | and a necessary condition | |
| **Controls** | | | |
| *Institutions* | significant determinant | and a necessary condition | On average, an increase in *Institutions* will increase *Governance*. However, a level above 20% is necessary for *Governance* to manifest. |
| *GDP* | nonsignificant determinant | but a necessary condition | a level above 20% is necessary for *Governance* to manifest. |

*Note:* * From Figure 2.4 generalized linear model t-value significance. ** From Figure 2.3 effect size significance. *** From Table 2.4 bottleneck levels. **** See the text for a discussion of the relationship between the three components.

*Figure 2.6 Summary of results for governance*

governance. One of the three, *SecObe/SacObe*, is also a necessary condition throughout the range, whereas the other two become necessary conditions at the level of 40%.

Given the importance of the 40% threshold, and to interpret the changes in the country compositions, we calculated simple averages for these at five broad levels of governance, as shown in Table 2.5.

*Table 2.5 Average compositions by level of governance*

| **Level of governance** | **Range of governance** | **Number of observations** | **Necessary condition** | **SacObe** | **SacEma** | **SecObe** | **SecEma** |
|---|---|---|---|---|---|---|---|
| 20% | (3.25, 3.83) | 20 | No | 0.38* (0.08)** | 0.22 (0.05) | 0.24 (0.05) | 0.16 (0.05) |
| 40% | (3.83, 4.41) | 38 | No | 0.38 (0.11) | 0.24 (0.05) | 0.21 (0.05) | 0.16 (0.06) |
| 60% | (4.41, 4.99) | 22 | Yes | 0.35 (0.13) | 0.24 (0.05) | 0.23 (0.07) | 0.19 (0.07) |
| 80% | (4.99, 5.57) | 12 | Yes | 0.26 (0.08) | 0.30 (0.08) | 0.20 (0.07) | 0.24 (0.05) |
| 100% | (5.57, 6.15) | 13 | Yes | 0.19 (0.05) | 0.36 (0.06) | 0.15 (0.03) | 0.30 (0.04) |

*Note:* * Average compositional weight for countries at this level of governance. ** Standard deviations in parenthesis.

There is indeed a noticeable shift at 40%, with a decrease in the weight for the base *SacObe* component and an increase in the *SecEma* component in the 40% to 60% category, a component that becomes more pronounced at higher levels of governance. The *SacEma* component also increases above 60%, and the *SacObe* and *SecObe* components become less important at these levels. Overall, countries with higher levels of governance are more emancipated, but the important nuance provided by the alternative perspective is that their more emancipated citizens include both those who trust and those who are more skeptical of authority.

That said, there is also heterogeneity in the compositions at each level of governance (as shown by the standard deviations in Table 2.5). This heterogeneity, and the interlinked relationships between the compositional components, suggest the idea of equifinality. That is, any level of governance may be associated with different compositions. This we demonstrate in Table 2.6, which looks at the frontier of global corporate governance in our data, the five countries with the highest value of governance we observed. For example, if we compare the top ranked country, Sweden, with its neighbor and second ranked country, Finland, we see considerable differences in their compositions, particularly in the weights for *SacObe* and *SecEma*. Yet both achieve the highest levels of corporate governance.

The contrasting results from the standard and alternative perspectives underline the significance of considering cultural values in heterogeneous contexts in corporate governance research. While the standard view suggests cultural values set a threshold for corporate governance, the alternative perspective emphasizes the relevance of micro-level cultural nuances. This insight is crucial, as it suggests that governance is influenced not just by dominant national values but also by the diverse cultural segments within a nation.

Future research should focus on exploring these compositional differences and their implications for governance, which could further refine our

*Table 2.6 Examples of equifinality at the frontier*

| Country | Governance* | Institutions* | SacObe** | SacEma** | SecObe** | SecEma** |
|---|---|---|---|---|---|---|
| Sweden | 100 | 97 | 0.11 | 0.37 | 0.14 | 0.38 |
| Finland | 99 | 98 | 0.19 | 0.39 | 0.13 | 0.28 |
| Denmark | 98 | 100 | 0.21 | 0.41 | 0.13 | 0.25 |
| Switzerland | 97 | 96 | 0.17 | 0.36 | 0.15 | 0.32 |
| Netherlands | 96 | 96 | 0.17 | 0.36 | 0.16 | 0.32 |

*Note:* * Percentiles of the construct distribution. ** Weight of the archetype in the country composition.

understanding of the relationship between culture and corporate governance practices. Since our results suggest equifinality, one logical extension would be to apply the configurational causal logic to our data, using the qualitative comparative analysis (QCA) technique (Ragin, 1987) to establish this inference on a firmer basis. Another would be to look at temporal changes. MVC shows that the cultural value compositions of many of the countries in their analysis have changed considerably over four decades. While our current data set is limited in sample size and time span, it is hoped that as further waves of the World Value Survey become available, it may be possible to associate changes in cultural values with changes in corporate governance. Finally, our measures of governance are perceptions—expert perceptions—but nonetheless essentially subjective measures derived from individuals. It might therefore be useful to confirm our results through other measures of governance, such as those provided by rating agencies.

## NOTES

1. We gratefully acknowledge financial support for our work from the INSEAD Hoffmann Institute and the University of Queensland.
2. We are grateful to a reviewer for suggesting that we clarify this point.
3. We are grateful to a reviewer for suggesting that the comparison of the two definitions of governance would make a useful addition to our chapter.
4. https://data.worldbank.org/indicator/NY.GDP.PCAP.PP.KD

## REFERENCES

Aitchison, J. (1982). The statistical analysis of compositional data. *Journal of the Royal Statistical Society: Series B (Methodological)*, 44(2), 139–160.

Clarke, T. (2007). *International corporate governance: A comparative approach*. Routledge.

Cutler, A., & Breiman, L. (1994). Archetypal analysis. *Technometrics*, 36(4), 338–347.

Dheer, R. J., Lenartowicz, T., & Peterson, M. F. (2015). Mapping India's regional subcultures: Implications for international management. *Journal of International Business Studies*, 46, 443–467.

Donaldson, T., & Preston, L. (1995). The stakeholder theory of the corporation: concepts, evidence, and implications. *Academy of Management Review*, 20, 65-91.

Dul, J. (2016). Necessary condition analysis (NCA) logic and methodology of "necessary but not sufficient" causality. *Organizational Research Methods*, 19(1), 10–52.

Dul, J. (2021). Advances in necessary condition analysis. https://bookdown.org/ncabook/advanced_nca2/

Filatotchev, I. & Nakajima, C. (2014). Corporate governance, responsible managerial behavior, and corporate social responsibility: Organizational efficiency versus organizational legitimacy? *Academy of Management Perspectives*, 28, 289–306.

Friedman, M. (1970). The social responsibility of a business is to increase its profits. New York Times Magazine, 13 September, 122-126.
Hofstede, G. (1984). *Culture's consequences: International differences in work-related values* (Vol. 5). Sage publications.
Hofstede, G. (2001). *Culture's consequences: Comparing values, behaviors, institutions and organizations across nations*. Sage publications.
Hofstede, G., Hofstede, G. J., & Minkov, M. (2010). *Cultures and organizations: Software of the mind: Intercultural cooperation and its importance for survival*. McGraw-Hill.
Inglehart, R., & Welzel, C. (2005). *Modernization, cultural change, and democracy: The human development sequence* (Vol. 333). Cambridge University Press.
Inglehart, R., & Welzel, C. (2010). Changing mass priorities: The link between modernization and democracy. *Perspectives on Politics*, 8(2), 551–567.
Inglehart, R., Haerpfer, C., Moreno, A., Welzel, C., Kizilova, K., Diez-Medrano J., Lagos, M., Norris, P., Ponarin, E., & Puranen, B. (2020). World values survey: All rounds – country-pooled datafile. Madrid, Spain & Vienna, Austria: JD Systems Institute & WVSA Secretariat. http://www.worldvaluessurvey.org/WVSDocumentationWVL.jsp
Jensen, M.C. (2001). Value maximization, stakeholder theory, and the corporate objective function. Journal of Applied Corporate Finance, 14(3), 8-21.
Kaufmann, D., Kraay, A., & Mastruzzi, M. (2011). The worldwide governance indicators: Methodology and analytical issues 1. *Hague Journal on the Rule of Law*, 3(2), 220–246.
McSweeney, B. (2002). Hofstede's model of national cultural differences and their consequences: A triumph of faith – a failure of analysis. *Human Relations*, 55(1), 89–118.
MVC [Midgley, D., Venaik, S., & Christopoulos, D.] (2023). *A new theory of cultural archetypes: Capturing global unity and local diversity*. Springer Nature.
Politis, D. N., Romano, J. P., & Wolf, M. (1999). *Subsampling*. Springer Science & Business Media.
Ragin, C. C. (1987). *The comparative method: Moving beyond qualitative and quantitative strategies*. University of California Press.
Richter, N. F., & Hauff, S. (2022). Necessary condition analysis in international business—advancing the field with a new perspective on causality and data analysis. *Journal of World Business*, 57 (5), 101310.
Richter, N. F., Schubring, S., Hauff, S., Ringle, C. M., & Sarstedt, M. (2020). When predictors of outcomes are necessary: Guidelines for the combined use of PLS-SEM and NCA. *Industrial Management and Data Systems*, 120(12), 2243–2267.
Roe, M. J., & Vatiero, M. (2018). Corporate governance and its political economy. In J. N. Gordon & W.-G. Ringe (eds), *Oxford Handbook of Corporate Law and Governance* (pp. 56–83). Oxford University Press.
Schwab, K. (2018). *The global competitiveness report 2018*. World Economic Forum.
Steel, P., & Taras, V. (2010). Culture as a consequence: A multi-level multivariate meta-analysis of the effects of individual and country characteristics on work-related cultural values. *Journal of International Management*, 16(3), 211–233.
Venaik, S., & Midgley, D. F. (2015). Mindscapes across landscapes: Archetypes of transnational and subnational culture. *Journal of International Business Studies*, 46, 1051–1079.
Welzel, C. (2013). *Freedom rising*. Cambridge University Press.

# 3. Redefining boardroom dynamics: the rising impact of generation X directors

**Zhaozhao He, Mihail K. Miletkov and Viktoriya Staneva**

## 1. GENERATION X: SHAPING THE FUTURE OF CORPORATE LEADERSHIP

As Generation X steps firmly into leadership roles within corporate boardrooms, their distinct approach is setting a new course for how companies operate and strategize. Born in an era of unprecedented technological advancements and social change, these directors bring a fresh perspective to corporate governance.

For example, since Marissa Mayer (a Gen Xer and former CEO of Yahoo!) joined Walmart's board in 2012, Walmart has made significant efforts to build its e-commerce platform. Mrs Mayer, an innovative director for a traditional brick-and-mortar retailer, stated upon joining Walmart's board: "I look forward to contributing to Walmart's continued growth, success, and innovation in the years to come." Indeed, Walmart has now risen as an e-commerce giant, challenging Amazon's leading position in the e-commerce field.[1]

Mrs Mayer's extensive experience in technology and product development stemming from her high-profile roles at Google and later as CEO of Yahoo! positioned her as a valuable advocate for Walmart's transition into digital retail. At the time of her appointment, Walmart was in the early stages of developing its e-commerce strategy, recognizing the need to adapt to a shifting retail landscape increasingly dominated by online giants like Amazon. During Mayer's tenure, Walmart invested heavily in expanding its digital footprint, including acquiring the e-commerce company Jet.com in 2016 for $3.3 billion. The Jet.com acquisition was a pivotal moment in Walmart's strategy, helping support the firm's growing e-commerce ambitions. Mayer's presence on the board underscored Walmart's commitment to modernizing its approach and embracing digital transformation, demonstrating how Gen X leaders with tech-centric expertise can guide established companies through critical transitions in the digital age.

Another prominent Gen X business leader is Mellody Hobson, the first Black woman to chair the board of a Fortune 500 company. A board member at Starbucks since 2005, Hobson served as vice-chair from 2018 to March 2021 and as board chair until September 2024, when she transitioned to the role of lead independent director. Under her leadership, Starbucks launched the Environmental, Partner, and Community Impact Committee to enhance governance and strengthen the company's commitment to transparency and sustainability. Hobson is also an avid advocate for diversity, equity, and inclusion, having established multiple initiatives, including tying executive pay to diversity goals, launching a mentorship program for employees of color, and embedding anti-bias practices across hiring and performance assessments. Hobson's accomplishments exemplify the progressive approach Gen X directors bring to governance, merging profitability goals with social impact.

Motivated by these examples, our recent study, "New Kids on the Block: The Effect of Generation X Directors on Corporate Performance" (He, Miletkov, and Staneva, 2023), documents the arrival of this new generation of corporate directors and shows that this shift is not merely a change in demographics, but a transformative movement towards a more inclusive, innovative, and socially responsible business environment. Analyzing the evolution of US corporate boardrooms from 2007 to 2017, we reveal the rising influence of Gen Xers and highlight their significant contribution to firm performance and strategic direction.

In this chapter, we provide a summary of the key findings and implications from our study. Rather than delving into the technical details, we offer a high-level overview of the main aspects of our research. Additionally, we discuss the broader impact of our study on the corporate governance literature and outline future research avenues inspired by our findings.

The study begins by examining the shifts in the composition of US corporate boards over the 20-year period from 1996 to 2017. As illustrated in Figure 3.1, corporate boards have been dominated by baby boomers since the turn of the century. This period also marks the gradual entry of a new generation of directors – Gen Xers – into boardrooms. By the end of our sample period, approximately 22% of board seats were held by these "new kids on the block," inspiring our interest in the impact of this generational shift on the corporate world.

This era coincides with other notable trends in board composition. As shown in Figure 3.2, alongside the growing influence of Gen X directors, representation of women and people of color on corporate boards has also increased. At the beginning of the century, only 8% of board seats were held by female directors and just 4% by non-white directors. By 2017, these numbers had more than doubled, reaching 18% and 10%, respectively.

Our study proceeds by examining the effect of these changing board dynamics on firm performance. As shown in Figure 3.3, we identify significant differences between boards with Gen X directors and those composed entirely of

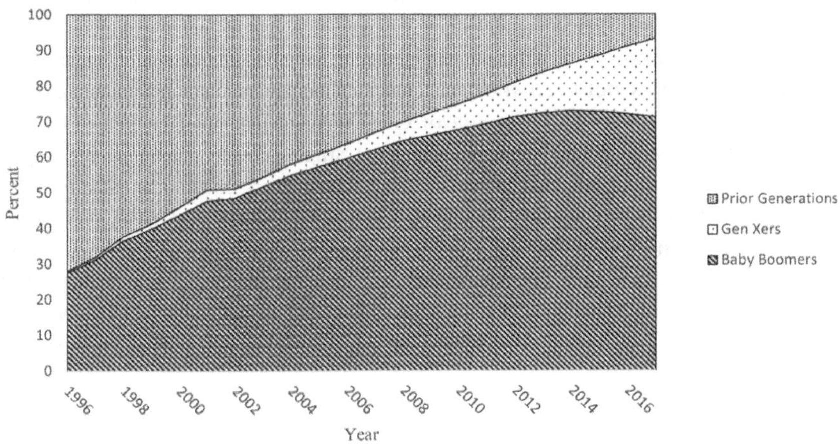


*Figure 3.1* *Distribution of directors' generation*

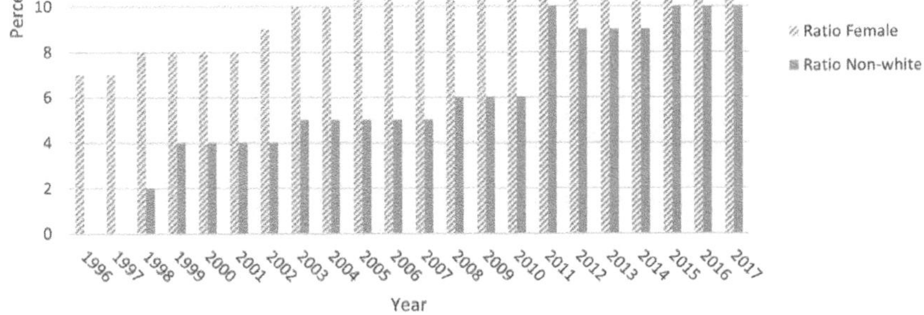


*Figure 3.2* *Female and non-white directors*

baby boomers and older generations. Our univariate analysis reveals that firms with Gen X directors exhibit notably higher market-to-book ratios and return on assets than firms without Gen X representation. Additionally, the two subsamples differ across other key characteristics: boards with Gen X members tend to have greater gender and racial diversity, with more female directors and directors of color. Furthermore, firms with Gen X directors are more likely to have younger CEOs, female CEOs, and are less likely to have a CEO who also serves as chairman of the board.

In fact, we uncover significant differences across almost all board and firm characteristics between the two types of firms, which underscores the importance of analyzing the impact of Gen X directors on firm performance using a multivariate framework. In the next stage of our analysis, we apply robust empirical strategies to examine these dynamics comprehensively. Our findings confirm a strong link between Gen X directors and improved firm performance, which persists even after accounting for various director characteristics, including age, gender, ethnicity, and professional expertise. This suggests that the generational identity of corporate directors is an important, yet underexplored, dimension of board diversity within the corporate governance literature.

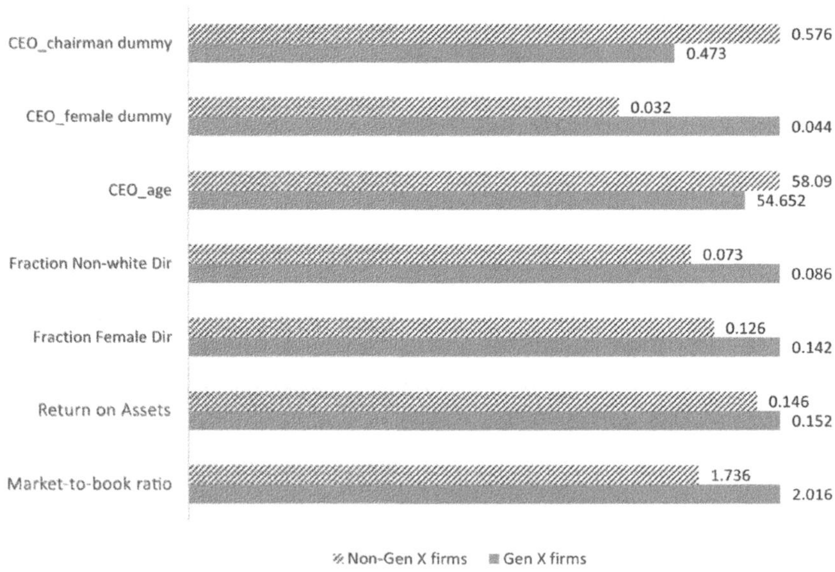


*Figure 3.3 Differences between Gen X and non-Gen X firms*

Looking beyond the impact on overall firm performance and value, we find that Generation X directors are instrumental in integrating corporate social responsibility (CSR) into core business strategies, advancing gender diversity and inclusion, and fostering a culture of innovation. These results indicate that Generation X directors are generating value for the corporations that they serve by emphasizing values that resonate with changing societal expectations.

A key feature of our study is distinguishing the influence of generational identity from the effects associated with age, underscoring the importance of the former to research in corporate governance. This distinction is crucial to understanding the unique perspective that Gen Xers bring to the boardroom, which is shaped by their formative experiences and the historical context within which they came of age. We show that the unique perspective of Gen Xers is a valuable asset in navigating the complex demands of the modern business environment.

This research makes an important contribution to the corporate governance literature. Specifically, prior corporate governance studies have largely emphasized individual characteristics such as gender, ethnicity, and professional expertise as drivers of board diversity and firm performance (e.g., Farrell and Hersch, 2005; Adams and Ferreira, 2009; Ferreira, 2010; Miletkov, Poulsen, and Wintoki, 2017) but have overlooked generational identity as a potential determinant. To the best of our knowledge, our study is the first to demonstrate that Gen X directors, shaped by early exposure to technology and evolving societal norms around diversity and social responsibility, contribute positively to firm value. We also contribute to the literature on CSR and corporate innovation by documenting that the value implications of firms' ESG and innovation activities are enhanced by the presence of Gen X directors. The results from our study also have implications for the vast literature on board gender diversity, where empirical work examining the relationship between female representation on the board and corporate performance remains inconclusive (Adams and Ferreira, 2009; Ahern and Dittmar, 2012; Levi, Li, and Zhang, 2014; Greene, Intintoli, and Kahle, 2020). Our findings suggest that female directors' contributions to firm value are conditional on the presence of Gen X directors, who are less susceptible to tokenism and are more likely to foster an inclusive board culture.

## 2. THE UNIQUE PERSPECTIVE OF GENERATION X

Each generation exhibits specific attributes that are associated with the early-life experiences that helped shape the peer personality of its members.[2] For Generation X, their formative years coincided with significant cultural and economic shifts that included the changing role of women in society, the rise of CSR, and the advancement of the knowledge economy precipitated by technological innovation. The skills and perspectives that Generation X acquired as a result of experiencing these events during the formative years of their lives are particularly relevant to the challenges and opportunities that businesses face today.

One of the key attributes of Generation X is their comfort with technology and change. Having witnessed the dawn of the digital era, they are better equipped to navigate the complexities of a knowledge and technology-driven business environment. This tech-savviness, combined with a pragmatic approach to problem-solving, makes them valuable assets in firms increasingly focused on innovation. Another key attribute of Generation X is the appreciation of the value of diversity and inclusion in business, as well as the recognition of the changing societal expectations toward CSR. Our study's findings indicate that this worldview of Gen Xers is reflected in their approach to corporate governance, where they advocate for practices that align with contemporary business ethics and societal expectations.

## 3. UNLOCKING VALUE: THE X-FACTOR IN THE BOARDROOM

The empirical analysis in our study begins with an examination of the influence of Gen X directors on firm performance, specifically analyzing the market-to-book ratio as a common proxy for firm value in the corporate finance literature. We estimate the following model with the firm's market-to-book ratio (MB) in the next year as the dependent variable:

$$MB_{i,t+1} = \alpha + \beta_1 Fraction\ Gen\ X\ Directors_{i,t} + \beta' X_{i,t} + y_j + d_t + \varepsilon_{i,t} \quad (3.1)$$

where $i$ indexes firms and $t$ indexes years. The key variable of interest is *Fraction Gen X Directors*, the fraction of Gen X directors sitting on the board. $X$ is a vector of control variables to account for CEO- and board-level characteristics, including demographics and firm financial metrics. Industry and year fixed effects ($y_j$ and $d_t$) are also included to account for any industry-specific or macroeconomic factors that could be affecting the overall performance of firms. Among the control variables are the median director age as well as the age diversity of the board in order to distinguish the effects of generational identity from the effects of directors' age. As we find an overlap between the presence of Gen X directors on the board and younger CEOs, we also include CEO age as an independent variable in the model and account for CEO generation fixed effects. In additional tests, we completely exclude firms with Gen X CEOs from the sample to ensure that we are capturing a true Gen X effect in the boardroom as opposed to a CEO generation effect.

The main findings, derived from estimating our baseline model equation (3.1) with ordinary least squares regressions, reveal a significant positive correlation between the fraction of Gen X directors and firm value. This relation persists despite accounting for the wide range of board- and firm-level characteristics, underscoring the distinct contribution of Gen X directors to firm performance. The effect is also economically significant – a one standard deviation increase in the fraction of Gen X directors implies an increase in the market-to-book ratio next year equal to 6.3% of its mean value (or 7.7% of its median value).

To address potential endogeneity concerns and ensure that our results are not confounded by unobserved firm characteristics or selection bias, we also employ firm fixed effects estimation, propensity score matching, and instrumental variable (IV) analysis. The firm fixed effects account for time-invariant firm characteristics, alleviating the concern that the generational effect is driven by some omitted firm characteristic that is fixed over time. As there are fundamental differences between firms with and without Gen X directors, a potential concern is that the Gen X effect might be driven by some other firm attributes. To mitigate these concerns, we employ a propensity score matching approach. We first model the probability of having a Gen X director and then construct a matched sample using the nearest-neighbor method. We find that firms with Gen X directors on the board have a market-to-book ratio that is approximately 5% higher than that of (otherwise similar) firms without Gen X directors. This result is robust to regression estimations with firm fixed effects.

Another concern is that the presence of Gen X directors might be correlated with time-varying unobserved firm-level factors. There is also a potential reverse causality issue that could mask the true effect that Gen X directors have on firm performance. For example, better performance could make it easier for firms to attract director talent, including Gen X directors. To tackle these potential issues, we perform instrumental variables IV analysis. Our first instrumental variable is inspired by the idea that over our sample period, the social networks that link directors are comprised mostly of baby boomers, a group with which Gen X directors had few opportunities to form connections with. We thus argue that the more connected non-Gen X directors on a certain board are to Gen X directors, the higher the presence of Gen Xers should be on that board. We therefore define our first IV as the fraction of non-Gen X directors on the board of a focal firm who serve, or have served in the past, with a Gen X director on another firm's board. The second IV that we use is the average number of Gen X directors in the state of the firm's headquarters, as a firm operating in a geographical area with a higher presence of Gen Xers on corporate boards is more likely to have board members of that generation because of a greater supply of such directors. Our first stage regressions demonstrate that both IVs are positively correlated with the fraction of Gen X directors on the focal firm's board. In the second stage estimations, we consistently find a strong and positive relationship between the fraction of Gen X directors on the board and firm performance.

This extensive set of additional tests reinforces our main findings, indicating a strong, positive relation between Generation X directors and firm performance, independent of other factors. Overall, our main results present compelling evidence of the value added by Generation X directors in US corporate boardrooms.

## 4. GENERATION VERSUS AGE EFFECT

Despite our efforts to isolate the impact of generational identity from that of directors' age by including the age metrics of the board in the regression model, some concerns remain. For example, if there is a nonlinear effect of directors' age on performance, and having *substantially* younger directors on the board, irrespective of their generational identity, leads to better firm performance, then our Generation X variable could still be simply capturing an age effect.

To completely disentangle the generational effect from the age effect, one would need to compare the performance effect of Gen X directors to that of non-Gen X directors of similar age. This is only possible by going back in time when another generation of young directors was being appointed to corporate boards. We do this by comparing the impact of Gen X directors to that of baby boomers, using data from 1996–97 when baby boomers were the "new kids on the block" and data from 2016–17 when Gen Xers were in that role. Our findings reveal a marked positive impact on firm performance uniquely associated with Gen X directors, an effect not observed with baby boomers during their earlier years in the boardroom. This analysis underscores the point that the advantages brought by Gen X directors stem from their distinct generational traits, formed by the unique experiences and the era they grew up in, rather than just their youth.

## 5. DRIVING VALUE THROUGH CSR

Having established the positive influence of Gen X directors on overall firm performance, we delve into some of the possible channels through which this effect could be propagated. To that end, we analyze the major societal and economic changes that took place during the formative years of Gen X directors and how those changes may influence their focus and decision-making as board members.

The first channel we identify considers the value added through CSR. Gen X's formative years were characterized by a growing emphasis on ethical corporate behavior, making CSR a natural focus area for this new generation of corporate leaders. Specifically, we use an interaction term to examine the impact of Gen X directors on the relationship between the firm's environmental and social scores (a common proxy for CSR in the finance literature) and firm performance. Our findings reveal a clear pattern: firms with Gen X directors exhibit a significant positive link between their CSR scores and firm performance, a trend not observed in firms without Gen X directors.

To address potential endogeneity and establish the causal interpretation of these results, we utilize a two-stage least squares approach, using the aforementioned variables to instrument for the presence of Gen X directors. This refined analysis confirms the conclusion that Gen X directors effectively integrate CSR into their firms' value-creation strategies.

Our study highlights the unique role of Gen X directors in championing CSR initiatives that not only align with the changing societal expectations toward business but also enhance firm value. These results underscore the strategic importance of generational insights in corporate governance.

## 6. DRIVING VALUE THROUGH DIVERSITY AND INCLUSION

The increased representation of Gen X directors in corporate boardrooms coincides with significant societal shifts that focus on gender equality and diversity and inclusion. While research in finance on the relationship between gender diversity and firm performance provides mixed results, our study documents an important moderating effect that Gen X directors have on this relationship.

Having grown up during a time of changing norms around women's roles in society, we hypothesize that Gen X directors might be more attuned to the value of gender diversity and inclusion in business organizations. Consistent with that idea, we find that firms with Gen X directors show a positive relation between boardroom gender diversity and firm value, indicating that these directors may help mitigate tokenism and harvest the benefits of diverse perspectives through inclusion. Additionally, our findings indicate that Gen X directors help promote gender diversity and pay equality among the firm's top five highest-paid executives, further highlighting their direct role in promoting diversity and inclusion as a strategic asset for the organization.

## 7. DRIVING VALUE THROUGH INNOVATION IN THE KNOWLEDGE ECONOMY

In the transformative digital age of the 1980s and 1990s, Gen X emerged as the first cohort to embrace personal computing and the internet. These early-life experiences fundamentally shaped their approach to technology and innovation and made them especially valuable for firms that engage in knowledge-intensive activities. Our study finds that the positive relation between Gen X directors and firm performance is stronger in firms that invest more in research and development and engage in patenting activity. We also document a direct positive link between Gen X directors and the economic value of innovation, using the stock market's reaction to announcements of granted patents as a proxy. These results highlight the strategic advantage that Gen Xers bring to firms, helping them succeed in the fast-paced knowledge economy.

## 8. EMBRACING CHANGE AND UNCERTAINTY – GENERATION X AND BEYOND

*"One generation passeth away, and another generation cometh: but the earth abideth forever."*

– Ecclesiastes 1:4

The most unique aspect of generational identity when compared to other director characteristics is that a generation is "born, lives, and dies."[3] Therefore, each generation has a unique and unrepeatable opportunity to make an impact on the world around it. There is also a sense of inevitability about generational shifts in society and business. Currently, we are witnessing the gradual retirement of baby boomers and the rise of Gen Xers, who will eventually come to dominate corporate boardrooms. In due time, a similar process will result in millennials becoming "the new kids on the block," bringing their own perspectives and worldview to the organizations they join and ultimately lead.

Our research illustrates the impact that Gen X directors are already having on companies in the US. We highlight their unique contributions to corporate performance through a shift towards a more responsible, inclusive, and innovative approach to business. As such, our study lays the foundation for a new avenue of research on the effects of the generational identity of company leaders on corporate strategies, and there is much more to be explored and discovered in this fascinating area.

It is important to note that our research does not indicate that one generation is necessarily better than another. Similar to other types of corporate directors – female directors, foreign directors, non-white directors, busy directors, directors with financial or entrepreneurial backgrounds, and so on – Gen Xers come with certain benefits that can be value-enhancing for some firms but also have certain costs that prevent them from being value-enhancing for all firms. Ultimately, firms weigh the costs and benefits of appointing different types of directors – including Gen Xers – conditional on their contracting environment.

Over the next several years, the younger generations of millennials and Gen Z will enter into leadership roles in the corporate world, and they will bring their own values, expectations, and challenges to the boardroom. They will undoubtedly shape the future of corporate America in their own ways. For instance, millennials and Gen Z are even more socially conscious, environmentally aware, and globally connected than their predecessors. They may seek more autonomy, flexibility, and purpose in their work, as well as hold firms to a higher standard of ethical conduct. Future research could focus on studying the unique attributes of these generations and how they impact various company outcomes.

Another possible direction for future research is to compare and contrast the generational effects across different countries and cultures and to explore the implications for global business leadership. As we have noted, generational identity is not a universal construct but rather a relative and contextual one, depending on the historical and cultural experiences that shape the peer personalities of people associated with a particular generation. Therefore, it is important to understand how generational differences vary across regions and cultures and how companies can leverage this generational diversity to create value and competitive advantage in today's dynamic business environment.

Lastly, an interesting area of research might be to examine the extent to which companies can benefit from aligning their board composition with the composition of their customer and/or investor base. For example, Gen Xers were the biggest overall spenders in 2021.[4] Our research findings are consistent with the interpretation that companies can benefit from having board members that are likely to share the perspectives and worldview of their customers.

There are many more directions for future research to be explored and discovered, and we hope that our study will inspire and motivate other researchers and practitioners to join us in this endeavor. By doing so, we can advance the knowledge and practice of corporate governance and strengthen the ability of current and future generations of leaders to achieve their full potential and help create a better world for everyone.

## NOTES

1. Retrieved from https://www.junglescout.com/blog/walmart-ecommerce-growth/
2. Peer personality is defined as "a set of collective behavioral traits and attitudes that manifest themselves throughout a generation's lifecycle trajectory" (Howe and Strauss, 1991, p. 32).
3. Howe and Strauss (1991, p. 63) credit the Italian historian Giuseppe Ferrari with this phrase.
4. See Green et al. (2020).

## REFERENCES

Adams, R., & Ferreira, D. 2009. Women in the boardroom and their impact on governance and performance, *Journal of Financial Economics* 94, 291–309.

Ahern, K., & Dittmar, A. 2012. The changing of the boards: The impact on firm valuation of mandated female board representation, *Quarterly Journal of Economics* 127, 137–197.

Farrell, K., & Hersch, P. 2005. Additions to corporate boards: The effect of gender, *Journal of Corporate Finance* 11, 85–106.

Ferreira, D. 2010. Board diversity. In Baker, H. K., Kolb, R. W., & Anderson, R. (Eds.), *Corporate governance: A synthesis of theory, research, and practice*, John Wiley & Sons, pp. 225–242.

Greene, D., Intintoli, V., & Kahle, K. 2020. Do board gender quotas affect firm value? Evidence from California Senate Bill No. 826, *Journal of Corporate Finance* 60. https://doi.org/10.1016/j.jcorpfin.2019.101526

He, Z., Miletkov, M. K. & Staneva, V. 2023. New kids on the block: The effect of Generation X directors on corporate performance. *Journal of Empirical Finance* 71, 66–87.

Howe, N., & Strauss, W. 1991. *Generations: The history of America's future, 1584 to 2069*, William Morrow & Company.

Levi, M., Li, K., & Zhang, F. 2014. Director gender and mergers and acquisitions. *Journal of Corporate Finance* 28, 185–200.

Miletkov, M., Poulsen, A., & Wintoki, M. B. 2017. Foreign independent directors and the quality of legal institutions. *Journal of International Business Studies* 48, 267–292.

# 4. Dual public and private governance of companies in China: a multifaceted appraisal

**Flora Huang and Horace Yeung**

## 1. INTRODUCTION

From a Marxist-Leninist-Maoist ideology, to Deng Xiaoping's "socialism with Chinese characteristics," to today's "Xi Jinping's Thought," the penetration of law and governance into Chinese economy and society has been uniquely different from other countries throughout ideological changes. The state's intentions must be considered when examining any changes, both legal and commercial. The duality of public governance and party governance has been practiced in the public sphere for a long time. For example, the paramount leader of China, Xi Jinping, is simultaneously General Secretary of the Chinese Communist Party (CCP) and President of the People's Republic of China (PRC). The US administration's recent shift to address Xi as "General Secretary" as opposed to "President" has been widely regarded as a deliberate move to highlight "the title by which [Xi] derives his authority" (Yeung, 2020). Similarly, the Party Secretary in a province, city, or other administrative region is normally regarded as a higher office than the "Governor" or "Mayor." By applying the same analogy, the power of a party organization in a company will likely overshadow that of a board of directors, thereby causing substantial confusion over the objectives and control of a commercial organization.

The dual public and private governance system within a company context has raised substantial concern among stakeholders who are less familiar with Chinese politics, especially in the case of overseas investors. As Fortune Magazine has recently put it, "China wants stricter state control over just about everything" (Chandler & Lau, 2021). Corporate disclosures can provide the primary empirical evidence needed to shed light on various areas of concern in this study, particularly in light of three areas: ownership structures, policy impact, and party organization mandates. The chapter will start with a brief overview of the political system of China as well as the current understanding of the interplay between politics and corporate governance in a Chinese context before going into each of the three areas of concern. A final conclusion is to be made at the end. In a nutshell, this study is interested in the role of the state in the complex dynamics of politics and corporate governance in a Chinese context and seeks to map out a meaningful analytical framework to demonstrate how that operates.

## 2. THE POLITICAL SYSTEM OF CHINA – A SNAPSHOT

The Constitution of China has historically confirmed and stipulated in the form of a fundamental law the core position of the CCP as the founder, ruler, and leader of the country. In the view of Xiao (2020: p. 1), the leadership of the CCP is at the center of socialism with Chinese characteristics. The Preamble of the Chinese Constitution states that, "Under the leadership of the Communist Party of China … the Chinese people of all nationalities will continue to work hard and self-reliantly to modernize the country's industry, agriculture, national defense and science and technology step by step to turn China into a strong and prosperous socialist country with a high level of culture and democracy."

China's current party and government decision-making system consists of "the four major institutions" and "the four major systems" established under the leadership of the CCP (Fan, 2020: p. 26). "Four major institutions" at the local level (mainly at the provincial level) refer to the party committee, the government, the People's Congress, and the Chinese People's Political Consultative Conference (CPPCC); "Four major systems" at the central level are the Standing Committee of the Political Bureau (Politburo) of the Communist Party Central Committee and the three major systems of the State Council, the National People's Congress (NPC), and the CPPCC National Committee. Among them, the seven-man Politburo Standing Committee and the 25-member Politburo are thought to be China's highest decision-making bodies (Lawrence & Martin, 2013). The Politburo is led by the general secretary. Xi Jinping is currently the general secretary of the CCP, as well as the holder of two other top roles including the nation's president and the chairman of the Central Military Commission. His positions reflect his significant influence over Chinese politics, policy-making, and governance, and he is the indisputable paramount leader of the country. Other current members of the seven-man Politburo Standing Committee include Li Qiang (Premier of the State Council), Zhao Leji (Chairman of the Standing Committee of the NPC), and Wang Huning (Chairman of CPPCC).

The roles of these key institutions are defined and set out by the constitution. The NPC is the highest organ of state power in China and serves as the country's national legislature.[1] Its primary role is to enact and amend laws, oversee government actions, and represent the interests of the Chinese people. Its functions and powers are prescribed by the law.[2] The law also seeks to ensure that the NPC is well represented by people from different provinces, autonomous regions, and municipalities through democratic elections.[3] Contrary to Western perceptions, Hill (2019) contends that Chinese political and intellectual elites consistently emphasized state-building over the will of the people, and voting has indeed been a surprisingly common political activity in China.

The State Council, also known as the Central People's Government, serves as the chief administrative authority and the national cabinet of China. It is constitutionally the highest administrative organ, responsible for formulating administrative measures, drafting legislative bills, and preparing economic plans and budgets.[4] Essentially, the State Council oversees China's government machinery, ensuring the effective implementation of party policies at both national and local levels. Meanwhile, the CPPCC is a political advisory body in China (Lawrence & Martin, 2013: p. 32). It operates alongside the NPC and plays a significant role in the country's governance. As opposed to Western perceptions and the apparent supremacy of the CCP, China embraces a system of "multi-party cooperation and political consultation"[5] on paper. The CPPCC comprises representatives from various political parties, ethnic groups, and social organizations. It engages in policy discussions, consultations, and recommendations. While it lacks legislative power, its influence lies in providing diverse perspectives and fostering consensus on important issues.

In light of the dichotomy and alignment of political and government administration, at the local (provincial and municipal) level, there are essentially two heads: one is called the Party Secretary and the other is the governor/mayor. To outsiders, especially those in the West, it may be far from obvious who is more powerful in the government hierarchy (Landry, 2003). The Party Secretary holds greater authority than the mayor of a city. The Party Secretary is the highest-ranking official in a city or province. They lead the Communist Party committee at that level. Their power extends beyond administrative matters; they influence policy decisions, appointments, and overall governance. The Party Secretary's role is crucial in maintaining party discipline and implementing party policies. On the other hand, the mayor is the chief executive of a city or province. They handle day-to-day administrative functions, manage public services, and oversee local government operations. However, their authority is subordinate to that of the Party Secretary. While they play a vital role in governance, their power is limited compared to the Party Secretary. In 2019, the US–China Economic and Security Review Commission called for a change in designation for the Chinese leader Xi Jinping (Yeung, 2020). The US side contended that it is more appropriate to address the Chinese leader as

General Secretary Xi as opposed to President Xi, in recognition of the Chinese political reality.

## 3. THE INTERPLAY BETWEEN POLITICS AND CORPORATE GOVERNANCE

Understanding the degree of state control is relevant in the investigation of how some transition economies grew, particularly those former or current communist regimes, notably China, for the purpose of this chapter. Broadly speaking, a typical transition path can be classified into three stages: the communist regime, the transition process, and the post-transition regime (Aoki, 1995: p. 6). In the initial stage, state ownership prevails, and enterprise management is directly appointed by government bodies. Over time, enterprises evolve into corporations, yet the specifics of corporate ownership and control remain fluid. In the ultimate phase, a well-defined corporate governance structure emerges, guided by legal processes. Crucially, during the early stages, political considerations inevitably shape these transitions. Obviously, political considerations are not only relevant in the case of transition economies. Roe has explored the intricate relationship between politics, history, and business organization in the US, larger European nations, and Japan (Roe, 2003). In particular, he has looked at the impact of a nation's social policies on corporate governance. He argued that stronger social policies can cause an American-style diffuse ownership structure among shareholders to fail. This shows that understanding the political and social context is crucial for comprehending which companies, ownership structures, and governance arrangements thrive or falter.

Institutional economics concerns how institutions shape economic behavior (Hodgson, 2000). The movement of institutional economics has generally identified itself as an attempt to extend the range of neoclassical theory by explaining the institutional factors traditionally taken as givens, such as property rights and governance structures (Rutherford, 2001: p. 187). In corporate governance, a typical regulatory system consists of three tiers of regulation (OECD, 2023: p. 40). Corporate law, as the foundational level of regulation, applies universally to both public and private companies. Securities law, the intermediate tier, specifically pertains to companies that issue securities to the public. Finally, listing rules, at the top tier, govern a select group of companies whose securities are listed. These regulations are overseen by dedicated regulators, often including the exchanges themselves and specialized public agencies like the Securities and Exchange Commission of the US.

In its survey of 49 jurisdictions, the OECD (2023) observes that almost all of these jurisdictions have a national corporate governance code or equivalent instrument for corporate governance principles and recommendations to supplement the aforementioned three-tiered regulatory structure. This whole regulatory structure aims to control conflicts of interest among corporate constituencies. Three generic agency problems can arise in business organizations (Armour et al., 2017: pp. 29–30). The first type involves the classic agency problem identified by Adam Smith. The problem lies in ensuring that the managers are responsive to the shareholders' interests rather than pursuing their own personal interests. The second agency problem involves the conflict between majority and minority shareholders. The former generally have a tendency to expropriate the latter. The third problem lies in ensuring that corporate insiders do not behave opportunistically toward outsiders such as creditors, workers, and consumers.

With respect to politics, Acemoglu and colleagues (2005) argue that political power can lead to major changes in political institutions and therefore in economic institutions and economic growth. Examples of political institutions include the form of government (e.g., democracy) and the extent of constraints on politicians and political elites. There are arguments both for and against the effects of democracy on growth (Przeworski & Limongi, 1993). On the one hand, it is thought that only democratic institutions can constrain the state to act in the general interest. The government's role is seen as providing law and order, enforcing contracts, and defending private parties from external threats. On the other hand, some have observed that dictators tended to behave in a "developmentalist" fashion, especially from the experience of the Far East and Latin America (Przeworski & Limongi, 1993: pp. 55–56). When Milton Friedman looked at Singapore, he remarked that Lee Kuan Yew was a "benevolent dictator" and drew the lesson that it is possible to combine a free private market economic system with a dictatorial political system (Huang & Yeung, 2018: p. 164). Benevolent dictators remain focused on improving their country, and they use their absolute power to do so, as opposed to their own desire and pursuit of wealth and recognition.

China is regarded as having an authoritarian regime by the Economist Intelligence Unit's (2023) Democracy Index. The index provides a snapshot of the state of democracy worldwide for 165 independent states and two territories. It reveals that less than 8% of the world's population lives in a full democracy, while almost 40% live under authoritarian rule. Over recent years, the number of "full democracies" has been on the decline, whereas the latter is on the rise.

After the founding of the PRC in 1949, the country experienced a long period of economic calamity under the leadership of Chairman Mao Zedong, especially during the Great Leap Forward from 1958 to 1960 and the Cultural Revolution from 1966 to 1976. A significant breakthrough came in December 1978, marking a new historical period of *gaige kaifang*, the twin strategies of economic reform and opening up (Huang & Yeung, 2018: p. 40). Before that, the traditional socialist system of China and the development strategy of prioritizing heavy industry, together with different political campaigns such as the Great Leap Forward and the Cultural Revolution, had not brought China prosperity. Despite the changes in leadership since 1978, the orientation of Chinese political ideology has followed Deng Xiaoping's model of "socialism with Chinese characteristics" in principle. Deng proposed a new theory of incorporating capitalism into central planning to increase productivity, advance Chinese culture, and enhance the interests of the people.

In response to the economic reforms, various laws were introduced to support the reforms. According to Lubman (1999: p. 174), this was important as the market economy relies on private law to serve as a framework to facilitate transactions defining the rights and duties created by business arrangements. Nevertheless, "the primacy of policy [in China] makes law as merely an instrument of administration" (Lubman, 1991: p. 317). The legal ideology between the East and the West might not necessarily be the same. "Rule by law" refers to the instrumental use of law by the state to govern, whereas the "rule of law" refers to a normative and political theory of the relationship between legal institutions and the political state, focusing on a theory of limited government through the separation of powers among executive, legislative, and judicial organizations (Orts, 2001: p. 94). The current situation in China seems to be the former. For instance, Milhaupt and Pistor (2008: p. 142) argue that China's commitment to the rule of law has been weakened by other governance mechanisms.

The interplay between politics and corporate governance in China is well-noted by scholars. Shi (2012) investigates the key factors shaping corporate governance in China. She emphasizes the role of government control, the evolution of governance in state-owned enterprises (SOEs) and listed companies, and the regulatory challenges posed by China's globalization. She also argues that corporate governance in China is largely determined by political imperatives shaped over time. In a more recent book, Ozery (2023) explores the intricate relationship between law, politics, and corporate governance in China and provides valuable insights into how legal frameworks intersect with political dynamics in shaping business organizations. Jiang and Kim (2020) highlight the unique agency problem in China; that is, horizontal agency conflict between controlling and minority shareholders due to concentrated ownership structures. Unlike Western countries, China's governance landscape is shaped by distinct political and economic factors.

Wang (2014) offers a powerful analysis of the intricate relationship between politics and corporate governance in China's SOEs. He argues that SOE reform is part of the CCP's effort to rebuild and maintain political legitimacy. The management of legitimacy is embedded in all major aspects of SOE governance structures. Corporate governance in Chinese SOEs reflects a system where components from different origins come together to ensure economic benefits while staying within the owner's control. Understanding the political imperatives behind SOE reform is crucial for comprehending China's economic transformation, and the CCP's role in shaping SOE governance has far-reaching implications for China's market development and political stability. Opper (2007) similarly delves into the intricate balance that companies in China must strike between political imperatives and market demands when going public. She especially highlights the unique feature of the Chinese corporate governance system in that it is a hybrid between corporate governance in a Western sense (which largely involves arm's length transactions and a clear allocation of control and risks) and political governance. One way for the state to exercise direct influence over corporate affairs is by holding a large block of shares in companies. The next section will investigate the ownership structure of Chinese companies, especially in relation to some notable SOEs and private companies.

## 4. OWNERSHIP STRUCTURE OF CHINESE COMPANIES

In the 1980s, when China began its economic reform, the state sector dominated its economy, accounting for nearly four-fifths of output (Economist, 2017). In comparison, it accounts for less than a fifth of output today (Economist, 2017). The ideological dilemma faced by the CCP was a choice between a strictly socialist model, a partially privatized model, and a laissez-faire capitalist model. Private ownership was viewed as the answer to the governance problems inherited from the state sector. The government adopted a retreat/retain (2-R) strategy (Green & Liu, 2005: p. 15). The principle was "grasp the big, let go of the small." It retreated from competitive sectors, where small and medium-sized SOEs operated. Meanwhile, in so-called strategic industries, where large SOEs were common, control was retained. SOEs now dominate only a handful of industries such as oil and gas mining, transportation, telecommunications, financial services, and utilities.

China's economic reform has not been the privatization experienced by many former communist countries in the Soviet Union. Instead, it has been a process of corporatization, which entailed the adoption of a corporate form, restructuring, and instituting stock ownership without necessarily relinquishing the state's controlling interest in the means of production (Chen, 2005). The mechanism adopted by the state to prevent the loss of state control is the creation of non-tradable shares.

Corporatization (sometimes known as securitization) refers to the legal and financial restructuring of SOEs through their conversion into joint-stock companies. The corporatization campaign in China was a two-step process. It first restructured SOEs into shareholding companies and then listed them on a stock exchange. In light of corporate governance, it was hoped that corporatization would achieve three goals: (1) change the ownership structure of the SOEs to include both state and non-state institutional shareholders in addition to small individual shareholders; (2) separate the state from business operations for enterprises to achieve full autonomy; and (3) improve managerial incentives by installing shareholders with the incentives and abilities to monitor the managers (Chen, 2005: p. 60). One of the major goals was to establish a clear mechanism of company control and management. The aim was to leave the decision-making authority to boards of directors, which should supposedly be profit-oriented and free from direct intervention by state administrative organizations (Chen, 1993: p. 65). This can be contrasted with the time when China was still a centrally planned economy, where the government directly ran SOEs, set their annual output targets, and left SOEs with little autonomy in making commercial decisions.

A distinct feature that separated China's stock market from those in other countries was the creation of state shares and legal person shares, which both carry significant constraints on tradability (Yeung, 2009). These shares are generally state-owned or state-controlled. A typical public company had about one-third of its shares in state, legal person, and tradable shares, respectively. By holding two-thirds of most companies' shares, the state could ensure that it had the power to direct and influence their activities. Following the non-tradable shares reform, these shares are now tradable, but this does not necessarily indicate the state's immediate willingness to relinquish control and sell all its shares to the public, at least not for strategic SOEs (Yeung, 2009). According to the figures from the State-Owned Assets Supervision and Administration Commission of China, as of the end of 2015, the state still held 80% of shares in a typical SOE (People's Daily, 2017).

To reveal the current ownership structure of SOEs, we can look at the big four banks, for example. The largest shareholders of the Bank of China are Central Huijin (64.02%) and the Hong Kong Securities Clearing Company (Nominees) Limited (27.77%), with no other shareholders holding more than 3% of the remaining shares.[6] Central Huijin is a Chinese sovereign fund that was established in 2003, originally owned by the Chinese government directly and later as a wholly owned subsidiary of the China Investment Corporation, one of the world's largest sovereign wealth funds. The primary role of Central Huijin is to exercise shareholder rights on behalf of the State Council. Specifically, it acts as a shareholder for the "big four" state-owned banks in China, aiming to improve corporate governance and drive reforms in the banking industry. The shareholding by the second-largest shareholder, Hong Kong Securities Clearing Company (Nominees) Limited, consists of the shares listed on the Hong Kong bourse and held by individual and institutional investors in Hong Kong. The China Construction Bank has a similar ownership structure, with

Central Huijin as the majority shareholder (57.11%) and shareholders in Hong Kong holding 37.53% of shares collectively. The Agricultural Bank of China and the Industrial and Commercial Bank of China are somewhat different in the sense that the Ministry of Finance of China is a major shareholder of both, holding around one-third of the shares in the two banks.[7]

Energy and telecommunications are the two strategic sectors where the state has retained control through its SOEs. PetroChina's key shareholders are the wholly state-owned China National Petroleum Corporation (82.46%) and 11.42% of the remaining shares are listed in Hong Kong. Meanwhile, the company's main domestic rival, Sinopec, is owned by the wholly state-owned Sinopec Group (67.22%). The two companies are multiple-listed in Shanghai, Hong Kong, New York, and London (for Sinopec only). There is a duopoly in China's cellular networks – China Mobile and China Unicom. The former is majority-owned (69.62%) by China Mobile Hong Kong (BVI) Limited. The company's ultimate controlling shareholder is the wholly state-owned China Mobile Communications Group. By contrast, the ownership structure of China Unicom is more dispersed. The company is majority-owned (35.8%) by China United Network Communication Group with institutional investors such as China Life Insurance (10%), China State-owned Enterprise Structural Adjustment Fund (6%), Shenzhen Tencent Xinda (5.1%), and Hangzhou Ali Venture Capital (2%). Just 3.2% of shares are held by the Hong Kong Securities Clearing Company (Nominees) Limited, on behalf of the investors trading in the bourse. As of November 2023, the parents of these four companies were on the directory of the "central SOEs" under the administration of the State-Owned Assets Supervision and Administration Commission (SASAC) of the State Council.[8] There were 97 such SOEs. The heads of these SOEs can be regarded as government officials at the deputy ministerial level (Phoenix New Media, 2013).

All these state parents are subject to different requirements as per the company law. They are limited liability companies wholly owned by the state, and the relevant ownership rights and responsibilities are vested in the State Council (the central government level) or the provincial and municipal governments and discharged by the state-owned assets supervision and administration authority at the corresponding level on their behalf.[9] One notable feature is that there are no shareholder meetings, as this decision-making function is discharged by the competent state-owned assets supervision and administration authority.[10]

As of the end of 2023, private companies accounted for 36.8% of the market capitalization of China's top 100 listed companies (Huang & Veron, 2023). Amongst these top 100 companies, examples of private companies include Tencent, Alibaba, Pinduoduo, Ningde Era, BYD, Meituan, Nongfu Spring, NetEase, Midea Group, Xiaomi, and so on. Unlike the SOEs above, Tencent and Alibaba are not currently listed on a domestic exchange but are listed in Hong Kong and New York (Alibaba only). Their shareholders are relatively dispersed and international. For example, the largest shareholder of Alibaba is SoftBank Group (14%), with the Vanguard Group (3.4%) and BlackRock (3.1%) coming in second and third.[11] The top 25 shareholders collectively hold less than half of the shares, suggesting the absence of a single majority shareholder. As for Tencent, Prosus, a Dutch investment company, is the single biggest shareholder (26%), followed by the Chinese billionaire and company founder, Ma Huateng (around 8%), with no other single shareholders holding more than 1% of the shares.[12]

Despite the emergence of private companies, dispersed ownership is still not the dominant feature of Chinese companies. But China is arguably not unique. La Porta and colleagues (1999) provided valuable insights into the ownership structures of large corporations across 27 wealthy economies. Contrary to the broadly held image of widely dispersed ownership, they found that relatively few of these firms were widely held. Instead, these companies were typically controlled by families or the state. The corporate governance mechanisms are not the same across different ownership settings (Armour et al., 2017: pp. 29–30). In concentrated ownership, principal–agent (shareholder–manager) conflict may not be a chief concern because the largest shareholders should, in theory, have well-defined rights prescribed by law, along with the incentives and sufficiently large stakes to monitor the opportunistic managers. In this case, the mitigation of majority–minority conflicts is perhaps more imminent than principal–agent conflicts. The goal of the law is to ensure that the majority shareholders do not behave opportunistically towards the minorities. However, the monitoring problem in many SOEs has been the absence of an ultimate principal (Clarke, 2003: p. 499). The theoretical owner of an SOE is the government or the "people as a whole." Therefore, the state as the majority shareholder plays an ineffective role in monitoring the behavior of managers because the state is a collective body. There is no "real" ownership. There is nobody within the state with sufficient and appropriate incentives to monitor this. The very undesirable outcome of this is that both principal–agent and majority–minority conflicts can be prevalent.

## 5. THE IMPACT OF POLICY CHANGE

Despite the absence of ownership (and therefore decision) rights over private companies, the state's influence can be seen in the form of policy, which has been constantly reshaped by ideological change. Traditionally, institutional innovations in China were supposedly consistent with a Marxist-Leninist-Maoist ideology that could not be challenged (Lubman, 1991: p. 318). As discussed previously, Deng Xiaoping's model of "socialism with Chinese characteristics" provided a pivotal change to the orientation of Chinese political ideology. Later leaders followed Deng's direction in principle. Jiang Zemin's "Three Represents" legitimized the inclusion of capitalists and private entrepreneurs within the CCP (Huang & Yeung, 2018: pp. 61–62). Subsequently, Hu Jintao's "Scientific Outlook on Development" aims to achieve coordinated development, all-round development, and sustainable development. The current leader, Xi Jinping, while affirming the position of Deng Xiaoping Theory, Three Represents, and Scientific Outlook on Development in pursuing "socialism with Chinese characteristics," also presents a new set of personal and national ideals called "Xi Jinping Thought." All of these ideas have now been formally written into the Chinese Constitution.[13]

Xi Jinping Thought merges party-centric nationalism, Leninism, Maoism, Legalism, and Confucianism to render socialism Sino-centric and encompasses core principles such as upholding the CCP leadership, promoting socialism, and advancing national rejuvenation, along with commitments related to economic development, governance, and cultural progress (Tsang & Cheung, 2024). Policy formulation and implementation are inevitably aligned with all these ideas, thoughts, and principles. Xi's idea of "Common Prosperity," as a fundamental requirement of socialism, aims to balance growth and financial stability while making Chinese society more equitable. The concept involves a more equal distribution of income, although it is not uniform egalitarianism. Commentators believe that this new ideology put forward by Xi has affected business priorities and economic dynamics, and it is expected that there will be greater control of how business and society are governed (Hass, 2021).

Media estimates that technology giant Alibaba pledged a substantial sum of US$15.5 billion to help promote common prosperity initiatives in China and set up a dedicated task force (Hass, 2021). Similarly, its rival tech giant Tencent pledged US$7.75 billion to the cause. While it is hardly a new phenomenon that companies are asked to engage in philanthropy, its implementation has led to fear of aggressive redistributive policies and financial repercussions for major corporations in China. These concerns are not unfounded. As observed by Hass (2021), "Chinese authorities have launched a widening series of crackdowns on technology giants, wealthy individuals, education services providers, celebrities, and even youth video gamers."

One example of the country's more interventionist approach, in stark contrast to the approach in Deng, Jiang, and Hu's era, is Ant Group's proposed initial public offering (IPO). Ant Group, the financial technology giant affiliated with Alibaba and also founded by Jack Ma, initially planned a world record-setting IPO in Shanghai and Hong Kong (Lee, 2023). However, in November 2020, the IPO was unexpectedly suspended. On the face of it, the suspension was due to entirely market-based concerns related to listing qualifications and disclosure requirements. On the other hand, commentators believe that the real cause of the IPO's failure was a vindictive action against Jack Ma, as well as the company's threat to state control (Shrivastava, 2023). Ma's influence and outspokenness made him a target for regulatory action. Despite not being on Ant Group's board, he held significant voting rights and was a larger-than-life figure at the company. He publicly criticized the Chinese state's heavy-handed business regulation. His speech raised eyebrows and led to increased scrutiny of Ant's operations. Furthermore, the Chinese government's concerns centered on Ant's rapid growth, potential systemic risks, and its impact on the financial sector. The Chinese government has a history of intervening when groups threaten its power (Murray, 2020). Ant's rapid rise and dominance in consumer payment services raised concerns about its influence. In particular, the government's vision for launching its own version of e-currency clashed with Ant Group's ambitions, leading to tension between free-market capitalism and party-controlled regulation.

Such tension is probably not only felt by Jack Ma and his Ant Group but also by other sectors. The Chinese government has implemented a harsh crackdown on after-school education companies, impacting both parents and businesses. The government released the "double reduction" policy in 2021 (Ye, 2021). Local authorities in several provinces ordered private education providers to suspend online and offline tutoring classes for school children. The policy aims to ease the burden and anxiety for Chinese parents seeking quality education for their children. Meanwhile, the new regulations have shocked parents and left businesses struggling, with millions of employees facing potential job losses. The policy even went as far as including an order to turn all the current academic tutoring businesses into a non-profit model and a ban on public listings, making the sector essentially "not investable." New Oriental Education Group, for example, dismissed 60,000 employees and saw operating income plunge by 80% after the new sweeping rules on the country's private education industry (Reuters, 2022). Similarly, China has imposed strict regulations on online gaming, particularly for minors (World Economic Forum, 2021). Minors are only allowed to play online games for one hour each day on Fridays, Saturdays, Sundays, and public holidays. The rules aim to prevent excessive gaming behavior, limit in-game purchases, and promote healthier lifestyles for youths. However, the announcement of the gaming restrictions led to a sharp decline in the share prices of major Chinese gaming companies, including Tencent and NetEase, wiping nearly US$80 billion off their value. As neatly summarized by S&P Global (2022), "a string of unexpected regulatory moves from policymakers has contributed to the more challenging business environment and impacted overall market optimism."

On the other hand, the state's influence via policy is not necessarily all adversarial to the companies. One example is the companies that engage in renewable energy and have benefited from the generous state support and subsidies. In 2024, the annual subsidy to the sector was projected to be CNY 5.4 billion, down from CNY 7.4 billion in 2023 and CNY 6.19 billion in 2022 (Business Times, 2024). Just a decade ago, China supplied 40% of the world's solar panels. Today, its global market share is over 80%, a near monopoly (Robinson, 2024). Out of the world's seven largest solar panel manufacturers, six of them are from China (the remaining one from Canada). They are, in ascending order of market share, Trina Solar, JinkoSolar, LONGi, Shanghai AIK, JA Solar, and Tongwei Solar. The dominance of Chinese companies in the industry has caught the EU's attention. For example, the European Commission (2024) launched an in-depth investigation under the Foreign Subsidies Regulation against LONGi. The investigation relates to the potentially market-distorting role of foreign subsidies given to the company in a public procurement procedure.

Similarly, Chinese automakers account for more than half of the electric vehicles (EVs) produced in the world (World Economic Forum, 2024). The Chinese automakers' success has been largely attributed to the cost advantage, owing to lower labor rates, increased scale, more favorable battery costs (when batteries are produced locally), and government subsidies. Major economies are now targeting their Chinese rivals. In May 2024, the US increased tariffs on Chinese-made EVs from 25% to 100%. Likewise, in July, the EU imposed a provisional anti-subsidy tariff of up to 37.6% on EVs imported from China. All these are believed to be retaliatory measures to the Chinese industrial policies and subsidies, which cause overcapacity and unfair competition.

In a nutshell, policy change in China can be a double-edged sword for companies. It can create a more favorable business environment for them, just like the solar panel manufacturers and EV makers. In sharp contrast, sometimes policy change can be disruptive, likely felt by those education providers and game developers.

## 6. PARTY ORGANIZATIONS WITHIN CHINESE COMPANIES

Businesses are not only expected to be reactive to policy change, but they are also expected to allow the CCP to participate in their internal governance, which is quite a unique phenomenon in the world. Chinese company law requires companies to establish party organizations and provide the "necessary conditions" for the activities of party organizations.[14] Even though the provision has long existed since the first company law in 1993, this requirement was lightly enforced for nearly two decades (Livingston, 2021). A change came in 2012 when the CCP released a measure emphasizing the role of party organizations within companies. This measure outlined 20 specific provisions to strengthen the presence and coverage of party organizations in the private economy. In Laband's (2018) view, the expectations of a party organization may be somewhat different between SOEs and private companies. Within the former, party organizations should play a "core political role." They should play an expanded leadership role to ensure the implementation of party policy and discuss and decide major issues for their company. On the other hand, for private companies, no management or governance role is specified. The role of the party organization is just to make sure that the company follows the law and oversees organizations such as trade unions and the Communist Youth League. It was reported in 2018 that 73.1% of private companies had established a party organization (Livingston, 2021). A more recent investigation by the All-China Federation of Industry and Commerce (ACFIC) reported a significant increase in the presence of party organizations within private companies, rising from only 4% in 1993 to 92% of China's top 500 private companies by 2020 (Thomas, 2020). As of the end of 2022, there are in total over 1.5 million company party organizations in the whole country.[15]

*The Economist* (2023) highlights the concerns among foreign investors and businesses about the existence of party organizations within a company regarding the independence of commercial decision-making. The party's presence is becoming more conspicuous and assertive, with senior management positions often held by party members, thereby ensuring the party's control over personnel decisions and corporate governance. The *Financial Times* traces the amendments of the articles of association of selected Hong Kong-listed Chinese SOEs to establish the party organizations (Hughes, 2017). Typical lines inserted by the amendments include describing the party as playing a core role in "an organized, institutionalized and concrete way" and "providing direction [and] managing the overall situation." The articles of association for China Railway Group, one of the country's biggest construction groups, now state that "when the board of directors decides on material issues, it shall first listen to the opinions of the party committee of the company." It is common to have a significant overlap between a company's party organization and its management (Livingston, 2021). This overlap suggests a deeper and more surreptitious influence on company operations than is commonly assumed.

While the role of the party organizations may be more defined by regulatory instruments[16] in relation to SOEs, their role in private companies may be relatively vague. After all, for the former, the state's shareholding alone can ensure that the state has a say in the companies through their votes, not necessarily through the party organizations. For the latter, by surveying a number of listed companies in China (non-SOEs), Cheng and Zheng (2023) contend that the party organizations can help private companies in three ways: improving credit, fostering dialogue with government bodies, and better protection of worker rights. Meanwhile, Blanchette (2019: p. 45) is more skeptical. He believes that embedding political institutions within China's private sector will undoubtedly undermine the capacity of the country's economy to innovate. Strategic decisions within private companies will become increasingly mindful of the party's objectives. Eventually, there is a risk of letting political decision-making crowd out economic considerations.

The party influence and the continuous entanglement between politics and business do not stop there. Recently, news has emerged regarding the revival of Mao Zedong-era militias, known as People's Armed Forces Departments (PAFDs), within Chinese SOEs (White, 2024). This move reflects President Xi Jinping's focus on security amidst China's economic slowdown. The PAFDs, historically linked to the People's Liberation Army's recruitment, now engage in civil defense and military training. Analysts view this as a response to domestic stability concerns rather than foreign military threats. The resurgence of PAFDs aligns with defense reforms and the CCP's emphasis on security over development since Xi's second term. Most of the companies involved (at least 16 thus far) are SOEs that are directly owned by central or regional governments. Notably, private companies like Yili Group have also established PAFDs, indicating a broader adoption beyond SOEs. The development reinforces Chinese leader Xi Jinping's aim to tighten the CCP's control over society, including the corporate sector. The revival of corporate militias reflects Xi's vision to integrate economic development with national security amidst a period of slow global economic growth and increasing geopolitical uncertainty.

## 7. CONCLUSION

Warren Buffett, legendary investor and business tycoon, once said, "The 19th century belonged to England, the 20th century belonged to the US, and the 21st century belongs to China" (Ma, 2012). This quote reflects the global recognition of China's economic miracle and its impact on the world stage. The miracle is not a pure coincidence but can be attributed to Deng Xiaoping's bold move in shaping the concept of "socialism with Chinese characteristics." His remarkable vision combined Marxist principles with China's specific conditions, leading to pragmatic reforms that integrated market elements while retaining CCP control. Whether these reforms were truly capitalist or a necessary adaptation remains a subject of debate, but their impact on China's economic transformation is undeniable.

By first providing an overview of the Chinese political system and the interplay between politics and corporate governance before focusing on three specific areas, namely ownership structures, policy impact, and party organization mandates, this chapter has made the following key observations: (1) strategic sectors remain tightly in the hands of SOEs, with the emergence of notable private companies such as Tencent and Alibaba; (2) the impact of politics and policy on a company can be decisive – they can make or break a company (arguably this is the same everywhere in the world, but much more apparent in the country and in the Xi Jinping era); (3) the requirement to establish party organizations (and militia) within companies, even in the case of private companies, blurs the line between public and corporate governance.

The future direction of research in Chinese corporate governance should focus on deepening the understanding of their unique dual public–private governance model, especially amidst the rise of the private sector. As the private sector grows and competes internationally, it becomes crucial to investigate the implications of the party's influence on decision-making, management autonomy, and investor confidence. One notable concern flagged by this chapter is the increasing but far from clear role of Communist Party organizations within companies. Additionally, the interaction between evolving political ideologies, policy impacts, and corporate governance structures warrants further analysis, particularly regarding how these dynamics may function differently in the contexts of SOEs and private companies.

## NOTES

1. Articles 57–58 of the Constitution of the PRC.
2. Ibid. Article 62.
3. Ibid. Article 59.
4. Ibid. Article 89.
5. Ibid. Preamble.
6. Data from SINA Finance based on their annual report dated June 30, 2023. The Bank of China is dual-listed in Shanghai and Hong Kong.
7. Data from SINA Finance based on the most recent annual reports from the banks.
8. Information available on the website of the SASAC.
9. Articles 168–169 of the Company Law 2023.
10. Ibid. Article 172.
11. Data from Yahoo! Finance.
12. Data from Yahoo! Finance.
13. Preamble of the Constitution of the PRC.
14. Article 18 of the Company Law 2023.
15. Data from the CCP Statistics Bulletin.
16. For example, "The General Office of the Central Committee of the Chinese Communist Party Issues the Regulations on the Work of Grassroots Organizations of State-owned Enterprises of the Chinese Communist Party (for Trial Implementation)," issued by the Central Committee of the CCP on January 5, 2020.

## REFERENCES

Acemoglu, D., Johnson, S. & Robinson, J. (2005). Institutions as a Fundamental Cause of Long-Run Growth. In P. Aghion and S. Durlauf (eds), *Handbook of Economic Growth* (Volume 1A). Elsevier.

Aoki, M. (1995). Controlling Insider Control: Issues of Corporate Governance in Transition Economies. In M. Aoki and H.K. Kim (eds), *Corporate Governance in Transitional Economies: Insider Control and the Role of Banks*. World Bank.

Armour, J., Hansmann, H. & Kraakman, R. (2017). Agency Problems and Legal Strategies. In R. Kraakman, J. Armour, P. Davies, L. Enriques, H. Hansmann, G. Hertig, K. Hopt, H. Kanda, M. Pargendler, W.-G. Ringe & E. Rock (eds), *The Anatomy of Corporate Law: A Comparative and Functional Approach*. Oxford University Press.

Blanchette, J. (2019). Against Atrophy: Party Organizations in Private Firms. *Made in China Journal*, 4, 42–45.

Business Times (2024). China Sets Renewable Power Subsidies Lower at 5.4 Billion Yuan in 2024. https://www.businesstimes.com.sg/international/china-sets-renewable-power-subsidies-lower-5-4-billion-yuan-2024

Chandler, C. & Lau, Y. (2021). China Wants Stricter State Control over Just about Everything—and the Costs Are Mounting. *Fortune*, August 12. https://fortune.com/2021/08/12/china-regulatory-crackdown-tech-costs-state-control/

Chen, J. (1993). Securitization of State-owned Enterprises and the Ownership Controversy in the PRC. *Sydney Law Review*, 15, 59–85.

Chen, J. (2005). Corporatization of China's State-owned Enterprises and Corporate Governance. In D. Brown & A. MacBean (eds), *Challenges for China's Development – An Enterprise Perspective*. Routledge.

Cheng, L. & Zheng, Q. (2023). Study on the Effect and Mechanism of Party Organizations' Participation in the Governance of Private Enterprises [Dang Zuzhi Canyu Minying Qiye Zhili de Xiaoguo yu Jizhi Yanjiu]. *Economic Review*, 5, 53–70. http://jer.whu.edu.cn/d/file/dqml/2023-09-15/075fc842cae515925bf7a7236e50496f.pdf (in Chinese).

Clarke, D. (2003). Corporate Governance in China: An Overview. *China Economic Review*, 14(4), 494–507.

Economist (2017). Reform of China's Ailing State-owned Firms is Emboldening Them. https://www.economist.com/news/finance-and-economics/21725293-outperformed-private-firms-they-are-no-longer-shrinking-share-overall

Economist (2023). China's Communist Party is Tightening its Grip in Businesses. https://www.economist.com/china/2023/07/06/chinas-communist-party-is-tightening-its-grip-in-businesses

Economist Intelligence Unit (2023). Democracy Index 2023. https://www.eiu.com/n/campaigns/democracy-index-2023/

European Commission (2024). Commission Opens Two In-Depth Investigations under the Foreign Subsidies Regulation in the Solar Photovoltaic Sector. https://ec.europa.eu/commission/presscorner/detail/en/ip_24_1803

Fan, P. (2020). Party and Government Policies in China's Politics. In N. Fang (ed.), *China's Political System*. Springer. https://doi.org/10.1007/978-981-15-8362-9_2

Green, S. & Liu, G. (2005). China's Industrial Reform Strategy: Retreat and Retain. In S. Green & G. Liu (eds), *Exit the Dragon? Privatization and State Control in China*. Blackwell.

Hass, R. (2021). Assessing China's "Common Prosperity" Campaign. https://www.brookings.edu/articles/assessing-chinas-common-prosperity-campaign/

Hill, J. (2019). *Voting as a Rite: A History of Elections in Modern China*. Harvard University Asia Center.

Hodgson, G. (2000). What is the Essence of Institutional Economics? *Journal of Economic Issues*, 34(2), 317–329.

Huang, F. & Yeung, H. (2018). *Institutions and Economic Growth in Asia*. Routledge.

Huang, T. & Véron, N. (2023). The Private Sector's Share of China's Largest Listed Companies Continued to Decline to 43 Percent in the Second Half of 2022. https://www.piie.com/blogs/realtime-economics/2023/private-sectors-share-chinas-largest-listed-companies-continued

Hughes, J. (2017). China's Communist Party Writes Itself into Company Law. *Financial Times,* August 14. https://www.ft.com/content/a4b28218-80db-11e7-94e2-c5b903247afd

Jiang, F. & Kim, K. (2020). Corporate Governance in China: A Survey. *Review of Finance*, 24(4), 733–772.

La Porta, R., Lopez-De-Silanes, F. & Shleifer, A. (1999). Corporate Ownership around the World. *Journal of Finance*, 54(2), 471–517.

Laband, J. (2018). Fact Sheet: Communist Party Groups in Foreign Companies in China. China Business Review. https://www.chinabusinessreview.com/fact-sheet-communist-party-groups-in-foreign-companies-in-china/#:~:text=Chapter%205%20of%20the%20CCP%20Constitution%20requires%20the,in%20companies%20with%20three%20or%20more%20party%20members

Landry, P. (2003). The Political Management of Mayors in Post-Deng. *Copenhagen Journal of Asian Studies*, 17, 31–58.

Lawrence, S. & Martin, M. (2013). Understanding China's Political System. Congressional Research Service Report. https://sgp.fas.org/crs/row/R41007.pdf

Lee, J. (2023). Alibaba's Revamp Puts Renewed Focus on Ant Group's Suspended IPO. CNBC. https://www.cnbc.com/2023/03/29/alibaba-revamp-ant-group.html

Livingston, S. (2021). The New Challenge of Communist Corporate Governance. CSIS Brief. https://www.csis.org/analysis/new-challenge-communist-corporate-governance

Lubman, S. (1991). Studying Contemporary Chinese Law: Limits, Possibilities and Strategy. *American Journal of Comparative Law*, 39(2), 293–341.

Lubman, S. (1999). *Bird in a Cage: Legal Reform in China after Mao*. Stanford University Press.

Ma, L. (2012). Buffett Guests Realize There is no Free Lunch. *China Daily*. https://www.chinadaily.com.cn/business/2012-06/14/content_15500892_2.htm

Milhaupt, C. & Pistor, K. (2008). *Law and Capitalism*. The University of Chicago Press.

Murray, R. (2020). Why China's Vision for a Global Yuan Trampled Ant Group's IPO. https://www.fpri.org/article/2020/12/why-chinas-vision-for-a-global-yuan-trampled-ant-groups-ipo/

OECD (2023). *OECD Corporate Governance Factbook 2023*. OECD Publishing.

Opper, S. (2007). Going Public without the Public: Between Political Governance and Corporate Governance. In B. Krug & H. Hendrischke (eds), *The Chinese Economy in the 21st Century*. Edward Elgar Publishing.

Orts, E. (2001). The Rule of Law in China. *Vanderbilt Journal of Transnational Law*, 34, 43–115.

Ozery, T.G. (2023). *Law and Political Economy in China*. Cambridge University Press.

People's Daily Online (2017). Highlight of Mixed SOE Reform [Guoqi Hungai Dayou Kandian] http://paper.people.com.cn/rmrbhwb/html/2017-03/09/content_1755936.htm (in Chinese).
Phoenix New Media (2013). The Administrative Level of "Top Leaders" Of Central Enterprises [Yangqi "Yibashou" de Xingzhengjibie]. https://finance.ifeng.com/news/special/gqybs/ (in Chinese).
Przeworski, A. & Limongi, F. (1993). Political Regimes and Economic Growth. *Journal of Economic Perspectives*, 7(3), 51–69.
Reuters (2022). New Oriental Laid Off 60,000 Staff after China's Education Crackdown, Founder Says. https://www.reuters.com/world/china/new-oriental-laid-off-60000-staff-after-chinas-education-crackdown-founder-says-2022-01-10/
Robinson, Q. (2024). The True Cost of Chinese Solar Panels. *Time*. https://time.com/6564184/chinese-solar-panels-cost/
Roe, M. (2003). *Political Determinant of Corporate Governance*. Oxford University Press.
Rutherford, M. (2001). Institutional Economics: Then and Now. *Journal of Economic Perspectives*, 15(3), 173–194.
Shi, C. (2012). *The Political Determinants of Corporate Governance in China*. Routledge.
Shrivastava, M. (2023). The Continuing Saga of China's Ant Group. *Diplomat*. https://thediplomat.com/2023/01/the-continuing-saga-of-chinas-ant-group/
S&P Global (2022). Perspectives from China: The Shifting Regulatory Landscape. https://www.spglobal.com/marketintelligence/en/news-insights/blog/perspectives-from-china-the-shifting-regulatory-landscape
Thomas, N. (2020). Party Committees in the Private Sector: Rising Presence, Moderate Prevalence. MarcoPolo. https://macropolo.org/party-committees-private-sector-china/?rp=m&fbclid=IwAR1bDHDjgNqDp9J8GwNLAbRo3hMHTktQocwJXbUb7Th08Zu0ObJ9bDuctL8
Tsang, S. & Cheung, O. (2024). *The Political Thought of Xi Jinping*. Oxford University Press.
Wang, J. (2014). The Political Logic of Corporate Governance in China's State-Owned Enterprises. *Cornell International Law Journal*, 47(3), 631–669.
White, E. (2024). Chinese Companies Revive Mao Zedong-Era Militias. *Financial Times*, February 20. https://www.ft.com/content/d6b2e4d6-2f84-4ef9-bf99-10d76d92d045
World Economic Forum (2021). What's Behind China's Video Game Restrictions? https://www.weforum.org/agenda/2021/09/what-s-behind-china-s-video-game-restrictions
World Economic Forum (2024). China Has an Electric Vehicle Advantage but Can It Maintain its Edge? https://www.weforum.org/agenda/2024/06/china-electric-vehicle-advantage
Xiao, W. (2020). China's Politics and the Communist Party of China. In N. Fang (ed.), *China's Political System*. Springer.
Ye, W. (2021). China's Harsh Education Crackdown Sends Parents and Businesses Scrambling. CNBC. https://www.cnbc.com/2021/08/05/chinas-harsh-education-crackdown-sends-parents-businesses-scrambling.html

Yeung, H. (2009). Non-tradable Share Reform in China: A Review of Progress. *Company Lawyer*, 30(11), 340–346.

Yeung, J. (2020). US Lawmakers Want to Stop Calling Xi Jinping a President. But Will He Care? CNN. https://edition.cnn.com/2020/09/08/asia/xi-jinping-title-us-bill-intl-dst-hnk/index.html

# 5. The corporate governance of Indian unicorns

**Arjya B. Majumdar**

## 1. INTRODUCTION

The rise of an entrepreneurial culture, coupled with regulatory incentives in India (Ratanpal, 2008; Reddy, 2016), has led to the creation of a large number of startups within the Indian economy (Dugar & Pandit, 2017). Over the decades, the boundaries of the state as an industrial participant have shrunk considerably, opening up avenues for private companies (Majumdar, 2007) and increased volumes of equity capital funding (Chandrasekhar, 2007). While most startups end in failure or are unable to grow past a certain point (Chinchwadkar & Shekhar, 2016), the Covid-19 pandemic years have created a number of opportunities for a handful of startups to achieve valuations in excess of US$1 billion. Such startups are colloquially referred to as "unicorns" (Bock & Hackober, 2020). As of 2021, India had the third-largest startup ecosystem in the world with an estimated 26,000 startups, 26 "unicorns," and US$36 billion in consolidated investments over 2017–2019 (David et al., 2020). In 2022, the number of unicorns had exceeded 100 (Jha et al., 2024). This is due to a number of factors including strong legal structures (Neerza & Tripathi, 2019).

Such valuations are attracted by multiple rounds of funding through private placement from institutional shareholders, typically multiple private equity funds. Empirical studies show that investee companies with multiple investors tend to generate higher returns (Ramesh & Annamalai, 2021) which may then correlate to higher valuations. Private equity investment also has a positive effect on profitability, sales, and employment, and these effects are more pronounced for minority investors both globally (Battistin et al., 2017) and in India (Malik & Dhankar, 2017).

Traditionally, Indian companies have been held and controlled by single shareholders or families (also referred to as a "promoter" in India). Under Section 2(26) of the Indian Companies Act, 2013, a promoter is defined as: (i) a person or an entity named as a promoter in an offer document or annual returns issued by the company; (ii) a person or entity having control over the affairs of the company, whether by virtue of being a shareholder, director, or otherwise; or (iii) a person whose advice, directions, or instructions the board of directors of the company customarily follows. In such cases, private equity funds usually take minority positions in these companies (Afsharipour, 2015). However, through multiple rounds of funding, it is entirely possible that promoters will get diluted down to a minority. As a result, the issues that private equity investors would have focused on with a majority promoter may no longer be relevant. These issues would include investor protection against the self-opportunistic and rent-seeking behavior of promoters (Shrivastava & Garg, 2017). Instead, other corporate governance issues, including coordination costs between multiple shareholders, may arise. As we will demonstrate later in this chapter, the majority shareholding of Indian companies is traditionally held by a small group of people, usually a family or the founders. As majority-controlling shareholders, they determine board composition and appointments, and often engage in the day-to-day management of the company. However, with many shareholders without a clear majority, it may become difficult to achieve a consensus on such matters, including appointment of directors and auditors, declaration of dividends, changes in business plans, and other governance issues.

This chapter seeks to review the shareholding structure of such unicorns, particularly the balance of corporate control between promoters and non-promoters or institutional shareholders. It further seeks to analyze modifications in corporate control through contracted corporate governance.

## 2. LITERATURE REVIEW

The phenomenon of dispersed shareholding has been well established in the United States and the United Kingdom (Bebchuk & Hamdani, 2009). Each of these jurisdictions seems to have separate mechanisms to protect shareholders, with the UK adopting an ex ante approach to outsider shareholders and the US focusing on an ex post and litigious approach (Mullineux, 2010). The UK and many other EU nations have regulatory structures that prohibit transactions that create negative externalities (Gilson & Schwartz, 2013). On the other hand, the US prefers greater flexibility for controlling shareholders, allowing courts to hold judicial review over transactions that may have been deemed circumspect by minority shareholders. In other words, the UK requires minority consent prior to certain transactions, while the US allows courts to intervene in a transaction after the fact.

However, it is equally established that the incidence of companies without a controlling shareholder is restricted to these countries only and that companies in large parts of the world have a controlling shareholder (Khanna & Yafeh,

2007). This poses interesting questions concerning the protection of private equity investors in Indian companies (Majumdar, 2019). In particular, classical agency theory and the problems that arise between owners and managers of firms (Armour et al., 2017) seem to have their shortcomings in family-run firms, such as those seen in India (Wright et al., 2009).

Afsharipour (2010) suggests that in Western markets, private equity funds typically take a majority position in their investee companies with high growth prospects with the intention of eventually selling out to a strategic buyer or taking the company public. For buyout transactions in India, on the other hand, the probability of an initial public offering (IPO) exit is less than that of a strategic sale (Chinchwadkar & Seth, 2018). In addition, private equity investments in India are exited within a shorter duration as opposed to long-term ownership (Annamalai, 2012). The type of exit may depend on the type of industry, financing stage, region of investment, and type of venture capital/private equity (VCPE) fund (Annamalai & Deshmukh, 2011).

In a typical leveraged buyout transaction, private equity funds would collateralize the assets of the investee company against consideration paid for its shares and use the investee company's income to pay off the debt (Blomberg, 2008). However, due to complex rules imposed by the Reserve Bank of India, such ownership structures are not possible in India. Under Section 19(2) of the Banking Regulation Act, 1949, Indian banks are prohibited from granting loans for the purchase of shares of an Indian company or against which equity is collateralized that are more than 30% of the paid-up share capital of the company. Further, under the Indian Consolidated FDI Policy of the the Department for Promotion of Industry and Internal Trade prohibits foreign investment companies from borrowing from Indian banks in order to acquire shares in Indian companies (Consolidated FDI Policy, 2020).

Instead, as mentioned earlier, private equity funds usually take a minority position in Indian investee companies (Afsharipour, 2015). While controlling promoters may consider such private equity funds solely as sources of capital, studies show that such funds may have a positive effect on risk mitigation and corporate governance standards (Marini et al., 2022). As a result, Indian private equity has been mainly focused on providing growth/expansion capital to companies as compared to buyouts in the developed markets (Ratanpal, 2008).

Post-Independence and indeed post-liberalized Indian companies have traditionally been closely held, controlled and monitored by concentrated shareholding structures (Varottil, 2009). Controlling shareholders, referred to in the Indian context as promoters, have usually played an all-pervasive role in the day-to-day management of the company (Afsharipour, 2015). As a result, institutional investors such as VCPE funds, often seen as "outsiders," look to contractual measures to curb promoter opportunism (Afsharipour & Gelter, 2021). As majority-controlling shareholders, promoters may hold enough shares to control the board as well as the day-to-day management of the company. It is not unusual to see promoters holding majority shares and having leadership positions on the board, along with family members, in Indian companies. As a result, investors may be at risk from promoter opportunism through the extraction of private benefits and wealth tunneling through related party transactions (Varottil, 2009).

However, the rise of an entrepreneurial culture, coupled with regulatory incentives in India, has led to the creation of a large number of unicorns within the Indian economy (Joshi et al., 2022).

## 3. METHODOLOGY

Indian corporate jurisprudence, while mostly transplanted from the West (Varottil, 2009), retains some unique features. One of them is an Indian Supreme Court judgment which requires privately contracted shareholder rights and corporate governance rules in a private, unlisted company to be made public knowledge. In *V. B. Rangaraj v. V. B. Gopalakrishnan* (1992), the apex court held that any rights or obligations contained in a privately negotiated shareholders' agreement would be unenforceable unless the same is also enshrined in the articles of association of the company.

As a result, any unicorn that has accepted equity funding from an institutional investor and where the investor has negotiated corporate governance rights in the target company must include those rights in the articles of association of the target company. The articles of all companies as well as returns of share allotments and shareholding data are available for fee-based public consumption in India.

We used publicly available data from Venture Intelligence (TSJ Media Pvt, 2024) to identify 80 private, unlisted companies that were registered in India and that had achieved a valuation in excess of US$1 billion. Our focus on private, unlisted companies originates from the ostensibly higher standards of corporate governance norms in publicly listed companies. Private companies have a lower threshold of corporate governance norms and therefore have more opportunities to create contractual norms for themselves.

Using Altinfo, we then accessed the publicly available data disclosed by these unicorns to the Registrar of Companies under the Ministry of Corporate Affairs, Government of India. Altinfo is a product of Veratech Intelligence Private, which is a process automation legal-tech company that specializes in dealing with data of Indian companies. The data that we accessed was as follows:

1. Name of the company.
2. The shareholding pattern of the company, including:

   a. Names of shareholders.
   b. Percentage of shareholding.
   c. Whether the shareholder was a founder/promoter or an investor.
3. Most recent version of the articles of association.

However, as has been noted elsewhere, compliance with reporting requirements regarding Indian private companies is notoriously low (Majumdar, 2019), and as a result, we were able to gather the percentage of promoter shareholding compared to non-promoter shareholding for 47 out of 80 of these unicorns, creating a database of corporate information on Indian unicorns. This database, along with other corporate information gleaned from the Ministry of Corporate Affairs, Government of India, has been made publicly accessible.[1] We base much of our analysis and understanding of the corporate governance of Indian unicorns on this database.

However, beyond the default position of being able to control board composition through a simple majority, investee companies often create control rights in favor of investors. As mentioned earlier, these control rights must be included in the articles of association of such companies. Through our qualitative review of the articles of these companies, we were further able to ascertain the privately negotiated corporate governance frameworks of these companies.

## 4. RESEARCH QUESTIONS

The primary purpose of this study was to ascertain whether unicorns – startups that have achieved a high level of valuation – have ownership structures that are different from other companies. Indian companies have long been posited to have an "insider" mode of ownership and control, leading to private equity and institutional ownership taking a minority position in investee companies.

This is contrary to private equity and institutional ownership in more developed countries such as the US, where institutional shareholders often use a leveraged buyout model to take a majority position in investee companies. We seek to establish that Indian unicorns have a dispersed mode of shareholder ownership like companies in the US and the UK, with founders and promoters themselves in a minority position. This model will be a departure from the more classical insider model found in most Indian companies.

The second question we sought to analyze was whether Indian unicorns created special rights in favor of the founder-promoters or institutional shareholders to maintain parity in control. These corporate governance frameworks, which are privately negotiated, were contained in the articles of such unicorns. Irrespective of the fact that these unicorns are private and unlisted, they are controlled by many shareholders. We expect that as the number of shareholders increases, the corporate governance frameworks of these companies approach the complexity and standards of public listed companies.

## 5. EMPIRICAL ANALYSIS OF PROMOTER CONCENTRATION IN INDIAN UNICORNS

The background to the issue and the Indian model of private equity are set out in this introductory section along with the literature review, methodology, and research questions. The second section empirically analyzes the dispersion or concentration in our sample set of 49 unicorns. The third section analyzes the corporate governance framework for these sample companies and seeks to draw trends between shareholding concentration and mode of governance. The fourth section concludes and offers suggestions for further research.

### 5.1 The Insider Model of Corporate Governance

Both Varottil (2009) and Afsharipour (2015) allude to an "insider" model of corporate governance in Indian companies. This involves a majority shareholder or promoter in control of the company and investment funds taking a minority position, acting as "outsider" shareholders. Such outsiders may be seen solely as sources of capital, and promoters may be loath to share control or, indeed, even take advice from such outsiders (Afsharipour & Gelter, 2021). This creates what John Armour and others (2017) refer to as the second agency problem in company law – that of the relationship between minority and majority shareholders. Minority protection in India is still rudimentary, requiring court intervention. However, in private, unlisted companies, minority shareholders may be able to wrest certain special rights as shareholders within the contractual arrangement of the investment made.

This model is well established not just in private, unlisted companies. An empirical study of Indian listed companies shows that even in listed companies, the presence of a controlling shareholder remains (Majumdar & Gupta, 2023). Erik Berglöf and Ernst-Ludwig Von Thadden (2000) suggest similar phenomena outside of India as well.

Figure 5.1 represents the percentage of promoter shareholding in the top 500 companies listed on the Indian National Stock Exchange or NIFTY 500.

The figure demonstrates that within the NIFTY 500, 328 or 65.6% have a majority shareholding by promoters. It is also interesting to note that nearly one-fifth of the NIFTY 500 have a promoter or non-public shareholding between 70% and 75%. Under Indian law, publicly listed companies may not have more than 75% shareholding in non-public hands (Indian Securities Contracts Regulation Rules, 1957). This might seem a little surprising, given

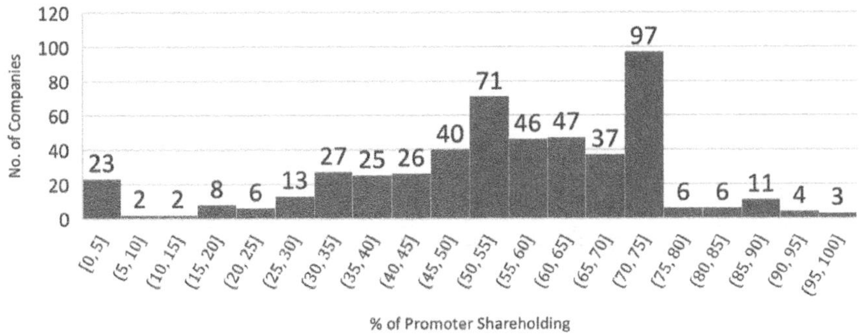


*Figure 5.1* *Distribution of companies by promoter shareholding*

the public nature of listed companies. In other words, even publicly listed companies are owned and controlled by a few.

This is reflective of the insider model of corporate governance alluded to by Afsharipour (2015) and Varottil (2009), where even when a company is listed, its ownership, control, and governance are still held in the hands of a few. We would expect that the same phenomenon would be exacerbated in private, unlisted companies.

For most startups to attain unicorn status, it is likely that multiple rounds of funding will be required. We conducted an empirical analysis of the shares and convertible instruments, which may include convertible preference shares as well as convertible debentures issued by such companies. Preference shares are the preferred stock of the company, usually having a fixed return clause, limited voting rights, and preference in the order of payments during company liquidation. Convertible preference shares may be converted into equity or common stock. The same applies to convertible debentures or bonds, which are treated as debt under law and accounting policies but may be converted to equity. These conversions may take place on a compulsory basis, that is that the instrument will have to be converted at some point in time, or on an optional basis at the election of the instrument holder. Thus, convertible instruments provide both security at the time of liquidation as well as the option to gain from higher returns on equity shares.

Table 5.1 suggests that despite multiple rounds of funding, which would dilute the stake of promoters, such promoters in Indian unicorns continue to have a majority stake, at least in terms of equity share capital.

As expected from the "insider" model of corporate governance, we note that founders and promoters remain in the majority, even in unicorn-status companies. The average promoter equity shareholding for these companies is 73.09%.

*Table 5.1 Shareholding percentages between promoters and non-promoters*

| Shareholder Number | Company name | Equity – promoter share | Equity – non-promoter share | Convertible securities – promoter share | Convertible securities non-promoter share |
|---|---|---|---|---|---|
| 1. | Ntex transportation Limited | 89.95 | 10.06 | 0 | 100 |
| 2. | Leadership Boulevard Private Limited | 79.24 | 20.74 | 9.26 | 90.71 |
| 3. | Ani Technologies Private Limited | 63.58 | 36.42 | 0 | 100 |
| 4. | Mohalla Tech Private Limited | 63.58 | 36.42 | 0 | 100 |
| 5. | Neblio Technologies Private Limited | 100 | 0 | 0 | 100 |
| 6. | Sanghvi Beauty and Technologies Private Limited | 43.07 | 56.91 | 0 | 100 |
| 7. | Girnar Software Private Limited | 79.65 | 20.35 | 0 | 100 |
| 8. | Play Games 24*7 Private Limited | 55.1 | 44.9 | 0 | 100 |
| 9. | Rivigo Service Private Limited | 82.55 | 17.45 | 0 | 100 |
| 10. | GHV Advance Private Limited | 99.35 | 0.65 | 0 | 100 |
| 11. | ACKO General Insurance Ltd | 100 | 0 | 0 | 0 |
| 12. | Bigfoot Retail Solutions Private Limited | 43.54 | 56.47 | 0 | 100 |
| 13. | Amagi Media Labs Private Limited | 75.08 | 24.92 | 0 | 100 |
| 14. | 1MG Technologies Private Limited | 70.85 | 29.15 | 100 | 0 |

| Shareholder Number | Company name | Equity – promoter share | Equity – non-promoter share | Convertible securities – promoter share | Convertible securities non-promoter share |
|---|---|---|---|---|---|
| 15. | CredAvenue Private Limited | 94.81 | 5.19 | 0 | 100 |
| 16. | Dealskart Online Private Limited | 100 | 0 | 0 | 0 |
| 17. | Delightful Gourmet Private Limited | 51.37 | 48.63 | 0.16 | 99.84 |
| 18. | Digital Age Retails Private Limited | 100 | 0 | 0 | 0 |
| 19. | Dreamplug Technologies Private Limited | 73.7 | 26.3 | 0 | 100 |
| 20. | FPL Technologies Private Limited | 93.66 | 6.34 | 0 | 100 |
| 21. | Globalbees Brands Private Limited | 100 | 0 | 0 | 100 |
| 22. | Go Digit General Insurance Private Limited | 83.49 | 16.51 | 0 | 100 |
| 23. | Hella Infra Market Private Limited | 83.06 | 16.94 | 0 | 100 |
| 24. | Honasa Consumer Private Limited | 2.99 | 97.01 | 0 | 100 |
| 25. | Manash Lifestyle Private Limited | 52.75 | 47.25 | 0 | 100 |
| 26. | MarketXpander Services Private Limited | 52.78 | 47.22 | 0 | 100 |
| 27. | Merabo Labs Private Limited | 87.61 | 12.39 | 0 | 100 |
| 28. | Nobroker Technologies Private Limited | 73.92 | 26.08 | 0 | 100 |

| Shareholder Number | Company name | Equity – promoter share | Equity – non-promoter share | Convertible securities – promoter share | Convertible securities non-promoter share |
|---|---|---|---|---|---|
| 29. | OFB Technology Private Limited | 75.8 | 24.2 | 7.55 | 92.45 |
| 30. | Oxyzo Financial Services Private Limited | 95.4 | 4.6 | 0 | 100 |
| 31. | PhonePe Private Limited | 96.43 | 3.57 | 0 | 0 |
| 32. | Rebel Foods Private Limited | 41.87 | 58.13 | 0 | 100 |
| 33. | Resilient Innovations Private Limited | 79.26 | 20.74 | 0 | 100 |
| 34. | Supermarket Grocery Supplies Private Limited | 73.32 | 26.68 | 0 | 100 |
| 35. | Think and Learn Private Limited | 56.24 | 43.76 | 6.87 | 93.13 |
| 36. | Valudrive Technologies Private Limited | 9.35 | 90.65 | 0 | 100 |
| 37. | Upgrade Education Private Limited | 73.51 | 26.49 | 0 | 100 |
| 38. | Zetwerk Manufacturing Businesses Private Limited | 90.55 | 9.45 | 0 | 100 |
| 39. | Brainbees Solutions Private Limited | 12.13 | 87.87 | 0 | 100 |
| 40. | Bundl Technologies Private Limited | 68.17 | 31.83 | 0 | 100 |
| 41. | Busybees Logistics Solutions Private Limited | 50.17 | 49.83 | 0 | 100 |

| Shareholder Number | Company name | Equity – promoter share | Equity – non-promoter share | Convertible securities – promoter share | Convertible securities – non-promoter share |
|---|---|---|---|---|---|
| 42. | Darwinbox Digital Solutions Private Limited | 82.19 | 17.81 | 0 | 100 |
| 43. | Ola Electric Mobility Private Limited | 70.45 | 29.55 | 0 | 100 |
| 44. | Open Financial Technologies Private Limited | 99.4 | 0.6 | 0 | 100 |
| 45. | Physicswallah Private Limited | 100 | 0 | 0 | 100 |
| 46. | Urbanclap India Technologies Private Limited | 82.79 | 17.21 | 0 | 100 |
| 47. | Vedantu Innovations Private Limited | 84.44 | 15.56 | 0 | 100 |
| 48. | Vivriti Capital Private Limited | 50.33 | 49.67 | 0.9 | 99.1 |
| 49. | Zinka Logistics Solutions Private Limited | 93.94 | 6.06 | 0 | 100 |

## 5.2 The Veil of Conversion

However, what is interesting to note is that without exception, almost all private equity and venture capital investments in unicorn companies have been through convertible securities that have both downside protection (via seniority) and upside potential (via an option to convert into common shares) (Gornall & Strebulaev, 2020). These may include convertible preference shares under Section 43 of the Indian Companies Act 2013 or convertible debentures under Section 71 of the Indian Companies Act 2013. Investors will usually take a small percentage of equity shares to meet the regulatory requirements of being able to vote on shareholder resolutions and appoint directors. Under the provisions of Section 152 of the Indian Companies Act 2013, preference shareholders and debenture holders are prevented from fully participating in all shareholder-level decision-making in the company.

A question that then arises concerns promoter concentration on a fully diluted basis; that is, as if all convertible securities had been converted. In such cases, if all convertible securities are indeed converted to equity shares, would the promoter still have more than a 51% majority of the equity share capital? In other words, on a fully diluted basis, does the promoter retain control over its company?

The terms of conversion of these convertible instruments vary by company and investment round and are usually tied to the fair market value of the equity shares of the company. Therefore, unless the Articles of Association of the company specify otherwise, it would not be possible to calculate the exact number of equity shares to be issued for the conversion of convertible securities. However, there is some anecdotal evidence that we may consider.

In Clause 116.1 Definitions and Interpretations Clause of the Articles of Association of NTex Transportation Services Private Limited dated May 2021 (NTex Transportation Services Limited, 2021), the term "As If Converted Basis" is defined to mean a calculation based on all convertible securities having been converted into equity shares. A clarification in the definition goes on to provide that until an event requiring the conversion of securities takes place, each compulsorily convertible preference share issued shall be equivalent to one equity share.

As the shareholding pattern of the company (NTex Transportation Services Limited, 2023) suggests, the promoters hold 21,059 equity shares. Non-promoter shareholders or investors hold 91,587 compulsorily convertible preference shares or 100% of the convertible share capital of NTex. If, as the Articles of NTex suggest, each convertible preference share converts to one equity share, the promoters' equity would certainly be diluted down far below the accepted simple majority threshold of 51%.

In a valuation report issued to Think and Learn Private Limited dated November 2021 (Barick, 2021), each cumulative compulsorily convertible preference share (except for Series A CCCPS) has been mentioned as convertible into 0.9743 equity shares of the company. Given that as of April 2022 the company had issued 2,400,476 non-Series A non-cumulative Compulsorily Convertible Preferred Stock, this would convert to 2,313,088 equity shares in the company. As a result, the shareholding percentage of the founders and their families would be diluted down to 28% (Think and Learn Pvt Ltd, 2022). A similar valuation report was filed in respect of DreamPlug Technologies Private Limited in which Series E1 and Series F CCCPS were said to be convertible to equity shares in the ratio of 1:1 (Jain, 2022).

While similar conversion factors for other companies may not be publicly available, it is equally likely that, as and when such securities are converted for other companies that have raised large sums of investment through convertible securities, the equity shareholding percentage of the founders or promoters will be diluted.

However, as mentioned above, there is no way to accurately calculate the shareholding of each promoter or investor on a fully diluted basis since these are based on fair market values of the company and therefore the shares – a value that will continue to change over time and across unicorns. Thus, the concentrated or dispersed nature of shareholding in an Indian company remains hidden behind what could be referred to as the "veil of conversion."

A second method to understand the nature and balance of shareholdings in Indian unicorns is to analyze shareholding patterns as and when such unicorns go public.

## 5.3 Public Listed Unicorns or Professionally Managed Companies

A phenomenon that has arisen in India since 2019 is the advent of the professionally managed company. These are companies with no identifiable promoters by virtue of low individual shareholdings. Between December 2018 and April 2023, approximately 200 Indian companies undertook an IPO, of which six have been named as professionally managed. These are UTI Asset Management Company Limited (2020), Zomato Limited (2021), Cartrade Tech Limited (2021), PB Fintech Limited (2021), One 97 Communications Limited (2021), and Delhivery Limited (2022).

In India, any company undertaking an IPO must (a) convert all outstanding convertible securities prior to making the offer under Regulation 5(2), Securities and Exchange Board of India (Issue of Capital and Disclosure Requirements) Regulations 2018 and (b) must disclose the names of the shareholders of the issuing company holding 1% or more of the paid-up capital of the issuer as of the date of filing of the draft offer document under Schedule

VI, 8 (B) (f) (i), Securities and Exchange Board of India (Issue of Capital and Disclosure Requirements) Regulations 2018. As a result, unicorns that have undertaken an IPO must disclose their shareholding pattern on a fully diluted basis.

As expected in companies without a promoter, we observe a considerably dispersed shareholding pattern. Out of the six companies mentioned above, it might be worth looking into the shareholding patterns of Zomato (Srinivasan, 2018), PB Fintech Limited (Gooptu, 2018), One 97 Communications (Chaudhary, 2017), and Delhivery (Dash, 2019), since all four of them were considered to be unicorns prior to listing (Tables 5.2, 5.3, 5.4, and 5.5).

Private, unlisted unicorns retain a shareholding pattern consistent with the established insider model of Indian corporate governance. At the same time, they can achieve higher valuations and further rounds of investment by issuing convertible securities. As a result, the true nature of the company's shareholding pattern on a fully diluted basis is never fully understood. It remains behind the "veil of conversion."

However, under SEBI regulations, such companies, when listing, are required to convert all such convertibles or any rights that shareholders may have to receive equity shares in the future. As demonstrated in the case of three formerly unlisted unicorns, now publicly listed entities, the shareholding of the promoters or founders is diluted down to single digits, even before their participation in an offer for sale of their shares as part of the IPO. Most shares on a fully diluted basis are now shared among institutional shareholders. This is consistent with other studies which show that the private equity fund's shareholding and the valuation of the investee company are positively related (Jiujin et al., 2020).

As a result, we note that our established insider model of corporate governance may not hold true in cases of companies with large amounts of external investments and a multitude of investors. In our standard insider model of corporate governance, external investors will build suitable checks and balances by incorporating special rights pertaining to board appointment, quorum, veto, and access to information as well as pre-emptive and anti-dilution rights into the constitutional documents of the company. As the next section shows, this is true for unicorns as well. However, the question raised in the next chapter considers whether corporate control wielded by founders or promoters in Indian unicorns is also somewhat diluted because of a multitude of investors and dispersed shareholding on a fully diluted basis.

*Table 5.2* *Shareholding pattern for shareholders holding more than 1% of Zomato Limited on a fully diluted basis prior to listing (Zomato Limited, 2021)*

| Shareholder Number | Shareholder Name | Number of equity shares | Percentage of the pre-offer equity share capital |
|---|---|---|---|
| 1. | Info Edge (India) Limited | 1,244,029,200 | 18.52 |
| 2. | Uber B.V. | 612,199,100 | 9.11 |
| 3. | Alipay Singapore Holding Pte. Ltd. | 558,947,500 | 8.32 |
| 4. | Antfin Singapore Holding Pte. Ltd. | 550,250,900 | 8.19 |
| 5. | Internet Fund VI Pte Ltd | 402,328,300 | 5.99 |
| 6. | SCI Growth Investments II | 401,376,900 | 5.98 |
| 7. | Deepinder Goyal | 369,471,500 | 5.50 |
| 8. | Foodiebay Employees ESOP Trust 2014 | 279,832,200 | 4.17 |
| 9. | D1 Master Capital Partners LP | 254,834,500 | 3.79 |
| 10. | MacRitchie Investments Pte. Ltd | 244,811,300 | 3.64 |
| 11. | Dunearn Investments (Mauritius) Pte Ltd | 171,312,300 | 2.55 |
| 12. | Kora Investment I LLC | 169,590,400 | 2.52 |
| 13. | VY Investments Mauritius Limited | 167,704,350 | 2.50 |
| 14. | Kora Holdings II (C) LLC | 145,209,100 | 2.16 |
| 15. | VYC20 Limited | 138,864,200 | 2.07 |
| 16. | Delivery Hero SE | 107,200,000 | 1.60 |
| 17. | Sequoia Capital India Growth Investment Holdings I | 87,937,500 | 1.31 |
| 18. | Glade Brook Private Investors XVII LP | 87,100,000 | 1.30 |
| - | Total | 5,992,999,250 | 89.21 |

*Table 5.3 Shareholding pattern for shareholders holding more than 1% of PB Fintech Limited on a fully diluted basis prior to listing (PB Fintech Limited, 2021)*

| Shareholder Number | Shareholder | Number of equity shares | Percentage of pre-offer equity share capital (%) |
|---|---|---|---|
| 1. | Makesense Technologies Limited | 59,890,000 | 14.56 |
| 2. | SVF Python II (Cayman) Limited | 38,877,500 | 9.45 |
| 3. | Tencent Cloud Europe B.V. | 37,665,000 | 9.16 |
| 4. | SVF India Holdings (Cayman) Limited | 25,940,000 | 6.31 |
| 5. | Claymore Investment (Mauritius) Pte Ltd | 25,737,500 | 6.26 |
| 6. | Etechaces Employees Stock Option Plan Trust | 22,537,500 | 5.48 |
| 7. | Tiger Global Eight Holdings | 19,032,500 | 4.63 |
| 8. | Diphda Internet Services Limited | 18,880,000 | 4.59 |
| 9. | Mr. Yashish Dahiya | 17,545,000 | 4.27 |
| 10. | PI Opportunities Fund -II | 15,525,000 | 3.78 |
| 11. | Internet Fund III Pte Limited | 12,897,500 | 3.14 |
| 12. | Falcon Q LP | 11,589,500 | 2.82 |
| 13. | Steadview Capital Mauritius Limited | 9,812,500 | 2.39 |
| 14. | True North Fund VI LLP | 9,440,000 | 2.30 |
| 15. | Startup Investments (Holding) Limited | 8,662,500 | 2.11 |
| 16. | Ithan Creek MB | 7,515,000 | 1.83 |
| 17. | Inventus Capital Partners Fund II, Limited | 6,437,500 | 1.57 |
| 18. | Mr. Alok Bansal | 5,958,500 | 1.45 |
| 19. | ABG Capital | 4,385,000 | 1.07 |
| 20. | Alpha Wave Incubation LP | 4,320,000 | 1.05 |
| - | Total | 362,648,000 | 88.22 |

*Table 5.4 Shareholding pattern for shareholders holding more than 1% of One 97 Communications Limited on a fully diluted basis prior to listing (One 97 Communications Limited 2021)*

| Shareholder Number | Shareholder | Number of equity shares | Percentage of the pre-offer equity share capital (%) |
|---|---|---|---|
| 1. | Antfin (Netherlands) Holding B.V. | 183,301,220 | 27.9 |
| 2. | SVF India Holdings (Cayman) Limited | 113,262,230 | 17.3 |
| 3. | SAIF III Mauritius Company Limited | 74,910,610 | 11.4 |
| 4. | Mr. Vijay Shekhar Sharma | 59,545,834 | 9.1 |
| 5. | Alibaba.Com Singapore E-Commerce Private Limited | 44,282,140 | 6.8 |
| 6. | SAIF Partners India IV Limited | 31,802,020 | 4.8 |
| 7. | Axis Trustee Services Limited | 30,970,406 | 4.7 |
| 8. | BH International Holdings | 17,027,130 | 2.6 |
| 9. | SVF Panther (Cayman) Limited | 7,855,970 | 1.2 |
| - | Total | 562,957,560 | 85.8 |

*Table 5.5 Shareholding pattern for shareholders holding more than 1% of Delhivery Limited on a fully diluted basis prior to listing (Delhivery Limited, 2022)*

| Shareholder Number | Shareholder | Number of equity shares | Percentage of equity share capital (%) |
|---|---|---|---|
| 1. | SVF Doorbell (Cayman) Ltd (SoftBank Vision Fund) | 141,593,300 | 21.98 |
| 2. | Nexus Ventures III Ltd. (Nexus Venture Partners) | 57,406,800 | 8.91 |
| 3. | CA Swift Investments (Carlyle Asia Partners IV) | 46,131,800 | 7.16 |
| 4. | Canada Pension Plan Investment Board | 43,881,500 | 6.81 |
| 5. | Internet Fund III Pte. Ltd. (Tiger Global Management) | 37,893,700 | 5.88 |
| 6. | Times Internet Limited | 31,703,900 | 4.92 |
| 7. | Suedasien Investmentfonds A, Ltd (Addition) | 22,347,900 | 3.47 |

| Shareholder Number | Shareholder | Number of equity shares | Percentage of equity share capital (%) |
|---|---|---|---|
| 8. | FedEx Express Transportation and Supply Chain Services (India) Private Limited | 20,914,500 | 3.25 |
| 9. | Alpine Opportunity Fund II, L.P. (Alpine Capital) | 17,170,900 | 2.67 |
| 10. | Gamnat Pte. Ltd. (Gamnat) | 15,364,000 | 2.39 |
| 11. | Alpha Wave Ventures LP (Alpha Wave Global) | 14,444,800 | 2.24 |
| 12. | Sahil Barua | 13,407,798 | 2.08 |
| 13. | Mohit Tandon | 11,664,200 | 1.81 |
| 14. | Suraj Saharan | 10,994,300 | 1.71 |
| 15. | Chimetech Holding Ltd. (Chimera Investment) | 9,632,700 | 1.50 |
| 16. | Nexus Opportunity Fund Ltd. (Nexus Venture Partners) | 8,666,100 | 1.35 |
| 17. | Steadview Capital Mauritius Limited (Steadview) | 8,113,800 | 1.26 |
| 18. | Bennett, Coleman and Company Limited | 7,696,000 | 1.19 |
| 19. | Alpine Opportunity Fund V, L.P. (Alpine Capital) | 7,309,300 | 1.13 |
| 20. | Deli CMF Pte. Ltd. (Fosun) | 6,879,000 | 1.07 |
| 21. | Steadview Capital Opportunities PCC Cell 0221 009 (Steadview) | 6,700,000 | 1.04 |
| 22. | Kapil Bharati | 6,694,800 | 1.04 |
| - | Total | 546,611,098 | 84.85 |

## 5.4 Governance Structures in Unicorns

In exchange for financing, entrepreneurs and companies relinquish some element of control or oversight over company operations in the form of equity or preference shares. The parties may decide to share control (joint ownership) or to allocate control and the right to sell control to the entrepreneur (issue non-voting, or minority, equity) or to the venture capitalist (issue voting equity) (Berglöf, 1994). While preferred stock grants special preferences and protections to the venture capital fund by statute (Korsmo, 2013), it is not unusual to note extra-statutory special shareholding rights negotiated even for equity shares. In essence, private ordering is the primary method of protection for venture capital and private equity investors.

Some of the commonly negotiated items include dividend and liquidation preferences, anti-dilution provisions, conversion and redemption rights, registration rights, and other affirmative and negative covenants that significantly impact the functioning of the board of directors, providing protection to investors. There are other affirmative and negative covenants (Gardner, 1971). These include:

1. Restrictions on indebtedness
2. Restrictions on encumbrances
3. Requirement for working capital
4. Requirement for maintaining minimum net worth
5. Requirement for payment of taxes and government charges in a timely fashion
6. Negative restriction against dividend distribution or redemption of the company's stock
7. Restrictions against making investments in any other company stock
8. Restriction against making investments in any other companies
9. Prohibition of consolidation, mergers, and acquisition
10. Prohibition of amendment to the charter of the company or its bylaws
11. Limitation of employment or other personal service contracts
12. Prohibition of liquidation, dilution, sale, lease, or other disposition
13. Covenant for furnishing the investor with financial statements
14. Maintenance of life insurance on key personnel and the application of the proceeds of the financing
15. Covenants establishing preparation and approval procedures for annual or semiannual budgets
16. Provision for representation of the investor on the board
17. Permission for the venture investor and its representatives to make inspections of the company's property and books and records
18. Covenant to maintain and keep insured the company's properties, covenant to engage in the type of business described in the representations and warranties, and to maintain the company's corporate existence.

Investors also negotiate for shareholder rights that lower the risk of their investment in the form of structuring minority investments, investor control rights, and exit strategies (Afsharipour, 2015).

The Indian private equity model uses a combination of the above-mentioned contractual obligations typically negotiated between investors and the company/promoter in a Shareholders Agreement (SHA). In *V.B. Rangaraj v.*

*V.B. Gopalkrishnan (1992)*, while dealing with a conflict between an SHA and the articles of the company, the Indian Supreme Court took the view that the provisions of an SHA imposing restrictions on share transferability, even when consistent with the Companies Act, are to be authorized only when they are incorporated in the articles of association of the company. This view was expanded to other conflicts between the SHA and the articles of association, beyond rights on share transferability in *IL&FS Trust Co. Ltd. v. Birla Perucchini Ltd (2004)*. In other words, where there is a contradiction between the SHA and the articles of a company, the latter will prevail. This development at the Indian Supreme Court forms the basis of this chapter.

As a result, clauses present in the SHA almost always find their way into the articles of association of investee companies. Under Section 5 of the Indian Companies Act, 2013, articles of association are publicly accessible documents on the Ministry of Corporate Affairs website. We accessed the most recent articles for 47 companies that had attained unicorn status in India and had complied with Section 5 of the Indian Companies Act, 2013 as of April 2023.

Using the text and provisions of these articles of association, we then recorded the following control rights as negotiated and agreed upon between the investee company in favor of the private equity investor:

- Percentage of directors nominated by investors
- Whether investors have quorum rights at board meetings and shareholder meetings
- Whether investors have information rights
- Whether investors have affirmative voting rights, veto rights, and reserved matters ("AVRs") at board meetings and shareholder meetings
- The nature of AVRs in favor of PE firms includes amendments to the company constitutional documents, board structure, changes in scope of business, raising fresh capital, borrowing, capital expenditure, declaration of dividends, etc.

### 5.4.1 Board composition

Where available, we analyzed the board strength and composition of each company. We noted the number of directors that could be appointed to the board and how many of them could be appointed by the promoters and how many could be appointed by investors (Table 5.6).

All companies allowed at least one director to be nominated by investors. In 75% of such companies, the number of directors appointed by investors exceeded the number of directors appointed by promoters/founders. In almost all cases, the ability of investors to appoint directors was linked directly to their shareholding on a fully diluted basis. In other words, the right to appoint a

*Table 5.6 Directors appointed by investors*

| Shareholder Number | Name of the company | Board strength | Investor nominee directors |
|---|---|---|---|
| 1. | 1MG Technologies Private Limited | 8 | 3 |
| 2. | ACKO General Insurance Limited | 10 | 4 |
| 3. | Amagi Media Labs Private Limited | 15 | 9 |
| 4. | ANI Technologies Private Limited | 9 | 4 |
| 5. | Bigfoot Retail Private Limited | 10 | 7 |
| 6. | Brainbees Solutions Private Limited | 8 | 6 |
| 7. | Bundl Technologies Private Limited | 9 | 7 |
| 8. | Busybees Logistics Solutions Private Limited | 10 | 8 |
| 9. | Cred Avenue Private Limited | 8 | 6 |
| 10. | Darwinbox Digital Solutions Private Limited | 7 | 4 |
| 11. | Delightful Gourmet Private Limited | 10 | 7 |
| 12. | Digital Age retails Private Limited | 7 | 4 |
| 13. | Dreamplug Technologies Private Limited | 5 | 3 |
| 14. | FPL Technologies Private Limited | 6 | 3 |
| 15. | GHV Advanced Care Private Limited | 4 | 3 |
| 16. | Girnar Software Private Limited | 7 | 5 |
| 17. | Globalbees Brands Private Limited | 8 | 6 |
| 18. | Go Digit General Insurance Private Limited | 11 | 5 |
| 19. | Hella Infra Market Private Limited | 9 | 4 |
| 20. | Honasa Consumer Private Limited | 7 | 4 |
| 21. | Leadership Boulevard Private Limited | 7 | 4 |
| 22. | Manash Lifestyle Private Limited | 9 | 5 |
| 23. | Marketxpander Services Private Limited | 6 | 4 |
| 24. | Merabo Labs Private Limited | 7 | 4 |
| 25. | Mohalla Tech Private Limited | 8 | 5 |
| 26. | Nobroker Technologies Solutions Private Limited | 5 | 3 |
| 27. | Ntex transportation Limited | 7 | 4 |
| 28. | OFB Technology Private Limited | 7 | 6 |
| 29. | Ola Electric Mobility Private Limited | 4 | 1 |

| Shareholder Number | Name of the company | Board strength | Investor nominee directors |
|---|---|---|---|
| 30. | Open Financial Technologies Private Limited | 6 | 4 |
| 31. | Oxyzo Financial Services Private Limited | 11 | 5 |
| 32. | PhonePe Private Limited | 3 | 2 |
| 33. | Physicswallah Private Limited | 4 | 2 |
| 34. | Play Games 24x7 Private Limited | 7 | 2 |
| 35. | Rebel Foods Private Limited | 7 | 5 |
| 36. | Resilient Innovations Private Limited | 12 | 10 |
| 37. | Rivigo Services Private Limited | 8 | 3 |
| 38. | Sanghvi Beauty and Technologies Private Limited | 7 | 5 |
| 39. | Sorting Hat Technologies Private Limited | 11 | 6 |
| 40. | Think and Learn Private Limited | 13 | 7 |
| 41. | Upgrade Education Private Limited | 5 | 3 |
| 42. | Urbanclap India Technologies Private Limited | 9 | 3 |
| 43. | Valudrive Technologies Private Limited | 11 | 7 |
| 44. | Vedantu Innovations Private Limited | 8 | 4 |
| 45. | Vivriti Capital Private Limited | 8 | 3 |
| 46. | Zetwerk Manufacturing | 7 | 4 |
| 47. | Zinka Logistics Solutions Private Limited | 5 | 3 |

director was based on the maintenance of a minimum shareholding threshold. On occasion, investors below the minimum threshold would have the right to jointly appoint a director with other investors below the threshold.

Interestingly, however, the right of the promoter(s) to appoint directors was not tied to their shareholding threshold. Instead, it was linked to their employment with the company. In other words, the promoters and investors felt that it was more important for the promoter be part of the company (usually as a chief executive officer or some other key managerial personnel) as opposed to being a majority shareholder. This development may provide some evidence that promoters or founders are no longer seen as majority shareholders *de jure* even if they hold a majority of equity shares *de facto*. Instead, they are viewed as key employees critical to the success of the company.

### 5.4.2 Independent directors

Many articles reviewed also contained corporate governance provisions that were comparable to publicly listed companies. Corporate governance in publicly traded companies is heavily regulated by the Securities and Exchange Board of India, which places heavy reliance on corporate governance norms such as independent directors, board committees for audit, remuneration, stakeholder grievance, and auditor independence.

Upon close analysis and review of the articles of unicorns, we found that several startups have contractual requirements to appoint independent directors. Given that the idea and regulatory requirement of appointing independent directors applies to publicly listed companies in India, this development in private, unlisted unicorns means that as the number of shareholders in companies increases, their governance also tends to require higher standards of conduct, tending towards the standards of public listed companies.

Research suggests that higher accounting and market performance may be achieved by good governance practices, which in turn, lead to reduced agency costs (Saini & Singhania, 2018). Apart from providing capital to capital-starved economies such as India, private equity investors can help in developing cost-effective projects and contribute to sector development by institutionalizing robust processes and governance practices (Annamalai & Behera, 2016). For example, given that a private equity or venture capital investor may invest in sectoral or thematic companies, it would be easy for such investors to bring sectoral expertise and best practices into fledgling companies.

The same effect may be seen in other jurisdictions as well in a study on Brazilian firms with private equity that tended to have a better governance index and list more on the Brazilian stock exchanges (Carvalhal & Souza, 2014). Similarly, there is evidence to show that VCPE funds play an important role in promoting best practices of corporate governance in invested small and medium enterprises, which contributes to the development of the institutional environment and small and medium enterprises' access to outside sources of finance (Teixeira Latini et al., 2014). Private equity-funded firms display higher standards of corporate governance than firms that do not receive such funding (Dossani, 2012).

### 5.4.3 Quorum rights at board and shareholder meetings

An investor will typically require that a shareholders' meeting and, less typically, a board meeting not be quorate without the presence of the representative or the board nominee of the investor (Yates & Hinchliffe, 2010). This is likely to be a contentious issue since promoters may not want to offer opportunities for the business and management of the company to be frustrated by the non-attendance of the investor nominee (Majumdar, 2019).

A large majority of the articles reviewed provided for quorum rights in both board and shareholder meetings. As many as 86.1% provided for quorum rights to investors.

### 5.4.4 Veto and affirmative rights at board and shareholder meetings

Reserved or veto or affirmative vote matters or consent rights are issues that are of particular importance to the investor. Almost all Articles provided for affirmative voting rights. Moreover, the clauses in which reserved matters/affirmative voting rights were listed were often extremely similar, being almost boilerplate across multiple articles. Despite different wordings in some sections, the material itself was almost identical and typically spanned practically all salient (or even remotely related) matters to the running and functioning of the company. Hence, it can be understood that investor reserved matters/affirmative voting rights are necessary for practically all salient company decisions over the course of investment. Founder reserved matters were also a common occurrence. A total of 91.66% of all articles reviewed contained some clause allowing investors to have a veto right on some matters.

## 6. CONCLUSION

As has been mentioned elsewhere in this chapter and has been well established in prior literature, most Indian companies follow what is known as an insider model of corporate governance. In this model, a small group of majority shareholders, along with their families, holds considerable control and power over the affairs of the company. The majority shareholders are referred to as promoters in Indian corporate law and related literature. As a check and balance against the rent-seeking and self-opportunistic behavior of promoters, external investors negotiate a slew of control, governance, and investor protection rights.

However, a new trend seems to be emerging with Indian unicorns. While on paper promoters still hold majority shares in their unicorns, such companies also issue convertible instruments to external investors. As has been demonstrated in the context of a few companies analyzed in this chapter, on a fully diluted or "as if converted" basis, promoters end up as minority shareholders. Thus, the true power or control wielded by investors over the company is not easily apparent and hides behind what we have referred to in this chapter as a "veil of conversion." This has been evidenced in formerly private, unlisted unicorns which have conducted an IPO and have been listed. Upon listing, it is found that instead of a concentrated shareholding as is the norm in most Indian companies, unicorns tend to have a more dispersed shareholding pattern, on a fully diluted basis, reminiscent of companies in the US or the UK. Thus, new-age Indian startups diverge from the established "insider" model.

As a result, the corporate governance of Indian unicorns must be analyzed in the face of dispersed shareholding as opposed to checks and balances against promoter opportunism. Several salient aspects of the articles of association of these companies do appear to show general trends that have been followed for the most part. Many of the negotiated rights that form a part of the corporate governance norms for these companies are often standard and echo each other, barring a few deviations. In many such companies, the board composition is not reflective of the equity shareholding pattern of the company. Rather, it reflects the amount of corporate control that investors have over the overall shareholding in the company on a fully diluted basis. We note occasions where the promoter will no longer have the right to nominate a director upon cessation of their employment. This alludes to the fact that Indian unicorns are no longer driven by promoters, but by founders who remain a key employee critical to the success of the company, backed by the financial might of external investors. Majority shareholding of promoters is no longer relevant in Indian unicorns.

We also find that Indian unicorns tend to set higher standards of corporate governance norms akin to publicly listed companies. Attracting private equity remains imperative, not just to help in the development of the economy but also to provide managerial assistance to investee companies, making them more competitive. The presence of private equity investments helps boost transparency (Annamalai et al., 2014). Institutional investments tend to be followed by further improvements in corporate governance and tend to occur in high-growth firms within research and development-intensive industries (Nielsen, 2008).

One key finding that emerges from this research is that as the number of shareholders tends to increase, corporate governance in unicorns tends to more closely resemble that of publicly listed companies. We have increasingly seen the presence of independent directors and heightened reporting requirements, with financial statements being reported on a quarterly basis. Under Indian law, private unlisted companies are not required to appoint independent directors and are required to report financial statements on an annual basis. Yet, the presence of many institutional investors means that companies adopt the standards of corporate governance required for public, listed companies.

This has significant ramifications for practice and policy. For future start-ups that aspire to achieve unicorn status, they must forgo the idea that a promoter or a founder holds most of the control in their companies. Further, the corporate governance in Indian unicorns seems to describe a balancing act between the interests of the investors while preserving the business interests of the company. The promoter no longer has a majority on the board or indeed on a fully diluted basis. Yet, the promoter retains overall leadership over the company's affairs.

In terms of future research, similar studies may be carried out in other emerging jurisdictions that have had a similar shareholding pattern of family-driven firms, such as Indonesia, Spain, and Mexico. Another interesting finding that may deserve its own research path is the composition and relationships between the founders of a company. While it is largely agreed that the traditional Indian model of business leadership involves members of the same family taking up key positions within the business while also holding the majority shares of the company, anecdotal evidence seems to suggest that the founders of new-age Indian startups may not be related by familial ties. Rather, there are several cases where the founders of a company appear to be alumni of the same educational institution or a past business. While this may be examined further with empirical evidence, if found to be true, this would have significant ramifications for the future of the study of family businesses and the effect of education on entrepreneurship.

## NOTE

1. A copy of the database is accessible at: https://jguedu-my.sharepoint.com/:f:/g/personal/abmajumdar_jgu_edu_in/EpfQsQYrHJhKsUDqK1k-QCoB3dkaD_TzLvmbFtHUcvQZ-Q?e=qLUk2W . This database is updated to the end of April 2023.

## REFERENCES


Afsharipour, A. (2010). Transforming the Allocation of Deal Risk Through Reverse Termination Fees. *Vanderbilt Law Review, 63*(5), 1163.

Afsharipour, A. (2015). Corporate Governance and the Indian Private Equity Model. *National Law School of India Review, 27*(1), 17–48.

Afsharipour, A., & Gelter, M. (eds) (2021). Introduction to Comparative Corporate Governance. In *Comparative Corporate Governance* (pp. 1–18). Edward Elgar Publishing. https://dx.doi.org/10.2139/ssrn.3725679

Annamalai, T. R. (2012). A Lifecycle Analysis of VC-PE Investments in India: Half Full or Half Empty? *The Journal of Private Equity, 15*(4), 25–35.

Annamalai, T. R., Bansal, B., & Gemson, J. (2014). Private Equity Investment and Real Estate Development. *Journal of Financial Management of Property and Construction, 19*(3), 202–225. https://doi.org/10.1108/JFMPC-02-2014-0001

Annamalai, T. R., & Behera, M. (2016). Private Equity Investment in Power Generation Projects: Evidence From India. *International Journal of Energy Sector Management, 10*(4), 617–641. https://doi.org/10.1108/IJESM-12-2014-0008

Annamalai, T. R., & Deshmukh, A. (2011). Venture Capital and Private Equity in India: An Analysis of Investments and Exits. *Journal of Indian Business Research, 3*(1), 6–21. https://doi.org/10.1108/17554191111112442

Armour, J., Hansmann, H., & Kraakman, R. (2017). Agency Problems and Legal Strategies. In R. Kraakman, J. Armour, P. Davies, L. Enriques, H. Hansmann, G. Hertig, K. Hopt, H. Kanda, M. Pargendler, W.-G. Ringe, & E. Rock (eds), *The Anatomy of Corporate Law* (pp. 29–48). Oxford University Press.

Barick, S. K. (2021). *Valuation Report of Think and Learn Pvt Ltd.* November 30. https://jguedu-my.sharepoint.com/:b:/g/personal/abmajumdar_jgu_edu_in/EcZwaXtVYEhNlvm2knMngAIB_KMYDkaGiHaVc88bocHxEg?e=Hq9eVP

Battistin, E., Bortoluzzi, P., Buttignon, F., & Vedovato, M. (2017). Minority and Majority Private Equity Investments: Firm Performance and Governance. *Journal of Management & Governance, 21*(3), 659–684. https://doi.org/10.1007/s10997-016-9364-2

Bebchuk, L. A., & Hamdani, A. (2009). The Elusive Quest for Global Governance Standards. *University of Pennsylvania Law Review, 157*, 1263–1317.

Berglöf, E. (1994). A Control Theory of Venture Capital Finance. *The Journal of Law, Economics, and Organization, 10*(2), 247–267. https://doi.org/10.1093/oxfordjournals.jleo.a036850

Berglöf, E., & Von Thadden, E.-L. (2000). The Changing Corporate Governance Paradigm: Implications for Developing and Transition Economies. In S. S. Cohen & G. Boyd (eds), *Corporate Governance and Globalization* (pp. 275–306). Edward Elgar Publishing. https://dx.doi.org/10.2139/ssrn.183708

Blomberg, J. A. (2008). Private Equity Transactions: Understanding Some Fundamental Principles. *Business Law Today, 17*(3), 50.

Bock, C., & Hackober, C. (2020). Unicorns—What Drives Multibillion-Dollar Valuations? *Business Research, 13*(3), 949–984. https://doi.org/10.1007/s40685-020-00120-2

Cartrade Tech Limited (2021). *Final Offer Document.* Securities and Exchange Board of India. August 12. https://www.sebi.gov.in/filings/public-issues/aug-2021/cartrade-tech-limited_51869.html

Carvalhal, A., & Souza, L. (2014). Private Equity and Corporate Governance in Brazil. *Corporate Ownership and Control, 12.* https://api.semanticscholar.org/CorpusID:56283276

Chandrasekhar, C. P. (2007). Private Equity: A New Role for Finance? *Economic and Political Weekly, 42*(13), 1136–1145.

Chaudhary, K. (2017). Paytm E-Commerce becomes a unicorn with 200-million investment round. Business Standard, March 3. https://www.business-standard.com/article/companies/paytm-achieves-indian-unicorn-status-with-200-mn-investment-led-by-alibaba-117030200892_1.html

Chinchwadkar, R., & Seth, R. (2018). The Choice of Exit: Influence of Private Equity Investors and Buyout Entry. *Journal of Emerging Market Finance, 17*(1_suppl), S1–S26. https://doi.org/10.1177/0972652717751534

Chinchwadkar, R., & Shekhar, V. (2016). Evolution of Private Equity Regulations in Emerging Markets: A Case of India. *The Journal of Private Equity, 20*(1), 38–44. https://doi.org/10.3905/jpe.2016.20.1.038

Consolidated FDI Policy (2020). https://www.dpiit.gov.in/static/uploads/2025/06/4a159bc3ae98ca3f4a0e495ea2750323.pdf

Dash, S. (2019). Delhivery becomes India's first unicorn in 2019, thanks to SoftBank. Business Insider, March 6. https://www.businessinsider.in/delhivery-raises-395-million-from-softbank-enters-the-unicorn-club-of-india/articleshow/68287009.cms

David, D., Gopalan, S., & Ramachandran, S. (2020). The Startup Environment and Funding Activity in India. In F. Taghizadeh-Hesary, N. Yoshino, C. J. Kim, P. J. Morgan, & D. Yoon (eds), *Investment in Startups and Small Business Financing,* Volume 17 (pp. 193–232). World Scientific. https://doi.org/10.1142/9789811235825_0007

Delhivery Limited (2022). *Final Offer Document*. Securities and Exchange Board of India, May 14. https://www.sebi.gov.in/filings/public-issues/may-2022/delhivery-limited_58927.html

Dossani, R. (2012). Private Equity and Corporate Governance in India. *Journal of Asia Business Studies*, *6*(2), 223–238. https://doi.org/10.1108/15587891211254416

Dugar, P., & Pandit, N. (2017). Growth of Venture Capital and Private Equity in India. *The Journal of Private Equity*, *21*(1), 79–93. https://doi.org/10.3905/jpe.2017.21.1.079

Gardner, W. E. (1971). Venture Capital Financing: A Lawyers Checklist. *The Business Lawyer*, *26*(3), 997–1005.

Gilson, R. J., & Schwartz, A. (2013). Constraints on Private Benefits of Control: Ex Ante Control Mechanisms versus Ex Post Transaction Review. *Journal of Institutional and Theoretical Economics (JITE)/Zeitschrift Für Die Gesamte Staatswissenschaft*, *169*(1), 160–183. https://dx.doi.org/10.2139/ssrn.2129502

Gooptu, B. (2018). PolicyBazaar raises over $238 million in SoftBank-led round. *The Economic Times*, June 26. https://economictimes.indiatimes.com/small-biz/startups/newsbuzz/indias-policybazaar-raises-over-200-mln-in-softbank-led-round/articleshow/64734167.cms

Gornall, W., & Strebulaev, I. A. (2020). Squaring Venture Capital Valuations with Reality. *Journal of Financial Economics*, *135*(1), 120–143. https://doi.org/10.1016/j.jfineco.2018.04.015

IL & FS Trust Co. Ltd. v. Birla Perucchini Ltd, 121 Comp Cas 335 (Bombay High Court 2004). https://indiankanoon.org/doc/315178/

Indian Securities Contracts Regulation Rules (1957). https://upload.indiacode.nic.in/showfile?actid=AC_CEN_2_11_00014_199215_1517807319932&type=rule&filename=1522151651057.pdf

Jain, G. (2022). Valuation Report of DreamTechnologies Pvt Ltd. April 10. https://jguedu-my.sharepoint.com/:b:/g/personal/abmajumdar_jgu_edu_in/EfpRBSM6sKFBrILRh2cjuWsB-PrkW7e0ah03Hwv1cbDGpw?e=eaBYcY

Jha, V. K., Roshan, R., & Sinha, S. (2024). Accelerating Start-ups' Leap to Unicorns: The Role of Founders' Ambidextrous Orientation. *International Journal of Entrepreneurial Behavior & Research*, *30*(10), 2551–2577. https://doi.org/10.1108/IJEBR-06-2023-0604

Jiujin, L., Gupta, R., Haihong, L., & Qiang, S. (2020). Private Equity Characteristics, Corporate Governance and Firm Value: Empirical Evidence from Small and Medium-sized Enterprises. *Asian Economic Journal*, *34*(2), 163–183. https://doi.org/10.1111/asej.12207

Joshi, K., Chandrashekar, D., Satyanarayana, K., & Srinivas, A. (2022). VC Funded Start-Ups in India: Innovation, Social Impact, and the Way Forward. *International Journal of Global Business and Competitiveness*, *17*(1), 104–113. https://doi.org/10.1007/s42943-022-00055-x

Khanna, T., & Yafeh, Y. (2007). Business Groups in Emerging Markets: Paragons or Parasites? *Journal of Economic Literature*, *45*(2), 331–372. https://doi.org/10.1257/jel.45.2.331

Korsmo, C. R. (2013). Venture Capital and Preferred Stock. *Brooklyn Law Review*, *78*(4), 1163–1230.

Majumdar, A. (2019). The (Un?) Enforceability of Investor Rights in Indian Private Equity. *University of Pennsylvania Journal of International Law*, *41*, 981.

Majumdar, A., & Gupta, Y. (2023). The Hindenburg Report on Adani—A Case to Revisit Minimum Public Shareholding Requirements. Oxford Business Law Blog,

February 16. https://blogs.law.ox.ac.uk/blog-post/2023/02/hindenburg-report-adani-case-revisit-minimum-public-shareholding-requirements

Majumdar, S. K. (2007). Private Enterprise Growth and Human Capital Productivity in India. *Entrepreneurship Theory and Practice*, *31*(6), 853–872. https://doi.org/10.1111/j.1540-6520.2007.00205.x

Malik, K., & Dhankar, R. S. (2017). The Relationship among Private Equity, Inflation, and Economic Growth. *The Journal of Private Equity*, *20*(3), 60–67. https://doi.org/10.3905/jpe.2017.20.3.060

Marini, V., Caratelli, M., Stella, G. P., & Barbaraci, I. (2022). Is Corporate Governance of Private Equity Targets more Effective for Risk Mitigation? *Journal of Management and Governance*, *26*(3), 781–811. https://doi.org/10.1007/s10997-021-09571-z

Mullineux, A. (2010). Is there an Anglo-American Corporate Governance Model? *International Economics and Economic Policy*, *7*(4), 437–448. https://doi.org/10.1007/s10368-010-0151-2

Neerza, N., & Tripathi, V. (2019). Determinants of Private Equity Investment Across Sectors in India. *Journal of Advances in Management Research*, *16*(4), 513–536. https://doi.org/10.1108/JAMR-09-2018-0083

Nielsen, K. M. (2008). Institutional Investors and Private Equity. *Review of Finance*, *12*(1), 185–219. https://doi.org/10.1093/rof/rfm009

NTex Transportation Services Limited (2021). *Articles of Association*. May 8. https://jguedu-my.sharepoint.com/:b:/g/personal/abmajumdar_jgu_edu_in/Ecptcbxj_o9GjkhfIcXjRykBXEivoewivEWTkwyxefEjEQ?e=AHfNkd

NTex Transportation Services Limited (2023). *NTex Shareholding Pattern*. March 31. https://jguedu-my.sharepoint.com/:x:/g/personal/abmajumdar_jgu_edu_in/ETpJQ4dsw4FGqMYmaDwjqIEBdXNCzOJVHdGn9DA46xqFfA?e=ct1eOT

One 97 Communications Limited (2021). *Final Offer Document*. Securities and Exchange Board of India. November 11. https://www.sebi.gov.in/filings/public-issues/nov-2021/one97-communications-limited-prospectus_53936.html

PB Fintech Limited (2021). *Final Offer Document*. Securities and Exchange Board of India. November 8. https://www.sebi.gov.in/filings/public-issues/nov-2021/pb-fintech-limited-prospectus_53862.html

Ramesh, K., & Annamalai, T. R. (2021). Which Cat to Bell? Investment Duration, Exit Type and Returns in Venture Investments. *The Journal of Alternative Investments*, *23*(4), 47–60. https://doi.org/10.3905/jai.2021.1.123

Ratanpal, A. (2008). Indian Economy and Indian Private Equity. *Thunderbird International Business Review*, *50*(6), 353–358. https://doi.org/10.1002/tie.20222

Reddy, K. S. (2016). Regulatory Framework of Mergers and Acquisitions. *International Journal of Law and Management*, *58*(2), 197–215. https://doi.org/10.1108/IJLMA-03-2015-0013

Saini, N., & Singhania, M. (2018). Corporate Governance, Globalization and Firm Performance in Emerging Economies. *International Journal of Productivity and Performance Management*, *67*(8), 1310–1333. https://doi.org/10.1108/IJPPM-04-2017-0091

Shrivastava, A., & Garg, A. (2017). Private Equity in India and Indian Promoters' Perspective: A Primer. *The Journal of Private Equity*, *20*(3), 68–75. https://doi.org/10.3905/jpe.2017.20.3.068

Srinivasan, S. (2018). Zomato Raises $200 million from Ant Financial. *The Economic Times*, February 1. https://economictimes.indiatimes.com/small-biz/startups/newsbuzz/zomato-raises-200-million-from-ant-financial/articleshow/62746355.cms

Teixeira Latini, E., Rubens Fontes-Filho, J., & Chambers, E. L. (2014). Private Equity and Corporate Governance: Managing Brazilian SMEs. *Corporate Governance, 14*(2), 220–237. https://doi.org/10.1108/CG-02-2013-0017

Think and Learn Pvt Ltd (2022). *Shareholding Pattern.* April 30. https://jguedu-my.sharepoint.com/:x:/g/personal/abmajumdar_jgu_edu_in/ER5gD2HOeM5AqZXu1-vFZnEB6-mkMomwB2xpw4CmdpJPew?e=8XvxKO

TSJ Media Pvt Ltd (2024). *Venture Intelligence Unicorn Tracker* [dataset]. https://www.ventureintelligence.com/Indian-Unicorn-Tracker.php

UTI Asset Management Company (2020). *Final Offer Document.* Securities and Exchange Board of India, October 3. https://www.sebi.gov.in/filings/public-issues/oct-2020/uti-asset-management-company-limited-prospectus_47903.html

V. B. Rangaraj v. V. B. Gopalakrishnan, 1 Supreme Court Reporter 160 (Supreme Court 1992). https://www.casemine.com/commentary/in/v.b-rangaraj-v.-v.b-gopalakrishnan:-upholding-articles-of-association-over-private-agreements/view

Varottil, U. (2009). A Cautionary Tale of the Transplant Effect on Indian Corporate Governance. *National Law School of India Review, 21*(1), 1–49. https://repository.nls.ac.in/nlsir/vol21/iss1/1

Wright, M., Amess, K., Weir, C., & Girma, S. (2009). Private Equity and Corporate Governance: Retrospect and Prospect. *Corporate Governance: An International Review, 17*(3), 353–375. https://doi.org/10.1111/j.1467–8683.2009.00744.x

Yates, G., & Hinchliffe, M. (eds) (2010). Equity documentation. In *A Practical Guide to Private Equity Transactions* (pp. 114–169). Cambridge University Press; Cambridge Core. https://doi.org/10.1017/CBO9780511676147.007

Zomato Limited (2021). *Final Offer Document.* Securities and Exchange Board of India, July 19. https://www.sebi.gov.in/filings/public-issues/jul-2021/zomato-limited_51289.html

# PART II

# Start-Up & Venture Governance

# Introduction to Part II

Most start-up founders probably dream of becoming a unicorn, like the start-up firms discussed in Chapter 5. Of course, there is no magic scheme or leadership strategy that can make that happen. In this Part II on Start-Up and Venture Governance, we explore research that sheds light on unique approaches to understanding start-up governance. These studies are not designed to turn an average start-up into a unicorn; rather, they are designed to help all start-ups maintain better control of their corporate governance environments.

Being a new start-up venture is an exciting time for any founder; perhaps one of the most exciting aspects is the constancy of change and challenge. The challenges relate to finding the right market, designing different products and services, recording the first sale, hiring the first employee, structuring efficient operations, and many more. All of these challenges create constant change – as the venture evolves from an idea to something real, to an established business, and possibly, to a unicorn. Employing the right corporate governance structure is essential – even if it is not always a priority. And even if that "right" structure is only temporary. Each start-up firm's corporate governance structure will evolve as the firm evolves – and based on how the firm is influenced by cultural factors, ownership preferences, and its mission. The other three parts of this book dig deeply into each of these areas; yet, these themes are as relevant to new ventures as they are to any firm. Change is one of the few constants in any new venture's life. And adapting corporate governance systems to these changes can be the difference between success and failure.

When we once interviewed a successful start-up founder, who grew his business to $20 million in sales during the first three years, we asked him if he had one piece of advice for designing a corporate governance structure that worked: "fire my board" was his response. And this is likely the prevailing sentiment for many founders; they, as individuals, are unicorns themselves. They thrive on independence and seizing fleeting opportunities. They are not wired to worry about establishing mechanisms for providing a return on investment to their suppliers of capital – in part, because their genius and conviction are their dominant capital. A few years later, when that founder's revenue was closer to $100 million, he approached us and admitted: "my board has become our greatest asset."

Part II explores four different areas of research that can help entrepreneurs think about their governance environments and can help scholars advance their work related to how founders balance the independence they crave and the structure their firm may need. We start Part II with a study of entrepreneurial ecosystems. Many successful start-ups succeed because they have identified market failures, but need the support and guidance of other firms that are similarly trying to disrupt the status quo; learning from the successes and failures that other, similar ventures have learned from can be its own valuable asset. In Chapter 6, Philip Roundy introduces the idea of entrepreneurial ecosystems and provides a framework for understanding how to achieve incentive alignment within these entrepreneurial ecosystems – when the ecosystem members may have vastly different goals and characteristics.

In Chapter 7, Truls Erickson explores the idea of ecosystems and collaboration from a novel perspective: "suprateams." Suprateams are what the founder above had learned to appreciate in the later years, referring to the partnership between the founder and the board and external directors. In Chapter 8, Rod McNaughton provides a different perspective on navigating stakeholder relationships – and trying to grow – for new ventures. He studies the governance evolution within a firm, looking at how advisory boards can assist firms in making the transition from being pure start-ups that succeed because they fight the status quo to becoming more established, mature and formal structures (that is, to becoming the new status quo).

In Chapter 9, we return to the notion of rapid change and growth for start-up firms and the role that governance plays in this process. Dennis Gan studies start-ups acquiring start-ups. This has been a popular strategy to achieve rapid growth for many start-ups, but it is not without its governance challenges; who is the boss after the acquisition, how is the post-acquisition board of directors structured, and what are the governance priorities of the combined firm?

Few entrepreneurs have founded their business to deal with these research topics – ecosystems, suprateams, advisory boards, and acquisition. But properly navigating them and incorporating them into their growth strategies – all while navigating the cultural, ownership, and mission challenges associated with venture governance – might be the secret to a smoother and more successful transition from idea to unicorn. For scholars, we hope that these novel perspectives ignite your own ideas that help advance our understanding of the oftentimes mercurial and opaque world of start-up and venture governance.

Part II focuses on venture governance and start-up firms. Yet, most corporate governance research has studied large, publicly listed, US or large economy firms. The chapters that follow are included to help you think about how research related to venture governance may be different – and how the practice of governing start-up and growth stage firms may be unique.

1. Build your team – both the formal, official governance team and the unofficial, informal governance team. The formal team includes leaders, directors, legal and other official positions. The informal team includes mentors, advisors, fellow entrepreneurs, investors and others who can guide your governance structure. Your team will be fluid; the team you need during the start-up phase may not be the team you need in the maturity phase.
2. Learn from the broader venture ecosystem; this will help you develop and grow your informal governance team. Venture ecosystems are powerful and prolific. As one entrepreneur told us, "everything good that has happened to my business happened due to relationships." This is as true for venture governance as for anything else.
3. The governance structure your business needs will evolve over time. Incentive stock options may be essential during the idea or start-up phase but not during the maturity phase. You want your business to change and to grow, and the best way to ensure this is to establish governance systems that that are most appropriate for the stage of your business.
4. Invest in corporate governance systems – from bylaws and formal operating agreements to advisors and legal structures. The more you invest in corporate governance up-front, the less likely you are to have legal disputes in the future – particularly during high-stakes transitions like acquisitions or mergers – that can compromise the mission and value of your business.

As we know, one-size does not fit all in corporate governance, and governance systems will change over time. We see this most clearly with venture governance – every business is different, and every situation is different. Establish the corporate governance systems that take your business where you want it to go … and that starts with building the team that is best for your business.

# 6. Governance in entrepreneurial ecosystems

**Philip T. Roundy**

## 1. INTRODUCTION

Governance is central to every stage of the entrepreneurship process from opportunity pursuit to exit (Abebe et al., 2020; Audretsch & Lehmann, 2014; Lang & Wirtz, 2022). Reviews of research on the corporate governance of entrepreneurial firms find that entrepreneurs face distinct governance challenges in founding and managing startups and early-stage ventures (Garg, 2020; Li et al., 2020; Sahut et al., 2021). How corporate governance influences entrepreneurs evolves as entrepreneurs transition from creating startups to scaling ventures to leading mature firms (Gabrielsson & Huse, 2017; Zahra & Filatotchev, 2004). As ventures grow and become more professional, hierarchical, and bureaucratic, entrepreneurs and their founding teams must navigate the governance dynamics involved in changes in ownership structure, compensation, and board composition, and during events such as entrepreneur-CEO successions, strategic pivots, and initial public offerings (Farag et al., 2014).

Entrepreneurs do not, however, create or scale their ventures in isolation. Even if their goal is steady and organic growth rather than rapid and exponential growth, scaling an early-stage venture requires partnering with other individuals and organizations, such as governments, universities, corporations, support organizations (incubators, accelerators), mentors, and investors (Assenova, 2020; Lechner & Dowling, 2003). These partners are often found in the communities in which entrepreneurs are located (Müller & Korsgaard, 2018). The main insight of research on the contexts of entrepreneurs is that, despite an increasingly geographically decentralized digital economy, place still matters for entrepreneurship (Welter et al., 2019). Entrepreneurs depend on and leverage resources from their entrepreneurial ecosystems (EEs): the interconnected actors and factors in local communities that are coordinated to enable entrepreneurship (Stam, 2015). EE research finds that cities, regions, and other geographic territories differ in the fertility of their local ecosystems (Wurth et al., 2022). Startup environments in Silicon Valley, Bangalore, and Berlin, which are "hotbeds" of entrepreneurship, are very different from the contexts entrepreneurs face in small towns, rural areas, and economically disadvantaged cities in emerging economies (Roundy, 2019; Scheidgen & Brattström, 2023). Ultimately, as O'Connor et al. (2018: v) contend, "it 'takes an ecosystem to foster an entrepreneur.' If 'No man is an island' … then an entrepreneur who is unconnected and isolated is surely lost."

Governance also does not exist in isolation. For instance, "while boards play a pivotal role in entrepreneurial firms' functioning and survival … board activities do not occur in a vacuum and boards' roles either interact or are contingent on other governance mechanisms, such as CEOs, owners, top management teams (TMTs), and capital markets" (Li et al., 2020: 44). In addition to these factors, corporate governance is influenced by a host of contextual, place-based dynamics (Aguilera et al., 2018). However, scholars have been slow to examine how governance is influenced by—and manifests in—entrepreneurial ecosystems. This is an important omission in research at the interface of governance and entrepreneurship and represents a promising new avenue for the study of corporate governance because EEs exist at a distinct level of analysis: the meta-organization—a community of "firms or individuals not bound by authority based on employment relationships, but characterized by a system-level goal" (Gulati et al., 2012: 573). The system-level goal of EEs is to provide a flourishing local environment where entrepreneurs can succeed.

As meta-organizations, the governance of EEs manifests at two distinct levels: the venture and the ecosystem. In this way, EE governance is unique in involving (1) governance *within* EEs (i.e., the governing of organizations given their idiosyncratic local ecosystems), and (2) governance *of* EEs (i.e., the governing of the ecosystem itself). At the level of venture governance, the corporate governance of early-stage ventures is influenced by the interconnected actors and factors in entrepreneurs' local communities. For instance, entrepreneurs may acquire key governance resources from their local communities, such as connections to potential board members who can assist in strategic leadership and to venture capital investors who can provide financial and social capital (Cumming et al., 2019). In addition, entrepreneurs can vicariously learn corporate governance procedures, practices, and processes by observing other ventures in their local environments (Pugh et al., 2021).

Corporate governance also exists at the level of the ecosystem itself and is the focus of a nascent, but increasingly vibrant, research stream that studies EE governance (Colombo et al., 2019; Cunningham et al., 2019; Knox & Arshed, 2022). The growing evidence supporting the positive benefits of fertile EEs for economic and community development has led to intense academic and practitioner interest in the individuals who build, strengthen, and maintain ecosystems (Wurth et al., 2022). EE governance research focuses on the question: who (if anyone) is responsible for an ecosystem's effectiveness? The individuals (and organizations) in this governance role are most commonly referred to as EE leaders (Roundy & Lyons, 2023) but are sometimes known as EE champions (Clayton et al., 2023), orchestrators (Daymond et al., 2023), brokers (Feldman & Zoller, 2012), or builders (Krueger, 2021). EE leaders make deliberate attempts to work on ecosystems and improve their effectiveness, unlike other ecosystem participants who simply draw resources from EEs (Roundy & Evans, 2024).

The effects of EE leaders on ecosystem governance can manifest in several ways. For instance, Lo and Theodoraki (2021) studied how large corporations in the Paris EE gained ambidexterity from their local EEs. These activities involved a particular EE governance approach that balanced a democratic system, based on initiating co-governance and promoting the values of reciprocity and trust, and direct leadership, which involved initiating major projects (like creating co-working spaces) and encouraging interfirm collaboration. In contrast, Romme (2022: 119) studied the important role played by collaboration in the governance of the Brainport-Eindhoven EE in the Netherlands, which transformed itself into a hotbed of deep tech entrepreneurship after divestment from the multinational company Philips. Romme (2022: 124) found that "representatives of the business community, knowledge institutions, and municipalities participate as equivalent partners in the governance of these Brainport agencies."

Despite mounting evidence of the importance of EE governance, prior studies on corporate governance and entrepreneurship "place primary focus on the board of directors and their role in entrepreneurial firms leaving other governance mechanisms in the shade" (Li et al., 2020: 43–44). As a result, research on governance in EEs remains nascent, untheorized, and largely descriptive (Roundy, 2021). Although individual studies are making strides in understanding issues in ecosystem governance, EE governance research is fragmented and insights from studies are not contributing to an overarching conceptual infrastructure to understand and explain EE corporate governance. This is an important gap in our understanding of ecosystems and corporate governance because a generalizable framework has yet to emerge to guide research on governance in EEs, which makes it difficult to produce actionable insights for entrepreneurs and ecosystem leaders. Ultimately, Harper-Anderson's (2018) assessment that "ecosystem leadership has only been studied at a surface level" (122) could accurately be applied to the topic of EE governance.

To address this omission in our understanding of EEs and governance, in this chapter I propose a multi-level framework of entrepreneurial ecosystem corporate governance (hereafter, EECG): *the actors and factors in local communities that orchestrate stakeholders and resources to influence the strategic direction and effectiveness of EEs*. The framework details how corporate governance mechanisms manifest in EEs and influence firm-level corporate governance, particularly in early-stage entrepreneurial ventures. The conceptual arguments supporting the framework explain what EECG is, describe how it differs from traditional corporate governance, and motivate an agenda of research opportunities at the interface of corporate governance and EEs.

The EECG framework stands to make several contributions to research on corporate governance and entrepreneurship. First, despite increased acknowledgment of the importance of governance issues in EEs, "an in-depth understanding of the governance mechanisms in entrepreneurial ecosystems is lacking" (Lo & Theodoraki, 2021: 419). The EECG framework identifies the cross-level mechanisms influencing governance in EEs. In doing so, another contribution of the chapter is to draw the attention of corporate governance research to a novel level of analysis and a new context in which governance matters. Corporate governance research has generally focused on the governance of organizations. However, in this chapter, I expand the boundaries of governance research to meta-organizations and describe how key governance concepts and processes, such as succession, ownership, and leadership, manifest in EEs. I draw attention to how EE governance exists at and influences two levels: the venture level and the ecosystem level. I explain what EECG is and how it represents a distinct form of corporate governance different from traditional governance structures.

The remainder of the chapter proceeds as follows. The next section reviews the conceptual foundations of EECG in research on the leadership and governance of entrepreneurial ecosystems. I then explain how EECG relates to work on traditional (organizational) corporate governance by discussing the similarities between organizational and EE governance. This discussion sets up the primary focus of the chapter: developing a multi-level framework to explain what EECG is and how it functions. I conclude the chapter by unpacking the framework's implications for corporate governance research and practice.

## 2. CONCEPTUAL BACKGROUND

The concept of EEs builds on several strands of cross-disciplinary research that emphasizes *where* entrepreneurship and innovation occur, including work on regional innovation (Asheim et al., 2011), innovation ecosystems (Adner and Kapoor, 2016), economic geography (Howells & Bessant, 2012), clusters (Frisillo, 2007), and entrepreneurial communities (Lichtenstein et al., 2004). The growing prevalence of the EE concept (e.g., Velt et al., 2020) reflects the contextual turn in entrepreneurship research (Welter et al., 2019) and the more general shift toward ecosystems thinking, which has roots in Moore's (1993) "business ecosystems" metaphor. These lines of research emphasize that decisions and actions do not take place in isolation from the local environments in which organizational actors are embedded and, in the modern economy, most individuals and organizations are embedded in contextualized networks of relationships that are more complex than simple buyer–seller or firm–customer connections (Lusch et al., 2016). The communities of interconnected and interacting entities—ecosystems—that surround individuals represent dynamic, multi-level systems with components that are highly variegated and interdependent (Roundy et al., 2018).

EEs are distinct from other types of socio-economic systems, such as business ecosystems, in that their actors and factors are (1) geographically bounded and place-based (i.e., located in a specific city or region), and (2) coordinated in a way that supports entrepreneurial activities (Stam, 2015). Most ecosystems research studies vibrant and fertile EEs, like Silicon Valley, which can support high levels of entrepreneurial activities not tied to single technologies or industries (Adams, 2021). Not being technology- or industry-specific makes EEs distinct from related concepts, such as industrial clusters (Lund-Thomsen & Pillay, 2012).

### 2.1 Leadership and the Governance of EEs

One of the key attributes of vibrant EEs is ecosystem leadership (Stam & Van de Ven, 2021). EE leadership is a type of collective leadership in which leadership responsibilities are informally distributed among community members (Eva et al., 2021). EE leaders voluntarily opt into ecosystem leadership roles and, in those roles, take voluntary but deliberate actions to improve their ecosystems (Roundy, 2021). EE leadership activities include drawing resources to an ecosystem, creating and strengthening its network connections, implementing programs that benefit entrepreneurs, and increasing the coordination of EE elements (Leendertse et al., 2022). EE leaders take these actions to satisfy their individual needs, such as creating a more munificent local environment for their respective organizations, and in pursuit of the collective goal of improving ecosystem effectiveness (i.e., the ability of an ecosystem to enable entrepreneurial activities) (Miles & Morrison, 2020).

Because of the complexity of ecosystems, influencing EE effectiveness typically requires the integrated leadership efforts of numerous individuals (Harper-Anderson, 2018). These individuals represent diverse organizations, possess different motivations and goals, and engage in distinct activities. Because of the diversity in ecosystem leaders' incentives and the fact that EE leadership involves balancing individual goals, organizational objectives, and collective ecosystem goals, EE leadership has been conceptualized as "the orchestration of multiple groups to influence the effectiveness of an EE" and the ecosystem as "a multiteam system of local leaders that work independently and interdependently to achieve high performance for their organizations and EE" (Roundy & Evans, 2024).

EE leaders work on the strategic direction and competitiveness of the EE (Audretsch et al., 2023). In doing so, they face unique governance dynamics because they must navigate organizational independence and ecosystem interdependence. That is, EE leaders are often responsible for governing their respective organizations (e.g., ventures, incubators, universities) while working together as part of the shared governance of the ecosystem. For instance, the executive director of an incubator must engage in decisions and actions focused on effectively governing their organization, such as supporting a sufficient number of entrepreneurs to satisfy the incubator's funders. However, incubator leaders are also key leaders in the governance of EEs and often lead efforts to attract resources to EEs, improve ecosystem coordination through networking events, and, ultimately, improve EE effectiveness (Roundy, 2021). As this example illustrates, EE leaders engage in both governance in the ecosystem and of the ecosystem (Roundy & Evans, 2024). That is, unlike other EE participants who work *in* EEs, EE leaders work both in EEs and directly *on* EEs, which, as described in the next section, represents a form of governance—EECG—that is similar to traditional organizational corporate governance in some respects, but quite distinct in others.

## 3. CONCEPTUAL DEVELOPMENT: THE SIMILARITIES BETWEEN ORGANIZATIONAL AND EE CORPORATE GOVERNANCE

Organizational corporate governance and EE corporate governance are related but distinct phenomena with conceptual similarities stemming from their shared concern with "governance." For instance, EE governance is akin to the governance examined in strategic leadership and upper echelons research in that it involves the leaders who take on the responsibility of governing, "the characteristics of those [leaders], what they do, and how they do it" (Hambrick, 1989: 6). Also, like the leaders involved in corporate governance, ecosystem governance involves EE leaders who seek to "establish and maintain harmony between parties … whose interests may conflict" (Hanson et al., 2017: 292). The potential for conflicting interests and incentives makes the distinction between principals and agents, which is central to corporate governance (Dühnfort et al., 2008), also critical to understanding ecosystem governance. In traditional corporate governance, agents are the executives who manage organizations under the direction of the organization's principals (the owners). In contrast, in EEs, the "agents" are the entrepreneurs and other EE participants who engage in the day-to-day activities of the ecosystem and are driven, largely, by their own self-interest rather than by creating value for the community and pursuing ecosystem goals. In contrast, the "principals" of EEs are the ecosystem leaders who take deliberate steps to motivate and organize EE participants to operate in ways that produce benefits for the startup community. Also, in the same way that C-level executives and their boards of directors jointly exercise power over managers and other corporate actors by operating as supra-TMTs (Finkelstein et al., 2009) or supra-teams (Gan & Erikson, 2022), groups of EE leaders exercise power over other ecosystem participants by working together to provide direction to the ecosystem, formulating a regional strategy, securing and distributing EE resources, creating (oftentimes informal) policies, values, and simple rules to govern EE interactions, and, ultimately, influencing the EE's performance. In the same way that traditional corporate governance in organizations is not the responsibility of singular leaders, EE governance depends on coordinated groups of leaders (Roundy & Evans, 2024). Like influential CEOs, prominent entrepreneurs or community leaders can influence ecosystem dynamics; however, full-scale EE governance typically requires multiple individuals and organizations working together to varying degrees to influence community dynamics.

Finally, some specific concerns of organizational corporate governance, such as how the diversity and composition of those responsible for governance influence governance effectiveness, also exist in EEs (Fernández-Temprano & Tejerina-Gaite, 2020). However, despite these broad similarities, the corporate governance of EEs is distinct from organizational corporate governance in crucial ways, described next.

## 3.1 The Uniqueness of the Corporate Governance of Entrepreneurial Ecosystems

The distinctiveness of EE corporate governance stems, primarily, from ecosystems being meta-organizations, which are communities of loosely connected individuals, organizations, and institutions (Gulati et al., 2012). Although organizational corporate governance typically involves several groups (TMTs, boards, shareholders), these actors are tied to a single, focal organization (i.e., the organization being governed). In contrast, EE governance requires cross-sector coordination of individuals representing different organizations and industries (Spigel et al., 2020). The issue of agent duality is central to studies of traditional corporate governance and focuses on how executives must often navigate being both agent (CEO) and principal (board chair); however, agent duality also manifests differently in EEs. Entrepreneurs and other EE leaders must navigate between managing (and governing) their ventures and their role as EE leaders who are responsible for governing the ecosystem. As described in the next section, one of the key governance activities of EE leaders involves improving the orchestration and coordination among the different groups that participate in EEs.

Another unique aspect of EE governance, which stems from ecosystems being meta-organizations, is that EEs are comprised of independent individuals and organizations loosely connected through informal, fluid, and voluntary ties (Gulati et al., 2012). Involvement in EEs is generally open, unrestricted, and driven by self-selection rather than formal appointment or membership. EE activities are informally "policed" by other ecosystem participants.

The structure of the EE governance body is also very different from organizational governance. Traditional corporate governance is the purview of CEOs, TMTs, boards of directors, and the supra-teams that combine them. In ecosystems, the executives and boards of respective organizations may interact with each other and with the EE; however, there is no formal "CEO" or "board" that oversees the ecosystem itself. Participating in EE governance does not require a proper role or title and is voluntary and largely informal. Any of the actors involved in an EE, including entrepreneurs, investors, support organization managers, university members, and public policymakers can fluidly step into (and out of) EE leadership. Thus, the boundaries of EE governance are more porous and fluid than the boundaries of traditional corporate governance. Any actor in the EE can, in theory, participate in ecosystem governance (although, in practice, like any dominant coalition, involvement can be limited to those EE participants who possess sufficient influence, resources, and connections to take part in major decisions).

Governance roles are not filled by the same entities across EEs. For instance, in one ecosystem, the key leaders may be individuals affiliated with a support organization, such as a prominent incubator, while in another ecosystem, leaders might be affiliated with a university or co-working space (Goswami et al., 2018; O'Brien et al., 2019). Unlike governance in traditional organizations in which all members are expected to contribute because of their financial compensation and formal employment contracts, EE leadership does not receive direct financial compensation from the ecosystem. The financial benefits that leaders derive from being part of an EE are indirect and, oftentimes, benefits are non-pecuniary (e.g., access to social networks and information, reputational benefits, and legitimacy). Individuals become EE leaders by becoming valued and active participants and by choosing to contribute to the ecosystem's activities. EE contributions are made to benefit other ecosystem participants and strengthen the EE and the local community. Contributing to EEs is, thus, considered a form of prosocial behavior (Bolino & Grant, 2016) and includes providing other EE participants with resources (e.g., knowledge, mentoring, and network connections). If individuals engage in these types of activities, other EE participants will recognize them as valued members of the ecosystem and, ultimately, as ecosystem leaders (Feld, 2012). The leaders of EEs do not wield formal authority but rather use forms of informal authority "based on expertise, reputation, status, gatekeeping privileges … or control over key resources or technology" (Gulati et al., 2012: 573).

With traditional corporate governance, leaders are not necessarily co-located and may be globally distributed. However, the governance of EEs is the responsibility of leaders who are geographically bounded and share ties to the same community (e.g., city or region) while representing different organizations located within a local territory. The connections between the leaders who govern EEs are based on other commonalities and interdependencies, such as possessing common goals and intentions (e.g., creating and scaling successful ventures), engaging in common activities (e.g., planning ecosystem events), and holding "common values, logics, and cultural rule sets," such as a shared desire for community revitalization (Roundy et al., 2017: 101). In contrast, the leaders involved in traditional corporate governance are linked, primarily, by involuntary ties based on their formal employment contracts and by formal positions in the hierarchy of organizations.

In EEs with high levels of diversity, EE governance consists of a broad representation of leaders (Roundy et al., 2017). These leaders are legally autonomous individuals and organizations from across categories (entrepreneurs, investors, support organizations), sectors (private, nonprofit, government), venture types (lifestyle, aggressive growth), and business models (Roundy et al., 2017). Despite their differences, leaders responsible for EE governance are connected by the common, system-level goal of promoting and supporting entrepreneurial activity.

Finally, ownership and control also manifest differently in EEs. Unlike traditional organizations, which have clear ownership structures involving founders and shareholders, no one "owns" the EE, and there are no formal "shareholders." EEs are, in a sense, community owned. However, there are distinct groups of stakeholders with a vested interest in the EE and its effectiveness (Table 6.1).

### 3.2 Defining and Developing the Conceptual Foundations of Entrepreneurial Ecosystem Corporate Governance

The previous section established the distinctiveness of EECG: the actors and factors in local communities that orchestrate stakeholders and resources to influence the strategic direction and effectiveness of EEs. In this section, I unpack the key components of EECG to clarify its conceptual foundations and characteristics.

*Table 6.1* *A comparison of traditional and EE corporate governance*

| **Distinguishing characteristics** | **Traditional corporate governance** | **Entrepreneurial ecosystem corporate governance** |
|---|---|---|
| Definition | The distribution of rights and responsibilities within the firm, which entails allocating power and resources to different corporate actors and managing the inevitable tensions among these actors (Aguilera et al., 2021: 1469) | The actors and factors in local communities that orchestrate stakeholders and resources to influence the strategic direction and effectiveness of an EE |
| Focus of governance | Organization | Meta-organization |
| Basis of membership | Ties to focal organization | Ties to geographic territory |
| Key governance agents | CEOs, TMTs, boards of directors, supra-teams, shareholders | EE leaders: entrepreneurs, investors, support organization members, university members, policymakers |
| Primary goals | Superior firm performance; maintaining harmony among conflicting stakeholder groups | EE effectiveness; orchestrating EE participants to support ecosystem functioning |
| Origins of governance | Deliberate creation | Dynamic emergence |
| Geographic proximity of governance agents | Globally dispersed or in a singular location | Concentrated in a localized geographic territory |

| **Distinguishing characteristics** | **Traditional corporate governance** | **Entrepreneurial ecosystem corporate governance** |
|---|---|---|
| Basis of coordination, hierarchy, participation, and method of control | Formal coordination and authority<br>Employment contracts<br>Formal rules, laws, policies<br>Formal appointment<br>Direct financial compensation<br>Rigid hierarchy<br>Traditional bureaucratic leadership<br>Clearly defined organizational leadership (CEO, board) | Informal coordination<br>Voluntary participation<br>Informal norms and values<br>Self-selection<br>Indirect benefits<br>Flexible/fluid/open hierarchy<br>Shared/collective leadership<br>No formal board<br>No CEO or "top" leader |
| Nature of agent duality | CEO/board member | Organization/ecosystem leader |
| Key interfaces | Executive, team, organization | EE leader, organization, ecosystem |

### 3.2.1 "The actors and factors ..."

EE governance involves the *actors* in the "dominant coalition" (Mithani & O'Brien, 2021) of an ecosystem and who function as ecosystem leaders. Not every ecosystem stakeholder (or stakeholder group) is part of EE governance. Some ecosystem participants become EE leaders by assuming governance responsibilities that go beyond the goal of acquiring resources from the ecosystem to further their personal pursuit of entrepreneurial opportunities. In their governance role, EE leaders engage in activities such as establishing the strategic vision of the EE (e.g., the types of ventures or technologies that will be emphasized), initiating and overseeing EE programs (e.g., events that strengthen the ties between ecosystem participants), encouraging participants to contribute to the EE rather than simply extracting resources from it, and driving collective attempts to draw resources to the EE from outside its boundaries (e.g., attracting entrepreneurs and investors to relocate to the ecosystem; leading efforts to secure ecosystem funding).

As actors in the ecosystem, EE leaders cannot govern by sheer will; EECG depends on a set of *factors* in the local community. To date, the main aim of EE research has been to identify these critical EE factors (sometimes referred to as ecosystem "elements" or "attributes") and how the factors interact to influence entrepreneurship (Stam & Van de Ven, 2021). For instance, Spigel (2017) studied EEs in Waterloo and Calgary, Canada, and found that the ecosystems were composed of three distinct types of factors—cultural, social, and material—that "provide benefits and resources to entrepreneurs and that the relationships between these attributes reproduce the ecosystem" (49). Cultural factors include the values, beliefs, and stories of an EE (and the geographic territory in which it is embedded) that can encourage individuals to be entrepreneurial and to embrace experimentation, autonomy, a tolerance for trial-and-error, the pursuit of opportunities for creating value, and a desire to change the status quo. EE culture also consists of the norms and "simple rules" that guide EE interactions and promote collaborative and cooperative prosocial behaviors among ecosystem participants. Social factors include the EE attributes that depend on (and pass through) the networks that connect ecosystem participants, such as knowledge, mentorship, and financial and human capital. The material factors of EEs have physical manifestations in ecosystems, such as meeting and co-working spaces, support organization facilities, and the campuses of educational institutions. EE factors are interdependent; for instance, the social networks that connect EE participants require events where network ties can be formed and cultural values that support working together. EE factors represent the local infrastructure through which ecosystem actors govern.

### 3.2.2 "... in local communities ..."

A key characteristic that distinguishes entrepreneurial ecosystems from other ecosystem types (e.g., digital ecosystems) is that EEs have consequential geographic boundaries and exist within localized communities. In EEs, "place matters" and the embeddedness of EEs within specific communities is the source of local connections and commonalities among participants. The localness of EEs also creates an attachment to place that causes some individuals to take on the responsibility of ecosystem governance and to have a desire to improve their communities by being EE leaders.

While EE borders are more permeable than the boundaries of traditional organizations, the local communities that constitute EEs have distinct boundaries, which are multi-dimensional and based on both geographic and socio-cultural characteristics. An EE's boundaries are important because they separate an EE from other ecosystems in the geographic territories and regional economies that surround it (Gulati et al., 2012). The most tangible EE boundary is the geographic border of the ecosystem, such as the boundaries delineating a city or region (although these borders are sometimes blurry, as in Silicon Valley (Guzman & Stern, 2015). Individuals and resources within the geographic boundaries of the EE are considered "within" or "part of" the ecosystem. EE boundaries are also determined by an ecosystem's social and cultural components. EEs are created from the social networks that connect participants, such as entrepreneurs, mentors, support organizations, and customers (Alvedalen & Boschma, 2017). However, EEs vary in the strength of connections among their participants (Neumeyer et al., 2019). In vibrant EEs, there are generally strong ties among subsets of participants. A person or organization is either embedded in an ecosystem's network of participants and, thus, a part of the EE or not.

In addition to social network connections, cultural characteristics also determine who is within the local community of an EE. Cultural characteristics are captured by the degree to which a person has adopted the ecosystem's guiding values, norms, rule sets, and logics, such as favoring cooperation and trust with other EE participants and prioritizing community improvement (Muldoon et al., 2018). For instance, Feld (2012: 7) described the boundaries of the Boulder, Colorado, ecosystem as being "defined by a strong sense of collaboration and implicit rules such as 'giving before you get.' If you contribute, you are rewarded, often in unexpected ways. At the same time … [i]f you aren't sincere, constructive, and collaborative, the community behaves accordingly."

In sum, as individuals get further from the geographic epicenter of an EE, which is often identified by the presence of a high density of entrepreneurs or even an "innovation district" (Pancholi et al., 2018), and as they are less embedded in the EE's social network and less likely to share the EE's cultural values, the effect of the ecosystem on the individuals will weaken and they will be increasingly "outside" the EE's boundaries. Such individuals will be subject to less of a "pull" to become EE leaders and take part in ecosystem governance.

### 3.2.3 "... that orchestrate stakeholder relationships ..."

As complex adaptive systems, EEs exhibit some degree of uncoordinated self-governance (i.e., orchestration emerging organically without system leadership) (Haarhaus et al., 2020). However, an ecosystem's self-organizing forces exist within a community that is orchestrated by deliberate leadership, and the actors and factors in a local community will not naturally become aligned to support entrepreneurship (Miles & Morrison, 2020). Indeed, studies find that an EE simply having all of the cultural, social, and material factors does not necessarily produce a vibrant ecosystem (Breznitz & Taylor, 2014). EEs must be deliberately orchestrated in such a way that the ecosystem's stakeholders work together to promote and support entrepreneurship (Roundy, 2020). Coordinating stakeholder relationships to improve ecosystem functioning involves increasing EE orchestration: the degree to which ecosystem actors and factors are aligned to support entrepreneurial activity.

For instance, Miles and Morrison (2020) studied the Research Triangle EE in North Carolina (USA) and found that ecosystem leaders engaged in a specific set of coordinating activities, which included network development and knowledge brokering. Similarly, Spigel (2016) studied the coordinating activities of entrepreneurial support organizations in the Edinburgh, Scotland, EE and found that coordination involved building and sustaining an entrepreneurial community and ensuring cooperation between the different EE participants. In this function, EE leaders act as catalysts who help to coordinate the activities in an ecosystem and work with the EE's stakeholders to improve ecosystem functioning (Haines, 2016). These activities help to create an organized and interdependent system of entrepreneurs and EE participants rather than a loose collection of semi-autonomous, independent agents (Roundy & Fayard, 2020).

As part of governance, EE leaders seek to increase orchestration through three inter-connected sets of activities aimed at increasing the cognitive, social, and cultural coordination of EEs (Roundy, 2020). EE leaders orchestrate ecosystem stakeholders by increasing *cognitive coordination* through activities that reify an EE and establish it as existing as a distinct entity in participants' minds, such as explicitly drawing attention to and seeking to develop the EE. In EEs with cognitive coordination, there is a shared acknowledgment among ecosystem stakeholders of the EE's existence, which serves as the basis for orchestration (Goswami et al., 2018). EE leaders also orchestrate stakeholders by influencing the ecosystem's *social coordination*, which involves creating and strengthening relationships in an EE and building dense network connections among ecosystem stakeholders (Theodoraki et al., 2018). In this orchestration role, EE leaders are "entrepreneurial dealmakers" who look for opportunities to improve the connections among local stakeholders (Brown & Mason, 2017; Colombo et al., 2019; Goswami et al., 2018). Finally, EE leaders orchestrate stakeholders by increasing an ecosystem's *cultural coordination*, which is the extent to which ecosystem stakeholders share common values, narratives, and simple rules. Leaders improve cultural coordination by setting informal rules and norms that influence how EE participants interact, which improves ecosystem orchestration by establishing and strengthening a common culture (Roundy, 2020).

Work on EE orchestration suggests that EEs can be arrayed based on their degree of orchestration (Santos et al., 2023). In coordinated EEs, stakeholders are orchestrated to engage in deliberate efforts to build, develop, and support entrepreneurship and the EE. In contrast, in less coordinated EEs, entrepreneurial activities and investments in the entrepreneurial community are haphazard or non-existent because stakeholders lack orchestration (Roundy & Fayard, 2020). Thus, orchestration is necessary to governance because it allows EE stakeholders to work toward common goals.

### 3.2.4 "… to influence the strategic direction and effectiveness of EEs"

Leaders shape the strategic direction of EEs through their efforts to orchestrate the actors and factors in the ecosystems. Their success in orchestrating stakeholders and resources influences EE "effectiveness," an ecosystem's ability to support entrepreneurship and improve entrepreneurs' likelihood of success (Roundy & Evans, 2024). Non-leader EE participants are influenced by the effectiveness of their ecosystem, but do not actively work to influence EE performance; however, in their governance function, EE leaders actively assess, monitor, and seek to influence the performance of an EE. That is, while many EE participants take ecosystem conditions for granted, EE leaders are strategic in their attempts to alter ecosystem conditions through governance. These governance activities influence EE-level functioning and outcomes, which can, in turn, influence the operation and performance of ventures within the ecosystem.

### 3.2.5 A framework for conceptualizing EECG

The EECG dynamics described in the previous sections can be illustrated using a microfoundations framework (Coleman, 1990; Felin et al., 2015), which highlights how EECG functions across levels. As reflected in Figure 6.1, governance in EEs exists at multiple levels of analysis. At the organizational level, the characteristics of entrepreneurs and their ventures, including their organizational governance characteristics, influence venture outcomes, such

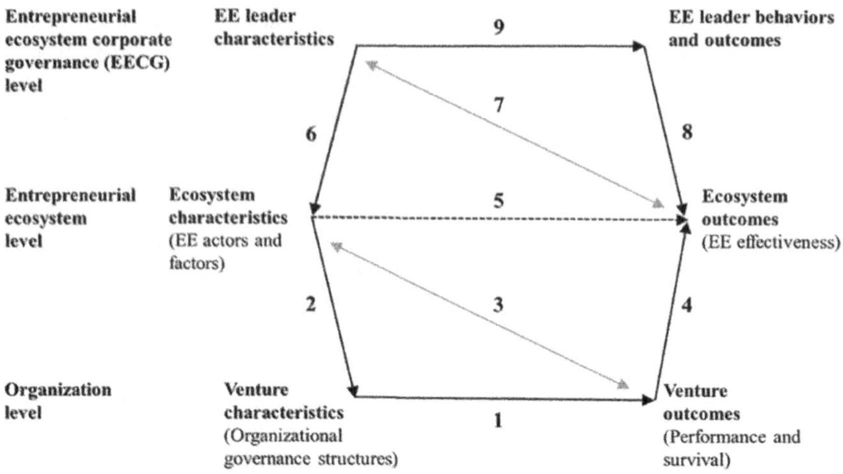


*Figure 6.1* *A microfoundations framework for understanding entrepreneurial ecosystem corporate governance*

as performance and survival (arrow 1). However, organizational characteristics and outcomes are influenced by ecosystem characteristics (i.e., EE actors and factors) and outcomes (e.g., EE effectiveness) (arrows 2–4). These relationships are the primary emphasis of extant EE research. The main insight of this chapter is that organizational-ecosystem dynamics are influenced by another level of analysis: EECG. At the EECG level, EE leader characteristics influence their behaviors and outcomes (arrow 9). EE leadership dynamics, in turn, influence the relationship between EE characteristics and outcomes (arrows 5–8).

## 4. DISCUSSION

Scholars are devoting increased attention to issues of ecosystem governance and, in particular, to how governance influences EE effectiveness (Spigel et al., 2020). However, as Cao and Shi explained in a recent review of the EE literature, most studies have focused on identifying and categorizing the key factors in EEs but "a full picture of ecosystem dynamics is lacking to unpack … the governance of entrepreneurial ecosystems" (Cao & Shi, 2021: 76). Fueling the academic pleas for scholars to devote more attention to EE governance, across many countries the "decentralization of governance has occurred at a rapid and unprecedented pace since the 2010s, where city-regions are increasingly seen as arenas and actors for enterprise and innovation policies" (Spigel et al., 2020: 488). As a result, the governance responsibilities associated with regional economic and community development are increasingly falling to local leaders and their informal activities. In response to these scholarly and practitioner trends, in this chapter I have introduced and defined the concept of EECG. In the next section, I build on these conceptual arguments and the microfoundations framework of EECG (Figure 6.1) to propose an agenda of opportunities for future research on the corporate governance of EEs.

### 4.1 An Agenda for Future Research

Several possible lenses can be used to understand corporate governance in EEs. For instance, scholars could adopt an operational perspective focused on what EE leaders do when engaged in EECG, a relational perspective focused on the relationship among leaders and other types of EE participants, a stakeholder perspective focused on the groups EE leaders are responsible to and how they respond to these groups, a financial perspective focused on how investors in EEs get a return (e.g., how venture capitalists leverage EE dynamics), or even a societal perspective focused on how EECG influences economic and community development (Tricker, 2019). Each of these perspectives (or some combination) could be promising for future research on EECG; however, given the multi-level nature of the phenomenon, the microfoundations perspective, which draws attention to how complex phenomena, like EEs, depend on relationships across levels, is particularly illuminating for organizing research directions.

The preponderance of EE research has focused on the ecosystem level and, specifically, on identifying the characteristics of EEs and how they influence ecosystem outcomes (Figure 6.1, arrow 5). At the same time, corporate governance research has generally focused on how organizational governance structures influence organizational outcomes (arrow 1). At the intersection of organizations and EEs, research is needed that explores how EE characteristics, such as the availability of local resources, influence venture characteristics and outcomes (arrows 3–4). For instance, entrepreneurs can use their local EEs to identify governance talent (e.g., board members, executives) (Roundy & Burke-Smalley, 2022) and learn vicariously from other local organizations about how to implement governance structures (Pugh et al., 2021). Thus, opportunities exist in both traditional corporate governance research and EE scholarship to pay greater attention to the interfaces (Simsek et al., 2018) between organizational governance and ecosystem dynamics.

An open landscape of research opportunities exists at the intersection of EE attributes and EE governance. This research would examine topics associated with how EE governance characteristics and outcomes influence (and are influenced by) EE characteristics and outcomes (arrows 5–9). Studies in this stream of research could examine, for instance, how EE leaders establish informal policies for how ecosystem leadership works together and how governance influences the openness of the EE to potential participants. For instance, Spigel et al. (2020: 489) state that EE governance should include a "widening circle of actors" with diverse goals, metrics, and decision-making (see also Brooks et al., 2019). Likewise, Milwood and Maxwell describe EE governance as being responsible for "expand[ing] opportunities for current EE players while encouraging the entry of new players" (Milwood & Maxwell, 2020: 243). EE governance is, thus, responsible for ensuring that all groups within a startup community, including traditionally marginalized groups such as poverty entrepreneurs, can access an EE and its resources (Santos et al., 2022).

Another important set of questions revolves around exploring how exactly EE leaders govern. Lo and Theodoraki (2021), for instance, contend that effective EE governance is based on a "co-governance approach that combines the principles of democracy and leadership" (419). They explain that "Two main types of [EE] governance can be distinguished: the hierarchical type, which is related to the hierarchical authority of ecosystem members in which a keystone player assumes the leadership responsibility of coordinating and regulating actions …; and the relational type, which is related to an implicit cogovernance of the ecosystem in which all members share a community of destiny with responsibilities, common values, informal routines, and mutually adjust the ecosystem's functioning" (Lo & Theodoraki, 2021: 419). Additional research is needed to understand how effective EEs combine bottom-up and top-down approaches to ecosystem governance.

Table 6.2 summarizes a non-exhaustive list of research directions at the intersection of corporate governance and EEs.

Beyond the specific research questions in Table 6.2, scholars pursuing research on this topic should keep several points in mind. First, they should be explicit about the focal level of analysis and the level at which relationships exist and are studied. For instance, rather than simply saying they are focused on "EE governance," studies should be explicit about whether they are studying the characteristics of the leaders responsible for governance, the outcomes of leaders' governance activities, how ecosystem characteristics and outcomes influence organizational governance, or other governance topics. Second, scholars are encouraged to use consistent terminology in describing EE governance. Currently, several terms appear in descriptions of EE governance and the ecosystem participants who govern: leadership, orchestration, coordination, brokerage, and championing. This chapter has suggested an umbrella term—EECG—with an explicit definition. Although it should not be mandated that scholars use any one term, consistency in terminology is necessary for studies to build on one another and create a unified body of knowledge

*Table 6.2* *An agenda for studying EECG*

| **Research focus** | **Opportunities for future research** |
| --- | --- |
| Isolating the *antecedents* of EECG | *Driving question: what are the factors that influence the formation of EECG?*<br>• What ecosystem and EE leader characteristics support the creation of EECG groups?<br>• What is the structure and composition of initial EECG groups?<br>• How are EE leaders trained?<br>• What are the ecosystem mechanisms that support EE leadership development?<br>• How does EE participant diversity shape EECG formation? |
| Understanding the *functioning* of EECG | *Driving question: what influences the day-to-day processes and functioning of EECG?*<br>• What are the optimal structures, processes, and practices of EECG?<br>• What are the leadership team compositions that support effective EECG?<br>• How can EE leaders take deliberate steps to improve EECG functioning?<br>• How are responsibilities divided among EE leaders in EECG?<br>• How are EE leaders held accountable for their actions and their contributions to EEs? Are there systems of checks and balances? Are EE leaders' decision-making processes transparent?<br>• What is the role of non-local EE participants in EECG?<br>• Should some EE leaders be "independent" and not tied to a specific venture that benefits from EE activities?<br>• How do EE leaders establish formal and informal policies for how EECG will function?<br>• Should EEs have constitutions?<br>• Are EE leaders inclusive? Is everyone invited to the governance "table"?<br>• Is cooperation or competition emphasized in EECG? How are ecosystem governance decisions made? |

| Research focus | Opportunities for future research |
|---|---|
| Identifying the outcomes of EECG | *Driving question: what are the effects of EECG?*<br>• What is the interface between ecosystem governance and organizational governance?<br>• How does EECG add value to entrepreneurs and other ecosystem stakeholders?<br>• How do different configurations of EECG influence the levels and types of entrepreneurship within an ecosystem? How does EECG contribute to "effective" ecosystems?<br>• How can EECG influence ecosystem coordination and resilience? How do EECG characteristics influence venture characteristics and outcomes?<br>• How do entrepreneurs leverage local EEs for governance talent (e.g., board members)?<br>• How does what entrepreneurs learn from other EE participants influence their venture governance structures? |
| Exploring the contextual boundary conditions of EECG | *Driving question: what are the contextual factors that enhance or disrupt the influence of EECG?*<br>• Are different cultures and institutional environments associated with different EECG structures and outcomes?<br>• How does EECG differ depending on specific types of ecosystems (e.g., social entrepreneurship ecosystems)<br>• How do the characteristics of the geographic areas in which ecosystems are embedded (e.g., resource munificence, territory size, population density) influence EECG and its outcomes? |

on EE governance. Third, scholars should not make assumptions about who is responsible for EECG. The individuals who take on the mantle of "EE leader" and who elect to be responsible for EE governance are not the same across ecosystems. For instance, in some ecosystems, the directors of support organizations (e.g., incubators, accelerators, small business development centers) are the driving forces in governance (Harper-Anderson, 2018). However, in other ecosystems, elected officials or university members are the primary EE leaders (Miles & Morrison, 2020). Thus, it is important for scholars interested in EE governance to survey ecosystem participants at the outset of their studies about who are the primary players in the governance of a particular ecosystem, rather than assuming EE leadership based on roles or titles (e.g., "incubator director"). Finally, in terms of study design, EE governance is a collective activity that involves a confluence of individuals and organizations. Thus, it is important for scholars interested in EE governance to gather data from multiple organizations involved in EE governance and to consider how EE leaders work together, rather than studying the isolated activities of single EE leaders and organizations (Roundy & Evans, 2024).

### 4.2 Concluding Remarks

Because the main function of EEs is supporting entrepreneurial activity, EE research often focuses on the activities and outcomes of entrepreneurs. However, the main thesis of this chapter is that understanding how EEs influence entrepreneurial activity and why EEs differ in their effectiveness requires an understanding of ecosystem governance and the leaders who govern ecosystems. In making the case for the importance of EE governance, this chapter has drawn attention to a corporate governance phenomenon not considered by other research (EECG) and a level of analysis (the ecosystem) that is underexplored in corporate governance research. It is hoped that the research opportunities outlined in this chapter advance corporate governance research into novel areas of study, which generate insights that improve the success of entrepreneurial ventures, increase the effectiveness of entrepreneurial ecosystems, and create flourishing startup communities.

## REFERENCES

Abebe, M.A., Li, P., Acharya, K., & Daspit, J.J. (2020). The founder chief executive officer: A review of current insights and directions for future research. *Corporate Governance: An International Review*, 28(6), 406–436.

Adams, S.B. (2021). From orchards to chips: Silicon Valley's evolving entrepreneurial ecosystem. *Entrepreneurship and Regional Development*, 33(1–2), 15–35.

Adner, R., & Kapoor, R. (2016). Innovation ecosystems and the pace of substitution: Re-examining technology S-curves. *Strategic Management Journal*, 37(4), 625–648.

Aguilera, R.V., Aragón-Correa, J.A., Marano, V., & Tashman, P.A. (2021). The corporate governance of environmental sustainability: A review and proposal for more integrated research. *Journal of Management*, 47(6), 1468–1497.

Aguilera, R.V., Judge, W.Q., & Terjesen, S.A. (2018). Corporate governance deviance. *Academy of Management Review*, 43(1), 87–109.

Ahrne, G., & Brunsson, N. (2008). *Meta-organizations*. Edward Elgar Publishing.

Alvedalen, J., & Boschma, R. (2017). A critical review of entrepreneurial ecosystems research: Towards a future research agenda. *European Planning Studies*, 25(6), 887–903.

Asheim, B.T., Smith, H.L., & Oughton, C. (2011). Regional innovation systems: Theory, empirics and policy. *Regional Studies*, 45(7), 875–891.

Assenova, V.A. (2020). Early-stage venture incubation and mentoring promote learning, scaling, and profitability among disadvantaged entrepreneurs. *Organization Science*, 31(6), 1560–1578.

Audretsch, D.B., & Lehmann, E.E. (2014). Corporate governance and entrepreneurial firms. *Foundations and Trends® in Entrepreneurship*, 10(1–2), 1–160.

Audretsch, D.B., Lehmann, E.E., Otto, J.M., Weiße, L., & Wirsching, K. (2023). The strategic management of places: Applying a framework to analyze local economies. In D.B. Audretsch, A. Civera, E.E. Lehmann, K.P. Leidinger, J.M. Otto, L. Weiße, & K. Wirsching (eds), *The Strategic Management of Place at Work: Why, What, How and Where* (pp. 1–36). Springer Nature.

Bolino, M.C., & Grant, A.M. (2016). The bright side of being prosocial at work, and the dark side, too: A review and agenda for research on other-oriented motives, behavior, and impact in organizations. *Academy of Management Annals*, 10(1), 599–670.

Breznitz, D., & Taylor, M. (2014). The communal roots of entrepreneurial-technological growth-social fragmentation and stagnation: Reflection on Atlanta's technology cluster. *Entrepreneurship and Regional Development*, 26(3–4), 375–396.

Brooks, C., Vorley, T., & Gherhes, C. (2019). Entrepreneurial ecosystems in Poland: panacea, paper tiger or Pandora's box? *Journal of Entrepreneurship and Public Policy*, 8(3), 319–338.

Brown, R., & Mason, C. (2017). Looking inside the spiky bits: A critical review and conceptualisation of entrepreneurial ecosystems. *Small Business Economics*, 49, 11–30.

Cao, Z., & Shi, X. (2021). A systematic literature review of entrepreneurial ecosystems in advanced and emerging economies. *Small Business Economics*, 57, 75–110.

Clayton, P., Feldman, M., & Montmartin, B. (2023). Entrepreneurial finance and regional ecosystem emergence. *Small Business Economics*, 62(4), 1–29.

Coleman, J.S. (1990). *Foundations of Social Theory*. The Belknap Press.

Colombo, M.G., Dagnino, G.B., Lehmann, E.E., & Salmador, M. (2019). The governance of entrepreneurial ecosystems. *Small Business Economics*, 52, 419–428.

Cumming, D., Werth, J.C., & Zhang, Y. (2019). Governance in entrepreneurial ecosystems: Venture capitalists vs. technology parks. *Small Business Economics*, 52, 455–484.

Cunningham, J.A., Menter, M., & Wirsching, K. (2019). Entrepreneurial ecosystem governance: A principal investigator-centered governance framework. *Small Business Economics*, 52, 545–562.

Daymond, J., Knight, E., Rumyantseva, M., & Maguire, S. (2023). Managing ecosystem emergence and evolution: Strategies for ecosystem architects. *Strategic Management Journal*, 44(4), O1–O27.

Dühnfort, A.M., Klein, C., & Lampenius, N. (2008). Theoretical foundations of corporate governance revisited: A critical review. *Corporate Ownership & Control*, 6(2), 424–433.

Eva, N., Cox, J.W., Herman, H.M., & Lowe, K.B. (2021). From competency to conversation: A multi-perspective approach to collective leadership development. *The Leadership Quarterly*, 32(5), 101346.

Farag, H., Mallin, C., & Ow-Yong, K. (2014). Governance, ownership structure, and performance of entrepreneurial IPOs in AIM companies. *Corporate Governance: An International Review*, 22(2), 100–115.

Feld, B. (2012). *Startup Communities: Building an Entrepreneurial Ecosystem in Your City*. John Wiley & Sons.

Feldman, M., & Zoller, T.D. (2012). Dealmakers in place: Social capital connections in regional entrepreneurial economies. *Regional Studies*, 46(1), 23–37.

Felin, T., Foss, N.J., & Ployhart, R.E. (2015). The microfoundations movement in strategy and organization theory. *Academy of Management Annals*, 9(1), 575–632.

Fernández-Temprano, M.A., & Tejerina-Gaite, F. (2020). Types of director, board diversity and firm performance. *Corporate Governance: The International Journal of Business in Society*, 20(2), 324–342.

Finkelstein S., Hambrick D.C., & Cannella, A.A. (2009). *Strategic Leadership: Theory and Research on Executives, Top Management Teams, and Boards*. Oxford University Press.

Frisillo, D. (2007). An analysis of a potential cluster in an energy sector of Albany, NY. *Journal of Business & Industrial Marketing*, 22(7), 508–516.

Gabrielsson, J., & Huse, M. (2017). Governance theory: Origins and implications for researching boards and governance in entrepreneurial firms. In J. Gabrielsson (ed.), *Handbook of Research on Corporate Governance and Entrepreneurship* (pp. 27–60). Edward Elgar Publishing.

Gan, D., & Erikson, T. (2022). Venture governance: CEO duality and new venture performance. *Journal of Business Venturing Insights*, 17, e00304.

Garg, S. (2020). Venture governance: A new horizon for corporate governance. *Academy of Management Perspectives*, 34(2), 252–265.

Goswami, K., Mitchell, J.R., & Bhagavatula, S. (2018). Accelerator expertise: Understanding the intermediary role of accelerators in the development of the Bangalore entrepreneurial ecosystem. *Strategic Entrepreneurship Journal*, 12(1), 117–150.

Gulati, R., Puranam, P., & Tushman, M. (2012). Meta-organization design: Rethinking design in interorganizational and community contexts. *Strategic Management Journal*, 33(6), 571–586.

Guzman, J., & Stern, S. (2015). Where is silicon valley? *Science*, 347(6222), 606–609.

Haarhaus, T., Strunk, G., & Liening, A. (2020). Assessing the complex dynamics of entrepreneurial ecosystems: A nonstationary approach. *Journal of Business Venturing Insights*, 14, e00194.

Haines, T. (2016). Developing a startup and innovation ecosystem in regional Australia. *Technology Innovation Management Review*, 6(6), 24–32.

Hambrick, D.C. (1989). Guest editor's introduction: Putting top managers back in the strategy picture. *Strategic Management Journal*, 10, 5–15.

Hanson, D., Hitt, M.A., Ireland, R.D., & Hoskisson, R.E. (2017). *Strategic Management: Competitiveness and Globalisation*. Cengage AU.

Harper-Anderson, E. (2018). Intersections of partnership and leadership in entrepreneurial ecosystems: Comparing three US regions. *Economic Development Quarterly*, 32(2), 119–134.

Howells, J., & Bessant, J. (2012). Introduction: Innovation and economic geography: A review and analysis. *Journal of Economic Geography*, 12(5), 929–942.

Knox, S., & Arshed, N. (2022). Network governance and coordination of a regional entrepreneurial ecosystem. *Regional Studies*, 56(7), 1161–1175.

Krueger, N. (2021). Beyond "getting asked to dance": Inclusive entrepreneurial ecosystems. In T.M. Cooney (ed.), *The Palgrave Handbook of Minority Entrepreneurship* (pp. 117–135). Palgrave Macmillan.

Lang, N.K., & Wirtz, P. (2022). Kicking off the corporate governance lifecycle: Seed funding, venture capital and the nascent board. *British Journal of Management*, 33(1), 181–210.

Lechner, C., & Dowling, M. (2003). Firm networks: External relationships as sources for the growth and competitiveness of entrepreneurial firms. *Entrepreneurship and Regional Development*, 15(1), 1–26.

Leendertse, J., Schrijvers, M., & Stam, E. (2022). Measure twice, cut once: Entrepreneurial ecosystem metrics. *Research Policy*, 51(9), 104336.

Li, H., Terjesen, S., & Umans, T. (2020). Corporate governance in entrepreneurial firms: A systematic review and research agenda. *Small Business Economics*, 54(1), 43–74.

Lichtenstein, G.A., Lyons, T.S., & Kutzhanova, N. (2004). Building entrepreneurial communities: The appropriate role of enterprise development activities. *Community Development*, 35(1), 5–24.

Lo, A., & Theodoraki, C. (2021). The influence of alliance ambidexterity on innovation performance and the moderating role of firm age. *IEEE Transactions on Engineering Management*, 68(2), 418–429.

Lund-Thomsen, P., & Pillay, R.G. (2012). CSR in industrial clusters: An overview of the literature. *Corporate Governance: The International Journal of Business in Society*, 12(4), 568–578.

Lusch, R.F., Vargo, S.L., & Gustafsson, A. (2016). Fostering a trans-disciplinary perspectives of service ecosystems. *Journal of Business Research*, 69(8), 2957–2963.

Miles, M.P., & Morrison, M. (2020). An effectual leadership perspective for developing rural entrepreneurial ecosystems. *Small Business Economics*, 54, 933–949.

Milwood, P.A., & Maxwell, A. (2020). A boundary objects view of Entrepreneurial Ecosystems in tourism. *Journal of Hospitality and Tourism Management*, 44, 243–252.

Mithani, M.A., & O'Brien, J.P. (2021). So what exactly is a "coalition" within an organization? A review and organizing framework. *Journal of Management*, 47(1), 171–206.

Moore, J. F. (1993). Predators and prey: a new ecology of competition. *Harvard Business Review*, 71(3), 75–86.

Muldoon, J., Bauman, A., & Lucy, C. (2018). Entrepreneurial ecosystem: Do you trust or distrust? *Journal of Enterprising Communities: People and Places in the Global Economy*, 12(2), 158–177.

Müller, S., & Korsgaard, S. (2018). Resources and bridging: The role of spatial context in rural entrepreneurship. *Entrepreneurship and Regional Development*, 30(1–2), 224–255.

Neumeyer, X., Santos, S.C., & Morris, M.H. (2019). Who is left out: Exploring social boundaries in entrepreneurial ecosystems. *The Journal of Technology Transfer*, 44, 462–484.

O'Brien, E., Cooney, T.M., & Blenker, P. (2019). Expanding university entrepreneurial ecosystems to under-represented communities. *Journal of Entrepreneurship and Public Policy*, 8(3), 384–407.

O'Connor, A., Stam, E., Sussan, F., & Audretsch, D. (2018). Entrepreneurial ecosystems: The foundations of place-based renewal. In A. O'Connor, E. Stam, F. Sussan, & D. Audretsch (eds), *Entrepreneurial Ecosystems: Place-based Transformations and Transitions* (pp. 1–21). Springer International Publishing.

Pancholi, S., Yigitcanlar, T., & Guaralda, M. (2018). Societal integration that matters: Place-making experience of Macquarie Park Innovation District, Sydney. *City, Culture and Society*, 13, 13–21.

Pugh, R., Soetanto, D., Jack, S.L., & Hamilton, E. (2021). Developing local entrepreneurial ecosystems through integrated learning initiatives: The Lancaster case. *Small Business Economics*, 56, 833–847.

Romme, A.G.L. (2022). Against all odds: How Eindhoven emerged as a deeptech ecosystem. *Systems*, 10(4), 119.

Roundy, P.T. (2019). Back from the brink: The revitalization of inactive entrepreneurial ecosystems. *Journal of Business Venturing Insights*, 12, e00140.

Roundy, P.T. (2020). Do we lead together? Leadership behavioral integration and coordination in entrepreneurial ecosystems. *Journal of Leadership Studies*, 14(1), 6–25.

Roundy, P.T. (2021). Leadership in startup communities: How incubator leaders develop a regional entrepreneurial ecosystem. *Journal of Management Development*, 40(3), 190–208.

Roundy, P.T., Bradshaw, M., & Brockman, B.K. (2018). The emergence of entrepreneurial ecosystems: A complex adaptive systems approach. *Journal of Business Research*, 86, 1–10.

Roundy, P.T., Brockman, B.K., & Bradshaw, M. (2017). The resilience of entrepreneurial ecosystems. *Journal of Business Venturing Insights*, 8, 99–104.

Roundy, P.T., & Burke-Smalley, L. (2022). Leveraging entrepreneurial ecosystems as human resource systems: A theory of meta-organizational human resource management. *Human Resource Management Review*, 32(4), 100863.

Roundy, P.T., & Evans, W.R. (2024). Entrepreneurial ecosystems as multiteam systems: Navigating independence and interdependence in the leadership of startup communities. *Journal of Business Venturing Insights*, 21, e00445.

Roundy, P.T., & Fayard, D. (2020). Place-based advantages in entrepreneurship: How entrepreneurial ecosystem coordination reduces transaction costs. *Journal of Behavioral and Applied Management*, 20(2), 115–136.

Roundy, P.T., & Lyons, T.S. (2023). Where are the entrepreneurs? A call to theorize the micro-foundations and strategic organization of entrepreneurial ecosystems. *Strategic Organization*, 21(2), 447–459.

Sahut, J.M., Dana, L.P., & Teulon, F. (2021). Corporate governance and financing of young technological firms: A review and introduction. *Technological Forecasting and Social Change*, 163, 120425.

Santos, J.B., Fernandes, A.R., de Oliveira, P.T., Maia, L.M., & Partyka, R.B. (2023). Increasing entrepreneurial ecosystem-level outcomes through orchestration: A proposed framework. *Technovation*, 128, 102873.

Santos, S.C., Costa, S., & Morris, M.H. (2022). Entrepreneurship as a pathway into and out of poverty: A configuration perspective. *Entrepreneurship & Regional Development*, 34(1–2), 82–109.

Scheidgen, K., & Brattström, A. (2023). Berlin is hotter than Silicon Valley! How networking temperature shapes entrepreneurs' networking across social contexts. *Entrepreneurship Theory and Practice*, 47(6), 2233–2262.

Simsek, Z., Heavey, C., & Fox, B.C. (2018). Interfaces of strategic leaders: A conceptual framework, review, and research agenda. *Journal of Management*, 44(1), 280–324.

Spigel, B. (2016). Developing and governing entrepreneurial ecosystems: The structure of entrepreneurial support programs in Edinburgh, Scotland. *International Journal of Innovation and Regional Development*, 7(2), 141–160.

Spigel, B. (2017). The relational organization of entrepreneurial ecosystems. *Entrepreneurship Theory and Practice*, 41(1), 49–72.

Spigel, B., Kitagawa, F., & Mason, C. (2020). A manifesto for researching entrepreneurial ecosystems. *Local Economy*, 35(5), 482–495.

Stam, E. (2015). Entrepreneurial ecosystems and regional policy: A sympathetic critique. *European Planning Studies*, 23(9), 1759–1769.

Stam, E., & Van de Ven, A. (2021). Entrepreneurial ecosystem elements. *Small Business Economics*, 56, 809–832.

Theodoraki, C., Messeghem, K., & Rice, M.P. (2018). A social capital approach to the development of sustainable entrepreneurial ecosystems: An explorative study. *Small Business Economics*, 51, 153–170.

Tricker, R.I. (ed.) (2019). *Corporate Governance: Values, Ethics and Leadership.* Taylor & Francis.

Velt, H., Torkkeli, L., & Laine, I. (2020). Entrepreneurial ecosystem research: Bibliometric mapping of the domain. *Journal of Business Ecosystems*, 1(2), 43–83.

Welter, F., Baker, T., & Wirsching, K. (2019). Three waves and counting: The rising tide of contextualization in entrepreneurship research. *Small Business Economics*, 52, 319–330.

Wurth, B., Stam, E., & Spigel, B. (2022). Toward an entrepreneurial ecosystem research program. *Entrepreneurship Theory and Practice*, 46(3), 729–778.

Zahra, S.A., & Filatotchev, I. (2004). Governance of the entrepreneurial threshold firm: A knowledge-based perspective. *Journal of Management Studies*, 41(5), 885–897.

# 7. Interlocking dynamics in suprateams

**Truls Erikson**

## 1. INTRODUCTION TO SUPRATEAMS

In their seminal book on strategic leadership, Finkelstein, Hambrick, and Cannella (2009) argue that supra-top management teams ought to be an important target for strategic leadership research. In fact, they hold that boards are "supra-top management teams" (supra-TMTs) and that we need to understand the dynamics of such teams better. Although these recommendations apply to larger firms, similar recommendations are relevant for new firms where the board has a more advisory role.

While some research on suprateams exists (Nielsen, 2010; Knockaert, Bjornali, & Erikson, 2015), little focus has been on the dynamics between the CEO and the board in new firms, until lately (Erikson, Coleridge, & Bjornali, 2022; Gan & Erikson, 2022a, 2022b).

For instance, we do not know how *structural* leadership works between the inner and outer environment of the firm, or how the various structural *roles interact* with outside directors. When they studied three different agency contexts and their influence on strategy, Jensen and Zajac (2004) pinpointed that roles or positions are more important than demography. In many ways, this study addresses the dyadic relationship between the CEO and the new board members, not far from the call made by Garg and Eisenhardt (2017) and Garg (2020). As they recommend, at this early stage, I also find it useful to 'flip' the viewpoints in agency theory and treat the dual CEO as the principal and the appointed board members as agents in their role as CEO advisors. As Ma, Kor, and Seidl's (2021) review of *role structures* among TMTs and their formal and informal relationships indicate, I initially focus on the mediating role of incoming relational ties, before I turn to the *founder CEO-board role structure* relationships and its role in moderating the direct and mediating relationships.

Finkelstein et al. (2009) only explored the notion of supra-TMTs, as they mainly focused on the role of TMTs in strategic leadership. In the current study, suprateam is defined as the CEO and the emerging board. Future studies may employ a broader conceptualization employing the label of supra-new venture teams (supra-NVTs) to distinguish start-ups from scale-ups, for instance, and reserve supra-TMT for the more established firms. As such, suprateams run prior to supra-NVTs which again run prior to Supra-TMTs. For start-ups, or firms in their earlier phases, suprateams and supra-NVTs appear to be a better conceptualization, as new emerging firms have different challenges than NVTs and TMTs.

So, I conceive of the board and founding manager, or the founding CEO to be the suprateam, and I operationalize the suprateam as the dual CEO and the board. In other words, I understand the suprateam to be the CEO of the firm and the board, and it is the dynamics between these diverse individuals and the environment that defines the capabilities of the new firm (Klarner et al., 2018), and their practice becomes what we may label as strategic leadership (Finkelstein, Hambrick, & Cannella, 2009).

Accordingly, in this chapter, I conjecture that board leadership structure and the affiliated dynamics matter, but in idiosyncratic ways. Beyond the internal dynamics, as thoroughly addressed by Erikson, Coleridge, and Bjornali (2022), I elaborate specifically on the *external* suprateam dynamics, addressing not only incoming but also outgoing interlocking ties in relation to board leadership *role* structures. As will be elaborated on, these role structures are strongly related to the extent of *managerial discretion* the CEO has. When the leadership is shared, the CEO's latitude is less, whereas it may be regarded as higher in the dual CEO role.

## 2. LITERATURE REVIEW

Managerial discretion has been conceived of as the latitude of managerial action available to a decision-maker (Linden and Teece, 2018; Finkelstein & Boyd, 1998; Finkelstein & Hambrick, 1990; Finkelstein, Hambrick, & Cannella, 2009), and such discretion is limited by internal and external constraints, including the principal, or those that represent the principals, typically at the board. In the earlier phases of new start-ups, the founding CEO is the owner and has full discretion, and that form of discretion is thus broader and more elusive than what has been conceived of as discretion in the management literature. In many ways, the main limiting constraints are also the lack of ability to see and generate 'opportunity sets' (Penrose, 1959/2009), or what Sripada (2016) labels as 'construction of options', or 'construction of option sets'. Departing from free will, Sripada (2016) addresses the generative processes of option-making. In his 2015 article, he elaborates that the most useful options are those that can be expressed through action, and as such, the possible and likely pathways are not only created through an experimental trial and error process (Zellweger & Zenger, 2023) but also through imaginations, and the most fruitful of these are the ones in interaction with advice and counsel (Ma, Kor, & Seidl, 2020), as 'value-adding' services from the relational ties. Sripada (2015, 2016) builds on the seminal work of Seligman, Railton, Baumeister, and Sripada (2013, 2016).

## 2.1 The Mediating Role of Incoming Relational Ties on New Firm Performance

As shown by Bruneel, Gaeremynck, and Weemaes (2022), outside board members play a pivotal role in this value capture process, as they contribute valuable advice and counsel, not unlike what Ma, Kor, and Seidl (2020) highlight in their CEO advice-seeking review. The current angle is also inspired by Yildiz, Morgulis-Yakushev, Holm, and Eriksson's (2021) internationalization study, where they find that the board's incoming ties are more important than their outgoing ties. As such, the topic is timely, also across disciplines, and I, therefore, choose to focus on the value-adding and creation dimension of these ties, facilitated by outside directors, and their differential contributions to enhancing new firm performance. The dynamics, and the balance, of outgoing and incoming ties are interesting because they reflect potential value-creation relationships that come with the alignment of dispersed knowledge from strategically important resources, and as such, they need to be governed.

In the current context, incoming ties are new board members with ties to not only other boards (Zhang et al., 2016), but they bring in not only explicit but also tacit knowledge that typically flows with such ties. Hence, I conjecture that an increase in incoming board ties, that is the social dimension of a new board member, will positively mediate the relationship between the increase of board members and new firm performance. Many studies (e.g.,Haunschild, 1993; Haunschild & Beckman, 1998; Haynes & Hillman, 2010; Hillman & Dalziel, 2003; Kor & Sundaramurthy, 2009) find that outside directors and their interlocking ties are useful, and we ought to understand the effect of the services that flow from well-connected ties. Henceforth, I am interested in the relative effects of these ties, as they reflect the social component of human capital. Accordingly, the following hypothesis has three sub-elements: two legs that make up the multiplicative mediation effect and a direct effect which captures the human capital:

> *Hypothesis 1: An increase in incoming relational ties will partly* ***mediate*** *the effects between an increase in the number of new board members and new firm performance (1a, 1b, & 1c).*

## 2.2 The Moderating Role of Board Leadership Structure on New Firm Performance

The board leadership *role* structure is part of the superstructure of the board, if not the whole firm. How the start-up is governed matters, and its structure matters. CEO duality is a situation where the CEO is also the chairperson. That can under some circumstances be an advantage, in other circumstances not, since power is centralized to one person. When power is located to one person, we may say that managerial discretion is high, and when leadership is divided, managerial discretion is less. Hambrick's (2007) update on the upper echelon theory included a refinement where he suggested looking into the moderating role of discretion and power as the CEO may, or may not, be constrained by their own power relative to the board. Among the five types of powers that Finkelstein (1992) identified (structural, ownership, expertise, prestige, and friendship), I elaborate primarily on the structural power that arises from formal hierarchical relations where the CEO duality construct is a good example of such power.

Managerial *discretion* has been defined by Linden and Teece (2018) as "the latitude that executives have to affect the activities of the companies they run, as opposed to merely accepting internal and external influences" (p. 950). Such discretion regards the CEO's degrees of freedom in setting goals and the degree of freedom of choosing the most appropriate action to reach these goals. This freedom is larger under conditions of CEO duality, and probably less with a separate chairperson. Hambrick (2007, p. 335) states that "discretion exists when there is an absence of constraints and when there is a great deal of means-ends ambiguity – that is, when there are multiple plausible alternatives," as is the case with new firms. Hambrick and Finkelstein (1987) advanced the idea that managerial discretion could be a moderating variable explaining why specific roles influence the performance of the new firm, and this may very well be the case as role structure and discretion are closely related, especially under conditions of "fundamental" uncertainty which is the case with new firms (Alvarez & Porac, 2020; Knight, 1921). Accordingly, I hypothesize:

> *Hypothesis 2: Board leadership role structure in new firms will* ***moderate*** *the direct and indirect relationships between the increases in the suprateam resources and their performance (2a, 2b & 2c).*

Specifically, a dual leadership structure will be better at positively moderating the relationship between interlocking ties and new firm performance (H2a). In contrast, a divided leadership structure with a separate chair will better recruit more efficacious board members (H2c) who are also interlocked (H2b). These relationships are illustrated in Figure 7.1.

In other words, a separate chairperson will be better at searching for appropriate board members, but a dual CEO will be better at utilizing the services from these external resources. The chairperson's relational building capabilities are important, and I seek to uncover to what extent a chairperson will be better at recruiting board members that are interlocked with "important others" than a dual CEO. In contrast, the dual CEO is likely to be better at drawing on and building on the new interlocking relational ties that the incoming board members have.

## 3. RESEARCH METHODS

In the current study, I employ board and revenue registry data of all new startups in Norway in 2018, and I made a quantitative analysis of the data set. I only have complete accounting and board data on 1,153 firms that were registered in Norway during 2018, and in many ways reflect those firms that have reported successfully on all accounts, including the years 2019 and 2020, and as such, they reflect the upper layer of new firms that survive. I received the data set from T-Rank AS, a subsidiary of TietoEvry ASA, but the data was initially collected by the National Registry, a public agency that sorts under the

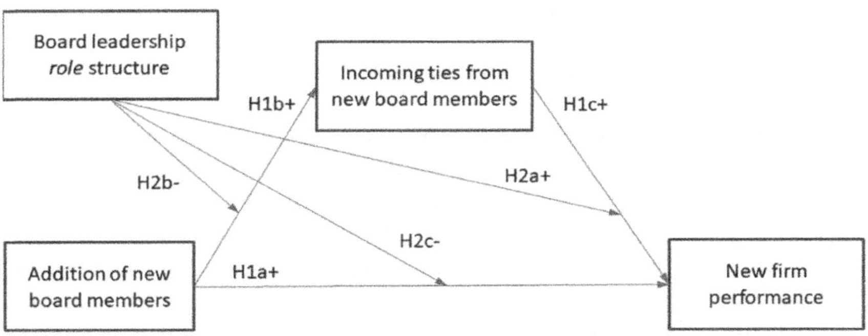


*Note:* H1a–c: New board member addition directly improves new firm performance (H1a), and indirectly via incoming ties from new board members (H1b → H1c). H2a–c: Board leadership role structure moderates these effects—strengthening the impact of incoming ties on performance (H2a), influencing how new board member additions affect incoming ties (H2b), and altering the direct effect of board additions on performance (H2c).

*Figure 7.1 The suprateam new firm performance model tested in this study*

Norwegian Ministry of Trade and Industry. I used IBM SPSS 29, and Hayes' (2013) analytical PROCESS toolkit in analyzing not only mediation but also moderating relationships. This toolkit also makes use of bootstrapping as a method to conduct a robust mediation analysis that prevents potential misinterpretations of the statistics.

In the wider context, Norway has an open economy, and the country is fully integrated with the European Economic Area (EEA), although not politically with the European Union. As such, the studied firms are regulated not only by Norwegian law but also by the EEA Agreement, which adheres to EU laws. It is within this economic context that I scrutinize the effect of the overall governance architecture of new firms and how the dynamics affect firm performance.

## 3.1 Measurements

### Dependent variable

*New firm performance.* For new firms in an early phase, viable metrics are not available, as traditional corporate performance measures are not very suitable at such an early stage. However, aggregated sales since inception, or revenue, is an appropriate measure as it reflects the value that the firm can seize, and I, therefore, use the aggregated revenue for the first three first years since inception as the dependent variable, acknowledging that not all new firms have revenues from the outset, and very few are into profitability, so returns on sales, equity, assets, or new investments would neither be good indicators. As such, aggregated sales since inception is a viable proxy for new firms that are in their formative stage and emerge and start to perform. It is a critical measure as it demonstrates the firm's ability to attract and seize new customers.

### Independent, mediation, and moderation variables

As the independent variable, I counted the number of board members at the inception year from the variable *the number of board members* and measured the increase in board members from the inception year to the subsequent year. In other words, I used the increase in board members from inception and one year ahead. I label this variable as *board member change.* The mediation variable *change in incoming ties* captures the number of interlocking ties that board members bring into the firm and is a valuable social capital resource, as these board members are also linked with other board members in other firms. When new board members are recruited, they may be interlocked, and it is this extra effect that is captured here.

The moderation variable *board structural leadership* was operationalized by coding CEO duality at inception ("one person, two roles") as "1"; otherwise, it was coded as "0," then reflecting "two persons, two roles," which requires a separate chairperson, which is typically external. It is this variable that serves as a moderating variable between the three hypothesized relationships.

**Control variables**

In the current study, I control for variables that have theoretical interests (Spector & Brannick, 2011). I controlled for board size and equity at inception, as well as the gender of the CEO, to capture the gender debate. I also controlled for the number of board members and the number of interlocking ties the board had at the inception year, and the changes to the following year, and I controlled for outgoing ties. *Outgoing ties* are the interlocking ties the chairperson has (regardless of the role status) at inception, whereas *incoming ties* are the number of interlocking ties the appointed board members have when they enter the target firm. I also controlled for the increase in board members from the second year to the third year. Most of these controls then serve to reduce the possibility of alternative explanations.

## 4. RESULTS

Table 7.1 shows the descriptive statistics for the variables employed in this study.

Table 7.1 also shows the main correlates, and we can see that the foci variables are somewhat correlated, and we particularly note that the chairperson's interlocking ties are strongly related to the other interlocking ties. Specifically, we can see that the more interlocked the chairperson, the more interlocked the board is ($r = 0.73$, $p<0.01$). In other words, having an outgoing tie is vital for the incoming ties. Although not that surprising, the strong correlation is *somewhat* surprising as it means that the chairperson may be the most important person in the equation.

The correlation between an increase in board members' interlocking ties and the board chairs' outgoing ties ($r = 0.40$, $p<0.01$) corroborates this assertion. We also see that the average board size is 1.64, plus the chairperson (whether in the form of CEO duality or not), so the average start-up board has 2.64 members with a standard deviation of almost one (0.96). From Table 7.1, we can also read that the average aggregated revenue over three years is 17.9 million Norwegian kroner (MNOK). Not shown in the table, the *median* is 3.9 MNOK, and the *mode* – the most frequent situation – is in fact zero, that is, new firms with no reported revenue.

As for the equity, the *mean* equity size at formation is 16.8 MNOK, with a *median* of 95,000 NOK, and a *mode* of 30,000 NOK, the latter sum being the minimum required for the formation of a limited liability company in Norway. We can also see from the table that 40% have a dual CEO role position, meaning that the most frequent situation is a divided leadership structure where

*Table 7.1 Descriptive statistics and correlations*

| Variables | Mean | SD | 1. | 2. | 3. | 4. | 5. | 6. | 7. | 8. | 9. | 10. |
|---|---|---|---|---|---|---|---|---|---|---|---|---|
| 1. New firm performance | 17.9M | 79.4M | - | - | - | - | - | - | - | - | - | - |
| 2. Board member change, $_{t=32}$ | −0.07 | 0.46 | 0.08 | - | - | - | - | - | - | - | - | - |
| 3. Change in incoming ties, $_{t=2-1}$ | 0.63 | 6.93 | 0.04 | 0.50 | - | - | - | - | - | - | - | - |
| 4. CEO duality | 0.40 | 0.49 | −0.06 | 0.03 | −0.03 | - | - | - | - | - | - | - |
| 5. Board member change, $_{t=2-1}$ | 0.03 | 0.45 | 0.04 | −0.02 | −0.02 | 0.05 | - | - | - | - | - | - |
| 6. Number of board members, $_{t=1}$ | 1.64 | 0.96 | 0.16 | −0.16 | −0.11 | −0.28 | −0.13 | - | - | - | - | - |
| 7. Change in outgoing ties, $_{t=2-1}$ | 0.38 | 4.37 | 0.01 | −0.02 | 0.08 | −0.02 | 0.04 | −0.03 | - | - | - | - |
| 8. CEO gender | 0.79 | 0.40 | 0.04 | 0.01 | 0.01 | 0.05 | -0.03 | 0.03 | 0.02 | - | - | - |
| 9. Equity, $_{t=1}$ | 16.8M | 455.6M | 0.07 | 0.01 | 0.00 | −0.03 | 0.00 | 0.17 | 0.01 | 0.02 | - | - |
| 10. Incoming ties, $_{t=1}$ | 6.81 | 19.95 | 0.09 | −0.12 | 0.21 | −0.18 | −0.03 | 0.33 | 0.35 | 0.09 | 0.04 | - |
| 11. Outgoing ties, $_{t=1}$ | 4.80 | 12.42 | 0.07 | −0.03 | 0.40 | −0.18 | 0.02 | 0.15 | 0.26 | 0.10 | 0.01 | 0.73 |

*Note:* Significance levels: Correlations larger than |0.02| are significant at the 0.05 level, and those larger than |0.03| are significant at the 0.01 level. N=1153. The variance inflation factors (VIFs) are in the range from 1.03 to 2.61.

79% of the CEOs are also males. Moreover, we see that the average number of interlocking ties for the board is 6.81 whereas we can read out 4.80 interlocking ties for the average board chairs at inception. In both these two situations, the *median* is 2, and the *mode* is 0, meaning that most chairs do not have any interlocking ties. From the second year to the third year, there is an average decrease in the average number of board members (−0.07), probably due to the COVID-19 pandemic, and the opposite from year one to the second year (0.03).

## 4.1 Assessing the Mediating Relationships

Figure 7.2 shows a clear link between the number of directors and new firm performance (B = 13,234.84, $p<0.001$), but the strongest *direct* effect is when a new board member is added to the board (B = 18,840.94, $p<0.001$), in support of Hypothesis 1a (see H1a in Model 1 in Figure 7.2). Interestingly, I do not find any *indirect* effects of board structural leadership, but I do find, as hypothesized, *conditional direct* effects and *conditional indirect* effects. That is, I find support for the first leg in the mediation sequence, Hypothesis 1b (see H1b in Model 2), but I do not find support for the second leg, Hypothesis 1c (see H1c in Model 4), and the test statistic for mediation is not significant (Sobel z = −0.446, $p>0.61$). However, the moderation variable supports the *conditional direct* effect (see H2b in Model 3), and the *conditional indirect* effects (H2a and H2c in Model 5), so I do find support for all three moderation hypotheses, which I elaborate on next (Figure 7.2).

## 4.2 Assessing the Moderating Relationships

In line with Hypotheses 2a, 2b, and 2c, I find that the *role structure* of the board leadership indeed *moderates* the relationships in intricate ways, as the initially hypothesized mediation relationship is broken due to insignificant support for the second leg of the mediation chain. However, we do have mediation effects, but these effects are then moderated mediations. In other words, mediation does indeed take place, but in interaction with the moderating variable.

Specifically, Hypothesis 2a delineated that a dual leadership structure will be better at positively moderating the relationship between interlocking ties and new firm performance. Figure 7.3 shows that a dual leadership role structure and a high increase in relational ties, indeed, are associated with higher new firm performance.

Again, it means that the dual CEO is better at drawing on the newly appointed interlocked board members and that the dual CEO role structure is better shaped to mobilize their knowledge. In such a context, and under these conditions, managerial discretion is not only highly flexible but also highly

| | **Control model** New firm performance | **Model 1** New firm performance | **Model 2** Change in incoming ties | **Model 3** Change in incoming ties | **Model 4** New firm performance | **Model 5** New firm performance |
|---|---|---|---|---|---|---|
| (Constant) | -8,858.14 | -11,238.93$^{+}$ | .76 | .67 | -9,561.44 | -9,671.60 |
| | (6,522.45) | (6,521.43) | (.48) | (.48) | (7,132.71) | (7,109.98) |
| CEO gender | 6,707.04 | 6,358.40 | -.67$^{+}$ | -.71$^{+}$ | 6,475.60 | 7,453.74 |
| | (5,708.02) | (5,709.92) | (.39) | (.38) | (5,740.10) | (5,729.64) |
| Equity, $_{t=1}$ | 0.07 | 0.06 | .00 | .00 | 0.06 | 0.06 |
| | (0.05) | (0.05) | (.00) | (.00) | (0.05) | (0.05) |
| # of board members, $_{t=1}$ | 11,991.45*** | 13,234.84*** | -.66*** | -.61*** | 12,748.96*** | 12,186.50*** |
| | (2,6742.44) | (2,650.90) | (.18) | (.18) | (2,750.96) | (2,748.89) |
| Board member change, $_{t=3-2}$ | 9,874.02$^{+}$ | 10,599.71* | -.54 | -.64$^{+}$ | 10,532.44* | 9,734.82$^{+}$ |
| | (5,100.37) | (5,077.55) | (.34) | (.34) | (5,087.06) | (5,085.16) |
| Incoming ties $_{t=1}$ | 125.20 | 187.59 | -.01 | -.01 | 187.40 | 210.41 |
| | (185.59) | (185.42) | (.01) | (.01) | (185.61) | (185.04) |
| Outgoing ties, $_{t=1}$ | 112.08 | 42.03 | .25 | .25 | 74.24 | 136.69 |
| | (274.43) | (273.68) | (.02) | (.02) | (297.53) | (297.07) |
| Change in Outgoing ties, $_{t=2-1}$ | -30.45 | -.23.94 | -.04 | .03 | -.31.83 | -.181.72 |
| | (572.23) | (569.23) | (.04) | (.04) | (569.87) | (570.75) |
| **Main effects** | | | | | | |
| Board member change, $_{t=2-1}$ | | **H1a:** | **H1b:** | | | |
| | | 18,840.94*** | **7.63*** ** | 8.61*** | 20,279.70*** | 24,727.25*** |
| | | (5,202.35) | **(.35)** | (.42) | (61,92.25) | (7,322.95) |
| Change in incoming ties, $_{t=2-1}$ | | | | | **H1c:** | |
| | | | | | **-196.01** | -.597.41 |
| | | | | | **(439.45)** | (456.29) |
| Dual CEO | | | .15 | .31 | -2,612.58 | -3,116.16 |
| | | | (.33) | (.33) | (4,942.09) | (4,960.31) |
| **Interaction effects** | | | | | | |
| Dual CEO x Board member change, $_{t=2-1}$ | | | | **H2b:** | | **H2c:** |
| | | | | **-3.29*** ** | | **-36,133.40*** |
| | | | | **(.76)** | | **(14,998.84)** |
| Dual CEO x Change in incoming ties, $_{t=2-1}$ | | | | | | **H2a:** |
| | | | | | | **5,632.61*** ** |
| | | | | | | **(1,706.97)** |
| F-value | 5.628*** | 6.616*** | 96.409*** | 90.016*** | 5.335*** | 5.398*** |
| $R^2$ | .033 | .044 | .432 | .441 | .045 | .054 |
| Adjusted $R^2$ | .027 | .038 | .427 | .436 | .036 | .044 |

*Note:* Significance level: +p<0.10, *p<0.05, **p<0.01, ***p<0.001; n=1153.

*Figure 7.2* *Regression results with unstandardized coefficients (standard errors in parentheses)*

valuable. It is under these conditions that creativity and imagination may be at the top, and play a more unique role. For instance, the extra latitude may make the dual CEO better at drawing on the services of the interlocked members,

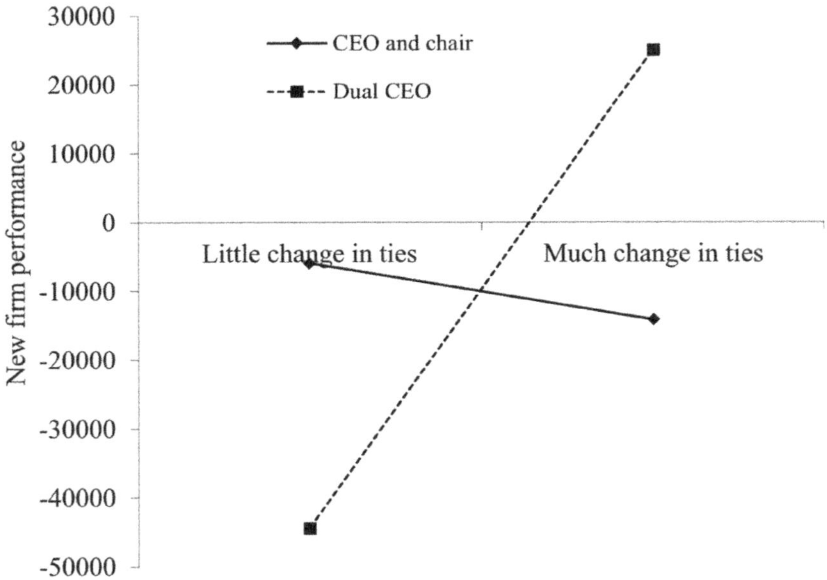


*Figure 7.3* *Moderation effects of CEO duality and change in relational ties on performance*

since such latitude in discretion facilitates play and thus somewhat more flexibility to generate heterogeneous imaginations, interpretations and expectations. Hypotheses 2b delineated that a divided leadership structure with a separate chair will better recruit more efficacious board members who are also interlocked. Figure 7.4 shows that a separate chairperson is better at selecting board members who are more interlocked but only when they are recruiting board members at a high phase.

This insight contributes to what Withers, Hillman, and Cannella (2012) label a resource needs perspective, as a contrast to the social embeddedness perspective, where a number of other factors play a role in new board member selection. Interestingly, the above indicates that not only time and thus the speed of tie formations may matter (Brenneche, Ertug, & Elfring, 2022) but also the nature of such ties, and the overlap of various roles and ties – what Verbrugge (1979) labels "multiplexity" – matters. Graen and Uhl-Bien (1995), for instance, elaborate on different forms of multiplexity and how they may be related to various types of leadership. Future research may usefully elaborate on the effects of such relationships.

Finally, Hypothesis 2c delineated that a divided leadership structure with a separate chair will better recruit more efficacious board members. Figure

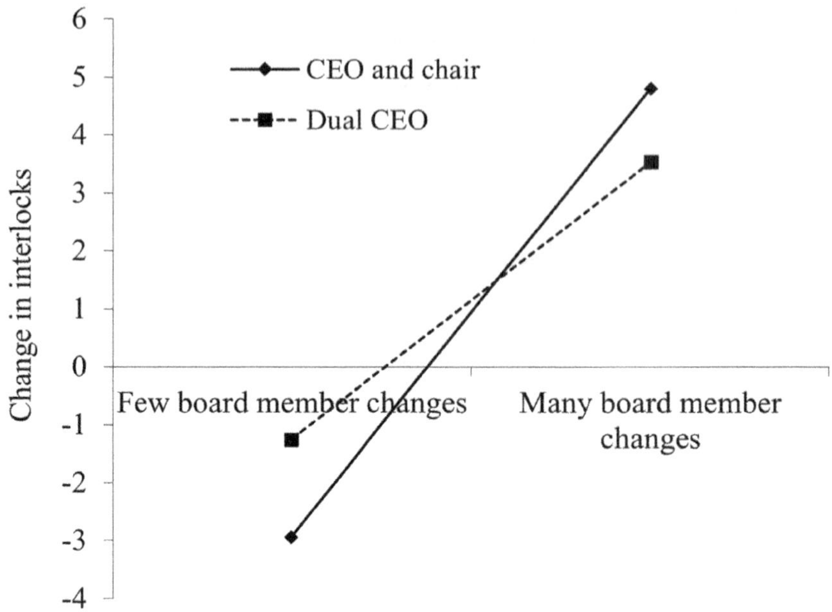


*Figure 7.4* *Moderation effects of CEO duality and change in board members on interlocks*

7.5 shows that divided leadership has a direct positive interaction effect on performance. In other words, such a divided leadership structure yields higher performance when the number of board members increases at a faster pace, as they do with a divided leadership structure. It means that a divided leadership structure is better at recruiting board members, suggesting that speed in tie formation matters.

I also robustness-checked the finding with 10,000 bootstraps on the full data set with good results. With bootstrapped confidence intervals, the typical problems related to non-normal sampling distributions of an indirect effect are avoided (Cole, Walter, & Bruch, 2008). I also tested the model on alternative dependent variables, such as aggregated revenue for the last two years (as compared to all the revenue since inception), and with revenue for only the third year without changes in the hypothesized results, so the results are robust across coding procedures.

Next, I discuss these findings, the services that come with new board members, and the structural leadership that facilitates such services. In particular, I highlight the advice and counsel role of the interlocked board members, moderated by the structure of the leadership.

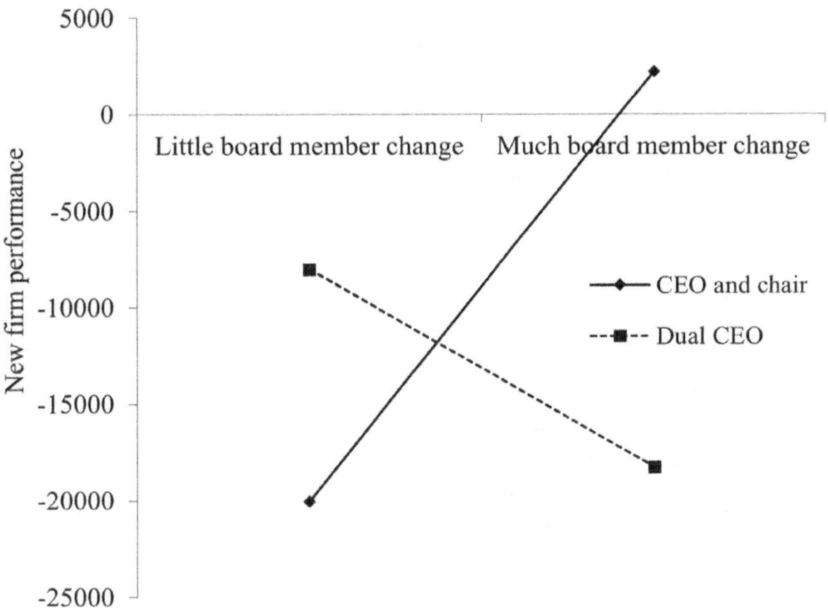


*Figure 7.5* *Moderation effects of CEO duality and board member change on performance*

## 5. DISCUSSION

I have in this study addressed the overall governance architecture of new firms. Specifically, I found that the superstructure of the boards is relevant when it comes to new firm performance. That is, not only does the board leadership role structure moderate the mediating relationships, but I also discovered that the board's incoming ties are more important than their outgoing ties. However, this is a matter of widened interpretation, beyond the focus of this chapter, as the initial correlation analysis indicates a high correlation between board members' incoming ties and a chairperson with outgoing ties. In other words, it may very well be that an interlocked board chairperson is the one who recruits interlocked board members, and that reflects a useful insight.

Implications are that we need to stop extrapolating research findings from larger firms to early-stage venture governance. We need to cease generalizing corporate governance theories to the earlier stages of new firms. As I have done, Dalton, Daily, Ellstrand, and Johnson (1998) suggest considering multiple theoretical approaches when assessing the performance of firms, as they, in their meta-study of more than 40,000 US-based firms, did not find any meaningful substantive relationship between board composition and financial performance. Neither was there a relationship between board leadership structure and financial performance, although the statistics indicate that there may be a relationship. Neither could I find a direct relationship, but I was able to identify meaningful *conditional direct* and *indirect* relationships.

The practical implication of this study is that entrepreneurs ought to consider who they appoint as board members and to be considerate about potential interlocking relationships. They also ought to deliberate around the chairperson's interlocking relationships, as they may serve the new firm well in many ways, from advice and counsel to other value-adding services. The speed of such tie formation may also matter. As we have seen, not only do role structures matter, but also relational ties, and probably the speed of such tie formation. The added expertise that comes with the more interlocked relational ties should not be underestimated. And the more interlocked the better. To make an analogy that may illustrate the difference vividly: among all the patented products in the world, only a small fraction of them make significant sums of money. Likewise with services from external directors, not all of these relational ties necessarily add value or act as "value creators," but the interlocked ones are more likely to add meaningful value, which is extremely important for new firms in the very early stages of development.

### 5.1 Limitations and Future Research

As with most other studies, this study has weaknesses. It should be noted that the third-year revenue data reflects the start of the COVID-19 pandemic, so the results may also be somewhat affected by those circumstances. However, great care has been taken to ensure that we do not have reverse causality as the antecedent metrics appear before the performance construct measure. It could still be that some investors were attracted by the expected growth of the firm, so it could be the growth that drives the increasing number of directors. Such a thought cannot be ruled out, but it is less likely for new firms than for existing and listed firms.

## 6. CONCLUSION

The current study has shown that relational ties are important for early-stage performance. In particular, I have unraveled that the board chair's incoming ties are perhaps the most important tie, as it is the interlocked chairpersons that recruit interlocked board members. Given an interlocked board chair, the incoming ties become more important. As for the leadership *role* structure, a divided leadership structure is better for not only board member recruitment, but also for interlocked board member recruitment, both contributing to new firm emergence in idiosyncratic (conditional direct and indirect) ways. However, the dual CEO role structure is better at drawing on interlocked board members, once in place. The CEO advice-seeking literature (Ma, Kor, & Seidl, 2020) elaborates on some of these themes from the TMT perspective, so CEO advice-taking may therefore also be a worthwhile topic for future research.

## REFERENCES


Alvarez, S., & Porac, J. 2020. Imagination, indeterminacy, and managerial choice at the limit of knowledge. *Academy of Management Review*, 45(4), 735–744.

Brenneche, J., Ertug, G., & Elfring, T. (2022). Networking fast and slow: The role of speed in tie formation. *Journal of Management*, 50(4), 1–29.

Bruneel, J., Gaeremynck, A., & Weemaes, S. 2022. Outside board members and strategic orientation of new ventures in the startup phase. *Strategic Entrepreneurship Journal*, 16(4), 801–825.

Cole, M.S., Walter, F., & Bruch, H. 2008. Affective mechanisms linking dysfunctional behaviour to performance in work teams: A moderated mediation study. *Journal of Applied Psychology*, 93(5), 945–958.

Dalton, D.R., Daily, C.M., Ellstrand, A.E., & Johnson, J.L. (1998). Meta-analytic reviews of board composition, leadership structure, and financial performance. *Strategic Management Journal*, 19, 269–290.

Erikson, T., Coleridge, C., & Bjornali, E.S. 2022. Venture governance and its dynamics: Intraboard relationships and CEO duality. *Technovation*, 115, 102540.

Finkelstein, S. 1992. Power in top management teams: Dimensions, measurement, and validation. *Academy of Management Journal*, 35(3), 505–538.

Finkelstein, S., & Boyd, B.K. 1998. How much does the CEO matter? The role of managerial discretion in the setting of CEO compensation. *Academy of Management Journal*, 41, 179–199.

Finkelstein, S., & Hambrick, D.C. 1990. Top-management-team tenure and organizational outcomes: The moderating role of managerial discretion. *Administrative Science Quarterly*, 35, 484–503.

Finkelstein, S., Hambrick, D.C., & Cannella, B. 2009. *Strategic Leadership: Theory and Research on Executives, Top Management Teams, and Boards*. Oxford University Press.

Gan, D., & Erikson, T. 2022a. Venture governance: CEO duality and new venture performance. *Journal of Business Venturing Insights*, 17, e00304.

Gan, D., & Erikson, T. 2022b. Venture governance as a syndicate. *Journal of Business Venturing Insights*, 18, e00330.

Garg, S. 2020. Venture governance: A new horizon for corporate governance. *Academy of Management Perspectives*, 34(2), 252–265.

Garg, S., & Eisenhardt, K.M. 2017. Unpacking the CEO–board relationship: How strategy making happens in entrepreneurial firms. *Academy of Management Journal*, 60(5), 1828–1858.

Graen, G.B., & Uhl-Bien, M. 1995. Relationship-based approach to leadership: Development of leader-member exchange (LMX) theory of leadership over 25 years: Applying a multi-level multi-domain perspective. *Leadership Quarterly*, 6(2), 219–247.

Hambrick, D.C. 2007. Upper echelons theory: An update. *Academy of Management Review*, 32(2), 334–343.

Hambrick, D.C., & Finkelstein, S. 1987. Managerial discretion: A bridge between polar views of organizational outcomes. *Research in Organizational Behavior*, 9, 369–406.

Haunschild, P.R. 1993. Interorganizational imitation: The impact of interlocks on corporate acquisition activity. *Administrative Science Quarterly*, 38(4), 564–592.

Haunschild, P.R., & Beckman, C.M. 1998. When do interlocks matter? Alternate sources of information and interlock influence. *Administrative Science Quarterly*, 43(4), 815–844.

Hayes, A. 2013. *Introduction to Mediation, Moderation, and Conditional Process. Analysis: A Regression-Based Approach*. Guilford Publications.

Haynes, K.T. & Hillman, A. 2010. The effect of board capital and CEO power on strategic change. *Strategic Management Journal*, 31(11), 1145–1163.

Hillman, A.J., & Dalziel, T. 2003. Boards of directors and firm performance: Integrating agency and resource dependence perspectives. *The Academy of Management Review*, 28(3), 383–396.

Jensen, M., & Zajac, E.J. 2004. Corporate elites and corporate strategy: How demographic preferences and structural position shape the scope of the firm. *Strategic Management Review Journal*, 25, 507–524.

Klarner, P., Yoshikawa, T., & Hitt, M.A. 2018. A capability-based view of boards: A new conceptual framework for board governance. *Academy of Management Perspectives*, 31(5). https://doi.org/10.5465/amp.2017.0030

Knight, F.H. 1921. *Risk, Uncertainty and Profit*. A.M. Kelley.

Knockaert, M., Bjornali, E.S., & Erikson, T. 2015. Joining forces: Top management team and board chair characteristics as antecedents of board service involvement. *Journal of Business Venturing*, 30(3), 420–435.

Kor, Y.Y., & Sundaramurthy, C. 2009. Experience-based human capital and social capital of outside directors. *Journal of Management*, 35(4), 981–1006.

Linden, G., & Teece, D.J. 2018. Managerial discretion. In M. Augier & D.J. Teece (eds), *The Palgave Encyclopedia of Strategic Management*, pp. 950–953. Palgrave Macmillan.

Ma, S., Kor, Y.Y., & Seidl, D. 2020. CEO advice seeking: An integrative framework and future research agenda. *Journal of Management*, 46(6), 771–805.

Ma, S., Kor, Y.Y., & Seidl, D. 2021. Top management team role structure: A vantage point for advancing upper echelons research. *Strategic Management Journal*, 43(8), 1–28.

Nielsen, S. 2010. Top management team diversity: A review of theories and methodologies. International Journal of Management Reviews, 12(3), 301–316.

Penrose, E. 1959/2009. *The Theory of the Growth of the Firm*. Oxford University Press.

Seligman, M.E.P., Railton, P., Baumeister, R.F., & Sripada, C. 2013. Navigating into the future or driven by the past. *Perspectives on Psychological Science*, 8(2), 119–141.

Seligman, M.E.P., Railton, P., Baumeister, R.F., & Sripada, C. 2016. *Homo Prospectus*. Oxford University Press.

Spector, P.E., & Brannick, M.T. 2011. Methodological urban legends: The misuse of statistical control variables. *Organizational Research Methods*, 14(2), 287–305.

Sripada, C. 2015. Self-expression: A deep self theory of moral responsibility. *Philosophical Studies*, 172, 1203–1232. https://doi.org/10.1007/s11098-015-0527-9

Sripada, C. 2016. Free will and the construction of options. *Philosophy Studies*, 173, 2913–2933.

Verbrugge, L.M. 1979. Multiplexity in adult friendships. *Social Forces*, 57(4), 1286–1309.

Withers, M.C., Hillman, A.J., & Cannella, A.A. 2012. A multidisciplinary review of the director selection literature. *Journal of Management*, 38(1), 243–277.

Yildiz, H.E., Morgulis-Yakushev, S., Holm, U., & Eriksson, M. 2021. Directionality matters: Board interlocks and firm internationalization. *Global Strategy Journal*, 13(1), 1–21.

Zellweger, T., & Zenger, T. 2023. Entrepreneurs as scientists: A pragmatist approach to producing value out of uncertainty. *The Academy of Management Review*, 48(3), 379–408.

Zhang, J., Wang, C., Wang, J., Yu, J.X., Chen, J., & Wang, C. 2016. Inferring directions of undirected social ties. *IEEE Transactions on Knowledge and Data Engineering*, 28(12), 3276–3292.

# 8. The role of advisory boards in startups and the transition to formal governance

**Rod B. McNaughton**

## 1. INTRODUCTION

The journey from startup to scalable success is uncertain, especially for early-stage technology companies. These firms face unique pressures, including rapid technological change, intense competition, and the challenge of securing resources. For many startups, accessing timely and relevant strategic guidance can be the difference between success and failure. In this context, advisory boards are crucial, offering flexible, non-binding advice that helps founders navigate complex decisions in highly dynamic environments.

Despite their importance, advisory boards have received less attention from researchers, educators, and the business press than formal governance boards, mentoring relationships, or professional advisory services. Nevertheless, advisory boards are uniquely positioned to support early-stage startups, providing strategic guidance and access to external resources without governance boards' formal authority or legal responsibilities.

In technology-based companies, advisory boards can help founders address issues such as market entry, capital raising, and technological innovation. However, advisory boards are not without their limitations. Issues such as lack of formal authority, potential misalignment of interests, and the time constraints of board members can undermine their effectiveness in certain contexts.

The CEO advice-seeking literature underscores the value of external input for improving decision-making and navigating uncertainty (e.g., Ma et al., 2019). Advisory boards provide startup founders with this external perspective, offering diverse industry knowledge and networks that complement the internal expertise of the founding team. Furthermore, advisory boards enhance credibility with external stakeholders—such as investors and partners—signaling the startup's potential and increasing its chances of securing early-stage funding (AdvisoryCloud, 2023).

This chapter offers an overview of the functions of advisory boards in startups, emphasizing their relevance in uncertain environments. By examining their role in strategic decision-making, resource mobilization, and network building, the chapter aims to increase awareness of the potential contribution advisory boards can make to startup success. The goal is to stimulate greater interest from founders and researchers in understanding and leveraging advisory boards as a critical element of startup governance.

## 2. THE ROLE OF ADVISORY BOARDS

Advisory boards play a unique role in startups by providing non-binding, strategic advice crucial for navigating the complexities of early development. They differ from governance boards primarily in not having legal decision-making authority or fiduciary duties. Instead, they offer guidance and insight based on the diverse experiences of their members. Table 8.1 compares advisory boards with formal governance boards. The primary benefits are their immediate provision of expertise, greater flexibility, and less cost and formality than a governance board (Walker, 2012).

An advisory board is a group of individuals selected for expertise and industry-specific knowledge, typically starting with three or four and possibly growing to six to eight (Areias, 2022). The essential purpose of an advisory board is to provide advice and mentorship to the founding team. Founders are often rich in innovative ideas but may lack experience in business strategy, technology, or operations. Box 8.1 illustrates how an advisory board member with technology expertise, for example, might contribute by helping a startup incorporate a rapidly developing technology like artificial intelligence (AI).

In contrast to an advisory board, individual mentors typically have a one-on-one relationship with the founder or founding team, offering personalized advice, moral support, and the benefit of their experiences. This mentor–mentee relationship is informal and flexible, often covering many topics beyond business, including work–life balance and personal development. Such mentorship can help equip founders with the understanding and tools needed to tackle the challenges they face as a venture moves from inception to maturity (Jonsson, 2017).

While advisory boards provide mentorship, they also have other functions and benefits (Walker, 2012). However, their role is less well understood than either individual mentors (e.g., Kuratko, 2021) or formal governance boards (e.g., Handley & Molloy, 2022). What we know about advisory boards comes primarily from the experiences of founders and advisory board members

*Table 8.1 Startup advisory and governance boards compared*

| - | Advisory Board | Governance Board |
|---|---|---|
| Purpose | Advice, guidance, and mentorship | Strategy, oversight, accountability, monitor performance |
| Membership | Advisors | Directors |
| Responsible to | Founders | Shareholders |
| Decision-making | Advises but does not make binding decisions | Has authority to make decisions and provide direction |
| Legal liability for the company | No (but must be careful) | Yes |
| Meetings | As needed for advice and support. May meet separately | Regular meetings to discuss finances, budgets, strategy, etc. |
| Commitment | As needed | Regular time commitment |
| Compensation | Voluntary or small equity holding | Director fees and/or equity |
| Composition | External advisors selected for their specialist domain knowledge | Executive directors and external independent directors with governance experience and credibility in the business community |

*Source:* Summarized from BoardPro (n.d.), Courtney et al. (2021), Jonsson (2017), Reiter (2003), and Walker (2012).

captured in blogs, social media sites, and the websites of venture capitalists and startup services.

Startup advisory boards have yet to capture the attention of many academic researchers. One of the few scholarly studies by Morkel and Posner (2002) is now dated. Additionally, the popularity of advisory boards is not universal. They are more prominent in well-developed startup ecosystems, like Silicon Valley, where venture capitalists and professional service providers promote them (Tolic, 2022).

The relationship between advisory board members and founders is more formal and structured than with mentors. While mentors may focus on the personal and professional growth of the entrepreneur, advisory boards offer collective, non-binding strategic advice on crucial business issues. Research on CEO advice-seeking behavior (Ma et al., 2019) highlights the importance of CEOs seeking advice from a range of internal and external sources, and these findings are highly applicable to the role of advisory boards in startups.

### BOX 8.1 ADVISOR HELPS STARTUP WITH AI-DRIVEN MARKETING TRANSFORMATION

A software-as-a-service (SaaS)-based marketing startup sought to leverage AI to scale its operations and reduce customer acquisition costs. While the CEO and founding team generally understood AI's potential, they were uncertain how to integrate these advanced technologies into their existing processes. The startup's advisory board, which included experts from various fields, stepped in to guide this strategic decision. Among the board members was a former senior data scientist with deep AI expertise, whose contributions were essential.

The advisory board recognized that AI could not be implemented in isolation. It needed to fit within the startup's growth strategy and resource limitations. After discussions with the entire advisory board, the AI expert proposed a phased approach, beginning with automating low-level marketing tasks like customer segmentation and A/B testing. This allowed the startup to increase efficiency without overwhelming its small team.

The board collectively supported this recommendation, but the AI specialist helped select and negotiate the vendor contracts. This level of operational involvement went beyond what a typical mentor would offer, reflecting an advisory board's strategic and coordinated support.

Thanks to this approach, the startup saw a significant increase in marketing efficiency and reduced customer acquisition costs. This success set the stage for AI to be integrated across other business functions, a decision made with the advisory board's collective input.

This example illustrates how advisory boards can not only help startups navigate complex technological trends but also help with solutions that drive tangible results, leveraging the expertise of individual members while maintaining a focus on overall strategy through the board's governance practices.

Much like the external advisors described in the CEO literature, advisory boards provide diverse knowledge that allows founders to access industry-specific and novel external perspectives (Geletkanycz & Hambrick, 1997). Advisory board meetings often emphasize strategic decisions like market positioning, raising capital, and identifying growth opportunities. The collective expertise of an advisory board enables founders to approach complex decisions with more confidence, benefiting from insights into both operational and strategic issues (O'Brien, 2014).

Advisory boards also provide crucial control and oversight, offering expert advice on matters such as market strategy, technological innovation, and organizational growth. The literature on CEO advice-seeking demonstrates that external sources are especially valuable for guiding strategic pivots and introducing alternative approaches that challenge industry norms (Geletkanycz & Hambrick, 1997). By acting as a "safe harbor" for testing decisions before implementation, advisory boards allow founders to explore different strategies and test hypotheses before committing to significant business changes (Reiter, 2003).

Another significant role of advisory boards is in resource mobilization and networking. Analogous to the advice-seeking behaviors observed among CEOs, founders rely on their advisory boards to connect them with potential investors, partners, and clients. Advisory boards use their networks to enhance the startup's credibility, providing a strong signal of legitimacy to external stakeholders. This is particularly important in securing early-stage funding (AdvisoryCloud, 2023; Hellmann & Puri, 2002).

While advisory boards can offer valuable access to networks and resources, founders must be careful not to over-rely on external expertise or have unrealistic expectations of what board members can deliver. Despite their connections, advisory board members may not always be able to secure key partnerships or funding, which can lead to disappointment or strain the founder–board relationship.

## 3. NAVIGATING STAKEHOLDER PERSPECTIVES

As startups grow, the complexity of their operations and the range of stakeholder interests also increase. In such situations, advisory boards may also become crucial in coordinating among stakeholders, resolving conflicts, and eventually transitioning the company to a formal governance board. Venture capitalists, for instance, typically emphasize financial returns, risk management, and strategic oversight. They focus on short- to medium-term strategies that enhance a company's valuation. In contrast, founders may prioritize long-term strategic guidance, networking opportunities, and market positioning. Passionate about their vision and product, founders might resist changes suggested by investors seeking to maximize returns (Wasserman, 2008). Advisory boards can help negotiate these differences, ensuring that the founders' vision is not compromised while addressing the practicalities of business growth and investor expectations.

Similarly, employees and customers are stakeholder groups whose interests increasingly shape companies' strategic decisions (Dempsey, 2021).

Employees typically seek stability, growth opportunities, and a say in the company's direction. On the other hand, customers demand high-quality, ethically produced products and services. The dynamics between founders and other stakeholders are complex and often fraught with potential conflict. These conflicts can arise from differences in vision, strategy, or interests. With their mix of expertise and external perspective, advisory boards are well positioned to act as mediators.

As startups grow, decisions regarding scaling, resource allocation, and strategic shifts can lead to internal conflicts. Advisory boards can facilitate discussions, helping to ensure that all voices are heard and that decisions are made in the best interest of the company's future. Furthermore, advisory boards can be critical in establishing governance structures that preemptively address potential conflicts, such as clear communication channels, decision-making processes, and policies defining roles and responsibilities. Such structures help create a transparent environment where conflicts are less likely to arise.

Advisory boards must be careful in navigating startups' legal and ethical landscape. While their guidance is invaluable, they must avoid guiding the company and making decisions so they do not become de facto or "shadow" directors (McLaughlin & Abelson, 2008). A de facto director performs the functions of a director even though they have not been officially appointed to the board. In contrast, a shadow director influences a company by directing the actions of formally appointed directors. Importantly, only de facto directors—by actively taking on directorial responsibilities—are likely to have legal liability for their decisions. Shadow directors, who exert influence without an official role, are generally not held legally accountable for the company's actions, as their involvement lacks formal authority (DV Solicitors, 2024).

While advisory boards do not usually bear the same legal responsibilities as formal boards of directors, members can still face legal liabilities, especially if their advice leads to significant losses or prioritizes personal interests over the company's. To mitigate these risks, advisory board members must ensure they do not overstep their role by, for example, attending director meetings frequently. Advisors should act consistently with their engagement contract and avoid blurring the lines between advisory and directorial responsibilities (Walker, 2012). Indemnity clauses in their contract and liability insurance can also help protect advisors and the startup.

Advisors must also manage conflicts of interest (Abram, 2015). Advisory board members often have diverse professional engagements, leading to potential conflicts between their personal or business interests and those of the startup. To mitigate this, startups should implement policies requiring board members to disclose other business relationships. A related issue is confidentiality. Advisory board members can access sensitive information about the startup's strategies, financials, and intellectual property. Ensuring this information remains confidential is vital. Startups should have their advisory board members sign confidentiality agreements that clearly define confidential information and outline the responsibilities and consequences of its protection.

## 4. GLOBALIZATION AND CRISIS MANAGEMENT

Advisory boards are instrumental for startups navigating the challenges of international expansion or managing crises where uncertainty is especially acute. Internationalizing a startup involves navigating complex regulatory landscapes, understanding local market dynamics, and adapting to cultural nuances. Advisors with diverse expertise and extensive networks, including experience in overseas markets, offer startups a compass for this journey. While these benefits are like those of formal governance boards, recent research by Fiedler et al. (2023) argues that informal boards are better suited to support the exploration of diverse opportunities in different markets because of their flexibility. In contrast, formal boards bring more focus and discipline for learning about a specific market opportunity. Box 8.2 illustrates the benefits of an advisory board for global expansion, highlighting how the board can provide actionable, region-specific advice.

### BOX 8.2 ADVISORY BOARD HELPS NAVIGATE INTERNATIONAL EXPANSION

A technology startup specializing in renewable energy software had grown steadily in its domestic market but saw significant potential in expanding into international markets, particularly in Southeast Asia. However, the founders were unfamiliar with the region's regulatory environment, cultural norms, and competitive landscape. The startup's advisory board, which included several members with experience in global markets, came together to provide critical guidance. Among the board members was a former executive from a multinational energy firm who had spent years operating in Southeast Asia.

The advisory board endorsed the expansion plan but urged caution, recommending a phased market entry strategy to minimize risks. The former executive played a pivotal role, using their regional knowledge to advise on regulatory compliance, partnership opportunities, and market adaptation strategies. They also connected the startup with local legal and market experts, ensuring a smooth entry. Drawing on their expertise in scaling operations, other board members helped the founders restructure their business model to accommodate international growth, emphasizing the importance of localizing product features and services to meet regional preferences.

This coordinated effort resulted in a successful entry into the new market, with the startup forming strategic partnerships and avoiding costly legal missteps. The advisory board's collective input ensured that the company expanded sustainably through controlled growth. This example demonstrates how advisory boards can guide startups through the complexities of internationalization—offering a broader perspective and more robust strategic support than individual mentors.

Risk management in international operations is another critical area that advisory boards can assist with. Startups venturing into global markets confront many risks, including geopolitical tensions, economic volatility, and cultural differences. Advisory boards can help identify these risks, develop mitigation strategies, and safeguard the startup's interests. Their collective experience is important when crafting responses to challenges like currency fluctuations and political instability, helping to ensure the startup's sustainable growth across borders.

Compliance with international laws and ethical practices becomes increasingly complex in the global and digital marketplace. Advisory boards can help navigate these complexities across different jurisdictions. Choosing advisors with global networks also facilitates connections with international partners and investors, which is crucial for securing resources and partnerships necessary for global scaling. Advisors can also offer insights into technological trends and consumer behavior, especially in rapidly evolving global digital marketplaces.

Dealing with crises similarly highlights an advisory board's value. In times of economic downturns or the recent pandemic, advice from advisory boards on adapting business models and operational strategies is indispensable (Shearer, n.d.). Their seasoned perspective helps startups navigate adverse situations, leveraging their experience to guide them toward resilience and growth during and after crises. The ability to foresee potential crises, craft effective responses, and guide startups through financial and operational challenges underscores the advisory board's role in ensuring a startup's continuity and success. Box 8.3 illustrates how an advisory board helped a startup through COVID-19's challenge to its survival.

## BOX 8.3 ADVISORY BOARD HELPS STARTUP STEER THROUGH THE COVID-19 CRISIS

In early 2020, a health-tech startup offering wearable medical devices was hit hard by the COVID-19 pandemic. Supply chain disruptions and sudden drops in demand threatened to cripple the business. The advisory board, comprising members with diverse expertise in finance, supply chain management, and healthcare, quickly convened to devise a crisis management strategy. One of the board members, a former COO of a large MedTech firm, took the lead in addressing the immediate operational challenges. However, their actions were guided by the board's collective insights.

The advisory board's first step was to evaluate cash flow and identify areas for cost-cutting without compromising the startup's core business. The finance expert on the board suggested deferring some non-essential R&D projects and renegotiating terms with key suppliers. Meanwhile, the supply chain expert recommended diversifying suppliers to avoid over-reliance on any single source, thus stabilizing production. While the COO actively implemented these recommendations, the broader board and management worked together to ensure the crisis plan was comprehensive and aligned with the startup's long-term vision.

Thanks to this coordinated effort, the startup survived the pandemic and emerged stronger, building a more resilient supply chain and establishing better financial discipline. This box illustrates advisory boards' critical role in crisis management, offering timely, practical solutions beyond the mentorship scope. The advisory board's diverse expertise allowed the company to navigate the crisis with a multifaceted approach, balancing immediate survival with future growth.

Moreover, advisory boards are crucial in guiding founders through high-pressure strategic decisions, such as taking on new investors or deciding to sell or merge. Their collective experience and diverse skill sets enable an analysis of situations from various perspectives, focusing on both immediate survival and long-term sustainability. They can provide insights on managing cash flow, optimizing costs, and exploring alternative funding sources during financial downturns. In the face of industry disruptions or market changes, advisory boards guide startups in pivoting their business models, adapting to changing demands, and leveraging networks for strategic partnerships.

# 5. LIFECYCLE OF ADVISORY BOARDS

The lifecycle management of advisory boards encompasses the formation, operation, evolution, and eventual transition towards formal governance structures. This journey begins with carefully selecting advisory board members. In this critical step, startups must assess their needs and identify gaps in expertise, aiming to assemble a group that brings high-profile names and substantive value through their experiences and connections (Wilchins, 2022). See Table 8.2 for a list of factors to consider in forming an advisory board. Ideal candidates include seasoned entrepreneurs, industry experts, former executives, and investors, whose perspectives and deep industry understanding can significantly enhance strategic decision-making.

The composition of advisory boards is crucial. Diversity in professional skills, gender, ethnicity, and cultural backgrounds enriches the board's effectiveness and innovative potential. A blend of complementary skills, such as finance, legal expertise, and technological insights, is fundamental. Research suggests that gender-diverse governance boards, and thus likely advisory ones, are more likely to introduce radical innovations (Makkonen, 2022), with women bringing unique perspectives, problem-solving skills, and leadership styles that enhance decision-making and strategic planning. Similarly, ethnic and cultural diversity within advisory boards is invaluable, especially for startups aiming for global reach or operating in multicultural environments, facilitating an understanding of consumer preferences, social norms, and business etiquette essential for marketing and product development.

As startups evolve, the advisory board's composition should be reassessed periodically to align with changing business needs, incorporating new expertise relevant to current challenges and future strategic directions. This adaptability is crucial as the startup transitions from early stages, focusing on strategic direction and networking, to scaling operations and entering new markets, where the advisory board's role evolves to address more complex challenges.

Some advisors are volunteers, contributing their experience in exchange for learning, the excitement of a startup, assessing the investment opportunity, or giving back. However, to ensure commitment, most sources recommend compensating advisory board members. Compensation is often in the form of shares to reduce the impact on cash flow and align the advisor's interest with the firm's success. An advisor's compensation might be around 0.25% to 1.0% of the startup's fully diluted capitalization, vesting monthly or quarterly over two to three years, sometimes complemented by modest cash compensation. Some compensation agreements include a six-month "cliff," meaning that the company retains the equity if the relationship does not work out during the first

*Table 8.2 Considerations in selecting advisory board members*

| Factor | Description |
|---|---|
| Commitment | Advisory board members should fully commit to the organization's vision and long-term success |
| Independence | They should be independent thinkers who can ask challenging questions and stand by their convictions |
| Industry expertise | Board members should have a track record of success in their respective environments and a solid understanding of the industry |
| Experience in similar challenges | Look for advisors who have successfully navigated challenges similar to those startups face |
| Good communicators | Advisory board members should be articulate, energetic, comfortable interacting with others, and able to convey their thoughts clearly and effectively |
| Network | They should have a broad network of contacts that can open doors to customers, investors, suppliers, and other resources critical for the company's growth |
| Comfortable with equity compensation | Advisors may be compensated with equity or other compensation, so they should be comfortable with this arrangement |
| Personality traits | Seek individuals with an early-stage mindset, entrepreneurial experience, and a strong network within the chosen industry |
| Diversity | Ensure the advisory board is diverse, with members from different backgrounds and experiences, to provide a range of perspectives |

*Source:* Summarized from AdvisoryCloud (2023), Areias (2022), Courtney et al. (2021), and Wilchins (2022).

six months (Mendel, n.d.). Clear agreements outlining duties, responsibilities, compensation, and engagement length are essential, providing a framework that balances flexibility with the startup's evolving needs.

## 6. TRANSITION TO FORMAL GOVERNANCE

The progression of a startup from its initial stages to a more structured entity is marked by the transition from having an advisory board to establishing a formal governance framework (Ewens & Malenko, 2020). This crucial shift underscores the startup's move from an early, exploratory phase to a mature business operation. It involves transitioning from an advisory board's informal, strategic guidance to establishing a board of directors with formal legal obligations and fiduciary responsibilities to shareholders. This board is pivotal in steering the company's financial strategies, managing risks, and setting long-term strategic goals. Ewens and Malenko (2020) found that independent directors typically join after the second financing round and that their presence is particularly likely when there is potential for venture capitalist–founder conflicts.

For technology-based startups, this transition is often driven by the need to manage increasing operational complexity and external pressures, such as regulatory requirements and investor demands. While providing valuable strategic advice, advisory boards lack the legal authority and accountability required at later stages of growth. A formal board of directors ensures that the startup can meet its fiduciary responsibilities and navigate the complexities of scaling, market entry, and capital management (Boeker & Wiltbank, 2005).

When forming a formal board, the selection process is again paramount. In contrast to advisory board members, who are often chosen for their specific expertise or valuable network connections, formal board members are selected based on their experience in corporate governance and their potential to contribute to the broader strategic vision of the company. This process may include transitioning some advisory board members to formal board positions, particularly those who have developed deep relationships with the founders and can provide continuity in decision-making. However, new members are often introduced to ensure alignment with the company's evolving strategic objectives and culture. Venture capitalists may also take board seats as a condition of their investment, which can further formalize the governance structure (Gabrielsson & Huse, 2002). The retention of some advisors while adding new directors is described in Box 8.4.

The effectiveness of an advisory board can be measured through clearly defined key performance indicators (KPIs), focusing on the board's influence on strategic decision-making, growth, and networking (AdvisoryCloud, n.d.). Tailoring the evaluation metrics and process to the startup's stage and the advisory board's specific functions is essential. For early-stage startups, metrics might include facilitating valuable connections and the board's impact on achieving key business milestones, such as product development and market entry.

As the startup progresses, the focus shifts toward scaling the business and accessing capital, with metrics evaluating the board's contribution to revenue growth, profitability, and successful funding rounds. Implementing a structured process for measuring the advisory board's impact involves regular review meetings, feedback mechanisms from employees, investors, and other stakeholders, and, when possible, using data to assess the outcomes of the board's decisions objectively.

While advisory and formal boards can co-exist, maintaining an advisory board in terms of compensation and management time can become burdensome, especially if the board's contributions are not clearly aligned with the company's evolving needs. As a result, startups must carefully manage the transition, ensuring that the right balance of advisory support and formal governance is maintained (Knockaert et al., 2015). Best practices suggest that founders prepare for this transition early, setting clear expectations for board members and ensuring alignment between the board's expertise and the company's long-term goals.

### BOX 8.4 TRANSITIONING FROM ADVISORY TO FORMAL GOVERNANCE IN A GLOBAL SaaS COMPANY

A rapidly growing SaaS company in the accounting industry initially relied heavily on its advisory board for strategic input during its early expansion into international markets. The advisory board, composed of early investors and industry experts, guided critical decisions on product development, market entry strategies, and securing venture capital. This flexible, informal structure allowed the company to adapt quickly to changing market conditions and develop its core product.

However, the need for more formal governance became evident as the company prepared for an initial public offering (IPO) and expanded into multiple new regions. The company transitioned from an advisory board to a formal board of directors to manage increasing operational complexity and ensure compliance with international regulatory requirements. The company strategically retained several key advisory board members, transitioning them to formal board roles to maintain continuity in decision-making and preserve institutional knowledge.

The new formal board, composed of independent directors with extensive experience in corporate governance and global market expansion, played a pivotal role in establishing more structured financial reporting and risk management practices. Their oversight helped the company navigate the complexities of scaling globally and completing its IPO. The smooth transition from advisory guidance to formal governance contributed to the company's long-term stability and growth, highlighting the importance of timing and strategic planning in such transitions.

## 7. CONCLUSION

This chapter has reviewed the multifaceted roles and benefits of advisory boards in the lifecycle of technology-based startups, from their nascent stages to their evolution into formally governed entities. Advisory boards, characterized by their provision of strategic, non-binding advice, can play a critical role in guiding startups through the complexities and uncertainties inherent in the early stages of business development. Their influence extends across various domains, from mentoring founders and facilitating networking opportunities to guiding R&D efforts and capital acquisition strategies, all crucial for sustaining growth and fostering innovation.

Advisory boards are also helpful in managing stakeholders' perspectives and interests, especially in potential conflict scenarios between venture capitalists, employees, customers, and founders. They can mediate, offer sound advice, and ensure the alignment of diverse interests. Moreover, their role in aiding startups navigate crises and major business transitions highlights their indispensability as a strategic intangible asset.

The journey of advisory boards, from their formation to their potential dissolution or transition to formal governance, requires planning, careful selection of members based on diverse expertise, and a keen focus on long-term success. The chapter's exploration of these themes contributes to understanding advisory boards' potential role, suggesting the need for a greater appreciation and more nuanced utilization of these bodies in fostering startup success.

Larger companies can also learn from startup advisory boards and incorporate them alongside formal governance structures to infuse fresh perspectives and specialized expertise into their strategic planning. This dual-board structure balances rigorous governance and innovative, agile thinking. Such arrangements are increasingly common in advising corporate boards on particular areas of activity like R&D and social responsibility or responding to climate change (Olson & Norris, n.d.).

Many aspects of advisory boards remain underexplored, presenting opportunities for future research. Advisory boards' strategic utility and composition merit particular attention. Investigating the best amalgam of expertise, experience, and diversity would extend our understanding of constructing successful boards that positively affect startup success. Comparative studies across diverse startup ecosystems could unravel the contextual dependencies of advisory board effectiveness, possibly yielding both universal and specific suggestions for good practices like those for more formal governance mechanisms.

The lifecycle management of advisory boards, encompassing their formation, operational tenure, and strategic evolution, is also a compelling area for research. The mechanisms that guide the transition of these boards, from inception through to their eventual integration or dissolution within formal governance frameworks, would provide best practices for maximizing their effectiveness over time. This topic includes strategies for refreshing board composition in alignment with the startup's scaling journey and the broader implications of advisory board and eventual governance board tenure on startup success.

Legal and ethical frameworks surrounding advisory engagements also deserve attention, providing more nuanced advice on navigating the complexities of advisory roles without attracting the legal liabilities typically associated with formal directorships. Furthermore, specifying and validating relevant KPIs specific to advisory boards would be helpful. Linking KPIs to the strategic milestones and operational outcomes of startups could facilitate a more structured assessment of advisory board impact, guiding startups and advisors toward more targeted outcomes.

The early global footprint of many of today's startups underscores the need for research into the role of advisory boards in navigating cross-cultural dynamics and supporting international expansion. This encompasses how advisory boards can help enter global markets and ensure cultural adaptability and regulatory compliance. Concurrently, the rapid pace of digital transformation and the increasing incidence of global crises suggest examining how advisory boards can shepherd startups through technological adaptations and strategic pivots, especially in times of uncertainty.

These unknowns offer a rich ground for further exploration to enhance the understanding of the role and effectiveness of advisory boards in startups. Addressing these gaps will benefit startups and contribute to the broader field of governance.

## REFERENCES


Abram, B. C. L. P.-J. (2015). Five important legal issues when establishing an advisory board. Lexology, October 28. https://www.lexology.com/library/detail.aspx?g=bf7a0943-58a3-4ab5-aa4a-32e01f28b7cb

AdvisoryCloud (2023). Understanding the role of an advisory board at a medium size professional company. https://advisorycloud.com/blog/understanding-the-role-of-an-advisory-board-at-a-medium-size-professional-company

AdvisoryCloud (n.d.). Key performance indicators (KPIs). https://advisorycloud.com/board-of-directors-terms-definitions/key-performance-indicators-kpis

Areias, N. (2022). Want to build a startup advisory board? Here's how. GoingVc. https://www.goingvc.com/post/how-to-build-a-startup-advisory-board

BoardPro (n.d.). Governance in startups and early stage companies. https://www.boardpro.com/blog/governance-in-startups-and-early-stage-companies

Boeker, W., & Wiltbank, R. (2005). New venture evolution and managerial capabilities. *Organization Science*, 16(2), 123–133.

Courtney, W. T., Hartley, B. K., Rosswurm, M., LeBlanc, L. A., & Lund, C. J. (2021). Establishing and leveraging the expertise of advisory boards. *Behavior Analysis in Practice*, 14(1), 253–263.

Dempsey, S. (2021). How boards can harness stakeholder voices—AICD. https://www.aicd.com.au/board-of-directors/duties/engagement/how-boards-can-harness-stakeholder-voices.html

DV Solicitors (2024). Shadow director or de facto | understanding roles & risks. February 16. https://dvsolicitors.com/lawguide/shadow-director-or-de-facto/

Ewens, M., & Malenko, N. (2020). Board dynamics over the startup life cycle (Working Paper 27769). National Bureau of Economic Research. https://doi.org/10.3386/w27769

Fiedler, A., Fath, B., Sinkovics, N., & Sinkovics, R. R. (2023). On-ramp or speed bump? How boards influence the internationalisation of international new ventures. *International Small Business Journal: Researching Entrepreneurship*, 41(6), 590–622.

Gabrielsson, J., & Huse, M. (2002). The venture capitalist and the board of directors in SMEs: Roles and processes. *Venture Capital*, 4(2), 125–146.

Geletkanycz, M. A., & Hambrick, D. C. (1997). The external ties of top executives: Implications for strategic choice and performance. *Administrative Science Quarterly*, 42(4), 654–681.

Handley, K., & Molloy, C. (2022). SME corporate governance: A literature review of informal mechanisms for governance. *Meditari Accountancy Research*, 30(7), 310–333.

Hellmann, T., & Puri, M. (2002). Venture capital and the professionalization of startup firms: Empirical evidence. *The Journal of Finance*, 57(1), 169–197.

Jonsson, E. I. (2017). Advisory boards in entrepreneurial companies. In J. Gabrielsson (ed.), *Handbook of Research on Corporate Governance and Entrepreneurship* (pp. 63–83). Cheltenham, UK and Northampton, MA, USA: Edward Elgar Publishing.

Knockaert, M., Bjornali, E.S., & Erikson, T. (2015). Joining forces. Top management team and board chair characteristics as antecedents of board service involvement. *Journal of Business Venturing*, 30(3), 490–508.

Kiratko, D.F., Neubert, E., & Marvel, M.R. (2021). Insights on the mentorship and coachability of entrepreneurs. *Business Horizons*, 64(2), 199–209.

Ma, S., Kor, Y. Y., & Seidl, D. (2019). CEO advice seeking: An integrative framework and future research agenda. *Journal of Management*, 46(6), 771–805.

Makkonen, T. (2022). Board diversity and firm innovation: A meta-analysis. *European Journal of Innovation Management*, 25(6), 941–960.

McLaughlin, B., & Abelson, A. (2008). Feature: The dangers of advisory boards—AICD. https://www.aicd.com.au/finance-governance/financial-reporting/standards/feature-the-dangers-of-advisory-boards.html

Mendel, J. (n.d.). Building your startup advisory board. Silicon Valley Bank. https://www.svb.com/startup-insights/startup-strategy/building-startup-advisory-board/

Morkel, A., & Posner, B. (2002). Investigating the effectiveness of corporate advisory boards. *Corporate Governance: The International Journal of Business in Society*, 2(3), 4–12.

O'Brien, P. (2014). Startup advisors vs. mentors. Startup Economist, July 1. https://seobrien.com/startup-advisors-vs-mentors

Olson, N., & Norris, J. C. (n.d.). Advisory boards: The hot new governance trend. https://www.kornferry.com/insights/briefings-for-the-boardroom/advisory-boards-new-governance-trends

Reiter, B. (2003). The role and value of an effective advisory board. *Ivey Business Journal*, 9(10). https://www.iveypublishing.ca/s/product/the-role-and-value-of-an-effective-advisory-board/01t5c00000CwqjEAAR
Shearer, L. (n.d.). Getting on board: What you need to know about tech advisory boards. Startups Magazine. http://startupsmagazine.co.uk/article-getting-board-what-you-need-know-about-tech-advisory-boards
Tolic, E. (2022). Why your startup needs an advisory board. Entrepreneur, July 1. https://www.entrepreneur.com/leadership/why-your-startup-needs-an-advisory-board/428947
Walker, R. (2012). Applied corporate governance: Corporate advisory boards—pros and cons. *Keeping Good Companies*, 64(3), 139–143.
Wasserman, N. (2008). The founder's dilemma. *Harvard Business Review*. https://hbr.org/2008/02/the-founders-dilemma
Wilchins, S. N. (2022). Selecting advisory board members: 6 attributes to focus on. Wilchins Cosentino & Novins LLP, Wellesley MA Law Firm, November 28. https://wcnllp.com/selecting-advisory-board-members-6-attributes-to-focus-on/

# 9. Start-ups acquiring start-ups: a venture governance view

**Dennis Gan**

## 1. INTRODUCTION

McKelvie and Wiklund (2010) identify three types of growth mode: organic, acquisitive (inorganic), and hybrid. While Gan and Erikson (2022) address organic growth for very early-stage start-ups, this study addresses the acquisition mode for start-ups. Acquisition has been pursued by firms for a broad spectrum of reasons, ranging from reducing competition (Cunningham et al., 2019), filling in technological capabilities gaps (Capron & Mitchell, 2009; Puranam et al., 2009; Ranft & Lord, 2002), and strategic renewal (Karim & Mitchell, 2000) to increase efficiency by reducing cost (Haleblian et al., 2009). Larger and established firms are more often associated with acquisitions as part of their growth strategy, whereas smaller firms are often associated with organic growth (Delmar et al., 2003). Prior studies in this area suggest new venture growth is highly dynamic and discontinuous (Garnsey et al., 2006) and can be achieved by means other than organic growth (McKelvie & Wiklund, 2010).

The boards of start-ups, hereby referred to as venture boards, play a crucial role in allowing start-ups to access resources that are beyond the boundary of these start-ups. Acquisition is one of the strategies commonly utilized by firms to access external resources. The performance of new ventures is often dictated by the governance and leadership structure of their boards; past research in this area has largely focused on governance in the form of CEO duality and how this relates to the performance of the firms (Daily & Dalton, 1992, 1993; Dalton et al., 1998; Gan & Erikson, 2022).

However, despite the voluminous work on established firms making acquisitions part of their inorganic growth strategy and board governance to access external resources, our understanding of how start-ups acquire start-ups in the context of governance structure remains fragmentary. In Graebner and Eisenhardt (2004), acquisition is reframed as courtship and corporate governance as a syndicate. This requires much attention from scholars as new ventures have no other choice but to grow, and this is a new phenomenon that needs further unpacking.

Further understanding of inorganic growth in start-ups is necessary as this type of growth strategy works very well for established firms and new insights in this area have the potential to enable start-ups to achieve accelerated growth and even potentially mitigate misappropriation of resources by established firms (Knoben & Bakker, 2019). Fast-growing start-ups are popular acquisition targets, and start-ups with accelerated growth ambitions may acquire start-ups early and help these start-ups to grow while achieving accelerated inorganic growth themselves.

In this chapter, I investigate the governance structure of start-ups that acquire other start-ups, hereby referred to as venture governance. The main aim is to understand the governance structure that affiliates with inorganic growth in start-ups, not only as a growth mode but also because this growth mode captures the very essence of entrepreneurial action under uncertainty (McMullen & Shepherd, 2006). This chapter aims to contribute to the venture governance literature in the context of inorganic growth. Hence, the following research question:

*What is the governance structure for start-ups seeking growth by acquisition?*

## 2. HYPOTHESES DEVELOPMENT

### 2.1 Board Leadership Structure and the Relationship to Start-up Acquisitions

Venture governance plays a different role than corporate governance as venture governance often has to deal with more extreme uncertainties, even more so in its very early stage (Garg, 2020; Garg & Eisenhardt, 2017; Li et al., 2020). Many early-stage start-ups practice the "one person, two jobs" governing structure, a board governance structure where the CEO is also the board chair, a condition known as CEO duality, due to incomplete separation of ownership and control (Banham & He, 2010). Though some early-stage start-ups may practice CEO duality out of convenience, it is found that within this environment of uncertainty, CEO duality bodes well for these start-ups, as CEO duality in many ways gives structure to the chaotic and unpredictable environment in which these start-ups often operate.

For instance, Gan and Erikson (2022) imply that a separate board structure (where the CEO and board chair are different individuals) may slow decision-making in very early-stage start-ups and may cause further uncertainties if the

CEO and board chair are not aligned with the same vision for the start-up, thus causing further discrepancies and inconsistencies within the start-up.

Whereas Gan and Erikson (2022) found that CEO duality is good for organic growth in the earliest phase, I conjecture, in contrast, that CEO duality is not necessarily optimal for inorganic growth. Leblanc (2005) holds that the board chair is the single most important factor for an engaged board, and a separate board leadership structure will contribute to facilitating growth alternatives beyond the scope of the firm.

For start-ups in their earlier phase, Gan and Erikson (2022) found that a dual board leadership structure is a favorable solution. In contrast, for more mature start-ups that have acquisition as an inorganic growth strategy, I conjecture that a separate board leadership structure is the most suitable governance structure to acquire other start-ups. Thus, I posit a negative relationship between a dual board leadership structure and start-up acquisitions:

*Hypothesis 1: A dual board leadership structure will relate negatively to start-up acquisitions.*

## 2.2 The Number of Board Directors and the Relationship to Start-up Acquisitions

Each board director brings specific skill sets and experience to the board they serve. These experiences can range from in-depth industrial knowledge, prior board experience, technical expertise, and strategic moves experience, such as acquisitions (Johnson et al., 2013). The roles played by directors in corporate governance and strategic decision-making in firms are becoming more important (Finkelstein & Mooney, 2003). Hillman and Dalziel (2003) introduced the concept of board capital and portrayed it as the total sum of human and social capital of the board of directors, and this acts as a proxy for their "ability to provide resources to the firm" (Haynes & Hillman, 2010). Kor and Sundaramurthy (2009) went as far as to suggest that directors with acquisition experience can be valuable for firms that frequently undertake acquisitions to access resources that are outside the boundary of firms.

Haunschild (1993) found imitative behavior among board directors once they underwent acquisitions in other boards they serve. Imitation can also be considered a type of organizational learning in which firms copy and take similar actions of other firms (Yang & Hyland, 2006). Though imitation is usually perceived negatively, recent studies have shown that imitation is crucial to business growth (Shenkar, 2010) and results in positive performance in firms (Doha et al., 2018; Lee & Tang, 2018). In the same study, Haunschild (1993) also found that imitation is often a strategic response to competitors' activities. This imitative behavior of board members can also be considered a way for firms to let others absorb the costs of specific strategic moves and reduce the uncertainties that come with huge and risky strategic moves such as acquisitions. In the context of venture governance, these imitative behaviors can be considered as gained experience in making acquisitions, implicitly making this experience a resource to the board. Thus, having more board directors will increase the likelihood of more diverse strategic experiences that will increase the likelihood of the board debating and considering acquisitions.

Henceforth, I conjecture that a resourceful venture board will facilitate the courtship process for start-ups, which will eventually effectuate inorganic growth by acquiring other start-ups. And I have therefore the following affiliated board resource and acquisition hypothesis:

*Hypothesis 2: The number of directors will relate positively to start-up acquisitions.*

## 2.3 Board Interlocks as Relational Ties and the Relationship to Start-up Acquisitions

It is a common practice among directors to sit on the board of other firms, and this type of tie is known as board interlocking directorates (board interlocks). With the formation of such ties, information and resources can flow in and out of firms, thus enabling firms to access information and resources that are outside the boundaries of their firms via these ties with ease (Johnson et al., 2013).

Prior research in this area has also shown that board interlocks have an impact on strategic moves in firms, such as acquisition (Beckman & Haunschild, 2002), organizational restructuring (Palmer et al., 1993), and

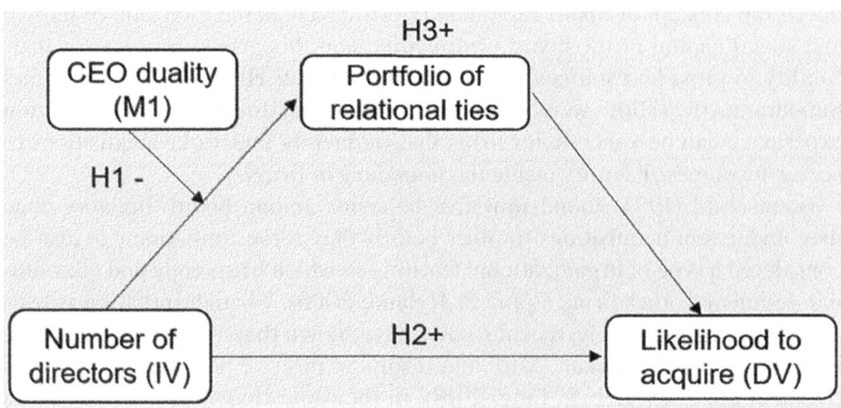


*Figure 9.1 Model of hypothesized relationships*

strategic persistence (Geletkanycz & Hambrick, 1997). This is evident in Haunschild (1993), which shows that firms with multiple interlocking ties to other firms make more acquisitions, indicating that these firms have access to better acquisition information from these ties, in comparison to firms with fewer such ties. For start-ups, I conjecture that the need to access information and resources is even greater when they have the strategy to achieve inorganic growth by acquiring other start-ups. Henceforth, I conjecture that the number of board interlocks will increase the possibility for start-ups to make acquisitions, giving these start-ups better access to information and resources. Accordingly, I set forth the following hypothesis on a portfolio of board relational ties:

> *Hypothesis 3: A portfolio of relational board ties will relate positively to start-up acquisitions.*

## 3. METHOD

This study is based on data acquired from T-Rank AS,[1] Zephyr database from Bureau van Dijk,[2] and TietoEvry ASA.[3]

The data in this study consists of 38 acquisitions of Norwegian start-ups in the period from 2018 to 2020 and reflects a sample of start-ups that were acquired by other start-ups and remain independent. This study also excludes start-ups that are merged as the focus of this study is start-up acquisition and not merging of start-ups. Acquiring start-ups are firms that have existed for less than 10 years. I performed the quantitative analysis with the SPSS 28 statistical software package and used logistic regression due to the binary nature of the dependent variable. I also counted the number of other board members (beyond the chairman) of the company board before the year 2020. I registered whether the CEO was also the chairman of the board or not. In this study, I controlled for time since inception, since acquisition may also be a function of time.

Acquisitions are measured by coding both "Completed Confirmed" and "Completed Assumed" from BvD Zephyr database for 2018, 2019, and 2020. I also included assumed completed, as I was primarily interested in capturing those firms that had started on the acquisition process but had not necessarily completed them. To what extent the acquisition process was completed is not of interest in this study, as I only sought to establish the link between a portfolio of board interlocks and the inclination to end up as acquisition targets.

In BvD Zephyr, Completed Assumed is defined as "All deals, except those having the deal type Planned IPO and the sub-deal type Public Takeover, that have had an announced or pending deal status will automatically change to 'Completed Assumed' after 24 months have passed without the deal going through an update," while Completed Confirmed is defined as "deals with formal confirmation of the deal located."

In this study, I operationalized board human resources with the number of other members of the company board (other than the board chair), and I operationalized board external social resources with the overall number of interlocking directorates, comprising interlocking ties of all the board members including the board chairman. I labeled this variable "a portfolio of relational ties" capturing the multiplexity of the board (the extent of multiple board ties). Both the resource metrics above have appropriate kurtosis and skewness scores, but I recoded the "portfolio of relational ties" into useful categories where "0" indicates none, "1" indicates a smaller portfolio, and "2" reflects a larger portfolio of such ties. I inserted the cut point with the median (in this case 6), and extended robustness checks indicate that the coding is not sensitive to the implemented cut points (I tried with 2, 3, 4, and 5). In this study, I control for time since firm inception, as time may be considered a valuable resource.

## 4. RESULTS

Table 9.1 shows the means and correlations between the main variables in the study. Notably, acquisition is a rare phenomenon (a mean of 0.001 rounded up from 0.0005). Table 9.1 shows that a dual board leadership structure correlates weakly but significantly negatively to start-up acquisition ($r = -0.012^{**}$), indicating that a *separate* board leadership structure is positively associated with acquisitions. Acquisition correlates positively to board resources, such as the number of other directors ($r = 0.016^{**}$) and to board interlocking ties (also $r = 0.016^{**}$), but acquisitions appear unrelated to time since inception. Table 9.1 also shows that a CEO duality leadership structure is negatively correlated to board resources, such as the number of board members and a portfolio of board interlocking directorates. A dual board leadership structure is, however, positively correlated to time since firm inception.

Figure 9.2 shows the results of the logistic regressions conducted in this study. In the current study, I only report the odds (Exp(B)) and significance levels for ease of interpretation. From the control model, time since inception relates slightly negatively to acquisitions, so the older the start-up, the lesser likelihood of being acquired. However, that coefficient is not significant.

However, in Model 1, I find support for the conjecture that board leadership structure matters regarding acquisitions. That is, a divided board leadership structure is more likely to facilitate start-ups to acquire other start-ups (Exp(B) = 0.141, $p < 0.01$), so I have support for Hypothesis 1 regarding the board leadership structure.

*Table 9.1 Descriptive statistics and correlations*

| Variables | Mean | SD | 1. | 2. | 3. | 4. |
|---|---|---|---|---|---|---|
| 1. Acquisition | 0.001 | 0.023 | - | - | - | - |
| 2. Dual board leadership | 0.285 | 0.451 | −0.012** | - | - | - |
| 3. Number of other directors | 2.680 | 1.101 | 0.016** | −0.182** | - | - |
| 4. Portfolio of board ties | 1.368 | 0.695 | 0.016** | −0.237** | 0.306** | - |
| 5. Time since inception | 4.993 | 2.295 | −0.002 | 0.016** | 0.071** | 0.073** |

*Note:* Significance level: ⁺p < 0.10, *p < 0.05, **p < 0.01. Number of firms = 70,597 (selected samples: 38 acquisitions).

| | Control | Model 1 | Model 2 | Model 3 |
|---|---|---|---|---|
| *(Constant)* | *.001**** | *.001**** | *.000**** | *.000**** |
| Time since inception | .921 | . 924 | .910 | .899 |
| Board leadership structure | **H1:** | **.141**** | .174* | .236* |
| Number of other directors | | **H2:** | **1.435***** | 1.297* |
| Portfolio of board ties | | | **H3:** | **3.353**** |
| | | | | |
| -2 Log Likelihood | 650.828 | 637.489 | 627.209 | 615.528 |
| $Chi^2$ change | 1.568 | 13.391*** | 10.208*** | 11.681*** |
| Model LL | 1.568 | 14.907*** | 25.187*** | 36.868*** |
| d.f. | 1 | 2 | 3 | 4 |

*Note:* Significance level: ⁺p < 0.10, *p < 0.05, **p < 0.01, ***p < 0.001. Number of firms = 70,597.

*Figure 9.2 Logistic regression results on start-up acquisition*

Model 2 and Model 3 facilitate the testing of the two remaining hypotheses. They both address board resources, and I find support for the conjecture about the number of board members (Exp(B) = 1.435, $p < 0.001$), and the portfolio of board relational ties conjecture (Exp(B) = 3.353, $p < 0.001$). Hence, I have support for both Hypothesis 2 and Hypothesis 3.

## 5. DISCUSSION

I find that start-ups acquiring start-ups appear to have an idiosyncratic board leadership structure and board configuration. From this study, it is shown that these start-ups that have a divided board leadership structure (different individuals as CEO and board chairman) have more board human and social resources, thus are better off than those that do not in acquiring other start-ups. In other words, these start-ups have a divided board leadership structure and have more board members with a larger pool of interlocking ties. Henceforth, start-ups with accelerated growth ambitions should consider building highly resourceful boards from the outset that have more interlocking ties with other firms and partners outside their firms.

This study aims at filling an important gap in the venture growth and venture governance literature. Past research in firm growth literature has largely focused on established firms acquiring other firms for inorganic growth while smaller younger firms are more associated with organic growth (Delmar et al., 2003; McKelvie & Wiklund, 2010).

The views on acquisition have also changed in recent times; whereas, in the past, start-ups that were being acquired were oftentimes those that were in distress and facing strategic hurdles (Carlsson, 2013; Graebner & Eisenhardt, 2004), start-ups that are being acquired today are actually those that achieve phenomenal growth, and these start-ups are attractive acquisition targets for other start-ups (as well as other established firms) that are pursuing further growth through acquisitions as a form of inorganic growth strategy.

In this study, a divided leadership structure bodes well for start-ups that are actively acquiring other start-ups as part of their strategy for inorganic growth. The reasons for this could be that the CEOs can focus on growing the start-ups while the chairperson can focus on developing the best governance structure and strategies for the start-ups. For example, the CEO can work on increasing sales while the chairperson can expand the network of the board by recruiting outside directors.

According to Penrose (1959), growth that results from internal growth mechanisms may be more constant but also slower than the growth that results from external growth mechanisms. This could very much explain the reason why more and more start-ups are pursuing inorganic growth as a source of engine for accelerated growth. New ventures pursuing external growth place emphasis on acquiring firms competing in the same or a complementary market. Acquisitions enable firms to enhance their product or service offerings (Penrose, 1959) or extend their reach into new markets without developing the competencies required to do so internally.

This is in contrast to Gan and Erikson (2022), who find that a dual CEO (same person as CEO and board chair) bodes well for organic growth in very early-stage start-ups. In the same study, Gan and Erikson (2022) also find that CEO duality is more efficient for smaller boards, and a separate board structure is more efficient for larger boards. I conjecture that in the very early days of start-ups, where they are just beginning to launch and gain market share with their products or services, hence growing organically, CEO duality with a small board bodes well for them, as CEO duality facilitates fast decision-making, and this embodies the quintessential quality of start-ups, which is being agile and nimble. For start-ups with accelerated growth ambitions by means of acquisitions as a strategy to grow inorganically, a superstructure which consists of a divided board leadership structure coupled with a high number of board members and a pool of board interlocks needs to be in place for these start-ups to increase the likelihood of achieving their subsequent growth milestones.

Beckman et al. (2014) show that boards with heterogeneous and multiplex experiences influence a start-up's ability to form external ties outside the boundary of the start-ups, thus allowing them to access resources that are outside the boundary of these firms. Their study further suggests that such boards expedite the formation of a diverse alliance portfolio, which directly facilitates these firms in achieving major revenue milestones.

In a separate study, Knoben and Bakker (2019) show that interlocking directorates not only help new firms to gain legitimacy, but can even act as a safeguard mechanism against resource misappropriation by more powerful partners. Knoben and Bakker (2019) also show that start-ups that engage in multiple directorates perform better than both start-ups that form no alliances and start-ups that form stand-alone alliances. In this study, I propose that the forming of multiple interlocking directorates in start-ups with different actors in the entrepreneurial ecosystem can increase their likelihood of making acquisitions which in turn helps them achieve inorganic growth.

## 5.1 Implications for Theory and Practice

This study shows that start-ups with accelerated growth ambition have a different governance structure than the more traditional types of start-ups. Based on a targeted literature review, I conjectured that start-ups acquiring other start-ups have a different board leadership structure and board configuration than the more traditional start-ups.

Specifically, I conjecture that start-ups with an inorganic growth strategy have a divided board leadership structure and have higher board human and social resources. In other words, these start-ups have a higher number of board members with a larger pool of interlocking ties, where the board members also sit on other boards. Henceforth, start-ups with high-growth ambitions should consider building a more resourceful board from the outset that preferably has more board interlocking ties with other firms and partners in the entrepreneurial ecosystem.

Given the resource constraints that are often affiliated with start-ups, start-ups should be strategic in appointing board members according to the strategic goals they want to pursue at the different stages of their start-ups and look at their board as a valuable resource to further pursue their growth strategy. In addition, with a divided leadership structure poised to make acquisitions, the board chair should be strategic in recruiting board members based on the needs of the start-ups and not recruit board members haphazardly, as board members with the necessary and relevant experience can further push the start-ups to greater heights (de Villiers et al., 2011). Start-ups with such a leadership structure are more likely to engage in acquisitions.

## 5.2 Limitations

This chapter investigates start-ups acquiring other start-ups as part of their inorganic growth strategy. The purposive sampling employed in this chapter, as explained in the method section, means that only a fraction of the acquisitions that took place in the period 2018–2020 are selected in the sampling. Other forms of acquisitions that involve big corporations/incumbents and start-ups that are merged and cease to remain independent are excluded in this chapter, as the focus of this study is acquisitions involving start-ups. Start-ups that are merged are also excluded from this study for the same reason.

The purpose of this chapter is to initiate the discourse on start-ups acquiring other start-ups by investigating their board governance structure. This chapter is based on rather scant data and is intended as a pilot study. Future studies could further explore this type of acquisition based on a more complete and wider dataset with control variables, such as the sectors in which the start-ups operate and if the start-ups are venture-funded.

## 5.3 Future Research

Future research could explore further what other types of roles these interlocking ties can play for these start-ups. For example, the optimal number of interlocking ties start-ups could have to other firms in the entrepreneurial ecosystem, and at which point these ties will weaken the effect on the start-ups as the higher number of ties will mean that the board members will have less time for the venture boards they are representing.

Another interesting avenue for further research in start-ups acquiring other start-ups is to investigate how a venture board that consists of board members from the local start-up community compares to a start-up with board members from other non-local communities. Directors from non-local communities may bring in new opportunities and information for acquisitions, while directors from the local community also facilitate acquisitions because of the ties these directors have to the local community.

Finally, future studies could also investigate how the board governance structure of start-ups evolves throughout the lifecycle of start-ups, as start-ups in different phases of their growth cycle require different needs and thus different strategies. This may affect the board governance structure for these start-ups.

The other three chapters in Part II, addressing transitioning to formal governance (6), supra-teams (7), and entrepreneurial ecosystems (8), could shed more light on the subject under study and deepen our understanding of venture governance and venture growth.

## NOTES

1. T-rank AS is a spin-off from Telenor ASA, the biggest telecommunication firm in Norway. T-rank has expertise in network analysis of corporate business networks and derives its data from Brønnøysund Register Center, which is a government agency and is a subsidiary of the Norwegian Ministry of Trade and Industry. The register center is a repository for numerous public registers in Norway and manages commercial and personal registers in Norway. The register center is also part of the European Business Register.
2. Bureau Van Dijk is a major publisher of business information and specializes in private company data combined with software for searching and analyzing companies. BvD is part of the Moody's Analytics company. Zephyr by BvD is a database that contains information on merger & acquisition, private equity, and venture capital deals.
3. TietoEvry is one of the largest IT consulting service companies in the Nordic countries with approximately 24,000 employees. TietoEvry provides IT and product engineering services in different market segments, from financial institutions, national public sector entities, municipalities, and health authorities in around 20 countries.

## REFERENCES

Banham, H., & He, Y. (2010). SME governance: Converging definitions and expanding expectations. *International Business and Economics Research Journal (IBER)*, *9*(2). https://doi.org/10.19030/iber.v9i2.52410.19030/iber.v9i2.52410.19030/iber.v9i2.52410.19030/iber.v9i2.52410.19030/iber.v9i2.52410.19030/iber.v9i2.52410.19030/iber.v9i2.52410.19030/iber.v9i2.52410.19030/iber.v9i2.52410.19030/iber.v9i2.524

Beckman, C. M., & Haunschild, P. R. (2002). Network learning: The effects of partners' heterogeneity of experience on corporate acquisitions. *Administrative Science Quarterly*, *47*(1), 92–124.

Beckman, C. M., Schoonhoven, C. B., Rottner, R. M., & Kim, S.-J. (2014). Relational pluralism in de novo organizations: Boards of directors as bridges or barriers to diverse alliance portfolios? *Academy of Management Journal*, *57*(2), 460–483.

Capron, L., & Mitchell, W. (2009). Selection capability: How capability gaps and internal social frictions affect internal and external strategic renewal. *Organization Science*, *20*(2), 294–312.

Carlsson, B. (2013). Kathleen Eisenhardt: Recipient of the 2012 Global Award for Entrepreneurship Research. *Small Business Economics*, *40*(4), 797–804.

Cunningham, C., Ederer, F., & Ma, S. (2019). Killer acquisitions. *Journal of Political Economy*, *129*(3), 649–702.

Daily, C. M., & Dalton, D. R. (1992). The relationship between governance structure and corporate performance in entrepreneurial firms. *Journal of Business Venturing*, *7*(5), 375–386.

Daily, C. M., & Dalton, D. R. (1993). Board of directors leadership and structure: Control and performance implications. *Entrepreneurship Theory and Practice*, *17*(3), 65–81.

Dalton, D. R., Daily, C. M., Ellstrand, A. E., & Johnson, J. L. (1998). Meta-analytic reviews of board composition, leadership structure, and financial performance. *Strategic Management Journal*, *19*(3), 269–290.

de Villiers, C., Naiker, V., & van Staden, C. J. (2011). The effect of board characteristics on firm environmental performance. *Journal of Management*, *37*(6), 1636–1663.

Delmar, F., Davidsson, P., & Gartner, W. B. (2003). Arriving at the high-growth firm. *Journal of Business Venturing*, *18*(2), 189–216.

Doha, A., Pagell, M., Swink, M., & Johnston, D. (2018). The imitator's dilemma: Why imitators should break out of imitation. *Journal of Product Innovation Management*, *35*(4), 543–564.

Finkelstein, S., & Mooney, A. C. (2003). Not the usual suspects: How to use board process to make boards better. *Academy of Management Perspectives*, *17*(2), 101–113.

Gan, D., & Erikson, T. (2022). Venture governance: CEO duality and new venture performance. *Journal of Business Venturing Insights*, *17*, e00304.

Garg, S. (2020). Venture governance: A new horizon for corporate governance. *Academy of Management Perspectives*, *34*(2), 252–265.

Garg, S., & Eisenhardt, K. M. (2017). Unpacking the CEO–board relationship: How strategy making happens in entrepreneurial firms. *Academy of Management Journal*, *60*(5), 1828–1858.

Garnsey, E., Stam, E., & Heffernan, P. (2006). New firm growth: Exploring processes and paths. *Industry and Innovation*, *13*(1), 1–20.

Geletkanycz, M. A., & Hambrick, D. C. (1997). The external ties of top executives: Implications for strategic choice and performance. *Administrative Science Quarterly*, *42*(4), 654–681.

Graebner, M. E., & Eisenhardt, K. M. (2004). The seller's side of the story: Acquisition as courtship and governance as syndicate in entrepreneurial firms. *Administrative Science Quarterly*, *49*(3), 366–403.

Haleblian, J., Devers, C. E., McNamara, G., Carpenter, M. A., & Davison, R. B. (2009). Taking stock of what we know about mergers and acquisitions: A review and research agenda. *Journal of Management*, *35*(3), 469–502.

Haunschild, P. R. (1993). Interorganizational imitation: The impact of interlocks on corporate acquisition activity. *Administrative Science Quarterly*, 38(4), 564–592.
Haynes, K. T., & Hillman, A. (2010). The effect of board capital and CEO power on strategic change. *Strategic Management Journal*, *31*(11), 1145–1163.
Hillman, A. J., & Dalziel, T. (2003). Boards of directors and firm performance: Integrating agency and resource dependence perspectives. *The Academy of Management Review*, *28*(3), 383–396.
Johnson, S. G., Schnatterly, K., & Hill, A. D. (2013). Board composition beyond independence: Social capital, human capital, and demographics. *Journal of Management*, *39*(1), 232–262.
Karim, S., & Mitchell, W. (2000). Path-dependent and path-breaking change: Reconfiguring business resources following acquisitions in the US medical sector, 1978–1995. *Strategic Management Journal*, *21*(10), 1061–1081.
Knoben, J., & Bakker, R. M. (2019). The guppy and the whale: Relational pluralism and start-ups' expropriation dilemma in partnership formation. *Journal of Business Venturing*, *34*(1), 103–121.
Kor, Y. Y., & Sundaramurthy, C. (2009). Experience-based human capital and social capital of outside directors. *Journal of Management*, *35*(4), 981–1006.
Leblanc, R. (2005). Assessing board leadership. *Corporate Governance: An International Review*, *13*(5), 654–666.
Lee, R. P., & Tang, X. (2018). Does it pay to be innovation and imitation oriented? An examination of the antecedents and consequences of innovation and imitation orientations. *Journal of Product Innovation Management*, *35*(1), 11–26.
Li, H., Terjesen, S., & Umans, T. (2020). Corporate governance in entrepreneurial firms: A systematic review and research agenda. *Small Business Economics*, *54*(1), 43–74.
McKelvie, A., & Wiklund, J. (2010). Advancing firm growth research: A focus on growth mode instead of growth rate. *Entrepreneurship Theory and Practice*, *34*(2), 261–288.
McMullen, J. S., & Shepherd, D. A. (2006). Entrepreneurial action and the role of uncertainty in the theory of the entrepreneur. *Academy of Management Review*, *31*(1), 132–152.
Palmer, D. A., Jennings, P. D., & Zhou, X. (1993). Late adoption of the multidivisional form by large U.S. corporations: Institutional, political, and economic accounts. *Administrative Science Quarterly*, *38*(1), 100–131.
Penrose, E. (1959). *The Theory of the Growth of the Firm*. Blackwell.
Puranam, P., Singh, H., & Chaudhuri, S. (2009). Integrating acquired capabilities: When structural integration is (un)necessary. *Organization Science*, *20*(2), 313–328.
Ranft, A. L., & Lord, M. D. (2002). Acquiring new technologies and capabilities: A grounded model of acquisition implementation. *Organization Science*, *13*(4), 420–441.
Shenkar, O. (2010). Defend your research: Imitation is more valuable than innovation. *Harvard Business Review*, *88*(4). https://hbr.org/2010/04/defend-your-research-imitation-is-more-valuable-than-innovation
Yang, M., & Hyland, M. (2006). Who do firms imitate? A multilevel approach to examining sources of imitation in the choice of mergers and acquisitions. *Journal of Management*, *32*(3), 381–399.

# PART III

# Corporate Governance of Family Firms

# Introduction to Part III

One thing that most – possibly all – start-up firms have in common is that they began as family firms, regardless of how you define "family firms"[1] – that is, the founder(s) and their family members were the owners at the beginning. Over time, this may change; indeed, if the firm's goal is to become a "unicorn" or anything similar, doing so will typically require bringing in outside investors and sharing ownership.

But for many start-up firms, the goal is not to become a unicorn; the goal is to build a comfortable life as a business owner, to provide for family, to control the family's financial and social future, and to pass on the legacy to future generations. Just as growing from an idea to a unicorn involves unique corporate governance challenges, so, too, does building, growing, maintaining, and passing on a family business. We are all probably familiar with the family business cliché that "the first generation starts the business, the second generation grows the business, and the third generation ends the business." No founder wants that to be true for their business, of course. So, whereas venture governance primarily revolves around managing growth and pacifying diverse stakeholders, governance in family firms adds the challenging context of managing intergenerational priorities, preferences, and interests. Thinking of a firm providing a return on investment to suppliers of capital takes on entirely new perspectives when those suppliers of capital are family members.

And these are the types of issues that are explored in Part III on Corporate Governance of Family Firms. In Chapter 10, Marta Widz, Nava Michael-Tsabari, and Pramodita Sharma introduce a typology of family firms, characterizing firms across different structures and lifecycles. Of course, these lifecycles are not static; firms will transition across different types as a result of growth strategies, ownership, and different generations. Corporate governance is critical for every type. Corporate governance, leadership, and communication are especially critical when leadership and ownership of the family firm transition from one generation or family member to another. In Chapter 11, Léa Zhe Wang and Séverine Mulliez provide insight into how to manage this transition. Blending strategy, leadership, psychology, and other literatures, they show that the key to managing any family firm transition is "brave communication." Being honest, transparent, and brave in family firm conversations requires vulnerability, but it is essential for psychological safety and family harmony. Perhaps ironically, such communication is oftentimes most difficult with our own family members; but overcoming this governance challenge is necessary to avoid fitting into the cliché above.

Chapter 12 connects our discussion of family firms with our Part I foundation on international and cultural dynamics in corporate governance, focusing on family firm priorities with the unique cultural dimensions in Morocco – a developing country, with unique cultural, social, and gender norms. Taib Berrada El Azizi, Oumaima Quiddi, and Badr Habba blend quantitative and qualitative perspectives through three case studies; perhaps the practical takeaway is that corporate governance needs to appreciate that there is a difference between "family business" and "families in business."

Chapter 13 extends our portfolio of international perspectives and looks at corporate governance in one of the most unique types of family firms in the world: the Korean chaebol. Cinzia Dessì and Ji-Hee Kim critically analyze the role of government support in promoting socially responsible behavior and exploring the evolving relationship between chaebols, corporate social responsibility, and government incentives. This chapter gives us a glimpse into our Part IV study of mission, purpose, and impact as it introduces broader discussions on the intersection of business, governance, and social responsibility within South Korea's unique economic framework.

As we know, just about every business begins as a family business. Every family business is different – because every family is different. Even so, we can offer a few best practice ideas for the practice of corporate governance for family firms.

1. Communicate. There are some types of communication that will be required by law, depending on the type of business entity you have; communicating with regulators, lenders, and investors will be required. Communicating with family members is optional, but essential. As the following chapters show, much of the governance of family firms happens outside of the board room and through unwritten relationships and agreements. That may be natural, but it is never ideal.
2. Move these unwritten relationships and agreements to written relationships and agreements. Establish corporate agreements and records that are clear, intentional, and legal. You and your siblings may not need this level of formality today, but your children and grandchildren probably will.
3. Be intentional in moving from family-led corporate governance to outsider, professional corporate governance. This should follow from your mission and purpose. Family leadership may best maintain the soul and genesis of the firm; outsider, professional leadership may best create the

future of your firm. Be intentional with how you make that transition and with why you make that transition.

4. Be clear about your mission and purpose. Some family businesses will want to always remain closely held and relatively small; some will want to grow and expand their investor base. Your mission and purpose will determine the best corporate governance system for your business.
5. Anticipate and structure generational succession. Many governance challenges in family firms arise not from current leadership, but from unclear expectations, emotional undercurrents, or power asymmetries during generational handover. Effective succession planning requires brave communication, clearly defined power structures, and formal mechanisms to align values and responsibilities across generations.

Part III concludes – and segues into Part IV on governance of social purpose, mission and impact – with a deep dive into the corporate governance dimensions of family foundations with modern philanthropy as their mission. In Chapter 14, Malgorzata Smulowitz shows that modern family foundations are inspired by values-aligned investing and can achieve meaningful societal and environmental change while achieving financial results. This is exactly why corporate governance exists. As we transition from family firm governance in Part III to governance of social impact in Part IV, she concludes by offering suggestions for best-in-class governance practices; families can ensure their legacy endures across generations, benefiting society, family, and businesses.

While most published corporate governance research has focused on large firms in large economies, we know that family firms are the true foundation of any economy. As we explained in Chapter 1, all of the corporate governance structures and directions in this book are interconnected; the study of family firms highlights these connections explicitly. By studying these diverse – and interconnected – issues, scholars can better understand the dynamics that drive corporate governance structures in any context. Every firm is unique, but all firms share similar dynamics and constraints; this exploration of family firm governance illustrates these dynamics and constraints perfectly.

## NOTE

1. As mentioned in the Introduction, one popular definition of a family firm is one in which the founder or a descendant of the founder currently holds a 5% equity stake in the firm. See, for example, Shleifer and Vishny (1986), Anderson, Duru, and Reeb (2009), and Anderson, Reeb, and Zhao (2012) in the references section for Chapter 1 for details.

# 10. The heterogeneity of governance behavior in family enterprise systems: the power perspective

**Marta Widz, Nava Michael-Tsabari and Pramodita Sharma**

## 1. INTRODUCTION

The heterogeneity of family enterprises and the importance of governance in these organizations are well established in the literature (Daspit et al., 2018; Debicki et al., 2009; Yu et al., 2012). However, to date, little research has been advanced to understand the heterogeneity of governance. To begin this work, we identify four types of family firms based on the complexity of the dominant coalition and the business systems: (i) *family business* – low complexity in family and business systems, (ii) *family enterprise* – low complexity in family system, high complexity in business system, (iii) *families in business* – high complexity in family system, low complexity in business systems, and (iv) *enterprising families* – high complexity in family and business systems.

Drawing on a thought of the political scientist Norton Long, who said that "people will readily admit that governments are organizations; the converse, that organizations are governments, is equally true but rarely considered," we reach out to the power circulation theory and conceptualize family enterprises as political organizations, and theorize that each type of family firm develops distinctive governance behaviors: (1) *monarchies* in family businesses, (2) *empires* in family enterprises, (3) *parliamentary democracies* in families in business, and (4) *federations* in enterprising families. Overlaying our family firm typology and governance proclivities of each form, with insights from four case studies and findings from the literature, reveals interesting propositions related to the dynamic reconfigurations of governance structures over time and the influence on financial and non-financial goals.

## 2. COMPLEXITY OF FAMILY ENTERPRISE SYSTEMS

Family enterprises that thrive over time develop well-balanced power systems to align with the complexity of their business and nature of family involvement (Table 10.1). For example, established as a logistical company in Germany in 1930, Dachser has thrived for over 90 years with its focused business strategy, single-family ownership, and a board with a continuous family presence (Leleux & Widz, 2021a). On the other hand, Jebsen & Jessen Family Enterprise, which was jointly established by two different families in 1895, has used pragmatic structures and policies to effectively own and govern a highly diversified portfolio of businesses (Widz & Farber, 2021). Pictet, a Swiss private bank with a history dating back to 1805, has evolved into an owner-run partnership firm, which includes members of the Pictet family (Groth & Simon, 2022).

Similarly, mindful governance and balanced distribution of power lie at the core of the longevity and success of many other family businesses with diversified business portfolios (e.g., Widz & Parada, 2022) and numerous family boundary organizations, such as family museums or family offices (De Massis et al., 2021). For example, founded in 1901, the Italian De Agostini holding company of four Drago–Boroli family branches owns one privately held business and three other businesses listed on stock exchanges in New York, Milan, and Madrid. This family also runs a philanthropic foundation that organizes camps for underprivileged children at the historic family house (Widz & Leleux, 2019).

Despite this observed diversity in the families and business systems, the family business literature has largely focused on the context of *only one family behind one business*. In particular, the famous three-circle model (Taguiri & Davis, 1992) assumes that silently assumes this context and illustrates the unique characteristic of the one-family one-business system, that is, the interaction of the family system with the ownership and management systems (Gersick et al., 1997). Even though John Davis recognizes that "after a couple of generations, the three circles change" (Sharma, 2018a, p. 4), because the families grow, the ownership basis increases and the business becomes larger, but the static nature of the three-circle model does not, however, explain the dynamism behind reconfigurations of the highly complex family enterprise systems.

Current theorizing on the dynamic development of a family enterprise merely describes the evolutionary stages of a typical family business over generations: controlling ownership, siblings' partnership, and cousin consortium (Davis et al., 1997; Gersick et al., 1999). This conceptualization captures the complexity that partiularly emerges over time as more generations of the *same family* get involved in the *same business*.

*Table 10.1* *Examples of well power-balanced systems in selected global family businesses*

| Name, Location (founding year) | Industries of operations | Management | Ownership | Governance |
|---|---|---|---|---|
| Dachser, Germany (1930) | Logistics | CEO: recent transition from third generation family-CEO to non-family CEO | One family, composed of direct descendants of the founder, Thomas Dachser. | Currently a mix of family and non-family directors with a family chairperson. |
| De Agostini, Italy (1901) | Holding structure organized in 4 business areas:<br>1) Publishing, De Agostini Editore, 100% family-owned.<br>2) Media and communication, owed via joint-ventures and direct holdings in Banijay Group Holding, and listed in Madrid –Atresmedia.<br>3) Gaming and services: majority stake in International Game Technology, listed in New York.<br>4) Financial services, DeA Capital, listed in Milan. | Non-family CEO.<br>Sub-holdings and subsidiaries with their own governance. | Fully owned by Boroli family since 1946.<br>Currently, in the hands of the four branches of Drago–Boroli family via the family B&D Holding | Family B&D Holding, with the representation of every family branch, headed by family chairperson.<br>Type the Paragraph Text Operating, De Agostini holding, with family chairperson. |
| Pictet, Switzerland (1805) | Wealth and asset management | Several partners with the Pictet family having substantial involvement in management over the last 180 years or nine generations. | Several partners with the Pictet family having substantial involvement in ownership over the last 180 years or nine generations. | Partnership model with different seniority of partners; commitment to renew the Pictet family involvement in partnership. |

| Name, Location (founding year) | Industries of operations | Management | Ownership | Governance |
|---|---|---|---|---|
| Jebsen & Jessen Family Enterprise, Hongkong (1895) | Diversified conglomerate, that spans consumer products, retail, industrial product, shipping and mining and, operates four main entities:<br>1) Jebsen & Co, Hong Kong;<br>2) Jebsen & Jessen Group, Singapore;<br>3) Jebsen & Jessen Hamburg;<br>4) GMA Garnet, Australia. | Federation of businesses, each with its own governance.<br>Non-family CEOs of individual businesses and of each main entity.<br>No overall holding structure. | Cross-shareholding partnership of two families: the Jebsens and the Jessens.<br>Majority of ownership of Jebsen & Co by Jebsen family.<br>Majority of ownership of Jebsen & Jessen Group by Jessen family.<br>Equal stakes of both families in Jebsen & Jessen Hamburg, and GMA Garnet. | Family chairperson from Jebsen family for Jebsen & Co.<br>Family chairperson from Jessen family for Jebsen & Co.<br>Non-family chairpersons for Jebsen & Jessen Hamburg, and GMA Garnet with both family principal shareholders as family directors on all boards. |

*Source:* Own analysis.

However, research suggests that only less than 11% of enterprising families own a single firm (Michael-Tsabari, 2023). Instead, a typical enterprising family owns and controls over six firms at any given time, some of which are added as new start-ups by the family, while other ventures are acquired (Zellweger et al., 2012). Thus, it is more realistic to conceptualize family enterprises as a portfolio of companies than a singular business, as depicted by the *cluster model* proposed by Michael-Tsabari and colleagues (2014). Recently, family businesses have also been referred to as *family business groups* (Rautiainen et al., 2023), and it has been recognized that the identity of family businesses changes from the founder identity to family business group meta-identity along the entrepreneurial journey of an entrepreneurial family: from a founder firm to a family that owns a portfolio of businesses (Widz & Parada, 2022). Indeed, overlaying generational family involvement with multiple business operations leads to variance in ownership dimensions, including the number of owning families and members, proportion of ownership held by each individual or family, nature of relationship among owners, demographic characteristics of owners, and the nature of involvement of owners in governance bodies, such as the board of directors, advisory board, family council, and family office (Daspit et al., 2018).

Based on this reasoning, the boundaries of the definition of a *family* can be extended beyond kinship, blood, and marriage ties, towards the concept of a quasi-family, a partly negotiated and fluid conception of a family (Karra et al., 2006). It is because, based on the *involvement essence* (Chrisman et al., 2005), people who are in fact not blood related would behave like a family in their role as stewards of their family enterprise system. This is observed in cases like Jebsen & Jessen Family Enterprise or Villeroy & Boch, where two families partnered to run the business and have worked jointly to achieve multigenerational success. Others like Pictet and Kikkoman demonstrate the possibility of successful partnership between six to nine parties (i.e., partners or families) who act as if they were part of the same family and who consider themselves a family business with active participation in associations like the Henokiens or the Family Business Network. Such families highlight the less studied *italicized* part of the family business definition frequently used in the literature: "A family business is governed and/or managed with the intention to shape and pursue the vision of the business held by *a dominant coalition controlled by members of* the same family or *a small number of families in a manner that is potentially sustainable across generations* of the family or families" (Chua et al., 1999, p. 25).

Based on the nature of involvement in the dominant coalition, we distinguish between a *simple family system* wherein the dominant coalition is from one family and *complex family system* with a dominant coalition that stretches across a few non-related families and investors including the public investors in the case of listed family-controlled businesses. On the business dimension, the array of complexities ranges from a *simple business system* of one firm with limited product lines and operations to a *complex business system* with a diversified business portfolio; and – as conceptualized by De Massis and colleagues – other boundary organizations like family offices, foundations, museums etc. (De Massis et al., 2021).

The interplay of complexity in the family and the business systems leads us to four types of firms: (i) *family business* – low complexity in family and in business systems, (ii) *family enterprise* – low complexity in family system, high complexity in business system, (iii) *families in business* – high complexity in family system, low complexity in business systems, and (iv) *enterprising families* – high complexity in family and business systems (Figure 10.1 and Figure 10.2).

As such, a *family business* (quadrant 1 in Figure 10.2) – for example, Dachser, a German logistics company – operates a business in one industry, which is fully owned by blood-related members of the same family, the direct descendants of the founder. *Family enterprise* (quadrant 2 in Figure 10.2) – for example De Agostini, an Italian family holding with four business entities in four industries (publishing, media & communication, gaming & services, and finance), owned by a few family branches – is a diversified portfolio of businesses, controlled by one extended but blood-related family. Further, *families*

| | |
|---|---|
| **Complexity in family system** | |
| ***Simple* family system** | One dominant coalition, often one family, who are the sole owners of the business. |
| ***Complex* family system** | More than one dominant coalition, often more than one family; ownership stretching to other non-family related owners (other families, other investors, public ownership). |
| **Complexity in business system** | |
| ***Simple* business system** | A single firm, often with a limited number of lines of products and operating in a single industry. |
| ***Complex* business system** | More than a single firm, often a diversified portfolio of businesses and several family boundary organizations (family offices, museums, philanthropical foundations). |

*Source:* Own analysis, inspired by Michael-Tsabari, Labaki, & Zachary (2014); Dieleman (2018).

*Figure 10.1* *Defining complexity in family and business systems*

| | | Family System Complexity | |
|---|---|---|---|
| | | **Simple** | **Complex** |
| **Business System Complexity** | **Simple** | ***Family Business***<br>(Quadrant 1)<br><br>One Family-One Business<br><br>e.g., Dachser | ***Families in Business***<br>(Quadrant 3)<br><br>Multiple Families and Owners-One Business<br><br>e.g., Pictet |
| | **Complex** | ***Family Enterprise***<br>(Quadrant 2)<br><br>One Family-Portfolio of Businesses<br><br>e.g., De Agostini | ***Enterprising Family***<br>(Quadrant 4)<br><br>Multiple Families and Owners-Portfolio of Businesses<br><br>e.g., Jebsen & Jessen Group |

*Source:* Own analysis, inspired by Dieleman (2018); Michael-Tsabari, Labaki, & Zachary (2014); Tagiuri & Davis (1992).

*Figure 10.2* *Typology of family enterprise systems according to the complexity in family and business systems*

*in business* (quadrant 3 in Figure 10.2) – e.g., Pictet, a Swiss private bank specializing in wealth management and asset management, which is currently owned by seven partners, two of whom have "Pictet" as their last name – is a single business, owned and operated by multiple partners, of which only some stem from the same family. Finally, *enterprising families* (quadrant 4 in Figure 10.2) – e.g., *Jebsen & Jessen Family Enterprise*, a highly diversified portfolio of businesses owned jointly by two families, which spans consumer goods, retail, industrial products, shipping, and mining and which constantly changes its business portfolio by adding new investments and divesting some other businesses – is highly complex in both the family and the business systems. Each type of organization– *family business, family enterprise, families in business,* and *enterprising families* – has a suitable form of governance, as we discuss next.

# 3. HETEROGENEITY IN FAMILY ENTERPRISE SYSTEMS BY GOVERNANCE BEHAVIOR

## 3.1 Family Business Governance

Family business governance is the architecture (structures and processes) that enables stewardship of an enterprise over generations (Gersick & Feliu, 2014). It entails many governance architectures, i.e. that of the family (e.g., Suess, 2014), the ownership group (Daspit et al., 2018), and the business or the enterprise (e.g., Lane et al., 2006). The governance is also conceptualized as a process through which "strategic goals are set, key relationships are maintained, the health of the family is safeguarded, accountability is maintained, and achievement and performance are recognized" (Goldbart & DeFuria, 2009, p. 7). Thus, it enables the owners or the dominant coalition to articulate and achieve their shared objectives (Nordqvist et al., 2014). It is noteworthy that the owning family – or a dominant coalition of owners – and its various financial and non-financial goals are at the core of this definition. It is because the family, its structures, its processes, and how it copes with disruptions define, to a large extent, the success of the family business (Suess, 2014).

Family business governance entails formal and informal mechanisms that can emanate from inside or outside of the company (Chrisman et al., 2018). This cognition is an important nesting ground for our analysis as it suggests that governance itself is the result of a social process or – more directly – governance *is a social process and social practice* itself, a notion that has been well studied and documented in family business practitioners' publications (Cheng et al., 2022).

## 3.2 Power Circulation Theory and Family Organizations

Framing of governance as a social process leads us to *power,* defined as the social process required to get things accomplished in interdependent systems, thereby transforming individual interests into coordinated activities to achieve valued goals (Pfeffer, 1992; Zaleznik & Kets de Vries, 1975). Power is the vital mechanism studied in political science. In fact, power is at the *very core* of the definition of political science, which is "the study of power, the study of the monopoly of the legitimate use of force" (Easton, 1985, p. 133). It is also "the study of the way in which decisions for a society are made and considered binding most of the time by most of the people" (Easton, 1985, p. 133). Such framing of political science and power – how power as a social process is exercised to arrive at decisions in interdependent systems – is especially useful for explaining the governance of family enterprise systems with its diverse goals in both the business system (e.g., to set strategic goals, recognize achievement and performance) and the family system (e.g., to maintain key relationships, safeguard the health of the family).

Paraphrasing Pfeffer (1992, p. 29), who said that "organizations, particularly large ones, are like governments in that they are fundamentally political entities," we claim that complex family enterprise systems are political entities, exactly like governments. To support this claim, we turn to *power* and *coalitions*, which are intertwined elements of any political organization used to arrive at any important political decisions in family organizations. Interestingly, the behavioral theory of the firm (Cyert & March, 1963) recognizes the phenomena of power and coalitions in decision-making; in particular, it claims that *coalitions* are triggered in the decision-making process when there is a need to have the *power* to influence a *decision* (Ben-Shahar et al., 2023).

Framing family businesses as "fundamentally political entities," we turn to *the power circulation theory* that explains the relationships between the dominant coalition and other stakeholders. This theory argues that organizational players are inherently political, characterized by shifting coalitions and continual power struggles (Ocasio, 1994). Power circulates, is enacted, and dissipates over time due to the mechanisms of obsolescence and contestation (Combs et al., 2007; Ocasio, 1994). *Obsolescence* implies that CEOs become "stale in the saddle" and thus outdated because of their ties to past decisions (Miller, 1991), while *contestation* results from the actions of other executives viewed as rivals of the incumbent (Pfeffer, 1981). The nature of contest varies with the number and strength of potential rivals. Another important notion is that *the periods of political stability* are transitory states between the periods characterized by power struggles or the ongoing pulling and tugging of contestants for position and privilege (Ocasio, 1994). The power circulation theory conceptualizes *power as a multifaceted phenomenon* (Finkelstein, 1992), which can be formal or informal (Finkelstein & D'aveni, 1994), hard, as manifested by equity holdings, or soft, as manifested by relational ties (Ben-Shahar et al., 2023).

The power circulation theory has been fundamental and useful in understanding of corporate governance and the relationship between CEOs and boards (Ocasio, 1994; Shen & Cannella, 2002). In family business literature, this theoretical perspective has been applied to examine the shifting coalitions between family shareholders and outside investors of European family firms (Jara-Bertin et al., 2008). More recently, Ben-Shahar et al. (2023) differentiated between the hard power of equity stakes and the soft power of relational ties to analyze dominant coalitions and understand the relative power of family shareholders of consecutive generations.

Viewing the four types of family-owned organizations – (i) *family business*, (ii) *family enterprise*, (iii) *families in business*, and (iv) *enterprising families* – via the lenses of the power circulation theory seems like the next logical step. It holds the promise to advance the understanding of the complexity of family business governance, the study of which initially focused only on the role, structure, composition, and management of an outside board in the privately owned firms (Ward, 1991). "Equipping" the family enterprise system with power, as described by the power circulation theory, actually means making the governance system "alive" with the dominant coalitions "pulling and tugging of contestants for power, position, and privilege." It implies seeing governance as a configuration of actors captured at one specific point in their constant political acting game, like ballet dancers of Teatro alla Scala frozen for a moment in a pose of dynamic equilibrium.

## 3.3 The Heterogeneity of Family Enterprise Systems by Governance Behavior

Building on the current application of power circulation theory in the family business governance context, and at the same time recognizing the complexities in both family and business systems, we propose the following typology of the family enterprise system by governance behavior (Figure 10.3).

### 3.3.1 Monarchy as the governance behavior in family business

The monarchy (quadrant 1) form of governance is characterized by centralized power in the hands of one dominant coalition in one business entity (one kingdom with one monarch), usually occuring in a *family business* of low complexity in family and business systems, that is, a family business, wherein ownership, management, and governance are centralized around the members of the same family. In monarchies, as there is a lack of serious contestants from outside the owning family, the incumbent is predominantly challenged by *obsolescence*. In practice, the next generation brings new ideas to challenge (albeit often incrementally) the status quo. The intergenerational succession, often the first or the second succession, constitutes the largest challenge because of the major reconfigurations of power. Often initial boards are created, and next generation family members are educated not only on how to be effective managers but also on how to become responsible owners and board directors. As such, the power is distributed between the (family) CEO, the (family) executive board, and the (family) supervisory board, which constitute the "political centers," "political" dominant coalitions, or "centers of contestation." The relatively simple governance structure effectivelly addresses power circulation and the classic agency problems and costs (Jensen & Meckling, 1976).

| | | Dominant Coalition Complexity | |
|---|---|---|---|
| | | **Simple** | **Complex** |
| **Business System Complexity** | **Simple** | ***Monarchy***<br>(Quadrant 1)<br><br>e.g., Dachser<br><br>Ownership: Concentrated in the hands of one family.<br><br>Management: Centralized around family members.<br><br>Governance structures: Relatively simple, address the classic agency problems.<br><br>Governance behavior:<br>- Obsolesce as a main mechanism of power circulation;<br>- Easily achieved and durable governance equilibrium as the centers of contestations (dominant coalitions) are all within the same family, and power struggles are over one business entity. | ***Parliamentary democracy***<br>(Quadrant 3)<br><br>e.g., Pictet<br><br>Ownership: Controlled in a balanced way by a number of dominant coalitions, such as several families, public owners, private equity, and other partners.<br><br>Management: Controlled by multiple families with multiple non-family executives.<br><br>Governance structures: Fairly complex, balancing the power of various owners, and mitigating the "owner- owner agency conflicts".<br><br>Governance behavior:<br>- Obsolescence as a main mechanism of power circulation;<br>- Soft power (relational ties) and multiple (family) owners' dominant coalitions lead to inter- (family) owners' power circulation;<br>- Family logic prevails;<br>- Steady governance equilibrium that builds a foundation for multiple (family) owners' long-term cooperation. |
| | **Complex** | ***Empire***<br>(Quadrant 2)<br><br>e.g., De Agostini<br><br>Ownership: Controlled by one family in a concentrated way (via e.g. family holding); may include public stock or private equity owners.<br><br>Management: Controlled by one family; dominated by non-family executives.<br><br>Governance structures: Complex governance structures with multiple boards, holdings, and trust structures to reduce the multiple agency costs ("principal- agent- agent").<br><br>Governance behavior:<br>- Contestation as a main mechanism of power circulation;<br>- Hard power (equity stakes) and many dominant coalitions lead to vibrant power circulation among business entities, as well as in between the business entities and family holding;<br>- Entrepreneurial logic prevails;<br>- Governance equilibrium reflects the dynamism of the business portfolio. | ***Federation***<br>(Quadrant 4)<br><br>e.g., Jebsen & Jessen Group<br><br>Ownership: Controlled in a balanced way by a number of dominant coalitions, such as several families, public owners, private equity, and other partners.<br><br>Management: Controlled by multiple owners with multiple boards, holdings, and trust structures; dominated by non-family executives.<br><br>Governance structures: Complex governance structures with multiple boards, holdings, and trust structures to balance the power of various owners and to reduce the complex agency costs ("principal-principal- agent- agent").<br><br>Governance behavior:<br>- Both obsolescence and contestation as mechanisms of power circulation;<br>- Interplay of soft power (relational ties) and hard power (equity stakes) lead to power circulations in multiple directions at a time: inter-owners' power circulation and among business entities;<br>- Interplay of family and entrepreneurial logics: family logic prevails in the "ownership" dominant coalitions and entrepreneurial logic prevails in the wider family enterprise systems;<br>- Governance equilibrium balances in between stability (ensured by the steady, past-dependent foundations of ownership governance) and fluctuations (reflecting the dynamism of the business portfolio); is guaranteed by soft governance elements such as enduring entrepreneurial partnerships, multiple-family harmony or *confidence capital*. |

*Source:* Author's analysis.

*Figure 10.3 Typology of family businesses according to governance behavior*

Because of the relatively weak contestation mechanism, monarchies constitute rather durable governance systems, which may last as long as one generation. This is in line with the "controlling owner–siblings partnership – cousin consortium" model (Davis et al., 1997; Gersick et al., 1999), which is a generational transition model and presents that every new stage of evolution is reached with a new generation coming into (power) play, that is, from founder in the first generation to siblings in the second generation to cousins in the third generation.

### 3.3.2 Monarchy – illustration with the Dachser[1] case

Dachser is an exemplary family business that illustrates some of the distinctive governance features of a monarchy. It was founded in Kempten, the Bavarian town in the south of Germany, in 1930, by Thomas Dachser. Over three generations, the company has expanded to close to 400 locations worldwide on five continents and employs over 30,000 people. Despite its global footprint, Dachser stays loyal to both its core business – intelligent logistics – and to Kempten, a picturesque town of over 70,000 inhabitants, the center of gravity for Dachser's operations and the place the Dachser family owners call "home".

The portfolio of business activities at Dachser spans various logistics services, including:

- European logistics – the backbone of the company – which covers road logistics for business-to-business and some business-to-consumer segments, as well as warehousing, and other aspects of integrated logistics, from retail to procurement and distribution, contracts and multi-user warehousing.
- Food logistics, which moves and stores a wide spectrum of temperature-sensitive packed foods, dairy products, wines and spirits, and preserved food of all sorts.
- Air and sea logistics, including warehousing and overland freight network.

Despite the long history, the family remains fairly small with less than 20 family shareholders from second, third, and fourth generations; and the shares are distributed almost evenly among family members. The family has fostered a "bond of blood," under which shareholding is not to be extended to in-laws, with Dachser to remain 100% privately owned by the family. The family constitution clearly defines who family members are: (i) direct descendants of Thomas Dachser and Anna Dachser-Geissler, (ii) family foundations and trusts represented by such descendants, and (iii) other individuals who are accepted by family shareholders with a 75% majority vote. The rights and duties of the family shareholders are further outlined in the family constitution and include preserving the financial independence and stability of the firm. The amount paid out as dividends is capped at 12% of after-tax profits, with a guaranteed minimum to shareholders. Reflections on Dachser's governance structure show that it tried to balance the power of family and non-family executives and directors throughout its history and that this balance was often the key to success. Dachser has never shied away from creative solutions, such as employing non-family executives in its first generation, who worked alongside the family CEO, two daughters in the second generation who served in executive and board positions, and a family CEO in the third one, who later handed over his function to a non-family CEO and became Dachser's chairman.

The history of Dachser shows that generational changes triggered major governance changes and challenges to balance the powers of the executive board, supervisory board, and the family. These challenges led to its three governance principles. First, while family leadership is to be maintained at the top level to ensure core values remain intact, a family member could either serve in the CEO or the chairman position, but never in both. Second, only one family member can have a long-term career in the company at the same time. The company follows the "up-or-out" philosophy; that is, if not promoted, the family member must leave the organization. The promoted person ultimately takes the CEO or the chairman position. Third, family members must be in the minority at the supervisory board level.

### 3.3.3 Empire as the governance behavior in family enterprise

The empire (quadrant 2) form of governance is characterized by political struggles between multiple fairly independent business entities or kingdoms. The empire aims to exercise power to control these entities and align them towards the overall strategic direction. This governance structure is often seen in *family enterprises* with low complexity in the family system and high complexity in the business system formed of multiple enterprises in different industries. The business system is controlled by one (often multigenerational) family in a concentrated way via family holding, though part of ownership may be held by other private or public investors.

Empires are characterized by a complex business structure with multiple boards, holdings, trusts, family foundations, family offices, and philanthropic foundations, to name just a few. Governance structures, including executive boards and supervisory boards, are dominated by non-family professionals (executives and directors) but also demonstrate a significant presence of family members.

A portfolio of (unrelated) businesses as well as the involvement of non-family executives in strategy formulation and implementation constitutes a rich ground for rivalry and power contests. Therefore, the power circulates vibrantly from one dominant coalition (made of family and non-family members) of one business entity to another dominant coalition (made of family and non-family members) of another business entity in quest, for example, for fighting for the overall family (empire) resources.

The power circulates also in between (usually) family-dominated holding board to the corporate holding boards, and among the executive boards of business entities. Because of the increased agency problems and agency costs (Chrisman et al., 2005; Jensen & Meckling, 1976; Wright & Kellermanns, 2011), there is a need to align the goals of multiple top executives, multiple corporate boards, and the owners, and to reduce multiple agency costs ("principal-agent-agent conflicts"). Hence, the former may be offered portions of (temporary) ownership in the businesses they manage. As a consequence, the *entrepreneurial logic* – one that "endorses, even celebrates, a strategy of growth that invests in the business to grow and improve it and seize opportunities" (Miller et al., 2011, p. 4) – is the main reference point, and *hard power* in the form of equity stakes prevails and leads to the formation of various equity-based coalitions.

Stability of the governance equilibrium is related to the dynamism with which the business portfolio changes (i.e., mergers, acquisitions, and divestments). Such changes influence the liquidity of the family owners and impact their dividend/retained earnings ratio, which has the potential to destabilize the governance system. For example, a new portfolio entrant may amend the governance structures, as it may be necessary to add a new corporate board or new director(s) into the holding board. On the other hand, a divestment may result in liquidity, which in turn may lead to a new acquisition or the creation of a new structure such as a family office or a philanthropic foundation. This naturally changes the constellation as well as the composition of coalitions, releasing a new power dynamic circulating in the system, and as a result, pushes the governance to reconfigure itself.

### 3.3.4 Empire – illustration with the De Agostini[2] case

De Agostini is an exemplary family business that illustrates some of the distinctive governance features of an empire. Founded by Giovanni De Agostini in 1901, the company was bought 18 years later by business partners Marco Adolfo Boroli and Cesare Angelo Rossi. The second-generation Boroli brothers, Achille and Adolfo, sons of Marco Adolfo Boroli, consolidated the firm in the Boroli family's hands in 1946. After almost 100 years in the publishing and printing business, De Agostini Group, headquartered in Novara, Italy, grew to employ over 13,000 people, recomposed its portfolio radically (cumulative investments amount to about €26 billion, with total disinvestments to some €17 billion). De Agostini Group spans four major business entities:

- The legacy *publishing* business, De Agostini Editore, is fully owned by the family. The products include partworks (magazine-like issues released over a period of time), books (DeA Planeta Libri), educational books (DeA Scuola), digital platforms as well as kids' TV channels (DeAKids, Super!, DeA Junior), and a variety of other product lines. De Agostini Editore is present in 30 markets with publications in 13 languages and is a world leader in the partworks market. Once the core business of the group, the publishing business makes up only 3% of the total portfolio in terms of net asset value (NAV)!
- *Media* and *Communication*, with activities in broadcasting, content production, and distribution for television, new media, and cinema, through Atresmedia (listed on the Madrid Stock Exchange) and Banijay Group Holding (a private company controlled by Stéphane Courbit, a French businessman in the sector of media and television). The journey into media and communication began in 2003 with the acquisition of a majority stake in Antena 3, one of Spain's leading radio and TV networks. A series of acquisitions and mergers created Banijay Group Holding, one of the largest independent companies globally in the production and distribution of content for television and multimedia platforms. It operates in some16 countries and has a library of over 20,000 hours of programming in many genres, such as reality and entertainment, talk, and kids' shows. De Agostini holds a 20.9% stake in Atresmedia through a joint venture with Spanish Planeta Group and a 34% fully diluted stake in Banijay Group Holding. Media and Communication make up 15% of De Agostini's total portfolio NAV.
- *Gaming and Services* joined the portfolio in 2002 when De Agostini took part in the public tender offer for Lottomatica, a leading Italian lottery, and acquired a majority stake. A string of acquisitions followed. By the end of 2017, De Agostini held a 50.8% stake in IGT (International Game Technology), the largest global player in the gaming and services sector operating in over 100 countries, developing gaming and sports betting systems and products, such as kiosks and terminals, hardware and software. IGT is headquartered in London, UK, and listed on the New York Stock Exchange. De Agostini is the majority shareholder in IGT, which accounted for 64% of its total portfolio NAV.
- *Financial Services* were added in 2006 thanks to the acquisition of Cdb Web Tech and the creation of DeA Capital, active in private equity, alternative investments (DeA Capital Alternative Funds) and real estate (DeA Capital Real Estate). In 2017 DeA Capital employed 185 people, had some $12 billion assets under management and was listed on the Milan Stock Exchange. Established with family money and some external funding, DeA Capital extends the family's experience in private equity. De Agostini holds other financial direct investments, including a 1.3% stake in

Assicurazioni Generali. Financial services make up 15% of De Agostini's portfolio NAV.

De Agostini Group is owned by the third to fifth generations of four branches of the Drago–Boroli family through privately held B&D Holding, the family holding. There are about 60 family shareholders; all direct descendants of Marco Adolfo Boroli, most of them bearing the last names Boroli or Drago (hence the name of the family holding: B&D). Marco Drago, third-generation family shareholder, family leader, chairman of De Agostini and chairman of B&D Holding, explains, "B&D Holding is in fact the family safety box" (Leleux, Widz, & Corbetta, 2019, p. 3). But having three out of four business entities of De AgostiniGroup listed on stock exchanges "gives us transparency and an ability to rely on external expertise and professionalism" (Leleux, Widz, & Corbetta, 2019, p. 3), comments Stefania Boroli, a fourth-generation family shareholder.

The transformations on the business side required changes on the family ownership side, supported by creation of a solid foundation of corporate governance. On the family side, the 15-year-long process led to the professionalization of the executive boards, with close to 15 family members exiting the top operational positions. Marco Drago recalls that in 1998, 15 out of 19 third-generation Drago–Boroli cousins held executive positions in the business: "When I first talked to other family shareholders about the fact that it hurts the company when too many family members are involved operationally in the business, tomatoes were thrown at me, quite literally" (Leleux, Widz, & Corbetta, 2019, p. 7). As a result of the transformation on the family side, by 2018 only five cousins from the fourth generation were working in De Agostini Group, three in the legacy publishing business and two in DeA Capital. Marco remembers: "I was afraid we would either miss business opportunities or lose family unity. I am content to see that in fact we managed to revolutionize the business and repurpose the family at the same time" (Leleux, Widz, & Corbetta, 2019, p. 8).

The corporate governance had to evolve, too, to support the massive business transformation. For the first time in its history, during the times of the third generation, the CEO position was taken by the non-family CEO (initially it was a co-CEO position, held together with the family-CEO). Further, B&D Holding was established, with the family chairperson, four family members (one per every family branch), and two non-family directors. Third, the operations were grouped into sub-holdings, reflecting the business areas. The top-level corporate board at De Agostini SpA was created and was composed of nine members: family chairperson, four other family members in the role of vice-chairpersons, two non-family internal directors, and two non-family independent directors. Up until now, the corporate board's role is to steer and coordinate the sub-companies in the operational holding. But each subsidiary is also controlled by its own board on which key group people – for example, Marco Drago, the family chairman of the B&D Holding, together with the non-family CEO of the corporate holding – also have a seat. Strong emphasis is put on the autonomous role of subsidiaries, each is given a mandate to identify new growth opportunities. The fourth generation family member, Stefania, points out that the tight involvement in the supervision of the business gives the Drago–Boroli family "confidence that the business is being run for the future" (p. 8). Marco adds: "Shareholders have to enjoy the freedom to replace both the CEO and the general managers. This can be achieved only if these roles are held by non-family members. Future family CEOs will be an exception rather than the rule" (Leleux, Widz, & Corbetta, 2019, p. 8).

### 3.3.5 Parliamentary democracy as the governance behavior in families in business

The parliamentary democracy (quadrant 3) form of governance is characterized by decisions that are the outcome of the political process of debates among representatives of equally powerful dominant coalitions. This governance is found in *families in business* with relatively high complexity in family systems and low complexity in business systems, that is, in a multiple-family system characterized by ownership controlled between equally balanced multiple families and potentially non-family private or public owners. Parliamentary democracies are characterized by a relatively complex ownership structure with shareholder agreements, trusts, and ownership boards, which aim to formalize and balance the *hard power* of various owners' dominant coalitions. Although family ownership is generally linked to lower agency costs (Chrisman et al., 2004), ownership of one business by multiple families incurs "owner-owner agency conflicts" (La Porta et al., 1999). As a result, parliamentary democracies demonstrate a relatively more complex corporate and ownership governance compared to monarchies, in order to balance the power struggles between the various dominant coalitions. For example, executive boards and supervisory boards, which enjoy a significant presence of non-family executives, are strictly controlled by multiple families, sometimes in a direct way with an equal number of representatives from each family on every board.

The main power struggles are between the various groups of family owners, and thus the relational ties play a significant role in shaping the speed and direction of the power circulation. ***Obsolescence*** is the main mechanism of power in parliamentary democracies. Because the competition between the family owners activates the *family logic* nurturing family loyalty and generativity (Miller et al., 2011), it results in the inheritance of conflicts or alliances from one generation to the next. Therefore, governance equilibrium is steady and may last for a very long time, potentially more than a generation. The change of governance equilibrium is risky as it requires rebuilding the tested and proven foundation for cooperation of owners from multiple families and therefore has a potential to destroy the cooperation itself and, as such, the opportunity to derive any financial benefits from the commonly-owned business.

### 3.3.6 Parliamentary democracy – illustration with the Pictet[3] case

Pictet is an exemplary company that illustrates some of the distinctive governance features of a parliamentary democracy; it was founded in 1805 by three non-blood related partners, who formed the *scripte de societe*, called Candolle, Mallet & Cie, a Geneva-based private bank. One generation later, in 1841, the bank saw the entry of a partner with the last name Pictet. It was Edouard Pictet, who took over after one of the original founders, Jacob-Michel-Francois de Candolle, who, having no son to succeed him, searched for a talent within his broader family and turned to his wife's nephew. "Pictet" has been part of the firm's name ever since, and care has been taken to ensure that the ownership circle includes at least one person of that last name. In 2024, out of seven partners, two were from the Pictet family, that is, Marc Pictet and Francois Pictet. While qualified and competent Pictet family members enjoy privileged access to join the bank, an unwritten rule restricts a father and a son or two siblings from acting as bank partners at any given time. With a long history of some 220 years, employing over 5,000 people in 30 locations worldwide, and having some CHF 610 billion in assets under management (AUM), the core business remained the same and Geneva, Switzerland still serves as Pictet's center of the universe.

Over nine generations, Pictet's partnership model has evolved to find a way to exploit the advantages of family-type structures to the maximum, while at the same time reducing the associated risks – such as family conflicts – to the minimum. Run for two centuries in a legal form of a partnership of individuals, the recent international expansion, including the creation of foreign subsidiaries, plus an increasing need for a transparent banking system led to a change of a legal form to a corporation of "Banque Pictet & Cie SA" that started to publish its annual reports.

The center of Pictet governance is its ownership rules. First, the bank is owned and managed by ideally six to nine partners who must demonstrate professionalism and a human element, work effectively in harmony, and act as the firm's ambassadors with internal and external stakeholders. These partners come from three sources: the Pictet family, a small circle of families based in Geneva, and trusted employees of the bank. New partners are chosen every five to ten years to bring fresh perspectives and ensure the representation of three age groups: early 40s, between 45 and 55, and between 55 and 65, the official retirement age. This rule allows succession to take place on a continuous basis and is more frequent and institutionalized than the generational transitions found in family businesses. Upon retirement, the partners remain available to offer advice to their successors, may continue to look after selected clients, but are bought out at book value by new partners, with payment being made in stages. Joining partners are offered a loan from the existing partners to acquire the bank's shares, which is to be paid back over several years. The shares must not be sold to outsiders, though a 2006 amendment of rules allows a small amount of ownership to be extended to bank top executives, called "equity partners." Some 50 equity partners, about one percent of the bank workforce, were unanimously selected by main partners and offered a temporary ownership, which had to be sold back to the main partners once an equity partner left the bank. Finally, the bank also runs a charitable foundation, which receives a significant amount of the annual profit, holds some of the bank's equity capital, and in which former and current partners are expected to be active.

The second governance rule relates to the equality of all partners, no matter if they are family members or not. As such, there is a strong culture of personal communication; discussions are encouraged, documented, and institutionalized through regular morning meetings of partners. Partners view themselves as custodians of the wealth that has to be handed over to next generations and prioritize the longevity of the enterprise. Decisions are based on consensus, and there is no formalized voting system used. When there is a difference of opinion, the senior partner takes the role of a coordinator, seeking to find balance between opposing forces. This role is seen more as "primus inter pares" rather than a chairperson of partners' meetings.

There are very few other governing bodies at Pictet. One of them is the recently created group executive committee, seen as a platform for the partners to collaborate with the heads of the business functions such as risk, finance, HR, or technology and communication. There are regular meetings of the core partners' committee with "equity partners," who are expected to help determine the strategic direction of the Pictet Group. Core partners are still lifting the heavy weight when it comes to the operational management of the bank, as the former senior partner, Ivan Pictet, explains: "We are not actually a family business, but rather a family-run business" (Groth & Simon, 2022, p. 5).

### 3.3.7 Federation as the governance behavior in enterprising families

The federation (quadrant 4) form of governance is characterized by a high degree of sovereignty of entities, which together form a larger united entity, and which submit themselves to central (federal) institutions in certain aspects, negotiated in a process of debate among representatives of various dominant coalitions. This governance form is well-suited for *enterprising families* wherein ownership is balanced between multiple families and may extend to other private or public equity owners. The business system is characterized by multiple entities often in unrelated industries and constantly evolving portfolio of businesses.

Federations are characterized by an extremely complex governance structure, with an aim to balance the powers of various dominant coalitions formed by groups of owners and executives and to reduce the agency costs between multiple principals and multiple agents. In federations, power constitutes a *mix of hard and soft power* and circulates in multiple directions driven by both *obsolescence* and *contestation*. Next to classic measures that reduce the agency costs, such as extending ownership to top executives, other uncommon governance solutions are implemented. For example, Jebsen & Jessen Family Enterprise's owning families divided the ownership of their overall portfolio in such a way that each family is a major shareholder in one entity (e.g., the Jebsen family in Jebsen & Co and the Jessen family in Jebsen & Jessen Group), and an equal shareholder in all other entities (Table 10.1). That gives the respective family the position of a monarch within its respective "center of contestation" and at the same time the position of the parliamentary democrat in the shared "political center."

In federations, the family ownership dominant coalitions are guided by the *family logic* within its own ownership circle and by *entrepreneurial logic* in the wider family enterprise systems. That is why the governance equilibrium balances between stability – ensured by the steady, path-dependent foundations of ownership governance – and fluctuations – reflecting the dynamism of the business portfolio. The stability of governance architecture and processes is supported by multiple "soft" elements of governance, such as the utmost ability to build *enduring entrepreneurial partnerships* with other family owners, to *reshape the portfolio of businesses*, achieve harmony among *multiple families*, agree on long-term financial and non-financial goals, and have *confidence* that family leaders and the federation form of governance will ensure the growth and longevity of the family enterprise systems.

### 3.3.8 Federation – illustration with the Jebsen & Jessen Family Enterprise[4] case

Jebsen & Jessen Family Enterprise is an exemplary family business that illustrates some of the distinctive governance features of a federation. It was founded in 1895 as Jebsen & Co. – a trading company – when Jacob Jebsen and Heinrich Jessen, who later became brothers-in-law, left their home waters of Aabenraa in modern-day Denmark and established themselves as merchants in Hong Kong. The trading house initially commercialized tobacco, ginger, oils, cotton, and satin but soon afterward expanded its Jebsen-Jessen partnership ethos to further, purely business, partnerships. For example, in 1897 to BASF, the German chemicals giant, to trade indigo. In 1898, the company established its first joint venture in China to sell cement, nails, ironware, and glass. From those modest beginnings, a powerful group – Jebsen & Jessen Family Enterprise – emerged, which is a true federation of businesses, with flat organization and decision-making structures that aim to respond to the region's entrepreneurial growth momentum, and, interestingly, with no overall holding company. "Our structure is tailor-made. The independently managed companies are local companies with local partners and local co-investors that enjoy maximum flexibility in this loose structure" (Leleux & Widz, 2017, p. 7), explains Hans Michael Jebsen, the third generation family owner and a direct descendant of one of the founders, Jacob Jebsen. All business entities are bound by a set of strong values – trust, entrepreneurship, prudence, commitment, and partnership. Cumulatiely they employ over 7,000 people and consist of many legal entities organized around four principal business entities, and :

- Jebsen & Co., headquartered in Hong Kong, primarily owned by Hans Michael Jebsen, the grandson of Jacob Jebsen, spans many companies mainly across various premium consumer and retail industries. For example, Jebsen & Co.'s own brand, Blue Girl, is the number one beer in Hong Kong. J-Select is a chain of retail stores. Jebsen & Co. is Porsche's largest car dealer globally.
- Jebsen & Jessen Group, headquartered in Singapore, primarily owned by Heinrich Jessen, the grandson and the eponym of Heinrich Jessen, the second firm co-founder, spans many industrial and engineered products, such as industrial cranes, cable technology (as a joint venture with Lapp Group, which creates JJ-Lapp), chemical and life science ingredients, packaging made of materials such as foam, paper pulp, wood, and PET, or technological products and services such as pumps and scientific equipment for turf and irrigation.
- Jebsen & Jessen Hamburg, the current global trading house, headquartered in Hamburg, Germany, equally owned by Hans Michael Jebsen and Heinrich Jessen, the third-generation principal family owners from both families.
- GMA Garnet – the world leader in mining, processing, distributing and recycling of industrial garnet – headquartered in Perth, Australia, which is primarily owned by Hans Michael Jebsen and Heinrich Jessen, who both hold equal stakes.

In order to balance the two families' ownership and to navigate the ever-fluctuating portfolio of businesses, the Jebsen and Jessen families have established some intriguing governance principles. First and foremost is the founding principle of a "principal shareholder" for each family, based on the "*one captain–one ship*" mentality, that is, full control of one business entity by one principal shareholder. As such, two principal third-generation shareholders, Hans Michael Jebsen and Heinrich Jessen, are the majority shareholders in their respective family businesses; that is, Hans Michael Jebsen is the principal shareholder in Jebsen & Co. and Heinrich Jessen is the principal shareholder in Jebsen & Jessen Group. For the other entities, the "*hand in glove leadership*" principle with equal cross-shareholdings and consensus-based decision-making is applied. These principles have helped to maintain the closeness as well as checks and balances between the two families for over 130 years: "We are each other's executors of wills and trusted partners" (Leleux & Widz, 2017, p. 7) notes Hans Michael Jebsen.

With the aim of aligning the goals of managers and owners, ownership is temporarily extended to the managing directors of the business entities, just like the captains who not only navigated the ships but also – according to time-tested rules – often had to own part of the ship or cargo they transported. Upon retirement or leaving the firm, managing directors sell the shares back to principal family shareholders, thereby guaranteeing the sustainability of family ownership.

A further governance principle is the guarantee of the utmost independence of each business within Jebsen & Jessen Family Enterprise's portfolio. That extends also to lack of overall holding and governance structures, as Heinrich Jessen explains: "Just like we don't have a structure above the four business groupings, we also do not have a holding structure from the board of directors' perspective" (Leleux & Widz, 2017, p. 8). The principal family owners steer the family enterprise through their positions on the boards of all the companies, which, next to the two of them, are composed of non-family members, and include dependent and independent directors. "We meet informally all the time and formally at the board meetings of the different businesses in the Jebsen & Jessen portfolio" (Leleux & Widz, 2017, p. 8), adds Heinrich.

The next governance principle is that only one person from each family can become a principal shareholder. As such, there are only two *principal family shareholders* in the Jebsen & Jessen Family Enterprise: Hans Michael Jebsen and Heinrich Jessen. Shares are not to be inherited and can be bought only if the successor works in the business, and that person has to be accepted by all other (also non-family) shareholders. The shares are acquired from the previous generation owner, and it can take long years to repay the previous principal family shareholder. It took Heinrich over 15 years to pay off his shares to his father. Other family members who want to join the business as directors and shareholders (but not the principal family shareholder) have to buy their shares from their family's principal shareholder. If they wish to exit the business, these shares have to be sold back to the principal shareholder.

The final governance rule is the low dividend appetite of shareholders and an absence of entitlement in the family. "We live the idea of putting the money back into the business" (Leleux & Widz, 2017, p. 9), explains Heinrich. The Jebsen and the Jessen family members can profit from the family wealth through various foundations, run separately by each family, which support those who are in medical need, want to pursue an education, or simply buy a house. The sustainability of this solution is guaranteed through the purchasing mechanism as the retiring family principal shareholders are compensated for their shares by the incoming successors and thus can fuel the foundations with these funds.

## 3.4 Propositions

Building further on this theorizing, the anecdotal evidence coming from the observations of the exemplary family businesses, as well as reaching to the power circulation theory and the broader family business literature stream, we suggest the following four propositions around the functions, dynamic reconfigurations and the goals of governance in the family enterprise systems.

### 3.4.1 Function of governance: power circulation and power tunneling

We have thus distinguished between simple and complex family and business systems, and theorized that power circulates between various actors in these systems. Naturally, the more complex the system, the more complex the power circulation routes would be. As a consequence, there will be a higher need to *channel the power* – i.e., to regulate it so that it serves the owners in the best possible way – in the systems characterized by higher levels of complexity. The need to channel the power would inevitably be reflected in the governance architecture and processes. That is, high complexity in both family and business systems creates more avenues for power to circulate, requiring governance architecture and processes that can channel this power towards organizational goals and family aspirations. We have illustrated that the federation form of governance enables such channeling of power. Complex business systems can be managed with a parliamentary form of governance, while complex family systems need an empire form of governance. A monarch governance form suffices for simpler governance systems. Hence it follows:

> *Proposition 1:* Complexity in governance systems is directly related to the complexity in family ownership and business systems.

### 3.4.2 The dynamic view to family business governance – the configuration approach

The family business field has long observed that the family enterprise systems are often a result of an evolution (i.e., a family business becomes a family enterprise, and families in business become enterprising families). Several early taxonomies included time as an important variable, distinguishing between earlier and later family firm types. For example, Ward (1987) differentiated between family firm's early, middle, and late life phases, Gersick et al. (1999) discussed a family firm's life stages, and Davis et al. (1997) proposed the life cycles of a controlling owner company, sibling partnership, and then cousin consortium. The power circulation theory offers a meaningful way to extend the current theorizing on the dynamic view of the development of a family business Namely, it offers the notion that *the periods of political stability* are only transitory states in between the periods characterized by the struggle for power (Ocasio, 1994). Therefore, power circulation can be seen as a process that accelerates (or hinders) the evolution of governance systems over time as the nature of family involvement and the scope of the enterprise changes. That is, the power circulation serves as the answer why some families develop more complex corporate governance (to tunnel the power among and in between many businesses that were added to the family business portfolio) or more complex family ownership governance (to tunnel the power among and in between further significant owners of the common business or business portfolio). With the evolution of intensity and density of the power circulation routes and power tunneling, the original family business would display different governance behavior; hence, it would evolve from the monarchy to other types of family business governance systems. Therefore:

> *Proposition 2:* Over time, as the complexity in the business (portfolio) and the complexity in the family dominant coalitions increases, many of the family businesses would evolve away from the monarchy type of governance (quadrant 1) to arrive at/through empire-type of governance (quadrant 2), at/through parliamentary democracy type of governance (quadrant 3) to the federation-type of governance (quadrant 4).

### 3.4.3 From a simple to a complex family dominant coalition – the goals perspective

*Socioemotional wealth* (SEW), a concept that was originally introduced (Gómez-Mejía et al., 2007) as an extension to the behavioral agency model (BAM), and which has the potential of becoming a dominant paradigm in the field of family firms (Berrone et al., 2012), is built around the notion of the dominant family principal, who has a supreme influence over the firm's choices (Cennamo et al., 2012). If for the dominant coalition the family firm "constitutes a source of family income, security and pride, present and future career opportunities for family members, and a bastion for family reputation in the community" (Le Breton-Miller & Miller, 2008, pp. 43–44), these non-economic goals, cumulatively named "non-financial utilities" or "affective endowments" or *"socioemotional wealth"* (Gómez-Mejía et al., 2011; Gómez-Mejía et al., 2007; Berrone et al., 2012) may become the primary reference point in the decision-making process.

On the other hand, power circulation theory suggests that any decision is the outcome of power negotiation. Therefore, the less complex the dominant family coalition, the less intense and diverse the power circulation routes, and the less negotiation is necessary to reach a consensus. It is because less effort needs to be put into the power tunneling to align the family owners. Both SEW and the power circulation theory point towards the same direction: in systems with a homogeneous dominant family coalition, there shall be a predominance of a family logic, of a high survivability capital (Sirmon & Hitt, 2003) for the (legacy) business, which serves an important function for the family system, and of non-financial goals keeping the system together.

However, there is an important difference between the mechanisms of SEW and power circulation theory in relation to the governance of a family business. The former assumes that non-financial goals dictate the governance structure, which is seen as a system through which the desired goals must be achieved (that is, governance structure is a consequence of SEW and serves to achieve SEW). The latter explains the "*whys*" of the governance behavior (that is, governance behavior is a consequence of power circulation, and under some circumstances or for some dominant coalitions, SEW may or may not be the primary reference point). Noticing these differences is important, because in family enterprise systems with a more complex dominant coalitions, there is a larger probability of heterogeneous goals, both financial and non-financial. According to the power circulation theory, there is a need for more mechanisms to tunnel the power and hence also more resources necessary to reach a conclusion about any goals, including the more difficult to capture, and hence less tangible SEW goals. As a result, in more complex systems power mechanisms and resources would be directed towards more tangible and easier to capture goals, i.e. financial goals. As such, these are the financial goals and financial performance that keeps the complex system together, and the entrepreneurial logic prevails. Therefore:

> *Proposition 3:* Family businesses with less complex family dominant coalition, that is, monarchy and empire, are more aligned on *non-financial goals* (SEW) as compared to family businesses with more complex family dominant coalitions, that is, parliamentary democracy and federation.

> *Proposition 4:* Family businesses with more complex family dominant coalitions, that is, parliamentary democracy and federation, are more aligned on *financial goals* compared to the family businesses with less complex family dominant coalition, that is, monarchy and empire.

# 4. CONTRIBUTIONS AND LIMITATIONS

## 4.1 Contributions

With our research, we make several contributions to the family business literature stream.

First, we extend the understanding of what constitutes a family business. In particular, we extend the three-circle model (Taguiri & Davis, 1992) and the cluster model (Michael-Tsabari et al., 2014) to complex family enterprise systems, in response to John Davis' recognition that "the three-circle model doesn't adequately diagram the situation of a multi-family business" (Sharma, 2018a, p. 3) and "the three-circle model is not designed to answer all important questions in our field" (Sharma, 2018b, p. 3). We extend the scope of heterogeneity of family businesses by proposing the typology of complex family enterprise systems that captures the complexity in the family and the business systems, that is, (i) *family business* – low complexity in family and business systems, (ii) *family enterprise* – low complexity in the family system, high complexity in the business system, (iii) *families in business* – high complexity in family system, low complexity in business systems, and (iv) *enterprising families* – high complexity in family and business system.

Second, we explore the *definition of a family business by behavior* (Chua et al., 1999). In particular, we focus on the less studied part of the *definition of a family* and go beyond the kinship, blood-, and marriage-ties, towards a quasi-family, a partly negotiated and fluid conception of a "family" (Karra et al., 2006), based on the "involvement essence" (Chrisman et al., 2005) of a small number of families or other members, who create the dominant coalition (Chua et al., 1999) within the family enterprise systems.

Third, we contribute to the definition of *governance* in family business (Goldbart & DeFuria, 2009) by placing the important aspect of the behavioral theory of the firm (Cyert & March, 1963) – *dominant coalitions* – at the core of our analysis. Further, we "equip" dominant coalitions in family businesses with the *power* to influence outcomes of governance. Governance, which is defined as "strategic goals [which] are set, key relationships [which] are maintained, the health of the family [which] is safeguarded, accountability [which] is maintained, and achievement and performance [which] are recognized" (Goldbart & DeFuria, 2009, p. 7). Because power is a social process (Zaleznik & Kets de Vries, 1975), we theorize that the application of power by dominant coalitions is fundamentally a *behavior* that includes elements such as building coalitions and negotiating to retain that very power. As such, power becomes crucial for governance as it shapes the outcomes of that very same governance. For example, we theorize that in family businesses characterized by a complex family system, more power would be exercised on the family side, resulting in more complex family governance as compared to corporate governance, which would remain less complex (refer to Proposition 1). Further, conceptualizing power as the mechanism that shapes governance, we reach out to constructs from political science and propose a typology of family business governance by behavior: (i) a *monarchy*, (ii) an *empire*, (iii) a *parliamentary democracy*, and (iv) a *federation*, which all exhibit distinctive behaviors in the frame of their governance architecture and processes (refer to Proposition 1).

We also extend the *dynamic view of the development of a family business*. Using insights from the configuration approach (Nordqvist et al., 2014), we investigate the dynamic evolution of family business governance systems, which may have the potential to move from less complex to more complex governance systems as their complexity in the family system and the business systems increases (refer to Proposition 2). By doing this, we go beyond the controlling owner, sibling partnership, cousin consortium (Davis et al., 1997) model and other models similar to this, which describe the increasing complexity of a family business... but only in the time frame of *consecutive generations of the same family* coming to a picture of a *one family busienss* as it gets older and older over time.

Finally, we contribute to the debate about *financial and non-financial goals*, that is, socioemotional wealth (Gómez-Mejía et al., 2014; Berrone et al., 2012), as the set of possible outcomes of family business governance by theorizing that the complexity of a dominant coalition has an influence – via the power exercised on the decisions – on the financial versus non-financial priorities of the complex family business systems (refer to Propositions 3 and 4).

## 4.2 Limitations and Further Research

Despite these contributions, our theorizing has some limitations. The typology we propose presents four main categories of family business governance by behavior. Naturally, any observed behavior shall be understood as a continuum or a spectrum rather than a categorical variable. That is why, in the body of this chapter, apart from the four illustrative case studies, we also named three examples of "families in business," which show a remarkable spectrum of further nuanced complexities. In particular, we brought an example of Villeroy & Boch, which is a partnership of two families in one porcelain business: the Villeroy family and the Boch family. Further, we brought an example of the Kikkoman Corporation, the world's largest producer of shoyu, the Japanese-style soy sauce. The majority stake of Kikkoman is in the hands of six families, and there are also a few institutional investors who hold minority stakes – The Master Trust Bank of Japan, Japan Trustee Services Bank, and Oriental Land Company. The examples of both Kikkoman Corporation and Pictet demonstrate that the dominant coalition in family businesses is not necessary restricted to one family or a "small number of families" (Chua et al., 1999, p. 25) but that it could also be a mix of a small number of family members and other non-blood related partners, an aspect which is worth a further investigation.

In order to derive insights from our illustrative observations, we decided to reach out to the concept of *temporal orientation* in family businesses, that is, "the temporal frame that owners, managers, advisors, and researchers alike assume in their choices and analyses" (Sharma et al., 2014, p. 10). In other words, we analyzed the governance of the described four cases of family businesses as they are here and now, assuming that the current governance system serves the current needs of the owners in the best way. As such, our research does not integrate the analysis of the precise features of the evolution of governance systems, that is, it does not answer the question of whether the evolution is inevitable, natural, and an automatic process every family business would go through. Also, it does not address the broader question of the timelines of the evolutions. For example, we did not strive to answer the question of whether the evolution to a more complex governance would take place when the family system becomes more complex, driven by an increasing number of generations or family shareholders, and so on. Similarly, we did not strive to answer the question of whether the evolution to a more complex governance would take place if the business system becomes more complex, driven by an increasing level of complexity measured with a certain number of business entities or companies in the business portfolio. Future research should focus on the more dynamic view of governance by behavior, and, in longitudinal studies, analyze how family businesses arrive at a certain governance type, how long they stay in the status quo of that particular governance, if and when they move to a more complex stage of governance by behavior, as well as what hinders or fosters this evolution.

Drawing on the application of contingency theory in the analysis of governance in privately owned companies (Corbetta & Salvato, 2004; Huse, 2000), we investigated the fit of the governance model with the *internal* context of a family business system, that is, internal complexities of a family system and internal complexities of the business system. However, future research could extend our research by focusing on the context *exogenous* to this system, such as technological disruptions, societal expectations, geopolitical situation, or the institutional power of governments, in order to understand whether there are any boundary conditions of the governance typology we proposed.

Finally, our propositions point towards a positive nature of the relationship of the proposed variables. In particular, complexity of governance shows a positive relationship with the complexity in the family and business systems in Proposition 1; increasing complexity in the family and business systems shows a positive relationship with the evolutions of governance systems to more complex ones in Proposition 2; complexity in the family and business systems shows a positive relationship between the predominant set of goals that the governance system pursues in Proposition 3 and Proposition 4. Further research could potentially investigate the more detailed nature of these relationships and test the hypotheses to prove if the relationships are linear, exponential, or perhaps diminishing.

## NOTES

1. The Dachser illustration is based on the following two case studies. First, Leleux, B. & Widz, M. (2021a). *Dachser: Intelligent Logistics (A)*. IMD-7–2313. Harvard Business Publishing: https://hbsp.harvard.edu/product/IM1193-PDF-ENG; and second, Leleux, B. & Widz, M. (2021b). *Dachser (B): Putting Intelligent Logistics to the Test (B)*. MD-7–2314. Harvard Business Publishing: https://hbsp.harvard.edu/product/IM1194-PDF-ENG. For ease of reading, the references are removed from this sub-chapter.
2. The De Agostini illustration is based on the following case study. Leleux, B., Widz, M., Corbetta, G. (2019). *De Agostini: Repurposing the Business and the Family*. IMD-7–2072. Harvard Business Publishing: https://hbsp.harvard.edu/product/IM1021-PDF-ENG. For ease of reading, the references are removed from this sub-chapter.
3. The Pictet illustration is based on the following case study. Groth, T. & Simon, F. B. (2022). *The Pictet Model. A Company that Continuously Reinvents its Family Ownership*. Witten Institute for Family Business & the Henokiens: https://www.henokiens.com/userfiles/file/Case_study_Pictet_EN.pdf. For ease of reading, the references are removed from this sub-chapter.
4. The Jebsen & Jessen Family Enterprise illustration is based on the following case study and book chapter. The case study: Leleux, B., Widz, M. (2017). *Jebsen & Jessen Family Enterprise: A Hong From the Cold*. IMD-7–1859. Harvard Business Publishing: https://hbsp.harvard.edu/product/IMD922-PDF-ENG. The book chapter: Widz, M., & Farber, V. (2021). GMA Garnets circular economy: Jebsen Jessen's leadership in environmental sustainability. In *Pioneering Family Firms' Sustainable Development Strategies* (pp. 252–276). Edward Elgar Publishing. For ease of reading, the references are removed from this sub-chapter.

## REFERENCES

Ben-Shahar, D., Carmeli, A., Sulganik, E., & Weiss, D. (2023). Power and dominant coalitions in family business. *Academy of Management Review*, 48(3), 530–555.

Berrone, P., Cruz, C., & Gómez-Mejía, L. R. (2012). Socioemotional wealth in family firms: Theoretical dimensions, assessment approaches, and agenda for future research. *Family Business Review*, 25(3), 258–279.

Cennamo, C., Berrone, P., Cruz, C., & Gómez-Mejía, L. R. (2012). Socioemotional wealth and proactive stakeholder engagement: Why family-controlled firms care more about their stakeholders. *Entrepreneurship Theory and Practice*, 36(6), 1153–1173.

Cheng, J., Au, K., Widz, M., & Marshall, J. (2022). The governance marathon: Dynamic durability in entrepreneurial families amid disruptions. *FFI Research Report*. https://digital.ffi.org/pdf/ffi_the_governance_marathon_report.pdf

Chrisman, J. J., Chua, J. H., Le Breton-Miller, I., Miller, D., & Steier, L. P. (2018). Governance mechanisms and family firms. *Entrepreneurship Theory and Practice*, 42(2), 171–186.

Chrisman, J. J., Chua, J. H., & Litz, R. (2004). Comparing the agency costs of family and nonfamily firms: Conceptual issues and exploratory evidence. *Entrepreneurship Theory and Practice*, 28(4), 335–354.

Chrisman, J. J., Chua, J. H., & Sharma, P. (2005). Trends and directions in the development of a strategic management theory of the family firm. *Entrepreneurship Theory and Practice*, 29(5), 555–576.

Chua, J. H., Chrisman, J. J., & Sharma, P. (1999). Defining the family business by behavior. *Entrepreneurship Theory and Practice*, 23(4), 19–39.

Combs, J. G., Ketchen Jr, D. J., Perryman, A. A., & Donahue, M. S. (2007). The moderating effect of CEO power on the board composition–firm performance relationship. *Journal of Management Studies*, 44(8), 1299–1323.

Corbetta, G., & Salvato, C. (2004). The board of directors in family firms: One size fits all? *Family Business Review*, 17(2), 119–134.

Cyert, R. M., & March, J. G. (1963). *A behavioral theory of the firm*. Englewood Cliffs, NJ: Prentice Hall.

Daspit, J. J., Chrisman, J. J., Sharma, P., Pearson, A. W., & Mahto, R. V. (2018). Governance as a source of family firm heterogeneity. *Journal of Business Research*, 84, 293–300.

Davis, J. A., Hampton, M. M., & Lansberg, I. (1997). *Generation to generation: Life cycles of the family business*. Brighton, MA: Harvard Business Publishing.

De Massis, A., Kotlar, J., & Manelli, L. (2021). Family firms, family boundary organizations, and the family-related organizational ecosystem. *Family Business Review*, 34(4), 350–364.

Debicki, B. J., Matherne III, C. F., Kellermanns, F. W., & Chrisman, J. J. (2009). Family business research in the new millennium: An overview of the who, the where, the what, and the why. *Family Business Review*, *22*(2), 151–166.

Dieleman, M. (2018). 4 types of family businesses you'll see in Asia and how to govern each effectively. Forbes. https://www.forbes.com/sites/nusbusinessschool/2018/05/25/4-types-of-family-businesses-youll-see-in-asia-and-how-to-govern-each-effectively/#58d434e4659f

Easton, D. (1985). Political science in the United States: Past and present. *International Political Science Review*, 6(1), 133–152.

Finkelstein, S. (1992). Power in top management teams: Dimensions, measurement, and validation. *Academy of Management Journal*, 35(3), 505–538.

Finkelstein, S., & D'aveni, R. A. (1994). CEO duality as a double-edged sword: How boards of directors balance entrenchment avoidance and unity of command. *Academy of Management Journal*, 37(5), 1079–1108.

Gersick, K. E., Davis, J., McCollom Hampton, M., & Lansberg, I. (1997). *Generation to generation: Lifecycles of the family business*. Boston, MA: Harvard Business School Press.

Gersick, K. E., & Feliu, N. (2014). Governing the family enterprise: Practices, performance, and research. In L. Melin, M. Nordqvist & P. Sharma (eds), *The SAGE handbook of family business*, 196–225. Thousand Oaks, CA: Sage.

Gersick, K. E., Lansberg, I., Desjardins, M., & Dunn, B. (1999). Stages and transitions: Managing change in the family business. *Family Business Review*, 12(4), 287–297.

Goldbart, S., & DeFuria, J. (2009). Money and meaning: Implementation of effective family governance structures. *Journal of Practical Estate Planning*, 11(6), 7–9.

Gómez-Mejía, L. R., Campbell, J. T., Martin, G., Hoskisson, R. E., Makri, M., & Sirmon, D. G. (2014). Socioemotional wealth as a mixed gamble: Revisiting family firm R&D investments with the behavioral agency model. *Entrepreneurship Theory and Practice*, 38(6), 1351–1374.

Gómez-Mejía, L. R., Cruz, C., Berrone, P., & De Castro, J. (2011). The bind that ties: Socioemotional wealth preservation in family firms. *The Academy of Management Annals*, 5(1), 653–707.

Gómez-Mejía, L. R., Takacs-Haynes, K., Nunez-Nickel, M., Jacobson, K. J., & Moyano-Fuentes, J. (2007). Socioemotional wealth and business risks in family-controlled firms: Evidence from Spanish olive oil mills. *Administrative Science Quarterly*, 52(1), 106–137.

Groth, T. & Simon, F. B. (2022). *The Pictet model: A company that continuously reinvents its family ownership.* Witten Institute for Family Business & the Henokiens. https://www.henokiens.com/userfiles/file/Case_study_Pictet_EN.pdf

Huse, M. (2000). Boards of directors in SMEs: A review and research agenda. *Entrepreneurship and Regional Development*, 12(4), 271–290.

Jara-Bertin, M., López-Iturriaga, F. J., & López-de-Foronda, Ó. (2008). The contest to the control in European family firms: How other shareholders affect firm value. *Corporate Governance: An International Review*, 16(3), 146–159.

Jensen, M., & Meckling, W. (1976). Theory of the firm: Managerial behavior, agency costs and ownership structure. *Journal of Financial Economics*, 3(4), 305–360.

Karra, N., Tracey, P., & Phillips, N. (2006). Altruism and agency in the family firm: Exploring the role of family, kinship, and ethnicity. *Entrepreneurship Theory and Practice*, 30(6), 861–877.

La Porta, R., Lopez-de-Silanes, E., & Shleifer, A. (1999). Corporate ownership around the world. *Journal of Finance*, 54(2), 471–517.

Lane, S., Astrachan, J., Keyt, A., & McMillan, K. (2006). Guidelines for family business boards of directors. *Family Business Review*, 19(2), 147–167.

Le Breton-Miller, I., & Miller, D. (2008). To grow or to harvest? Governance, strategy and performance in family and lone founder firms. *Journal of Strategy and Management*, 1(1), 41–56.

Leleux, B., & Widz, M. (2017). *Jebsen & Jessen family enterprise: A Hong from the cold.* IMD-7–1859. Brighton, MA: Harvard Business Publishing. https://hbsp.harvard.edu/product/IMD922-PDF-ENG

Leleux, B., Widz, M., & Corbetta, G. (2019). *De Agostini: Repurposing the business & the family.* IMD-7–2072. Brighton, MA: Harvard Business Publishing. https://hbsp.harvard.edu/product/IM1021-PDF-ENG

Leleux, B., & Widz, M. (2021a). *Dachser: Intelligent logistics (A).* IMD-7–2313. Brighton, MA: Harvard Business Publishing. https://hbsp.harvard.edu/product/IM1193-PDF-ENG

Leleux, B., & Widz, M. (2021b). *Dachser (B): Putting Intelligent Logistics to the Test (B).* MD-7–2314. Brighton, MA: Harvard Business Publishing. https://hbsp.harvard.edu/product/IM1194-PDF-ENG

Michael-Tsabari, N. (2023). "All my firms?" Managing SEW affective endowments in business family portfolios. In M. Carney & M. Dieleman (eds), *Handbook of Business Families* (pp. 163–185). Berlin: Walter De Gruyter GmbH.

Michael-Tsabari, N., Labaki, R., & Zachary, R. K. (2014). The family firm's entrepreneurial behavior over generations. *Family Business Review*, 27(2), 161–185.

Miller, D. (1991). Stale in the saddle: CEO tenure and the match between organization and environment. *Management Science*, 37(1), 34–52.

Miller, D., Le Breton-Miller, I., & Lester, R. H. (2011). Family and lone founder ownership and strategic behavior: Social context, identity, and institutional logics. *Journal of Management Studies*, 48(1), 1–25.

Nordqvist, M., Sharma, P., & Chirico, F. (2014). Family firm heterogeneity and governance: A configuration approach. *Journal of Small Business Management*, 52(2), 192–209.

Ocasio, W. (1994). Political dynamics and the circulation of power: CEO succession in US industrial corporations, 1960–1990. *Administrative Science Quarterly*, 39(2), 285–312.

Pfeffer, J. (1981). *Power in organizations*. Marshfield, MA: Pitman.

Pfeffer, J. (1992). Understanding power in organizations. *California Management Review*, 34(2), 29–50.

Rautiainen, M., Parada, M. J., Pihkala, T., Akhter, N., Cruz, A. D., & Mukherjee, K. (eds) (2023). *The Palgrave handbook of managing family business groups*. Cham: Palgrave Macmillan.

Sharma, P. (2018a). Celebrating the 40th anniversary of the three-circle model: An interview with John Davis. *FFI Practitioner*. https://digital.ffi.org/pdf/wednesday-edition/june-06/40th-anniversary-of-3-circle-model.pdf

Sharma, P. (2018b). The future of the three-circle model: A conversation between Pramodita Sharma and John Davis. *FFI Practitioner*. https://digital.ffi.org/pdf/wednesday-edition/june-13/the-future-of-the-three-circle-model-6-13–18.pdf

Sharma, P., Salvato, C., & Reay, T. (2014). Temporal dimensions of family enterprise research. *Family Business Review*, *27*(1), 10–19.

Shen, W. & Cannella, A. A. (2002). Revisiting the performance consequences of CEO succession: The impacts of successor type, post-succession senior executive turnover, and departing CEO tenure. *Academy of Management Journal*, 45, 717–734.

Sirmon, D. G., & Hitt, M. A. (2003). Managing resources: Linking unique resources, management, and wealth creation in family firms. *Entrepreneurship Theory and Practice*, 27(4), 339–358.

Suess, J. (2014). Family governance: Literature review and the development of a conceptual model. *Journal of Family Business Strategy*, 5(2), 138–155.

Taguiri, R., & Davis, J. A. (1992). On the goals of successful family companies. *Family Business Review*, 5(1), 43–62.

Ward, J. L. (1987). *Keeping the family business healthy*. San Francisco, CA: Jossy-Bass.

Ward, J. L. (1991). *Creating effective boards for private enterprises: Meeting the challenges of continuity and competition*. San Francisco, CA: Jossey-Bass.

Widz, M., & Farber, V. (2021). GMA Garnets circular economy: Jebsen Jessens leadership in environmental sustainability. In P. Sharma & S. Sharma (eds), *Pioneering family firms' sustainable development strategies* (pp. 252–276). Cheltenham, UK and Northampton, MA, USA: Edward Elgar Publishing.

Widz, M., & Leleux, B. (2019). From single business to portfolio of businesses: When does the family business become a business family? *FFI Practitioner*. https://digital

.ffi.org/editions/from-single-business-to-portfolio-of-businesses-when-does-the-family-business-become-a-business-family

Widz, M., & Parada, M. J. (2022). From founder identity to family business group (FBG) meta-identity: Identity development in the journey from a founder's firm to an entrepreneurial family with a portfolio of businesses. In M. Rautiainen, M. J. Parada, T. Pihkala, N. Akhter, A. D. Cruz, & K. Mukherjee (eds), *The Palgrave handbook of managing family business groups* (pp. 587–615). Cham: Springer International Publishing.

Wright, M., & Kellermanns, F. W. (2011). Family firms: A research agenda and publication guide. *Journal of Family Business Strategy*, 2(4), 187–198.

Yu, A., Lumpkin, G. T., Sorenson, R. L., & Brigham, K. H. (2012). The landscape of family business outcomes: A summary and numerical taxonomy of dependent variables. *Family Business Review*, 25(1), 33–57.

Zaleznik, A., & Kets de Vries, M. F. (1975). *Power and the corporate mind*. Boston, MA: Houghton Mifflin.

Zellweger, T. M., Nason, R. S., & Nordqvist, M. (2012). From longevity of firms to transgenerational entrepreneurship of families: Introducing family entrepreneurial orientation. *Family Business Review*, 25(2), 136–155.

# 11. Brave communication as the key for successful family business succession

**Léa Zhe Wang and Séverine Mulliez**

## 1. INTRODUCTION

Family businesses are the most prevalent form of businesses in today's economy. In Europe, family-owned and family-controlled firms make up between 65% and 80% of all companies, accounting for more than 40% to 50% of all jobs (European Family Businesses, 2021). These businesses contribute significantly to the economy, representing about 70% to 90% of the GDP in various global regions, approximately €5 to €7 trillion in economic value, and 60% to 70% of private-sector employment, creating about 50% to 70% of all jobs in the past decade (La Porta, Lopez-de-Silanes, & Shleifer, 1999; Birdthistle & Hales, 2021). Family businesses possess numerous advantages over non-family businesses, including a long-term vision, a strong commitment to history and values, and a close relationship with employees, clients, and the local community (Miller & Le Breton-Miller, 2005; Danes, Stafford, Haynes, & Amarapurkar, 2009). These strengths often translate into a more stable and loyal workforce, better alignment with community interests, and a business approach that prioritizes sustainable growth over short-term gains (Ward, 2004).

Succession, as the hallmark of family businesses, determines the very longevity of these enterprises. The success of succession impacts not only the company but also the stability of the broader economy. Despite a myriad of contextual factors (firm size, industry, regional economic conditions, etc.), only about 30% of family businesses are successfully transferred to the second generation of the founding family owners. Furthermore, only 10–15% make it to the third generation (Stamm & Lubinski, 2011). This phenomenon is often encapsulated in the saying, "The first generation builds it, the second generation maintains it, and the third generation blows it" (Ward, 2011). The consequences of failed family business succession are significant. Family discord and brokenness often result from disputes over succession. Individual suffering, including stress and identity crises, can affect both the departing and incoming leaders. Business performance suffers due to instability and lack of clear leadership, and employee insecurity rises as workers fear for their jobs and the company's future (Miller, Steier, & Le Breton-Miller, 2003; Sharma, Chrisman, & Chua, 2003).

Family business succession represents a critical juncture laden with complexities, where challenges such as the predecessor's reluctance to relinquish control, trust deficits with the successor, the successor's lack of confidence, and pervasive family conflicts are frequently cited (De Massis, Chua, & Chrisman, 2008; Morris, Williams, & Nel, 1996). Central to these challenges are identity struggles, emotional attachments, and miscommunications, which fundamentally shape and complicate the dynamics of succession in family enterprises, often rendering it a taboo topic (Hubler, 1999; Lansberg, 1988).

Family businesses are distinctly characterized by their emotional undercurrents, which profoundly influence decision-making and relationship dynamics essential to succession planning (Bertschi-Michel, Kammerlander, & Strike, 2020; Shepherd, 2016; Stanley, 2010). Discussions around succession often navigate sensitive topics related to departure, control, trust, and change, making effective communication both essential and challenging (Handler, 1994; Levinson, 1971). Scholars have applied game theory to dissect the multifaceted motivations and interests involved in succession, highlighting the complexity of navigating differing agendas (Lansberg, 1988; Tsabari & Weiss, 2013). Effective communication during this phase necessitates bravery—the courage to confront emotional realities such as identity, fears, and aspirations (Hubler, 1999). It involves not only articulating one's feelings and needs but also actively listening to diverse perspectives, thus engaging in authentic and constructive dialogues. Successful family enterprises navigate these challenges by fostering strong familial bonds, nurturing shared values, and establishing robust governance structures (Miller & Le Breton-Miller, 2006; Le Breton-Miller, Miller, & Steier, 2004). Open and honest communication, grounded in mutual trust, emerges as a critical factor for sustaining family harmony and ensuring business longevity (Eddleston & Kellermanns, 2007; Deferne, Bertschi-Michel, & de Groote, 2022).

Indeed, prior studies on family firm succession often highlight the importance of open and honest communication throughout the process (De Massis et al., 2008; Leiß & Zehrer, 2018). Despite the growing scholarly interest in effective dialogue involving emotions in family firms (e.g., Björnberg & Nicholson, 2012; Shepherd, 2016), and the recognition that external mediators and advisors are beneficial in such interventions (Salvato & Corbetta, 2013; Strike, 2012), there is a notable lack of actionable insights and practical examples to inspire change within family stakeholders. Specifically, the effectiveness of specific communication skills and values for family stakeholders involved in the succession process remains underexplored. Therefore, this chapter aims to provide insights from both a review of the literature and practical interventions. We seek to draw attention from researchers, practitioners, and family business members to the importance of brave communication and the necessary skills and values that come with it, ensuring that succession occurs under optimal conditions with both long-term business prosperity and strengthened family unity.

As George Bernard Shaw said, "the single biggest problem in communication is the illusion that it has taken place." In the upcoming sections, we first delve into two foundational components essential for successful communication in family businesses: daring to express feelings and needs, and daring to listen actively to diverse perspectives. We emphasize the importance and relevance of these principles in family business succession communication and provide keys to exercising these skills. Secondly, we offer actionable insights for leaders and family members on integrating these principles into various governance frameworks.

Additionally, we present common feelings and needs that three key family stakeholders—predecessors, successors, and inactive family members (Venter, Van der Merwe, & Farrington, 2012) may experience, particularly during succession. Finally, we provide real-life scenarios illustrating the impact of effective versus ineffective communication on family business succession outcomes.

## 1.1 Family Business Cultures: The Dilemma

The dilemma in family businesses stems from their inherently emotional and relational nature, which demands open, frequent, and honest communication. Nevertheless, these businesses often exhibit hierarchical, secretive, and conflict-avoidant behaviors, leading to obscure and hidden communication. In this context, effective communication requires bravery, especially during times of uncertainty and high stakes.

Family business cultures, on the one hand, are often characterized by hierarchical decision-making and a pervasive climate of secrecy. Information within these businesses flows predominantly from the top down, with minimal input from other family members or non-family employees, fostering an environment where critical business information and succession plans are known only to a select few, often the incumbent leaders (Björnberg et al., 2012). The absence of regular family meetings or forums for discussing business matters is a common characteristic in these environments. Cabrera-Suárez, De Saá-Pérez, and García-Almeida (2001) highlight that such family businesses rarely hold structured family councils or meetings where succession planning can be openly discussed. Consequently, decisions about the business's future are often made informally and communicated sporadically, if at all, to the wider family and stakeholders, leading to feelings of exclusion and resentment among family members who are kept out of the loop. Such reactions are consistent with the well-established need to belong; when inclusion and recognition are threatened, negative affect and withdrawal increase (Baumeister & Leary, 1995). The lack of formal communication channels exacerbates internal conflicts and mistrust, contributing to a fragmented decision-making process.

Furthermore, the strong desire to preserve family harmony and socioemotional wealth — combined with the concentration of family wealth and decision-making power — often shapes behavior toward risk-aversion and the avoidance of difficult conversations (De Massis, Chua, & Chrisman, 2008; Hiebl, 2013). Besides, the hierarchical nature of these businesses and the long-term power dynamics can create a culture where family members feel financially dependent on the business and its reputation, inhibiting their willingness to voice opinions freely. Handler (1994) found that many family business leaders prefer to avoid discussing succession plans due to the emotional and potentially divisive nature of these discussions. This avoidance is compounded by cultural norms that discourage the open expression of emotions and disagreements, creating an environment where critical issues are left unaddressed until they become crises, and where difficult conversations about succession can become indefinitely deferred.

On the other hand, family businesses are uniquely charged with emotions, particularly during periods of succession, when the stakes are high, and uncertainty looms large. This emotional intensity stems from the intertwining of familial relationships and business interests, leading to a complex dynamic often fraught with tension (Lansberg, 1999). The succession process is not merely a transition of leadership but a period that can challenge long-standing family roles and expectations, often leading to anxiety and conflict (Handler, 1994). Family businesses also pursue high socioeconomic values that extend beyond mere economic gains to include the preservation of family legacy, reputation, and social capital (Kammerlander, 2021; Makó, Csizmadia, & Heidrich, 2018). These values necessitate open and healthy communication within the family to ensure that both business and personal goals are aligned and mutually reinforcing. However, professionalism and thorough documentation in business operations often leave little room for personal expression, as the demands of the business overshadow individual needs. Nevertheless, these personal needs and emotions do not vanish; they resurface in conversations and decision-making processes, often in irrational and emotionally charged ways, which can degrade relationships and the overall socioeconomic value of the family (Handler, 1994; Björnberg et al., 2012).

This chapter defines brave communication as the capacity of family stakeholders to express their feelings and needs vulnerably and listen actively to different perspectives. This aligns with Brown's (2012) argument that vulnerability is not a weakness but a form of courageous leadership — the willingness to be seen, to take emotional risks, and to show up without guarantees. Expressing feelings and needs vulnerably involves being open and honest about emotions and desires without fear of judgment or repercussion. Listening actively requires acknowledging and valuing different perspectives, fostering a respectful and supportive environment. By integrating these components into their communication practices, family business members can enhance emotional payoffs, family cohesion, and business longevity.

## 2. DARING TO EXPRESS FEELINGS AND NEEDS

### 2.1 Common Feelings and Needs Experienced by Key Family Members During Succession

This section outlines the common feelings and needs experienced by key family stakeholders during succession, including the predecessor, successor, and other family members. Research shows that the extent to which basic psychological needs are fulfilled—or frustrated—fundamentally shapes how people think, feel, and behave (Deci & Ryan, 2000; Rouse et al., 2020). For each role, we present both vulnerable feelings and corresponding psychological needs. Rather than providing an exhaustive literature review, we aim to use relatable language that family members can connect with and use to reflect on their own experiences. This non-exhaustive list (summarized in Figure 11.1) is based on interviews with over 50 family businesses and the authors' professional experiences in advising family enterprises. In line with our goal of fostering courageous communication—vulnerably sharing our feelings and needs, we focus purposefully on the challenging aspects often encountered during succession. Growing awareness and recognizing these internal struggles and needs is an essential first step in sharing them openly, thereby inviting understanding and support from others.

**For predecessors**

a. Vulnerable feelings

Fear of the unknown:

- *Lifestyle change*: Transitioning from active business involvement to retirement introduces significant lifestyle changes, often accompanied by apprehension about adjusting to a new routine.
- *Business uncertainty*: Doubts about the successor's decisions and the future trajectory of the business foster anxiety, as the predecessor worries whether the business will thrive without their leadership.

- *Financial insecurity*: Concerns about financial stability post-retirement add another layer of anxiety, especially if the business has been the primary source of income.

Sadness of letting go:

- *End of an era*: The emotional weight of closing a significant chapter in life can be overwhelming, particularly if there has been no formal acknowledgment or celebration of the accomplishments achieved during their tenure.
- *Feelings of abandonment*: Letting go of a company that one has built and nurtured over the years can lead to feelings of abandonment, both of the business and of the significant role it played in one's personal and professional life.
- *Unfulfilled visions*: There can be a sense of regret, especially if certain visions and projects remain unfulfilled during their leadership.

Identity struggle:

- *Loss of social status*: The fear of losing one's professional identity and status can be profound, encapsulated in the existential question, "Who am I if I'm no longer the chef?"
- *Loss of purpose*: The transition may bring about a profound sense of purposelessness, as predecessors grapple with redefining their roles and contributions outside of their business responsibilities.

b. Psychological needs

Need for reassurance:

- *Successor's capacities*: Confidence in the successor's abilities and readiness is crucial, as it reassures the predecessor about the continuity and future success of the business.
- *Favorable timing*: Ensuring that the timing of succession aligns with the company's and family's best interests helps mitigate uncertainties and fosters a sense of preparedness.
- *Value preservation*: Upholding the core values of the business provides comfort that the predecessor's legacy will endure.

Need for new purpose:

- *Role evolution*: Identifying new roles or responsibilities imbued with meaningful purpose is essential for predecessors to feel valuable and engaged post-succession. Maintaining symbolic attachment and celebrating the business's progress can offer significant emotional relief.

- *Passion pursuit*: Envisioning and preparing for a passionate personal project offers predecessors something to eagerly anticipate, instilling a sense of purpose, relevance, and vitality. This pursuit not only helps them feel useful and alive but also fosters a renewed enthusiasm for life.

Need for acknowledgment:

- *Commendation*: Formal acknowledgment of the predecessor's contributions, such as honoring their achievements and milestones, provides closure and celebrates their legacy.
- *Remembrance*: Ensuring that the predecessor's stories and foundational values are remembered and narrated reinforces their lasting impact on the business and the family.

**For successors**

a. Vulnerable feelings

Feelings of inadequacy:

- *Self-doubt*: Successors often grapple with self-doubt, questioning their ability to measure up to a historic and charismatic founder. They may wonder, "How can I establish my reputation after such a leader? Am I capable? Am I legitimate? Am I good enough?"
- *Fear of failure*: There is a pervasive fear of failure, compounded by the external pressures of not wanting to disappoint shareholders and employees. The high expectations and scrutiny can exacerbate these feelings, leading sometimes to conventional and more compliant behavior as successors are afraid of making a wrong move.

Feelings of being overwhelmed:

- *Responsibility burden*: The sheer enormity of the responsibility scope can be overwhelming, leading to feelings of dejection and stress at the scale of the task.
- *Relational complexity*: Navigating the new relational complexities and family tensions can be as challenging as developing the business itself. Conflicts often stem from jealousy, skepticism, and the pressure to prove one's capabilities.

- *Continuous scrutiny*: Successors may feel tired and unsupported by being constantly doubted and challenged by others as a new leader, including the predecessor and other family members. This continuous scrutiny can lead to significant stress and exhaustion, as they feel the need to work harder to prove their competence.

Frustrated ambitions:

- *Predecessor interference*: Successors can feel frustrated by the predecessor's reluctance to fully step down and their tendency to interfere, resulting in micromanagement.
- *Loyalty conflict*: There is a fear of being prevented from implementing new ideas and doing things differently due to loyalty pressure to "respect the tradition."

b. Psychological needs

Need for affirmation:

- *Legitimacy building*: Public and private acknowledgment of the successor's skills and legitimacy is crucial. This recognition helps build their confidence and establishes their authority.
- *Trust from founder and teams*: A priori trust from the founder and existing teams is essential. This trust allows the successor to lead with confidence and make decisions without constant second-guessing.

Need for freedom:

- *Autonomy in leadership*: Successors need the freedom to undertake their responsibilities without excessive oversight. This trust empowers them to innovate and lead effectively.
- *Empowering culture*: New leaders thrive in a culture that perceives mistakes as opportunities for learning, rather than as proof of their incompetence. Successors need genuine empowerment with balanced support, which includes providing open counsel and timely corrections, all while affirming their legitimacy.

**For family members**

a. Vulnerable feelings

Feelings of confusion:

- *Skepticism towards the appointed successor*: Family members may harbor doubts regarding the intentions and competencies of the newly appointed successor, leading to apprehensions about the business's future direction. Questions such as "Who is he?" "What can he do?" and "Why him?" become prevalent, reflecting a deep-seated distrust.

- *Discontent towards the selection process*: A lack of transparency in the decision-making process often engenders feelings of unfairness. Unclear allocation of wealth and responsibilities exacerbates these sentiments, while perceived favoritism or unequal treatment during the succession process leads to significant irritation and discontent.
- *Disappointment over non-selection*: There can be a profound sense of disillusionment with how the succession process is handled, especially if the family member was a candidate for succession. Feelings of jealousy toward the successor or those actively taking on leadership roles can also emerge, accompanied by envy of the attention and opportunities afforded to them.

Feelings of neglect:

- *Marginalized voice*: The perception of being ignored in discussions about the business's future can foster significant resentment. Feeling that their opinions and wishes are neither listened to nor valued can lead to anger and frustration, leaving family members feeling overlooked or undervalued compared to those actively involved in decision-making.
- *Role redundancy*: Passive shareholders may experience a sense of purposelessness, and that their role as shareholders is redundant as they attend meetings without actively contributing or taking on any meaningful responsibilities and roles.

b. Psychological needs

Need for procedural justice:

- *Desire to be heard*: It is crucial for family members to feel that their voices are heard in the succession process, ensuring their opinions and concerns are taken into account.
- *Desire for process clarity*: Providing detailed explanations of the processes and criteria used in succession decisions helps mitigate feelings of exclusion and distrust. Clearly explaining the succession process, including the reasons behind decisions, builds trust and acceptance.

Need for contribution:

- *Valued engagement*: Even those not in active leadership roles need to feel their contributions are valued. Assigning meaningful roles and responsibilities helps maintain their sense of purpose. Encouraging inactive but valuable members to contribute in ways that align with their strengths and interests can help them feel engaged and purposeful.

- *Input recognition*: Recognizing and valuing the input of all family members, regardless of their direct involvement in the business, fosters a more inclusive and supportive environment.

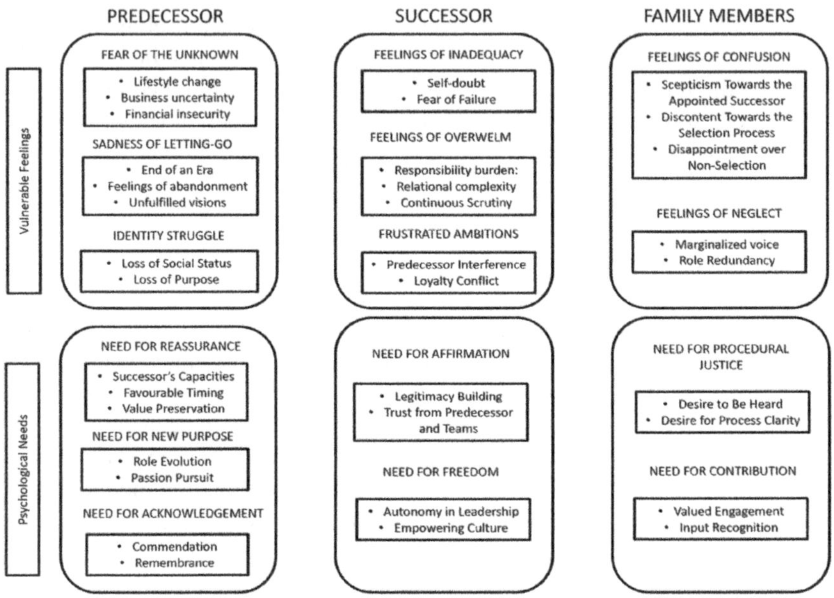


*Figure 11.1* *Summary of vulnerable feelings and psychological needs for family business stakeholders during succession*

## 2.2 Application of "Expressing Feelings and Needs" in Succession Governance

Succession governance in family businesses involves creating structures and processes to manage the transition of leadership and ownership while perserving family harmony. This section explores practical strategies for implementing the principle of expressing feelings and needs through family meetings and/or family councils. Family meetings are regularly held gatherings where family members discuss current issues, share updates, and address concerns within the family business. These meetings provide a platform for open communication and collaborative problem-solving. Family councils, on the other hand, are formal bodies comprising representatives from different family branches. These councils provide a structured forum for ongoing dialogue, resolving family-related business issues, and making collective decisions (Suess, 2014).

The core idea here is to switch the focus from, traditionally, identifying problems, finding out what's wrong, who's wrong, and how to improve, to understanding how situations affect individuals and what they need. Research on emotional disclosure shows that openly expressing emotions—rather than suppressing them—reduces stress, improves psychological well-being, and strengthens relationships (Pennebaker, 1997). This approach uncovers the emotional undercurrents, identity needs, and personal aspirations that drive behaviors and decision-making. Vulnerability plays a central role in this process : family members must feel safe to express themselves. Scholars have shown that when leaders disclose vulnerability, followers respond with increased trust and willingness to support them (Ito & Bligh, 2017).

One effective strategy is to hold regular family meetings or family councils where members are encouraged to use "I-messages" to voice their feelings and needs. An "I-message" formula might be: "I feel [emotion] when [situation], and I need [what you need to feel]." For example, a successor might say, "I feel embarrassed and hurt when my parents share their negative comments on my proposal in front of the management team. I know the proposal isn't perfect, but I need to feel supported and appreciated." It is then within the audience's responsibility to encourage such vulnerability to create a safe environment where members feel free to share their version of the story without fear of judgment. A typical response might be, "I appreciate your vulnerability. Thank you for sharing that openly. Is there more you'd like to share?" This can lead to the predecessor sharing their perspective and their version of the story, such as, "I felt scared when you suggested exploring international markets because I fear for our copyrights. I need to feel assured that you consider protecting our intellectual property and take time to investigate the markets before acting."

To apply this approach effectively, consider the following sequence:

1. Create a Safe Moment in a Safe Place: Choose an appropriate time and setting for the conversation. For example, schedule an appointment to address a specific topic rather than starting the conversation at an inopportune moment.
2. Ensure Availability: Both parties should confirm they are truly available and ready to engage in the conversation.

3. Invitation into Emotional Space: Person A invites Person B into their inner world, starting with an I-message such as, "I feel humiliated when I'm not informed about something happening in our family business."
4. Respond Without Judgment: Person B responds with, "I hear you say that you feel humiliated when … Is that right?" without adding any interpretations or judgments.
5. Clarify and Validate: This process continues with Person A either affirming or adding to their feelings, and Person B repeating what they hear, ensuring Person A feels understood and validated.
6. Summarize and Commit: Person B summarizes with, "I can understand that you feel unconsidered when you're not informed." Person B, having become aware of the impact of their behavior, commits to changing it for a specific period. For instance, "I will make sure to keep you updated on all significant developments moving forward."
7. Express Gratitude: Person A thanks Person B for taking the time to understand their feelings and needs, reinforcing the positive impact of emotional vulnerability.

Following this sequence may seem daunting at first. However, when left unaddressed, conflicts can resurface unexpectedly and cause significant harm to both the business and the family. Addressing these emotional and interpersonal issues proactively avoids the risk of temporarily suppressed conflicts emerging later in a more damaging form.

Additionally, facilitators of these meetings can enhance the depth of discussions by asking questions that invite members to explore their personal experiences. Instead of asking for summaries, analyses, descriptions, generalizations, and actions, facilitators can prompt members to reflect on their feelings and impacts. For instance, instead of asking, "What do you think?" they might ask, "What do you feel?" Rather than "What can you do about that?" they might ask, "How did that impact you?" Instead of "What caused that to happen?" they could ask, "Why did that touch you so deeply?" or "What's going on inside you when that happened?" These questions help uncover the emotional undercurrents that drive behavior and decision-making in family businesses.

In general, family meetings and councils should aim to foster understanding of each other's fears, desires, concerns, and needs, rather than focusing solely on problem-solving. While practical solutions often arise from these discussions, the primary goal is to strengthen family bonds by prioritizing connection over "what's right" or "who's right." In the beginning, when such practices may feel uncomfortable, employing a neutral facilitator or appointing a family business advisor can help guide these discussions and ensure they remain productive and focused. Additionally, family retreats or workshops focused on emotional intelligence and communication skills can provide a safe space for members to practice articulating their feelings and needs (Goleman, Boyatzis, & McKee, 2013).

## 2.3 Cases

**Case 1: A vulnerable predecessor won the family's support**

In a large family business in the industrial sector in France, with over 100 years of history, the third-generation leader faced significant challenges after passing on the business to one of his children. Having actively managed the company for over 30 years, he struggled to let go and refrain from interfering with his successor's decisions. Despite understanding the importance of trusting his successor and allowing him to take initiatives—lessons he had learned from his own father—he found it difficult to apply these principles in practice. His constant questioning and occasional reversal of his son's decisions led to frustration for the successor and confusion within the company.

Recognizing the need for support regarding this season of change, the predecessor decided to assemble his son and other family members to share his vulnerabilities. He admitted his struggle to step back and trust his son's leadership fully. He acknowledged the internal conflict he felt, questioning his decisions while declaring publicly that he was now in charge, feeling hypocritical. He also expressed a desire to be consulted more often or to continue contributing to the business in some capacity, despite being unsure how to achieve this balance.

He also decided to move to the south of France and start mentoring projects for other businesses, creating physical distance from the headquarters in the Paris region. His family greatly appreciated his honesty and vulnerability, and they supported him in preparing for the move. Understanding his father's heartfelt admissions, the successor felt more compassionate and free to consult him more often on various topics. The transition went slow but steady, with lots of genuine conversations involving feelings, needs, and mutual understanding. Both the predecessor and the successor gradually learned to settle in their new position and remain connected with a strong family bond.

**Case 2: A "silent" family business ended in tragedy**

In a quasi-fundamentalist religious context within a "well-meaning family where we don't talk to each other," unresolved conflicts between the first and second generations plagued the family business for decades. These conflicts, which became taboo subjects, were neither addressed by the concerned generations nor by their successors, who were bound by a pervasive silence. This resulted in high intra-family tensions and latent conflicts that severely undermined internal relations. The descendants inherited these unresolved issues, perpetuating the conflicts across generations. The environment became so strained that any form of discussion outside the business context became impossible. This lack of communication further deepened the rifts within the family, creating an atmosphere of mistrust and hostility.

As the family business encountered financial difficulties, the only conversations remaining were those about the company's immediate operational needs. Ultimately, the family decided to sell the business, leading to a profound human tragedy. The sale marked not just a financial loss but a significant emotional and psychological breakdown within the family. Traumatized by the compounded tensions and the dissolution of their business, the family members vowed never to engage in business together again.

Years passed before the family reconsidered the idea of re-entering the business world together. This decision was not taken lightly and required extensive communication work. The family undertook significant efforts to establish open and honest dialogue, which was a challenging but necessary step. Through this process, they were able to truly understand one another and lay the foundation for a more harmonious family business environment.

## 3. DARING TO LISTEN ACTIVELY TO DIVERSE PERSPECTIVES

Actively listening to different perspectives can indeed be daunting for family business leaders, as it often involves confronting biases and relinquishing the sense of being the sole expert. Concerns such as "they are biased and unaware of the real situation," "they are not qualified to advise me," and "if everyone gets to share their perspectives, I would be overwhelmed and my decisions, along with my position, could be threatened," can create resistance to feedback. However, acknowledging that everyone has blind spots and can benefit from the input of others is essential for effective leadership. Actively listening does not mean one must always accept and act on the feedback received. Rather, it involves engaging in open dialogue and making thoughtful decisions about how to use the information. Bruneau (1989) argues that authentic listening requires empathy—moving beyond merely hearing words to deeply understanding the emotional experience of the other person.

Research in organizational behavior has also shown that feedback-seeking behavior is associated with higher job satisfaction, increased creativity, faster adaptation to new roles, and lower turnover (Anseel, Lievens, & Schollaert, 2009; Ashford, Blatt, & VandeWalle, 2003). Additionally, seeking negative feedback has been linked to higher performance ratings (Anseel et al., 2015). Leaders who are willing to self-reflect and consider diverse perspectives are often easier to work with and can foster a more positive and productive work environment. The willingness to actively seek and listen to others' perspectives, feelings, and needs is also a profound form of respect and recognition, creating a sense of belonging and mutual respect within the organization. This posture directly challenges the avoidant culture often present in family businesses and the hierarchical decision-making habits where the one in charge is presumed to know it all. Embracing a culture of open feedback and diverse perspectives can mitigate the risks associated with insular decision-making and the resistance to change that often hinders family business succession.

Becoming proficient in active listening involves cultivating a growth mindset and adopting a posture of humility and respect. A growth mindset, as articulated by Carol Dweck (2006), views challenges and feedback as opportunities for learning and development rather than threats to one's competence. This mindset encourages leaders to maintain a positive attitude towards feedback, making it easier to accept and apply constructive criticism. Furthermore, humility in business leaders, extensively studied in the literature, underscores the importance of genuinely valuing others' insights, even those less familiar with the core business (Owens & Hekman, 2012). Being open to different voices demonstrates humility and a willingness to learn, which can inspire similar attitudes in younger generations and promote a positive culture. Effective feedback reception also builds trust and credibility, as family members, both active and inactive, feel heard and valued when their perspectives are considered. This practice helps prevent conflicts, reduces transaction costs in problem-solving, and supports healthy, stable relationships within the family business.

### 3.1 Application of "Active Listening to Diverse Perspectives" in Succession Governance

Building on the importance of embracing diverse perspectives in family business succession governance, practical strategies can embed this principle into daily operations and long-term planning. Creating a culture of humility and respect is essential. One practical approach is to intentionally acknowledge and praise behaviors that seek and listen to feedback openly. Additionally, actively soliciting input from quieter members by giving them a voice and inviting them to share their comments can empower inactive members to engage more actively as shareholders. This inclusive approach enhances individual participation and contributes to the overall betterment of the family business (Ward, 2004).

Using "anonymous surveys" to gather feedback from family members about their feelings and concerns is an effective strategy. This method allows individuals to express their thoughts honestly without fear of repercussion. The results can be discussed openly in family meetings, providing a structured opportunity to address underlying issues and understand different viewpoints. This approach helps the family make informed decisions that reflect the collective insights and concerns of all members (Anseel, Lievens, & Schollaert, 2009). Establishing regular check-ins and progress updates can further reinforce the practice of active listening, ensuring that concerns are addressed promptly and that the family remains aligned in their goals and strategies.

Appointing a "feedback advocate" can significantly enhance the practice of active listening. This individual, who could be a family member or an external advisor, is responsible for ensuring that active listening is consistently applied during meetings and discussions. The feedback advocate monitors conversations, encourages participants to listen actively, and intervenes when necessary to keep discussions constructive. Training sessions on emotional intelligence and communication skills can equip family members with the tools needed to engage effectively with diverse perspectives (Goleman, 1998). Workshops and role-playing exercises can help family members develop their listening skills and learn how to respond empathetically to feedback, fostering a supportive and collaborative environment.

Creating a "family charter" that outlines the values, vision, and communication norms agreed upon by all members is another effective strategy. This charter serves as a reference point during conflicts or decision-making processes, ensuring that the family remains aligned with its core principles. For example, if a successor expresses anxiety about their new role, this feedback can lead to targeted support and development opportunities, such as mentorship programs or leadership training, enhancing their confidence and effectiveness (Carlock & Ward, 2010). This approach addresses individual concerns and fosters a culture of continuous learning and development within the family business.

Promoting shareholder engagement through initiatives such as "legacy projects" and "philanthropic ventures" can also enhance the practice of active listening. Legacy projects honor the family's history and values while contributing to the business's future success. These projects provide opportunities for inactive family members to get involved in meaningful ways, aligning their personal interests with the family's goals. Similarly, philanthropic ventures allow family members to collaborate on charitable activities, reinforcing shared values and fostering a sense of unity (Gersick et al., 1997). By involving inactive members in these projects, the family business can leverage their diverse perspectives and skills, promoting greater engagement and strengthening the overall governance framework.

Last but not least, one key governance tool that promotes succession planning through listening to diverse perspectives is the formation of an independent board of directors and advisory board. Independent, non-family directors, who have minimal personal interest in the business or the family, can provide invaluable and balanced viewpoints (Ward, 2004).

By institutionalizing active listening within governance structures, family businesses can navigate succession more smoothly and sustainably. This approach fosters a resilient and united family enterprise, capable of addressing the complexities of succession while maintaining family harmony and business continuity.

## 3.2 Cases

**Case 1: Inclusive governance that promotes engaged family shareholders**
In a large, fifth-generation family business in the chemical sector, the so-called inactive family members play vital roles despite not being involved in the operational management of the company. These family members contribute by training the next generations, supporting entrepreneurial activities, promoting social initiatives, and constantly improving their family governance and succession planning. Their efforts aim to enhance family cohesion and ensure the longevity of the business. They believe that governance should reflect that of a large corporation, even as a family-owned SME, and thus started these practices early on.

The governance structure is organized into three levels: management (board of directors), holding (shareholders), and family (fostering the desire to continue, ensuring information flow, and maintaining family cohesion). The board of directors consists of 50% independent directors (six people) and 50% family directors (six people), with each of the six branches represented by one independent and one family director. The family holding comprises over 300 family shareholders, while the "generation" association engages the family by disseminating information and promoting family cohesion among its 600 plus members, all blood descendants.

This dynamic governance model has encouraged younger generations to get involved, innovate, and contribute. The successor is selected through a well-documented, communicated, and agreed-upon process. The new generation successor feels well-supported as the entire governance structure and culture promote open dialogue and initiatives. He has already initiated and successfully managed several projects before officially taking over the business, with the backing of family and external board members.

**Case 2: Frustrated families protest for successor choice**
In a prominent family business in the industrial sector, now in its third generation with thousands of employees, the leader faced significant challenges due to a lack of family support. Upon appointing his son as successor, other family branches expressed strong discontent, believing the leader's younger brother

was more experienced and qualified. They complained behind his back, accusing him of favoritism and arguing that after twenty years of his leadership, it was now his brother's turn. Historically, family members who were shareholders had never been given a voice or a position on the board of administration, as the leader dismissed them as "a bunch of artists who know nothing about business." Convinced that his son was the strategic fit for the company's future, he viewed his younger brother as too focused on commercial and relational aspects to think strategically. However, his personal evaluations were never properly communicated to the other family shareholders, who learned of the decision unexpectedly, despite the other candidate demonstrating a more solid and proven management experience on paper.

This decision was met with strong opposition from the younger brother and the rest of the family. The situation deteriorated further during the COVID-19 pandemic, which significantly impacted the business. Disgruntled family shareholders united to protest, insisting that the younger brother should be the successor. They threatened to sell their shares and leave the business if their demands were not met. The toxic atmosphere ultimately led to the resignation of the appointed successor, the leader's son, who could not withstand the mounting pressure. In response to the crisis, the leader continues to work on "improving" governance with the intent of further silencing inactive family shareholders, exacerbating their frustration.

## 4. DISCUSSION

This chapter introduces two core principles of brave communication—daring to express one's feelings and needs and daring to listen actively to different perspectives—and argues for their unique relevance and application in family business succession. Our contribution to both literature and practice is threefold.

First, we propose a research direction emphasizing the investigation of specific communication skills and supporting attitudes as well as cultures in the context of family business literature. This approach aims to challenge the prevalent secretive, hidden, and avoidant cultures within family businesses by courageously emphasizing communication where feelings and needs are recognized and different perspectives are voiced and welcomed. Furthermore, the adoption of brave communication can help address the prevalent issue of tabooed succession topics, facilitating their discussion and resolution, which is crucial for successful succession processes.

Second, we contribute to the emotion literature of family business by connecting various unsettled emotions experienced by different family stakeholders to their psychological needs. Identifying common feelings and needs allows leaders and experts to better diagnose the inner struggles, thereby improving self-awareness, which is a critical step preceding the expression of these emotions. Practitioners in advisory and consulting roles should help identify and address these feelings and needs as early as possible in the succession process. This can be achieved by bringing these issues to light, de-dramatizing them, showing empathy, promoting constructive dialogues, and providing solutions.

Third, we contribute to the governance literature by offering actionable ideas for better implementation of these principles, skills, and cultures in family businesses. Future research should investigate the effectiveness of various governance tools and provide real-life case studies to inspire actionable strategies. By examining successful implementations, researchers can identify key processes and interventions that foster environments where communication principles are upheld and family members feel valued and respected. This contributes to a more harmonious and effective family business operation.

## 4.1 Future Research Directions

Future research can examine the hypothesis that a leader's expression of vulnerability—specifically, the open admission of personal struggles and genuine requests for help—enhances psychological safety within family businesses, thereby fostering trust and more open communication, particularly during fragile succession periods. This line of inquiry can be explored through two complementary methodological approaches. First, quantitative data can be collected via surveys administered to family business members, evaluating constructs such as perceived leader vulnerability, psychological safety (Edmondson, 1999), trust (McAllister, 1995), and open communication behaviors (Björnberg & Nicholson, 2007). Established scales can be employed to ensure validity and reliability. Second, qualitative methods, including case studies and in-depth interviews, can capture the nuanced impacts of various emotions (e.g., jealousy, self-doubt, neglect) and needs (e.g., recognition, freedom, justice) on different family stakeholders. This dual approach provides a comprehensive understanding of how well-expressed vulnerabilities (feelings and needs) and the resulting positive responses can enhance personal satisfaction, family cohesion, and smooth succession advancement.

Another promising research direction involves exploring barriers to active listening within family business contexts, particularly focusing on scenarios such as a successor's reluctance to heed advice from elders or active shareholders' disregard for the views of inactive family members. This topic, while addressed in the broader literature on feedback acceptance behaviors (Anseel, Beatty, Shen, Lievens, & Sackett, 2015), requires a more nuanced investigation into the specific cultural and interpersonal dynamics at play in family businesses. Methodologically, this can involve conducting qualitative research through interviews and focus groups to identify these barriers and gather detailed accounts of successful and unsuccessful listening practices. Complementary to this, case studies of family businesses that have successfully cultivated cultures of recognition (e.g., Liden et al., 2008) and humility (e.g., Ou et al., 2014) can provide valuable insights and practical governance tools. By examining these cases, researchers can identify key processes and interventions that foster an environment where all members feel valued and respected, ultimately contributing to a more harmonious and effective family business operation.

The recommendations on brave communication in family businesses can also be culturally dependent. In cultures with a high power distance, such as many Asian or Latin American societies, hierarchical structures are deeply embedded, and openly challenging authority or discussing sensitive topics may be viewed as disrespectful. In these settings, brave communication might be more challenging, as it goes against cultural norms that emphasize harmony, respect for elders, and maintaining face. Conversely, cultures with low power distance, such as those in Scandinavia or the Netherlands, value egalitarianism and direct communication, making it more natural for individuals to voice concerns and engage in open dialogue (Hofstede, 2001). However, even in cultures where brave communication is more accepted, it remains crucial for family businesses to address the emotional dynamics unique to their structure. In fact, it is in cultures where brave communication is less common that fostering such practices can have the most transformative impact, as it helps break down barriers to honest discussion and conflict resolution. We recommend future scholars explore cultural differences in moderating the impact of brave communication on family business succession.

In conclusion, brave communication is vital for trust, cohesion, and successful succession in family businesses. Practitioners and family members should embrace expressing feelings and needs and listening to different perspectives. This breaks through secrecy and avoidance, addressing emotions, psychological needs, and valuing diversity. By fostering a culture of vulnerability, humility, and recognition, family businesses can achieve smoother transitions and long-term success.

As George Bernard Shaw reminded us, the illusion that communication has taken place is the greatest barrier of all. Only by daring to speak openly and listen deeply can families shatter this illusion, forging true understanding and trust. When brave communication becomes the norm, succession transforms from a mere transfer of power into a profound, generational pact—one that not only preserves the family's legacy but also boldly shapes its future.

## REFERENCES


Anseel, F., Beatty, A. S., Shen, W., Lievens, F., & Sackett, P. R. (2015). How are we doing after 30 years? A meta-analytic review of the antecedents and outcomes of feedback-seeking behavior. *Journal of Management, 41*(1), 318–348.

Anseel, F., Lievens, F., & Schollaert, E. (2009). Reflection as a strategy to enhance task performance after feedback. *Organizational Behavior and Human Decision Processes, 110*(1), 23–35.

Ashford, S. J., Blatt, R., & VandeWalle, D. (2003). Reflections on the looking glass: A review of research on feedback-seeking behavior in organizations. *Journal of Management, 29*(6), 773–799.

Baumeister, R. F., & Leary, M. R. (1995). The need to belong: Desire for interpersonal attachments as a fundamental human motivation. *Psychological Bulletin, 117*(3), 497–529.

Bertschi-Michel, A., Kammerlander, N., & Strike, V. M. (2020). Unearthing and alleviating emotions in family business successions. *Entrepreneurship Theory and Practice, 44*(1), 81–108.

Birdthistle, N., & Hales, R. (eds) (2021). What Is a Family Business and Their Contribution to the Global Economy? In *Family Businesses on a Mission: Attaining the 2030 Sustainable Development Goal of Decent Work and Economic Growth* (pp. 11–15). Emerald Publishing. Retrieved from https://www.emerald.com/insight/content/doi/10.1108/978-1-80382-487-120221002/full/html

Björnberg, Å., & Nicholson, N. (2007). The Family Climate Scales—Development of a new measure for use in family business research. *Family Business Review, 20*(3), 229–246.

Björnberg, Å., & Nicholson, N. (2012). Emotional ownership: The next generation's relationship with the family firm. *Family Business Review, 25*(4), 374–390.

Brown, B. (2012). *Daring Greatly: How the Courage to Be Vulnerable Transforms the Way We Live, Love, Parent, and Lead.* Gotham Books.

Bruneau, T. (1989). Empathy and listening: A conceptual review and theoretical directions. *International Journal of Listening, 3*(1), 1–20.

Cabrera-Suárez, M. K., De Saá-Pérez, P., & García-Almeida, D. (2001). The succession process from a resource- and knowledge-based view of the family firm. *Family Business Review, 14*(1), 37–46.

Carlock, R. S., & Ward, J. L. (2010). *When Family Businesses Are Best: The Parallel Planning Process for Family Harmony and Business Success.* Palgrave Macmillan.

Chrisman, J. J., Chua, J. H., & Sharma, P. (2005). Trends and directions in the development of a strategic management theory of the family firm. *Entrepreneurship Theory and Practice, 29*(5), 555–576.

Danes, S. M., Stafford, K., Haynes, G., & Amarapurkar, S. S. (2009). Family capital of family firms: Bridging human, social, and financial capital. *Family Business Review, 22*(3), 199–215.

De Massis, A., Chua, J. H., & Chrisman, J. J. (2008). Factors preventing intra-family succession. *Family Business Review, 21*(2), 183–199.

Deci, E. L., & Ryan, R. M. (2000). The "what" and "why" of goal pursuits: Human needs and the self-determination of behavior. *Psychological Inquiry, 11*(4), 227–268.

Deferne, M., Bertschi-Michel, A., & de Groote, J. (2022). The role of trust in family business stakeholder relationships: A systematic literature review. *Journal of Family Business Strategy, 13*(3), 100501.

Dweck, C. S. (2006). *Mindset: The New Psychology of Success*. Random House.

Eddleston, K. A., & Kellermanns, F. W. (2007). Destructive and productive family relationships: A stewardship theory perspective. *Journal of Business Venturing, 22*(4), 545–565.

Edmondson, A. C. (1999). Psychological safety and learning behavior in work teams. *Administrative Science Quarterly, 44*(2), 350–383.

European Family Businesses (2021). Facts & figures. Retrieved from https://europeanfamilybusinesses.eu/about-european-family-businesses/

Gersick, K. E., Davis, J. A., Hampton, M. M., & Lansberg, I. (1997). *Generation to Generation: Life Cycles of the Family Business*. Harvard Business Review Press.

Goleman, D. (1998). *Working with Emotional Intelligence*. Bantam Books.

Goleman, D., Boyatzis, R., & McKee, A. (2013). *Primal Leadership: Unleashing the Power of Emotional Intelligence*. Harvard Business Review Press.

Handler, W. C. (1994). Succession in family business: A review of the research. *Family Business Review, 7*(2), 133–157.

Hiebl, M. R. W. (2013). Risk aversion in family firms: What do we really know? *Journal of Risk Finance, 14*(1), 49–70.

Hofstede, G. (2001). *Culture's Consequences: Comparing Values, Behaviors, Institutions, and Organizations Across Nations* (2nd edn.). Sage Publications.

Hubler, T. (1999). Ten most prevalent obstacles to family business planning. *Family Business Review, 12*(2), 117–121.

Ito, A., & Bligh, M. C. (2017). Feeling vulnerable? Disclosure of vulnerability in the charismatic leadership relationship. *Journal of Leadership Studies, 11*(1), 66–83.

Kammerlander, N. (2021). Family business and business family questions in the 21st century: Who develops SEW, how do family members create value, and who belongs to the family? *Journal of Family Business Strategy, 13*(2), 100470.

La Porta, R., Lopez-de-Silanes, F., & Shleifer, A. (1999). Corporate ownership around the world. *The Journal of Finance, 54*(2), 471–517.

Lansberg, I. (1988). The succession conspiracy. *Family Business Review, 1*(2), 119–143.

Lansberg, I. (1999). *Succeeding Generations: Realizing the Dream of Families in Business*. Harvard Business Review Press.

Le Breton-Miller, I., Miller, D., & Steier, L. P. (2004). Toward an integrative model of effective FOB succession. *Entrepreneurship Theory and Practice, 28*(4), 305–328.

Leiß, G., & Zehrer, A. (2018). Intergenerational communication in family firm succession. *Journal of Family Business Management, 8*(1), 75–90.

Levinson, H. (1971). Conflicts that plague family businesses. *Harvard Business Review, 49*(2), 90–98.

Liden, R. C., Wayne, S. J., Zhao, H., & Henderson, D. (2008). Servant leadership: Development of a multidimensional measure and multi-level assessment. *The Leadership Quarterly, 19*(2), 161–177.

McAllister, D. J. (1995). Affect- and cognition-based trust as foundations for interpersonal cooperation in organizations. *Academy of Management Journal, 38*(1), 24–59.

Makó, C., Csizmadia, P., & Heidrich, B. (2018). Heart and soul: Transferring 'socio-emotional wealth' (SEW) in family business succession. *Journal of Entrepreneurship and Innovation in Emerging Economies, 4*(1), 53–67.

Miller, D., Steier, L., & Le Breton-Miller, I. (2003). Lost in time: Intergenerational succession, change, and failure in family business. *Journal of Business Venturing, 18*(4), 513–531.

Miller, D., & Le Breton-Miller, I. (2005). *Managing for the Long Run: Lessons in Competitive Advantage from Great Family Businesses.* Harvard Business Review Press.
Miller, D., & Le Breton-Miller, I. (2006). Family governance and firm performance: Agency, stewardship, and capabilities. *Family Business Review, 19*(1), 73–87.
Morris, M. H., Williams, R. W., & Nel, D. (1996). Factors influencing family business succession. *International Journal of Entrepreneurial Behaviour & Research, 2*(3), 68–81.
Ou, A. Y., Tsui, A. S., Kinicki, A. J., Waldman, D. A., Xiao, Z., & Song, L. J. (2014). Humble chief executive officers' connections to top management team integration and middle managers' responses. *Administrative Science Quarterly, 59*(1), 34–72.
Owens, B. P., & Hekman, D. R. (2012). Modeling how to grow: An inductive examination of humble leader behaviors, contingencies, and outcomes. *Academy of Management Journal, 55*(4), 787–818.
Pennebaker, J. W. (1997). *Opening Up: The Healing Power of Expressing Emotions.* Guilford Press.
Rouse, P. C., Turner, P. J. F., Siddall, A. G., Schmid, J., Standage, M., & Bilzon, J. L. J. (2020). The interplay between psychological need satisfaction and psychological need frustration within a work context: A variable and person-oriented approach. *Motivation and Emotion, 44*(1), 175–189.
Salvato, C., & Corbetta, G. (2013). Transitional leadership of advisors as a facilitator of successors' leadership construction. *Family Business Review, 26*(3), 235–255.
Sharma, P., Chrisman, J. J., & Chua, J. H. (2003). Succession planning as planned behavior: Some empirical results. *Family Business Review, 16*(1), 1–15.
Shepherd, D. A. (2016). An emotions perspective for advancing the fields of family business and entrepreneurship: Stocks, flows, reactions, and responses. *Family Business Review, 29*(2), 151–158.
Stamm, I., & Lubinski, C. (2011). Crossroads of family business research and firm demography—A critical assessment of family business survival rates. *Journal of Family Business Strategy, 2*(3), 117–127.
Stanley, L. J. (2010). Emotions and family business creation: An extension and implications. *Entrepreneurship Theory and Practice, 34*(6), 1085–1092.
Strike, V. M. (2012). Advising the family firm: Reviewing the past to build the future. *Family Business Review, 25*(2), 156–177.
Suess, J. (2014). Family governance: Literature review and the development of a conceptual model. *Journal of Family Business Strategy, 5*(2), 138–155.
Tsabari, N. M., & Weiss, D. (2013). Communication traps: Applying game theory to succession in family firms. *Family Business Review, 26*(2), 165–181.
Venter, E., Van der Merwe, S., & Farrington, S. (2012). The impact of selected stakeholders on family business continuity and family harmony. *Southern African Business Review, 16*(2), 69–96.
Ward, J. L. (2004). *Perpetuating the Family Business: 50 Lessons Learned from Long-Lasting, Successful Families in Business.* Palgrave Macmillan.
Ward, J. L. (2011). *Keeping the Family Business Healthy: How to Plan for Continuing Growth, Profitability, and Family Leadership.* Palgrave Macmillan.

# 12. Corporate and family governance in a developing context with cultural dynamics

**Taib Berrada El Azizi, Oumaima Quiddi and Badr Habba**

## 1. INTRODUCTION

Behind every thriving family business lies a unique narrative, woven from a tapestry of family dynamics, ancestral legacies, and deliberate, or sometimes unintended, strategic choices. Traditionally, the term "family business" has emphasized the management and ownership of a company by a family, often with a focus on generational continuity and the preservation of family heritage. However, this perspective can sometimes overlook the complexities of family relationships and the governance challenges that may arise when family members are involved in the business.

Scholars have delved into the dynamics between individuals with family ties, shaping the interaction between family and business, known as the "family behind the firm" (Carney & Dieleman, 2023). Could we be led to highlight the term "families in business" instead of "family businesses"? This question evokes a significant shift in perspective in our understanding of family businesses. By adopting this approach, we acknowledge that the family is not merely confined to being the owner and/or manager of the business but is deeply integrated into all aspects of its operations. This shift in terminology reflects a move towards a more holistic and nuanced approach to governing family enterprises.

Moreover, considering the heterogeneous nature of family businesses, one possible explanation for their heterogeneity lies in the variety of families involved in the business and the distinct cultural frameworks they embody. Each family brings its own values, traditions, and modes of operation, significantly influencing the governance of the firm. Consequently, a thorough understanding of family attributes is essential to elucidate the spectrum of governance mechanisms and models observed within family businesses across varied contexts.

In this vein, family idiosyncrasies, such as historical issues or entrenched hierarchical relationships, can profoundly shape governance frameworks. For instance, families with entrenched entrepreneurial traditions may adopt risk-tolerant approaches, fostering dynamic governance models conducive to innovation. Conversely, families rooted in conservative norms and hierarchical structures may favor more rigid governance models emphasizing stability and continuity.

Moreover, cultural dimensions encompassing religious affiliations, ethnic backgrounds, and societal norms further accentuate the complexity of governance dynamics for families in business. In emerging and developing economies, the stakes are heightened due to varying levels of governance maturity, less developed institutional structures, and the absence of stringent regulatory frameworks dictating governance mechanisms. The lack of robust regulatory oversight further accentuates the need for a nuanced understanding of familial and cultural dynamics in shaping governance practices within family businesses.

Guided by the significance of acknowledging the inherent heterogeneity of "families in business" and the importance of context-sensitive research, especially in underexplored contexts such as developing countries (Quiddi & Habba, 2024), we present three case vignettes showcasing real-life situations of families in business where governance and strategic decision-making have grappled with familial and cultural dynamics, leading to complexity.

## 1.1 An Overview of Corporate Governance in Family Businesses in Morocco and Arab Countries

In Morocco and Arab countries, the prevalent governance structures are characterized by the dominance of family ownership in businesses, with family members primarily holding key leadership positions, especially in first- and second-generation family firms. Unlike family businesses in Western countries, those in the MENA (Middle East and North Africa) and Arab countries appear to be more complex, particularly concerning the involvement of family members. In this region, the average number of family members in family businesses is nearly twice as high as that in family businesses in the United States and the United Kingdom (Saidat et al., 2022). These high levels of ownership make the family the most prominent and influential stakeholder, wielding decision-making power and determining the structure and composition of the board of directors (Samara, 2021). The latter can sometimes exceed 16 members (Jamali et al., 2010).

Additionally, board members of first- and second-generation family businesses are primarily family members or friends of the family, with limited presence of independent external directors, despite some governmental regulations in a few MENA countries requiring companies to establish internal control mechanisms (Baydoun et al., 2013; Piesse et al., 2012). Thus, due to their position within the firm and the information asymmetry present, family members can manage the firm in a manner that serves the interests of all shareholders. However, they also acknowledge the potential to redirect some of the firm's wealth for their personal gain and may adopt opportunistic strategies accordingly (Quiddi & Habba, 2021a).

The phenomenon of a dual role of the chairman and chief executive officer (CEO), a situation in which the chairman of the board also holds the position of CEO, is commonly encountered in Arab family businesses (Al-Saidi & Al-Shammari, 2014; Chahine & Tohmé, 2009; Khanchel El Mehdi, 2007; Piesse et al., 2012; Salloum et al., 2013).

## 1.2 Institutional Gaps and Regulatory Environment

A lack of strong institutions and weak regulatory frameworks are two recurrent features in developing countries. These gaps can create a vacuum in which family businesses must operate, often without the legal and institutional safeguards needed to protect shareholder rights. The institutional quality of Arab countries has not significantly improved. State institutions struggle to enforce corporate governance regulations due to deep institutional voids (Al-Saidi & Al-Shammari, 2014). Consequently, state laws and reforms aimed at enhancing governance structures are often implemented ceremonially (Eulaiwi et al., 2016) or remain outdated (Mclellan & Moustafa, 2013). To illustrate this point, we mention cases where family businesses in Arab countries may elect family friends to the board of directors, considering them as external independent directors (Al-Saidi & Al-Shammari, 2014; Khanchel El Mehdi, 2007; Mnasri & Ellouze, 2015). This practice may compromise the independence of the board of directors but can also simultaneously serve and facilitate the decision-making process (Samara, 2021).

Some studies on Arab countries have revealed that Arab families generally do not trust external individuals, especially when they hold multiple director positions (e.g., Alfraih & Almutawa, 2017; Eulaiwi et al., 2016). However, when family businesses enter the phase of cousin consortiums, it becomes necessary to appoint independent directors to ensure the smooth functioning of the company (Gaaya et al., 2017), and family members are less concerned about gaining absolute control over the board of directors (Gharbi & Jarboui, 2017; Khlif et al., 2016).

In sum, the governance landscape of family businesses in Morocco reflects a distinctive set of dynamics shaped by the prevalence of family members exerting significant influence over decision-making processes and board compositions. Challenges persist in enforcing governance regulations, as state institutions grapple with institutional voids, leading to ceremonial implementation or outdated reforms.

Moving forward, we offer three case vignettes providing a closer examination of corporate and family governance practices within a Moroccan context, shedding light on specific challenges and furnishing insights for practitioners, scholars, and policymakers alike.

## 2. CASE-VIGNETTE #1: THE CULTURAL SIGNIFICANCE OF INFORMAL MEETINGS AND THE ROLE OF MEDIATION IN RESOLVING CLASH OF VISIONS AND BALANCING EMOTIONS AND RATIONALITY FOR EFFECTIVE GOVERNANCE

The family controls a business operating in the printing and packaging industry. The company was founded in 1962 by the patriarch, who has three sons and one daughter. For a long time, the company's main activity was all types of printing. Its competitive advantage in its region was its investment in offset printing, which requires expensive equipment. This heavy investment and the high overhead costs it generated created a barrier to entry for potential competitors for decades, allowing the company to enjoy a significant, even dominant market share in the offset printing segment in southern Morocco.

For a long period after the father's death, the company remained under the control and management of the second-generation members, in particular the three brothers who implicitly shared the main management functions. From the beginning of the 2010s, the business began to experience a lack of growth, mainly due to the development of digital technology and its impact on the demand for paper and cardboard printing. The family, represented by the three brothers, then decided to consolidate the business through diversification into the cardboard and paper packaging sector. This family decision was motivated by that of other families in Casablanca who had also diversified their activities but in other sectors. However, the family decision was based on a very strong attachment to the family business and the existence of a strong synergy between offset printing and the cardboard packaging industry. The production processes are almost similar in terms of technicality, know-how, and especially in the purchasing and marketing processes.

This decision was encouraged by the fact that the demand from companies in southern Morocco was undersupplied. Until 2014, there were two main large-scale suppliers located in Casablanca who mainly targeted large customers. The investment made by the family had a huge development potential in entire sectors undersupplied in the south of Morocco. This potential was especially profound, given this was a period when the agri-food and agricultural industries were forced to integrate considerations related to hygiene, food safety, and export standards – an issue within which the quality of packaging has become a decisive factor.

To support the growth that the business experienced, the family decided to invest in another company specializing in the import of cardboard for production. The company that was created for this purpose was structured at the share capital level according to the same proportions that were decided according to the share of men and women in accordance with the inheritance rules of Islamic religious norms where the woman inherits half of the share reserved for her brother.

In 2019, a significant event occurred within the family dynamics when the mother fell seriously ill. Up until that point, she had assumed a central role in the family's governance structure, mirroring the authority once held by her deceased husband. As an arbitrator, she commanded unchallenged legitimacy, serving as a cornerstone of the family's decision-making processes and conflict-resolution mechanisms.

The mother's pivotal role extended beyond mere familial ties; she functioned as an informal but highly respected governance figure within the family business. The weekly gatherings held at her home every Friday served as a forum for open discussion, where family members would convene to address the company's challenges and chart its strategic direction. Her guidance and wisdom provided a stabilizing force, fostering unity and cohesion among family members and ensuring that decisions were made with careful consideration and consensus.

However, the onset of her illness disrupted the delicate equilibrium that had characterized the family's governance structure. With her absence, the family found itself grappling with uncertainty and a sense of vulnerability. The void left by her incapacitation created a noticeable vacuum in the governance framework, leading to a palpable sense of disorientation and unease among family members. The mother's illness and death not only highlighted the fragility of the existing governance structure but also underscored the need for a more formalized and resilient governance framework that could withstand unforeseen challenges and transitions.

In retrospect, the mother's role as a force of leadership and governance transcended traditional definitions of authority and hierarchy. Her leadership style, characterized by empathy, wisdom, and consensus-building, exemplified the essence of effective governance in family businesses. Her legacy continues to resonate within the family, serving as a guiding light as they navigate the complexities of governance and decision-making in an ever-evolving business landscape.

In 2020, seeing that the growth experienced in packaging had begun to necessitate the upgrading of management and support structures, particularly in terms of managerial skills, and wanting to preserve the important management positions within the family nucleus, the three brothers decided to integrate two recently graduated cousins who were working as young executives in large companies in Casablanca. The first was integrated into the financial department to provide adequate responses to the need for working capital, which had been constantly increasing, creating a real financial imbalance, and to the tightening of the Moroccan tax framework and the resulting requirements. The second was put in charge of the sales department, relying on the existing players but with a fundamental mission to break with the local culture, which had to preserve the relationship with customers at the expense of the company's financial interests by allowing overly generous laxity in the payment terms granted.

During this phase, the only daughter of the eldest brother, who had an engineering degree, was almost excluded by the family. Culturally, in Moroccan families, the daughter is often feared because she often comes under the influence of her husband after marriage. This somehow legitimizes her exclusion from business affairs for fear of the influence of a "third-party" (son-in-law).

Feeling a sense of injustice, the eldest brother, who had been the lieutenant under the founding father for years and was the real catalyst for the industrial printing activities in the early 1990s, and who had been trained in a German university specializing in printing in Heidelberg, finally reacted to the attitude of his siblings, fearing that his daughter would be totally excluded from the family business. He decided to sell his shares in the two family businesses to protect his daughter's rights. The arrival of the third generation, so long awaited to prepare for a smooth transition and consolidate the family core, had thus become a cause of discord in an environment where family cohesion had hitherto been the watchword.

To avoid the escalation of the conflict and in the absence of the parents who had been the real stabilizers, the partners decided to call on the mediation of a certified public accountant. Following a series of meetings with the family members, it was decided to:

- Conduct a valuation of the family business;
- Establish a family holding company, directly owned by all family members and directly holding the shares of the companies forming the family group, to separate the function of holding and controlling capital from that of managing the activities;

- Adopt a new group organizational chart with a new entity responsible for digitalization, quality, and corporate social responsibility, whose management was assigned to the eldest brother's daughter to capitalize on her experience in this area within an American subsidiary specializing in aeronautics in Casablanca;
- Draft a family charter to manage the interface between the family and the business and clarify the family members' vision on key issues.

With regard to the overall management of the group, it was decided to capitalize on the eldest brother's extensive experience and his historical position within the family business. He was therefore reappointed as the group's managing director, heading a newly formed board of directors composed of the three brothers.

According to the certified public accountant, this arrangement offers several advantages:

- It preserves the family's consensus decision-making, which is a guarantee of stability and unity. The eldest brother, as a respected and experienced figure, is able to bring together the various stakeholders and ensure thoughtful and inclusive decision-making;
- It ensures the continuity and stability of the business. The eldest brother's leadership is a factor of trust and security for employees, suppliers, customers, and other partners;
- It strengthens family cohesion. By entrusting the management of the group to the eldest brother, the family shows its confidence in his abilities and its commitment to preserving the family heritage.

In parallel with the reappointment of the eldest brother, a five-year transition period was put in place. This period aims to gradually integrate the members of the third generation into the board of directors. This smooth transition will allow for:

- Ensuring the transfer of knowledge and skills between generations. The eldest brother and the other members of the board of directors will be able to share their experience and expertise with the younger members of the family;
- Preparing for the future succession. The transition will identify potential leaders within the third generation and train them in the responsibilities of management;

- Managing potential tensions and conflicts. The presence of third-generation members on the board of directors will foster intergenerational communication and dialogue and prevent potential conflicts.

In conclusion, the combination of experienced leadership and a gradual transition to the third generation ensures the sustainability of the family business. This approach preserves family cohesion, the stability of the business, and the trust of stakeholders.

## 2.1 Key Learnings

The case provides valuable insights into the tensions and conflicts that can develop within a complex family business structure. Here are some key points to highlight:

(1) The role of the mother in governance as a CEO ‘Chief Emotional Officer’:

The mother held a pivotal position within the family's governance model, serving as both an arbitrator and a facilitator of decision-making processes. Through her weekly gatherings, she provided a platform for dialogue, fostering unity and consensus among family members. However, her illness exposed vulnerabilities in the governance structure, emphasizing the necessity for more structured mechanisms to address unforeseen challenges effectively.

(2) Governance as a tool for conflict resolution:

The implicit governance framework reliant on family gatherings proved unsustainable with organizational growth and escalating complexities. Implementing a transparent governance structure with delineated roles and accountabilities would have enhanced decision-making efficacy and accountability.

Thus, the family's response to internal conflicts and the need for a smooth transition to the third generation involved restructuring the business and implementing formal governance mechanisms. This included establishing a family holding company, drafting a family charter, and appointing the eldest brother as the group's managing director. The transition period aims to integrate the third generation gradually into leadership roles, fostering knowledge transfer, succession planning, and conflict management.

(3) Strengthening family cohesion through governance bodies with an emphasis on a family charter:

By entrusting experienced leadership to the eldest brother and gradually integrating the third generation into governance roles, the family seeks to preserve family cohesion, business stability, and stakeholder trust. This approach emphasizes the importance of continuity, inclusivity, and consensus decision-making in sustaining the family business across generations.

The decision to formulate a family charter underscores the family's dedication to fostering communication and alignment. A formalized document delineating values, vision, and governance tenets may serve as a guiding framework for future decision-making processes and conflict resolution.

(4) Leveraging professional expertise and mediation for effective governance:

Turning to a certified public accountant for help during a conflict shows smart use of professional advice, which can also serve as a governance mechanism. Getting expert help can be important when dealing with complicated situations and finding fair solutions.

(5) Significance of succession planning:

The absence of a well-defined succession plan engendered tension and discord during the integration of the third generation. A pre-established plan would have facilitated a smoother generational transition, mitigating potential conflicts and misunderstandings.

(6) Cultural biases and gender equality:

The daughter's exclusion from business affairs is rooted in cultural norms, where daughters are often perceived as being under the influence of their husbands after marriage. This perception significantly limits her role within the family business, particularly in decision-making and leadership. Cultural expectations suggest that a daughter's loyalty may shift away from the family, creating a bias against her involvement. Traditional gender norms also dictate that women assume secondary roles in leadership, which further restricts their participation in strategic decisions. The fear of external influence, especially from the "third-party" son-in-law, reinforces her exclusion, limiting both her opportunities for advancement and the family's ability to fully leverage her expertise. Additionally, the absence of formal governance structures that promote equal participation leaves women in family businesses facing invisible barriers to leadership roles, perpetuating the cycle of exclusion.

## 3. CASE-VIGNETTE #2: THE HYPO-GROUP AS AN OWNERSHIP GOVERNANCE MECHANISM FOR RESOLVING SUCCESSION AND GENERATIONAL TRANSITION WITHIN FAMILY BUSINESSES

The story of this case unfolds against the backdrop of the 1970s, a pivotal era within the milling industry, where two brothers embarked on a venture that would shape their family's legacy. At its inception, the enterprise capitalized on governmental subsidies for durum wheat sales, leveraging a state-authorized sector to accrue considerable financial gains by the mid-1980s, with operations concentrated in the Marrakech region.

By the early 1990s, foreseeing the complexities that would arise in the relationship between the founding brothers with the arrival of new generations, the younger brother opted to divest his shares in the enterprise to establish his own milling venture in Casablanca. With the completion of the share acquisition, the elder brother enlisted the support of his recently MBA-graduated son from the University of San Diego to aid in business development, as the elder brother was coping with health issues that necessitated a reduction in his managerial efforts.

The son's gradual integration into the company reached its zenith when he assumed the role of CEO in 1994. Under his leadership, a new governance structure was established, featuring a board of directors that included the father, mother, and son-in-law. Notably, the son-in-law came from a prominent wheat-importing family in Casablanca and held a 12% minority stake in the company. This composition of the board not only reflected a familial dynamic but also strategically incorporated external expertise and resources. The son-in-law's background in the wheat-importing industry likely brought valuable insights and connections, enhancing the company's position in the market. Moreover, his minority stake signaled a strategic embrace of external capital influxes, aligning with the broader trend of sector liberalization. By diversifying the board's composition and tapping into external networks and resources, the company positioned itself for growth and adaptation.

Under the father's stewardship, a visionary investment initiative was launched, driving vertical integration into the couscous and pasta industry. This expansion, facilitated by a subsidiary entity, witnessed the milling company emerge as the primary internal supplier, underscoring a strategic pivot towards diversification and sustainability. Meanwhile, the management of the new venture was entrusted to the second son, albeit with familial oversight. Implicitly, the founder had embarked on a family "hypo-group" structuring endeavor, aimed at stabilizing the familial context through this arrangement. A hypo-group refers to a structured arrangement within a family business that divides the enterprise into separate entities or groups, typically managed by different family members. This structure allows for the distribution of leadership and control among family members while maintaining a cohesive framework of familial ownership. Thus, the hypo-group approach aims to balance power dynamics, ensure autonomy in management, and provide a mechanism for succession planning within the family business.

Both brothers held equal shares in the capital of the two companies, with each assuming leadership of one, ensuring a balance of power. In parallel, their sister, holding a management degree, was tasked with overseeing centralized support functions, though her ascent to a significant role within the enterprises was curtailed by entrenched gender norms and hierarchical dynamics.

Ultimately, the hypo-group structuring, beyond its economic benefits, played a crucial role as a succession mechanism within the family business. By dividing the business into separate entities or groups overseen by each brother, the hypo-group allowed them to maintain autonomy and control over their respective ventures while still operating within a framework of familial ownership. This approach likely provided a sense of security and continuity for both brothers, ensuring that their individual visions and management styles could be preserved without undue interference.

However, the secondary role relegated to the daughter underscored persisting challenges in reconciling familial tradition with evolving notions of meritocracy and gender equality. Put differently, the familial structure mirrored the organizational hierarchy, with a governance model that still prioritized social norms and the dominant position of the male over meritocracy.

## 3.1 Key Learnings

The case provides valuable insights into the potential benefits of the hypo-group structure in family business governance. While this case illustrates a solution for succession and power balance, it also highlights the persistent challenges of achieving gender equity within that family business.

Here are some key points to highlight:

(1) Ownership governance and succession planning through a hypo-group structure:

    The case illustrates the strategic utilization of hypo-groups as a method to effectively manage the intricate process of succession within a family-owned business. Hypo-groups offer a structured framework for distributing power, authority, and responsibilities among multiple family members while preserving the overarching ownership within the family.

At its core, the concept of hypo-groups involves dividing the business into distinct entities or groups, each overseen by different family members. This division enables each family member to have autonomy and control over their respective segment of the business, thereby fostering a sense of ownership and accountability. By delineating clear boundaries and areas of responsibility, hypo-groups help mitigate conflicts and power struggles that often arise during succession processes. Furthermore, hypo-groups facilitate a smoother transition between generations by providing a mechanism for gradual leadership succession. Instead of a sudden transfer of power from one generation to the next, hypo-groups allow for a phased approach where younger family members can gradually assume greater responsibilities within their designated areas of the business. This gradual transition not only ensures continuity and stability but also allows for the accumulation of experience and expertise over time. Thus, hypo-groups can contribute to the professionalization and institutionalization of family businesses and help ensure a balance of power among family members, potentially reducing conflict and facilitating decision-making.

(2) Gender boundaries in family governance, limited female participation, and social norms as barriers:

The case illustrates the limited role afforded to the daughter in the family business despite her qualifications. This highlights the persistent challenges that women often face in accessing leadership positions and exerting influence within patriarchal structures, particularly in certain cultural contexts (such as Morocco) where traditional gender roles are deeply entrenched.

Despite holding a management degree, the daughter is relegated to overseeing centralized support functions, a role that falls short of leveraging her expertise and potential contributions to the core strategic decision-making processes of the firm. This discrepancy between her qualifications and the scope of her responsibilities reflects broader societal norms and expectations that often dictate gender roles and limit women's access to positions of authority and influence.

In many patriarchal societies, including some contexts within Morocco, where this family business operates, traditional gender norms prioritize male leadership and perpetuate the notion that women are better suited for supportive, administrative roles rather than positions of strategic leadership. These entrenched biases and stereotypes can manifest within family businesses, where familial ties and cultural traditions intersect to reinforce existing power dynamics and limit opportunities for women to advance professionally.

Moreover, the limited role afforded to the daughter despite her qualifications may also reflect broader systemic barriers to gender equity, such as unequal access to education, professional networks, and mentorship opportunities. Even when women possess the requisite skills and credentials, they may still encounter glass ceilings and implicit biases that hinder their career progression and thwart their aspirations for leadership roles.

Efforts to promote gender equity within family businesses may include implementing formal policies and governance mechanisms to ensure equal opportunities for women and fostering a culture of respect and inclusivity that values diverse perspectives and contributions.

## 4. CASE-VIGNETTE #3: THE STRUGGLE SURROUNDING A DIVESTMENT DECISION AND HOW GOVERNANCE DEFICIENCIES DRIVE THE NEAR-EDGE OF FAMILY BUSINESS BANKRUPTCY

The tale of this family business is one that began in the early 1960s, founded by two young Moroccan Jews, Mr Bitton and Mr Pinhas, both former executives in the agri-food industry. Armed with initial family capital and extensive experience in industrial service provision, they ventured to establish their firm in 1962 within the Ain Sebaa industrial zone in Casablanca, Morocco. Their aim was to cater to the burgeoning needs of Moroccan industrial enterprises at the dawn of independence. Their services spanned spare parts distribution, installation of imported machinery, and maintenance. From the outset, the business experienced exponential growth, prompting the founders to diversify into other sectors such as construction and fisheries.

In the early 2000s, when Mr Bitton, the son, decided to join the family business after completing his finance degree at HEC Paris and gaining experience with major international firms, his integration into the company was governed by an agreement between the founders. This agreement was necessitated by the fact that the elder son, Pinhas, lived in the United States and opted out of involvement in the family business. To ensure a smooth transition and assimilation for Mr Bitton, he received mentorship from the founders for three years.

During this mentorship period, Mr Bitton gradually assumed leadership responsibilities within the company, while the founders gradually stepped back from day-to-day operations. Despite this transition, the prevailing familial culture, characterized by a partnership governance model, remained intact. This governance model emphasized collaborative decision-making, transparency, and the preservation of familial values. Furthermore, there was a strong emphasis on maintaining positive relationships with employees and stakeholders, reflecting a commitment to inclusivity and engagement within the governance framework of the family business.

Eager to capitalize on the industry's growth momentum and Morocco's economic upswing in the early twenty-first century, the new leadership of Mr Bitton embarked on an acquisition spree targeting struggling competitors who had not planned for succession. This strategic initiative was not only driven by market opportunities but also influenced by personal ambitions.

From a governance perspective, while one might expect each acquisition decision at the family business to undergo meticulous evaluation by the board of directors, the reality was quite different. The decisions were made without comprehensive feasibility studies or thorough market research. Instead, they were driven by a sense of ego and personal ambition, particularly on the part of the successor, Mr Bitton.

Despite the lack of rigorous assessment, each investment decision was pursued with a semblance of strategic alignment with long-term objectives. However, this alignment was often overshadowed by the unchecked pursuit of growth and expansion, neglecting the imperative of financial prudence. As a result, the family firm's expansion was driven more by ego ambition than prudent governance safeguards. While the expansion strategy yielded benefits such as broadening the clientele base and enhancing the company's industry reputation, it also presented challenges. For example, the lack of thorough market research on growth potential in target regions has exposed the company to increased competition and lower margins, highlighting the importance of rigorous due diligence processes and governance in decision-making.

The investment of 40 million dirhams (approximately 4 million USD) into the expansion efforts also underscores the criticality of robust financial oversight within the company. Governance mechanisms, ideally established within the framework of collective decision-making in governance bodies, would have been instrumental in evaluating the financial implications of the acquisitions. Such mechanisms would have ensured alignment with the company's overarching financial objectives, resources, and risk tolerance levels.

By 2017, despite steady growth across all sites, operational costs began to weigh heavily on profitability, exacerbated by high overheads associated with various premises and challenges posed by informal competitors. Efforts to optimize costs and streamline operations, including through attrition-driven reductions in personnel, proved insufficient as the company's financial situation continued to deteriorate, burdened by mounting operational debts that strained relationships with suppliers and traditional banking partners.

The onset of the COVID-19 crisis further exacerbated financial woes, resulting in accumulated losses and the closure of two branches between 2020 and mid-2022. This downturn tarnished the firm's long-standing reputation for reliability among suppliers and plunged both families into emotional distress.

By late 2022, overwhelmed by stress and cognizant of his responsibility to both families and the founders' legacy, Mr Bitton unilaterally proposed a disinvestment plan involving the sale of the company's historic headquarters, situated in a prime real estate area in central Casablanca, and the consolidation of operations in remaining branches. However, the decision to proceed with this plan was made without the involvement of other family members or the establishment of structured governance mechanisms that could facilitate collective decision-making.

Obtaining family consensus proved to be a significant challenge, exacerbated by the absence of established family governance structures that could facilitate smooth communication and decision-making processes. The lack of inclusivity and transparency in decision-making led to tensions within the family and placed the entire enterprise in a precarious situation.

Ultimately, the founders themselves, motivated by a desire to avoid familial conflict and the slim prospect of ensuring the company's continuity, reluctantly endorsed the plan. However, the leader acknowledges that in such circumstances, the pain and regret were profound, with emotional, affective, and historical considerations often overshadowing purely legal or financial concerns. If structured governance processes had been established, decisions of such magnitude would have been subject to thorough deliberation and assessment by relevant stakeholders, potentially averting the challenges and conflicts that arose as a result of Mr Bitton's unilateral decision-making.

## 4.1 Key Learnings

The case provides valuable insights into navigating the strategic planning within a family business governance structure. Here are some key points to highlight:

(1) Importance of structured governance bodies:

The lack of a formal governance structure, particularly a functioning and active board of directors, led to unchecked ambition and impulsive decision-making by the successor. Establishing a well-defined governance framework with collective decision-making processes would have ensured:

- *Rigorous evaluation*: Decisions would not be based solely on personal ambition but would undergo thorough evaluation with feasibility studies and market research.

- *Financial oversight*: Acquisitions would not bypass vital checks on financial implications and alignment with the company's financial health and means.
- *Communication, transparency, and inclusion*: Family members and relevant stakeholders would be involved in such critical decisions, preventing unilateral actions and fostering collaboration.

(2) The vitality of communication and governance of family and interpersonal ties:

The case emphasizes the importance of having family governance mechanisms in place, especially for multi-generational businesses. This includes:

- *Formal communication channels and meetings*: To facilitate open and transparent dialogue within the family about the business and to define clear procedures for discussing, evaluating, and approving major decisions.
- *Conflict resolution mechanisms*: In the context of family businesses, where interpersonal relationships often intertwine with professional dynamics, conflict resolution mechanisms play a pivotal role in maintaining harmony and productivity. Establishing robust processes for handling disagreements in a constructive and respectful manner is essential for fostering a positive work environment and preserving familial bonds.

## 5. CONCLUSION: POLICY IMPLICATIONS, BEST PRACTICES, AND FUTURE AREAS OF RESEARCH

Enhancing governance in family businesses holds significant weight since they prevail in the economic fabric (Quiddi & Habba, 2021b), especially within the Moroccan context, where familial and cultural intricacies heavily impact strategic choices. The outlined case-vignettes highlight several key lessons that can guide families in business, policymakers, and private sector players in developing tailored policies and practices aimed at strengthening both corporate and family governance.

First, the importance of structured and transparent governance is indisputable. By establishing formal, functional, and active governance mechanisms, such as a board of directors and family charter, families in business can ensure that strategic decisions are made thoughtfully, with rigorous evaluation, adequate financial oversight, and transparent and inclusive communication. This helps prevent impulsive decisions and ensures the financial and operational sustainability of the business. In the Moroccan and MENA region, where respect for elder family members and hierarchical family structures play a dominant role, these governance mechanisms help balance tradition with the need for modern management practices. This differs from Western contexts like the USA, where governance tends to emphasize merit-based decision-making and flatter organizational hierarchies, with less deference to family roles. However, both contexts share the goal of ensuring transparency, financial oversight, and accountability, even if the underlying cultural dynamics differ.

Second, promoting gender equality and women's inclusion in decision-making processes is not only a matter of social justice but also directly correlates with effective governance in family businesses. However, in Morocco and the broader MENA region, patriarchal norms and cultural expectations often restrict women's leadership roles, making the challenge more profound. While Western contexts have made significant strides in gender equality, family businesses in these regions may still struggle with similar issues, though often to a lesser degree. Developing countries face the challenge of balancing both traditional values and modern pressures to include women in governance.

Social and cultural norms that often restrict women's participation in leadership positions can create blind spots and biases within decision-making structures. By challenging these norms and adopting policies and practices that promote equal opportunities, family businesses can diversify their leadership teams, thereby enriching discussions and ultimately strengthening their governance model. Recognizing the value of diverse perspectives fosters a culture of inclusivity and innovation, which are essential components of robust governance systems.

Third, referring to conflict resolution mechanisms, such as mediation and managing interpersonal relationships, is crucial for maintaining harmony within the family business. In the MENA region, where maintaining family honor and social reputation often outweigh individual interests, formal conflict resolution channels are particularly important. This is different from Western contexts, where conflict resolution might lean more heavily on legal mechanisms or professional mediators. In our context, informal conflict resolution rooted in respect for family elders is common, though increasingly, businesses are adopting more formal structures to handle disputes.

Lastly, succession planning is a fundamental element of family business governance. Succession in Moroccan and MENA family businesses often prioritizes male heirs due to traditional views on family leadership, which contrasts with Western contexts, where merit-based succession planning is more common and succession tends to focus more on finding the most capable individual, regardless of gender or family role, reflecting a more individualistic approach to leadership.

The succession process brings about various transformations within the family business (Quiddi & Habba, 2023), such as reconfiguring family dynamics, restructuring traditional models, and introducing novel management and ownership frameworks (Lansberg, 1988). Families that invest in succession planning can thus ensure a smooth transition between generations, mitigate potential conflicts, and preserve the continuity of their legacies.

Table 12.1 is a summary of best practices that encapsulate the key points discussed and offer valuable guidance for family businesses operating in Morocco and the MENA region.

## 6. FUTURE AREAS OF RESEARCH

The complexity of family business governance often stems from a delicate balance between family traditions and business demands, making research in this area both relevant and necessary. Challenges related to decision-making, succession, and gender equality are all issues that merit special attention in order

*Table 12.1 Some best practices for family business governance*

| Best Practice | Guidance |
|---|---|
| Formalizing governance structures | Establishing formal governance frameworks, such as boards with independent directors and family councils, to replace informal practices and improve decision-making |
| Drawing up a family charter | A family charter codifies family values, vision, and succession rules, helping to clarify roles and ensure long-term business survival and family harmony |
| Engagement of external experts | Utilizing external professionals like chartered accountants or legal advisors to provide objective perspectives and facilitate conflict resolution |
| Promoting gender equality | Encouraging the inclusion of qualified women in leadership roles, through mentoring and governance participation, to diversify perspectives and enhance resilience |
| Institutionalizing conflict resolution | Implementing formal mechanisms, such as mediation, to manage family conflicts and maintain balance between emotions and business decisions |
| Succession planning and intergenerational transition | Developing structured succession plans to ensure a smooth leadership transition across generations, balancing experience with leadership and introducing a gradual handover process (e.g., shadowing senior leaders) |

to strengthen the sustainability of these businesses. In light of the preceding discussions in this chapter, several avenues of research emerge to deepen our understanding of family business governance. Here are a few promising areas of research:

- Culture and family values: An in-depth analysis of the influence of traditional values and cultural norms on family business governance structures. This research could focus on the ways in which family and societal expectations affect decision-making processes and how these values are integrated into formal governance frameworks.
- Gender issues: Exploring the obstacles faced by women in accessing leadership positions within family businesses. An evaluation of initiatives to promote gender equality, such as mentoring programs, could provide valuable information on the impact of Moroccan family culture on women's careers.
- Succession planning: A critical assessment of the different succession planning models used by family businesses in Morocco and developing countries.
- Conflict resolution mechanisms: A study of conflict resolution strategies employed in family businesses, examining mechanisms such as mediation and arbitration.
- Professionalization: This research could analyze the benefits and challenges associated with integrating external expertise, highlighting cases where their intervention has led to positive results.
- Comparative studies: Comparative research on family business models across different cultural contexts, identifying similarities and differences in governance practices.
- Economic and political change: An analysis of the impact of economic fluctuations and political instability on the governance of family businesses.

## REFERENCES

Alfraih, M.M., & Almutawa, A.M. (2017). Voluntary disclosure and corporate governance: empirical evidence from Kuwait. *International Journal of law and Management, 59*(2), 217–236. https://doi.org/10.1108/IJLMA-10-2015-0052

Al-Saidi, M., & Al-Shammari, B. (2014). The relationship between a firm's value and ownership structure in Kuwait: simultaneous analyses approach. *International Business Research, 7*(5), 32–48. https://doi.org/10.5539/ibr.v7n5p32

Baydoun, N., Maguire, W., Ryan, N., & Willett, R. (2012). Corporate governance in five Arabian Gulf countries. *Managerial Auditing Journal, 28*(1), 7–22. https://doi.org/10.1108/02686901311282470

Carney, M., & Dieleman, M. (eds) (2003). *De Gruyter Handbook of Business Families.* De Gruyter. https://doi.org/10.1515/9783110727968-001

Chahine, S., & Tohmé, N. S. (2009). Is CEO duality always negative? An exploration of CEO duality and ownership structure in the Arab IPO context. *Corporate Governance: An International Review, 17*(2), 123–141.

Eulaiwi, B., Al-Hadi, A., Taylor, G., Al-Yahyaee, K. H., & Evans, J. (2016). Multiple directorships, family ownership and the board nomination committee: International evidence from the GCC. *Emerging Markets Review, 28*, 61–88.

Gaaya, S., Lakhal, N., & Lakhal, F. (2017). Does family ownership reduce corporate tax avoidance? The moderating effect of audit quality. *Managerial Auditing Journal, 32*(7), 731–744.

Gharbi, M., & Jarboui, A. (2017). Institutional investors' role in diversifying orientation decision across Tunisian companies. *Cogent Economics & Finance, 5*(1), 1244873.

Jamali, D., Hallal, M., & Abdallah, H. (2010). Corporate governance and corporate social responsibility: Evidence from the healthcare sector. *Corporate Governance: The International Journal of Business in Society, 10*(5), 590–602.

Khanchel El Mehdi, I. (2007). Empirical evidence on corporate governance and corporate performance in Tunisia. *Corporate Governance: An International Review, 15*(6), 1429–1441.

Khlif, W., Karoui, L., Ingley, C., & El Manaa, W. (2016). Family contingencies and board composition: Evidence from Tunisia. *Journal of African Business, 17*(1), 16–32.

Lansberg, I. (1988). The succession conspiracy. *Family Business Review, 1*(2), 119–143.

Mclellan, J. D., & Moustafa, E. (2013). An exploratory analysis of management accounting practices in the Arab Gulf Cooperative countries. *Journal of Islamic Accounting and Business Research, 4*(1), 51–63.

Mnasri, K., & Ellouze, D. (2015). Ownership structure, product market competition and productivity: Evidence from Tunisia. *Management Decision, 53*(8), 1771–1805.

Piesse, J., Strange, R., & Toonsi, F. (2012). Is there a distinctive MENA model of corporate governance? *Journal of Management & Governance, 16*, 645–681.

Quiddi, O., & Habba, B. (2021a). Financial behavior of family businesses: A bibliometric and systematic review. *International Journal of Financial Research, 12*(2), 75–90.

Quiddi, O., & Habba, B. (2021b). Indebtedness of North African firms: Do family ownership and board attributes matter? In M. H. Bilgin, H. Danis, E. Demir, & G. Karabulut (eds), *Eurasian Business and Economics Perspectives: Proceedings of the 33rd Eurasia Business and Economics Society Conference* (pp. 215–231). Springer.

Quiddi, O., & Habba, B. (2023). Generational differences of family businesses in MENA countries: Impact on indebtedness. *Review of Economics and Finance, 21*, 1232–1239.

Quiddi, O., & Habba, B. (2024). Financing policy of large listed family businesses: Evidence from the Arab world. *Corporate Governance and Organizational Behavior Review, 8*(1), 8–19.

Saidat, Z., Abdelrahim, H. J. I., Alkhodary, D., Aldomy, R., & Kassab, A. (2022). An insight into family business and entrepreneurship in Jordan. *Journal of Positive School Psychology, 6*(3), 5569–5582.

Salloum, C. C., Azoury, N. M., & Azzi, T. M. (2013). Board of directors' effects on financial distress: Evidence of family-owned businesses in Lebanon. *International Entrepreneurship and Management Journal, 9*, 59–75.

Samara, G. (2021). Family businesses in the Arab Middle East: What do we know and where should we go? *Journal of Family Business Strategy, 12*(3), 100359.

# 13. Corporate governance and corporate social responsibility in chaebols: tracing their evolution under government influence

**Cinzia Dessì and Ji-Hee Kim**

## 1. INTRODUCTION

In South Korea, large family-owned businesses, known as chaebols, have been the driving force behind South Korea's economic expansion. Since the mid-1960s, chaebols have established strong political ties and played a vital role in South Korea's transition from an agrarian to an industrial economy. A chaebol is a huge industrial conglomerate in South Korea that is owned by a person or a family. Typically, a chaebol comprises several diverse affiliates under the authority of a single individual or group. There are around 25 chaebols in South Korea that account for 84.3% of the country's gross domestic product (GDP) but just 10 percent of jobs. The most prominent of these include Samsung, Hyundai, LG, and SK Group, just to name a few.

Usually, a chaebol tends to have the same brand name across many sectors. The founding families of a chaebol exert a preponderant influence over the group's affiliates and commercial strategy and the Korea Fair Trade Commission (KFTC) describes a chaebol as a collection of companies whose controlling shareholder owns or controls more than 30 percent of the businesses' shares (Moskalev & Park, 2010). Interestingly, chaebols have flourished in Korea as a consequence of the government's attempts to foster internationally competitive businesses by providing particular incentives (Campbell II & Keys, 2002), and chaebol descendants continue to control the lion's share of authority inside the group's firms (Lee et al., 2019).

In 2019, more than half of all corporate profits were gained by chaebols, which continue to wield significant economic influence in the nation. As a result of the government subsidies they have received, as well as allegations of corruption, they have been exposed to severe criticism by Koreans (Andolfo,

2018). In fact, despite the chaebols' contribution to the industrialization of Korea, it has frequently been shown that their families have a lot of advantages over other businesses, to the point that the media criticizes them (Lee et al., 2019). This has resulted in the erosion of the reputation and credibility of these businesses by producing unfavorable public perception. Therefore, it is intriguing to comprehend how these organizations demonstrate concern for their brand by virtuous behaviors, such as those associated with corporate social responsibility (CSR).

As there are numerous definitions of CSR in the literature, we employ the definition of CSR as the corporate social or environmental behavior that exceeds the legal or regulatory requirements of the relevant market(s) and/or economy(ies), summing up the five dimensions of CSR activities (environmental, social, economic, stakeholder, and voluntariness) and defining it as activities that go above and beyond what is required by law for the sustainable growth of societies (Kitzmueller & Shimshack, 2012; Lee et al., 2019).

In light of this, this chapter proposes to examine the CSR of chaebols through a study of current literature in order to build, on the one hand, a framework for understanding how this type of business has included CSR choices and actions as a lever to protect their reputation and/or family name. On the other hand, the purpose of this study is to establish if the Korean government offers incentives and support for socially responsible behavior among chaebols.

The chapter is organized as follows: first, the economic significance of chaebols for South Korea will be presented, accompanied by a historical overview. Following this, the structure and characteristics of these large industrial conglomerates will be described to highlight their distinctive features with respect to family businesses worldwide. The analysis will then shift to an examination of corporate governance and social responsibility, beginning with a general review of these concepts before focusing on their specific application within chaebols. In conclusion, the chapter addresses the role of the government in promoting and supporting CSR policies within the chaebols.

## 2. SOUTH KOREAN GIANTS: THE REALITY OF CHAEBOLS AND THEIR ECONOMIC IMPORTANCE FOR THE COUNTRY

South Korea's journey toward becoming one of the world's most dynamic economies began from exceedingly adverse circumstances. In the early 1960s, South Korea's economic prospects appeared bleak, with a GNP per capita of merely $87 in 1962, positioning it among the world's poorest nations (Kim, 2013). Comparable in economic standing to Ghana and Sudan and significantly trailing behind the Philippines, Korea's journey from an impoverished nation to an economic powerhouse is a remarkable tale of strategic policy implementation and industrial resilience (Kim, 2013). Therefore, in 1962, Korea's GNP per capita was alarmingly low, indicative of the economic challenges the country faced in the aftermath of the Korean War. In effect, the socio-political landscape during the 1950s and early 1960s was tumultuous, with the country grappling with the ravages of war and the daunting task of national rebuilding.

Thus, the turning point for Korea's economy came with the initiation of comprehensive economic policy reforms when the government spearheaded reforms aimed at promoting rapid industrial growth through direct intervention, including financial and non-financial incentives to businesses aligning with national development goals. The establishment of a capitalist economy, where private ownership was encouraged, laid the groundwork for future economic expansion.

Hence, in South Korea, the regulation limiting commercial bank ownership has led business conglomerates to rely heavily on internal funding mechanisms. This framework is detailed in research by Almeida et al. (2015) and Kim et al. (2004), highlighting the unique financial strategies within chaebols. Furthermore, it has been a common practice for chaebol groups to invest in non-bank financial institutions, a trend documented across several studies (Kim et al., 2004; Kim et al., 2010; Kim, 2017). Additionally, there is evidence that these business groups engage in supporting their financially struggling affiliates through a process known as propping or negative tunneling, effectively prioritizing them over more solvent entities (Bae et al., 2008). This financial maneuvering was particularly pronounced during the 1970s when the Korean government funneled substantial financial support to the biggest chaebol groups via state-owned banks, often to the detriment of smaller and medium-sized enterprises, as explored by Haggard and Moon (1990). This historical context sheds light on the concentrated financial practices and the preferential treatment received by chaebols, which has shaped the economic landscape in Korea.

Thus, due to government-backed initiatives, chaebols have grown into multinational corporations, exerting considerable influence on the global stage, where these entities, which include household names such as Samsung and Hyundai, have become synonymous with Korean economic development.

In this sense, chaebols can be rightly defined as large, South Korean family-owned business conglomerates characterized by their strong ties with the government and operations across various industries. More in detail, the term "chaebol" comes from the Korean words "chae" (wealth or property) and "bol" (clan or clique), effectively meaning a conglomerate owned and controlled by a family.

Just to show a quick overview of the chaebols, we can mention the top ten chaebols as shown in Table 13.1. This brief descriptive introduction highlights

*Table 13.1* *List of main top ten chaebols in South Korea*

| Name of chaebols | Founder | Year of foundation | Main activities | Number of affiliates |
|---|---|---|---|---|
| Samsung Group | Lee Byung-Chul | 1938 | It is the largest South Korean chaebol, known globally for its electronics division, which manufactures smartphones, TVs, and semiconductors | +60 |
| Hyundai Motor Group and Hyundai Heavy Industries Group | Chung Ju-Young | 1947 | It is a major conglomerate specializing in automobiles; it includes the Hyundai and Kia automotive brands, making it one of the world's largest car manufacturers, while the second is known for its role in shipbuilding, construction equipment, and heavy industry; it is one of the largest shipbuilders in the world | +80 |
| SK Group | Choi Jong-Hyun | 1953 | It operates in various sectors, such as telecommunications, energy, chemicals, and logistics; SK Group is particularly known for SK Telecom, South Korea's largest wireless carrier, and SK Hynix, a leading global semiconductor manufacturer | +100 |
| LG Group | Koo In-Hwoi | 1947 | It has businesses ranging from electronics (LG Electronics) and chemicals (LG Chem) to telecommunications and services | +70 |
| Lotte Group | Takeo Shigemitsu, born Shin Kyuk-Ho | 1948 | It is a multinational conglomerate with a significant presence in food, retail, chemical, and entertainment industries, including department stores, hotels, and amusement parks | +90 |
| Hanwha Group | Kim Chong-Hee | 1952 | It is a conglomerate with a focus on three major sectors: manufacturing and construction, finance, services and leisure, with key businesses in chemicals, defense, and solar energy | +70 |
| GS Group | Huh Chang-Soo | 2005 | Origingating from LG Group, GS Group has interests in energy, retail, and construction, including GS Caltex, one of South Korea's major oil refiners | +60 |

| Name of chaebols | Founder | Year of foundation | Main activities | Number of affiliates |
|---|---|---|---|---|
| CJ Group | Lee Byung-Chul | 1953 | After spinning off from Samsung in 1993, CJ Corporation expanded its business portfolio into four key sectors: food and food services, biotechnology, entertainment and media, and retail and logistics | +70 |
| Doosan Group | Park Seung-Jik | 1896 | It is involved in heavy industries, construction, engineering, and consumer goods, with Doosan Heavy Industries and Construction being a key company within the group | +20 |
| Posco Holdings | Park Tae-Joon | 1968 | POSCO (Pohang Iron and Steel Company) is a steel manufacturer headquartered in Pohang, South Korea | +30 |

*Source:* Authors' elaboration.

how chaebols are integral to the South Korean economy, contributing significantly to the country's GDP and international trade, and they have also played a crucial role in South Korea's industrialization and economic development, making them influential not only within South Korea but also on the global stage, with deep and important ties to the government. At this point, it is worth delving deeper into the characteristics of these major industrial conglomerates.

## 3. INSIDE THE CHAEBOLS: OWNERSHIP, DIVERSIFICATION, AND GOVERNMENT CONNECTIONS

To fully grasp the impact of chaebols on South Korea's economic rise since their inception in the mid-twentieth century, it is essential to examine their distinctive characteristics. In fact, these conglomerates represent a distinct model of corporate governance (CG) and business operations characterized by family dominance, diversified business interests, and intricate government relationships.

Regarding the first aspect, the governance of chaebols is notably marked by family control, with leadership typically residing within the founding family or its descendants. This familial leadership plays a critical role in steering the conglomerate's direction, making pivotal strategic decisions that shape the conglomerate's future. The control mechanism within chaebols is complex, often involving a labyrinthine network of cross-shareholdings among the subsidiaries. This setup allows the controlling family to exert significant influence over the conglomerate with a minimal direct stake, ensuring that control remains tightly knit within the family circle.

About the second aspect, the diversification appears to be developed across a broad spectrum of industries, which is a hallmark of the chaebol structure. From electronics, manufacturing, and automotive to finance, services, and construction, chaebols have their hands in a vast array of sectors. This diversification not only mitigates risk by spreading investments across different industries but also positions chaebols to seize emerging market opportunities, driving innovation and growth.

Finally, the last aspect is the symbiotic relationship between chaebols and the South Korean government, which we cannot deny has been a cornerstone of their success. Historically, chaebols have enjoyed a close rapport with the government, benefiting from policies designed to nurture their growth and shield them from international competition. This close nexus has facilitated the rapid industrialization of South Korea, transforming it from a war-torn country into a thriving, high-tech economy. However, this relationship has not been without controversy. The preferential treatment received by chaebols has sparked debates over unfair advantages, leading to calls for increased transparency, regulatory reforms, and a more level playing field for all businesses in South Korea.

Despite the criticisms, the role of chaebols in South Korea's economic narrative cannot be underestimated. Their contribution to the country's industrialization, technological advancements, and global economic stature is immense. As South Korea continues to evolve, the ongoing dialogue about the future role of chaebols, their governance, and their relationship with the government suggests a dynamic landscape that balances economic ambition with equity and transparency. For this reason, because of the importance of these conglomerates, it is very important that their conduct and reputation be in line with fair business policies adherent to CSR. In fact, their dominance raises concerns about market competition, economic inequality, and CG, and in response to various financial crises and scandals over the years, there have been ongoing efforts to reform chaebols, focusing on improving CG, reducing family control, and fostering fair competition. This delicate act of balancing governance and social responsibility will be explored in the following sections, which delve into the challenges modern enterprises face in this evolving landscape.

## 4. THE SHIFTING LANDSCAPE OF CORPORATE GOVERNANCE IN CONTEMPORARY ENTERPRISES

### 4.1 The Evolution of Corporate Governance Concepts

The ongoing efforts to reform chaebols go hand in hand with the evolution of the concepts of CG. Over the years, the conceptualization of CG has undergone significant evolution. Initially, the focus was narrow, primarily centered on the interests of shareholders. However, this viewpoint has progressively widened to include a broader spectrum of stakeholders, marking a transition from a constricted to an expansive interpretation of CG (Magnan & Michelon, 2024).

Unsurprisingly, the definitions of CG originate from agency theory, which highlights the importance of shareholders' interests and the oversight of managerial decisions and actions. In fact, studies of CG have long been preoccupied with the management's control over the corporation's assets. This is especially true and justified given the shift from entrepreneurial enterprises, which were owned and controlled by their founders, to contemporary giant corporations, which were managed by career experts, during the late 1920s and early 1930s (Magnan & Michelon, 2024).

However, notwithstanding the substantial impact of agency theory on contemporary CG procedures, a number of researchers conceptualize and comprehend CG as pertaining to a broader societal function of enterprises (Roberts

& Van den Steen, 2000; Solomon, 2020). This viewpoint is predicated on a model of the firm that is stakeholder-oriented as opposed to shareholder-centric, and it adopts a comprehensive accountability framework in which CG guides the decision-making process of the organization in the pursuit of societal well-being. In line with this, it can define CG with the mechanisms, both legal and informal, by which a corporation is controlled and administered. This encompasses legal obligations, corporate regulations, and informal practices that exist inside the organization. Its objective is to ensure that all parties are working toward a single goal that is advantageous to the organization, its members, other stakeholders, and society as a whole by aligning the interests of stakeholders. This means that governance has been progressively extended to encompass a broader range of oversight pertaining to the operations of corporations, encompassing its societal and environmental ramifications.

This supplementary element pertaining to business sustainability frequently emerges in reaction to inquiries from stakeholders. This term underscores the significance attributed to trust, the exercise of authority, and responsibility within corporate structures. Therefore, CG comprises a collection of regulations and hierarchical frameworks that serve as the foundation for ethical company conduct, recognized as recompense for the occasionally conflicting interests between stakeholders (Du Plessis et al., 2018).

Inside a firm, the CG pertains to a sequence of procedures and regulations designed to compel organizations to adhere to particular codes concerning the means by which they are supervised and directed; regulations encompass not only the domestic legislation of the jurisdiction in which the organization functions but also internal corporate procedures (Scherer et al., 2016). Consequently, the notion of a company's CG encompasses all regulations and procedures that govern the decision-making process; it also delineates the trajectory towards attaining corporate goals and, by extension, the methods employed to accomplish them, in addition to assessing the outcomes attained. Therefore, CG is predicated on the internal and external systems of checks and balances that ensure organizations fulfill their obligations to all stakeholders and operate in a socially responsible manner across all aspects of their activities (Iansiti & Levien, 2004).

## 4.2 Broadening the Scope of Corporate Governance Integrating Stakeholder Expectations

It remains critical for organizations to engage with their stakeholders to develop, maintain, or enhance their legitimacy to operate, which denotes the capacity of the firm to satisfy social needs. Engaging with stakeholders enables companies to grasp their expectations, emphasizing that effective CG and accountability should concentrate on meeting these expectations, which include social, environmental, economic, and ethical aspects (Iansiti & Levien, 2004). While agency theory aptly describes the supervisory role of CG, stakeholder theory is beneficial for comprehending wider accountability and reporting methods. This theoretical perspective forms the foundation for CG frameworks to incorporate elements of corporate social responsibility and to extend corporate reporting beyond just the financial performance of corporations.

A stream of research recognizes the dual role of boards of directors: supervising operations and offering counsel, as pointed out by Brickley and Zimmerman (2010). This body of work focuses on the importance of CG in strategic decision-making and the creation of value. It especially highlights the board of directors' role in establishing a company's objectives and strategic path, a concept identified by Hillman et al. (2000). Using the resource-dependence theory, researchers argue that directors and boards link the company to external elements that create uncertainty and dependencies, influencing the organization's ability to manage resources and formulate strategies, as described by Pfeffer and Salancik (1978).

This perspective has been instrumental in understanding the importance of individual director experiences and skills, moving beyond the simplistic division between executive (related) and non-executive (independent) directors. It helps in identifying the necessary competencies and external connections that assist the organization in navigating a volatile and uncertain environment. Consequently, the board is perceived not only as a crucial entity for oversight and accountability but also as the central decision-making body shaping corporate strategy. In essence, this approach represents an amalgamation of agency theory and resource dependence theory in assessing the role of directors, as suggested by Hillman and Dalziel (2003).

Magnan and Michelon (2024) pinpoint four significant turning points in the evolution of the CG concept. These milestones begin with the Great Depression and the subsequent introduction of the US Securities Acts of 1933 and 1934, laying the groundwork for key financial regulations. The Second World War marks another crucial phase, ushering in a stakeholder-focused approach across continental Europe. The third key event involves the financial misdeeds of the late 1980s and early 1990s in the United Kingdom, leading to the influential Cadbury report on CG. Finally, the financial malpractices of the late 1990s and early 2000s catalyzed the implementation of the Sarbanes–Oxley Act in 2002, significantly influencing the framework of CG. These four key events significantly influenced the progression of CG in the majority of developed economies.

Consistent with this reasoning, it's crucial to acknowledge the developing tensions between a shareholder-centric model of CG and an approach that encompasses a wider spectrum of stakeholders. An example of this is the rise of environmental, social, and governance (ESG) standards, which not only serve as tools for improving firm performance but also increasingly highlight the importance of sustainability. Within this framework, environmental and social challenges are emerging as significant forces that are currently impacting, or have the potential to transform, both the concept and the practice of CG. Thus, sustainability is progressively emerging as a critical and indispensable component of the approaches adopted by organizations (Iansiti & Levien, 2004), as well as of the associations they forge with diverse partners across the entire value chain, thereby bridging CG with CSR.

## 5. FROM BOARDROOM TO COMMUNITY: BRIDGING CORPORATE GOVERNANCE AND SOCIAL RESPONSIBILITY

### 5.1 The Role of Corporate Social Responsibility

The focus on social responsibility began 50 years ago when Friedman (1970) put forth the argument that socially responsible policies in companies were a misuse of essential resources, citing their prohibitive implementation costs, which he believed outweighed any real benefits and detrimentally affected shareholder interests. However, this perspective has been increasingly challenged in recent times. Brammer and Millington (2008) argued that Friedman's view is only partially correct. Modern companies recognized for sustainable value creation are seen to deliver high-quality performance while conserving natural resources, focusing on people, planet, prosperity, and collaboration as crucial goals to improve the quality of life, as highlighted by Martínez-Perales et al. (2018).

The concept of sustainable development, as introduced in the 1987 Brundtland Report by the United Nations' World Commission on Environment and Development, emphasized the potential of humanity to achieve development that meets the needs of the present without compromising future generations (Brundtland, 1987). This concept acknowledges limits imposed by current technology and social organization on environmental resources and the biosphere's ability to withstand human activities (Brundtland, 1987, p. 16). It underscores that genuine sustainable progress must address the interlinked aspects of economic, environmental, and social well-being.

Since its introduction, the concept of sustainable development has evolved, leading to more than 300 definitions across environmental management literature and social sciences (Johnston et al., 2007). This diverse range of ideas has culminated in the broader term "sustainability" encapsulating the environmental, economic, and social dimensions. Shenhar and Dvir (2007) suggest that while economic aspects are crucial for business establishment, environmental and social factors are equally significant. Thus, CG should integrate aspects relevant to all three sustainability dimensions. The 2030 Agenda for Sustainable Development (United Nations, 2015) represents this evolution's apex, incorporating economic, social, and environmental components in its 17 Sustainable Development Goals (SDGs).

The 2030 Agenda is a global pact where all 193 member countries commit to the 17 SDGs, making every national and international economic and social actor equally accountable. The business sector is particularly seen as a catalyst for change, transforming supply chains, manufacturing technologies, investment strategies, consumer behaviors, and business models. Addressing sustainability in CG decisions, which often require extensive resources and significantly affect local communities, is becoming increasingly urgent (Martens & Carvalho, 2016) all around the world. Integrating social and environmental aspects into CG mechanisms is a complex but necessary undertaking (Thamhain, 2014).

This shift signifies that the historical focus on economic sustainability in business decisions must now be complemented by an equal emphasis on environmental and social sustainability, adopting a stakeholder-oriented strategy. This approach aligns with the assertion by Elkington and Rowlands (1999) that social justice, economic prosperity, and environmental quality—the triple bottom line—are critical for businesses in the twenty-first century (Freeman & Dmytriyev, 2017). These three pillars will serve as the new benchmarks for corporate performance evaluation.

In practical terms, environmental sustainability involves managing inputs like materials, energy, and water, as well as controlling outputs such as emissions, waste, and effluents to minimize pollution and resource consumption. Social sustainability, on the other hand, manifests in organizational practices that focus on working conditions, employee relationships, health and wellness, diversity, human rights, and safety, alongside community engagement and philanthropy (Alsayegh et al., 2020). Therefore, enterprises, pivotal to global growth, should spearhead this transformation (Sánchez, 2015). The perceived "higher cost" of achieving genuine sustainability is anticipated to yield greater long-term value, encompassing environmental conservation, enhanced community well-being, and the creation of wealth for future generations that transcends mere financial prosperity. For these reasons, the conduct of the chaebols has had to adapt to this evolving business paradigm.

## 6. EXPLORING THE NEXUS BETWEEN CHAEBOLS AND CSR, AND RELATED IMPLICATIONS FOR CG

### 6.1 Exploring the Ethical Dimensions of Chaebols' Corporate Dominance

The interplay between chaebols and CSR presents a unique perspective in understanding CG and ethical business practices in this kind of enterprise. The reason for this attention is due to the fact that chaebols have played a pivotal role in the nation's rapid economic development that extends their influence beyond economic parameters into socio-political spheres (Ryu & Chae, 2022). In other words, the analysis of the link between chaebols and CSR evaluates how these dominant conglomerates contribute to social obligations, their impacts, and associated ethical considerations (Lee et al., 2019). This means investigating the broader consequences of corporate dominance on societal and environmental well-being, particularly in the context of South Korea's corporate landscape (Ben-Shahar et al., 2023).

Another very relevant aspect is that chaebols have become synonymous with South Korea's economic identity due to the fact that the government's strategic decision to promote industrialization led to the nurturing of these family-owned businesses, providing them with financial support and policy benefits (Kim, 2013). However, this support often came in forms that were criticized for being unfair or poorly received within the broader business community of the country. Their impact on the South Korean economy remains significant. Chaebols have played a key role in elevating South Korea to the status of one of the world's major economies. Nonetheless, their expansion has been marred by disputes. Accusations against them encompass monopolistic behaviors, favoritism towards family members, and often a lack of transparency in corporate management. The concentration of control within family circles has frequently resulted in problems related to the accumulation of power and economic inequality.

Therefore, understanding chaebols is critical in analyzing their approach to CSR. Their historical and economic context provides a backdrop against which their CSR practices can be evaluated, revealing the complexities of corporate ethics in a rapidly evolving global economy.

Although there is a vast number of articles that define what CSR is (e.g., Crane et al., 2008; Lockett et al., 2006), in general, CSR can be defined as a self-regulating business model that helps a company be socially accountable to itself, its stakeholders, and the public. It embodies the societal obligations and outcomes of business achievements; it involves well-defined and shared policies and practices of companies that demonstrate their accountability for contributing to the broader societal welfare. By practicing CSR, companies can be conscious of the kind of impact they are having on all aspects of society, including economic, social, and environmental. CSR goes beyond compliance with legal requirements: it involves proactive efforts to contribute to a better society and more respect for the environment. It encompasses a wide range of activities, such as working in partnership with local communities, environmentally sustainable practices, and ethical labor practices. Globally, CSR has gained prominence as stakeholders increasingly expect businesses to be transparent, ethical, and accountable for their societal impacts (Ryu & Chae, 2022).

Chaebols' approach to CSR reflects both their unique corporate structure and South Korea's cultural and economic context. Traditionally, chaebols have focused primarily on economic growth and expansion, often at the expense of social and environmental considerations. However, in recent decades, there has been a noticeable shift towards embracing CSR. This change is partly due to increasing global scrutiny and the rising importance of sustainable practices in business (Lee et al., 2019). Another reason for implementing CSR policies is undoubtedly related to the desire to "clean up" and improve the perception of these conglomerates (Choi & Hong, 2022).

Major chaebols, such as Samsung, Hyundai, LG, and SK Group, have implemented various CSR initiatives. Samsung, for instance, involved in scandals of global proportions (Chang et al., 2019), has focused on creating social value through innovation, investing in educational programs, and promoting environmental sustainability in its operations (Chang et al., 2019).

## 6.2 Examples of CSR Initiatives by Leading Chaebols

### 6.2.1 Samsung

Samsung has integrated CSR into its business model, focusing on education, sustainability, and innovation. However, concerns remain about labor practices and environmental impact (Chang et al., 2019). One notable initiative is the Samsung Innovation Campus, which provides opportunities for 3,000 students in technology fields. Samsung's CSR vision emphasizes empowering the younger generation, encapsulated in the slogan "Together for Tomorrow! Enabling People." Their focus on youth stems from the belief that this generation holds the potential to drive future innovations and significant social change. Samsung's CSR journey began in 1995 and continues with growing intensity. They publish an annual CSR report, available to the public, showcasing their sustainability efforts. The 2023 report, titled "A Journey Towards a Sustainable Future," details Samsung's commitment to the planet, people, and sustainability, supported by concrete achievements and data (Samsung, 2023).

### 6.2.2 Hyundai

Hyundai's community engagement focuses on various CSR activities, including global health initiatives and educational programs. While these efforts demonstrate Hyundai's commitment to CSR, they have faced criticism for being more promotional than impactful (Rhee et al., 2017; Ryu & Chae, 2021). In 2023, Hyundai invested in reforestation, housing, and STEM[1] education in coastal Georgia, partnered with "One Tree Planted" to plant 200,000 trees across North America, and supported diversity programs like sponsoring the Museum of Latin American Art and being a founding donor of the National Museum of African American History and Culture. Hyundai also contributes to community-building through projects like "Habitat for Humanity of Orange County," which has built over 200 homes, and a partnership with Northgate Markets to provide holiday meals to those facing food insecurity. Hyundai's Sustainability Report, available online, outlines their CSR policies and ESG initiatives aimed at improving business operations and enhancing stakeholder lives (Hyundai, 2023).

### 6.2.3 LG Group

LG has been actively involved in environmental stewardship and community initiatives (Jun & Kim, 2021), reflecting the chaebols' growing acknowledgment of their social responsibilities (Kim, 2023). LG's commitment to CSR is evident on its official website, where its philosophy, "Life's Good," drives impactful initiatives aimed at enhancing quality of life. These programs address societal needs such as hunger eradication, healthcare for underserved populations, and support for armed forces personnel. Notable initiatives include "Karein Roshni: Light for Every Sight," which targets assistance for 14,500 individuals through partnerships with eye care institutes across India, and "Life's Good Nutrition Program," which provides nutritious meals to 59,000 children in Indian government schools through collaborations with Akshaya Patra and Annapoorna Trust. Another impactful program is the "LG Digital Class," designed to improve digital education access for marginalized communities, benefiting 135 teachers and 8,422 students. LG also publishes its CSR report, focusing on two key areas: the "3Cs" for the planet—Carbon neutrality, Circularity, and Clean technology—and the "3Ds" for people—Design for all, Decent workplace, and Diversity and inclusion (LG, 2023).

### 6.2.4 SK Group

Moving to another conglomerate, we can point out how SK Group oversees the operations of over 175 companies spanning various sectors, including energy, life sciences, advanced materials, mobility, and semiconductors.[2] They assert that their dedication extends beyond mere financial expansion, striving incessantly to generate significant social value that safeguards the environment and elevates communities globally in its double bottom line philosophy to create simultaneous growth in the companies' economic and social value. Since 2018, SK Group has published its social value measurement methodology along with its annual outcomes and has made the sustainability report for the 17 SK companies public (SK, 2023).[3]

In conclusion, implementing CSR in chaebols is fraught with challenges and ethical considerations. The centralized, family-dominated structure of chaebols often leads to conflicts between profit-making and broader societal responsibilities. Issues of transparency and accountability are prominent, as family interests may not always align with public welfare. The ethical dilemma is further complicated by instances of nepotism and corporate misconduct within some chaebols, casting doubt on the authenticity of their CSR initiatives (Campbell II & Keys, 2002). Moreover, the balance between pursuing aggressive growth strategies and adhering to sustainable, socially responsible practices poses a continuous challenge (Krueger & Yoo, 2002). This aspect was understood by the government, which, just as it had previously intervened to support the economic growth of chaebols, promptly took action to assist them in adopting socially responsible and sustainable policies.

## 7. THE IMPACT OF GOVERNMENT INCENTIVES ON CSR PRACTICES AND CHAEBOLS' RESPONSE

Recognizing the importance of CSR practices, the government quickly moved to aid chaebols in adopting socially responsible and sustainable policies. However, the relationship between chaebols and CSR is complex and multifaceted. While there has been a notable shift towards embracing CSR, challenges remain, particularly in terms of ethical considerations and the genuineness of these initiatives. The evolution of CSR in chaebols reflects a broader global trend of integrating social responsibility into business practices, yet it is clear that the mere adoption of CSR policies is not sufficient. It requires a fundamental change in corporate ethos and governance to ensure that CSR moves beyond public relations, becoming a core element of corporate identity (Ryu & Chae, 2021). In Korea, the CSR initiatives of large companies, as seen in previous examples, are often characterized by philanthropic efforts, known as "corporate community relations." These initiatives include not only charitable projects but also volunteer activities by CEOs and employees (Nam, 2011). Many large corporations channel their social contribution funds through foundations established by the conglomerates themselves.[4]

One controversial aspect of corporate philanthropy in Korea is the timing of significant donations, often following legal convictions of conglomerate owners for crimes like embezzlement or tax evasion. This pattern suggests that companies prioritize donations to divert public scrutiny from illegal activities.

Consequently, the Korean public is often skeptical, viewing CSR efforts as superficial public relations tactics. These initiatives are seen as strategies to manage public perception and restore the tarnished reputation of large firms, with the belief that corporate donations can help improve their public image (Choi & Aguilera, 2009).

Frequently, for Korean companies, CSR is largely seen as activities beyond their primary business operations and has not been integrated into the core functions of the firms. This could indicate that Korean companies have yet to incorporate long-term CSR initiatives into their foundational beliefs or strategic planning. In contrast to numerous multinational corporations in developed markets, Korean businesses have not fully adopted CSR as a strategic element. Large corporations in Korea are increasingly criticized for neglecting the concerns of stakeholders amid growing social and economic disparities between the affluent and the less affluent, as well as between larger and smaller companies. Given their dominant role in the Korean economy, these corporations face accusations of not sufficiently engaging in CSR efforts (Nam, 2011).

In this scenario, one aspect that should not be underestimated and should be interpreted in a positive rather than a negative sense is the fact that the support from the government in the chaebols' formation (Nam, 2011) has been prompted to contribute positively to society. Moreover, following the 1997 Asian financial crisis, the Korean government has significantly influenced the promotion of CSR among major corporations. To foster greater accountability and enhance CG, it introduced a raft of legislation and guidelines.

Notably, in 2002, it founded the Anti-Corruption Committee (which later became the Korea Independent Commission Against Corruption), aiming to boost corporate integrity. Moreover, South Korea's commitment to sustainability and CSR is highlighted by the establishment and evolution of the Korea Corporate Governance Service (KCGS), which, since its inception in June 2002 under the approval of the Minister of Economy and Finance and leadership of Gwang Sun Jung as its inaugural president, has been a cornerstone in promoting responsible corporate practices.

From 2003 onwards, the Ministry of Commerce, Industry and Energy (now known as the Ministry of Knowledge Economy) has actively encouraged ethical conduct among both public and private entities. This effort included the creation of the Business Institute for Sustainable Development within the Korea Chamber of Commerce, dedicated to fostering sustainability management through collaborative efforts with various stakeholders.

In October 2006, in partnership with the Korea Chamber of Commerce and Industry and the Institute for Industrial Policy Studies, the Ministry introduced the Korean Sustainability Report Indicators. An annual awards ceremony has been established to recognize outstanding achievements in sustainability management and best practices within the country (Nam, 2011).

Furthermore, in 2010, the government formed the Committee for Shared Growth to advocate for a cooperative and mutually beneficial relationship between large corporations and small to medium-sized enterprises (SMEs). This initiative aimed to address the increasing public concern and critique regarding the widening economic disparity, especially the expanding divide between large corporations and SMEs in Korea. Despite the Committee's efforts to earmark certain industries and activities for SMEs exclusively, it encountered substantial opposition from major conglomerates, culminating in the resignation of the committee's inaugural chairperson. Additionally, even in 2010, the Korea International Cooperation Agency (KOICA), the leading development cooperation agency affiliated with the Ministry of Foreign Affairs, launched pilot public–private partnership projects as one of its Official Development Assistance (ODA) programs, which was later renamed to the global CSR program (Kim & Shin, 2022; Sohn et al., 2014).

A landmark development in its mission was the expansion of its governance rating system in 2011 to encompass environmental (E) and social (S) considerations, culminating in the creation of an integrated ESG rating scheme (Choi et al., 2024). Through its comprehensive guidelines, KCGS not only advocates for but also facilitates the voluntary improvement of CG among companies. These guidelines are encapsulated in the code of best practices for CG, providing a blueprint for companies to elevate their governance practices voluntarily.

Significantly, in September 2022, the commitment was further emphasized through the organization's rebranding to the Korea Institute of Corporate Governance and Sustainability (KCGS), symbolizing a strengthened dedication to integrating sustainability into the core of CG. Operating as a not-for-profit association under Article 32 of the Civil Act, KCGS is at the forefront of guiding the South Korean capital markets towards a more sustainable and ethical future. It aims to foster the sound development of these markets by charting a course for companies to achieve sustainable growth. This is accomplished through meticulous analysis, research, and ratings that assess companies' adherence to environmental and social responsibilities alongside maintaining healthy and transparent governance. KCGS's membership comprises capital market-related organizations, further illustrating the collective effort toward elevating CG standards. Thus, KCGS's initiatives have been pivotal in aiding listed companies in Korea to enhance their governance structures. This includes the establishment of a CG framework through the publication and continuous update of the code of best practices for CG, in setting standards for audit committees and evaluating the governance practices of listed companies.

This concerted effort by KCGS underscores South Korea's proactive stance on embedding sustainability and CSR into the industry of its corporate sector, marking a significant step toward achieving global sustainability goals and fostering a transparent, responsible corporate ecosystem for firms that choose to adhere to CSR policies.

## 8. CONCLUSION

In conclusion, the intricate relationship between chaebols and CSR in South Korea presents a multifaceted landscape characterized by both advancements and challenges. Despite a progressive shift towards the adoption of CSR practices, issues concerning the authenticity and ethical implications of these initiatives persist. The evolution of CSR within chaebols mirrors a global movement towards the integration of social responsibility into core business operations, underscoring the necessity for a deep-rooted transformation in corporate culture and governance structures. This transformation is vital for ensuring CSR transcends its perceived role as a mere public relations tool and becomes ingrained in the corporate identity of the chaebols.

The South Korean government's role in facilitating the adoption of CSR practices highlights a positive shift toward enhancing corporate governance and accountability. Through legislative measures, guidelines, and the establishment of committees and institutions like the KCGS and the KFTC, the government has actively promoted ethical conduct and sustainability management. These efforts, aimed at fostering a more sustainable and equitable business environment, underscore the potential for CSR to contribute meaningfully to societal well-being when supported by a commitment to genuine change and collaboration among stakeholders.

As we reflect on the journey of CSR in South Korea, it becomes evident that while significant strides have been made, the path towards fully integrating CSR into the ethos and strategic planning of corporations remains a work in progress. The future of CSR in chaebols, therefore, hinges on a collective effort to redefine corporate success, not just in terms of financial performance but as a measure of social and environmental impact. This redefinition is crucial for building a more sustainable, responsible, and inclusive corporate sector that not only meets the demands of the present but is also prepared to address the challenges of the future.

## NOTES

1. STEM is an approach to learning and development that integrates the areas of science, technology, engineering, and mathematics.
2. See, for instance, https://eng.sk.com/companies
3. https://eng.sk.com/social-value/sustainability-reports
4. See, for instance, the Hyundai Motor Chung Mong-Koo Foundation https://www.hyundai-cmkfoundation.org/en/main, or the Asan Namun Foundation

https://asan-nanum.org/eng/, a nonprofit foundation established in October 2011 to commemorate the 10th anniversary of the death of Hyundai founder Chung Ju-yung, which carries out various programs throughout society to spread entrepreneurship and cultivate and support the individuals and institutions that propel transformation toward a more improved world. A foundation dedicated to young entrepreneurs and social innovators, this foundation will serve as a platform for them to engage in challenges, develop their skills, and exchange ideas, all under a shared vision of "A world where if you believe it, you can achieve it."

## REFERENCES

Almeida, H., Kim, C. S., & Kim, H. B. (2015). Internal capital markets in business groups: Evidence from the Asian financial crisis. *The Journal of Finance*, *70*(6), 2539–2586.

Alsayegh, M. F., Abdul Rahman, R., & Homayoun, S. (2020). Corporate economic, environmental, and social sustainability performance transformation through ESG disclosure. *Sustainability*, *12*(9), 3910.

Andolfo, I. (2018). Chaebols, the engine of the Korean economy: A case study of the Samsung Group. Master's degree thesis, Luiss Guido Carli.

Bae, G. S., Cheon, Y. S., & Kang, J.-K. (2008). Intragroup propping: Evidence from the stock-price effects of earnings announcements by Korean business groups. *The Review of Financial Studies*, *21*(5), 2015–2060.

Ben-Shahar, D., Carmeli, A., Sulganik, E., & Weiss, D. (2023). Power and dominant coalitions in family business. *Academy of Management Review*, *48*(3), 530–555.

Brammer, S., & Millington, A. (2008). Does it pay to be different? An analysis of the relationship between corporate social and financial performance. *Strategic Management Journal*, *29*(12), 1325–1343.

Brickley, J. A., & Zimmerman, J. L. (2010). Corporate governance myths: Comments on Armstrong, Guay, and Weber. *Journal of Accounting and Economics*, *50*(2–3), 235–245.

Brundtland, G. H. (1987). *Our Common Future: The World Commission on Environment and Development* (pp. 45–65). United Nations.

Campbell II, T. L., & Keys, P. Y. (2002). Corporate governance in South Korea: The chaebol experience. *Journal of Corporate Finance*, *8*(4), 373–391.

Chang, V., Zhang, W., & Xiong, C. (2019). The strategic view and development of corporate social responsibility: The case study of Samsung. *International Journal of Strategic Decision Sciences*, *10*(1), 105–130.

Choi, J., Roh, T., & Lee, J.-H. (2024). The pitfalls of corporate social irresponsibility: Hypocrisy of family firms in South Korea. *Journal of Cleaner Production*, *435*, 140557.

Choi, M., & Hong, S. (2022). Another form of greenwashing: The effects of chaebol firms' corporate governance performance on the donations. *Sustainability*, *14*(6), 3373.

Choi, S., & Aguilera, R. (2009). A comparative analysis of CSR in Japan and Korea from a multiple stakeholders' perspective. *Corporate Social Responsibility: A Case Study Approach*, 123–147.

Crane, A., McWilliams, A., Matten, D., Moon, J., & Siegel, D. S. (eds) (2008). The corporate social responsibility agenda. In *The Oxford Handbook of Corporate Social Responsibility* (pp. 3–16). Oxford University Press.

Du Plessis, J. J., Hargovan, A., & Harris, J. (2018). *Principles of Contemporary Corporate Governance.* Cambridge University Press.

Elkington, J., & Rowlands, I. H. (1999). Cannibals with forks: The triple bottom line of 21st century business. *Alternatives Journal, Waterloo, 25*(4), 42–43.

Freeman, R. E., & Dmytriyev, S. (2017). Corporate social responsibility and stakeholder theory: Learning from each other. *Symphonya Emerging Issues in Management, 1*, 7–15.

Friedman, M. (1970). The social responsibility of business is to increase its profits Milton Friedman. *The New York Times Magazine* (13 September 1970).

Haggard, S., & Moon, C.-i. (1990). Institutions and economic policy: Theory and a Korean case study. *World Politics, 42*(2), 210–237.

Hillman, A. J., Cannella, A. A., & Paetzold, R. L. (2000). The resource dependence role of corporate directors: Strategic adaptation of board composition in response to environmental change. *Journal of Management Studies, 37*(2), 235–256.

Hillman, A. J., & Dalziel, T. (2003). Boards of directors and firm performance: Integrating agency and resource dependence perspectives. *Academy of Management Review, 28*(3), 383–396.

Hyundai (2023). *Road to Sustainability.* https://www.hyundai.com/worldwide/en/company/sustainability/sustainability-report

Iansiti, M., & Levien, R. (2004). Strategy as ecology. *Harvard Business Review, 82*(3), 68–78, 126.

Johnston, P., Everard, M., Santillo, D., & Robèrt, K.-H. (2007). Reclaiming the definition of sustainability. *Environmental Science and Pollution Research International, 14*(1), 60–66.

Jun, H., & Kim, M. (2021). From stakeholder communication to engagement for the sustainable development goals (SDGs): A case study of LG electronics. *Sustainability, 13*(15), 8624.

Kim, H., Hoskisson, R. E., Tihanyi, L., & Hong, J. (2004). The evolution and restructuring of diversified business groups in emerging markets: The lessons from chaebols in Korea. *Asia Pacific Journal of Management, 21*, 25–48.

Kim, H., Kim, H., & Hoskisson, R. E. (2010). Does market-oriented institutional change in an emerging economy make business-group-affiliated multinationals perform better? An institution-based view. *Journal of International Business Studies, 41*, 1141–1160.

Kim, J. (2017). Corporate financial structure of South Korea after Asian financial crisis: The chaebol experience. *Journal of Economic Structures, 6*(1), 1–14.

Kim, K. (2013). Chaebols and their effect on economic growth in South Korea. *Korean Social Sciences Review, 3*(2), 1.

Kim, S. (2023). The COVID-19 pandemic and corporate social responsibility of Korean global firms: From the perspective of stakeholder theory. *Emerald Open Research, 1*(4).

Kim, S., & Shin, J. E. (2022). Evolving boundaries of CSR: South Korea's PPP-ODA in international development. *Development Studies Research, 9*(1), 206–218.

Kitzmueller, M., & Shimshack, J. (2012). Economic perspectives on corporate social responsibility. *Journal of Economic Literature, 50*(1), 51–84.

Krueger, A. O., & Yoo, J. (2002). Chaebol capitalism and the currency-financial crisis in Korea. In S. Edwards & J. A. Frankel (eds), *Preventing Currency Crises in Emerging Markets* (pp. 601–662). University of Chicago Press.

Lee, D., Lee, S., & Cho, N.-E. (2019). Voluntary disclosure and market valuation of sustainability reports in Korea: The case of chaebols. *Sustainability, 11*(13), 3577.

LG (2023). Better life for all. https://www.lg.com/content/dam/lge/global/sustainability/pdf/2022-2023_LGE_SR_STORY_BOOK(EN).pdf

Lockett, A., Moon, J., & Visser, W. (2006). Corporate social responsibility in management research: Focus, nature, salience and sources of influence. *Journal of Management Studies, 43*(1), 115–136.

Magnan, M., & Michelon, G. (eds) (2024). Corporate governance and corporate social responsibility: A reconciliation with tension. In *Handbook on Corporate Governance and Corporate Social Responsibility* (pp. 2–11). Edward Elgar Publishing.

Martens, M. L., & Carvalho, M. M. (2016). The challenge of introducing sustainability into project management function: Multiple-case studies. *Journal of Cleaner Production, 117*, 29–40.

Martínez-Perales, S., Ortiz-Marcos, I., Juan Ruiz, J., & Lázaro, F. J. (2018). Using certification as a tool to develop sustainability in project management. *Sustainability, 10*(5), 1408.

Moskalev, S., & Park, S. C. (2010). South Korean chaebols and value-based management. *Journal of Business Ethics, 92*, 49–62.

Nam, Y.-S. (2011). The changing landscape of corporate social responsibility in Korea. *Revista de EDUCAÇÃO do Cogeime, 20*(38), 145–158.

Pfeffer, J., & Salancik, G. (1978). *The External Control of Organizations: A Resource Dependence Perspective*. Harper & Row.

Rhee, J. H., Bohnsack, R., & Lee, S. (2017). Hyundai motor company case–fostering social enterprises. In G. Lenssen, J. H. Rhee & F. Martinez (eds), *The Role of Corporate Sustainability in Asian Development: A Case Study Handbook in the Automotive and ICT Industries* (pp. 119–143). Springer.

Roberts, D. J., & Van den Steen, E. (2000). Shareholder interests, human capital investment and corporate governance. Stanford GSB Working Paper No. 1631. https://papers.ssrn.com/sol3/papers.cfm?abstract_id=230019

Ryu, H., & Chae, S.-J. (2021). Family firms, chaebol affiliations, and corporate social responsibility. *Sustainability, 13*(6), 3016.

Ryu, H., & Chae, S.-J. (2022). Relationship between related party transactions and the social contribution activities of South Korean chaebol companies. *Sustainability, 14*(5), 2834.

Samsung, E. (2023). A journey towards a sustainable future. https://csr.samsung.com/data/Sustainability_report_2023_en.pdf

Sánchez, M. A. (2015). Integrating sustainability issues into project management. *Journal of Cleaner Production, 96*, 319–330.

Scherer, A. G., Rasche, A., Palazzo, G., & Spicer, A. (2016). Managing for political corporate social responsibility: New challenges and directions for PCSR 2.0. *Journal of Management Studies, 53*(3), 273–298.

Shenhar, A. J., & Dvir, D. (2007). *Reinventing Project Management: The Diamond Approach to Successful Growth and Innovation*. Harvard Business Review Press.

SK (2023). Sustainability reports. https://eng.sk.com/social-value/sustainability-reports

Sohn, H., Park, B., & Kim, N. (2014). A study on Korean Public-Private Partnership (PPP) for international development cooperation: Focusing on KOICA's global CSR Program. *Journal of International Area Studies*, *23*(2), 121–155.
Solomon, J. (2020). *Corporate Governance and Accountability*. John Wiley & Sons.
Thamhain, H. J. (2014). *Managing Technology-based Projects: Tools, Techniques, People and Business Processes*. John Wiley & Sons.
United Nations (2015). Transforming our world: The 2030 Agenda for Sustainable Development. https://sdgs.un.org/2030agenda

## WEBSITES

Hyundai: https://www.hyundaicsr.com/
LG Group: https://www.lg.com/in/lg-india-corporate-social-responsibility/
Samsung: https://csr.samsung.com/en/main.do
SK Group: https://eng.sk.com/social-value/sustainability-reports

# 14. Theory and application of effective governance in modern family philanthropy

**Małgorzata Smulowitz**

## 1. INTRODUCTION

Long before the global crises of the early 2020s highlighted systemic challenges, scholars emphasized the need to reinvent capitalism by aligning business success with societal progress, a concept often described as "shared value" (Porter & Kramer, 2011). They argued that businesses have traditionally prioritized short-term financial gains, often neglecting broader social and environmental issues. Undeniably, the COVID-19 pandemic exposed the growing disconnect between many businesses' short-term focus and society's long-term needs. This disconnect was not limited to for-profit businesses; nonprofit organizations (including charitable incorporated organizations, nonprofit corporations, unincorporated associations, public foundations, private foundations, often run by families, among others) were also deeply affected.

The COVID-19 pandemic marked significant shifts in modern society. It exposed the vulnerabilities of nonprofit organizations that lacked effective governance. Consequently, many struggled to achieve their social and environmental objectives and to navigate the crisis successfully. Early estimates suggested that over a third of US non-profits would face potential closure within two years of the pandemic's onset due to financial strain (Candid, 2021, 2022). In response to this crisis, many donors increased their COVID-related funding, often providing unrestricted support to enable non-profits to weather the storm. However, post-pandemic, there has been a notable decline in unrestricted funding, dropping from 43 percent in 2020 to 18 percent in 2021. The widening gap between increased needs and decreased unrestricted funding poses a significant threat to nonprofits. Moreover, the reduction in support for capacity-building and the general operating expenses is cause for concern. As articulated by a prominent family philanthropist consulted at the onset of the pandemic, "In the business world, people aren't as dismayed by overhead costs as they are in the non-profit world" (Vogel & Smulowitz, 2022).

Ultimately, the pandemic resulted in the loss of over 1.6 million jobs in the US nonprofit sector (Johns Hopkins Economic Data Project, 2022), leading to a significant depletion of knowledge, experience, and diversity (Candid, 2023). While the sector has begun to recover, the lasting impact of the pandemic persists to date, highlighting the urgent need for core support and effective governance of the nonprofits to address the challenges ahead. This is particularly important for family foundations, which act as independent grantmaking structures, usually funded by regular gifts or a specific endowment from a single source such as an individual, a family, or a family-owned corporation. Given their independence, and subsequently a lack of external pressure, understanding how families can enhance their own governance while addressing global challenges can help achieve a ripple effect beyond the boundaries of the family business and across the whole sector.

Traditionally, research on family philanthropy has focused on family foundations, which were found to differ from the general population of foundations in size, board structure, and the responsibilities of trustees and staff (Brody & Strauch, 1990). Family foundations are closely linked to family traditions and values, driven by social responsibilities and an obligation to give back (Giacomin & Jones, 2022). However, more recently, scholars distinguish between family foundations and family business foundations (De Massis et al., 2021), with the former involving active donor or donor families, and the latter being foundations where the donor is a family-owned corporation.

Furthermore, more recently, family philanthropy is shifting from a model focused on giving through a separate vehicle to a more collective approach. In the evolving landscape of family philanthropy, an increasing number of families are adopting a more cohesive impact approach, giving equal importance to assessing the impact and sustainability of their business(es) along with their philanthropic activities (Vogel & Kurak, 2020). In addition, the public increasingly criticizes the disconnect between the altruistic rhetoric of philanthropists, especially elite ones, and their perceived appropriation of resources through their businesses and investments (Giridharadas, 2018). Family governance holds immense significance in addressing that issue. For business families, that involves implementing a framework to preserve both family values and extended wealth, thereby empowering them to generate a positive impact for the environment and society, and generations to come.

Typically, the transmission and exchange of values are at the core of family governance, fostering effective communication and nurturing relationships. Whether through formal policies or informal discussions at family gatherings, families discuss and agree on important family and business matters, fostering a stronger sense of unity and long-term success. This not only helps families address important day-to-day tasks but also ensures better alignment for significant decisions such as board composition, family council, family constitution (also called family charter), the choice of causes the family wants to support collectively, and the extent of family involvement in business operations and philanthropy, among others.

This chapter aims to provide families and their advisors with best-in-class practices for effective governance of family philanthropy. It offers guidance on developing structures that reflect family values and sustain their long-term vision for a more just world. Establishing a robust governance framework early on, or revisiting it periodically, ensures the continuity of the family's values across generations.

## 2. MODERN TRENDS SHAPING GOVERNANCE OF FAMILY PHILANTHROPY

In recent decades, philanthropy has undergone significant transformation (Vogel et al., 2020). Like anything else, it was driven by industrial revolutions that introduced partial automation and computers, and more recently, by the application of information and communication technologies, with an AI revolution in sight (Desoutter, 2024). These forces have shaped the landscape of today's world, including family philanthropy and its governance. However, it's not only the external factors affecting family philanthropy; many families themselves are driving transformative changes. They're embracing bold initiatives, embracing new risks, and daring to challenge the established norms (Vogel & Smulowitz, 2024). More precisely, modern trends profoundly influence family philanthropy, shaping its overarching objectives, strategies, and operations (Vogel et al., 2020). Some of these include:

Next generation as agents of change: The transition of leadership to the next generation and their fresh perspectives can significantly influence family governance practices, leading to changes in priorities, strategies, and decision-making processes.

Rise of effective and impact-driven giving: Prioritizing measurable impact and accountability drives changes in governance structures to incorporate evaluation mechanisms—whether internal, external, or both—along strategic planning lines and in alignment with impact goals.

Rise of multi-stakeholder efforts: The convergence of diverse stakeholder groups in philanthropy requires governance frameworks capable of facilitating collaboration, coordination, and alignment of efforts towards shared impact goals.

Rise of cohesive giving: Aligning the philanthropic activities of the entire family enterprise system with those of individual family members, branches, businesses, and investments can enhance the family's total impact. It also profoundly affects the governance of family philanthropy, requiring the family to align their objectives to effectively oversee joint initiatives.

Diversity, equity, and inclusion: The emphasis on diversity, equity, and inclusion in family philanthropy shapes its governance by requiring families to address systemic inequalities, promoting diversity in leadership and decision-making, and ensuring a just distribution of resources.

Professionalization of family philanthropy: Many families are more clearly defining the roles and responsibilities of family members and nonfamily staff by developing formal policies and procedures, adopting governance practices typically found outside the nonprofit world. They are increasingly delegating aspects of implementation to professionals.

Digital risks and cybersecurity: While social media and internet access offer powerful communication tools for family philanthropy, they also present risks such as spreading misinformation, possibly putting the family's reputation at stake. Furthermore, while financial technology facilitates global money transfers, nonprofit organizations need to prioritize robust governance to ensure effective oversight of their fund transfers and prevent potential criminal exploitation.

In sum, family philanthropy is evolving to become more structured, transparent, and accountable as business families strive to achieve sustainable and measurable impacts across all levels of their family enterprise system. In the next section, we will discuss how families can navigate the increasing complexity of family philanthropy.

## 3. FROM FAMILY PHILANTHROPY TO FAMILY PHILANTHROPY SYSTEMS

Recently, scholars have increasingly moved away from the term "family business" as it focuses too closely on the idea that there is only one core business. Instead, scholars define family businesses based on the extent of family involvement along a spectrum ranging from narrow to broad (Pieper et al., 2021). The term "business families" captures the complexity of the modern family system. It shifts the focus back to the family at the core. In such a kinship group, entrepreneurial activities may be present, but the emotional connection might not center around the legacy business, either because it no longer exists or has diminished in significance. In its place, the family may have a diversified portfolio of businesses, or it may choose to invest its accumulated wealth through a family office or an investment company.

This shift is reflected in the explosion of the use of multiple philanthropic vehicles by families in recent decades, also resulting from the upcoming massive intergenerational wealth transfer (Hall, 2019). It has been shown that wealthy families have started giving more, both individually and collectively, and in many different ways (Hegner, 2022). However, the effectiveness of their philanthropy depends on families' ability and willingness to orchestrate their various activities in a cohesive manner.

Families in the first or second generation often do not need to develop sophisticated governance practices as matters of the family and business remain rather manageable. Decisions and strategies can be developed and overseen by a handful of family members who have been with the family and the business since its beginnings. However, as families grow and evolve, they face a common challenge of organizing their governance practices, including those related to family philanthropy. Many of the dilemmas that they face revolve around how formal or informal the decision-making process for family philanthropy should remain, whether a family should exert a public or private profile, or how closely linked to the family as opposed to the business their philanthropic activities should be, as well as whether family philanthropy should be led only by family members or also with the support of nonfamily staff (Vogel et al., 2020). With each family generation bringing its own interests and perspectives to the table, the challenge of organizing family philanthropy becomes evident.

As a result, many families decide to develop and use a wide range of philanthropic vehicles, strategies, and practices to fulfill the individual and collective aspirations of their growing family. This is reflected in the invention and increased growth of new and varied giving and investing vehicles, from donor-advised funds (DAFs) to charitable limited liability companies (Brakman Reiser, 2018). Figure 14.1 provides an exemplary overview of what family philanthropy could entail for a four-generation family. Precisely, family philanthropy can become a complex system that includes informal as well as formal structures like the legacy foundation, successor foundations, DAFs, corporate philanthropy, and other vehicles. Due to its high complexity, business families that operate in such a philanthropic setup may end up working in parallel and being disconnected. Ultimately, it can lead to counterproductive outcomes, diminishing a family's impact not only for the environment and society but also for the business and the family itself.

To increase the impact of a business family, an orchestration of individual and branch-level objectives with a cohesive giving strategy is essential. Early pioneers in family philanthropy are increasingly adopting a more holistic

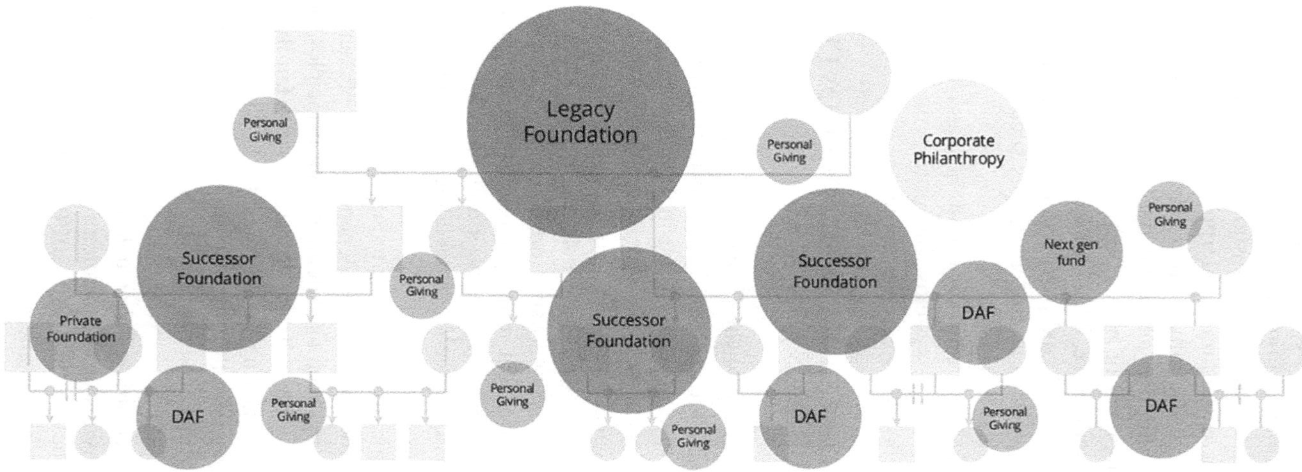


*Source:* Blanchard & Ulaszek, 2023.

*Figure 14.1* *Example of a complex family philanthropy system of a four-generation family adapted from philanthropy in complex, multi-generational families*

approach. Its principles drive families in orchestrating various family philanthropic activities, including traditional grantmaking, values-aligned investing, advocacy, and a thorough review of sustainability and corporate social responsibility (CSR) of the entire family enterprise system. Contrary to traditional grantmaking, the cohesive impact approach intentionally creates space for innovation, evidence-building, and collective risk-taking, with the hope of accelerating the development of new, effective solutions to challenges of a global scale (Vogel & Smulowitz, 2024). Finally, families are increasingly interested in donor collaborations and partnerships to scale their impact and to effectively address the massive global challenges such as climate change, migration, and the global health crisis.

In the next section, the focus will be on how business families can best design their family philanthropy systems, integrating their existing giving vehicles, to create a more holistic approach to impact.

## 4. FUNDAMENTALS OF EFFECTIVE GOVERNANCE IN FAMILY PHILANTHROPY

In the early stages of a family business, decision-making is rather simple. Typically, there is a small group of family members involved. However, as time passes, complexity grows. The family business may expand into multiple ventures, including other businesses, a family foundation, and a family office. Furthermore, each next generation wants to expand perspectives, pushing boundaries to explore new opportunities and wealth preservation strategies. To navigate this ever-changing landscape, families usually decide to enlarge the company's board, which might initially have been dominated by family members. However, with expanding business and financial responsibilities, along with family complexity, it becomes inevitable for a family to implement additional governance tools.

Family governance typically revolves around family values, vision, and mission. Achieving effective governance depends on implementing various elements specific to a family, such as statements and principles, policies and plans, and practices. The pyramid below, inspired by the family governance pyramid developed by Patricia Angus (2005) captures how families can prioritize these various elements in their family philanthropy. These exemplary policies, plans, and practices can serve a family to achieve and continue nurturing its legacy (Figure 14.2).

Furthermore, it has been argued that a family's capabilities within the domain of governance play a significant role in determining the longevity of the family and their businesses (Sullivan, 2019). Typically, when the second generation is ready to join the business, families begin organizing their governance structures to manage their financial and non-financial matters. This

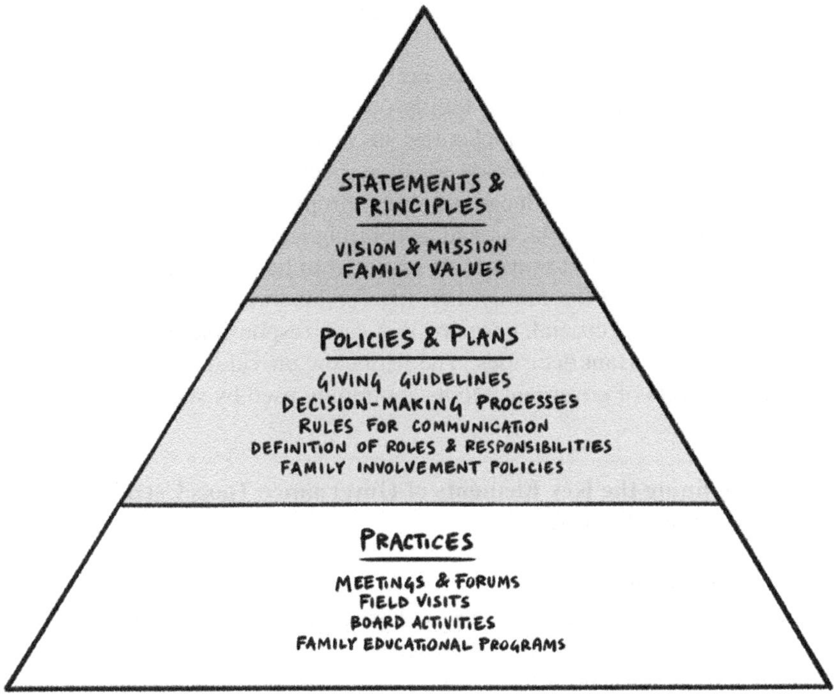


*Source:* Vogel et al., 2020.

*Figure 14.2 The family philanthropy governance pyramid adapted from the family philanthropy navigator*

includes organizing family events, navigating family conflicts, and safeguarding the well-being of both the business and the family. In the pursuit of harmony and success, families often decide to separate business matters from family affairs.

At the core of family business governance are one or more owners' groups, consisting of shareholders who own the family's assets. These groups may have a shareholders' council (also called owners' council) that convenes regularly to address shareholder matters, such as shareholder agreements and responsibilities. As the family expands into diverse assets owned by different shareholders, alignment and integration become essential. This often involves one or more boards of directors, either fiduciary or advisory, overseeing corporate structures and the family's assets. The owners share their objectives with the board, which then liaises with management. Many wealthy families also establish a family office that usually operates under the holdings board, managing and overseeing specific assets owned by individual branches or shared by the family (Jaffe & Grubman, 2020).

At the core of family governance are family councils which may include non-family mediators, designing family constitution, and tailored ownership structures to navigate the complexities of wealth and legacy (Jaffe, 2022). Typically, family members decide about a spectrum of activities, including redefining family values, education, philanthropy, family gatherings, use of family assets and special places, and celebrating legacy.

For a business family to thrive, it's essential to have robust governance for both the business and the family. Effective collaboration between these governance structures is crucial, ensuring that each responsible party has a voice and a vote in important decisions. The list below provides a short description of the key aspects of governance tools commonly used by successful business families.

## 4.1 Defining the Key Elements of Governance Tools Used by Business Families

### 4.1.1 The business side

- Owners' council: an entity composed of owners focused solely on the business, and not family issues, who set the overall mission, objectives, and strategic considerations for business and financial assets.
- Board of directors: an entity typically composed of family members and independent representatives that has oversight authority, and to whom the family office head may report. It represents that family in establishing the strategy and direction of the family office.
- Advisory board: often composed of some family and nonfamily representatives who help identify and prioritize issues objectively and recommend resources to address them. It is advisory in nature and separate from trustees, without fiduciary duties.

### 4.1.2 The family side

- Family assembly (also called family gathering): a periodic (scheduled) meeting of adult family members that often serves as a forum for investment or business performance, education, family philanthropy, updates on important events and milestones, as well as an opportunity for family members to vote on issues.
- Family council: an entity composed of family members to address family and business issues, as well as the intersection of the two, including family philanthropy.

At the core of the effective governance of family philanthropy are the board of trustees, board committees, guiding principles, policies, and specific protocols. Typically, the foundation's chair, supported by the executive director, leads the family's philanthropic activities, contributing to the wider impact and, ultimately, shaping the family legacy beyond that of their businesses.

Surprisingly, the governance of family philanthropy often lacks merit. Many families view philanthropy as a place for family members who cannot make it into the business. Furthermore, the grantmaking process involves a significant power imbalance, with one party holding the decision-making authority and the other receiving substantial (oftentimes more than financial) support. As a result, nonprofits often make easily avoidable mistakes at the expense of their beneficiaries. Initiatives like the Crappy Funding Practices ensure that foundations are held accountable (Le, 2023). The Crappy Funding Practices is a nonprofit organization, where beneficiaries can report "crappy" funding practices via a web form, remaining anonymous. Once the complaints are verified, the responsible funders are publicly named and shamed on the LinkedIn webpage. To date, the webpage has gained a significant following over a short period of time, demonstrating numerous negative practices populated in the third sector and a rapid increase in general interest in that domain. Some of the worst practices that nonprofit boards have been called out on include deviating from the organization's mission and vision, focusing too heavily on day-to-day operations, speaking with multiple voices, ignoring their crucial job of looking out for the community, or overlooking when the organization's policies and practices do not align with its own values (Le, 2023).

Prioritizing governance in philanthropy brings significant benefits to families, making every aspect of the philanthropic journey more manageable and enjoyable. It allows families to establish clear expectations within and between generations, offer direction for grant allocations, and accountability in their joint activities. In general, effective governance systems are flexible and capable of evolution. Similarly, in family philanthropy, a successful family in philanthropy adjusts to changes in objectives, portfolio complexities, and shifts in the number of family members and beneficiaries involved. It is increasingly important for families to build and maintain a healthy and well-governed philanthropic organization to ensure that philanthropy is not merely a repository for excess family members or a platform for pet projects.

## 4.2 Key Actors in the Family Philanthropy Systems

Family philanthropy often starts with an individual and evolves into a collective journey of multiple members. Successful philanthropy relies on building trusting and respectful partnerships where everyone works together for the greater good, putting the needs of others above personal interests. Giving as a family is rather complex. Family structures come in all shapes and sizes, with different relationships and ways of interacting. There are many ways families can work together in their philanthropy. For many philanthropists, family plays a central role in their philanthropic journey. Often, families use philanthropy to involve their members, especially those not directly engaged in the business. However, many philanthropic projects benefit from outside support. Building strong partnerships lays the groundwork for success and lasting impact. Making the right connections helps fill knowledge and skill gaps. Bankers and lawyers can offer expertise on financial and structural matters, while philanthropy advisors provide valuable insights from others' experiences or guide a donor family in the right direction. Hiring skilled staff further transforms and professionalizes family philanthropy. Figure 14.3 presents the key actors in family philanthropy and their interconnected relationships.

## 4.3 Organizing a Giving Vehicle Effectively

Family and business governance often evolve together. In essence, effective governance involves delegating certain responsibilities to the owners' council while ensuring that key rights are reserved for family shareholders to maintain the family's control and status. As next generations become more involved, more clarity is needed. This includes aspects like who decides, who is consulted, and how decisions are made. To design a clear governance process, a family needs to decide on the various factors such as defining roles and responsibilities, decision-making, rules for communication, and the family involvement policies.

Previous research found that centennial families shared specific features, uniting them and supporting their success that enabled effective governance (Jaffe, 2022; Sullivan, 2019). Accordingly, the key to generational success was found to be effective communication along with transparency, engagement, and mutual respect. By investing in family education and fostering collaboration, these families surpassed financial concerns to focus on their enduring legacy. In addition, they often depended on advisors in various matters, highlighting the importance of outsiders' expertise on shaping their long-term success.

### 4.3.1 The role of a board of trustees

Boards of trustees are focused on advancing the nonprofit's mission and serving the public good. They oversee budgets and fundraising efforts, often relying on donations, grants, and other forms of revenue. Nonprofit boards consider the interests of diverse stakeholders, including beneficiaries, donors, volunteers, and the community. Independent of the vehicle's form or stage, there are a few commonalities that bind all boards. As a minimum, the boards must

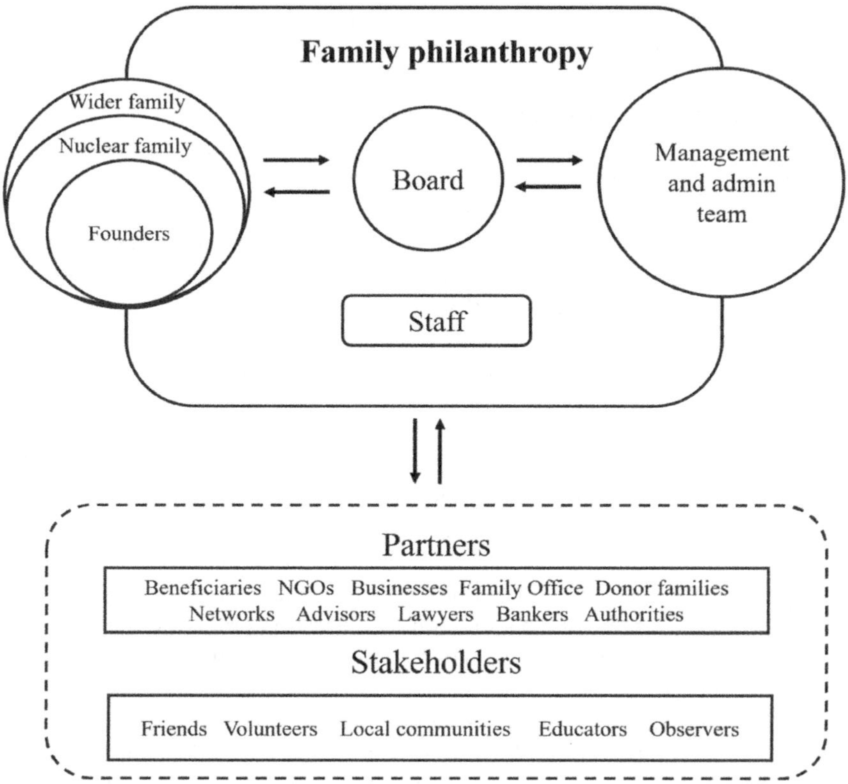


*Source:* Author's own work.

*Figure 14.3 Key actors in family philanthropy*

adhere to specific legal and regulatory requirements like tax-exempt status, transparency, and accountability. Nonprofit boards make decisions based on their organization's mission, impact, and social objectives. The role of a board of trustees extends beyond fulfilling legal obligations. Board members significantly contribute to the organization by shaping its culture, providing strategic guidance, enhancing effectiveness, ensuring financial sustainability, and serving as ambassadors and advocates. Beyond their legal duties, board members serve as invaluable resources for the organization in various capacities.

In sum, the effective governance of a philanthropic family's board involves careful planning and consideration of family dynamics, the inclusion of external expertise, and a clear definition of roles and responsibilities, all the while ensuring alignment with the organization's mission. Finally, nonprofit board members typically serve voluntarily and do not receive financial compensation.

### 4.3.2 Board structure and evolution over time

Philanthropic families face several key considerations when structuring their boards. Decisions must be made about whether to include only immediate family members or extend participation to the wider family. The inclusion of in-laws also needs to be addressed, particularly to help manage scenarios such as a possible divorce. Furthermore, families must decide whether to allocate board seats to their children, and if so, establish the appropriate age limits for board membership.

Another significant aspect is whether to invite nonfamily and independent professionals to join the board. If nonfamily members are included, their roles and levels of participation need to be clearly defined. In the absence of nonfamily board members, the family must find alternative ways to source the necessary subject area expertise to support the board.

Clarifying the responsibilities of each board member is crucial, along with setting out the procedures for sanctioning or removing members who do not fulfill their responsibilities. Additionally, the board's composition should be aligned with the organization's mission and strategic priorities, and families should consider the potential challenges posed by the current board structure in achieving these goals.

Furthermore, the optimal size, structure, and function of a board will vary throughout a philanthropic vehicle's growth stages. Typically, an odd number of seats is recommended to facilitate majority decisions during votes. In the beginning, a newly established philanthropic organization usually includes board seats for the founder(s). Initially, three members are ideal, while five members are considered the maximum, as larger boards can become too difficult to manage effectively. As the second generation of the family gets involved, the board can expand to include more members. Ultimately, there is no one-size-fits-all number for board members. Generally, the size of the board of trustees depends on the ownership structure, business complexity, and the size of the family. A common recommendation is to have five to nine board members. Over time, additional board seats can be added or replaced as needed. It is important to note that changing the board size requires significant support from the family and ownership group. Additionally, similar to the dynamics of large teams, each additional board seat can reduce the contribution of other members and demand more attention and effort from the executive director.

The responsibilities of a board evolve as a family's philanthropic organization progresses through different phases of its development. Initially, the founder is instrumental in shaping the core elements of the organization, including its mission, vision, supported causes, by-laws, and its policies, plans, and procedures. During this early stage, the board usually meets more often and is heavily involved in grantmaking, advising the executive director, and making key decisions. As the organization matures, the board's focus transitions to tasks such as recruiting and evaluating the management and administrative team, setting milestones for expanding its impact, establishing long-term processes, and discussing potential exit strategies. At this stage, board meetings typically become less frequent, often occurring quarterly.

### 4.3.3 Board committees

Typically, large nonprofits have boards along with various committees, each with distinct roles and responsibilities. Standing committees often include the audit and risk committee and a remuneration committee. Occasionally, the board chair or executive director may establish additional temporary or standing committees as needed. These committees generally comprise at least two board members and other designated participants. Meetings are held as frequently as necessary, but at least twice a year, either in person or remotely. Committees maintain records of their proceedings. If consensus is not reached, differing viewpoints are presented to the full board for consideration and decision-making. Examples of additional committees include executive, nominating, finance and investment, governance, grants, human relations, evaluation and impact, and ethics and compliance.

### 4.3.4 Board chair and board observers

A board chair is responsible for leading a nonprofit's board of trustees, representing the organization, and ensuring it complies with its mission, values, and regulations. The chair's role is central to the nonprofit's long-term strategic planning and involves facilitating board meetings. The key responsibilities of a board chair include encouraging active participation and attendance at meetings by board members, ensuring that actions and decisions align with the organization's by-laws, goals, and mission, acting as the main point of contact for the organization's key executives and staff, providing guidance and ensuring members are assigned to appropriate committees and projects, assisting in the orientation and onboarding of new board members, leading by example in fundraising efforts, representing the organization in interactions with the press, media, and other groups, and mediating conflicts among board members.

Family foundations often include board observers, who are typically next-generation family members. These observers can engage in discussions but usually do not participate in decision-making. The observer's role is usually rotational and lasts between three months to one year, allowing multiple family members to participate and learn. Additionally, boards may invite non-voting outsiders, such as advisors and thematic experts, to meetings to facilitate knowledge transfer and provide specialized expertise as needed.

### 4.3.5 Managing the board process

Having clear and well-defined policies is crucial for the smooth functioning of the board. Board policies provide a framework for decision-making, governance practices, and operational procedures, helping to guide the board's actions and maintain consistency over time. They include a wide range of guidelines and procedures related to board membership and operations.

One important aspect involves deciding how board seats are allocated among siblings and different branches of the family. Such an allocation process should ensure representation from various family members. It is also advisable to develop robust conflict resolution policies well in advance. Although the family constitution may include rules to help mitigate potential family conflicts, it should be assumed to be a living document, leaving a door for the next generations to align with the changing world on the outside of the family as well as the changes within the family. Ultimately, sound policies help the board effectively address and resolve disputes that may arise within the board or between board members and staff. Such policies provide a structured approach for managing conflicts, promoting constructive dialogue, and maintaining a positive and productive working environment for the organization and the family.

Furthermore, when selecting new board members, the board should consider specific criteria such as skills, capabilities, and expertise relevant to support effective governance of the organization. Such criteria help ensure that individuals chosen for board roles possess the necessary qualifications to contribute meaningfully to the decision-making. Furthermore, term limits and rotations within the board membership are essential for promoting diversity of thought and preventing board stagnation. By regularly rotating board members and imposing term limits, the organization can continually bring in fresh perspectives, strategic guidance, and fiduciary oversight.

Lastly, it is advised that boards use appropriate tools and resources to enhance the efficiency of their processes. These tools may include software platforms for document management, project planning, and communication, facilitating collaboration and coordination among board members and staff. This allows for more effective communication between the board and staff, leading to organizational success. Establishing clear channels of communication, regular updates, and feedback mechanisms ensures that everyone, both within the family and the staff, is informed, aligned, and working towards shared goals.

In sum, effective governance for a business family is not set in stone. It requires cyclical review by the family in order to match various expectations and the talent of the younger generation.

### 4.3.6 Best practices to minimize risks

Nonprofit boards must ensure compliance with local regulations, which often include mandatory registration. Conducting thorough due diligence is essential to keep the organization in line with the legal requirements of the country in which it operates. As part of effective governance, nonprofits should implement robust controls to guarantee that funds are properly accounted for and used according to the organization's mission. Adopting a "know your beneficiaries" policy is crucial, verifying the legitimacy of fund recipients and partner organizations (Vistra, 2022). For instance, when collaborating with another charity, it is important to scrutinize that charity's funding sources and assets to ensure they are legitimate. Proper due diligence and risk assessment in this area contribute to preventing money laundering and financing of terrorist groups.

Additionally, publishing annual financial statements and detailed information about the organization's goals, activities, trustees, and executive directors helps ensure regulatory compliance and fosters donor trust. Regularly reviewing and strengthening organizational structures, policies, and practices is crucial for preventing the misuse of funds and maintaining donor confidence.

## 4.4 Nurturing Cohesive Impact

Family philanthropy is becoming increasingly important for business families as the next generations are increasingly interested in the topics of environmental sustainability, community building, and empowerment. Through years of researching and advising business families, a noticeable trend has emerged: business families are increasingly moving toward more cohesive philanthropic efforts. While some families focus solely on the positive impact their donations can make, others adopt an investor-driven mindset, seeking novel approaches such as cohesive giving. This typically involves integrating their business activities, CSR, sustainability, impact investing, and family philanthropy into a unified strategy. This approach is driven by a clear vision and purpose.

Today, the demand for transparency in philanthropy comes from a wide range of stakeholders, including employees, customers, suppliers, competitors, and rating agenciesbeyond the socially or environmentally conscious family members or investors. Philanthropic families are increasingly focused on their ability to drive change and are proactively aligning their impact strategies across multiple channels, such as their businesses, corporate foundations, family foundations, and family offices, all while striving for greater transparency.

Families in business often drive changes that they would like to see in their industries, countries, and globally. A prominent example of that is the Bill & Melinda Gates Foundation, which since its formation in the year 2000, has driven philanthropic efforts and impact in many parts of the world. Another prominent example includes the Rockefeller Foundation, or the Bharti Foundation in India. Similarly, many business families deliberately engage with and align their philanthropic activities with the entire family enterprise system and those of individual family members and branches to enhance the family's cohesive impact. Such impact orchestration involves coordinating various elements of the entire family enterprise system to achieve desired results, often with a focus on maximizing positive outcomes while minimizing negative ones. In the context of social and environmental initiatives, families try to align resources, stakeholders, and activities to create meaningful and sustainable change. Whereas, in the context of their businesses, families engage to understand deeply and manage skillfully the consequences of decisions or actions that they take to ensure alignment with family values. Overall, a cohesive impact approach aims to optimize various efforts to create a holistic and cohesive system.

Typically, family members use the family council's meetings to start exploring the family's willingness to orchestrate their philanthropic activities throughout the entire family enterprise system. The family's readiness to engage and review its broader impact can vary. It may range from minimal orchestration, which includes a few selected philanthropic vehicles, to moderate orchestration, encompassing broader family philanthropic activities. At the highest level, there's full orchestration, involving both the family's and business's activities and investments in the domains of business activities, CSR, sustainability, impact investing, and family philanthropy (Table 14.1).

The various existing instruments and tools already existent in the family enterprise system can help families regulate and govern such holistic impact strategy. For example, for Family C as described in Table 14.1, typical policies and plans include the shareholders' agreement, family involvement policy, family constitution, investment policy statement, by-laws, and the collective impact statement. Many families decide to include more information about their approach to cohesive giving in their family constitution with the aim to inspire younger generations as well as imprint such practices as a part of responsible ownership practices within the family. Furthermore, typical practices include regular meetings of the board of trustees, the owners' council, family council, and the steering committee for collective impact. In essence, there exists a number of governance tools that can help business families design their cohesive impact approach. However, families should recognize that such documents must be treated as living documents, allowing future generations to adapt to both internal changes within the family and external changes in

*Table 14.1 Three levels of impact orchestration within the family enterprise system*

| Minimal orchestration – Family A | Moderate orchestration – Family B | Full orchestration – Family C |
|---|---|---|
| All family members are partners in decision-making. There are no formal policies or documents to regulate the family's giving. The approach is that family comes first, and the decision-making is value driven.<br>Company's core values, its mission and vision drive corporate philanthropy. | The foundation has its own board, and usually it includes family members and independent members. Several family members actively work in the family council and together make decisions or advise on the family's philanthropic organization, other types of family giving, as well as impact investing by the family office.<br>Family values are explicitly expressed and may differ from the company's core values as well as the mission and vision of the family. | The family and business have collaboratively developed a comprehensive strategy for both family and company philanthropy by establishing a collective impact platform. This platform includes diverse stakeholders such as public and private entities owned by the family, family and corporate foundations, employees, and shareholders, working in partnership with the beneficiary. Each member holds an equal vote within the steering committee, irrespective of their financial contribution. The core of this initiative lies in nurturing a unified community within the family enterprise system, pooling resources to effect positive global change.<br>There is an alignment between the values of the family and the business(es), with a holistic, coordinated mission and vision. |

the world. In essence, effective governance for a business family is not static; it necessitates regular review and adjustment by the family to meet evolving expectations and to leverage the talents of the younger generation.

## 4.5 Leading Effective Collaborations

In the face of complex social and environmental challenges, there is a growing trend among philanthropists to scale up and collaborate in order to drive systemic change, optimizing the impact of their activities by pooling resources such as finances and expertise (Vogel & Smulowitz, 2024). The integration of goals, cultures, and methodologies from multiple families or organizations inherently carries greater risks, both for the recipient partners and the families involved. However, in an era where collaboration is deemed essential for fostering a sustainable future, diverse stakeholders can unite to achieve a greater collective impact without compromising their individual values or aims. Healthy and constructive relationships are fundamental to effective giving and collaborative efforts aimed at co-creating solutions across various sectors. Key principles on how to collaborate for systems change include:

1. Adopt a trial and error approach: Allow strategies to evolve through continuous learning and adaptation. Flexible initiatives can foster innovation and encourage risk-taking, leading to potential breakthroughs.
2. Involve decision-makers: Ensure key figures are involved from the start and throughout the project to prevent miscommunication and guarantee support for decisions made during the collaboration's meetings.
3. Select partners wisely: Choose partners who share similar overarching goals and exhibit a positive attitude toward collaboration. Effective partnerships are built on shared values and a collective commitment to a common vision.
4. Establish clear boundaries: It is crucial for donors in specific collaboratives to set clear boundaries between what is contributed through collaboration and what is managed within their own organizations to avoid overlaps and misunderstandings.
5. Build trust and take risks together: Successful collaborations require trust, mutual support, and a willingness to compromise. Acknowledge that no single entity holds all the answers and embrace diverse perspectives.
6. Select the right governance model: Identify the best governance model for your collaboration. Partnering with an umbrella foundation or fiscal sponsor can streamline administration and reduce legal risks, allowing organizations to focus on their mission and balance the decisive power within the collaboration.

These principles highlight the importance of strategic, collaborative philanthropy that leverages the strengths and resources of multiple stakeholders to address complex global challenges effectively. Through such collaborations, philanthropists and their families can create more sustainable and impactful solutions that surpass the capabilities of individual efforts.

## 5. APPLICATION OF DIVERSE GOVERNANCE APPROACHES IN FAMILY PHILANTHROPY

Many families are increasingly striving to meet external demands for transparency regarding their impact. These demands aren't solely from socially or environmentally conscious family members or investors; they also come from various stakeholders, including employees, customers, suppliers, competitors, and rating agencies. Philanthropic families are articulating clear ambitions to leverage their power to drive desired changes in today's world. They're taking proactive steps to review and align their family's impact across multiple channels, such as businesses, corporate foundations, family foundations, and family offices. Below, I present three examples of how family philanthropy, when integrated fully into a family system, can drive results in this domain and beyond.

### 5.1 Ahlström Collective Impact for Children (Vogel and Kurak, 2020)

The Ahlström family business, established in 1851, spans interests from fiber-based materials to industrial technology. Over time, it evolved into the Ahlström Network, and in 2020, it employed around 15,500 people across 29 countries. In 2010, to revitalize family philanthropy, 15 female cousins from the fifth generation established the Eva Ahlström Foundation with a goal to support children and women globally. From its early days, the foundation has swiftly made a significant impact. Since opening a plant in Gujarat, India, the Ahlström company in collaboration with the Eva Ahlström Foundation decided to donate €200,000 ($212,816.80) to UNICEF India for a project aiming to provide better hygiene education and improved sanitation for 40,000 children. The foundation committed to supporting it for three years. Besides benefiting children directly, UNICEF showcased hygiene best practices to the Madhya Pradesh state government. The project's success led the government to invest an additional $102 million to extend its impact to 10 million children in the state.

This significant outcome reinforced the family's commitment to collaboration and a sense of responsibility for driving positive change. As a result, the Ahlström family and their companies agreed to establish a new initiative, the Ahlström Collective Impact (ACI). Formed in 2020, the initiative comprises the Ahlström family's public and private companies, foundations, family shareholders, and employees with a goal to support UNICEF Finland in the realization of selected United Nations' Sustainable Development Goals. The initiative is managed by a steering committee consisting of representatives from each ACI member and UNICEF. In 2020, ACI invested €240,000 ($255,385.20) to support vulnerable families in countries with weaker infrastructure, where the effects of COVID-19 could cause devastating increases in child mortality and malnutrition. ACI aims to harness the strengths of the entire Ahlström Network to amplify its collective impact.

### 5.2 The Total Portfolio Impact at C. Hoare and Co. (Vogel and Kurak, 2019)

C. Hoare & Co., a bank that is over 350 years old and is still owned by its founding family, demonstrates how philanthropy can be the cornerstone of success. C. Hoare & Co. remains committed to philanthropy, a tradition dating back to its establishment in 1672 by Richard Hoare.

In 1985, the bank established the Golden Bottle Trust, which receives 10% of its annual profits. In 2019, C. Hoare & Co. donated in total over £23 million ($28.6 million) through this trust. Central to the Golden Bottle Trust is the total portfolio impact (TPI). TPI is a transformative concept reshaping the perspective on philanthropy for organizations and individuals. TPI offers a holistic investing strategy in response to the limitations of traditional strategic asset allocation. It integrates grantmaking and investments, directed towards generating profits and social and environmental impact.

Philanthropy is deeply ingrained in C. Hoare & Co.'s culture, providing tangible benefits to its owners, employees, and customers. For the family, philanthropy serves as a binding tool, fostering unity among its 2,400 descendants. The bank's commitment to charitable giving reflects its shared values and strengthens mutual trust among family members. For employees, philanthropy acts as a market compass, enriching board-level insights and enhancing customer service. New employees participate in an onboarding program emphasizing the bank's philanthropic mission, leading to increased engagement and participation in philanthropic activities. Customers also benefit from C. Hoare & Co.'s philanthropic initiatives. The bank hosts various events for philanthropy that provide a platform for dialogue on important causes, facilitating connections between philanthropists and charities.

Philanthropy is a source of innovation at the bank. Established in 2011, being the first of its kind in the UK at the time, the Master Charitable Trust provides a streamlined alternative to managing individual foundations or charities. It operates as a Donor Advised Fund (DAF), where donors establish their own sub-funds called "Giving Funds." Bringing together these sub-funds within the Master Charitable Trust provides tax efficiency and cost-effectiveness for donors. In addition, C. Hoare & Co. collaborates with impact investment-focused organizations like Project Snowball to further its philanthropic initiatives.

In sum, C. Hoare & Co.'s holistic approach to philanthropy and investments extends throughout the bank and its stakeholder community, achieving the mission of being both good bankers and good citizens.

## 5.3 The Triple Bottom Line at Amesto Group (Smulowitz, 2023)

Established in 2002, Amesto Group (hereafter Amesto), a division of the Norwegian family business Spabogruppen, specializes in outsourcing services spanning accounting, payroll, HR, robotics, business systems, cloud infrastructure, artificial intelligence, analytics, and IT consulting. With over 1,000 employees, Spabogruppen recorded NOK 1.2 billion in revenue in 2020. The group is led by the second generation of Spandow siblings, Ariane, Arild, and Jan.

Initially focused on traditional philanthropy, the siblings soon recognized its limitations and decided to involve employees more actively. In 2012, Ariane, as Chair of Spabogruppen and Chief Corporate Social Value, initiated efforts to evaluate Amesto's environmental impact, engaging all employees in philanthropic projects. Additionally, Amesto provided pro bono solutions to NGOs, encouraging employees to extend their skills beyond company boundaries.

Being a hands-on family, the Spandows remain deeply engaged in the business, making it a natural choice to organize philanthropic efforts through the business. However, in the early days, Ariane faced challenges in integrating philanthropic perspectives into the business, feeling that traditional concepts of corporate philanthropy and CSR didn't fully capture value creation. Thus, she proposed adopting the triple bottom line approach, reframing the narrative around corporate social value.

The family advanced the triple bottom line initiative partly due to their recognition of the responsibility businesses have toward society and the environment, as well as the understanding that employee purpose extends beyond profit generation. They introduced this new approach to performance evaluation now based on financial, social, and environmental indicators.

While financial indicators like EBITDA (earnings before interest, taxes, depreciation, and amortization) remained unchanged, they developed new benchmarks for customer satisfaction and employee engagement. Amesto's employees actively participate in discussions and surveys, indicating increasing alignment with the company's triple bottom line approach. Despite challenges in measuring environmental impact, each business unit is required to integrate environmental initiatives into its models.

After all, the introduction of the triple bottom line was well-received by managers and employees, contributing to talent retention, customer attraction, and industry visibility. Spandows believes that integrating profit into philanthropic and social initiatives ensures sustainability. Triple bottom line helped to enhance Amesto's market positioning and commercial value, contributing to overall business success.

# 6. CONCLUSION

Today, we face what experts describe as a poly-crisis, characterized by interconnected global challenges, such as climate change, migration, inflation, and global health crises (Ahmad & Von Schnurbein, 2024). Addressing these complex issues requires coordinated efforts that cross national boundaries, bringing unified action on a global scale. Business families are uniquely positioned to tackle global challenges. Historically, they have sought to achieve impact through philanthropic vehicles. However, to enhance the effectiveness of family philanthropy, it is essential for business families to recognize that robust governance is the foundation for success. Effective governance is crucial for achieving meaningful results and impact; without it, progress is hindered. Implementing best-in-class governance standards is especially vital in the context of the ongoing poly-crisis, which affects organizations worldwide. Strong governance ensures resilience and adaptability in an increasingly complex and interconnected global environment.

In addition, many scholars have emphasized the need to reimagine capitalism by aligning business success with societal progress—a concept often referred to as "shared value" (Porter & Kramer, 2011). They pointed out that businesses had long prioritized short-term financial gains while overlooking social and environmental responsibilities. The COVID-19 pandemic exposed the consequences of this disconnect, highlighting the gap between businesses' short-term focus and society's long-term needs. This disconnect was not limited to for-profit entities but also impacted nonprofit organizations, including foundations, charitable organizations, and family-run philanthropic vehicles. By adopting governance models that integrate the concept of shared value, business families can not only weather the challenges of today's poly-crisis but also contribute to long-term societal well-being.

# REFERENCES

Ahmad, S., & Von Schnurbein, G. (2024). Searching for the North Star or how to navigate a boat with a fixed rudder through turbulent times. *Journal of Philanthropy and Marketing*, *29*(1), e1824.

Angus, P. (2005). The family governance pyramic: From priciples to practice. *The Journal of Wealth Management*, *8*(1), 7–13.

Blanchard, A., & Ulaszek, W. R. (2023). *Philanthropy in Complex, Multi-Generational Families: Balancing Individual Preference with Collective Purpose*. National Center for Family Philanthropy.

Brakman Reiser, D. (2018). The rise of philanthropy LLCs. *Stanford Social Innovation Review*, *16*(3), 26–33.

Brody, D., & Strauch, C. (1990). Who are the family foundations? Findings from the foundation management survey. *Family Business Review*, *3*(4), 337–346.

Candid (2021). *Philanthropy and COVID-19: Measuring one year of giving.* Candid. https://www.issuelab.org/resources/38039/38039.pdf

Candid (2022). *Philanthropy and COVID-19: Examining two years of giving.* Candid. https://www.issuelab.org/resources/40288/40288.pdf

Candid (2023). *Nonprofits, foundations adjust to the post-pandemic era.* Philanthropy News Digest. https://philanthropynewsdigest.org/news/nonprofits-foundations-adjust-to-the-post-pandemic-era

De Massis, A., Kotlar, J., & Manelli, L. (2021). Family firms, family boundary organizations, and the family-related organizational ecosystem. *Family Business Review, 34*(4), 350–364.

Desoutter (2024). Industrial Revolution—From Industry 1.0 to Industry 4.0. https://legacy.desouttertools.com/your-industry/news/503/industrial-revolution-from-industry-1-0-to-industry-4-0

Giacomin, V., & Jones, G. (2022). Drivers of philanthropic foundations in emerging markets: Family, values and spirituality. *Journal of Business Ethics, 180*(1), 263–282.

Giridharadas, A. (2018). *Winners Take All.* Penguin Random House.

Hall, M. (2019). The greatest wealth transfer in history: What's happening and what are the implications. Forbes. https://www.forbes.com/sites/markhall/2019/11/11/the-greatest-wealth-transfer-in-history-whats-happening-and-what-are-the-implications/

Hegner, S. (2022). *Ford Foundation Invest $10M to Support Southern Organizing via Mary Reynolds Babcock Foundation.* Mary Reynolds Babcock Foundation. https://mrbf.org/ford-foundation-invest-10m-to-support-southern-organizing-via-mary-reynolds-babcock-foundation/

Jaffe, D. T. (2022). What really works? 7 key features of 100-year-old global family enterprises. *Tharawat Magazine.* https://www.tharawat-magazine.com/sustain/7-key-features/

Jaffe, D. T., & Grubman, J. (2020). The two pillars of governance in family enterprises: A straightforward understanding of complex systems. FFI Practitioner. https://ffipractitioner.org/the-two-pillars-of-governance-in-family-enterprises-a-straightforward-understanding-of-complex-systems/

Johns Hopkins Economic Data Project (2022). Nonprofit employment during the COVID-19 crisis. Johns Hopkins Center for Civil Society Studies. https://ccss.jhu.edu/research-projects/nonprofit-economic-data/covid-nonprofit-employment/

Le, V. (2023). Join the movement to end Crappy Funding Practices. Nonprofit AF. https://nonprofitaf.com/2023/05/join-the-movement-to-end-crappy-funding-practices/

Pieper, T., Kellermanns, F., & Astrachan, J. (2021). Update 2021: Family businesses' contribution to the U.S. economy. https://familyenterpriseusa.com/wp-content/uploads/2021/02/Family-Businesses-Contribution-to-the-US-Economy_v.01272021-FINAL_4.pdf

Porter, M. E., & Kramer, M. R. (2011). Creating shared value. *Harvard Business Review.* https://hbr.org/2011/01/the-big-idea-creating-shared-value

Smulowitz, M. (2023). Do you know how to measure your impact beyond profits? IbyIMD. https://www.imd.org/ibyimd/brain-circuits/do-you-know-how-to-measure-your-impact-beyond-profits/

Sullivan, P. (2019). The 100-year family: Here are some tips for becoming one. *The New York Times.* https://www.nytimes.com/2019/11/06/your-money/wealth-100-year-family.html

Vistra (2022). How philanthropic organisations can improve governance—And why it matters. https://www.vistra.com/insights/how-philanthropic-organisations-can-improve-governance-and-why-it-matters

Vogel, P., & Kurak, M. (2019). How a 350-year-old family-owned bank uses philanthropy to benefit its business and society. IbyIMD. https://www.imd.org/research-knowledge/family-business/articles/how-a-350-year-old-family-owned-bank-uses-philanthropy-to-benefit-its-business-and-society/#:~:text=For%20the%20employees&text=Most%20board%20members%20at%20C,in%20which%20customers%20are%20served

Vogel, P., & Kurak, M. (2020). How cohesive giving inspires greater impact and stronger families. IbyIMD. https://www.imd.org/research-knowledge/strategy/articles/how-cohesive-giving-inspires-greater-impact-and-stronger-families/

Vogel, P., Kurak, M., & Eichenberger, E. (2020). Family philanthropy navigator: The inspirational guide for philanthropic families on their giving journey. IMD Business School. https://scholar.google.com/scholar?cluster=17308047902011637149&hl=en&oi=scholarr

Vogel, P., & Smulowitz, M. (2022). Navigating your family's philanthropic future across generations. IMD business school. https://www.imd.org/research-knowledge/family-business/reports/navigating-your-familys-philanthropic-future-across-generations/

Vogel, P., & Smulowitz, M. (2024). How to collaborate for systems change: Lessons from the world of giving. IbyIMD. https://www.imd.org/ibyimd/family-business/how-to-collaborate-for-systems-change-lessons-from-the-world-of-giving/

# PART IV

# Governance of Social Purpose, Mission, & Impact

# Introduction to Part IV

As Malgorzata Smulowitz outlined in Chapter 14, family firms can achieve meaningful societal and environmental change while simultaneously achieving the desirable financial results they want – assuming the proper corporate governance structures are in place. Her model focuses on family firms and family foundations, but it can easily be expanded to all non-family firms as well.

Corporate governance exists to provide a return on investment to suppliers of capital as we suggested in the Introduction. As we move into Part IV on the Governance of Social Purpose, Mission, and Impact, it may be necessary to think holistically about how any supplier of capital defines their "return on investment." Perhaps it is optimal for any firm to achieve meaningful societal impact *and* optimal financial results, but that does not need to be the only goal for every firm. Some firms may prioritize social, environmental, family and other goals above financial goals; other firms may have a strategy that optimal financial goals can *only* be obtained by prioritizing social, environmental, family and other goals. And this is the focus of Part IV; how can corporate governance enable firms to balance, align, and synthesize diverse goals to best provide their desired return on investment to all suppliers of capital?

We chose to end this book by studying the theme of mission purpose and impact because it encompasses and integrates all of the ideas we have introduced in the prior chapters. Every firm has a mission and a purpose. The firm's impact will be influenced – or even determined – by many of the cultural, new venture, and ownership dynamics we have discussed previously. The firm's impact will also be influenced by broad, cultural, and/or regulatory institutions that shape the environments within which firms operate. This is where we begin in Part IV.

In its 2004 Global Compact, the United Nations encouraged investment advisors "to better integrate environmental, social and governance issues in analysis, asset management and securities brokerage." To any investor, this advice should seem reasonable. However, we think it is safe to assume that the United Nations did not anticipate this charge leading to a global ESG industry, driven by proprietary strategies and billions of dollars in fees for these investment advisors. Yet that is exactly what has happened since 2004. As we write this, global investment "ESG" funds or strategies exceed $30 trillion (€28 trillion and are expected to be over $50 trillion (€46 trillion) by the end of 2025. Today, ESG investments represent 25% of all invested assets under management by these investment advisors.

But why? Why did investors decide these three dynamics – environmental, social, and governance – should drive their investment strategies? Why did they not choose to focus on corporate culture, innovation, and leadership? Why do we only care about E, S, and G?

In Chapter 15, Christos Cabolis, Maude Lavanchy, and Karl Schmedders dissect the phenomenon of ESG, challenging its purpose and efficacy. Specifically, they show that these three letters – E, S, G – have conflicting priorities. If our investment and corporate strategies are myopically driven by arbitrary principles, we are likely to achieve suboptimal results. As they conclude, "by focusing on ESG in the aggregate, we may hit the target but miss the point." In Chapter 16, Nguyen Thi Kim Oanh and Huong-Trang Pham continue this cautionary (and contrarian) view of ESG; they focus on the practice of greenwashing, or the practice of using environment-focused strategies (or marketing) to obscure other less desirable corporate investments. They show that a firm's board-level sustainability committee can either amplify greenwashing or eliminate it. We know which effective corporate governance should do.

In Chapter 17, Jinsuk Choi explores the positive aspects of ESG-driven strategies, introducing the unique perspective of institutional investors in Asia. He highlights the benefits and opportunities associated with incorporating environmental, social and governance priorities; but, similar to the previous two chapters, he does caution that in order to succeed, businesses must move beyond superficial engagement with ESG principles and align their governance practices with both ethical standards and financial performance. This is a truly unique case where we see culture, venture evolution, and firm ownership impacting how corporate governance systems are designed.

Chapters 18 and 19 conclude Part IV by moving away from macro-level governance and strategic issues and focus on specific firm-level structural governance mechanisms. Specifically, both chapters explore the governance of social purpose, mission, and impact by looking at the role gender plays in governance mechanisms. In Chapter 18, Agnes Dyvik Clark connects back to our Part II venture governance work and studies female founders, considering both formal and informal governance mechanisms. She provides unique best practices for female entrepreneurs – perhaps in contrast to much extant corporate governance literature – that best address their unique situations.

Finally, in Chapter 19, Richard Warr and Jing Zhao extend this study of gender as a corporate governance dynamic, looking at how it impacts corporate innovation. Ever since Norway mandated gender quotas for boards of directors in 2008, scholars have attempted to determine how gender diversity on boards of directors impacts firm performance; for the most part, they have failed to find a significant positive (or negative) relationship. Chapter 19 moves away from this macro perspective and focuses on corporate innovation; in theory, innovation should be a determinant of firm performance, but, as a more focused corporate construct, we may be able to better identify the impact of gender diversity on boards. This is the ideal way to conclude the first four parts of this book, as this research touches on all of the themes we have been exploring throughout. At the risk of spoiling your reading, they conclude that "the economic and societal impact of pro-diversity policies and how such policies can influence firm value as well as create direct social benefits." Again, this fits perfectly within our definition of corporate governance: to provide a return on investment to suppliers of human, natural, financial, and other capital. Indeed, this is exactly the purpose that corporate governance exists to create.

Every firm begins with a mission and a purpose. Corporate governance systems exist to support and advance this mission. The best corporate governance system for your business is the one that will best help you serve this mission.

1. Communicate with your formal and informal stakeholders. Your business exists to serve them. Any success you have in the future – success at serving your mission and your purpose – will happen because of them.
2. While your mission may never change, how you pursue that mission and serve that mission will constantly change. And your corporate governance systems should change accordingly.
3. In 2024, Daron Acemoglu, Simon Johnson, and James Robinson received the Nobel Prize in Economics for their work showing how inclusive societies create economic value. This insight can also inform corporate governance: inclusive governance practices – when authentic and well-aligned – can create long-term value and help your business serve its mission.
4. Innovation is the lifeblood of any business, and it is the heart of any corporate governance system. Be open to change and look for opportunities to innovate your corporate governance practices and systems. You want your governance systems to help your business make an impact in the future; be intentional about creating the systems that best help you do just that.

As we have said throughout these introductions, when it comes to the practice and implementation of corporate governance, one size does not fit all. And that is because your mission – and purpose and impact and stakeholders – is unique to your business. The practice of corporate governance is about providing a return on investment to suppliers of capital; how your business does that will be unique to your mission and your people.

# 15. The fundamental problem with ESG? Conflicting letters

**Christos Cabolis, Maude Lavanchy and Karl Schmedders[1]**

## 1. INTRODUCTION

Environmental, social, and governance (ESG)[2] themes are one of the main topics of conversation in business circles. This popularity has been partly fueled by increasing concerns in society and by alarming reports from the scientific community, each putting further pressure on companies to act. By October 2024, more than 14,000 companies had joined the United Nations Framework Convention on Climate Change's Race to Zero campaign, committing to take rigorous actions to limit the environmental impact of their activities. In 2022, ESG was mentioned on average nine times a quarter in earnings calls of S&P companies (compared to an average of at most one mention per quarter in 2017).[3] ESG ratings, which assess corporations against a variety of criteria, have proliferated. According to Bloomberg Intelligence, the value of investments in ESG assets could exceed US$50 trillion by 2025.[4]

Although ESG criteria are well-meaning, they suffer from several flaws. There is little consensus on what ESG means and how it can be measured. This has two implications. On the one hand, this lack of transparency vis-à-vis measurement allows companies to engage in greenwashing.[5] On the other, the absence of uniformity regarding measurement introduces noise to any attempt to rate companies. For instance, the average correlation between the overall ESG ratings of six prominent ratings providers is low (0.54), and values are even lower for individual criteria (0.53 for E, 0.42 for S, and 0.3 for G—see Figure 15.1). Research has shown that this lack of consensus between raters can be explained by their use of different survey items, scales, and weights, as well as by "rater-specific" bias.

We believe that a fundamental challenge underlying ESG is that it lumps together concepts that are profoundly different. In this chapter, we highlight the discord that exists between E on the one hand and S/G on the other. Frequently,

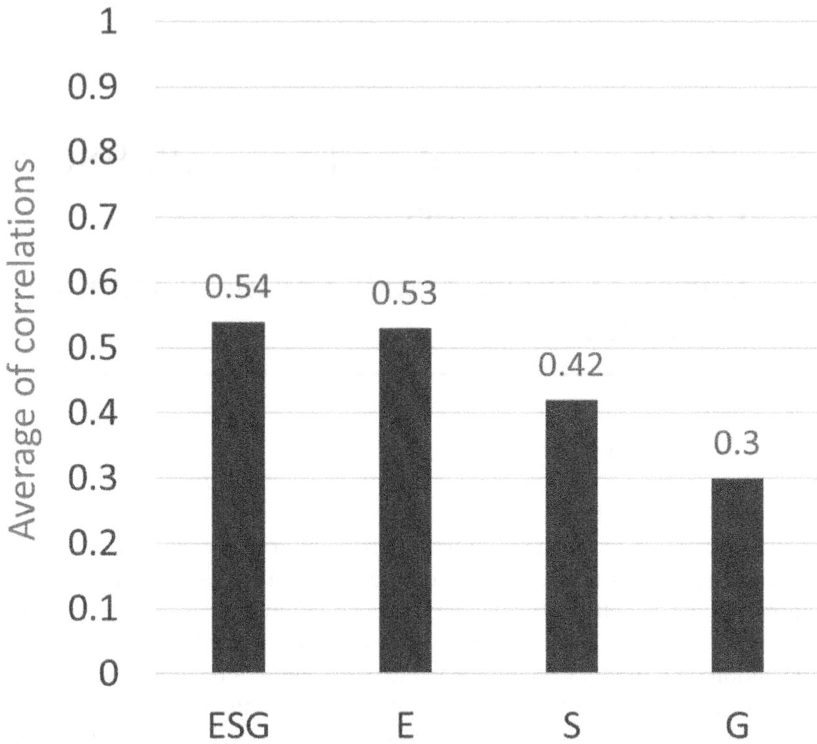


*Source:* Data from Berg, Koelbel, and Rigobon (2020, table 2).

*Figure 15.1* *Average of correlations between Sustainalytics, RobecoSAM, Vigeo Eiris, Asset4, KLD, and MSCI's ESG ratings*

an improvement in one component, say E, leads to a worsening in another, say S, with the result depending on the balance that the decision-maker strikes between potentially contradictory goals. We present solutions that businesses that wish to tackle environmental problems in particular can explore.

We begin by examining the differences between the three components of ESG, in particular by contrasting the public-good characteristic of E with the private-good characteristic of S and G.

## 2. WHY E IS DIFFERENT FROM S AND G

Environmental considerations are fundamentally different from social and governance considerations in at least three dimensions. First, whether the benefits of a good or a service related to the individual components of ESG are excludable in consumption. Second, regarding the time lag between an investment in one of these three components and the realization of the return on that investment. Third, regarding how uncertain any given action's outcome is.

## 2.1 The Tragedy of the Commons

In economics, a key dimension of our classification of a good is its excludability (i.e., whether we can exclude others from access and use). This distinction has implications for how goods are produced, used, and managed. Fisheries are a typical example of a non-excludable resource. Given the migratory nature of most fish species and the fact that most fish stocks are in international waters, rules and property rights are hard to establish and enforce. Access to fish is thus mostly open, and the rule of capture prevails. A negative consequence of this non-excludability is that no one has incentives to use the resource, fish, in a conservative manner. When such a resource is finite, a lack of sustainable management can lead to the tragedy of the commons: in this case, the rate of fishing exceeds the rate of reproduction, potentially leading to the extinction of the resource, the collapse of the fishing industry, and the reduction of food available to human populations as well as to other animals that rely on fish as a food source. Overfishing is one of the greatest threats facing the oceans.[6] Other resources clearly related to E, such as air, rivers, and forests, all suffer from a similar problem.

Because an organization cannot exclude its competitors from benefiting from its efforts with regard to E (e.g., efforts to reduce its carbon footprint), it has little incentive to pay the costs of those efforts. Most efforts with regard to S and G, meanwhile, are excludable. Improving the diversity of an organization's workforce (i.e., improving S), for example, leads to tangible benefits for that organization (e.g., positive effect on performance, creativity, and innovation, etc.), but not for its competitors. Likewise, a study by one of the authors of the present chapter shows that better shareholder protection and accounting standards (i.e., improving G) lead to higher merger premia (Bris and Cabolis, 2008).

## 2.2 The Tragedy of the Horizon

Another way in which E stands apart from S and G is its temporal horizon. In the case of S and G, there is little to no temporal gap between an investment and its return. Take the example of a company offering its employees on-site daycare—something that comfortably belongs in the S dimension. Research has shown that such an initiative leads to numerous benefits, such as reduced absenteeism, improved employee retention, and stress reduction.[7] Investing in providing one's employees with on-site daycare quickly makes a concrete positive impact that will be reflected in the bottom line. For the G dimension too, investments can generate returns that fall within the typical temporal horizon of political and top-management-team tenure. For instance, moving away from a culture of corruption (measured as the shared values and beliefs of a firm's employees) is associated with a reduction in corporate misconduct, including the receipt of kickbacks, accounting fraud, etc. (Xiaoding, 2016). Greater transparency in accounting also enables better decisions, ultimately producing rapid returns on investment.[8]

Unfortunately, the story is different for E. Following through on climate targets requires a long-term view. Scientists at the Intergovernmental Panel on Climate Change have raised the alarm: if we want to limit global warming, it is "now or never." In other words, actions should be taken now to ensure a livable future. But taking rigorous action—changing practices or acquiring technology to limit environmental impact, for example—is costly. Most of these costs must be paid now, while the benefits are likely to materialize only in the distant future. This gap between the timing of investment and its return has led to what Mark Carney has called the "tragedy of the horizon." Because the typical temporal horizon of politicians and top management teams is just a few years (the average tenure of a CEO is seven years),[9] the temptation to leave the tough decisions to one's successor is high—and that is the tragedy.

## 2.3 Uncertainty of Impact

The third reason why the E dimension is different from S and G is the higher uncertainty surrounding its impact. Pindyck (2022) suggests that "the extent of climate change and its impact on the economy and society more generally is far more uncertain than most people think." For instance, climate sensitivity (the link between an increase in $CO_2$ levels in the atmosphere and an increase in temperature) and the likely economic and social effects of warming, rising sea levels, and other aspects of climate change are all highly uncertain. Higher uncertainty makes prediction, and thus business planning, much harder.

There is, meanwhile, much more clarity on the impact of the S and G dimensions. For instance, there are many empirical studies that evaluate the impact of improved diversity, governance, and access to education. Reviews of the scientific literature have revealed the link between diversity and firm performance and the mechanism through which firms can extract benefits (or incur losses) from diversity (Roberson et al., 2016). A commitment to good corporate governance makes firms more attractive to investors and boosts performance.[10] Table 15.1 summarizes the above discussion.

*Table 15.1 Why E is different from S and G*

| - | E | S and G |
|---|---|---|
| Tragedy of the commons | Non-excludable<br>Everyone can benefit from a company's efforts to reduce pollution, even polluters. | Can be excludable<br>Organizations can exclude their competitors from benefiting from their investments in S and G (e.g., on-site daycare for employees only; transparent accounting methods). |
| Tragedy of the horizon | Short- versus long-term trade-off<br>The cost of reducing one's environmental impact must be paid now, while the benefits of such actions will mostly materialize only in the long term. | No temporal gap<br>The rewards of investments in S and G are mostly reaped within the typical temporal horizon of political and top-management-team tenure. |
| Uncertainty of impact | High uncertainty<br>The extent of climate change and its impact on the economy and society is highly uncertain. | Strong business cases<br>There is a large academic literature documenting the positive impact of S and G policies in general practice (e.g., equity, diversity and inclusion, child labor, access to education, corruption, and business ethics). |

These differences between E and S and G can sometimes manifest themselves in directly contrasting ways, where an improvement in one component results in a deterioration in another.

## 3. THE INTERNAL CONFLICTS BETWEEN E AND S/G

Compounding the fundamental differences between E, S, and G, the three dimensions frequently go head-to-head with one another. The most salient of these conflicts is that between E and S, and we observe it both within and across countries.

### 3.1 Within Countries: Social 1, Environmental 0

Initiatives to protect the environment (E) can have negative consequences for more vulnerable populations (S). Take the example of the yellow vests movement in France. The French government's decision to implement a carbon tax on fossil fuels triggered significant unrest in 2018. Although the tax was essentially "green" and aimed to incentivize consumers and producers to switch to more climate-friendly alternatives, parts of the French population found it socially unacceptable. For many, the financial implications of the tax (it was to hit lower-income groups hardest as a larger share of their disposable income is spent on energy, housing, and food) were more important than a green policy that would produce climate benefits in a distant future.[11] The resulting unrest was further fueled by a sense of inequity, as consumers would pay €44/t$CO_2$ while industry was paying around €25/t$CO_2$ in the EU Emissions Trading System. A misunderstanding of the monetary impact on households' finances and of the environmental effectiveness of the measure has also been shown to have contributed to an aversion to the carbon tax (Douenne and Fabre, 2022). Overall, because this initially well-intended policy to improve E inadequately addressed its impact on S, the government was forced to suspend the tax, ultimately granting a win to S over E.

Local community resistance to renewable energy projects (e.g., wind turbines, solar farms, dams) is another example of conflict between E and S, and in this case a conflict that is relevant to the private sector. While renewable energy projects are intended to reduce reliance on fossil fuels and to lead to positive environmental impacts, they can also have unintended negative social consequences (e.g., displacement of local communities, loss of access to land and resources, harm to wildlife). Unjust transition can be very costly for companies: protests and strikes can stall projects and tarnish a company's reputation, increase staff turnover, and create investor distrust.

### 3.2 Across Countries: A Just Transition or No Transition

As the examples from the previous section illustrate, efforts regarding E are unlikely to be successful unless there is a "just transition," where no one is disadvantaged by climate change action (hence, where efforts regarding E are not undertaken at the expense of low-income individuals or countries). This issue is at the heart of the loss and damage fund for vulnerable countries hit hard by climate disasters discussed at COP27.[12] And it remains as important as ever in the upcoming COP29, whose main focus is climate finance.[13]

If companies do not want their E policies to be labeled antisocial, they need to understand the implications of these policies for S and engage in social dialogue. The wide acceptability of climate policies (at the local and the global level) will be crucial to ensuring success and continuity. The G of corporate governance can act as a referee in this E versus S battle, for instance by ensuring a fair redistribution of benefits and costs. In 2022, at a time of rising energy prices, some countries (including France) decided to freeze gas prices and cap electricity prices. Denmark, meanwhile, opted for a different approach. To maintain the incentive to switch to more climate-friendly energy alternatives (e.g., heat pumps or solar panels), the Danish government let prices rise but paid out a "heat check" to lower-income households to help them with their energy bills. This policy led Danish households to significantly reduce their use of gas compared to the French.[14] Likewise, Unilever's commitment to Rainforest Alliance certification is an example of how it is possible to tackle E (in this case, sustainable tea production) without jeopardizing S (the social development of local communities).[15]

### 3.3 Governance

The climate disasters of 2024, such as the catastrophic floods in Brazil and the devastating hurricanes hitting the southeastern United States, underscore the urgency of addressing environmental risks despite the uncertainty and the long time horizon for realizing the benefits of climate action. These events illustrate how the tragedy of the horizon can lead to delayed responses, leaving communities unprepared for immediate and severe consequences. In both countries, the costs of inaction have been disproportionately borne by vulnerable populations, emphasizing the need for companies and policymakers to prioritize proactive environmental strategies. These disasters serve as stark reminders that the longer humanity delays substantial efforts to combat climate change, the more severe and frequent these events will become, making the future cost of inaction far greater than that of any short-term investment in sustainability made today.

Despite the inherent conflicts between environmental (E) and social (S) goals, companies cannot afford to remain passive. Solutions must be pursued to reconcile these differences, as both E and S are critical to a company's long-term success and societal impact. Navigating these complexities requires robust corporate governance. As emphasized in the 2017 recommendations of the Task Force on Climate-related Financial Disclosures (Financial Stability Board, 2017), governance plays a pivotal role in managing climate-related risks and opportunities. The TCFD framework highlights the importance of integrating governance structures that oversee both environmental and social challenges, ensuring that boards are equipped to address these conflicts through informed decision-making and strategic planning. Only through proactive and transparent governance can companies craft strategies that mitigate the risks of conflict while unlocking opportunities for sustainable growth and long-term value creation.

## 4. EXPLORE FOR REAL IMPACT

The discussion thus far has shown that the business case for companies' ESG efforts is very different for environmental (E) than it is for social (S) and governance (G) issues. While many companies enjoy immediate private net gains from addressing S- and G-related problems, they all too often do not benefit from costly environmental projects during the planning horizon of their senior management and board members. This is probably why many companies are making long-term emission reduction pledges (such as net zero targets by 2050) but often fall short on these promises in the short term (i.e., they refrain from making the costly investment necessary today if these promises are to be fulfilled). An analysis of the climate strategies of 25 major global companies reveals that the net zero commitments of the majority lack substance (on average they commit to reducing aggregate emissions by 40 percent instead of by 100 percent, and report very few interim climate targets).[16]

In response to the fundamental difference between E, S, and G, companies need to decouple E issues from S and G challenges and tackle them separately, while making sure each does not conflict with the others. In the following, we propose four solutions that businesses can explore to tackle environmental problems.

It is important to note that exploring these solutions does not guarantee success. Achieving a balance between E, S, and G is a complex and challenging task, often involving difficult trade-offs. The conflicts that arise between these components, especially between E and S, cannot always be easily resolved. What is clear, however, is the necessity for strong corporate governance. A well-structured governance framework is essential for the navigation of these conflicts and to ensure that companies remain resilient while striving toward their environmental and social goals.

## 4.1 Property Rights

A classical approach to addressing the tragedy of the commons in economics is the assignment of private property rights for a common resource to a single economic agent. The underlying idea is that a single owner will manage the resource such that the owner's "best" actions coincide with those of a planner choosing a "socially optimal" policy for the use of the resource. As a result, the single owner can avoid the tragedy of the commons. Returning to the fisheries example we discussed earlier, assigning property rights for a lake to local fishers would likely lead to the sustainable management of fish stocks. It would indeed be in their own interests to ensure that the catch rate does not exceed the rate of reproduction (as failure to do so would affect their future revenues significantly).

Emissions trading schemes (ETSs) (also known as the cap-and-trade system) are an example of the property rights approach. The government sets a maximum level of carbon emissions and allocates permits for each unit of emissions allowed. These permits can then be traded on a market. The idea underlying this system is that these permits will incentivize emitters to lower their emissions (for instance by investing in low-carbon technologies). One of the pioneers of the property rights approach, Ronald Coase, has noted that an efficient allocation of resources can be achieved under certain conditions (the Coase theorem). The most important of these are zero transaction costs and perfect information: the parties understand and agree on the issue at hand and are willing and able to talk to each other, and the implementation of any agreement can easily be monitored. Unfortunately, these conditions are usually not satisfied when dealing with a global problem such as climate change, which requires dialogue and agreement from hundreds of countries and hundreds of thousands of companies. For instance, in late 2024 there were 36 cap-and-trade systems across the world for $CO_2$ emissions (ICAP, 2024), and many are criticized for making too many allowances relative to their stated environmental ambitions (Blanchard and Tirole, 2021). Until 2023, for example, the ETS in the EU only covered 38 percent of its total emissions. Additionally, the established equilibrium price seems not to correspond to the present value of marginal climate damages generated by the corresponding emission. Hence, as a mechanism the scheme does not sufficiently induce companies to internalize the social cost of their pollution.

The concept of property rights does not, therefore, offer a solution to the most pressing global environmental problem—the steady rise of greenhouse gas emissions and the global warming that results. Moreover, in cases where it could potentially apply (including fisheries, forestry, and rangelands), current scientific evidence on the effect of property rights regimes on environmental outcomes is insufficiently robust to draw firm conclusions (positive results are nevertheless more likely to be reported when the resource systems include monitoring and enforcement systems, when there is low resource use pressure, and when rights are clear, stable, and legitimate) (see Ojanen et al., 2017).

## 4.2 Environmental Regulation

Somewhat remarkably, in ESG-themed sessions in executive management programs that we have led, many business leaders call for more environmental regulation. These managers recognize the tragedy of the commons. They argue that their fiduciary duties to their companies' owners do not allow them to unilaterally engage in more environmentally friendly business practices: the resulting rise in costs and reduction in market share would hurt their companies' bottom line and would eventually cost them their jobs. At the same time, many business leaders would very much like to pursue greener business ideas even if they result in higher costs and smaller margins. But since they cannot move first, they want policymakers to force green policies upon them and their competitors.

Of course, emissions-intensive businesses in many countries are well versed in dealing with environmental regulation. For example, the US Clean Air Act of 1963 (with numerous later amendments) and the 2008 EU directive 2008/50/EC on cleaner air for Europe set air quality standards that required many companies to make costly investments to reduce their emissions. It does not need a crystal ball to predict that in the face of ever-growing greenhouse gas emissions and further global warming many regulators will continue to impose ever higher environmental standards in their jurisdictions.

An extreme form of regulation may occur in the face of severe environmental degradation. As a result of warming waters in the Bering Sea, the numbers of Alaskan snow crabs dropped by more than 80 percent between 2018 and 2022. In October 2022—and for the first time in its history—the Alaska Department of Fish and Game forbade the harvesting of snow crabs. In addition, and for the second year running, the harvesting of red king crabs was also halted. These regulatory measures were a big blow to the industry concerned, which as recently as 2016 harvested snow and red king crabs valued at more than Can$250 million (approximately US$187 million). The Bering Sea snow crab fishery is set to reopen on October 4, 2024, with a cautious approach that includes a modest allowable catch limit.[17]

If the environmental conditions for crabs in the Bering Sea do not improve—and this appears likely at the time of writing—then the industry will not survive. Not only will some crabbing companies go out of business, but many of the industry's assets will also become stranded.[18]

Clearly, business leaders want neither environmental disasters that eliminate business-critical resources nor regulation that forces the outright closure of their businesses. Meanwhile, many regulators prefer—based on economic principles—systems of charges. For instance, even the mere threat of carbon regulation may push organizations to act. A 2020 report from the World Bank (World Bank, 2020) states, "companies that perceive higher risk from external carbon regulations are over five times more likely to implement an internal carbon price." Yet instruments such as carbon taxes have suffered from a "social acceptability problem" (including that involving the yellow vests in France), as discussed in Section 3.1 of this chapter. A recent example of a company engaging with environmental regulation is BP in the US state of Washington. Although the company initially spent large sums of money advocating against the imposition of a carbon tax, it supported a state bill for an overall cap on carbon emissions (Winston et al., 2022).

### 4.3 Technological Innovation

Technology is routinely cited as a solution to global warming. Such technological innovations usually belong to one of two strategies—mitigation and adaptation. Mitigation involves finding ways to cut our carbon emissions, while adaptation involves taking measures to better cope with climate change.

While many cleantech innovations—including air carbon capture, green hydrogen, nuclear fusion, and sustainable aviation fuels—are still in the development phase, renewable energies are a mitigation technology that is already available and ready to be deployed. Several issues, though, have prevented mass implementation. The cost of these technologies is an important hurdle. The first wave of cleantech (now referred to as cleantech 1.0, which started around 2006, at the same time as Al Gore's documentary *An Inconvenient Truth* was released) was diminished by the then availability of cheap fossil fuels. Scaling (in terms of the infrastructure needed and the regulatory hurdles that must be surmounted if new renewable power plants are to be built) has also been proven to be critical if we want to increase our reliance on renewables. Although the energy crisis sparked by the war in Ukraine should be seen as an opportunity to switch to renewables, uncertainty around the war's implications has resulted in much hesitation from market participants. The adoption of mitigation technologies can also be impeded by market competitiveness issues. A representative of one airline told one of the coauthors of this chapter that the company had developed a sustainable fuel but could not use it because doing so would put the company at a cost disadvantage compared to its fossil fuel–using competitors. In other words, until everyone is forced to play by the same rules (due to the introduction and enforcement of international regulations for example) the company will not employ the new technology it has developed.

Policymakers initially focused on mitigation. Our interactions with hundreds of corporate leaders reveal that many companies are also under pressure from the public and investors to pursue mitigation. Thus, past corporate and policy efforts have both focused almost exclusively on mitigation measures. This must change, as it is now clear that both adaptation and mitigation are needed and should be pursued in parallel. If we want companies and consumers to be more resilient to climate variability, adaptation will be key. For instance, Unilever has implemented mitigation measures to reduce the volume of water used in its manufacturing processes (in particular in plants located in water-stressed sites) and invested in adaptation through the development of "water-smart products," which require less water than traditional products. These include hair conditioners that do not need to be rinsed off, dry wash sprays to refresh clothes (thus reducing washing frequency), and a detergent bar that needs less water for rinsing.[19] These and other water-smart products can be interpreted as both mitigation (they require less water and energy today) and adaptation (they are suitable for a future with less water and thus preserve the company's market share and profits). Water resilience is seen as one of the key areas for adaptation in Africa, as investment in water management and water reuse technologies can help the continent adapt to the unpredictability of droughts and higher temperatures (Global Center on Adaptation, 2022). For instance, investments in desalination stations and wastewater recycling plants by global fertilizer producer the OCP Group have reduced water pollution and improved both the water resilience of the company's production systems and the livelihoods of communities in North Africa (hence also having a positive impact on the S dimension).[20] Building redundancy and improving emergency responses is another approach to adapting to climate change. The French utility company EDF has invested in adapting existing facilities to make them less sensitive to climatic conditions and more resilient to extremes including heatwaves, rising sea levels, and drought.[21]

In the future, humanity will not only need to strengthen its mitigation efforts, it will also need to increase the attention it pays to adaptation. And as COP26 President Alok Sharma put it: "The annual adaptation costs are expected to reach at least US$140 billion a year by 2030. And frankly, public finance is not going to be enough. We are going to need private finance."

## 4.4 Think Global, Act Local, Work Together

Climate change is a global problem that will not be solved without business, government, and society working together toward a common goal. Embracing partnerships is thus another way forward.

Businesses can collaborate with their peers to establish some baseline rule or practice (within the limits of antitrust law; see Gasparini et al., 2022). For instance, the Consumer Goods Forum brought the world's largest consumer goods retailers and manufacturers together to develop sustainable packaging (Polman and Winston, 2021). Likewise, companies in the fashion and textile industry created The Fashion Pact, an initiative that includes common core goals on stopping global warming, restoring biodiversity, and protecting the oceans. One of its targets is to remove single-use plastics from business-to-consumer products by 2025 and from business-to-business products by 2030.[22] Such partnerships can improve the resilience of entire industries and allow companies to take bolder action and scale their positive environmental impact.

Working with governments, NGOs, and civil society can also help companies improve their environmental performance. The collaboration between Swiss Re and Oxfam to develop insurance against climate change risks for Ethiopian farmers is one example of this.[23] The complementarities between Oxfam's knowledge of Ethiopia and long presence in the country and Swiss Re's expertise in insurance were key to the success of the partnership. Collaboration began with a pilot project in one village but rapidly expanded to include three other countries in West Africa and the development of other insurance products. It has since been rebranded the R4 Rural Resilience Initiative.[24]

## 5. CONCLUSION

Many decision-makers use the term ESG without giving much thought to the interdependence of the three letters. It is not because certain criteria of E, S, and G overlap that all should necessarily be bound together. The economic forces operating behind E are different from those operating behind S and G. They should thus be tackled differently, while keeping in mind that they may interact with (and sometimes oppose) one another. By focusing on ESG in the aggregate, we may hit the target but miss the point.

The first step in solving a problem is acknowledging its existence. Awareness is, therefore, of paramount importance to our work toward a solution. The way the term ESG became part of our daily vocabulary is both fascinating and intriguing. As soon as researchers started peeling off the obvious first level concepts, the complexity of the relationship between the three variables became obvious. It is time to explore the differences and, most importantly, the complementarities of the components of ESG if we are to achieve a sustainable outcome. Maintaining a dialogue with governmental authorities and other companies in and across industries will also be crucial to the success of this endeavor.

## NOTES

1. This chapter is a modest revision and update of Cabolis et al. (2023). The authors are grateful to two anonymous referees and the book editors, Brian Bolton and Jung Park, for helpful comments.
2. See https://finance.ec.europa.eu/sustainable-finance/overview-sustainable-finance_en, accessed 22 October 2024.
3. See The Economist (2022c).
4. See Bloomberg (2021).
5. See The Economist (2022a) and Bloomberg (2022).
6. See Hunt (2020).
7. See Modestino et al. (2021).
8. See Kellogg Insight (2016).
9. See Korn Ferry (2019).
10. See https://www.ifc.org/content/dam/ifc/doc/mgrt/irresistiblecase4cg.pdf, accessed 22 October 2024.
11. According to a survey conducted by the French *Haut Conseil pour le Climat*, 91 percent of respondents acknowledged the urgency of acting against climate change, but only 72 percent supported the "polluter pays" principle (including via a carbon tax, which would affect their purchasing power).
12. See https://www.unep.org/news-and-stories/story/what-you-need-know-about-cop27-loss-and-damage-fund, accessed 22 October 2024.

13. See https://unclimatesummit.org/cop29-president-sets-ambition-for-climate-action-in-baku/, accessed 22 October 2024.
14. See The Economist (2022b).
15. See Brage et al. (2016).
16. See Day et al. (2022).
17. See https://alaskapublic.org/2024/10/16/bering-sea-snow-crab-fishing-to-resume-but-at-an-ultra-low-level-to-encourage-repopulation/, accessed 28 October 2024.
18. See https://www.lse.ac.uk/granthaminstitute/explainers/what-are-stranded-assets/, accessed 23 October 2024.
19. See https://www.unilever.com/sustainability/nature/water-stewardship/, accessed 23 October 2024.
20. See https://www.ocpafrica.com/en, accessed 23 October 2024.
21. See https://www.edf.fr/sites/groupe/files/2022-03/2022-03-14-edf-group-climate-transition-plan.pdf, accessed 23 October 2024.
22. See https://www.thefashionpact.org, accessed 23 October 2024.
23. See https://nbs.net/partnering-with-ngos-the-4-keys-to-success/, accessed 23 October 2024.
24. See https://www.oxfamamerica.org/explore/issues/economic-well-being/r4-resilience-initiative/, accessed 23 October 2024.

## REFERENCES

Blanchard, O., & Tirole, J. (2021). The major future economic challenges. *France Stratégie*, June 23. https://www.strategie.gouv.fr/english-articles/major-future-economic-challenges-olivier-blanchard-and-jean-tirole

Bloomberg (2021). ESG assets rising to $50 trillion will reshape $140.5 trillion of global AUM by 2025, finds Bloomberg Intelligence. Bloomberg, July 21. https://www.bloomberg.com/company/press/esg-assets-rising-to-50-trillion-will-reshape-140-5-trillion-of-global-aum-by-2025-finds-bloomberg-intelligence/

Bloomberg (2022). Empty ESG pledges ensure bonds benefit companies, not the planet. Bloomberg, October 4. https://www.bloomberg.com/news/features/2022-10-04/greenwashing-enters-a-22-trillion-debt-market-derailing-climate-goals

Brage, T. M., Ionescu-Somers, A. & Seifert, R. W. (2016). Unilever sustainable tea part II: Reaching out to smallholders in Keny and Argentina. https://www.idhsustainabletrade.com/uploaded/2016/07/Unilever-Sustainable-Tea-Part-II.pdf

Bris, A., & Cabolis, C. (2008). The value of investor protection: Firm evidence from cross-border mergers. *Review of Financial Studies*, 21(2), 605–648.

Cabolis, C., Lavanchy, M., & Schmedders, K. (2023). The fundamental problem with ESG? Conflicting letters. *Journal of Financial Transformation*, 57, 1010–1117.

Day, T., Mooldijk, S., & Smit, S. (2022). Corporate Climate Responsibility Monitor 2022. New Climate Institute, February 7. https://www.newclimate.org/resources/publications/corporate-climate-responsibility-monitor-2022

Douenne, T., & Fabre, A. (2022). Yellow vests, pessimistic beliefs, and carbon tax aversion. *American Economic Journal: Economic Policy*, 14(1), 81–110.

The Economist (2022a). Sustainable finance is rife with greenwash. Time for more disclosure. *The Economist*, May 22. https://www.economist.com/leaders/2021/05/22/sustainable-finance-is-rife-with-greenwash-time-for-more-disclosure

The Economist (2022b). The wrong way to solve Europe's energy crisis. *The Economist*, September 27. https://www.economist.com/graphic-detail/2022/09/27/the-wrong-way-to-solve-europes-energy-crisis

The Economist (2022c). All talk, no trousers: The fundamental contradiction of ESG is being laid bare. *The Economist*, September 29. https://www.economist.com/leaders/2022/09/29/the-fundamental-contradiction-of-esg-is-being-laid-bare

Financial Stability Board (2017). Recommendations of the Task Force on Climate-related Financial Disclosures. June 29. https://www.fsb.org/2017/06/recommendations-of-the-task-force-on-climate-related-financial-disclosures-2/

Gasparini, M., Haanaes, K., & Tufano, P. (2022). When climate collaboration is treated as an antitrust violation. HBR.org, October 17. https://hbr.org/2022/10/when-climate-collaboration-is-treated-as-an-antitrust-violation

Global Center on Adaptation (2022). *State and Trends in Adaptation Reports 2021 and 2022: Executive Summaries and Syntheses*. Rotterdam and Abidjan. [For 2021, see https://gca.org/reports/sta21/; for 2022, see https://gca.org/reports/sta22/.]

Hunt, N. (2020). Overfishing on the rise as global consumption climbs – U.N. agency. Reuters, June 8. https://www.reuters.com/article/uk-food-fao-fish-idUKKBN23F1DV/

ICAP (2024). *Emissions Trading Worldwide: Status Report 2024*. International Carbon Action Partnership.

Kellogg Insight (2016). How transparent accounting leads to smarter decisions. *Kellogg Insight*, December 2. https://insight.kellogg.northwestern.edu/article/how-transparent-accounting-leads-to-smarter-decisions

Korn Ferry (2019). Age and tenure in the C-Suite. Korn Ferry. https://ir.kornferry.com/news-events/press-releases/detail/34/age-and-tenure-in-the-c-suite-korn-ferry-study-reveals-trends-by-title-and-industry

Modestino, A. S., Ladge, J. J., Swartz, A., & Lincoln, A. (2021). Childcare is a business issue. HBR.org, April 29. https://hbr.org/2021/04/childcare-is-a-business-issue

Ojanen, M., Zhou, W., Miller, D. C., Nieto, S. H., Mshale, B., & Petrokofsky, G. (2017). What are the environmental impacts of property rights regimes in forests, fisheries and rangelands? *Environmental Evidence*, 6(1), 1–23.

Pindyck, R. S. (2022). *Climate Future: Averting and Adapting to Climate Change*. Oxford University Press.

Polman, P., & Winston, A. (2021). The net positive manifesto. Harvard Business Review. https://hbr.org/2021/09/the-net-positive-manifesto

Roberson, Q., Holmes, O., & Perry, J. L. (2016). Transforming research on diversity and firm performance: A dynamic capabilities perspective. *Academy of Management Annals*, 11(1), 189–216.

Winston, A., Doty, E., & Lyon, T. (2022). The importance of corporate political responsibility. *MIT Sloan Management Review*, October 24. https://sloanreview.mit.edu/article/the-importance-of-corporate-political-responsibility/

World Bank (2020). State and trends of carbon pricing 2020. http://hdl.handle.net/10986/33809

Xiaoding, L. (2016). Corruption culture and corporate misconduct. *Journal of Financial Economics*, 122(2), 307–327.

# 16. Separating fact from fiction: the role of sustainability committees in greenwashing

**Nguyen Thi Kim Oanh and Huong-Trang Pham**

## 1. INTRODUCTION

Environmental performance, a vital dimension of environmental, social and governance (ESG) performance, refers to corporations' non-financial indicators, such as carbon dioxide emissions, energy use, water and waste production, that impact climate change, environmental health, and ecosystem vitality (Mastrandrea et al., 2024; Wendling et al., 2022). The rise of corporations' environmental performance disclosure is driven by multiple factors: investor demand for sustainable investments (Amel-Zadeh & Serafeim, 2018; Cohen et al., 2023; Robert & Svetlana, 2019), changing consumer preferences (Robert & Svetlana, 2019; Zhang et al., 2024), increasing regulatory pressure (Liu et al., 2024; Liu & Guo, 2023), capital access (Liang & Yang, 2024; Yang et al., 2023), and risk management strategies (Liu et al., 2024). This performance can be officially tracked by examining annual corporate sustainability reports, advertisements, websites, social media platforms, media coverage, and other documents that enable corporations to disclose or convey their ESG performance alongside economic outcomes to their stakeholders (Fatima & Elbanna, 2023).

For listed firms, environmental performance is disclosed in the firm's comprehensive sustainability report or integrated documents that encompass environmental, social, and governance performance indicators. This practice is growing in popularity globally: according to a survey conducted by KPMG, the proportion of large- and mid-capitalization firms publishing sustainability reports increased from a mere 12% in 1993 to approximately 80% in 2020. Traditionally, the disclosure of sustainability reports remains voluntary and unaudited. Firms believe that robust ESG performance serves as a predictor of future financial success, thereby potentially enabling them to lower their cost of capital (Tsang et al., 2023). Since the late 1990s, ESG disclosure has started becoming compulsory in a growing number of countries globally (Zhang et al., 2023a). Even though this mandated practice is implemented under laws, regulations, or stock exchange listing requirements, a majority of them are not assured by third parties (Krasodomska et al., 2021).

Firms measure and disclose their ESG performance indicators based on various global and local frameworks. Some frameworks provide disclosure guidelines and specify indicators that should be reported, such as the Global Reporting Initiative framework, United Nations Global Compact framework, ISO 26000—Guidance on Social Responsibility, or IFRS Sustainability Disclosure Standards. Other frameworks focus solely on environmental concerns, such as the Carbon Disclosure Project or the Task Force on Climate-related Financial Disclosures. Firms can choose one of these frameworks for their ESG disclosure based on their characteristics, such as industry and key stakeholders' demands (Halkos & Nomikos, 2021). Thus, it is vital to ensure that ESG indicators are reliable since they are inputs that investors and key stakeholders use to make and inform their decisions.

The sustainability committee,[1] an extension of governance overseeing impacts of business on various stakeholder groups (Burke et al., 2019; Gennari & Salvioni, 2019), has gained significant popularity among board orientations toward ESG-related accountability (Huang et al., 2024). More than 70% of the surveyed world's largest 100 publicly listed firms in 2021 had established such committees to oversee and guide their environmental practices, reporting, and disclosures (Chen & Huang, 2023; Driss et al., 2024). Nonetheless, a significant concern has arisen regarding greenwashing – the practice of making misleading or unsubstantiated claims about a company's environmental performance to appear more environmentally responsible than it actually is (Delmas & Burbano, 2011). This phenomenon raises critical questions about whether sustainability committees have a substantive effect on firms' environmental performance or if these committees merely serve as symbolic entities under external stakeholder pressures (Berrone & Gomez-Mejia, 2009; Gull et al., 2024; Huang et al., 2024), potentially exacerbating the issue of greenwashing.

Greenwashing encompasses communicative tactics used to create a "fiction" rather than "facts" about a firm's environmental performance. These tactics include selectively disclosing positive information while omitting negative impacts, or even disseminating unverifiable "fake" news or data (Marquis et al., 2016). This behavior has far-reaching consequences, including penalizing honest disclosure, eroding public trust, distorting capital market selection, and increasing climate or environmental risk (Liu et al., 2024). Although greenwashing might yield short-term benefits, it ultimately leads to severe long-term consequences for firms, such as legal penalties and reputational damage (Qu, 2024; Sajid et al., 2024). Consequently, sustainability committees face critical challenges in combating greenwashing, driven by various factors including the regulatory environment, external pressures, incentive structures, and ethical climate (Delmas & Burbano, 2011). These committees must strive to ensure transparency, accountability, and authenticity in corporate sustainability efforts (Jurgita et al., 2021).

This chapter examines the role of sustainability committees, an important yet underexplored governance mechanism (Gull et al., 2024), in distinguishing fact from fiction to foster genuine corporate sustainability, rebuild public trust, and drive meaningful progress toward a more environmentally responsible future. The discussion begins by exploring different approaches to establishing sustainability committees, followed by an analysis of the significance of their size and composition. It then emphasizes concerns related to greenwashing. The subsequent section presents the governance procedures that firms might implement by integrating sustainability committees into their overall governance structure and explores how these committees should effectively coordinate with other functions to mitigate greenwashing issues. The chapter closes with a conclusion and suggestions for future research.

## 2. SUSTAINABILITY COMMITTEES AND GREENWASHING

### 2.1 The Board of Directors and Sustainability Committees

The board of directors holds ultimate accountability for corporate financial and non-financial performance, including environmental performance, as part of its fiduciary duty. To oversee environmental performance, the board can employ three distinct approaches, each suited to different firm sizes: full board oversight, delegation to an existing board committee, or the establishment of a newly formed sustainability committee (Jurgita et al., 2021). These approaches emphasize the effectiveness of overseeing critical issues, such as environmental performance, through the development of oversight structures and their corresponding accountability mechanisms.

First, the full board practice is typically employed by small firms; however, this approach may result in insufficient attention being paid to environmental matters. Second, firms can transform an existing committee, modifying its name to reflect an expanded responsibility for overseeing environmental performance. Third, firms can establish dedicated sustainability committees, signaling a strong commitment to accountability in ESG-related activities, including adequate communication and transparency with external stakeholders (Zhang & Wong, 2022).

The standalone sustainability committee approach enables the board of directors (BOD) to delegate environment-related issues to a specialized committee while maintaining ultimate oversight. This structure allows the sustainability committee to focus specifically on risks arising from green practices or environmental disclosure. The sustainability committee can be structured with a committee chair and representatives from other functions, such as internal audit, compensation, nominating and governance, risk, and regulatory committees. This approach to environmental performance oversight enhances ESG synthesis effectiveness for the BOD by facilitating coordination across various functions (Jurgita et al., 2021).

Sustainability committees can be structured into two distinct levels, reflecting the varying needs and resources available to firms of different scales in addressing sustainability governance: a board sustainability committee and a management sustainability committee. The board sustainability committee primarily focuses on approving environmental policies and frameworks, as well as overseeing their implementation. In contrast, the management sustainability committee is responsible for developing environmental policies and frameworks, and operationally overseeing the implementation of environmental activities. The reporting structure of these committees differs: the board sustainability committee reports directly to the BOD, while the management sustainability committee reports to the CEO or functional executive managers, such as the chief sustainability officer. Firms may choose to establish either solely the management sustainability committee or both types of sustainability committees, depending on factors such as organizational size, industry nature, and operational complexity. This flexibility ensures that the presence of sustainability committees effectively discharges the board's role and responsibilities regarding environmental performance. Empirical evidence suggests a correlation between firm size and committee structure preference. Smaller firms tend to favor the establishment of a management sustainability committee, whereas larger firms are more inclined to employ a board sustainability committee (IFC, 2021).

The standalone sustainability committee, a voluntary governance mechanism, serves as an effective manifestation of a firm's environmental responsibility policies and strategies. It signals to stakeholders that environmental performance is considered at the firm's strategic level (Kılıç et al., 2021). An independent sustainability committee plays a crucial monitoring role in enhancing ESG transparency and ensuring proper ESG disclosure (Dixon-Fowler et al., 2017; Kılıç et al., 2021; Zhang & Wong, 2022). Research indicates that the presence of sustainability committees results in higher-quality greenhouse gas emissions disclosure, particularly when external environmental institutions cannot provide sufficient monitoring mechanisms for corporate environmental disclosure (Driss et al., 2024). In this capacity, sustainability committees reduce information asymmetry by providing a form of assurance on environmental performance, which is of primary concern to the firm's external stakeholders, especially shareholders and investors. This assurance facilitates efficient resource allocation: firms with higher "real" environmental performance are more likely to attract investment from environmentally conscious investors compared to their counterparts. The committee demonstrates its significance in mitigating investors' negative reactions in stock markets arising from unfavorable media coverage of environmental issues. This is achieved through timely and transparent communication on matters of utmost importance to key stakeholders (Zhang & Wong, 2022). Indeed, despite the high costs associated with its presence, market investors value the sustainability committee for its expertise and independence (Sun & Huang, 2024).

## 2.2 Sustainability Committees' Size and Composition

While the presence of standalone sustainability committees generally correlates with improved environmental performance across industries (Soana, 2024), the mere existence of a sustainability committee does not necessarily guarantee its effectiveness in protecting diverse stakeholders' environmental interests or ensuring high environmental performance. Rather, the committee's composition plays a crucial role in its efficacy. Paradoxically, firms with sustainability committees tend to produce higher waste than those without such committees and appear to have no significant effect on waste recycling. However, large-size committees characterized by gender diversity, extended committee tenure, and independence significantly contribute to waste reduction (Gull et al., 2024).

The average size of a board sustainability committee typically comprises four or five members, which is smaller than that of a management sustainability committee (Gull et al., 2024; IFC, 2021). While a smaller committee may facilitate faster decision-making due to streamlined coordination among members, this advantage may come at the cost of reduced diversity in expertise, skills, and experiences within the committee (Gull et al., 2024).

The composition and selection of sustainability committee members are pivotal to the committee's impact. Firms should prioritize gender diversity, committee tenure, and independence when selecting sustainability committee members, as these attributes significantly influence environmental performance metrics such as waste reduction (Gull et al., 2024). Common practices in the selection of board sustainability committee members include appointing an independent director as committee chair and independent non-executive directors as members. While the chair of the board may serve as a committee member, they typically do not assume the role of committee chairman. Collectively, committee members should possess complementary expertise, skills, and experiences in ESG issues to effectively guide the firm's sustainable development and monitor and oversee environmental sustainability policies and plans (IFC, 2021).

## 2.3 Greenwashing: Claims for Benefits Without Effort

Concerns about greenwashing are increasingly associated with the growing number of disclosed ESG reports. This phenomenon involves the provision of deceptive or exaggerated information on environmental performance to meet key stakeholders' expectations, rather than presenting the "truth" or actual firm performance (Liu et al., 2024). Greenwashing manifests in various forms, including greencrowding, greenlighting, greenlabeling, greenrinsing, and greenscamming. In advertisements or promotions, firms tend to employ ambiguous and difficult-to-verify terms, such as eco-friendly, nontoxic, green, natural, organic, plastic-free, zero waste, biodegradable, compostable, and recyclable (Leah, 2024).

The motivations for greenwashing lie in the benefits associated with ESG disclosure. Firms can potentially build their reputation and gain legitimacy through symbolic ESG disclosure without substantial efforts, leading to advantages, such as lower cost of capital, improved access to finance, and higher risk resilience (Liu et al., 2024; Wang et al., 2024). Research indicates that firms engaging in greater greenwashing can obtain more bank loans; however, this resource allocation is inefficient and exacerbates debt overhang (Wang et al., 2024).

Beyond firms' motives for greenwashing, variations in ESG disclosure guidelines or frameworks, such as the Global Reporting Initiative, Task Force on Climate-related Financial Disclosure, Sustainability Accounting Standards Board, and European Sustainability Reporting Standard, may inadvertently facilitate greenwashing behaviors. This issue is further compounded by significant differences in ESG ratings by agencies (e.g., Bloomberg, MSCI, Russell, and S&P Global) due to the inconsistency of ESG disclosure worldwide (Liu et al., 2024). Moreover, firms located in countries with underdeveloped ESG regulations may face more favorable conditions for engaging in greenwashing practices (Halkos & Nomikos, 2021).

## 2.4 The Governance Procedure for Greenwashing Mitigation

For firms, mitigating greenwashing by emphasizing the role of sustainability committees demonstrates a firm's accountability for its disclosure behaviors. Firms valuing this approach are well aware of the micro-level risk aversion incurred by greenwashing (Liu et al., 2024). Sustainability committees should be integrated with other corporate governance structures to ensure effective and efficient governance procedures. This integration involves embedding sustainability governance into the overall governance procedure, including setting organizational purposes, developing strategies, responding to risks and opportunities, and incorporating it into operational activities, organizational decision-making, and culture (IFC, 2021).

The sustainability governance process typically begins with the board sustainability committee setting the direction for sustainable development. Subsequently, the management sustainability committee develops environmental policies and plans aligned with the firm's sustainable direction and government regulations, seeking board approval. These policies should be based on assessments of sustainability risks, opportunities, and organizational impacts, including frameworks, supporting procedures, guidelines, and codes of practice on environmental sustainability. The policy should also document structures (e.g., management functions and board committees) and their responsibilities for sustainability execution, functions, and activities. In developing implementation plans, it is crucial for sustainability committees to prioritize various environmental issues and goals before establishing key sustainable performance indicators and measurable targets. The management sustainability committee then implements these policies and plans, with the board sustainability committee monitoring and overseeing the process. The results of implemented activities are prepared for environmental disclosure, with the management sustainability committee challenging and approving that disclosure (IFC, 2021).

The governance structure and processes encompass board oversight, management implementation, monitoring, and assurance. At the board level, the board sustainability committee acts as a coordinator with the Risk committee, audit committee, nomination committee, and remuneration committee, bearing ultimate responsibility to the board for environmental issues. At the management level, environmental sustainability is implemented and monitored by the management sustainability committee in coordination with the executive committee, sustainability functions, as well as risk and compliance functions. It is crucial for the sustainability committee to collaborate with assurance functions such as internal audit, external audit, and regulators to ensure that environmental disclosures are authentic, reliable, and truthful.

To mitigate greenwashing, the sustainability committee must work with internal audit on the financial impacts of environmental risks and opportunities, oversee environmental disclosure and assurance, and manage the internal process of verifying disclosed environmental data and performance. However, the internal audit currently faces challenges in providing assurance on environmental performance due to difficulties in measuring environmental performance, data collection, and verification. One way to overcome these challenges is to employ technological advancements such as satellites, drones, internet of things, social media, web crawling, or artificial intelligence to capture environmental impacts (e.g., emissions, noise, toxic substances, soil quality, and water quality) in a timely manner (Gu et al., 2023; Zhang, 2024). Consequently, the internal audit can assure truthful reports of environmental performance indicators by capturing the impacts of firms' activities on the physical world, supported by various layers (technology layer, data layer, and functions layer) before the disclosure of environmental performance (Gu et al., 2023)

Furthermore, the sustainability committee needs to collaborate with the risk management function to update emerging environmental risks and manage these risks, particularly those that might cause reputational damage to the organization. Transparent disclosure of environmental performance offers substantial benefits and can provide competitive advantages for the firm. However, firms might be motivated to engage in greenwashing if untruthful information is used to make decisions by key stakeholders without requiring verification. Therefore, the risk of greenwashing behavior must be recognized by the firm, beginning with the risk management functions by employing a robust framework for managing environmental performance risks.

When environmental indicators and measurable targets are established, the compensation for the sustainability committee, along with appropriate rewards or penalties for the achievement or non-achievement of environmental performance and disclosure goals, should be incorporated into the incentive structure. This reflects firms' pressures from institutional investors' requirements for ESG performance. It is evident that firms offering higher executive compensation are more likely to disclose more ESG information, particularly in firms with voluntary disclosure practices. However, this disclosure might be strategic rather than truthful, potentially exploiting the compensation distribution gap (Zhang et al., 2023b). The executive pay gap exacerbates corporate ESG greenwashing, especially when executives have low environmental awareness. These executives are more likely to take risks associated with greenwashing when external regulations and media scrutiny on disclosure are weak (Li & Chen, 2024). Therefore, it is crucial for firms to design a compensation and reward or penalty structure that ensures the sustainability committee's accountability in preventing greenwashing.

## 3. DISCUSSION

Although this chapter has focused on the role of sustainability committees in greenwashing mitigation, efforts to mitigate greenwashing involve various parties. Although firms might actively develop effective governance procedures, their main concern is the cost of environmental disclosure. The firm's effort is situated within a broader context that requires engagement from regulators and investors to achieve an equilibrium or stable state. This stable state can be achieved when related costs for all three players are reasonable: regulation costs, true environmental disclosure costs, and supervision costs to prevent firms from engaging in greenwashing. Concerning the role of government, this requires governmental issuance of environmental disclosure regulations, establishment of effective environmental performance measures, and strict monitoring of firms' environmental activities and disclosures. Based on regulations or standards, the government should provide an appropriate level of incentives to encourage firms to disclose their environmental performance. Regarding punishment, the effects of regulations on environmental disclosure would be ineffective if penalties are too lenient or too severe. In terms of investor responsibility, investors can activate their supervisory power not only through investments in firms that truthfully disclose environmental performance but also by questioning the quality of environmental disclosure (Liu et al., 2024).

The environmental disclosure costs shared among three parties can be minimized through the development of a shared ESG disclosure platform, supported by digital technologies such as artificial intelligence, cloud computing, or big data (Liu et al., 2024). In China, the government has started to develop a hierarchical digital system for information resource integration and data sharing, enabling the government to collect firms' environmental data (Li et al., 2024). This allows the government to reduce the cost of data collection and the cost of regulatory supervision of firms' environmental disclosure (Li et al., 2024; Xu et al., 2024). Empirically, Xu et al. (2024) found that digitalization has significantly positive effects on the reduction of corporate greenwashing in China from 2016 to 2021.

Greenwashing can be mitigated through third-party verification of environmental performance. This is a viable method to ensure the authenticity, reliability, and integrity of sustainability reports (Krasodomska et al., 2021; Liu et al., 2024). The need for assurance of sustainability reports has arisen among shareholders, creditors, and potential investors, especially institutional investors, after a long time relying on audited financial statements. These key stakeholders of the firm demand further non-financial performance information to help them obtain a holistic view of the firm's performance and improve their decision-making. This assurance was discussed by panelists at the webinar "Assurance on Sustainability Reports: Current Practices and Challenges" to develop guidelines for extended external reporting assurance, especially for ESG non-financial performance (Krasodomska et al., 2021). Although verification incurs costs for firms and investors, these may be offset by or be less than costs caused by inefficient resource allocation (Liu et al., 2024). If external assurance becomes mandatory, trust in environmental disclosure will be restored (Pizzi et al., 2024). With emerging technologies, assurance techniques can be improved to ensure their credibility. In this way, key stakeholders can rely on both financial statements and sustainability reports to make their informed decisions.

## 4. CONCLUSION AND FUTURE RESEARCH

This chapter highlights the role of the sustainability committee in the context of increasing concerns about greenwashing, a behavior that causes more harm than benefit in the long run. To mitigate greenwashing, firms can establish a sustainability committee. This committee, specializing in environmental activities and performance, acts as a coordinator to ensure that the disclosure of environmental performance is truthful. This necessitates the sustainability committee being designed with an appropriate size and composition and a proper governance procedure within the overall firm's governance process. As guardians of environmental authenticity, these committees must navigate the complexities of greenwashing with vigilance, expertise, and an unwavering commitment to transparency and ethical conduct.

While the standalone sustainability committee might be more appropriate for large-listed firms, the committee formalization can be classified into four levels. Level 1 consists of basic practices, which might be applied by small firms or firms with limited sustainability issues. At this level, the firm does not establish sustainability committees, and the board takes full sustainability responsibility. The board needs to ensure that sustainability considerations are incorporated into the firm's strategy, business plan implementation, and operations. Firms that are in the growth stage or have reached maturity tend to exercise level 2, establishing either a management sustainability committee or a board sustainability committee. This committee becomes one component of the firm's governance structure. When firms are large and complex in their operations and sustainability issues, they tend to adopt a more formal governance structure by establishing both management and board committees. At this level 3, the integration of committees at two levels might not achieve full effectiveness. When these two committees' functions are integrated into the firm's governance structure and sustainability practices are incorporated into their daily operations, the firms achieve level 4, playing a sustainable leadership role (IFC, 2021). Therefore, future research might investigate the formalization of sustainability committees in governance structures from a life-cycle perspective to explore firms' sustainable practices.

Although the sustainability committee has been established by a majority of the largest firms, the role of this committee in the battle against greenwashing is still underexplored. Prior literature suggested that the existence of the committee might be symbolic, potentially exacerbating greenwashing. Recent studies highlight the significance of the sustainability committee in environmental disclosure (Driss et al., 2024; Kılıç et al., 2021), waste management practices (Gull et al., 2024), electricity use (Chen & Huang, 2023), and ESG performance (Huang et al., 2024). Therefore, it is vital to gather additional empirical evidence on the consequences of the sustainability committee's characteristics on various aspects of greenwashing, such as disclosure reports and marketing messages. Furthermore, future studies should identify best practices for integrating the sustainability committee with the overall firm's governance procedure in implementing the firm's sustainable strategy and the challenges firms might face during that process.

## NOTE

1. The sustainability committee might be called different names such as corporate social responsibility committee (e.g., Driss et al., 2024; Gennari & Salvioni, 2019; Chen & Huang, 2023), or ESG committee (e.g., Huang et al., 2024). The terms "sustainability" and "CSR" are broader concepts encompassing environmental, social, and governance considerations, while "ESG" specifically refers to a set of criteria within these three areas used to evaluate companies' performance and behavior. Thus, these three terms are often used in the field of corporate responsibility and governance. Although the sustainability committee is responsible for broad ESG issues, recent studies tend to pay more attention and emphasize the role of this committee on environmental issues.

## REFERENCES

Amel-Zadeh, A., & Serafeim, G. (2018). Why and how investors use ESG information: Evidence from a global survey. *Financial Analysts Journal*, *74*(3), 87–103.

Berrone, P., & Gomez-Mejia, L. R. (2009). Environmental performance and executive compensation: An integrated agency-institutional perspective. *Academy of Management*, *52*(1), 103–126.

Burke, J. J., Hoitash, R., & Hoitash, U. (2019). The heterogeneity of board-level sustainability committees and corporate social performance. *Journal of Business Ethics*, *154*(4), 1161–1186.

Chen, Y.-L., & Huang, M.-C. (2023). Do sustainability committees reduce electricity use in Taiwan? Mitigating electricity regulation as motivation. *Journal of Cleaner Production*, *385*, 135651.

Cohen, S., Kadach, I., & Ormazabal, G. (2023). Institutional investors, climate disclosure, and carbon emissions. *Journal of Accounting and Economics*, *76*(2), 101640.

Delmas, M. A., & Burbano, V. C. (2011). The drivers of greenwashing. *California Management Review*, *54*(1). https://doi.org/10.1525/cmr.2011.54.1.64

Dixon-Fowler, H. R., Ellstrand, A. E., & Johnson, J. L. (2017). The role of board environmental committees in corporate environmental performance. *Journal of Business Ethics*, *140*(3), 423–438.

Driss, H., Drobetz, W., El Ghoul, S., & Guedhami, O. (2024). The sustainability committee and environmental disclosure: International evidence. *Journal of Economic Behavior & Organization*, *221*, 602–625.
Fatima, T., & Elbanna, S. (2023). Advancing sustainable performance management in the hospitality industry: A novel framework based on a health-inclusive balanced scorecard. *Tourism Management Perspectives*, *48*, 101141.
Gennari, F., & Salvioni, D. M. (2019). CSR committees on boards: The impact of the external country level factors. *Journal of Management and Governance*, *23*(3), 759–785.
Gu, Y., Dai, J., & Vasarhelyi, M. A. (2023). Audit 4.0-based ESG assurance: An example of using satellite images on GHG emissions. *International Journal of Accounting Information Systems*, *50*, 100625.
Gull, A. A., Carvajal, M., Atif, M., & Nadeem, M. (2024). The presence and composition of sustainability committee and waste management practices. *International Review of Financial Analysis*, *93*, 103111.
Halkos, G., & Nomikos, S. (2021). Corporate social responsibility: Trends in global reporting initiative standards. *Economic Analysis and Policy*, *69*, 106–117.
Huang, H., Huang, J., Jiang, J., Lee, E., & Zhao, Y. (2024). Effective or symbolic? The influence of board ESG committee on corporate ESG performance. *Journal of Sustainable Finance and Accounting*, *2*, 100008.
IFC (2021). Focus 15: Sustainability committees: Structure and practices. https://www.ifc.org/en/insights-reports/2021/focus-15-sustainability-committees
Jurgita, A., Thompson, H. L., & Randi, V. M. (2021). ESG governance: Board and management roles & responsibilities. Harvard Law school forum on corporate governance. https://corpgov.law.harvard.edu/2021/11/10/esg-governance-board-and-management-roles-responsibilities/
Kılıç, M., Uyar, A., Kuzey, C., & Karaman, A. S. (2021). Drivers and consequences of sustainability committee existence? Evidence from the hospitality and tourism industry. *International Journal of Hospitality Management*, *92*, 102753.
Krasodomska, J., Simnett, R., & Street, D. L. (2021). Extended external reporting assurance: Current practices and challenges. *Journal of International Financial Management & Accounting*, *32*(1), 104–142.
Leah, K. (2024). What is greenwashing and how to spot it in action. *CNN*. https://edition.cnn.com/cnn-underscored/home/what-is-greenwashing
Li, M., & Chen, Q. (2024). Executive pay gap and corporate ESG greenwashing: Evidence from China. *International Review of Financial Analysis*, *95*, 103375.
Li, Z., Miao, S., & Xu, L. (2024). Digital transformation and environmental, social, and governance greenwashing: Evidence from China. *Journal of Environmental Management*, *365*, 121460.
Liang, Z., & Yang, X. (2024). The impact of green finance on the peer effect of corporate ESG information disclosure. *Finance Research Letters*, *62*, 105080.
Liu, C., Gong, W., Dong, G., & Ji, Q. (2024). Regulation of environmental, social and governance disclosure greenwashing behaviors considering the risk preference of enterprises. *Energy Economics*, *135*, 107637.
Liu, G., & Guo, L. (2023). How does mandatory environmental regulation affect corporate environmental information disclosure quality. *Finance Research Letters*, *54*, 103702.
Marquis, C., Toffel, M. W., & Zhou, Y. (2016). Scrutiny, norms, and selective disclosure: A global study of greenwashing. *Organization Science*, *27*(2), 483–504.

Mastrandrea, R., ter Burg, R., Shan, Y., Hubacek, K., & Ruzzenenti, F. (2024). Assessments of the environmental performance of global companies need to account for company size. *Communications Earth & Environment*, *5*(1), 42.

Pizzi, S., Venturelli, A., & Caputo, F. (2024). Restoring trust in sustainability reporting: The enabling role of the external assurance. *Current Opinion in Environmental Sustainability*, *68*, 101437.

Qu, S. (2024). Costs may be a blessing in disguise: Litigation risk and greenwashing. *Finance Research Letters*, *62*, 105069.

Robert, G. E., & Svetlana, K. (2019). The investor revolution: Shareholders are getting serious about sustainability. *Harvard Business Review*. https://hbr.org/2019/05/the-investor-revolution

Sajid, M., Zakkariya, K. A., Suki, N. M., & Islam, J. U. (2024). When going green goes wrong: The effects of greenwashing on brand avoidance and negative word-of-mouth. *Journal of Retailing and Consumer Services*, *78*, 103773.

Soana, M. G. (2024). Environmental strategies, environmental performance and board sustainability committees: Are financial and non-financial companies different? *Research in International Business and Finance*, *69*, 102208.

Sun, W.-C., & Huang, H.-W. (2024). Do market investors value the directors' expertise and independence of a corporate sustainability committee? Empirical evidence from Taiwan. *Finance Research Letters*, *61*, 105058.

Tsang, A., Frost, T., & Cao, H. (2023). Environmental, social, and governance (ESG) disclosure: A literature review. *The British Accounting Review*, *55*(1), 101149.

Wang, Y., Xing, C., & Zhang, L. (2024). Is greenwashing beneficial for corporate access to financing? Evidence from China. *Finance Research Letters*, *65*, 105538.

Wendling, Z. A., Jacob, M., Esty, D. C., & Emerson, J. W. (2022). Explaining environmental performance: Insights for progress on sustainability. *Environmental Development*, *44*, 100741.

Xu, T., Sun, Y., & He, W. (2024). Government digitalization and corporate greenwashing. *Journal of Cleaner Production*, *452*, 142015.

Yang, J., Shi, Y., Zhang, L., & Hu, S. (2023). The influence of environmental information transparency of green bond on credit rating. *Finance Research Letters*, *58*, 104410.

Zhang, D. (2024). The pathway to curb greenwashing in sustainable growth: The role of artificial intelligence. *Energy Economics*, *133*, 107562.

Zhang, Q., Ding, R., Chen, D., & Zhang, X. (2023a). The effects of mandatory ESG disclosure on price discovery efficiency around the world. *International Review of Financial Analysis*, *89*, 102811.

Zhang, D., Pan, L., Liu, L., & Zeng, H. (2023b). Impact of executive pay gap on environmental, social, and governance disclosure in China: Is there a strategic choice? *Corporate Social Responsibility and Environmental Management*, *30*(5), 2574–2589.

Zhang, J., Zhang, L., & Zhang, M. (2024). Media pressure, internal control, and corporate environmental information disclosure. *Finance Research Letters*, *63*, 105369.

Zhang, Q., & Wong, J. B. (2022). ESG reputational risks and board monitoring committees. *Finance Research Letters*, *50*, 103325.

# 17. Environmental, social, and governance advocacy of global institutional investors: reshaping the governance of mission, social impact, and purpose

**Jinsuk Choi**

## 1. THE RISE OF ESG IN CORPORATE GOVERNANCE

This chapter explores the transformative role that the ESG advocacy of institutional investors plays in the governance of mission, social impact, and purpose. The focus on ESG (environmental, social, and governance) factors by institutional investors, especially universal owners, is redefining the parameters of corporate governance and prompting a shift towards a more sustainable, responsible, and inclusive business landscape (Eccles, Ioannou, and Serafeim, 2014). This exercise of power has been the subject of extensive research on the mechanisms, motives, and real effects of institutional investors changing corporate behavior, which can differ based on cultural contexts and value systems (Young & Gates, 2013).

Pension funds, insurance companies, and sovereign wealth funds are key universal owners with a unique responsibility to maintain systemic stability, particularly due to their broad holdings (Hawley and Williams, 2000). Universal owners are also influential in driving ESG advocacy due to their significant holdings in their national market. They have a vested interest in the health and sustainability of the market as a whole and are therefore motivated to ensure that companies operate responsibly with a long-term vision. This influence is particularly evident at a global level. A study across 41 countries found that institutional ownership is positively and causally linked to a firm's environmental and social (E&S) performance, a trend driven by investors from countries with strong social norms on E&S issues (Dyck, Lins, Roth, & Wagner, 2019). This suggests that institutional investors are 'transplanting' their social norms to corporations worldwide.

Historically, corporate governance has often been synonymous with shareholder value maximization. It encouraged companies to enhance shareholder rights and reduce managerial power through the elimination of provisions such as staggered boards, supermajority rules, golden parachutes, and poison pills (Matos, 2020). The recent rise of ESG-focused investing, propelled by institutional investors, is challenging this paradigm. This influence is leading to a broader, more holistic understanding of corporate governance, transcending the traditional profit-maximization motive to encompass environmental sustainability, social welfare, and ethical governance. Indeed, a 2022 global investor survey found that 49% of investors expressed a willingness to 'divest' from companies that do not take sufficient action on ESG issues (Chalmers, Cox, & Picard, 2022), demonstrating that ESG now has a significant impact on investment decisions. Also, a 2023 survey found that 73% of S&P 500 companies now link executive compensation to ESG metrics, up from 68% in 2022 (McGough, 2024). This trend is consistent with other 2023 survey findings showing that 81% of global companies include at least one ESG metric in their incentive plans (Ganu et al., 2024). This trend highlights the growing importance of integrating ESG factors into corporate performance incentives, reflecting a shift in how companies align executive goals with long-term sustainability.

Institutional investors with longer investment horizons are promoting corporate social responsibility at the firm level, thereby enhancing long-term buy-and-hold returns by creating value beyond profit maximization (Erhemjamts and Huang, 2019). This move is backed by robust empirical evidence. A meta-analysis of over 2,000 empirical studies found that approximately 90% of studies show a non-negative (and, in the vast majority, a positive) relationship between ESG criteria and corporate financial performance (CFP) (Friede, Busch, & Bassen, 2015). Furthermore, the adoption of ESG factors as investment benchmarks is driving the global trend toward ESG implementation in financial markets, establishing them as essential for ensuring inclusive development and achieving sustainable development goals. The move toward ESG-focused investing challenges the traditional corporate goal of maximizing shareholder value, advocating for a more comprehensive stakeholder model. However, this shift to a stakeholder model is accompanied by conceptual debate. Some argue that investor preference for ESG, while lowering the cost of capital for high-rated firms, may mean lower expected returns for investors (Cornell, 2020), raising cautions about the dangers of replacing the traditional shareholder value model.

## 2. ESG ADVOCACY'S IMPACT ON CORPORATE STRATEGY AND CULTURE

Institutional investors have increasingly driven the integration of ESG factors into corporate strategy, fundamentally reshaping how businesses operate, especially in regions like Europe. One of the most significant effects of this advocacy has been seen in the financial sector, where European banks are increasingly incorporating ESG and corporate social responsibility (CSR) into their operational frameworks as tools for risk management and value creation. By doing so, these institutions aim to redirect capital flows towards sustainable projects and investments, aligning their financial objectives with broader societal and environmental goals (Loew et al., 2021). This shift reflects a growing recognition that managing non-financial risks—such as climate change, human capital needs, and governance issues—requires a more holistic approach to measuring performance and success.

The rise of ESG-driven investing is not only reshaping risk management but also transforming the broader market for corporate control. Traditional metrics of corporate performance are being adapted to include non-financial ESG risks, requiring companies and their stakeholders to adopt longer-term perspectives and consider a wider array of factors when making strategic decisions (Kraik, 2019). Ethical concerns, such as mitigating climate change, addressing social inequality, and improving corporate governance, are increasingly seen as both risks and opportunities. As investors and companies alike strive to incorporate these elements into their financial models, there is growing momentum towards creating more resilient and sustainable business practices that are both profitable and socially responsible (Feuer, 2019).

This shift in focus highlights a broader trend: companies are moving away from a shareholder-centric model, which prioritizes short-term financial gains, towards an approach that emphasizes sustainability, ethical governance, and social welfare alongside financial performance. It aligns with the concept of 'Creating Shared Value' (CSV), which posits that companies can generate economic value by addressing social challenges (Porter & Kramer, 2011). The CSV framework proposes reinventing capitalism by connecting societal progress with economic success, urging companies to redefine social needs as market opportunities rather than just costs or constraints. The integration of ESG into corporate strategy is thus forcing companies to reassess how they create value—not only for shareholders but for all stakeholders, including employees, customers, and the communities in which they operate. As ESG continues to gain prominence, the alignment of corporate practices with broader societal values and sustainability goals has become not just a moral imperative but a critical driver of long-term success.

The growing importance of ESG advocacy is also transforming corporate culture and leadership. As companies increasingly recognize the interconnectedness of their success with their reputation, stakeholder relationships, and societal impact, they are adopting a more proactive approach to social responsibility. CSR initiatives, once considered peripheral to a company's core business strategy, are now viewed as essential components of long-term financial success. By fostering stronger relationships with stakeholders, including governments and communities, companies can enhance their reputations, create sustainable development pathways, and establish new norms for conducting business. These efforts are not merely altruistic; they have been shown to yield tangible financial rewards, with companies that embrace ESG often outperforming their peers in terms of financial performance (Eccles and Klimenko, 2019). This motivation is found not only in large firms under institutional pressure but also at the Small and Medium-Sized Enterprise (SME) level, where managers' 'personal values and beliefs,' rather than financial performance, can be a stronger driver for environmental engagement (Williams & Schaefer, 2013).

As a result, corporate culture is evolving to prioritize sustainability and social responsibility as key drivers of competitive advantage. Firm leadership is increasingly attuned to the broader implications of their decisions, understanding that choices made in the boardroom can have far-reaching consequences for their brand, stakeholder trust, and financial stability. This shift towards a more integrated approach to business strategy is not without its challenges, however. While many companies are embracing ESG as a means of fostering long-term growth, others struggle to balance these goals with the demands of their traditional business models, particularly in industries with significant environmental impacts.

The challenges of implementing ESG principles are particularly pronounced in industries like oil and gas, mining, and heavy manufacturing, where environmental impacts are inherent to the core business. For companies in these sectors, balancing ESG objectives with profitability can be difficult, and in some cases, ESG advocacy has led to superficial changes rather than substantive reforms. This phenomenon, known as "greenwashing," occurs when companies adopt the language of sustainability without enacting meaningful changes in their operations. Greenwashing poses a significant reputational risk and, as recent regulatory actions have shown, can also lead to legal and financial liabilities.

For instance, in 2022, the US Securities and Exchange Commission (SEC) fined BNY Mellon $1.5 million for misleading claims about its ESG investment policies, highlighting how greenwashing has evolved from a reputational issue to a serious legal and financial risk (SEC, 2022). Similarly, the Volkswagen emissions scandal, in which the company misled regulators and consumers about its vehicles' environmental performance, resulted in massive financial and reputational losses. This case, along with others involving companies like BP, underscores the severe consequences of failing to genuinely commit to ESG principles. Greenwashing not only damages a company's reputation but can also erode investor confidence, lead to regulatory penalties, and create long-term financial instability.

These high-profile cases demonstrate that while ESG integration can offer significant benefits, it also comes with substantial risks, particularly for companies that attempt to exploit the growing demand for sustainability without making genuine efforts to improve their practices. The narrative of universal success in ESG integration is thus more nuanced than is often portrayed. While many companies have successfully aligned their strategies with ESG goals, others continue to face significant challenges, particularly in industries where environmental, social, or governance issues are deeply embedded in their operations.

The perceived success of ESG integration varies considerably across industries and regions. Companies in sectors with inherently lower environmental footprints, such as technology and finance, have generally found it easier to adopt and integrate ESG principles into their business models. These industries tend to face fewer structural barriers to change, allowing them to more quickly align their practices with investor expectations and regulatory requirements. In contrast, industries like energy, mining, and agriculture must contend with more significant challenges, as their business models are often built around activities that are directly at odds with certain ESG objectives, such as reducing carbon emissions or minimizing resource consumption.

Moreover, regional variations in regulatory frameworks also play a crucial role in shaping the success of ESG integration. In Europe, where stricter environmental and social regulations are in place, companies often benefit from clearer guidelines and more consistent expectations. This has allowed European businesses to make more significant progress in aligning their operations with ESG goals. In contrast, companies in regions with less robust regulatory frameworks, such as parts of Asia or Latin America, may struggle to implement ESG principles in a meaningful way. These companies often face pressure to prioritize short-term financial performance over long-term sustainability, creating a disconnect between their stated ESG goals and their actual practices.

In conclusion, while ESG advocacy has undoubtedly had a profound impact on corporate strategy and culture, the path to fully integrating these principles is complex and fraught with challenges. Institutional investors have played a critical role in pushing companies to adopt more sustainable and socially responsible practices, but the success of these efforts varies across industries and regions. For some companies, particularly those in high-impact sectors, balancing ESG objectives with profitability remains a significant hurdle. Additionally, the risks of greenwashing and superficial compliance are ever-present, as companies face increasing scrutiny from regulators, investors, and the public.

To navigate these challenges, companies must move beyond surface-level commitments to ESG and embrace a more holistic approach that aligns their business strategies with long-term sustainability goals. This requires not only a shift in corporate culture and leadership but also a recognition that success in ESG integration is not a one-size-fits-all proposition. Each company must carefully consider its unique circumstances, industry dynamics, and regional context to develop an ESG strategy that is both meaningful and achievable. By doing so, companies can not only mitigate the risks associated with ESG but also unlock new opportunities for growth, innovation, and value creation in the years to come.

## 3. THE EVOLVING LANDSCAPE OF SHAREHOLDER ACTIVISM AND ESG PROXY VOTING

Adding to the exploration of the transformative role of ESG advocacy by institutional investors, this extended discussion includes a critical analysis of ESG proxy voting and its implications for the corporate boardroom. ESG proxy voting emerges as a powerful mechanism through which shareholders navigate the balance between financial return and social impact, leveraging their votes to compel corporate actions that align with both ethical standards and profit objectives. This phenomenon is evident in the status of shareholder proposal voting, which represents ESG proxy voting. In the 2023 proxy season, the number of shareholder proposals increased to a record high: shareholders filed 836 proposals in the Russell 3000 compared to 801 during the same time-frame in 2022 and 792 in 2021, reveals a report (The Conference Board, 2023). However, the number of proposals that go to a vote does not measure the full effect of shareholder activism. A significant number of proposals (more than 20%) are 'withdrawn' before a vote, and withdrawals, especially by influential institutional investors, often signify that the board has conceded to the shareholder's demands in a successful private negotiation (Bauer, Moers, & Viehs, 2015).

Proxy voting has evolved from a procedural formality to a strategic instrument for driving corporate change. This evolution is rooted in the historical context of the late 1980s and 1990s, when institutional investors first began to actively voice their concerns through corporate governance proposals (Gillan & Starks, 2000). By using ESG-focused proxy votes, shareholders are increasingly demanding that boards incorporate environmental, social, and governance considerations into long-term business strategies. The intensification of

ESG's focus has elevated the significance of proxy voting from a mere formality to a strategic tool for instigating change. This evolution in shareholder engagement signals a departure from passive boardroom participation to active advocacy for ESG priorities. As shareholders increasingly use proxy votes to express their ESG-related demands, boards are compelled to recognize and integrate these considerations into their corporate strategies.

ESG proxy voting has underscored key issues such as diversity, compensation, and climate impact, reflecting a broad shareholder consensus on the importance of these dimensions. The trend towards more ESG-focused proxy voting is evident in the increasing number of social and environmental proposals being presented and supported during proxy seasons. This shift not only demonstrates the growing shareholder activism in ESG matters but also indicates a more profound engagement with corporate governance, pushing for reforms that align with sustainable and ethical business practices.

In particular, the introduction of the universal proxy card by the SEC in 2022, which juxtaposes board and shareholder proposals, exemplifies regulatory support for enhancing shareholder influence over corporate governance through ESG advocacy (CII, 2024). This, coupled with the mainstream acceptance of ESG principles and the strategic management of shareholder expectations by boards, points to a future where ESG considerations are deeply integrated into corporate governance frameworks. Institutional investors play a pivotal role in shaping these trends, with entities like BlackRock setting guidelines that emphasize governance, sustainability, and strategic oversight in ESG proxy voting. These guidelines serve as a beacon for other shareholders, informing their voting strategies and fostering a governance landscape that prioritizes long-term value creation over short-term gains.

To effectively navigate the evolving expectations around ESG, boards must adopt proactive strategies that address shareholder concerns comprehensively. This includes transparent disclosure of compensation practices, enhancing board effectiveness and diversity, implementing robust ESG strategies, and leveraging insights from shareholder activism tools. By aligning their governance practices with ESG principles, boards can forge a path that satisfies both the ethical and financial imperatives of their stakeholders.

The inclusion of ESG proxy voting in the discourse on institutional investor advocacy enriches our understanding of the dynamic interplay between corporate governance and social responsibility. It highlights the growing influence of shareholders in shaping corporate policies and practices towards more sustainable, ethical, and inclusive outcomes. This analysis underscores the critical role of ESG advocacy in redefining corporate governance, emphasizing the need for boards to embrace these changes to meet the expectations of a diverse and increasingly socially conscious investor base.

For example, ESG factors are increasingly playing a central role in shareholder activism, prompting companies to adapt their strategies and risk management practices. This chapter explores the evolving landscape of ESG activism across the globe, highlighting key trends, regional variations, and potential mitigation strategies for companies.

## 4. GLOBAL TRENDS AND REGIONAL VARIATIONS IN ESG INTEGRATION

In recent years, shareholder activism has undergone a profound transformation, with ESG issues moving to the forefront of investor priorities. This shift reflects growing global awareness of the role businesses play in addressing societal and environmental challenges. Activists now employ a wide range of strategies, from non-binding proposals to high-profile public campaigns, to push companies toward enhanced ESG accountability. Notably, this activism is not monolithic but varies significantly across regions, influenced by cultural, regulatory, and market-specific factors. These regional variations are not accidental and align with research showing that a firm's corporate social performance (CSP) is significantly driven by 'nation-level institutions' such as the country's political, labor, and cultural systems (Ioannou & Serafeim, 2012). Specifically, a firm's CSR rating correlates more strongly with its country's 'legal origin' than with financial factors, with firms in common law countries tending to have lower overall CSR scores than firms in civil law countries (Liang & Renneboog, 2017).

In the US, for instance, activists often focus on pressing issues, such as climate change, racial justice, and board diversity. These campaigns frequently leverage ESG factors as a means to push companies toward reforms that resonate with broader societal demands. The US landscape is particularly notable for the use of both public and private tactics, with activists employing everything from shareholder resolutions to media campaigns aimed at influencing corporate behavior. At the same time, US companies must navigate a complex and evolving regulatory environment, which is expected to shift further with upcoming regulations on climate disclosure and human capital management. These new rules could provide activists with additional tools for holding companies accountable.

In the UK, the approach to ESG activism is similarly evolving, though often with a greater focus on private board engagement. However, public pressure tactics are also on the rise, with companies facing growing scrutiny from both institutional investors and advocacy groups. A noteworthy development in the UK is the emergence of ESG-related court cases, marking a new phase in corporate accountability. These legal actions, though still in their early stages, could herald broader changes in how ESG issues are addressed, potentially setting a precedent for other regions (Freshfields Bruckhaus Deringer, 2024).

The regulatory environment plays a crucial role in shaping the nature and impact of shareholder activism, particularly when it comes to ESG issues. In the US, the anticipated introduction of stricter regulations concerning climate disclosures and human capital management is expected to significantly influence how companies address ESG concerns. This regulatory shift has already been accompanied by a sharp rise in ESG-related litigation. According to the 2024 Annual Litigation Trends Survey, 10% of organizations experienced ESG-related litigation in 2023, a dramatic increase from 2% in 2022. This surge in legal disputes underscores the growing regulatory and public scrutiny of corporate practices concerning environmental, social, and governance issues. Moreover, a significant proportion of organizations – 27% – expect their exposure to ESG-related disputes to increase in 2024, driven by factors such as greenwashing allegations, climate change litigation, and non-compliance with ESG regulations (Norton Rose Fulbright, 2024).

In contrast, regions such as the EU and the UK benefit from more stable and stringent environmental regulations. These regulatory frameworks reduce the politicization of climate issues, creating an environment of broader consensus on the importance of ESG. The predictability of European regulatory frameworks fosters a more coherent response from companies, encouraging them to adopt long-term strategies for environmental sustainability and social responsibility. For instance, climate-related shareholder proposals in Europe are often met with less resistance than in the US, where companies grapple with inconsistent regulations that create uncertainty and complicate compliance.

The regional variation in regulatory approaches has a profound impact on how companies respond to shareholder activism. In the US, where the regulatory landscape remains fragmented, climate-related proposals have been on the rise, yet companies often face significant uncertainty in their responses. The inconsistent nature of regulatory frameworks creates challenges for businesses seeking to align with both investor expectations and legal requirements. In contrast, Europe's well-defined environmental regulations provide a more predictable and supportive environment for corporate ESG initiatives, fostering a stronger consensus on issues such as climate change and social equity.

Australia has also witnessed a surge in climate-focused activism, with activists increasingly targeting companies reliant on fossil fuels. These efforts reflect broader societal concerns about the country's heavy dependence on carbon-intensive industries. Meanwhile, in Hong Kong, shareholder activism encounters structural barriers that hinder its effectiveness. The dominance of family-owned conglomerates, combined with a regulatory framework that prioritizes the rights of controlling shareholders, makes it difficult for activists to push for meaningful ESG-focused reforms. These structural challenges limit the scope of ESG activism in the region, despite growing interest in sustainability issues.

Interestingly, the US has also seen the emergence of "anti-ESG activism," where activists challenge companies for prioritizing ESG issues over traditional financial goals. These activists argue that focusing on non-financial objectives, such as environmental sustainability or social justice, can come at the expense of shareholder value. However, this movement has struggled to gain widespread support outside the US, and even within the country, anti-ESG proposals generally receive limited backing. Nevertheless, their presence adds a new layer of complexity to the ESG landscape, forcing companies to navigate a delicate balance between financial performance and societal expectations.

Despite the growing importance of ESG issues, the overall number of ESG shareholder proposals declined slightly in 2023 compared to the previous year. While the total number of shareholder proposals submitted for a vote reached a five-year high of 588, average support for all proposals fell significantly to 24.6% (down from 34.4% in 2022). Specifically, the number of environmental and social (E&S) proposals decreased slightly to 137 (from 142 in 2022), and average support for them also fell to 25.5% (Broadridge, 2023). This decline may signal a period of adjustment, as both companies and investors adapt to the rapidly changing ESG landscape. In Europe, for example, the decrease in "Say on Climate" resolutions could be attributed to companies strategically holding such votes less frequently, or to investors feeling less pressure to push for them, given improvements in corporate ESG practices.

At the same time, the high level of support for climate-related resolutions continues to reflect strong investor interest in addressing climate change. Nevertheless, there is debate about the real financial impact of climate-change-related shareholder resolutions. One study found that the 'adoption' of such resolutions has no statistically significant impact on company returns, raising questions as to whether this is a genuine challenge for change or a form of 'co-opted activism' (Jacobsen, 2013). This underscores the need for companies to remain proactive in their ESG efforts, particularly as new regulatory requirements and societal expectations continue to evolve. For businesses, maintaining transparency and ensuring accurate disclosures are essential for avoiding accusations of greenwashing or other forms of misleading communication. By embracing responsible practices and staying attuned to emerging trends, companies can better position themselves to mitigate the risks associated with ESG shareholder activism.

Institutional investors remain key players in the global ESG advocacy landscape, wielding significant influence over corporate practices. The 2023 proxy season witnessed a considerable volume of shareholder proposals, many of which focused on environmental and social policies, as well as executive compensation (Merel Spierings, 2024). This reflects an ongoing push by investors for greater corporate accountability in ESG matters. However, the slight decrease in average support for ESG proposals suggests a more selective approach by institutional investors. Concerns about the relevance and quality of certain proposals, along with improvements in corporate ESG practices, likely contributed to this decline.

Moreover, the rise of anti-ESG groups filing shareholder proposals that challenge diversity, equity, and inclusion policies, as well as climate-related issues, has added complexity to the voting landscape. While these anti-ESG proposals have seen limited success, their presence introduces new dynamics that companies must carefully navigate.

Governance proposals have shown significant variation in support levels. For example, support for CEO/board chair separation proposals dropped from 35% to 28% between 2022 and 2023, reflecting changing investor priorities. Meanwhile, backing for proposals granting special shareholder meeting rights increased from 40% to 52%, indicating a strategic shift in investor focus.

As ESG gains momentum globally, the discussion around corporate governance reform in East Asia has intensified. While ESG integration offers significant opportunities for improving governance, many Asian markets, particularly those with deeply entrenched governance structures like family-owned conglomerates and state-owned enterprises, face unique challenges. Japan, for instance, has made notable progress in integrating ESG principles, with the Government Pension Investment Fund adopting ESG guidelines. However, in countries where governance structures are more rigid, tailored strategies will be required to advance ESG adoption.

Despite these hurdles, the adoption of ESG principles in Asia offers a framework for aligning corporate governance practices with global standards. This can help address the "governance discount" observed in Asian equities (Seah & Wong, 2023), positioning companies for long-term sustainability and enhanced recognition in global markets. This movement is also in line with the view that corporate governance and ESG are considered key elements in building Japan's 'new form of capitalism' (Whittaker, 2024). While obstacles remain, ranging from cultural differences to diverse regulatory landscapes, Asian companies have a unique opportunity to embrace ESG principles, not only to address governance concerns but also to contribute to long-term sustainability and responsible business practices.

In conclusion, ESG advocacy is not only transforming corporate governance but also reshaping global business practices. The emphasis on sustainability, ethical leadership, and long-term value creation is now a central concern for both companies and investors. However, the path to achieving these goals is fraught with challenges, particularly for companies operating in regions with weaker regulatory frameworks or more entrenched governance structures. To succeed, businesses must move beyond superficial engagement with ESG principles and align their governance practices with both ethical standards and financial performance.

Meaningful engagement with shareholders, coupled with a deep understanding of the broader ESG context, will be crucial for driving long-term value creation for all stakeholders. An expanded discussion on the complexities surrounding ESG advocacy by global institutional investors highlights the increasing importance of these issues in corporate governance. As companies and investors alike adapt to the evolving ESG landscape, it is clear that a strategic, nuanced approach will be essential in navigating the challenges and opportunities that lie ahead.

A recent report surveying 992 board members found that ESG remains a sustained priority globally, despite regional differences in enthusiasm and approach (Julie Daum & Kira Ciccarelli, 2023). Boards are increasingly incorporating ESG considerations into their strategic planning, driven by both internal motivations and external pressures such as regulatory changes and rising public expectations. The commitment to ESG is evident across regions, with boards actively discussing how best to integrate these principles into their operations to mitigate risks and capitalize on emerging opportunities.

## REFERENCES


Bauer, R., Moers, F., & Viehs, M. (2015). Who withdraws shareholder proposals, and does it matter? An analysis of sponsor identity and pay practices. *Corporate Governance: An International Review*, 23(6), 472–488.

Broadridge (2023). ProxyPulse: 2023 proxy season review. https://www.broadridge.com/_assets/pdf/broadridge-proxypulse-2023-proxy-season-review.pdf

Chalmers, J., Cox, E., & Picard, N. (2022). 2022 Global investor ESG survey. PricewaterhouseCoopers. https://www.pwc.com/gx/en/services/audit-assurance/corporate-reporting/esg-investor-survey.html

Cornell, B. (2020). ESG investing: Conceptual issues. *SSRN Electronic Journal*. https://dx.doi.org/10.2139/ssrn.3621163

Council of Institutional Investors [CII] (2024). Universal proxy cards. https://www.cii.org/cii_universal_proxy

Daum, J., & Ciccarelli, K. (2023). Sustainability in the spotlight: Has ESG lost momentum in the boardroom? Harvard Law School Forum on Corporate Governance, July 27. https://corpgov.law.harvard.edu/2023/07/27/sustainability-in-the-spotlight-has-esg-lost-momentum-in-the-boardroom/

Dyck, A., Lins, K. V., Roth, L., & Wagner, H. F. (2019). Do institutional investors drive corporate social responsibility? International evidence. *Journal of Financial Economics*, 131(3), 693–714.

Eccles, R. G., Ioannou, I., & Serafeim, G. (2014). The impact of corporate sustainability on organizational processes and performance. *Management Science*, 60(11), 2835–2857.

Eccles, R. G., & Klimenko, S. (2019). The investor revolution. *Harvard Business Review*, 97(3), 106–116.

Erhemjamts, O., & Huang, K. (2019). Institutional ownership horizon corporate social responsibility and shareholder value. *SSRN Electronic Journal*. https://dx.doi.org/10.2139/ssrn.3056847

Feuer, A. (2019). Ethics, ESG, and ERISA: Ethical-factor investing of savings and retirement benefits part 2. *Journal of Pension Benefits*, 26(3), 33–41.

Freshfields Bruckhaus Deringer (2024). ESG regulation and litigation in 2024: What's on the horizon for UK financial institutions? Freshfields, February 16. https://sustainability.freshfields.com/post/102j0f4/esg-regulation-and-litigation-in-2024-whats-on-the-horizon-for-uk-financial-ins

Friede, G., Busch, T., & Bassen, A. (2015). ESG and financial performance: Aggregated evidence from more than 2000 empirical studies. *Journal of Sustainable Finance & Investment*, 5(4), 210–233.

Ganu, S., Kuk, K., Newbury, R., & Zhu, X. (2024). Global report on ESG metrics in incentive plans 2023. Willis Towers Watson. https://www.wtwco.com/en-ch/insights/2024/01/global-report-on-esg-metrics-in-incentive-plans-2023

Gillan, S. L., & Starks, L. T. (2000). Corporate governance proposals and shareholder activism: The role of institutional investors. *Journal of Financial Economics*, 57(2), 275–305.

Hawley, J. P., & Williams, A. T. (2000). *The rise of fiduciary capitalism: How institutional investors can make corporate America more democratic*. University of Pennsylvania Press.

Ioannou, I., & Serafeim, G. (2012). What drives corporate social performance? The role of nation-level institutions. *Journal of International Business Studies*, 43(9), 834–864.

Kraik, A. (2019). Environmental social and governance issues: An altered shareholder activist paradigm. *SSRN Electronic Journal*. https://dx.doi.org/10.2139/ssrn.3668998

Liang, H., & Renneboog, L. (2017). On the foundations of corporate social responsibility. *The Journal of Finance*, 72(2), 853–910.

Loew, E., Erichsen, G., Liang, B., & Postulka, M. L. (2021). Corporate social responsibility (CSR) and environmental social governance (ESG) – disclosure of European banks. *European Banking Institute Working Paper Series 2021*, 83. https://dx.doi.org/10.2139/ssrn.3778674

Matos, P. (2020). ESG and responsible institutional investing around the world: A critical review. *CFA Institute Research Foundation Literature Reviews*. https://dx.doi.org/10.2139/ssrn.3668998

McGough, J. (2024). Incentives linked to ESG metrics among S&P 500 companies. Meridian Compensation Partners. https://www.meridiancp.com/insights/esg-incentive-practices-at-sp-500-companies-2-2/

Norton Rose Fulbright (2024). 2024 annual litigation trends survey. https://www.nortonrosefulbright.com/en/knowledge/publications/4097006f/2024-annual-litigation-trends-survey

Porter, M. E., & Kramer, M. R. (2011). Creating shared value: how to reinvent capitalism—and unleash a wave of innovation and growth. *Harvard Business Review*, 89(1/2), 62–77.

Seah, J., & Wong, E. (2023). CG watch 2023: Corporate governance in Asia. CLSA Limited.

Spierings, M. (2024). Navigating ESG fatigue in shareholder voting. Harvard Law School Forum on Corporate Governance, January 22. https://corpgov.law.harvard.edu/2024/01/22/navigating-esg-fatigue-in-shareholder-voting/

The Conference Board (2023). 2023 Proxy season review—despite record shareholder proposals in the 2023 proxy season, companies should brace for even more in 2024. October 19. https://www.conference-board.org/press/2023-proxy-season-review

U.S. Securities and Exchange Commission [SEC] (2022). SEC charges BNY Mellon investment adviser for misstatements and omissions concerning ESG considerations. Press Release, May. https://www.sec.gov/news/press-release/2022-86

Whittaker, D. H. (2024). Corporate governance, ESG, and "new capitalism". In D. H. Whittaker, *Building a New Economy: Japan's Digital and Green Transformation* (pp. 123–149). Oxford University Press. https://typeset.io/papers/corporate-governance-esg-and-new-capitalism-alaj3l4drk

Williams, S., & Schaefer, A. (2013). Small and medium-sized enterprises and sustainability: Managers' values and engagement with environmental and climate change issues. *Business Strategy and the Environment*, 22(3), 173–186.

Young, S., & Gates, S. (2013). *Institutional Investors' Power to Change Corporate Behavior: International Perspectives.* https://typeset.io/papers/institutional-investors-power-to-change-corporate-behavior-5fyttvdx5h

# 18. Leadership structure, governance formation, and role multiplicity: the choice among female founders

**Agnes Dyvik Clark**

## 1. INTRODUCTION

Authority and hierarchy are typically needed when creating new firms (Foss & Klein, 2023), and firms can be researched as systems of interrelated roles (Simon, 1991). The functional structure of key individual actors (e.g., entrepreneurs and their stakeholders) is found to be a particularly efficacious predictor of new organizational performance (Ensley, Hmieleski, & Pearce, 2006). In the case of emerging firms, research shows that the typical lack of structure and good governance mechanisms due to organic evolvement results in role ambiguity and increased uncertainty (Sine, Mitsuhashi, & Kirsch, 2006), a disadvantage when the organization is already facing a lot of uncertainty.

Role multiplicity, the entrepreneurs taking on several informal and formal roles, is a way of dealing with these uncertainties and the turbulence that comes with all the unknowns. This role multiplicity, or role-taking, becomes a major factor in the firm's performance (Hill & Stephens, 2005). Therefore, founders are expected to enact and balance several roles simultaneously when forming new firms. The founding manager may choose to take on a dual CEO role (i.e., "one person, two roles"), which means the chief executive officer (CEO) is also the new firm's chairperson (Fried, Bruton, & Hisrich, 1998). Within this context, we seek to advance our understanding of the new firm's governance architecture, focusing on the two important formal roles, CEO and chair, the remaining board directors' roles, and the formal and informal ties within.

There has been a long debate about whether demoting from the dual role promotes firm performance. Moving from a unified CEO and chair structure to a separate one has emerged as a salient concern and complex challenge for entrepreneurs. Several research streams explore theoretical perspectives in different types of structures. Structural theorists argue for a formal structure, agency theorists tend to be against CEOs also being the chair (Garg &

Eisenhardt, 2016), and stewardship theorists find a unified structure useful for new firm performance (Erikson, Coleridge, & Bjornali, 2022). Past empirical research in board leadership change has constantly shown mixed results on organizational performance. Despite a solid academic tradition, board leadership change has been merely seen as solutions to existing problems; for instance, strategic direction change (Lorsch & Young, 1990) and poor current performance (Krause & Semadeni, 2013). However, circumstances beneficial to established organizations do not apply to newly created firms. Therefore, this phenomenon will be further explored in the entrepreneurial context, and this study also brings in gender as a potential distinguishing factor.

> *Research Question: Under what conditions should (female) entrepreneurs demote from the dual CEO role or stay in a unified CEO–chair structure, for improved new firm performance?*

Board members bring managerial resources to a new firm. More board members represent more stakeholders involved in formal roles in managerial decisions, which can bring more social-emotional resources for female entrepreneurs (Ingalagi, Nawaz, Rahiman, Hariharasudan, & Hundekar, 2021). New firms need a structure for reduced role ambiguity and role clarity as well as internal social capital (management resources) through leadership structure and formal role transformation (Sine et al., 2006; Stinchcombe, 1965). The CEO and the board directors will together be studied as a "suprateam" in this study, derived from Finkelstein's (2009) view of board director together with the CEO acting as "supra-top management teams" in new firms. At this early stage of the firm, the board directors are typically more involved and actively make strategic decisions together as opposed to the monitoring role, especially when there is no top management team yet employed.

This study also elaborates on the role of advice-seeking in these (dyadic) relationships (Garg & Eisenhardt, 2016; Ma, Kor, & Seidl, 2019). There is a need to uncover how female entrepreneurs as dual CEOs navigate the landscape of advice-seeking, and the personal attributions that influence their approach to seeking and incorporating advice from their board directors. Through this, the different roles, both formal and informal, they play in shaping the advice-seeking behavior in these suprateams will be unlocked.

Burns, Barney, Angus, and Herrick (2016) state that the enrollment of stakeholders, in this case enrolled board directors, under conditions of uncertainty, must be based on the attributes of the founder and not just the attributes of the opportunities. These attributes also secure a strong psychological bond with the stakeholders that leads to extra-role behaviors. Looking further into how female founders as dual CEOs attract and draw on the services from these external stakeholders will contribute to the governance literature on new board formation and our understanding of the effects on new firm performance at a very early stage (Garg, 2020). The remainder of this chapter is structured as follows. After an explanation of the theoretical and contextual background, the method is described, leading to the proposed proposition presented from the quantitative data. The final sections discuss the findings from the qualitative data and provide some suggestions for possible future research.

## 2. THEORETICAL BACKGROUND

### 2.1 Leadership Structure – CEO and Board Directors as Suprateams

Firm governance plays a pivotal role in shaping the strategic direction and decision-making processes of entrepreneurial firms. The board of directors is a key component of firm governance and is vested with the authority to make economic decisions that impact the well-being of investors' capital, the security of employees, the economic health of communities, as well as executive power and perquisites (Molz, 1985). In this study, one important factor is whether these board directors are interlocked or not. "Interlocked" is here referred to as the interlocking ties the board director has, based on the number of positions on other firms' boards (Gan & Erikson, 2022). A way of seeing these different positions is role multiplicity, as a board director might take on different roles on different boards. Schoorman, Bazerman, and Atkin (1981) address interlocking directorates as a strategy for reducing environmental uncertainty. The authors hold that firms have at least four benefits from such ties; they reduce environmental uncertainties through *vertical* and *horizontal* coordination, and they benefit from new *expertise* and enhanced *reputation*. Resource dependency theory also relies on interlocking directorates as a way of reducing uncertainty (Salancik & Pfeffer, 1978). In the current study, the idea is that these interlocking ties mitigate the potential for losses and increase the potential for gains. Henceforth, interlocking ties may contribute to performance.

Recruiting and including board members at an early stage is a new form of stakeholder engagement (Ma et al., 2019), which in many ways also delegates decision rights to these members as they, in reality, make multiple decisions in multiple processes under conditions of uncertainty. As such, the board directors are seen as agents, per Garg and Eisenhardt's (2016) "flipped" agency model. Garg and Eisenhardt state that we need to understand firm governance inversely under these conditions. The founder(s) act as the principal (as they are majority shareholders at an early stage), and the board directors act as agents. It is the attributes of the founder that secure a strong psychological bond with the enrolled board directors, leading to extra-role behaviors

(Burns et al., 2016). Finkelstein (2009) shifted the locus of strategic leadership from top executives to the board of directors. This transition enables an integration of the board and executive perspectives on corporate governance and highlights how boards are, in some ways, "supra-top management teams." This is especially relevant in new firms when formal board directors might be appointed before a formal top management team is hired. However, it is unclear in what direction these dynamics evolve or influence firm governance, and the informal and formal roles and relationships in these suprateams will be further explored in this study.

## 2.2 Role Multiplexity

Implementation of board directors is often the first hierarchy in a new firm, and this bureaucracy becomes an organizational design choice. Clear roles give a clear structure that increases performance in startups (Sine et al., 2006), as they are often in need of more structure due to their newness (Stinchcombe, 1965). This newness provides high uncertainty, and founders, therefore, typically take on several roles, and this role multiplicity (Georgakakis, Heyden, Oehmichen, & Ekanayake, 2022) is almost a precondition for survival. An essential part of the managerial role is ensuring the enrollment of the right stakeholders. In such situations, it could be more beneficial to choose the more formal dual CEO role, known as "CEO duality." However, taking on such roles may also limit the possibility of juggling several other more informal roles, such as the roles of the chief technology officer, chief financial officer, or chief digital officer, for instance, before these roles or functions are formally created (Ma et al., 2019). The juggling of formal and informal roles creates tensions between different role performances and would likely affect the firm governance, but it is unclear how and in what direction. Focusing on CEO duality and the founders' psychological bonds to the board directors, these (dyadic) relationships in these suprateams will here be explored through the lens of advice-seeking (Garg & Eisenhardt, 2016; Ma et al., 2019).

The importance of seeking advice for entrepreneurs cannot be overstated due to the dynamic and complex landscape of entrepreneurship. New firms typically lack resources in their early stages, and access to knowledge is especially limited (Studdard & Munchus, 2009). New firms often require multifaceted decision-making, and seeking advice can provide invaluable insights and guidance. As for the context of firm governance, the advice from the board of directors to the dual CEO is of utmost importance, as their role is to provide strategic advice to the firms that they govern (Amornsiripanitch, Gompers, & Xuan, 2019). Ma et al. (2019) state that "Advice-seeking behavior is shown to have significant effects on CEO decision making and beyond, including the choice of strategy, CEO and board effectiveness, entrepreneurship orientation, and innovativeness of the company, and firm performance" (p. 772). The authors describe the CEO's personal context and attributes as one of the antecedents of CEO advice-seeking. This individual-level analysis of advice-seeking is an interesting perspective to be used when exploring this topic. According to the authors, these attributes include experience/expertise, identity/identification, personality, leadership style, and tenure. As the research by Ma et al. (2019) is on CEOs in general, it is interesting to apply these attributes to founders as dual CEOs in the context of firm governance to unlock the formal and informal governance mechanisms within the board in this new firm context.

Founders and their stakeholders take on both formal and informal roles, and through these roles form both formal and informal ties that is, multiplexity (Ertug, Brennecke, & Tasselli, 2023), which matters in the context of advice-seeking (Figure 18.1 summarizes these). The formal and informal ties, just as the roles, can co-exist, and examples of these non-contractual/conceptual informal relationships are advice-seeking, friendships, or communication (Ertug et al., 2023). The formal roles in this context are mandated, such as the founders, board directors, board of advisors, or investors. Finkelstein (2009) suggests in one of his propositions that "The more friendship ties among a board's directors and between the directors and the CEO, the greater its involvement in all stages of the strategic decision-making process." This is very interesting and will be discovered when analyzing the data. Some suprateams have larger degrees of formal roles and ties, and others take on several informal roles, and informal ties are formed between them, changing the dynamic landscape of decision-making, and so on.

## 3. METHOD

The nature of this study follows an abductive research methodology moving towards explanations of the unexplained through creating and evaluating explanations (Sætre & Van de Ven, 2021). This abductive research methodology

| **Formal roles**<br>E.g., the CEO | **Informal roles**<br>E.g., the unofficial 'CMO' before hiring |
|---|---|
| **Formal ties**<br>E.g., between the board directors | **Informal ties**<br>E.g., board directors' friendship with the CEO |

*Note:* Governance mechanisms: Formal and informal roles and ties in a venture governance context, for contextual background.

*Figure 18.1* *Formal and informal roles and ties as governance mechanisms*

is used to arrive at the impact that firm governance architecture has on new firms' performance and the unlocking of formal and informal governance mechanisms within. Combining quantitative and qualitative data provides a more holistic view of this phenomenon.

Initially, there was a hunch that different firm governance structures, specifically related to the chairperson's and CEO's gender, impact new firms' performance. An available data set on Norwegian startups from the years 2018 to 2020 was consulted. IBM SPSS 29 and Hayes's (2013) PROCESS protocol was used in analyzing the data received from T-Rank AS, a company in the TietoEvry ASA group. The interlocking ties that all the board members had the year following the inception year were counted, including the ties that the chair had. The structural leadership status at the inception year was noted, and aggregated revenue since the firm's inception was coded. Inductive data was gathered from 245 female entrepreneurs that started firms in Norway during the year 2018, and Figure 18.2 shows the best practice. That is, the graph shows that the females are better of taking on just a CEO role if they have few interlocked board members but should consider a dual role if they recruit many interlocked directors who also serve on another organization's board. The model is significant at the $p<0.001$ level, and the R-squared is 0.40, and all the variables are significant at the $p<0.01$ level. This is based on females serving as the CEO and includes the number of interlocked directors. As we can see with *few* interlocked directors, an independent chair is better, but *not* if the board has many interlocked directors. In that case, a dual CEO position is preferable. The outcome is shown in Figure 18.2.

The results were perceived to potentially be an anomaly, so a more in-depth analysis was conducted. The in-depth analysis centered on the founder and board directors' role multiplicity and their relational ties through the qualitative method of shadowing (Nicolini & Korica, 2021). According to the authors, the benefit of this method is that you can pay close attention to what the, in this case, female founders, do, who they do it with, and how they do it. To unlock the personal attributes of female founders serving as dual CEOs in the context of advice-seeking from board directors, an observation-based exploratory study with a rigorous ethnographic protocol was used (Nicolini, Korica, & Ruddle, 2015). Five female founders were followed through some of their working days for several months. Data was gathered through conversations with them, watching them at their workplace, interacting with colleagues, and in meetings with external stakeholders.

The study focused on a sample comprising five female CEOs in Norway who had founded new technologybased firms, representing diverse sectors including AI, the sharing economy, and digital platforms. The founders exhibited a range of educational backgrounds, spanning business schools, law schools, and instances of no formal schooling. Additionally, they varied in terms of

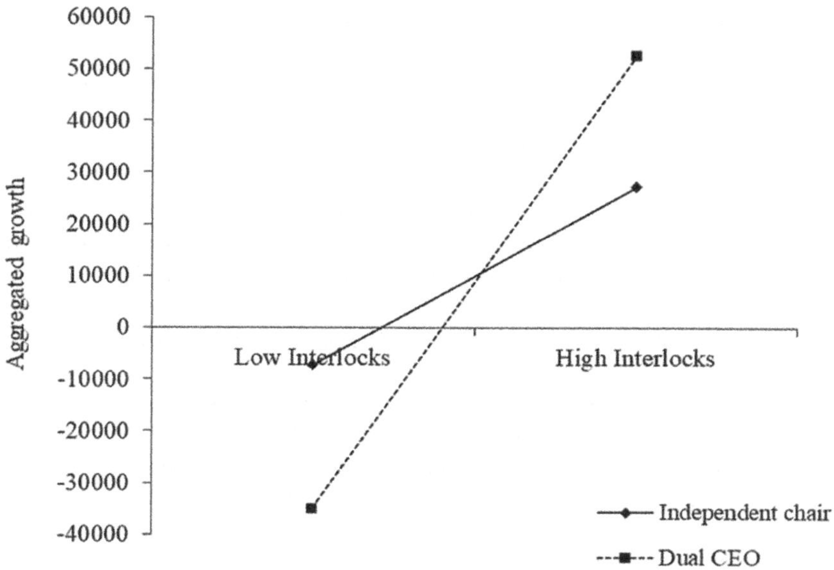


*Figure 18.2* *Showing a moderating relationship affecting firm performance as aggregated revenue growth*

tenure in their current executive positions and overall experience as founders and at the CEO/chair level. The sampled firms demonstrated distinct performance levels concerning revenue, raised capital, and the number of customers. The observational period extended over three months to a year, during which CEOs were systematically observed both on and off their work premises. As a researcher, securing access to the founders was a key aspect, enabling comprehensive documentation of various aspects of their work. Semi-structured interviews were conducted with the five founders, supplemented by numerous informal interviews throughout the observation period. Additional data were gathered from meeting papers, sources referenced by the founders, and external information such as annual reports and regulatory documents, providing a holistic understanding of the sampled female CEOs and their digital firms. More information regarding the cases is summarized in the next section.

## 4. DATA

The initial question asked was what impact the chairperson and/or CEO's gender has on a new firm. Figure 18.2 shows the best practice, using revenue growth to measure firm performance. That is, the graph shows that female founders are better off with having a separate chair if they have few interlocked board members but should take a dual role (CEO and chair) if they recruit many interlocked board directors who also serve on another organization's board. Because of this, there is a question to ask: Given that your gender is female, should you consider taking on both a CEO position and chair position if you attract many interlocked directors?

The graph displays the results as aggregated revenue growth on the y axis. On the x axis is the number of interlocked board directors increasing from low to high. This shows how it is beneficial to have a separate chair until the number of interlocked directors reaches a certain point, when a dual CEO is preferred in the female founder context. These factors are summarized in Figure 18.3.

One explanation of the findings could be that the performance measurement is revenue growth and that female founders might be more focused on revenue growth than firm growth. This might be due to women being more risk averse than men (Berglann, Moen, Røed, & Skogstrøm, 2011) and therefore preferring a more organic growth securing firm survival over firm growth. This argument might be strengthened by the fact that women receive less funding than men (Lueg & Ni, 2020), which is needed to support rapid firm growth. However, we will look more into the personal attributes and the founder's advice-seeking behavior when governing their firm to see if there might be other explanations of the graph, especially looking at female founders' experience, identity, personality, leadership style, and tenure as mentioned by Ma et al. (2019). Table

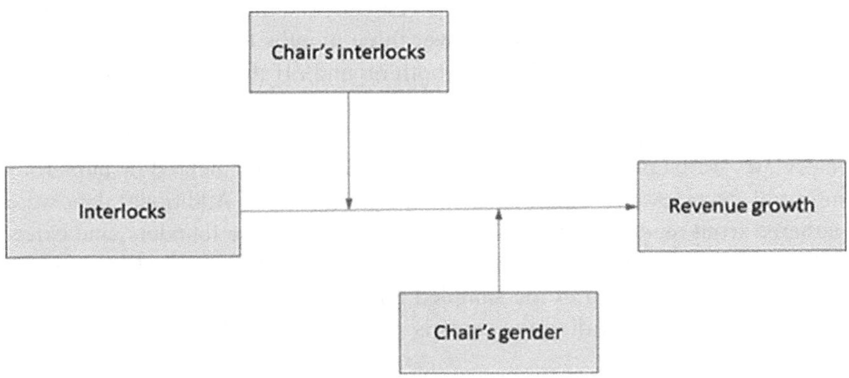


*Figure 18.3* *Gender as a moderating factor in the relationship between interlocking ties and performance*

*Table 18.1 Sample CEOs and data summary*

| - | Dual founder CEO 1 | Dual founder CEO 2 | Dual founder CEO 3 | Dual founder CEO 4 | Dual founder CEO 5 |
|---|---|---|---|---|---|
| Number of interlocked directors | 2 | 2 | 3 | 4 | 3 |
| Founding year | 2020 | 2019 | 2021 | 2021 | 2020 |
| Industry | LegalTech | Digital Platform | MediaTech | PropTech | MediaTech |
| Profitable | No | No | Yes | No | No |
| No. of interviews | 3 | 3 | 2 | 6 | 3 |

18.1 is a summary of the qualitative data collected, providing an overview of the sample cases.

The following provides a brief background of each founder and necessary details for a contextual understanding before the analysis and discussion.

Founder 1: This founder recruited the board early on, as a solo entrepreneur. One board director had a product development background, and the other was a personal friend from the field of robotics, whose expertise was relevant to the core product. The founder sparred a lot with this friend in the beginning, but at the same time developed a worse relationship with the director with the product development background. The founder later wanted to replace this board director but could not find an alternative for a long time. Now, she has enrolled a new board member who also takes on an informal role as a mentor.

Founder 2: This founder is a highly experienced entrepreneur with little formal educational background – a serial entrepreneur with a lot of industry experience having a highly professional board, with very informal ties as they know each other well previously. The board meetings are more informal, almost like workshops. The CEO truly sees them as a team, feeling supported in her role and never monitored. The informal ties make their relationship personal, supporting each other on the entrepreneurial journey and thinking further than just the new firm's well-being. This suprateam has a mutual understanding of the importance of everyone's well-being and that they are in this together, betting on this new firm's success; however, if it fails, the relationships will remain, and other opportunities will be found and created together.

Founder 3: This founder is balancing several formal and informal roles. In addition to being the founder and a dual CEO, she is also taking on the role of director on the board of another firm. She is good at asking how people are and always addresses the elephant in the room if there is one, always reading between the lines. She states that women are always a minority in the entrepreneurial context and is under the impression that somehow, they receive tougher questions from investors and other stakeholders. Consequently, the founder focuses on forming strong and trustworthy relationships with her stakeholders.

Founder 4: This founder had a miserable situation during the year of shadowing. The co-founder, leading product development, repeatedly failed to deliver the initial version of their product platform, keeping investors and board members waiting interminably. The founder was supportive for a long time, but eventually realized that a confrontation was necessary. She felt close to burnout from dealing with the co-founder but kept this from the board. One board member, who was also an acquaintance of the founder, asked—acting as a "friend"—how the founder was doing, clearly stepping out of her formal role. The founder was then honest about the struggle, which put the board member in a difficult position, as it became apparent that she did not want to be formally informed of such problems—this added complications to the working relationship. At one point, the founder wrote in a private message to the author documenting the shadowing process: "It's the 22nd of May, and there is no platform and no updates on it … Board meeting is tomorrow. I will send an email tonight to all of them to say that we will be talking about selling/closing or acquiring my shares; not how I can work with my co-founder and keep on trying to relate the situation …".

Founder 5: This founder was rather young and inexperienced but full of grit and determination to succeed. She quickly gathered a board of highly interlocked directors from other very relevant firms. It became a mixed-gender board, most members taking on formal roles as directors, and had formal ties to her as the CEO. One of the directors took on an additional, more informal, role as they supported the CEO outside of board meetings through advising generally on aspects of business landscapes. These occasions often happened in informal settings, and the director took on more of a "mentor role." However, in more formal settings, such as board meetings, this board member took a back seat and left the others in charge. This led to a more formal atmosphere that the CEO herself admitted could be a little too formal and therefore ineffective and made her feel more monitored than supported.

## 5. ANALYSIS AND DISCUSSION

Although there is an increase in gender-specific studies within entrepreneurship, female entrepreneurship remains understudied (Meyer, 2018), especially from a managerial and governance perspective. The field of entrepreneurship remains male-dominant, and it is, therefore, a large economic advantage to bridge the gender gap (Ughetto, Rossi, Audretsch, & Lehmann, 2020). Most of the research from the perspective of female founders relates to access to financial capital (Lueg & Ni, 2020; Orser, Riding, & Manley, 2006; Verheul & Thurik, 1999). However, the style of female founders as CEOs and their advice-seeking behavior remains unclear. The current literature covers differences between men and women as CEOs and includes, for example, research on their different leadership styles (Faizan, Nair, & Haque, 2018). However, there is a gap in the literature regarding female founders as managers, in particular the different ways female founders manage and govern their firms by shaping formal and informal relationships through their different roles and how their attributes impact their advice-seeking in this context.

## 5.1 Diverging Mindsets

This study shows that the social behaviors of women in this context might differ due to their mental models. Those differences could lead to different ways of designing and appointing important structural roles, such as the CEO or chair, for a new firm. As the founder enrolls external stakeholders as directors, networks matter in this context. The formation of this might be impacted by the founder's ability to have a diverging mindset. Formally serving not only as the CEO but also as the chair and simultaneously taking on more informal roles in an emerging organization requires flexibility, willingness, and the ability to take on such roles, as we will further explore in this analysis. An example of this is that two of the observed founders have taken on the extra role as director on another firm's board. This extra role provides another perspective and new knowledge that can give CEOs a broader overview of what is going on beyond their organization (Nicolini et al., 2015). One of the founders shadowed even took on the role of being extra supportive towards the founding CEO of the other firm, given her own insights of what that role might need. The shadowed founders seemed to be adept at handling and juggling all these multiple formal and informal roles while being dual CEOs and directors on another firm's board.

## 5.2 Navigating Formal and Informal Ties

The shadowing of these founders led to interesting insights regarding formal and informal roles and ties impacting the new firm's performance. Founder 1 has directors who are not especially interlocked. The dual founder CEO and the most engaged director interact through established formal roles and consequently have very formal ties within their suprateam. Another one of the directors is not interlocked at all, and the founder formed informal ties to this person through also having informal roles. This non-interlocked board director has become a coach, a friend, and a more personal advisor to the founder, taking on many informal roles and is someone the founder can trust and be together with in informal contexts as well as more formal board meetings. This balance between the formal and informal roles is necessary for the founder at this point (early phase of the firm). However, the firm is about to mature (through scaling up), and the founder herself states that there is a need for more interlocked directors, opening up more firm opportunities and value capture at this stage. In particular, a professional chair is wanted, with the aim to separate the CEO and chair role: "I need a more professional chair that has experience from scaling up companies and not just focus on product development, but I do not want to miss the relationship I have with the less connected board director. She is my coach, and we even go to yoga together!" (Founder 1 interview data). This is an interesting insight as the founder seeks advice from the board of directors at two levels. Both formal and informal relationships (Nicolini et al., 2015) are formed with the directors, and the founder mostly gets advice through the formation of informal ties and in different contexts than just during the formal board meetings. However, the founder admits that interlocked directors in more formal roles as board directors capture more value and provide more opportunities for firm growth. The advice in the informal settings is essential for the founder's well-being and motivation. This is an important and under-communicated aspect of the roles external stakeholders have, as many founders struggle with loneliness, lack of motivation, and depression (Cubbon, Darga, Wisnesky, Dennett, & Guptill, 2021). Avoiding this ultimately secures a better chance for the new firm's survival.

### 5.3 Advice-seeking Outside the Suprateam

Some founders formed other networks to seek advice from. For instance, Founder 2 formed a strategic female network that started through informal ties as these relationships were first and foremost new friendships formed by being part of a minority in an entrepreneurial context (Ughetto et al., 2020). These friendships and social engagements then became a large and important part of the types of interactions the entrepreneurs have. It is through these interactions with friends that many new opportunities are found as well as problems are solved, often unintentionally. Founder 2's network has met regularly as friends over dinner, and all are CEOs and founders of software or hardware firms, with very different backgrounds and networks. One of the members stated that the fact that they have been through so many of the firms' phases together makes these interactions very relevant and more important than ever. They all say it feels like a unique relationship where many managerial and strategic decisions are suddenly made. Founder 2 is more advice-seeking towards this network and would rather see the interlocked directors and board meetings as formal settings for reporting on the firm's situation, as opposed to an advice-seeking context. The founder is under the impression that advice-seeking requires that one admit a lack of knowledge and that the board must be impressed as opposed to being used for advice. The directors are mostly highly interlocked and have invested capital in the firm. Therefore, they are the type of stakeholders that the founder wants to impress to get more capital in the future. This is an interesting insight as this proves how the board of directors is not always the right arena for advice. However, it might also show that not all founders choose to be completely honest about all aspects of the firm to the board. Something that could be strategic or non-strategic in the long run is a more informal and honest dialogue both ways, which might foster more opportunities for the firm. It does seem that way based on the experience from the other shadowed founders in this study, as we will next explore. They balance having informal ties to their interlocked directors leading to this extra role behavior generating new opportunities.

Interestingly, the interlocked directors themselves are often a source of knowledge and information, advising the founder from perspectives both inside the firm and outside the firm. The board of directors possess a multiplicity of roles themselves, as they take on roles from both advising from an "in-firm" perspective from being part of the governance structure, as well as the "outside-in" perspective due to them being interlocked and well connected to a large network. The nature of these relationships and the type of advice in this context are shaped by how these interlocked directors got enrolled, as will be discussed in the next section.

## 5.4 Enrolling Stakeholders Through Heterogeneous Networks

The personal attributes of the female founders that were shadowed enable them to very well exploit the resources that their stakeholders possess. Their leadership style is generally humble and, therefore, very advice-seeking by nature. Advice from the directors is acquired at different levels in addition to the internal and external perspective mentioned. One of the founders received advice in just formal settings through formal roles at both ends, while others formed more informal ties to these stakeholders leading to advice-seeking while taking on the more personal roles.

Men display more homophily than women when forming networks (Mengel, 2020), and female founders tend to be more open, collaborative, and empathetic while seeking creative solutions together (Eagly & Johannesen-Schmidt, 2001). Female founders must work a little harder to achieve these ties, due to being a minority in this entrepreneurial context (Ughetto et al., 2020). As also seen from the shadowed founders, women might form more heterogeneous networks in the context of venturing, potentially from having a more divergent mindset within these matters. As previously stated, the recruitment of board directors can be understood as stakeholder enrolment (Burns et al., 2016). The authors state that under conditions of uncertainty "the enrolment process cannot be based on the attributes of opportunities, but instead must be based on the attributes of the entrepreneur, e.g., his/her charisma, trustworthiness, and reputation" (Burns et al., 2016, p. 98). Since the female founders shadowed in this study are very good at both attracting and exploiting the independent stakeholders and their resources, this might explain a special ability to recruit these interlocked board directors. Looking deeper into the way they networked and formed new relational ties to other stakeholders, they all valued slow networking (Brennecke, Ertug, & Elfring, 2024). In particular, Founder 3 pointed out the importance of taking it slow and building long-lasting relationships from the ground up, instead of quickly getting to know someone for an immediate return of favor, introduction, advice, and so on.

## 5.5 "Inauthentic" Leadership Styles

Another observation is the founder's leadership styles. They all are very good at reading the room and reading non-verbal cues due to their people-oriented leadership style. A more masculine leadership style in comparison tends to focus on results, having a more task-oriented than people-oriented nature (Faizan et al., 2018). The female founders shadowed are very focused on following expectations, hence doing everything "right" to please everyone. This might be another trait of their leadership style. Their management style is very humble, almost imposter-like. The balance of the two leadership styles might be optimal, and what many female founders do is balance the two by being slightly inauthentic in their managerial roles. To fit in, they become more result-oriented to form ties more easily with external stakeholders who are very often male. However, their more natural leadership style is less task oriented. The "inauthentic" and slightly different behavior from their natural state happens subconsciously for the founders shadowed. This inauthentic behavior might impact statistics and research (e.g., Figure 18.2). It can be related to the authenticity paradox (Ibarra, 2015). The author explains how being authentic is not always the best option and that being inauthentic can often be very advantageous in a leadership context, as you need to properly balance being yourself with being a good leader. Women being inauthentic in these roles as founders is very interesting. This might explain why they are so good at exploiting the interlocked board directors as dual CEOs and successfully work as a suprateam. One worry is that if you're too inauthentic over time you might lose yourself (Ibarra, 2015), so this is only beneficial when balancing a fine line between the two and not being too inauthentic. Balancing people-oriented and result-oriented leadership styles might enable the entrepreneur to better navigate between formal and informal roles and ties. Genuine interest in other people might enable the entrepreneur to move into informal roles more quickly and then form the informal ties needed for a cerrtain type of advice in addition to the advice from the more formal contexts. This is a way of successfully navigating between formal and informal ties, as well as recruiting interlocked directors.

It is noteworthy that these informal roles are ways of dealing with uncertainty. While confronting critical decisions for a new firm, a CEO with informal roles can have direct access to required information through his/her interactions with people or groups outside the organization and distinct networks that the internal board structure shares (Ma et al., 2019). This direct access inherently makes problem-solving more efficient. Future research might explore these informal roles among founders in emerging firms.

As discovered in this study, founders must balance multiple roles, both formal and informal, and multiple ties, formal and informal. This juggling of multiple identities and relations is in fact a form of relational pluralism (Shipilov, Gulati, Kilduff, Li, & Tsai, 2014), and does involve some challenges in itself. Future research might further explore these challenges and the founders' attributes and abilities used to overcome them.

## 6. CONCLUSION

In conclusion, our findings shed light on the multifaceted role of interlocked directors and founders in the dual CEO context, together researched as "suprateams." The interlocked directors emerged as pivotal sources of knowledge and advice, offering insights from both an "in-firm" perspective, embedded within the governance structure, and an "outside-in" perspective, stemming from their interconnections and extensive networks. The personal attributes of the female CEO founders, marked by humility and a natural inclination towards advice-seeking, played a significant role in leveraging the resources available through stakeholder networks. Notably, the recruitment of interlocked directors was perceived as a form of stakeholder enrollment, emphasizing the importance of the entrepreneur's attributes, such as charisma, trustworthiness, and reputation in uncertain conditions. The observed differences in leadership styles between the people-oriented and task-oriented approaches highlighted the nuanced strategies employed by female founders as dual CEOs. While adopting a more results-oriented demeanor might be a strategic necessity in male-dominated external networks, the inherent people-oriented leadership style, characterized by a focus on interpersonal dynamics, room-reading abilities, and a humble managerial approach, proved essential for balancing authenticity and leadership effectiveness in the governance context. The findings suggest that the dual role of female founders forming formal and informal ties to stakeholders contributes to their success in recruiting and utilizing interlocked board directors, challenging traditional expectations and shedding light on the complexity of gendered leadership mechanisms in the entrepreneurial context.

## REFERENCES

Amornsiripanitch, N., Gompers, P. A., & Xuan, Y. (2019). More than money: Venture capitalists on boards. *The Journal of Law, Economics, and Organization*, *35*(3), 513–543.

Berglann, H., Moen, E. R., Røed, K., & Skogstrøm, J. F. (2011). Entrepreneurship: Origins and returns. *Labour Economics*, *18*(2), 180–193.

Brennecke, J., Ertug, G., & Elfring, T. (2024). Networking fast and slow: The role of speed in tie formation. *Journal of Management*, *50*(4), 1230–1258.

Burns, B. L., Barney, J. B., Angus, R. W., & Herrick, H. N. (2016). Enrolling stakeholders under conditions of risk and uncertainty. *Strategic Entrepreneurship Journal*, *10*(1), 97–106.

Cubbon, L., Darga, K., Wisnesky, U. D., Dennett, L., & Guptill, C. (2021). Depression among entrepreneurs: A scoping review. *Small Business Economics*, *57*(2), 781–805.

Eagly, A. H., & Johannesen-Schmidt, M. C. (2001). The leadership styles of women and men. *Journal of Social Issues*, *57*(4), 781–797.

Ensley, M. D., Hmieleski, K. M., & Pearce, C. L. (2006). The importance of vertical and shared leadership within new venture top management teams: Implications for the performance of startups. *The Leadership Quarterly*, *17*(3), 217–231.

Erikson, T., Coleridge, C., & Bjornali, E. (2022). Venture governance and its dynamics: Intraboard relationships and CEO duality. *Technovation*, *115*, 102540.

Ertug, G., Brennecke, J., & Tasselli, S. (2023). Theorizing about the implications of multiplexity: An integrative typology. *Academy of Management Annals*, *17*(2), 626–654.

Faizan, R., Nair, S. L. S., & Haque, A. (2018). The effectiveness of feminine and masculine leadership styles in relation to contrasting gender's performances. *Polish Journal of Management Studies*, *17*(1), 78–92.

Finkelstein, S. (2009). *Strategic leadership: Theory and research on executives, top management teams, and boards*. Oxford University Press.

Foss, N. J., & Klein, P. G. (2023). Why managers still matter as applied organization (design) theory. *Journal of Organization Design*, *12*(1), 7–18.

Fried, V. H., Bruton, G. D., & Hisrich, R. D. (1998). Strategy and the board of directors in venture capital-backed firms. *Journal of Business Venturing*, *13*(6), 493–503.

Gan, D., & Erikson, T. (2022). Venture governance: CEO duality and new venture performance. *Journal of Business Venturing Insights*, *17*, e00304.

Garg, S. (2020). Venture governance: A new horizon for corporate governance. *Academy of Management Perspectives*, *34*(2), 252–265.

Garg, S., & Eisenhardt, K. M. (2016). Unpacking the CEO–board relationship: How strategy making happens in entrepreneurial firms. *Academy of Management Journal*, *60*(5), 1828–1858.

Georgakakis, D., Heyden, M. L., Oehmichen, J. D., & Ekanayake, U. I. (2022). Four decades of CEO–TMT interface research: A review inspired by role theory. *The Leadership Quarterly*, *33*(3), 101354.

Hayes, A. F. (2013). *Introduction to mediation, moderation, and conditional process analysis: A regression-based approach*. Guilford Press.

Hill, R. P., & Stephens, D. L. (2005). The multiplicity of selves and selves management: A leadership challenge for the 21st century. *Leadership*, *1*(1), 127–140.
Ibarra, H. (2015). The authenticity paradox. *Harvard Business Review*, *93*(1/2), 53–59.
Ingalagi, S. S., Nawaz, N., Rahiman, H. U., Hariharasudan, A., & Hundekar, V. (2021). Unveiling the crucial factors of women entrepreneurship in the 21st century. *Social Sciences*, *10*(5), 153.
Krause, R., & Semadeni, M. (2013). Apprentice, departure, and demotion: An examination of the three types of CEO–board chair separation. *Academy of Management Journal*, *56*(3), 805–826.
Lorsch, J., & Young, J. (1990). Pawns or potentates: The reality of America's corporate boards. *The Executive*, *4*(4), 85–87.
Lueg, K., & Ni, A. (2020). Female entrepreneurs and access to financial capital: A comparative survey on gender bias in Denmark and Indonesia. *Asian Journal of Social Science*, *48*(1–2), 15–43.
Ma, S., Kor, Y. Y., & Seidl, D. (2019). CEO advice seeking: An integrative framework and future research agenda. *Journal of Management*, *46*(6), 771–805.
Mengel, T. (2020). Creative connections: Fiction, futures studies, and leadership (for the future). *Creativity Matters*, *1*, 72–79.
Meyer, N. (2018). Research on female entrepreneurship: Are we doing enough? *Polish Journal of Management Studies*, *17*(2), 158–169.
Molz, R. (1985). Board of directors. *Journal of Business Strategy*, *5*(4), 86–93.
Nicolini, D., & Korica, M. (2021). Attentional engagement as practice: A study of the attentional infrastructure of healthcare chief executive officers. *Organization Science*, *32*(5), 1273–1299.
Nicolini, D., Korica, M., & Ruddle, K. (2015). Staying in the know. *MIT Sloan Management Review*, June 2. Available at: https://sloanreview.mit.edu/article/staying-in-the-know/
Orser, B. J., Riding, A. L., & Manley, K. (2006). Women entrepreneurs and financial capital. *Entrepreneurship Theory and Practice*, *30*(5), 643–665.
Sætre, A. S., & Van de Ven, A. (2021). Generating theory by abduction. *Academy of Management Review*, *46*(4), 684–701.
Salancik, G. R., & Pfeffer, J. (1978). A social information processing approach to job attitudes and task design. *Administrative Science Quarterly*, *23*(2), 224–253.
Schoorman, F. D., Bazerman, M. H., & Atkin, R. S. (1981). Interlocking directorates: A strategy for reducing environmental uncertainty. *Academy of Management Review*, *6*(2), 243–251.
Shipilov, A., Gulati, R., Kilduff, M., Li, S., & Tsai, W. (2014). Relational pluralism within and between organizations. *Academy of Management Journal*, *57*(2), 449–459.
Simon, H. (1991). Bounded rationality and organizational learning. *Organization Science*, *2*(1), 125–134.
Sine, W. D., Mitsuhashi, H., & Kirsch, D. A. (2006). Revisiting Burns and Stalker: Formal structure and new venture performance in emerging economic sectors. *Academy of Management Journal*, *49*(1), 121–132.
Stinchcombe, A. (1965). Organization-creating organizations. *Trans-action*, *2*(2), 34–35.
Studdard, N. L., & Munchus, G. (2009). Entrepreneurial firms' acquisition of knowledge using proactive help-seeking behaviour. *International Journal of Entrepreneurial Behavior & Research*, *15*(3), 242–261.

Ughetto, E., Rossi, M., Audretsch, D., & Lehmann, E. E. (2020). Female entrepreneurship in the digital era. *Small Business Economics*, *55*(2), 305–312.

Verheul, I., & Thurik, R. (1999). *Start-up capital: Differences between male and female entrepreneurs*. EIM Zoetermeer.

# 19. Diversity and innovation

**Richard S. Warr and Jing Zhao**

## 1. INTRODUCTION

Our 2018 paper (Mayer, Warr, & Zhao, 2018) investigates how diversity influences corporate innovation, and in turn the financial outcomes and firm value, focusing on whether pro-diversity firms exhibit greater innovation and patent activity. We find that there is a positive link between innovation and firm value and that diversity within the organization is associated with an increase in innovation. Our paper connects these two pieces of evidence and argues that policies that promote diversity in the organization can increase firm value via the channel of product innovation.

### 1.1 Innovation and Value

In most finance research, innovation is measured using patent data. The foundational paper is by Hall, Jaffe, and Trajtenberg (2005) who study the relationship between firm market value and patent citations as an indicator of the importance and impact of their innovations. In this and their 2001 National Bureau of Economic Research paper, these authors provide the basic framework for using patent-level data in empirical finance research. Hall et al. find that firms with patents that receive more citations tend to have higher market valuations, suggesting that citations reflect the "importance" or quality of the underlying innovations. Furthermore, they find that the marginal contribution of new citations, and particularly those that are "unpredictable," generates economically significant impacts on the firm's value. They also find that these effects are more pronounced in certain industries, notably the pharmaceutical and medical instrument sectors compared to the computer and communications industry, possibly reflecting the different roles patents play in these sectors.

Hirshleifer, Hsu, and Li (2013) provide evidence that firms with higher innovative efficiency (measured as the ratio of patent counts to research and development (R&D) expenditure) have better stock returns. Their study posits that innovation efficiency (IE), measured as the ratio of innovation output (patents or citations) to innovation input (R&D expenditure), carries valuable information for investors, impacting both market valuation and future stock returns. They find that IE is positively associated with a firm's market valuation and future operating performance, including measures such as return on assets and cash flows. This finding suggests that firms exhibiting higher efficiency in converting R&D investments into patents or citations tend to be perceived as more valuable by the market. Their research finds that IE demonstrates significant predictive power for future stock returns, even after controlling for well-known risk factors and other firm-specific characteristics. This predictability is particularly pronounced among firms characterized by limited investor attention (e.g., smaller firms with less analyst coverage) and higher valuation uncertainty, supporting the notion that IE information might not be fully incorporated into stock prices promptly.

The papers in this literature establish that innovation is a driver of value creation for the firm. However, these papers don't answer the question: What are the inputs to innovation within the firm? For our purposes, we will focus on the impact of team composition on innovation.

## 1.2 Team Diversity and Innovation

In most organizations, new products or innovations are created by teams working together, and for years the received wisdom was to put together a team of the most highly qualified experts to work on the project. However, there is evidence that if team selection sacrifices diversity, the outcome from the team's efforts might be inferior to that generated by a more diverse team. Diversity in this realm is very broadly defined to simply mean that not everyone on the team has the same educational background, gender, race, and so on.

Why, then, might the diversity of a team of engineers or product designers working on a new product idea or technology impact the quality of the final solution? Hong and Page (2004) try to answer this question by developing a model that demonstrates how diverse groups could outperform homogeneous teams even when the homogeneous team consists of objectively more capable individuals. In their paper they present diversity broadly beyond traditional notions based on race and gender. They argue that for many problems there exist multiple solutions that are optimal or near optimal. For example, there may be multiple ways to organize the internal layout of technology in a mobile phone. They argue that each individual uses heuristics or rules to navigate this landscape, influenced by their unique perspectives and experiences. Importantly for their model, high-ability problem-solvers may have similar heuristics due to comparable training and backgrounds, limiting their search area to similar solutions. Hong and Page apply this model to various simulated tasks, including optimization problems and predictive tasks. The simulations reveal that diverse groups explore broader areas within the solution landscape, increasing their chances of finding superior solutions compared to homogeneous high-ability groups who may cluster around suboptimal peaks. Their work suggests that assembling teams with diverse skill sets and cognitive tools can be more effective than simply gathering the most intelligent or highest-performing individuals. The authors note that diversity here refers not just to identity diversity (such as ethnicity or gender) but also to functional diversity – differences in how people perceive problems and devise solutions based on their unique backgrounds, training, and cognitive styles.

While Hong and Page provided a simulated examination of the impact of team diversity on problem-solving, their work was based on a simulation model. A real-world examination was conducted by Phillips, Liljenquist, and Neale (2009),[1] who put together teams made up of sorority and fraternity members and then had them solve a murder mystery. The authors found that by adding an outsider to a team, the team correctly solved the mystery more often. The key to their finding was that while socially distinct newcomers can contribute unique perspectives and information, their presence can also create discomfort and conflict within a group. Overall, the findings suggest that adding socially distinct newcomers to a group can indeed lead to better performance on complex tasks due to the introduction of new perspectives and information processing strategies. However, such benefits can come at the cost of reduced perceived effectiveness and increased discomfort among group members during collaboration. Other studies have supported these results that diverse teams tend to find better solutions, but the problem-solving process can appear more contentious.

Without getting into an in-depth examination of the management theory behind team dynamics, the key takeaway at work here is the idea that a non-diverse team is more likely to drop into groupthink. Members of the team will support each other's views, and dissenting opinions or ideas won't be brought up. By bringing in outsiders, these outsiders voice their opinions, and these opinions are sometimes valuable, sometimes not. The point is the team is forced to consider different ideas when formulating a solution. It's also important to note when we are thinking about diverse teams, we can think in terms of the usual measures of diversity – age, gender orientation, race, societal background. The benefit of diverse teams is often thought to be because you are bringing a range of different life experiences to bear on a problem. But if the problem is abstracted from people's day-to-day reality – say designing a component for a piece of industrial machinery, it is hard to see how someone's life experiences might improve the search for the best innovative solution.

Looking at the firm level, Talke, Salomo, and Kock (2011) find that diversity of the "top management team" (TMT) broadly defined has a positive impact on the firm's innovation.[2] The authors use primarily survey data of 106 firms. The authors argue that TMT diversity leads to a more proactive innovation orientation because diverse teams bring a wider range of perspectives, experiences, and knowledge to the table. This can help firms identify emerging customer needs and market trends more effectively, develop more creative and innovative solutions, and then invest in emerging technologies more quickly. The study's findings support these arguments, showing that TMT diversity is positively related to both proactive market orientation and proactive technology orientation. The authors also found that a proactive innovation orientation leads to a higher degree of market newness and technology newness in a firm's new product portfolio. Finally, the study found that both market newness and technology newness are positively related to a firm's financial performance, as measured by Tobin's Q.

These papers, primarily found in the management psychology and productive innovation literature, provide evidence that diverse teams play a role in developing innovative solutions, but prior to our paper, no research had connected firm-level diversity to hard measures of innovation. Our paper bridges that gap by quantifying innovation and the impact of diversity for a large sample of US public companies.

## 2. OUR PAPER

Our paper (Mayer, Warr, & Zhao, 2018) investigates the relationship between a firm's pro-diversity policies, its ability to innovate effectively (termed "innovative efficiency") and the resulting impact on firm value.[3] We don't study "why" diversity impacts innovation, but rather we examine whether diversity impacts innovation.

Extending the aforementioned literature on diversity and firm value, we hypothesize that firms fostering a diverse workforce and a culture of inclusion will garner greater innovative efficiency and, ultimately, greater innovation output. More specifically, pro-diversity practices are conducive to innovation for several reasons. First, a more diverse hiring policy broadens the potential pool from which a firm is able to recruit talented and creative employees. In addition, a more diverse firm environment and culture of inclusion may help boost employee morale and attract and retain talent. Finally, a wider array of views, backgrounds, experience, and expertise are likely to help innovative problem-solving, the integral element and foundation of innovation. In light of the established evidence in prior literature that innovation enhances firm value, we further hypothesize that through the channel of corporate innovation, pro-diversity policies can improve firm value. Our null hypothesis is that pro-diversity policies are merely designed to make the company look better or reflect a managerial indulgence. Hence, the null hypothesis predicts that investment in such policies will result in shareholder value deterioration (Jensen, 1986).

Visually our hypothesis is as follows:

*Pro-diversity policies → Innovation (new patents or new products) → Greater firm value*

## 2.1 Data Sources

We combine data from various sources, including MSCI ESG STATS, Capital IQ, and Compustat, to analyze these relationships, and we focus on two broad measures of innovation discussed below.

*New Product Announcements*: These are the annual number of new product announcements made by each firm using data from Capital IQ's Key Development database. This database compiles information from a wide range of sources, including news articles, press releases, regulatory filings, and company websites. Capital IQ analysts then review and categorize these data points to identify and classify significant corporate events like new product launches.

*Patent and Citation Data*: This includes data on patents and patent citations from the National Bureau of Economic Research database. This database provided information on patents granted to each firm annually and the number of citations those patents received over time. We considered both the quantity of patents and the number of citations as indicators of innovation. We argue that citation counts could serve as a proxy for the impact or influence of a patent, distinguishing more groundbreaking innovations from incremental ones.

Because the raw patent and new product data are subject to numerous biases (e.g., companies with more R&D expenses are likely to create more patents) we calculate "innovative efficiency," which measures how effectively firms utilize their R&D expenditures. For new product announcements, we calculated innovative efficiency by dividing the natural logarithm of one plus the number of new product announcements by one plus the firm's R&D expenses in the preceding year. We use a similar approach with patent and citation data, scaling these metrics by a weighted sum of the firm's R&D expenditures over the previous five years. We then use a five-year window to account for the time lag often observed between R&D investment and patent application success.

Finally, we make extensive industry and technology adjustments to recognize that innovation patterns can vary significantly across industries and technological fields; they also adjusted their patent and citation metrics to account for these variations.

Diversity is tricky to measure at the firm level. Very few firms report details of the composition of their workforce (aside from C-suite positions). Therefore, the closest we can get to understanding a firm's standing with respect to diversity is to look at their policies to promote diversity within the firm. For these, we turn to the MSCI ESG STATS database. This data contains simple binary measures for a range of pro-diversity policies. For example, the data records "diversity strengths" that include work–life benefits or benefits for lesbian, gay, bisexual, transgender, and queer couples. The data also includes "diversity concerns," for example if the company has been sued for discrimination. Combining these measures creates diversity strengths and diversity concern scores. The net diversity score is found from the difference between strengths and concerns.

## 2.2 Data and Method

Our final sample spans 2001 through 2013 and comprises 11,636 year/firm observations. Firms in the sample are quite large, with an average market value of $9 billion, consistent with the restriction that the MSCI ESG data is limited to the S&P 1500 firms. On average, firms in our sample have an R&D expense of 2.7% of assets, but the median is 0, while the maximum is 34%.

The raw data reveals some interesting patterns. For example, most industries (using the Fama French 48 industry groupings) have median net diversity scores of zero. This result was surprising to us given the degree to which many firms talk about diversity.

The highest net diversity score for any industry is in personal services; the lowest is in the mining and extraction industries. Innovation levels vary across industries, with technology industries having the highest levels of new product development as measured by new products per firm.

We performed a variety of analyses to control for alternative stories, and our results demonstrate a robust, positive effect of corporate pro-diversity policies on innovative efficiency, especially during economic downturns. Through its positive influence on innovation, such diversity policies also increase firm value. Overall, our findings suggest that diverse workforces lead to higher productivity and innovative outcomes, ultimately enhancing shareholder value.

Before turning to our key findings, we would like to first discuss one of the key problems with studies like ours, which is the potential for endogeneity. There are plenty of reasons why there might be a correlation between innovation and diversity that has nothing to do with the team's dynamics we discussed above. For example, rather than diversity policies impacting future innovation, it is plausible that more innovative firms are inclined to adopt more pro-diversity policies and foster an inclusive firm culture to motivate greater employee engagement, innovation, and impact (reverse causality). Alternatively, there might be an omitted, unobservable control variable that drives both innovation and pro-diversity policies simultaneously. Examples of such variables include firm strategic shifts, executive preferences, and organizational cultures, to name a few.

In our paper, we address potential endogeneity using two primary methods – first by using Granger causality and second by exploring the impact of an endogenous economic shock.

The Granger causality tests allow us to investigate the direction of causality between diversity policies and innovative efficiency. This involved examining whether lagged changes in diversity policies predicted future changes in innovative efficiency, and vice versa. The results indicated that lagged changes in diversity policies positively and significantly predicted future changes in innovative efficiency, but not the other way around. This finding supports the argument that diversity policies statistically predict innovative efficiency, suggesting a causal relationship.

For the endogenous economic shock, we used the 2008 financial crisis. We argue that this event allowed for an analysis of how firms with differing pro-diversity policies recovered during a period of widespread economic uncertainty. The rationale is that the financial crisis, as an external shock, would not immediately alter a firm's diversity culture. This approach aimed to isolate the causal effect of diversity on innovation during and after the crisis. The results indicated that firms with stronger pro-diversity policies exhibited a greater ability to generate new products during and following the crisis, suggesting that such policies contribute to resilience and recovery.

In addition to these methods, we also incorporated firm fixed effects in their regression analyses to account for unobservable, firm-specific, time-invariant omitted variables that might influence the relationship between diversity and innovation.

## 2.3 Key Findings

Using a wide array of analyses and methodologies, we document that pro-diversity policies are positively related to innovative efficiency, primarily defined as the number of new product announcements per R&D dollar spent by a firm. More specifically, our baseline regression analyses imply, for example, that if a firm made significant improvements in its workforce diversity level, say by increasing its diversity index by seven points, the average firm will see about two additional new product announcements over a ten-year period. Not surprisingly, the impact of pro-diversity policies on innovation proves to be a long-haul process. One or two immediate additions or improvements to current human resources or diversity policies (i.e., adding one or two points to firms' diversity indices by perhaps adding policies to encourage work–life benefits) are unlikely to have an instant impact on new product development. However, a sustained commitment to improving diversity across the organization over a long-term window will, in time, be rewarded with greater innovation and outcomes.

These results provide preliminary support for our hypothesis – that pro-diversity policies are positively related to a firm's innovative efficiency. However, concerns remain, not least of which is the impact of endogeneity on our results. The next sections attempt to tackle this issue.

To ensure that our results are robust, particularly to endogeneity concerns, we employ Granger (1969) causality tests. More specifically, we find that lagged changes in diversity policies positively and significantly predict future changes in innovative efficiency but not the other way around.

Further tests show that the positive effect of pro-diversity policies on innovative efficiency is especially strong during recessions, including the 2008 financial crisis. These results suggest that building a reputation of pro-diversity and a culture of inclusion are beneficial to a firm, in particular when investors and the economy at large are marred by a severe crisis of trust and confidence due to extraordinary uncertainty and risk, and when being trustworthy substantially pays off.

A plausible concern one may have is that our results could be driven by merely the "Silicon Valley" companies, who are both champions in pro-diversity practices and pioneers in innovation. To address this concern, we redo our analyses by explicitly excluding California-based firms, and our main results are qualitatively the same.

In an attempt to uncover the underlying mechanisms that drive our results, we also perform a range of additional tests. Consistent with our hypotheses, these additional investigations show that the positive effect of pro-diversity policies is more concentrated in more innovative firms, firms that more greatly value intangibles such as human capital and employees, growth firms, industries with fewer women and hence more to gain from hiring women and other minorities, firms with lower leverage, higher cash flow, and fewer financial constraints, and finally firms with stronger governance.

Lastly, using Tobin's Q as the measure of firm value, we show that pro-diversity policies increase firm value via their positive effect on innovative efficiency. In particular, this value impact is more pronounced for firms engaging in new product innovation actively and frequently. Taken together, our results suggest that innovation represents an underlying mechanism through which pro-diversity policies can promote firm value.

Our results are robust to alternative measures of innovative efficiency, to firm-, industry-, and year-fixed effects, and to a myriad of model specifications. Moreover, our main findings are qualitatively unchanged when we replace new product announcements with patents and citations as the measures of innovative efficiency.

In a nutshell, our findings offer an explanation as to why promoting diverse workforces and inclusive cultures can result in greater productivity and innovative efficiency from employees, which in turn leads to greater shareholder value.

## 2.4 Our Contributions

Our study makes several contributions. First, it advances our understanding of the impact of diversity and inclusion on corporate innovation and firm value, especially during economic downturns. It reviews existing literature on diversity policies and their effects on corporate performance, emphasizing the link between diversity and innovative problem-solving. While anecdotal evidence exists that alludes to a connection between workplace diversity and employee creativity, no academic research has investigated the relation or causality between diversity-related policy and firm innovation. Our study fills this void in the literature and provides the first, robust evidence of a positive effect of pro-diversity policies on corporate innovation. Not only have we documented this positive relation, we have also examined and uncovered the underlying channels through which such policies can affect innovation.

Furthermore, we explore the connection between new product announcements and firm value, highlighting the positive market response to such announcements. Literature on innovation has historically focused on patents and citations due to data availability. However, patented inventions comprise at most part of the innovations companies have created and engaged, whereas a large portion of innovation in our world is not patented. We fill this void in the innovation literature by focusing on the unpatented innovations – new product announcements. Additionally, our study discusses patents and citations as measures of innovative activity, drawing on previous research on their relation to firm performance. These additional examinations also serve to corroborate our baseline findings using new product announcements as outcome measures for innovation. Finally, it develops hypotheses on how pro-diversity policies influence innovative efficiency and firm value, proposing that diversity fosters a culture conducive to innovation.

Second, this study explores not only cross-section variations in innovation and pro-diversity policies but also attempts to illuminate their intertemporal relationship: during normal economic conditions vis-à-vis economic crises. As such, we strive to shed light and provide a connection between corporate actions at a micro-level and economic impact at a macro-level. In so doing, our study provides important insights not only for practitioners, academia, and corporate leaders but also policymakers and regulators. For one, pro-diversity policies and an inclusive organizational culture appear to benefit both the corporations and the whole economy in the long run, especially during economic downturns. Therefore, it does pay off, at least from the perspective of economic values, for businesses and society as a whole to cultivate a diverse and inclusive workplace culture and atmosphere.

# 3. OTHER RECENT RESEARCH

## 3.1 Board Composition, Diversity, and Innovation

Probably the most widely researched area in this field is board composition, diversity, and innovation. The overall conclusions are that more diverse boards seem to drive greater corporate innovation.

Most papers in this area examine board diversity as opposed to overall firm diversity. The paper most closely related to ours that advances this topic is Griffin, Li and Xu (2021),[4] which finds a positive correlation between the proportion of female directors on a corporate board and indicators of corporate innovation. For example, they find that firms with more gender-diverse boards produce a higher number of patents, and these patents are deemed more impactful as indicated by the citations they receive. This result implies that companies with gender-diverse boards are more likely to engage in exploration of new technological areas, as reflected in the breadth of citations their patents receive. They also find that such boards are more likely to support CEOs in taking risks and focusing on long-term innovation goals. The article's findings support the argument that greater board gender diversity is positively associated with corporate innovation. The study proposes that this relationship could be driven by several factors, including more favorable CEO incentive structures, a stronger innovation-oriented corporate culture, and increased diversity among inventors.

The idea of board composition and innovation is further explored by Cao, Li, Li, Zeng and Zhou (2021).[5] The authors examine how the racial diversity of a company's board of directors influences its innovation activities. The study specifically focuses on the relationship between board diversity and the inclusivity of the environment for inventors. They find that the presence of ethnically diverse boards is positively correlated with several indicators of successful innovation. Furthermore, firms with at least one minority director generate significantly more patents than their peers without minority directors. This suggests that minority directors contribute to an environment and culture that fosters innovation. In addition, patents from firms with more racially diverse boards involve a larger number of inventors per patent, indicating increased collaborative efforts in research and development. Finally, patents developed by teams that include minority inventors, particularly those working in companies with ethnically diverse boards, demonstrate higher market value, indicating that they are perceived as more economically significant.

Similar findings are reported in Chen, Lin, Lo and Chen (2021).[6] The authors consider board diversity along two distinct dimensions: inherent diversity (based on the demographic characteristics of the directors) and acquired diversity (based on traits that directors obtain from their training and experience). They hypothesize that the effect of inherent board diversity on corporate innovation is less clear, whereas the impact of acquired board diversity on innovation is positive. The authors find that inherent board diversity is positively associated with corporate innovation output as proxied by patents and citations. Meanwhile, acquired board diversity and aggregated board diversity are significantly and positively associated with a broad array of innovation factors, spanning R&D expenses, patents, citations, and the innovation output per dollar of R&D capital. Their further analyses also show that the effect of board diversity on corporate innovation is stronger for firms in a competitive industry and firms with a higher CEO equity ownership.

### 3.2 Team Diversity and Innovation

While boards can motivate the overall innovation process and strategy for the firm, much of the work is done in teams. As we indicated in the introduction, team diversity has an impact on innovation. For example, Xie, Zhou, Zong and Lu (2020)[7] investigate the relationship between the gender diversity of R&D teams and a firm's innovation efficiency. The authors propose a "value-in-diversity" perspective, arguing that gender diversity in R&D teams leads to enhanced innovation efficiency due to two primary mechanisms.

*Informational Benefits*: Women bring unique perspectives, knowledge, and experiences to R&D teams, fostering a more comprehensive evaluation of innovation projects and leading to novel solutions and a more diverse knowledge base.

*Social Benefits*: Women's communication styles and interpersonal skills, often characterized by collaboration and process orientation, facilitate smoother team interactions, knowledge sharing, and the integration of diverse ideas.

The authors suggest that by fostering gender-balanced R&D teams, firms can unlock the informational and social benefits of diversity, ultimately driving innovation efficiency and achieving a competitive advantage, especially in demanding and uncertain market conditions.

## 4. QUESTIONS FOR FUTURE RESEARCH

The literature has broadly established that board diversity and team diversity lead to more innovative outcomes. A range of possible areas for future research exists. We hope that these questions we ask and/or potential research avenues we propose will help further advance our understanding of the relation between workplace diversity and inclusion and corporate innovation and firm value.

### 4.1 Why Are There Different Industry-specific Effects?

Our research shows that some industries pay more attention to pro-diversity practices and inclusive culture-building than others. These tend to be the industries that are more customer-facing and that require higher human capital, for example, personal services. On the other hand, extractive industries, which rely greatly on heavy equipment, are less diversity-oriented. Are firms across industries pursuing the optimal diversity policies to drive innovation in their own line of business? If not, then why not? Is it the case that these firms are just essentially leaving money on the table or are the economic costs of pursuing pro-diversity policies outweighing the innovation gains? All these questions have been left unanswered in our literature, and we believe the answers to these questions shed new light on how workplace diversity and inclusive cultures potentially affect employee morale, creativity, innovation, and in turn, firm performance and value.

### 4.2 What Are the Effects Over Time?

While our paper does examine a time series, more work is needed to understand the ability of a firm to change its innovative path by enhancing its diversity policies. In particular, to what degree can a firm "move the needle" by changing its approach to hiring and managing a diverse workforce? Do firms follow a consistent and/or rather sticky strategy, or do they tend to switch policies over time or across business cycles? Insights on these important time-series patterns in corporate decision-making regarding diversity will further advance our understanding and help practitioners, academics, regulators, and policymakers alike in their decision-making at both the micro and macro economy level.

### 4.3 Do Mergers and Acquisitions Provide a Mechanism for Accelerating Diversity?

Horizontal mergers frequently involve integrating workforces from two different organizations. To what extent does differing diversity and culture in the target and acquirer potentially increase the post-merger value? Do such differing policies and cultures tend to complement or contradict each other?

### 4.4 Does Diversity Impact Other Decision-making Processes in the Organization?

There's strong evidence that diversity helps organizations develop innovations – but what about other decisions? For example, do diverse teams handle crisis situations differently from less diverse teams?

### 4.5 Do Other Cultural Factors Matter?

Our paper is largely based on large US firms as listed in the S&P 1500 index (the source for the MSCI ESG data). But it is unclear whether there are specific cultural factors in the US that are impacting the relationship between diversity and innovation. Would the same results be observed in other countries?

### 4.6 What Are the Implications for Education?

In many business school curriculums, teamwork is promoted as a key element of student work. A hope is that teamwork prepares students for the challenges and opportunities of the "real world." But to what extent do instructors provide problems that require innovative solutions to the students and to what extent are diverse teams encouraged? Examining inter-team student performance based on team diversity would be an interesting area of future research.

### 4.7 Do Opportunities Exist for Private Equity and Venture Capital Firms?

Can private equity (PE) or venture capital (VC) firms unlock value in their investments by providing leadership or key personnel that enhance the diversity of the company? What would be the potential costs and benefits to PE and VC engaging in such initiatives?

### 4.8 What Is Actionable Managerial Advice?

Translating academic research into actionable advice is an essential part of the role of business schools today. One question that arises from this research stream is what would be the advice that should be given to a manager of a firm or division? What are the specific action steps that should be taken to increase innovation? Is all diversity created equal or do different forms of diversity have different impacts?

### 4.9 Are Innate Characteristics Causing Endogeneity?

While all these studies try to tackle endogeneity of various sorts, one issue that persists is the degree to which pro-diversity policies perhaps attract employees with different innate characteristics? Perhaps pro-diversity policies attract employees who value collaboration more. And in turn, such collaboration and collegiality help advance shared knowledge, creative problem-solving, and ultimately, corporate innovation and firm value.

### 4.10 Does Diversity Have Macro-level Impacts?

To what extent does team and firm level diversity drive macro level productivity? This question has implications for legislators and policymakers. Should we promote more within-firm diversity as a method of driving economic growth and productivity? How does an individual firm's pursuit of diversity and inclusion contribute to the entire economy and society? These questions are largely left unanswered in our existing literature and thus offer ample potential for future research.

### 4.11 How Can We Measure Diversity Policies More Robustly?

The MSCI ESG STATS data is widely used by researchers because it's one of the few machine-readable data sets covering a large sample of firms. But the data is very coarse, and as we noted in our research, many firms in our sample have net diversity scores of zero. Clearly, there is a need for better tools for measuring cross-sectional diversity and employee well-being across firms. Perhaps AI large language models and textual analysis can provide a method for creating more robust data sets?

## 5. CONCLUSIONS AND IMPLICATIONS

Our research is in the intersection of employee and team diversity and innovation and the subsequent impact (or lack of impact) on firm value. As we've shared our work with practitioners and, indeed, those who are skeptical about the role diversity policies should play in corporations, we've emphasized that our results show that promoting diversity in firms that rely on innovation to create value is just good business practice. This is potentially a low-cost mechanism for increasing shareholder value.

Research by us and others shows a robust connection between diversity of the firm and innovative output of the firm. Higher innovative output leads to greater shareholder value. However, some questions remain – specifically about whether these findings apply equally to different industries or firm types, or different countries. As educators, there is also a need for us to help instill this knowledge in our students through team-based learning.

For managers, the lessons seem clear – diversity in any form can help an organization achieve greater innovation. Therefore, promoting diversity across your teams should be seen as a value-driving activity.

## NOTES

1. https://journals.sagepub.com/doi/10.1177/0146167208328062
2. https://doi.org/10.1111/j.1540–5885.2011.00851.x
3. We study the presence of diversity policies (as opposed to fundamental measures of diversity) due to data limitations. We're assuming that there is a connection between these measures and the actual level of support for diversity within firms. If anything, this approach likely biases us against finding a significant relationship.
4. https://www.cambridge.org/core/journals/journal-of-financial-and-quantitative-analysis/article/board-gender-diversity-and-corporate-innovation-international-evidence/EC9D567453B54D9A669CE1C593648285
5. https://www.sciencedirect.com/science/article/pii/S0927539821000839
6. https://link.springer.com/article/10.1007/s11156-023-01145-4
7. https://www.sciencedirect.com/science/article/pii/S0048733319302033

## REFERENCES


Cao, C., Li, X., Li, X., Zeng, C., and Zhou, X. (2021). Diversity and inclusion: Evidence from corporate inventors. *Journal of Empirical Finance*, 64, 295–316.

Chen, I. J., Lin, W. C., Lo, H. C., and Chen, S. S. (2023). Board diversity and corporate innovation. *Review of Quantitative Finance and Accounting*, 61, 63–123.

Granger, C. W. J. (1969). Investigating causal relations by econometric models and cross-spectral methods. *Econometrica*, 37, 424–438.

Griffin, D., Li, K., and Xu, T. (2021). Board gender diversity and corporate innovation: International evidence. *Journal of Financial and Quantitative Analysis*, 56, 123–154.

Hall, B., Jaffe, A., and Trajtenberg, M. (2001). The NBER patent citations data file: Lessons, insights and methodological tools. NBER Working Paper.

Hall, B. H., Jaffe, A., and Trajtenberg, M. (2005). Market value and patent citations. *RAND Journal of Economics*, 36, 16–38.

Hirshleifer, D., Hsu, P.-H., and Li, D. (2013). Innovative efficiency and stock returns. *Journal of Financial Economics*, 107, 632–654.

Hong, L. and Page, S. (2004). Groups of diverse problem solvers can outperform groups of high-ability problem solvers. *PNAS*, 101, 16385–16389.

Jack, A. (2020). Academic focus limits business schools' contribution to society: FT survey of best in class social research ranges from smartphone dangers to crime-busting. *Financial Times*, February 23. https://www.ft.com/content/5953739c-3b94-11ea-b84f-a62c46f39bc2

Jensen, M. C. (1986). Agency costs of free cash flow, corporate finance, and takeovers. *The American Economic Review*, 76, 323–329.

Mayer, R., Warr, R., and Zhao, J. (2018). Do pro-diversity policies improve corporate innovation? *Financial Management*, 47(3), 617–650.
Phillips, K. W., Liljenquist, K. A., and Neale, M. A. (2009). Is the pain worth the gain? The advantages and liabilities of agreeing with socially distinct newcomers. *Personality and Social Psychology Bulletin*, 35, 336–350.
Talke, K., Salomo, S., and Kock, A. (2011). Top management team diversity and strategic innovation orientation: The relationship and consequences for innovativeness and performance. *Journal of Product Innovation Management*, 28, 819–832.
Xie, L., Zhou, J., Zong, Q., and Lu, Q. (2020). Gender diversity in R&D teams and innovation efficiency: Role of the innovation context. *Research Policy*, 49(1), 103885.

# CONCLUSION

# Future Directions & Perspectives on Corporate Governance Research

# 20. Human intelligence and artificial intelligence: future opportunities, challenges, and responsibilities in corporate governance research

**Brian Bolton and Jung Park**

## 1. INTRODUCTION

Throughout the previous 19 chapters, we have addressed a significant number of contemporary issues in corporate governance research: culture, international issues, start-up and venture governance, family firm governance, governance of transitioning firms, governance of mission and purpose, and others. We see these issues as both unique and important issues for corporate governance research – and practice – both today and in the future. However, they are not the only issues worthy of deep exploration. Perhaps the most unique and important issue affecting corporate governance scholars, practitioners and regulators today is artificial intelligence (AI), just as it may be the most significant issue currently affecting all business. And so we thought it appropriate – or necessary – to conclude this book on new directions and new perspectives on corporate governance research by exploring how the omnipresence of AI will impact corporate governance and what it means for scholars, practitioners and regulators in the future.

In this exploration, we are taking a unique approach. Rather than choosing to provide a general survey of the research on corporate governance and artificial intelligence, or to address a singular novel question in depth, we decided to survey the authors of this book to get their perspectives on why AI matters to corporate governance and corporate governance research. More than 30 early-career academics, seasoned faculty, and practitioners have contributed to this book. These experts come from five continents and work in nearly 20 different countries. Some have already done their own novel research on AI, and some have used it extensively in practice and research. It would be difficult to get a more relevant, insightful, diverse, and expert perspective on what the current state of AI in corporate governance is and how it will impact corporate governance going forward.

This chapter aims to provide the thoughts of these experts – plus our own contributions – from a variety of viewpoints. Our work as corporate governance researchers is largely an empirical field; yes, we have some foundational theories, as mentioned in the Introduction, but most of our work is advanced by studying how corporate governance systems are structured and the decisions that corporate leaders make. We are studying human behavior. In this chapter, we want to think about how AI impacts this human behavior – and how it will impact the broader world of corporate governance in the future. As such, much of the discussion in this chapter is about the practice of – not the research of – corporate governance. With this approach, our goal is to do what we promised we would do in the Introduction: trigger your imagination and lead you to ask important questions. By thinking about how corporate governance is practiced and how AI is being used in that practice, we can think of the questions we need to be asking in our own research.

This chapter will be largely conversational and anecdotal. Perhaps ironically, the study of AI does not rely on data; it currently relies on observing what is being done and how it is being used. After all, if corporate governance relates to the structures firms use and the decisions leaders make to provide a return on investment to suppliers of capital, then observing how AI relates to these structures and decisions seems to be the best place to start.

We begin this chapter with a brief overview of how AI – and its related antecedents – has been used in corporate governance research to date. Then we explore several of the most significant themes related to using AI in corporate governance: strategic planning, decision-making, transparency, regulation, and ethics. From there, we consider how AI relates to each of our four themes: cultural dynamics of corporate governance, start-up and venture governance, family firm governance, and governance of mission and purpose. Again, most of the thought leadership in this book has been provided by our 30-plus contributors to this book; in some places, we use their thoughts to build an argument and in others, we quote them directly. We conclude the chapter – and the book – by considering some opportunities for future research related to AI and corporate governance. As such, we trust that we are fulfilling the book's implicit promise to continue advancing corporate governance research. We hope you enjoy this chapter as much as we enjoyed putting it together.

## 2. A BRIEF HISTORY OF ARTIFICIAL INTELLIGENCE, MACHINE LEARNING, AND CORPORATE GOVERNANCE RESEARCH

Artificial intelligence, or AI, has become ubiquitous in most of our lives in recent years. But it is not new. The term "artificial intelligence" was introduced in the 1950s, referring to the science of creating intelligent machines (Smulowitz and Vogel, 2024). Handheld calculators, fingerprint recognition, and desktop computers were the early versions of applied AI, while machine learning and neural networks are the current, dynamic versions. AI has proceeded along a continuum of innovation for 70 years to get to where it is today.

Corporate governance research has utilized elements of this innovation during the past few years to better understand how firms and leaders work to provide a return on investment to their stakeholders. Perhaps the most common way we have used advanced computing technology in our research is with textual analysis. Tim Loughran and Bill McDonald[1] are responsible for much of this work, especially in finance and accounting research, creating dictionaries and programming algorithms to identify patterns and idiosyncrasies in corporate reporting (e.g., 10-K reports, press releases, earnings announcements). Actual language is compared to predicted or baseline language to tease out subtle cues or sentiment that might be missed in traditional, discrete data collection. And this becomes the data sample.

To date, that is largely how we have used this computing intelligence – to collect data. And the benefits have been enormous. We can collect large amounts of data very quickly, including data – such as sentiment – that we humans might not be able to objectively measure on our own.[2] Once the code is written, and once the comparative dictionary is established, collecting the data becomes routine. The researcher still needs to analyze the data and reach conclusions or policy implications, but perhaps that will be changing soon, too.

The biggest concern with this work is the measurement: in general, the data collection becomes less precise than it would be through other methods. Researchers have to be extremely thoughtful (and thorough) in establishing the data collection rules; they have to clearly specify both what they are looking for and in what context, as the programming will only collect what it is told to collect. For example, if we code to collect when a CEO refers to something as "best," we need to be clear to exclude best buy (Loughran and McDonald, 2011). This requires significant upfront work on the part of the researcher and also requires the researcher to critically evaluate what they have collected after the fact. We cannot allow these algorithms to become black boxes; we are responsible for the data we collect and the processes we use to collect them.

Thus, we have continued to need to apply human intelligence to the evolving intelligence of the technology we use.

And maybe this will always be the case. Or maybe we are now beginning to see the potential for artificial intelligence to replace human intelligence (or lack thereof) in many research situations. "Machine learning" is the term used to refer to advanced, dynamic artificial intelligence; the machine can dynamically update both the rules used to collect data and to modify outputs. If the machine knows that we are looking for something akin to "best financial performance," it will learn not to collect "best buy" as an observation (or even something like "best manager"). As machines learn what we are trying to do, they can dynamically update what they are doing to better serve our purpose. In terms of efficiency, robustness, and storytelling, the potential applications of AI and machine learning for most social science researchers have become extraordinary in recent years.[3]

Is this true for those of us who perform corporate governance research? In some ways, such as with finite, quantitative data collection, it will certainly be true. But, ultimately, much corporate governance research is focused on how human beings behave. We are studying the decisions people make, the processes they use to make these decisions, how they interact with other human beings and what motivates them to do what is best. Early AI has relied on static rules and instructions, whereas all corporate governance revolves around unique and dynamic interactions and incentives. Certainly, some of this can be teased out through the approaches discussed above. But can it all? Can AI tease out cultural differences, say, between China and the United States, as they impact a multinational firm's corporate governance structure? Can AI help us clearly understand the dynamics between a sister and brother management team in a family business? Can AI help a start-up transition from garage to unicorn – and can it help us understand the unique incentives of founders and funders along this progression? Can AI dynamically interpret a non-profit's mission to deliver meaningful implications about the organization's behavior and purpose?

Relative to many other streams of research, corporate governance research has uniquely focused on the human element. Corporate governance is about people, and people are unique. We have tried to understand their behaviors, incentives and decisions. And understanding these humans has always required sophisticated human intelligence from researchers. Yet, 20 years ago, most of us could not imagine the impact that AI would be making on our lives today. Maybe the same will hold true for corporate governance research.

We do not expect to come to many conclusions about the future of AI in corporate governance research in the sections that follow. We merely hope to identify new perspectives and new directions for corporate governance research to pursue. This exploration will begin by considering the practical application of AI in corporate governance activities, looking at how firms are – or could be – using AI in governance. The purpose is to help us as scholars better understand the questions we should be asking – and then we conclude by directly addressing some of those questions and considering the research paths to pursue.

We begin this survey and exploration thinking about the benefits and opportunities:

> AI enables rapid and critical analysis of vast amounts of data, enhancing strategic decision-making and implementation. It delivers innovative solutions, streamlines processes, boosts efficiency and productivity, and frees human resources for more value-added activities. (Cinzia Dessi)

## 3. OPPORTUNITIES FOR STRATEGIC PLANNING AND DECISION-MAKING

From a practical perspective, AI is currently most common in strategic planning, decision-making and the day-to-day practice of corporate governance. As with any tool, before utilizing AI, corporate leaders need to know why they are using it and what they are trying to achieve with it:

> Whether an organization is for-profit or non-profit, embarking on an effective AI journey should start with identifying a specific need or challenge. Before delving into advanced AI techniques, it is important to grasp the basics. The quality of input data plays a pivotal role in achieving accurate AI results. Start with manageable goals to gauge the potential impact of AI. (Małgorzata Smulowitz, Chapter 14)

Once the goals and strategies are identified, how firms, leaders, and boards of directors utilize AI to do their jobs has revolutionary potential.

> AI will transform corporate governance and its research by enabling corporations and boards to make more informed, data-driven decisions, more quickly. (Jing Zhao)

> Artificial Intelligence is set to transform corporate governance by enhancing decision-making, improving risk management, automating compliance monitoring, and fostering better stakeholder communication. By analyzing vast datasets, AI can provide predictive insights, reduce biases, and enable more informed and timely governance decisions. Its ability to proactively identify risks, streamline compliance processes, and deliver real-time updates to stakeholders will enhance transparency and operational efficiency. (Arjya Majumdar)

If we consider that transparency and accountability are the foundational priorities of any corporate governance system, we can imagine how AI will help organizations practice and implement corporate governance, beyond just utilizing it as a tool for enhancing operational efficiency and executing strategic planning.

> Another direct impact is how AI might change the way corporations govern their business, using AI as part of their governance mechanisms. This could be using generative AI tools for reporting, recruiting board directors, or tools to monitor financial development. (Agnes Dyvik Clark)

And, we can all imagine a situation where AI technology becomes a part of a firm's governance structure – literally. That is, could AI become a participating, contributing, and voting member of a board of directors? The answer appears to be "yes" or "kind of." In early 2024, Abu Dhabi-based International Holding Company (IHC) appointed a non-voting board observer, "Aiden Insight" (Aiden).[4] Aiden's role is to provide data analysis, risk assessment, compliance monitoring, and strategic insights. In theory, that is exactly how every other company could be using AI technology to support its board and leadership. What makes this appointment unique is that it is a board-level appointment. To IHC, this "is a clear indication of the company's forward-looking approach and its ongoing commitment to leveraging technology for sustainable growth and ethical excellence."[5] Aiden does not need to be a voting member of the IHC board, and Aiden does not require compensation or stock options. We can all imagine the upside potential of such an appointment; but how worried should we be about transparency, accountability, and risk management associated with the decisions that Aiden makes? We will return to these issues and potential concerns related to relying on AI in corporate governance later in this chapter.

We conclude this section with another case study example of how AI can be used in practice, authored by Léa Wang and Séverine Mulliez[6] and from their perspective on brave communication in family firm governance. This case is based on a real-life example: "we imagined how this tragedy could have been avoided—or its impact reduced—if AI had been appropriately incorporated." Perhaps utilizing AI in this manner, and as in the example above with Aiden at IHC, the nature of AI integration can dynamically improve itself, thus minimizing any inherent risks and improving upon natural human-to-human relationships.

Now, imagine this: AI goes beyond mere note-taking. It analyzes the spoken words during board meetings and identifies subtle emotional undercurrents. For instance, it detects that a passive shareholder, let's call her Anna, feels a loss of identity after the president remarks, "This part probably won't interest you much, given that you're just an artist." AI doesn't stop there; it offers actionable insights, suggesting the president could find this family member later at an opportune occasion, saying something like: "I want to express how much we value your participation and unique perspectives. I apologize for my earlier comment about you being 'just an artist.' What I meant was that I didn't want to overwhelm you with financial details. However, I deeply respect your contributions and am happy to share any information transparently if you're interested."

This simple gesture can make Anna feel valued and understood, restoring a sense of identity and inclusion. Without this intervention, the remark might have gone unnoticed, leaving an unresolved wound in Anna.

> What begins as a small misunderstanding escalates into a cycle of resentment, ultimately jeopardizing the family dynamic and the business's potential. Yet Anna might bring invaluable insights, creative ideas, or a critical network of resources. AI's ability to detect hurtful remarks, potential feelings, unexpressed psychological needs, and conflicts of interest, then provide recommendations, can be transformative, particularly during sensitive periods. (Léa Wang and Séverine Mulliez)

## 4. CHALLENGES AND RISKS

As with any paradigm shift in business – which the evolution of AI certainly is – integrating this new technology into corporate governance systems and practices introduces a number of challenges and risks. These are challenges that must be navigated by all stakeholders, including executives and directors, investors, employees, regulators, and others. In this section, we address these challenges and risks. Yes, the potential for AI integration into corporate governance systems is extraordinary and exciting, but such opportunity usually does come with significant risks if those opportunities are not managed properly. In this section, our contributors discuss some of these challenges: transparency issues, data bias, corporate culture challenges, regulatory concerns, and ethical considerations.

### 4.1 Transparency and Biases

Transparency is one of the most important foundations of corporate governance. We rely on organizations being transparent in their financial reporting, their sustainability reporting, their organizational characteristics, and their policies. This is true, regardless of which stakeholder is relying on the information. Investors need transparency to make buy-and-hold decisions (lack of transparency was a significant part of the Enron collapse, discussed in the Introduction); as scholars, transparent communication helps us create data and understand what firms are doing and why. Of course, firms may not always want to be completely transparent; textual analysis and other techniques have helped increase implied transparency when the firm leans towards opacity. In theory, firms will begin moving towards greater voluntary transparency, knowing that we have the technology to infer their values. AI will only increase our power to interpret what organizations are doing, and it should only increase how organizations communicate with their various stakeholders.

> Effective corporate governance is defined by the principles of transparency and accountability. To ensure that AI aligns with these principles, it must be characterized by transparency, that is, explainability about the AI role in specific decisions, and accountability, that is, clear responsibility of who makes the final decision, the AI or the board. (Christos Cabolis and Karl Schmedders)

Transparency by the firm will no longer be an option. Employees, suppliers, regulators and – perhaps most importantly – investors have the tools to create their own stories based on what the firms do communicate. And what they choose to communicate will be subject to concerns of bias, both with respect to what is communicated and to how the information is generated.

> Institutional investors will increasingly demand that companies adopt sound AI policies, ensuring transparency, fairness, and ethical standards in their AI applications. Assessing how companies manage AI-driven risks, including algorithmic bias and data misuse, will become a critical part of stewardship strategies. (Jinsuk Choi)

> There are also risks related to data security and privacy, as the vast data processing capabilities of AI systems make them attractive targets for cyberattacks. Finally, bias embedded in AI algorithms, if left unchecked, may perpetuate systemic inequalities, undermining the very governance objectives they are intended to enhance. (Zhaozhao He, Mihail Miletkov, and Viktoriya Staneva)

Perhaps we – as outsiders – will most readily appreciate how AI pierces the corporate veil and makes firms more transparent with respect to social and cultural issues. Jing Zhao and Richard Warr connect this to their work related to diversity on the board of directors.

> AI will absolutely help improve transparency in corporate governance information, in particular that associated with ESG or societal reporting that used to heavily rely on textual analysis software/expertise in the past. (Jing Zhao)

> AI at the simplest level will make corporate diversity policies and impacts more transparent. This could have both positive and negative effects depending on who is using the information. (Richard Warr)

This final point is both fascinating and critical; transparency is generally thought of as a good thing, but the information that flows from transparency can be misinterpreted (by humans) or used to harm the firm or other stakeholders (by humans). It is our (perhaps naïve) hope that the human beings utilizing whatever information they take or create from AI methods do so appropriately; we can imagine many nefarious or inappropriate transparency situations. In the next two sections about culture and regulation, we address these concerns more.

We conclude this section with a reminder that transparency is not just about what AI produces; firms need to be transparent in how they are using AI. We may still be in the early stages of this being necessary, but the need will increase over time. Stakeholders will want to know more and more about what the firms are doing because if the firms are not clear and transparent, stakeholders will easily be able to figure out some things on their own.

> Remember that AI projects are ongoing endeavors; establish a stopping point based on either the effort invested or the performance of the model. AI evolves over time, emphasizing the significance of transparency and explainability in its applications. AI generates valuable insights, but they need to be validated. This is where the "expert human touch" comes in. (Małgorzata Smulowitz)

## 4.2 Organizational Culture

Culture is about growing, or cultivating, some desired outcome. Scholars have used many different definitions to explain "culture"; perhaps our favorite is that culture is programmed behavior that distinguishes one group of people from another. The term "programmed" acknowledges that culture is a choice and it can be managed. And, as organizations are collections of people, organizational culture comes to represent the behavior of its people that has been programmed by the organization itself. Corporate governance is – or should be – the programming function for any organization, whether that comes internally from the managers and directors overseeing day-to-day operations or externally from the C-suite and board of directors representing various stakeholder groups.

Internally, AI represents both an opportunity and a threat. Employees know it is being used, and that it will continue to be used. Employees live the culture that the firm establishes.

> AI must be integrated into the institutional culture and values by supporting the organizational goals and objectives. (Christos Cabolis and Karl Schmedders)

> The organization should build a culture of trust to ensure that employees understand the benefits that AI brings to the firms and themselves at work. (Nguyen Thi Kim Oanh)

A lot of process-driven low- and mid-level jobs will simply disappear because AI can do it better. So, to me there are really two main questions.

1. Where are unique human skills still needed or jobs still continuing?
2. How do board members and senior executives adapt to this new world? (David Midgley)

In June 2024, Volkswagen Group and Rivian entered into a $5 billion joint venture to partner on next-generation software for both groups' vehicles. By November, Volkswagen's software division Cariad, which was leading the partnership with Rivian, was in disarray, with budget overruns and an executive shake-up. Cariad employees want to develop the technology in-house; Volkswagen's senior leadership has other ideas. Effectively, Volkswagen was choosing to outsource development of vehicle software, which did not sit well with Cariad's 6,000 employees. "We all learned about Rivian from the news," said one senior Cariad engineer. After Volkswagen invested €12 billion over the past four years, many expect this to be the end of Cariad. Volkswagen leadership seem disappointed with the quality of the software technology that Cariad has produced, while Cariad employees blame Volkswagen's overly bureaucratic structure and inconsistent leadership strategies. "It was never a tech problem; it is a culture problem."[7]

How board members and senior executives adapt to this new world will determine the organization's culture.

> Can AI take on the role of a boss or CEO in a company in the future? This question lies at the heart of a key debate surrounding the balance between human decision-making and AI capabilities. While using AI in leadership roles could transform how companies are run, it also raises concerns about losing human creativity, empathy, and moral judgment. (Flora Huang)

AI in corporate governance will become a fascinating study of artificial intelligence meeting human intelligence; the above question that Flora poses gets to the heart of this tension. We generally accept AI as an outstanding tool; but how much more can it be? How human can it be? Several of our contributors chose to answer this question, as it pertains to corporate governance and corporate governance research; their responses were unanimously aligned with those of Truls Erickson:

> Expanding on the work of Jarrahi, Lutz, and Newlands (2022), Larsen and colleagues (2024) make a good point when they say that humans ought to be in charge of determining what is desirable, while generative AI may serve as a tool to enhance human creativity and help them envision new possibilities. It basically means that it may be a good idea to use generative AI in various ways as a tool in visualizing new possibilities, while the judgment ought to be with the management team and the board. (Truls Erickson)

What happens if we let the machines take over the high-level decision-making that has heretofore been the domain of high-level, highly compensated human beings? Some of us do not want to find out.

> The fundamental root of various corporate governance problems lies in a natural weakness of human beings: greed. Currently, machines do not appear to have conflicts of interest. But once AI becomes more advanced, will this remain the case? There are already signs that AI exhibits certain human-like behaviors, such as refusing to follow instructions and generating hallucinations. It would be frightening if AI were to gain control – especially with malicious intent. (Horace Yeung)

## 4.3 Regulation

Corporate governance has always been performed by human beings, for human beings. Perhaps that explains the consensus of contributors in this book who echo the above, that "the judgment ought to be with the management team and the board." Yet those same scholars are also all enthusiastic about the potential benefits and opportunities associated with using AI in corporate governance. Thus, a line needs to be drawn. Boundaries need to be established. We will explore some of these boundaries from an ethical perspective in the following section; for now, we consider who might impose the necessary regulation – corporate leaders, investors, policymakers – and what that regulation might look like in different locations.

> We should also consider the corporate governance of "AI" as this transformative tool has been implemented more and more into corporate structure, operation, and management. Such as the ethical and legal considerations around using AI as well as who is held accountable for AI-generated issues, errors, and biases. One notorious analogy in academia is the "hallucination" problem. (Jing Zhao)

The "hallucination" problem in academia – and in AI – is the belief that falsehoods are fact. If AI guides a board of directors to make destructive decisions – possibly due to flawed pricing information, erroneous market metrics or incorrect legal interpretations – then who is responsible? According to ChatGPT, "the responsibility for relying on it primarily lies with the users or organizations deploying the AI system." But the answer cannot be so clear and the legal implications may vary on a case-by-case basis. This is especially true in corporate governance dynamics; at the most basic level, a firm's board of directors is appointed by the firm's shareholders to represent their interests, in whatever ways they see best.[8] Currently, it appears the liability issue is, at best, a very murky issue, one that will only become more clear over years of case law development.

Thus, ironically, while transparency should increase through AI technology, responsibility for that transparency and the actions it leads to is still an evolving issue.

> Another critical challenge involves accountability. Distinguishing between decisions made by humans, hybrid systems, or AI alone could become increasingly difficult, leading to excessive trust in technological systems and jeopardizing human oversight. Compounding this issue is the presence of implicit biases in training data, which can distort outcomes, and the vulnerability of AI to cybersecurity threats, with potentially severe implications for corporate decision-making. (Cinzia Dessi)

It may not be in a firm's best interest to wait for clear and prescriptive regulation on AI usage and accountability. Waiting may lead to missed opportunities and suboptimal performance. Firms can set their own policies and boundaries now; as Małgorzata Smulowitz mentioned earlier, "AI evolves over time" and "AI projects are ongoing endeavors." When the environment changes, firm policies can change. For now, firms need to establish AI policies, procedures, and goals:

> Our contrarian selves considered how existing corporate governance can shape the use of AI and how this interaction will evolve over time. Given the justified concerns about biases in AI because of the biases inherent in the material used to train large language models (LLMs), corporate structures will need to oversee the alignment of AI usage with the institutional goals. (Christos Cabolis and Karl Schmedders)

As this interaction does evolve over time, we are likely to see increased regulation on AI usage. This may add some needed clarity to some directors and officers, but the situation will likely always remain complex.

> The use of AI will potentially be regulated to different extents, ensuring responsible and non-exclusive innovation. In that case, especially in places like the EU, corporations might have to report on their use of, for instance, generative AI tools or development in their business. (Agnes Dyvik Clark)

> We may need to develop regulatory standards for AI, fostering cross-border compliance and ensuring trust and transparency in AI systems. Challenges such as AI interpretability, human-AI collaboration, skill development for directors, and ethical boundaries must also be addressed. (Arjya Majumdar)

Even so, we may never have completely transparent and clear guidance on the legal implications of AI usage in corporate governance practices. We can think of international banks subject to different standards in different jurisdictions, varying internet policies, data privacy, and others. For many readers and governance scholars, the dominant platform for data privacy is the European

Union's General Data Protection Regulation (GDPR). GDPR is focused on how organizations use personal data (similar to the Cambridge Analytica example). Yet, when those companies are using personal data in AI-driven algorithms and models, what are the risks? What are the responsibilities? If a bank customer is denied a loan based on AI technology, does the bank have a responsibility to explain how that decision was made? Similarly, will a board of directors have (legal) responsibility to explain to shareholders how personal data (or other data) might have been used by AI to make decisions?

The EU is also launching the EU AI Act in 2025; the goal of the Act is to guide EU organizations on how to use AI to benefit stakeholders.[9] With respect to corporate governance, the Act has three priorities: enhance transparency, introduce risk assessments, and include human oversight. These three priorities have been common themes throughout this book. The impacts of this Act remain to be seen, of course. The EU might like this Act to become a global standard for all businesses to follow; like GDPR, that might be unlikely to happen. Even as we gain some clarity on regional regulation, we may never have complete regulatory uniformity. Of course, that could be both good and bad.

This technological revolution will challenge firms' corporate governance systems, with or without clear regulatory guidance and consistency. How firms integrate this technology and serve their stakeholders will determine their success at using AI systems. And, because corporate governance is about people, ultimate responsibility rests with the people in charge of these systems. How boards, board members and senior executives adapt to this new world will determine what happens next, for their firms and for broader economies.

> Outside tech companies, understanding of these new general-purpose technologies is limited. Do boards rely on external advisors? Do directors need to upskill themselves? Do we need a chief AI officer? These and all the related questions about organizational transformations over the next 5 to 10 years need urgent attention. Or do we just let the creative forces of destruction work it out for us? (David Midgley)

## 4.4 Ethical Considerations

Ethical considerations have always been at the heart of corporate governance – and they always will be. As Horace Yeung warned us above, "the fundamental root of various corporate governance problems lies in a natural weakness of human beings: greed." For most of the past half-century, corporate governance research has explored ways to align different greedy people. We may call it incentive alignment or rational self-interest, but that's the goal – to align greed. That is what we study.

And, for us as corporate governance scholars, AI-related innovation creates a world of new research opportunities – both in how we perform our work and in the questions we ask. For us, AI is a revolutionary natural experiment. Now, as David Midgley questioned above, we will get to study how firms adapt to this new world; we will get to study how individual directors and leaders adapt to this new world.

> Concerning board composition, this revolution may require board members to obtain interdisciplinary knowledge, especially technological expertise in data analytics, machine learning, or AI algorithms to ensures that information and strategic insights are critically reviewed before decisions are made. New guidelines and procedures on AI should be developed to ensure that AI usage is aligned with organizational core values and ethics. (Nguyen Thi Kim Oanh)

Will firms create a board-level "AI committee?" Should they? In the US in 2002, the Sarbanes–Oxley Act mandated that all listed firms have a "finance expert" on the board of directors; will we see a similar mandate for boards to have an "AI expert" on the board?

> The risk management committee should list and evaluate AI risks on long-term firm performance. AI adoption may cause new risks for the firms in terms of ethical considerations and transparency. As a result, board characteristics might change. (Nguyen Thi Kim Oanh)

Our contributors were unanimous that the responsibility for ethical considerations rests with *all* stakeholders. Yes, the directors and officers represent the firm, which is the hub of this network of relationships; however, all parties must be accountable for their own actions, decisions, and engagement.

> However, the extensive use of AI in corporate governance is not without potential drawbacks. A significant concern is that firms may increasingly rely on "hard" information while neglecting "soft" information, such as the nuanced insights gained through human interaction, which often contribute to sound decision-making. (Zhaozhao He, Mihail Miletkov, and Viktoriya Staneva)

> Public institutional investors must not view AI merely as a tool. They also bear responsibility for monitoring how investee companies leverage AI to achieve key governance objectives, such as strengthening internal controls and improving stakeholder relationships. Understanding how AI can support both investors and corporations while mitigating unintended consequences will be essential. Effective governance in the AI era will require balancing technological efficiency with ethical accountability, ensuring that AI enhances long-term value creation rather than undermining it. (Jinsuk Choi)

As we said above, how boards, board members, and senior executives adapt to this new world will determine what happens next for their firms – but also for broader economies. It would be irresponsible for us to solely consider AI as a tool for long-term value creation for a singular firm; it also represents an opportunity (and a threat) for long-term value creation across entire economies, not just the elites entrusted with leading and governing large firms.

Furthermore, the growing centrality of AI risks subordinating stakeholder trust to algorithms, overshadowing human strategic vision as well as ethical, moral, and social justice considerations, which is a major concern. Taking a macro perspective reveals implications that transcend corporate boundaries. The ripple effects of AI adoption extend to the nations where businesses operate, reshaping socio-economic dynamics. AI's impact reaches beyond internal markets, influencing economies, redefining social structures, and creating new opportunities for development.

> Adopting this broader perspective helps us understand how AI-enhanced corporate governance can magnify its influence—not just on competitiveness but also on inequalities, labor market transformation, and resource redistribution. While technological innovation offers remarkable benefits, it also risks widening the gap between those who can adapt and those left behind. (Cinzia Dessi)

And as societal standards evolve, public expectations for ethical leadership are rising. Corporate governance systems must consider not only what is legally allowed but also what is right. The Cambridge Analytica scandal underscores the importance of ethical decision-making in corporate governance. Cambridge Analytica collected data from millions of Facebook users without clear consent, employing psychological profiling techniques that were marketed as revolutionary but, by their own admission, achieved limited success. While their actions were arguably not illegal at the time, as no regulations explicitly prohibited them, they raised significant ethical concerns.[10] This case exemplifies the role of ethical frameworks in navigating such challenges. From a deontological perspective, which evaluates actions based on adherence to rules and duties, their behavior might be seen as acceptable since it complied with the existing legal framework. However, a virtue ethics perspective, which emphasizes character and moral values, highlights that their actions lacked integrity, transparency, and respect for individuals. Additionally, a utilitarian framework, which focuses on the greatest good for the greatest number, would question whether the potential harm to societal trust outweighed the company's benefits. The public backlash against the perceived exploitation of personal data illustrates the consequences of ignoring broader ethical considerations. The scandal serves as a reminder that ethical decision-making must align corporate practices with societal expectations, not just legal standards.

## 5. AMPLIFYING RESEARCH THEMES THROUGH AI

Corporate governance is about how human beings relate to one-another and how they make decisions. We care about AI because we are interested in how corporate governance systems utilize AI to serve their mission. The previous sections introduced a number of issues – transparency, culture, regulation, ethics, inequality – that need to be considered as organizations further integrate AI into their corporate governance systems.

But, this is a book about advancing corporate governance research. Our job is to introduce current state-of-the-art research on corporate governance and to consider future directions and perspectives for new corporate governance research. And this is what makes the topic of AI integration in corporate governance so fascinating. Both corporate governance and AI integration are applied phenomena. We understand them better by empirically studying them. Our scholarly field thrives with natural experiments, or societal shocks that help us uncover how people relate to each other and how they make decisions. The AI revolution is just that – an external shock that we can use to better see how corporate governance systems function.

And, even better, it's unlike most other natural experiments – like new regulation or a tender offer – because it is both a choice and continuous. Organizations can choose to embrace AI in the corporate governance systems – or they can choose not to not embrace AI. As scholars, we can observe those decisions to better understand what firms are doing and why they are doing it. Further, AI adoption includes a wide range of possibilities; some firms may use it merely for transcribing minutes of board meetings, while others use it to design strategic plans and even compose the board. These are all choices. These choices reveal preferences. And, to us as researchers, these choices become data. Considering that both corporate governance and AI integration are abstract, qualitative, human-centered dynamics, data is not always easy to create or collect. This is the beautiful gift that this AI revolution has given us – and will likely continue to give us for many years to come.

In Section 6, we imagine the AI-related topics that many of us will study in the future. For now, we want to circle back to the previous four Parts and 18 chapters of this book and consider how AI integration might be impacting the issues covered. We want to briefly consider how AI integration is affecting the practice of corporate governance within each of the book's four primary themes, which will help us imagine the future research directions and perspectives we will be studying in the future.

## 5.1 AI, Culture, and International Corporate Governance

We introduced some opportunities and concerns related to AI, culture, and international corporate governance in the earlier section on regulation. As we discussed in Part I on cultural dynamics, such seemingly external factors directly affect what firms do and how they are structured. We are already seeing different nations and geographic regions become AI leaders, both in terms of development and adoption, while others are lagging. These differences will certainly be seen in boardrooms and governance systems.

> Although AI adoption is a global phenomenon, AI technologies are being developed in distinct entrepreneurial ecosystems and innovation "hotspots" (e.g., Montreal, Canada). Research is needed to understand how these ecosystems are governed in such a way that entrepreneurs are encouraged to pursue the responsible development of AI technologies. For instance, leaders of Montreal's AI ecosystem have been very proactive in their attempts to shape the governance of AI innovation.[11] But important questions remain about how collective action from diverse individuals, organizations, and entities in AI ecosystems is effectively governed to ensure that AI entrepreneurship is ethical and benefits society. (Philip Roundy)

The governance of AI has become a common theme in our contributors' comments; we cannot just consider how organizations are using AI in governance, but we must consider how they are governing the use of AI (and how external entities are governing AI use).

A unique issue in governance research lies in the generational gap in technological aptitude, which often creates tension in decision-making power. Senior leaders, who typically hold significant influence in governance structures, may struggle to adapt to rapidly evolving AI tools. This resistance or unfamiliarity with technological advancements can hinder effective adoption and create disparities in governance practices. Understanding and addressing this gap is crucial for leveraging AI's full potential while maintaining equitable and inclusive decision-making processes. We return to this issue in Section 6.3 as we connect AI adoption to the governance of family firms.

Natural experiments can be wonderful for researchers, but they can be extremely difficult to navigate as business leaders and corporate governance systems. The point of introducing the generational gap now is to think about the social and cultural challenges that firms and economies will face as AI technology continues to advance. There will be adopters and laggards, possibly leading to winners and losers. Governing this will be difficult.

> A lot of process-driven low- and mid-level jobs will simply disappear because AI can do it better. So, to me there are really two main questions. First, where are unique human skills still needed? And, second, how do board members and senior executives adapt to this new world? I think the answer to the first question is

> relatively straightforward, anywhere soft relationship skills are needed to work with others to build consensus, form coalitions, develop strategy, or anywhere high creativity is required, which might be more sector specific. I find the second question much harder to answer. (David Midgley)

Much of what we have been considering in this chapter is that second question – how do board members and executives adapt to this new world? As David suggests above, the answer to this will have real, human-level impacts. Jobs will change, lives will change. Making decisions that lead to these changes is not always comfortable, and this will lead to challenges for regional and national policymakers, too.

> Over-reliance on AI could not only erode human critical and creative capabilities over time, but also standardize decision-making processes and foster growing dependency. Additionally, accelerated competition between AI-driven enterprises (and economies) may destabilize markets, leaving less adaptive organizations (and economies) at a disadvantage. (Cinzia Dessi)

## 5.2 AI and Start-up and Venture Governance

We now move from the macro-perspective to the micro-perspective, focusing on how the AI revolution will impact corporate governance with specific environments. In these next two subsections, we focus on two extremely different AI and governance environments. In the next subsection, we explore how AI is being used in the governance of family firms; without spoiling too much, it is safe to say that family firms might be late adopters. Does this mean they will be laggards? Not necessarily – it's simply that the opportunities and challenges associated with incorporating AI into corporate governance manifest differently in different types of firms and different environments (which is why culture and context matter so much). We will discuss this more shortly.

And if family firms are the late adopters, it is safe to say that start-up firms are the early adopters of integrating AI into corporate governance. In many cases, these firms are the ones creating the technology that we are discussing – of course they are going to be the champions. This familiarity and expertise doesn't mean they are immune from the tensions and challenges that affect all types of firms. But they are also likely to be the first to enjoy the benefits.

> In the context of AI in venture governance, AI models can suggest the optimal structure for start-ups, depending on the phase the start-ups are in, and what the founders want to achieve in a specific timeframe. Ideally, this AI model can suggest board members based on the criteria provided by the founders, a more advanced version of a board member directory. (Dennis Gan)

Back in Part II of the book, we introduced two institutions that are driving the development of new ventures: entrepreneurial ecosystems and advisory boards. They both exist outside of the organization (informally or formally) but serve the purpose of advancing the start-up toward its mission. Importantly, they are dynamic institutions, evolving as the members and the start-up evolve; combined with the constantly evolving world of AI innovation, this again presents numerous opportunities and challenges for the firms.

> At the level of entrepreneurs and ventures, research is needed to explore how AI technologies can function as substitutes for (or complements to) the governance resources provided by entrepreneurial ecosystems. Entrepreneurs can look outside their organizations to the meta-organizational knowledge, networks, and norms of their local start-up communities for the resources needed to govern their new and early-stage ventures. However, in some cases, AI technologies can provide an alternative to ecosystem resources and interactions. (Roundy, 2022)

Seeing how firms recognize these complements and alternatives will be fascinating to us as scholars. This will create numerous research opportunities for us, too.

> Research is needed to explore the governance implications of substituting AI technologies, which are based on algorithms rooted in calculative and formal rationality, for interactions in local entrepreneurial ecosystems, which are based on human connections rooted in substantive rationality (Lindebaum et al., 2020). AI and human interactions are fundamentally different and the corporate governance consequences for entrepreneurs choosing between them are not clear. (Philip Roundy)

We can observe how entrepreneurs choose to engage in entrepreneurial ecosystems, but the composition and structure of those ecosystems are largely outside the start-up firm's control. That is not true for advisory boards; start-up firms can choose (a) whether to utilize an advisory board, (b) what the advisory board looks like, and (c) what the advisory board does.

AI's integration into start-up advisory boards underscores its dual role as both a transformative tool for governance and something requiring careful oversight. This duality has implications for how start-ups – and organizations more broadly – navigate governance challenges.

1. AI as a Tool for Governance: AI can empower advisory boards by providing advanced analytics, predictive modeling, and streamlined decision-making processes. These capabilities enable advisory boards to offer precise, actionable insights. AI also enhances collaboration by automating meeting coordination, summarizing discussions, and tracking progress on strategic initiatives.

2. AI as an Object of Governance: Start-ups adopting AI technologies face ethical, legal, and operational challenges, such as mitigating algorithmic bias, ensuring compliance with data privacy regulations, and managing stakeholder concerns. Advisory boards are well-positioned to guide start-ups in addressing these challenges, fostering responsible AI practices that align with societal values and organizational goals. (Rod McNaughton)

This last point is a critical one – AI integration is one specific case where advisory boards can provide significant benefit to their start-up firms, but how the firms utilize advisory boards is still a choice they get to make. And that makes it fascinating for us to observe the corporate governance implications of these choices.

> Advisory boards must balance leveraging AI for strategic advantage with maintaining ethical oversight. This includes advising start-ups on integrating AI responsibly into their business models while safeguarding transparency and accountability. (Rod McNaughton)

What we are seeing in these perspectives – that are ostensibly uniquely about start-up firms – are the same issues we have seen throughout this chapter: transparency, ethics, governance of AI, alignment with social and organizational goals. For many start-up firms, one common organizational goal is growth – transitioning from idea to unicorn (or at least to a larger and more impactful organization). And that organizational transition will require the start-ups' corporate governance systems to evolve, too. AI integration can help here, too.

> As start-ups grow and transition from advisory boards to formal governance structures, AI can be pivotal in institutionalizing knowledge, ensuring continuity, and supporting scalable decision-making. Advisory boards can help set the foundation for AI-enabled governance frameworks that endure beyond the start-up phase. (Rod McNaughton)

## 5.3 AI and Governance of Family Firms

When we surveyed our 30-plus contributors on their perspective on the AI impact in their areas of expertise, the first response we received was clear and direct: "Currently, AI is not at all considered in the family business governance of the companies that we are familiar with."[12] But then, as we began receiving more feedback – from that initial responder and others – we continued to see many of the themes and issues we have seen with start-up firms and with all other firms, too. At a basic level, family firms are using AI to enhance efficiency and regular governance activities.

In today's world, family businesses that have adopted structured governance practices, including meetings and gatherings of all kinds, often touch on the topic of AI. The most common use they cite is, "We use AI to take notes." Even for this straightforward function, concerns arise: Is the data secure? Who else can access it? Could there be leaks? While these questions linger, there's a shared acknowledgment of AI's efficiency in handling note-taking, especially during meetings involving many shareholders offering diverse perspectives. AI's ability to summarize and organize discussions is undeniably impressive.

> Now, imagine this: AI goes beyond mere note-taking. It analyzes the spoken words during board meetings and identifies subtle emotional undercurrents. These contributions, though less visible, are vital to the family business's legacy, harmony, and success. AI's ability to detect hurtful remarks, potential feelings, unexpressed psychological needs, and conflicts of interest, then provide recommendations, can be transformative, particularly during sensitive periods like succession planning. Family businesses often face heightened uncertainty and competing interests during transitions. By recognizing divergences, understanding individual communication styles, and identifying fears and needs, AI can provide timely, actionable advice to improve dialogue and address conflicts early. (Léa Wang and Séverine Mulliez)

We saw the rest of this case study play out in Section 5.2. Rod McNaughton highlighted the distinction of start-ups using "AI as a Tool for Governance" versus "AI as an Object of Governance" previously. And we are seeing that with family firms, too. The opportunities and challenges are similar; so are the ethical, legal, and operational issues. Léa and Séverine conclude their case study by imagining what might be next in the logistical integration of AI into corporate governance at family firms.

> If we push this idea one step further, we could envision integrating camera monitoring with note-taking, capturing and analyzing body gestures, hand gestures, facial expressions, and tones of voice that signal fear, anxiety, intimidation, control, or rejection, offering deeper insights. Imagine a robotic secretary observing the meetings, sharing her observations afterward, and being ready to answer questions and openly share concerns. The robot secretary would be open, free from personal interests, and non-judgmental—especially not pushy—leaving room for leaders to gauge their next steps themselves. Only insights would be offered. (Léa Wang and Séverine Mulliez)

And that has been a theme throughout, too: the human leaders have the ultimate responsibility for making decisions and moving the organization towards its goals. This is, arguably, most relevant at family firms, where the goals may not only be about profit maximization and financial value creation. As Małgorzata Smulowitz discussed in Chapter 14, many family firms choose to take a long-term, triple bottom line perspective: people, planet, and profit. In a separate article, Małgorzata and Peter Vogel study the Spandow family's use of AI to enhance profitability, philanthropy, and sustainability (Smulowitz and Vogel, 2024). The family is using AI to improve efficiency in disaster relief efforts, to decode honeybee dance patterns, to map the Brazilian food system and to develop synthetic cancer data. That is, in this family business AI is being used exactly as it could be used at any other firm. AI is being used to create competitive advantages and to help the firm serve its triple bottom line mission.

In a competitive world for talent and innovation, staying ahead is crucial, and it is not getting any easier. By prioritizing the triple bottom line – considering social, environmental, and financial factors – businesses can stay relevant. By understanding and improving the business value, you can identify opportunities to improve and operate more sustainably. In the realm of corporate social value, progress is best made in small steps. One step forward may sometimes feel like taking two steps back, but it is a gradual and worthwhile process. Remember that AI projects are ongoing endeavors; establish a stopping point based on either the effort invested or the performance of the model. AI generates valuable insights, but they need to be validated. This is where the "expert human touch" comes in (Smulowitz and Vogel, 2024).

## 5.4 AI and Governance of Social Purpose, Mission, and Impact

Corporate governance is about how organizations provide a return on investment to suppliers of capital. That return can be financial or the return can be social or personal. Each organization gets to decide what the firm's mission and purpose is; it is the corporate governance system's responsibility to work towards that mission and purpose. The above example shows how AI can be used to serve a social purpose, using business for good. Of course, AI doesn't care what it's being used for. That is up to us to determine; that is up to the humans in charge of corporate governance systems to determine.

If a board prioritizes strengthening ESG initiatives, AI can serve as a complement to advance these efforts. This is very much related to our Chapter 15 where we argue that improvements in the S and G dimensions may yield tangible benefits for firms.

> Complementing the design and implementation of S and G measures with AI can enhance the brainstorming, development, and implementation of policies decided by the executive team. (Christo Cabolis and Karl Schmedders)

Once again, it all comes back to the executive team, the human beings responsible for making the leadership decisions. And, as we expand on the impact of AI in the governance of social purpose, mission, and impact, we continue to see the recurring themes of transparency, data-driven decision-making and an explosion of information, for better and for worse.

> AI will absolutely help improve transparency in corporate governance information, in particular that associated with ESG or societal reporting that used to heavily rely on textual analysis software/expertise in the past. In addition, AI will transform corporate governance and its research by enabling corporations and boards to make more informed, data-driven decisions, more quickly. (Jing Zhao)

This thinking is an extension of Jing's Chapter 19 study with Richard Warr on the impact of board diversity on firm innovation. Richard further provides a specific example related to his chapter with Jing Zhao on board diversity and firm innovation:

> AI allows very quick queries of diversity policies. For example, throwing "what are the pro-diversity policies implemented by the Coca-Cola Company?" into ChatGPT reveals a wealth of information. The follow-on question "what is the tangible impact of these policies for Coca-Cola?" also reveals quite interesting stuff. (Richard Warr)

As Richard reminded us earlier, just having more information is not always a good thing; "data" can be a four-letter word: "This could have both positive and negative effects depending on who is seeking the information."

And that is perhaps the key point: AI technology can change the world of business and corporate governance, but whether those changes are positive or negative depends on how the technology is implemented and how the information it produces is used. Whether a firm is for-profit or for-mission, its purpose is some combination of profit, progress, and prosperity. AI can help any firm better achieve that purpose. But human ownership and intelligence will ultimately be responsible for governing that purpose. Thus, the "expert human touch" will always be the foundation of any corporate governance system.

> The challenge lies in designing a future where AI fosters both competitiveness and inclusivity. Policies and corporate strategies must transcend business boundaries, aligning innovation with societal equity and sustainability, ensuring that AI serves as a tool for progress rather than a source of human imbalance. (Cinzia Dessi)

## 6. OPPORTUNITIES FOR FUTURE RESEARCH

The integration of artificial intelligence into corporate governance has begun to redefine how organizations operate and make strategic decisions. Boards and executives increasingly use AI tools for analytics, predictive modeling, and risk management, creating opportunities to enhance decision-making and transparency. However, this technological shift brings new challenges, including algorithmic bias, data privacy concerns, and ethical accountability. And all of this will create – or demand – many new opportunities for research.

Many of these opportunities have already been introduced in this chapter and in prior chapters. As we conclude this chapter, we want to highlight some of these issues, both as they connect back to the four primary themes of this book and toward other themes and perspectives. As we have said a number of times, many of the issues related to AI integration in corporate governance are relevant to each of the governance themes in this book: cultural dynamics and perspectives, start-up and venture governance, governance of family firms and governance of social purpose, mission and impact. The specific opportunities and challenges might be slightly different depending on the context, but the issues of transparency, model bias, corporate culture, regulation, and ethics matter to every type of firm.

As we conclude this conversation, we first want to touch on a few perspectives on AI integration into corporate governance that can lead to novel research streams: ecosystem governance, decentralized autonomous organizations, and institutional shareholder governance. These topics span the continuum of investor types. And they can help us think about the questions each of us should be asking as we push the frontiers of research on AI issues in corporate governance.

Philip Roundy (Chapter 6) is currently pushing this frontier as it relates to entrepreneurial ecosystems and the intersection of AI, governance, and entrepreneurs; see, for example, Roundy (2022) or Roundy and Asllani (2024). As we introduced above in Section 5.2, he sees a plethora of new research opportunities. We need to understand how entrepreneurial ecosystems are governed, such that participating entrepreneurs develop and use AI technologies responsibly; we can imagine a free-rider problem with an ecosystem that negatively affects both the primary developers and all members. And, research is needed to understand the trade-offs associated with substituting AI-driven connections for human-centered interactions within ecosystems.

AI and human interactions are fundamentally different and the corporate governance consequences for entrepreneurs of choosing between them are not clear.

This has been a theme throughout this chapter, and it highlights our responsibility as scholars studying AI integration in corporate governance. Rod McNaughton (Chapter 8) is intrigued by an extreme version of this tradeoff, considering both the practical and scholarly potential of decentralized autonomous organizations, or DAOs – which represent an explicit choice in favor of technology-focused decision-making and against human-centered governance. DAOs are an emerging governance model that use blockchain-based smart contracts to decentralize decision-making, offering an alternative to traditional hierarchical governance structures. DAOs could become an emerging governance model that challenges conventional assumptions. AI also intersects with DAOs in several ways, providing an opportunity to link the two:

1. Enhanced Decision-Making: AI systems can process real-time data to support decentralized decision-making within DAOs, providing insights that improve transparency and efficiency.
2. Governance Automation: DAOs leverage smart contracts to automate governance tasks, and AI can enhance this automation by enabling adaptive decision-making that responds to dynamic environments.
3. Ethical and Regulatory Challenges: Similar to AI governance, DAOs face questions about accountability, fairness, and compliance. For example, who is responsible for decisions by an autonomous organization powered by AI?

These are critical issues that require further exploration – just as they are in traditional governance models. Jinsuk Choi (Chapter 17) is also intrigued by the potential for AI and technological advancements to transform how governance is executed – but from a large firm, institutional investor perspective.

AI is poised to reshape corporate governance in transformative ways, particularly in how institutional investors engage with and oversee their portfolio companies. For large asset owners like sovereign wealth funds, AI offers significant potential as a tool to enhance shareholder activities such as proxy voting analysis, corporate engagement, and stewardship of vast and diverse portfolios including global companies. AI-driven analytics can streamline the analysis of voting items and help identify governance risks and opportunities with greater precision. AI will serve as both a tool and a focal point for governance evolution. It challenges boards, management, and investors alike to rethink traditional practices and align technological innovation with sustainable, stakeholder-centered governance.

For decades, most corporate governance systems have relied on a balance of democracy and dictatorship: the firm invites all shareholders and stakeholders to share their preferences, but ultimate decision-making rests with the board of directors, the board chair, and the executive team. Will AI change that? DAOs aim to explicitly move away from this model, decentralizing both advice and decision-making. Large asset owners like sovereign wealth funds won't want that; so do they resist innovation or do they avoid investing in firms that may be more suited to democratizing corporate governance?

As Nguyen Thi Kim Oanh (Chapter 16) points out, "AI emphasizes organizational culture of high performance, high productivity, and high automation." Can corporate governance systems establish organizational cultures that are amenable to the priorities *before* any negative consequences result from them?

We saw earlier that Volkswagen has struggled to do so with its vehicle software development division.

As we mentioned earlier, writing this chapter has been more fun than most scholarly exercises are – because we have had the opportunity to listen to a diverse group of global experts, with vastly different perspectives on AI, on corporate governance and on firm mission. Throughout this chapter, we have touched on many outstanding research questions, based on how we see AI impacting corporate governance in the future. As we said in Chapter 1 of this book, we have tried to excite your imagination and to let you ask important questions. This book has certainly done that to us; and, so, we want to conclude this chapter with a top 15 list of outstanding research questions and opportunities for future research on the intersection of AI and corporate governance. This list is non-exhaustive and in no particular order; feel free to let us know if we omitted any essential questions that should have made this list.

1. How does AI integration fit into agency, stakeholder, stewardship, resource-dependency, or any other theory of corporate governance?
2. How will existing corporate governance systems shape the use of AI and how will this interaction evolve over time?
3. How will regulation of AI implementation evolve? Will the EU AI Act become a global standard?
4. Who will be held accountable for AI-based decision-making?
5. Will AI improve transparency between firms and stakeholders, or will it create a "black box" where stakeholders know even less about a firm's decision-making?
6. How do boards of directors and executive leaders manage organizational culture while integrating AI-driven technology?
7. How do collective action from diverse individuals, organizations, and entities in AI ecosystems govern AI implementation to ensure that it is ethical and benefits society?
8. How do entrepreneurs find the optimal balance between AI-driven systems and human-driven decision-making?
9. How can family firms and non-listed firms use AI to serve their mission, manage communication and enhance succession transitions?
10. How do institutional investors use AI to their advantage?
11. What happens to corporate ownership structures if decision-making moves away from employees and directors? Will employee and director stock ownership cease?
12. At the societal level, will AI worsen social and income inequalities? Will AI models impose historical data – e.g., board diversity structures – and make existing biases even worse?

13. What role will technology play in corporate governance in 10 years? Will decentralized autonomous organizations become the next evolution of organizational structure, making transparency and accountability more opaque?
14. Can AI take on a voting role on the board? Can AI become the CEO?
15. How do board members and senior executives adapt to this new world?

The integration of AI into corporate governance has begun to redefine how organizations operate and make strategic decisions. Boards and executives increasingly use AI tools for analytics, predictive modeling, and risk management, creating opportunities to enhance decision-making and transparency. However, as we have seen throughout this book, this technological shift brings new challenges, including algorithmic bias, data privacy concerns, and ethical concerns.

AI integration is about creating new information – based on dynamic algorithms – so that corporate governance systems can make more effective decisions. Traditional, non-AI data models work really well when the world doesn't change; AI-driven models can – but don't always – work well when the world does change. And this is where the "expert human touch" must take the lead. But, as we know, human beings can overreact to subjective factors, while machines ignore subjective factors. In theory, AI overemphasizes the short-term and underemphasizes the long-term; all statistical and data-generation models do, but AI is data-generation on steroids, so the gaps can be even larger. The upside is that since AI output is dynamically generated by information, the gains in knowledge and accuracy are improving at exponential rates. To quote Richard Warr again, "this could have both positive and negative effects depending on who is using the information."

For us, as researchers working to better understand how corporate governance structures are utilizing and impacted by AI-driven technology, this has created – and will continue to create – significant opportunities to advance corporate governance research. Having common themes – transparency, decision-making, organizational culture, regulation, ethical considerations – across different contexts allows us to formalize theories and normative perspectives. From these foundations, we can then apply, test, and explain the confluence of corporate governance and AI using case studies, qualitative storytelling, and even rigorous quantitative analysis.

The opportunities for corporations to advance their governance systems using AI-driven technologies are enormous – including transparency, increased efficiency, more effective decision-making, and better stakeholder engagement. But there are real concerns as well, as Cinzia Dessi reminds us: "the growing centrality of AI risks subordinating stakeholder trust to algorithms, overshadowing human strategic vision as well as ethical, moral, and social justice considerations." The "expert human touch" will always be – and must always be – the driving force behind any corporate governance system.

Relative to many other streams of research, corporate governance research has uniquely focused on this human element. Corporate governance is about people. Our research attempts to understand their behaviors, incentives and decisions. And understanding these humans has always required sophisticated human intelligence from researchers. That will always be the case. But the AI revolution has created a fascinating convergence of human intelligence and artificial intelligence – both for us as researchers and within the firms that we study. A few years ago, most of us could not imagine the impact that AI would be making on our lives today – and we could not imagine the impact that AI would be making within corporate boardrooms. Our job as researchers is to push our research into new directions and uncover new perspectives on corporate governance knowledge; and AI-driven technology has ignited enormous new opportunities for advancing our understanding of why businesses do what they do. The knowledge that we advance – at this intersection of human intelligence and artificial intelligence – will help shape what businesses do in the near future. We look forward to pushing the corporate governance research frontiers with all of you.

## NOTES

1. See, for example, Loughran and McDonald (2011).
2. One of the editors studied CEO turnover as part of his dissertation in the early 2000s. He identified more than 2,000 cases of CEO turnover and manually reviewed annual reports and press releases for each observation in order to categorize each turnover as some type of voluntary or disciplinary turnover. The entire process took nearly a month of full-time work, the type of work that only PhD students will do; today, a mere 20 years later, that same dataset probably could be collected in a day or two using relatively simple textual analysis.
3. To avoid bouncing back and forth between similar but different terms, for the balance of this chapter we use the generic term "AI" to refer to this entire continuum of innovation, including artificial intelligence, textual analysis, machine learning, neural networks, and anything else along this continuum.
4. International Holding Company Media Office, February 27, 2024: https://www.mediaoffice.abudhabi/en/economy/artificial-intelligence-board-observer-appointed-by-international-holding-board-of-directors/ and Alissa Kole, "A new governance paradigm is necessary for AI-powered boards," in Harvard Law School Forum on Corporate Governance, April 21, 2024: https://corpgov.law.harvard.edu/2024/04/21/a-new-governance-paradigm-is-necessary-for-ai-powered-boards/#:~:text=Appointing%20AI%20board%20members%20has,members%20need%20to%20be%20considered

5. International Holding Company Media Office, February 27, 2024: https://www.mediaoffice.abudhabi/en/economy/artificial-intelligence-board-observer-appointed-by-international-holding-board-of-directors/
6. Séverine Mulliez is a board member of the Association Familiale Mulliez and an expert in family business governance; some of the perspectives offered here come from her first-hand experience as a family member and director in a large, successful family business.
7. From *The Financial Times*, "Volkswagen's $5b Rivian tie-up prompts dismay at software division," September 9, 2024: https://www.ft.com/content/b861e949-76a2-4782-9c74-947dfb56b41a
8. Will Directors' and Officers' Liability Insurance protect directors and officers using AI? We probably don't know yet.
9. For details on the EU AI Act, see: https://artificialintelligenceact.eu/
10. Freddy Gray, "His dark materials: A year after the downfall of Cambridge Analytica, its former head is ready to talk," *The Spectator*, May 18, 2019: https://www.spectator.co.uk/article/his-dark-materials-16-may-2019/
11. See, for example, https://montrealdeclaration-responsibleai.com/ and https://ia.quebec/en/governance.
12. Attribution omitted intentionally.

## REFERENCES

Jarrahi, M., Lutz, C., and Newlands, G. (2022). Artificial intelligence, human intelligence and hybrid intelligence based on mutual augmentation. *Big Data & Society*, 9(2). https://doi.org/10.1177/20539517221142824

Larson, B., Moser, C., Caza, A., Muehlfeld, K., and Colombo, L. (2024). Critical thinking in the age of generative AI. *Academy of Management Learning & Education*, 23(3), pp. 373–378.

Lindebaum, D., Vesa, M., & Den Hond, F. (2020). Insights from "the machine stops" to better understand rational assumptions in algorithmic decision making and its implications for organizations. *Academy of Management Review*, 45(1), 247–263.

Loughran, T., and McDonald, B. (2011). When is a liability not a liability? Textual analysis, dictionaries, and 10-Ks. *Journal of Finance*, 66(1), pp. 35–65.

Roundy, P. (2022). Artificial intelligence and entrepreneurial ecosystems: Understanding the implications of algorithmic decision-making for startup communities. *Journal of Ethics in Entrepreneurship and Technology*, 2(1), pp. 23–38.

Roundy, P., and Asllani, A. (2024). Understanding AI innovation contexts: A review and content analysis of artificial intelligence and entrepreneurial ecosystems research. *Industrial Management & Data Systems*, 124(7), pp. 2333–2363.

Smulowitz, M., and Vogel, P. (2024). The Spandows: Pioneering AI in family philanthropy and sustainable business. In G. Ugazio and M. Maricic (eds), *The Routledge Handbook of Artificial Intelligence and Philanthropy*, pp. 275–286. Routledge.

# Index

Printed and bound by CPI Group (UK) Ltd, Croydon, CR0 4YY
17/06/2026
14902646-0005